HOUSING FINANCE

DAVID GARNETT AND JOHN PERRY

Chartered Institute of Housing
Policy and Practice Series
in collaboration with the
Housing Studies Association

The Chartered Institute of Housing

The Chartered Institute of Housing is the professional organisation for people who work in housing. Its purpose is to maximise the contribution housing professionals make to the well-being of communities. The Institute has 19,000 members across the UK and the Asian Pacific working in a range of organisations, including housing associations, local authorities, the private sector and educational institutions.

Chartered Institute of Housing
Octavia House, Westwood Way
Coventry CV4 8JP
Telephone: 024 7685 1700
Fax: 024 7669 5110
Website: www.cih.org

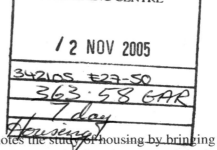

The Housing Studies Association

The Housing Studies Association promotes the study of housing by bringing together housing researchers with others interested in housing research in the housing policy and practitioner communities. It acts as a voice for housing research by organising conferences and seminars, lobbying government and other agencies and providing services to members.

The CIH Housing Policy and Practice Series is published in collaboration with the Housing Studies Association and aims to provide important and valuable material and insights for housing managers, staff, students, trainers and policy makers. Books in the series are designed to promote debate, but the contents do not necessarily reflect the views of the CIH or the HSA. The Editorial Team for the series is: General Editors: Dr. Peter Williams, John Perry and Professor Peter Malpass, and Production Editor: Alan Dearling.

Cover photographs: Aster Group

This publication has been sponsored by the Aster Group

ISBN 1 903208 53 X

Housing Finance
David Garnett and John Perry
Published by the Chartered Institute of Housing © 2005

Printed by Latimer Trend and Co. Ltd., Plymouth

Whilst all reasonable care and attention has been taken in compiling this publication, the authors, the publishers, the Editorial Team and its advisers regret that they cannot assume responsibility for any error or omission that it contains.

Contents   3, 45,

Foreword

An often overused expression is to say that housing is about far more than bricks and mortar, it's also about people and communities.

Whilst that is manifestly true, good people and sound finances are the foundation on which good quality housing and services are built. For an organisation to deliver successfully you need a strong and committed team, confident in their knowledge and capability; and they need to control and understand the financial resources so essential to producing effective and efficient organisations.

Like many other aspects of life, housing finance has become increasingly complex over the years. Too often, reforms are built upon reforms rather than a fundamental reappraisal being undertaken. This makes a good working knowledge of finance even more vital for modern practitioners. In an era in which there is an underlying assumption that proposals will be firmly tested against value-for-money criteria, those working in the sector need to understand just how the figures stack up. This broad understanding is important, not only in relation to your own organisation. An understanding of the financial basis on which other stakeholders and your many partners work, is also vital if you are to maximise the resources available for investment in homes and services.

Good use of financial resources is a key part in achieving our objectives of providing decent affordable homes and safe neighbourhoods. Getting the housing right provides a platform for maximising life chances, delivering social inclusion and creating sustainable communities. Financial resources are a key tool in meeting these objectives, and practitioners who understand the valuable housing finance principles in this book have the opportunity to help their organisations succeed.

Richard Kitson
Group Chief Executive
Aster Group

Acknowledgements

In writing this book we have received considerable help on some chapters from a range of people, many named below and none, of course, responsible for what we have finally written.

Sam Lister of the Chartered Institute of Housing wrote the new versions of Chapters 18 and 19, using his considerable expertise on the private rented sector and on housing benefits. Other colleagues at CIH – notably Merron Simpson and Mark Lupton – commented on particular chapters.

Peter Williams (of the Council of Mortgage Lenders), Peter Malpass (University of the West of England) and Alan Dearling formed the editorial team for the book and Alan took the project through the difficult editing and production process.

Richard Kitson of the Aster Group readily agreed to our proposal that the Group be the book's sponsors.

Finally, the following commented on individual chapters or were otherwise helpful with material that we used:

James Berrington, Housing Corporation
Ross Buchanan, ODPM
Alison Clements, CIH Cymru
Andrew Dench, Housing Corporation
Trevor Emmott, ODPM
Ross Fraser, HouseMark
Philip Hall, Audit Commission
Helen Jones, Scottish Executive
Bob Line, consultant
Stephen Mcallister, ODPM
Hal Pawson, Heriot-Watt University
Patrick McCarthy, Wirral Partnership Homes
Tamsin Stirling, consultant
Mick Warner, Housing Corporation
Steve Wilcox, University of York
Jeff Zitron, Tribal HCH

David Garnett
John Perry
May 2005

PART ONE

Housing finance: conceptual context

Introduction to Part One

The first four chapters of this book provide a conceptual introduction to the more descriptive and analytical material that follows. By drawing on aspects of economic theory and social policy, these early chapters seek to establish a way of thinking and talking about housing finance that will help the reader to develop a critical understanding of some of the enduring problems and issues that surround the topic. The more 'factual' material that constitutes Part Two makes constant references back to the ideas and definitions outlined in Part One. This means that impatient readers may, if they wish, initially skip Part One and turn straight to the book's substantive content that is located in Part Two. The serious student of the subject is, however, encouraged to begin at the beginning.

CHAPTER 1:
Housing and value

Finance is not an end in itself, but a means to an end. It is an instrument of action that allows modern societies to produce, consume and exchange the range of goods and services people demand and need. With respect to housing, finance provides the means to design, construct and acquire new dwellings, to maintain, repair and renew existing dwellings, and meet the day-to-day running costs associated with occupancy. Because for any particular household or housing agency their means are limited, people are concerned to make the best use of the financial resources at their disposal. Be they occupiers, landlords, politicians or practitioners, the primary concern of those with an interest in housing finance is to achieve value-for-money. It is for this reason that we will begin by confronting the question of what is meant by *value* in the context of housing provision, consumption and exchange.

In this introductory chapter we will consider the nature of housing as a commodity by analysing the legal, economic and social characteristics that distinguish it from the other things we produce and use. *Proprietary analysis*[1] will be used to make the point that it is not what housing is that matters, so much as how it is valued. In other words, our ultimate concern is with the question of what housing does for and to people. We will consider this question by seeking to understand how people value the housing in which they have some sort of interest.

Before beginning our discussion we must define some basic terms.

Agreeing a vocabulary

Because the term 'family' carries such strong social and cultural connotations, it is the convention to refer to the occupiers of housing as 'households'. A household can be an individual or a group. In either case, what distinguishes it as a distinct and separate household is its exclusive use of a sitting-room and its joint catering and general housekeeping arrangements.

The terms 'housing', 'houses' and 'house' are sometimes used generically to cover all types of residential unit. However, they can be used more specifically to describe a particular class of domestic property; in this way houses are sometimes

---

1   The notion of *proprietary analysis* used in this book is based on work done at the Department of Land Economy in the University of Cambridge. Readers interested in this approach to analysis might refer to Denman and Prodano, (1972), *Land Use: An Introduction to Proprietary Land Use Analysis*, Allen and Unwin; or Denman, D.R., (1978), *The Place of Property*, Geographical Publications Ltd.

distinguished from bungalows, maisonettes, flats, etc. To overcome this potential confusion, governmental and other official publications use the term 'housing' to describe habitation in general or the stock of accommodation in a defined area and they use the term 'dwelling' to describe an individual unit of accommodation; we will follow this convention.

In using the term 'dwelling' we will take it to apply to any building or part of a building used as a unit of habitation and which has its own separate entrance. To be a 'self-contained' dwelling it must afford the occupier access to the outside world without having to invade some other household's private living space. If a dwelling is shared by more than one household, it is said to be in 'multiple occupation'.

A dwelling can be in a number of *physical forms* and, in the UK, these are generally classified as houses, (detached, semi-detached or terrace), bungalows, maisonettes, flats, high or low rise, or mobile homes, sometimes called park homes. Dwellings in multiple occupation can include bed-sits, old people's homes, student residences, homeless persons' hostels and hotels. The legal terms on which a dwelling is held as property is referred to as its *tenure*. For the purposes of our analysis we will distinguish between three broad tenure arrangements: owner-occupation (freehold or long leasehold[2]); short leasehold; and rented (secure, assured, and assured shorthold). These three broad tenure sectors can be classified further by reference to the *proprietary interests* that individuals and organisations have in a particular dwelling.

The socio-economic nature of a dwelling

The three primary characteristics of a dwelling

We are going to argue that a dwelling is at one and the same time a consumer commodity, private investment, and a social good. These primary characteristics exist simultaneously in all dwellings irrespective of tenure.

Figure 1.1: The socio-economic characteristics of dwellings

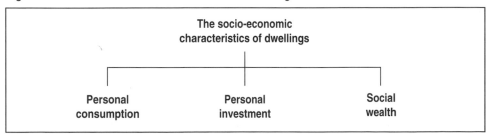

___

2   Legally leaseholders are tenants; however, in this text we are classing long leaseholders along with freeholders as owner-occupiers because typically they pay for their occupancy rights by means of a single 'purchase' payment rather than by periodic 'rental' payments. We will take the term of a 'long lease' to be a period long enough to make the exchange value of the lease more-or-less the same as the freehold value of the property.

That dwellings constitute both personal consumption and private investment highlights the point that people have *proprietary interests* vested in residential properties. The fact that dwellings can be partly or wholly funded from the public purse and that society as a whole is concerned about what happens to the housing stock, highlights the point that there are also *non-proprietary interests* vested in residential properties. Proprietary interests refer to the concerns of those who have a direct and private stake in a property – such as tenants, landlords and owner-occupiers. Non-proprietary interests refer to the concerns that the wider community have for the property. These indirect, wider public interests are sometimes referred to as *externalities* (see Figure 1.2).

Figure 1.2: The socio-economic characteristics of dwellings

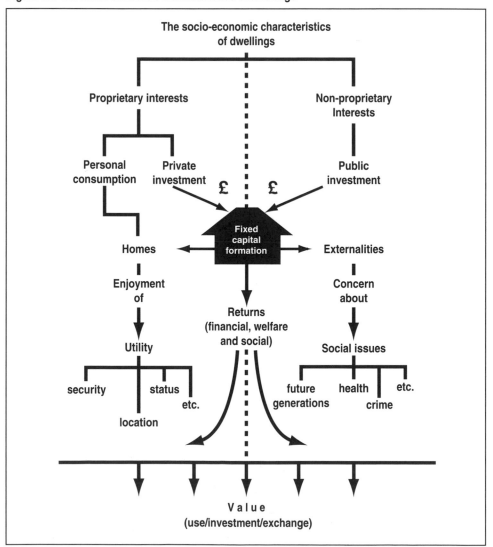

Proprietary interests

When considering the legal and economic relations associated with land and landed property it is more useful to talk of 'proprietorship' than of 'ownership'. This is because people or organisations other than just the freeholder may have some sort of stake in an individual plot or building.

Legal proprietorship is about tenure. In legal terms, a proprietor is someone who has a right or title to something that enables him or her to hold it as property. Although in everyday speech the term 'property' is commonly used to indicate the physical object to which various legal rights relate, in proprietary analysis the word is used to denote the legal relations appertaining to such an object. In this way, property is not conceived of as a concrete 'thing' but as a condition of belonging to some person or persons and is best thought of as comprising a bundle of rights relating to the possession, use and disposal of an object such as a building.

There may be a number of different legal proprietary interests attached to a particular dwelling. In addition to the freehold interest (*fee simple*)[3], individuals may possess leasehold or tenancy interests in the dwelling[4] and neighbouring households may have rights to use, enter or cross part of land or building(s) in order to carry out certain functions.[5] See Figure 1.3.

As well as a legal interest, a proprietor will have private welfare and economic interests vested in the property. Whereas a legal interest specifies the nature and scope of a proprietor's rights and authority to use or physically alter a particular dwelling, a welfare/economic interest determines their motivation for using or altering it in some way. It can be said that legal proprietary interests are about power and welfare/economic proprietary interests are about intent.

It is welfare/economic interests that underlie a proprietor's attitude towards the property and provide the rationale for making use of it or looking after it in a

---

3   The term 'fee' comes from the Anglo-Saxon *feoh* meaning cattle – cattle being in early times a chief part of a person's possessions and a common medium of barter or exchange and, as such, came to signify transferable property. A freehold interest is the nearest thing to an 'absolute, transferable ownership' of real estate.

4   A leaseholder has temporary possession of the land and building(s) for a term of years from a freeholder or superior leaseholder who may be a private individual or an organisation, a local authority or a housing association. The term could be *specific* (e.g. for '99 years') or *periodic* (i.e. recurring – renewable monthly, annually, etc.). This means that we are reserving the term 'tenant' to apply to those who pay a regular rent and whose tenancy rights are defined by Act of Parliament. Leaseholders whose tenancy rights extend into the distant future are here treated as owner-occupiers and those with a short or 'periodic' lease agreement are regarded as a separate category.

5   For example, rights of *easement* establish rights of way or access (e.g. to maintain pipes, wires, fences); and rights of *profits a prendre* establish rights to take something from the property (e.g. grazing rights). Rights and restrictions may also be established by positive or restrictive covenants.

Figure 1.3: Proprietary interests

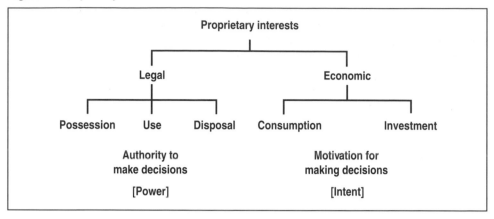

particular way. The welfare/economic stake that someone has in a dwelling can take the form of a *consumption interest* or an *investment interest*.

Housing as consumption

A dwelling is a consumer item in that it generates utility in the form of a stream of housing facilities that individuals and families need or want. Indeed, the primary reason that most people seek access to housing is to consume and enjoy all the various things it provides that together go to constitute a 'home'. These include *shelter* in the form of protection from the elements, *location* in the form of convenient proximity to work, shops, schools, countryside, etc., *physical security* in the form of safety and security from the outside world and, less tangibly, benefits such as *status* that may relate to the siting, size or design of the dwelling.

It is sometimes said that housing, like food and clothing, is a *primary* consumer good because without it a reasonably decent life is not possible. In other words, it is argued that housing is no ordinary consumer item, but a *consumer necessity*. This argument is, however, limited as the quantity and quality of the housing enjoyed by many better off households is more than that needed to satisfy what society currently regards as its minimum housing standards. Over the last hundred years or so society has used central and local government machinery to establish and enforce minimum housing standards and it is the desire to maintain such standards that is often pointed to as an underlying explanation of why housing is subsidised.

Another reason given for subsidising the consumption of housing is that it is expensive relative to disposable incomes. The price of a dwelling is almost invariably equivalent to a multiple of the purchaser's annual income, and for those who rent, the rental charge is likely to represent a high proportion of their expenditure relative to other items in their household budget.

The recognition of the fact that some minimum standard of housing is necessary for all people, and that it is expensive relative to income, has had a profound effect on the way in which the system of housing finance has evolved. When households with a preference for ownership are unable to purchase outright they must either rent their homes from landlords or borrow the money for purchase. Two consequences resulting from the nature of housing as a consumer commodity have been the establishment of a rented sector, and the development, alongside the market for owner-occupied housing, of a parallel money market providing long-term loans to purchasers in the form of mortgages. In subsequent chapters we will describe how, at different times, the state has intervened in different ways to encourage housing consumption by reducing both the price of renting and the price of borrowing.

In making a decision about where to live, a household will judge each dwelling's utility features in relation to its rental or purchase price. It is important to note, however, that to some extent, these features will be valued in terms of personal preferences. Just as different people like different types of music, different people like different types of home. This means that in choosing a home, a household will seek to balance a number of factors. On the one hand they will take account of the price or rent of the dwelling and its utility features, and on the other hand they will consider whether it suits their needs and expectations and whether or not they can afford to occupy it.

As well as being a home and generating utility, a dwelling will also have the features of an investment and, as such, have the potential to generate a financial or social 'return' on the money capital committed to its production or acquisition.

Housing as real capital investment

Investments can be held in the form of paper titles such as share certificates or bonds, or in the form of physical, utilisable artefacts such as plant, machinery or buildings. This latter category of investment is sometimes referred to as *real capital* or *fixed capital formation*. The term *fixed capital formation* is used to distinguish real capital from other, more liquid, types of assets such as stocks and shares. Although buildings are usually immobile, the word *'fixed'* here is not meant to imply that the asset itself cannot be moved but refers to the fact that the investor's money capital is 'tied up' and is in a sense 'fixed into' the physical asset. We therefore say that a building such as a house is an item of 'fixed capital' – that is, if needed, it will take the proprietor some time to 'unlock' the money they invested in it.

A dwelling can be regarded as an item of *personal investment* insofar as it is a durable asset with a potential to earn a yield in the form of a rental income or a capital gain. A dwelling can be regarded as an item of *social investment* insofar as it has a potential to yield social gains valued by society. In either case, the value of the investment is determined by its potential to generate utility to some current or future end user. This means its type, size, condition and geographical location will affect an asset's relative value.

Housing yield and the concept of 'capital value'

In the housing field, private and public investment generate additions to real capital in the form of improvements and additions to the existing stock of dwellings.

Consumption and investment are related categories that are linked through the concept of value. The word 'value' comes from the Latin *valere* – to be strong – to be relied upon – to have worth. So the 'value' of something is that attribute that makes it, in some sense, worthy of use. If something has no use it is worthless and if it is worthless, it has no value.

The economic value of any capital asset is composed of three interrelated factors; namely, its potential selling price, or its *exchange value*, its potential usefulness, its 'utility' or *use value*, and its potential to yield a return on money capital committed, its *investment value*. At any time, a building's exchange value will be determined by the perceptions of potential purchasers about its current use and/or future investment value. *The real, underlying, fundamental economic value of a building is determined by what it does – its usefulness*, and in the final analysis, it is this that determines both its investment value and its exchange value. In the end, all economic value is grounded in current or potential use value.

The exchange value of a building is represented by its selling price. Exchange is the mechanism by which use or investment value is realised. By selling the proprietary interests in a property, its use and investment values are exchanged for cash; that is, they are 'liquidated'.

Proprietorial motivations

The potential of a unit of accommodation to generate utility and a financial or social return affects a proprietor's attitudes towards spending money on its acquisition, improvement or maintenance. What people or organisations choose to do with or to a dwelling depends partly on their financial resources and partly on the nature of their proprietary interests. If the property is regarded as an item of consumption the proprietor will weigh up the price of buying, renting, repairing or maintaining it and compare this with the utility they would expect to acquire in return for such an outlay. If, however, a dwelling is regarded as a private or social investment then the proprietor will weigh up any proposed expenditure and compare it with the anticipated yield resulting from the investment outlay.

A tenant will have a predominantly consumption interest in a dwelling and will tend to be motivated to spend money on it with a view to gaining or maintaining its utility as a *home*. In contrast, a private landlord will have a predominantly investment interest and will be largely motivated to spend money on a dwelling with a view to maximising its rental income or capital value. An owner-occupier has a consumption and an investment interest in a property and will tend to bear both of these characteristics in mind when purchasing, improving or maintaining it. An understanding of the nature and scope of these private proprietary interests is a key concern of this text and will be considered in subsequent chapters.

Like other proprietors, local authorities and housing associations have clear legal interests in the stock they manage. In contrast with other proprietors, however, their economic *raison d'être* emphasises the need to generate politico-welfare returns for public expenditure and charitable investments. These returns are not simply measured in terms of rental flows and capital appreciation, but also take account of how the housing stock serves the needs of low-income or vulnerable households.

The provision, allocation and maintenance of decent, affordable housing constitutes the welfare/economic interest of local housing authorities and housing associations. The aims and policy pronouncements of the authority or association will determine the precise nature of this proprietary interest. Public sector and charitable landlords may regard the return on investment in social and political, rather than commercial, terms. To the extent that these 'returns' are specified (e.g. in the form of statutory duties, mission statements, performance targets, etc.), their achievement constitutes part of the organisation's proprietary interest. Because such agencies have to balance a number of objectives, such as the well-being of prospective as well as actual tenants, their proprietary interests will not necessarily be the same as those of their current tenants. The identification, creation and measurement of politico-welfare returns to social landlords are key concerns of this text and will be considered in detail in subsequent chapters. For the time being we will simply say that local housing authorities and housing associations have an interest in providing cost-effective housing for households deemed to be in some form of 'housing need'.

The social returns on housing investment extend beyond the specific concerns of the landlords and tenants of social housing. People and organisations that have no immediate, direct legal stake in a dwelling may still have concerns about its use or condition. These other-party concerns we term *'non-proprietary interests'* or *'externalities'*.

Non-proprietary interests

To say that someone has an 'interest' in a property is to say that they have some *stake in* or *duty for* the way in which it is produced, used and looked after. To the extent that its provision, use and maintenance is seen to be of concern to the wider community, housing possesses characteristics that can lead to it being classified as a *social commodity* in which non-proprietary as well as proprietary interests are vested.

Society as a whole may have concerns about the housing stock that go beyond, or are even in conflict with, the interests of those with proprietary stakes in the properties. For example, a housing association or a private company may wish to pursue their welfare or commercial objectives by developing a plot of land with a view to providing dwellings to let. The resultant development might obscure a view, create traffic congestion, destroy a wildlife area, or in some other way affect the interests of others.

Other examples of the ways in which we might consider housing to be a social good include the following:

1. Because nearly all dwellings in all tenures are built to a standard that ensures that they outlive their initial occupiers, housing production caters for future as well as current housing needs and demands. In this sense housing can be regarded as a national social asset, held in trust by one generation for the next.

2. Research findings have long demonstrated a clear link between homelessness, poor housing and people's health and vulnerability to crime.[6] Furthermore, there is a recognised, albeit ill-defined, link between housing conditions and educational performance. The research report, *More than somewhere to live* (1996), commissioned by the National Housing Forum with sponsorship from the Joseph Rowntree Foundation, produced evidence showing that these problems are particularly acute in the rented sector and among the poorest and most vulnerable.[7]

3. Together with roads, schools, hospitals, etc., housing constitutes part of an area's infrastructure and as such, plays a part in the promotion of its economic growth and prosperity. In particular, an appropriate supply of good quality housing is needed to attract a skilled and qualified workforce.

4. Because the condition of an individual dwelling has a 'spill-over effect' on the use values and exchange values of neighbouring properties, how one proprietor maintains or uses their property can affect the interests of neighbouring proprietors. It is in recognition of the interconnected nature of property interests that society gives local planning authorities powers to approve both new construction and alterations to existing buildings. In some instances, the externality interests of neighbours are internalised into the legal interests of a proprietor by means of positive or restrictive covenants.

---

6   For selected examples of nineteenth century parliamentary reports see Pike, E.R., (1966), *Human documents of the Industrial Revolution in Britain*, Allen & Unwin. Refer also to commentaries on the influential report into *Inequalities in Health* by Sir Douglas Black and others: e.g. Anderson, J. and Ricci, M. (Eds), *Society and Social Science: A Reader*, The Open University, 1990.

7   There has been an historical reluctance on the part of governments to accept the links between poor housing and social issues. When the Black Report on inequalities in health was completed in 1980 the government rejected its findings on poverty and argued that its recommendations for housing were unrealistic. However, after the Black Report other evidence mounted and in 1994 the Health Secretary, Virginia Bottomley announced a research project into the links between poverty and health, paying particular attention to socio-economic conditions, geography, and ethnicity.

For all these reasons it is possible to argue that community interests exist in the housing stock that are external to those of proprietors. The existence of external, non-proprietary, community interests in the size and condition of the housing stock is pointed to as yet another reason for directing public expenditure into the housing system.

Housing as a social service

We will end our discussion on the nature of housing as a commodity by considering the extent to which it might be regarded as a social service. It is often argued that some basic goods and services should be made available to every household irrespective of their ability to pay. This discussion normally focuses on the proposition that the state needs to provide what economists refer to as 'public goods' and 'merit goods'.

Public goods. Pure public goods and services are those things that are provided collectively by the state because individuals operating in a market cannot sensibly pay for them. In other words, by their very nature, their consumption is indivisible: in providing them for one they become available to all. Good examples would be national defence, sewers, and street lighting. Some goods and services *could* be marketed to individuals but society may decide that such an arrangement would be administratively cumbersome or in some other way inconvenient or inappropriate. These are referred to as '*quasi-public goods and services*' and might include roads, a police and fire service, and education. The extent to which quasi-public goods and services are financed or administered by the state will to some extent depend upon the political ideology of the government in power.

Dwellings, whether rented or owned, and housing services, such as advice, repairs, maintenance and improvements, are capable of being supplied on an individual basis and therefore do not display the features of pure public goods and services. This means that whether they are provided by the state or by the price system will be a matter of political judgement. Council houses are therefore quasi-public goods and a local authority's housing advice centre is providing a quasi-public service.

Merit goods. These are quasi-public goods and services that society regards as being too important to be left to market forces to provide. The state intervenes to subsidise or regulate their provision or to provide them directly because the community regards them as being particularly meritorious. If left to the market they might be 'under-consumed' or be of an 'inappropriate' type or standard. Education is a good example of a merit service. Society has come to believe that it is in the national interest that all children to be educated to some minimum standard and in ways that society, rather than the market, decides.

It might be argued that some minimum standard of housing should be regarded as a *merit service* because the quantity and quality of housing affects the general national interest. This is so because the under-consumption of decent housing impinges on such things as health, educational performance, crime, and the mobility of labour.

The case for state intervention

The case for state intervention in the housing system is usually made in terms of the following logical argument. A completely free-enterprise system of market provision and consumption is inappropriate because the housing market is intrinsically imperfect. Furthermore, some minimum level of 'shelter' is a *necessity* for a humane and civilised life and therefore welfare *ideology* dictates that we should guarantee a basic level of housing to all. In addition to the welfare argument, an agreed minimum level of housing for all should be provided because it is *meritorious*: that is, it is in the general national interest that all people are decently housed. This national interest relates to such issues as public health, civil stability, and an effective economy.

In contemporary Britain there is a general consensus that for social, political and economic reasons, it is desirable that everyone should have access to some minimum level of shelter. However, it follows from what has been argued above, that housing at the level which most people consume it, cannot be regarded as a 'necessity'. Just because food and shelter are basics to life, it does not follow that a person's steak dinner or penthouse apartment should be regarded as necessities.

Summary

Housing is an unusual and complex commodity in that it simultaneously possesses the features of personal consumption, private investment and social capital. Various proprietary and non-proprietary interests are associated with each of these features. As we will see in subsequent chapters, these characteristics, together with their associated interests, have important consequences for the ways in which we finance the production, consumption, management and exchange of housing.

CHAPTER 2:
Housing finance, accountability and value-for-money

Because the operational practices and procedures associated with the financing of owner-occupation and the various forms of renting all differ somewhat, much of the later material of this book is organised around a tenure framework. However, we need to recognise that the underlying principles governing the provision, distribution and utilisation of housing finance are independent of tenure. This chapter will therefore consider various ways of categorising housing finance that are not tenure-specific and it will confront the central issues of 'accountability' and 'value-for-money'. These ways of thinking about, and assessing the effects of, housing finance need to be grasped at the outset because they permeate the tenure analysis that follows and they provide a cross-tenure coherence to our subsequent descriptions and arguments.

The system of housing finance

One way of appreciating the nature and scope of housing finance is to regard it as a mechanism for linking money inputs (sources of finance) to money outputs (expenditure). Treating housing finance as a system of bridging money inputs and outputs is useful on two counts. First, it highlights the functions to which the finance is eventually put and thereby acts as a reminder that raising and spending money are not ends in themselves; it underlines the point that financial arrangements exist to facilitate proprietary plans and public policies. Second, it provides us with a simple conceptual framework and vocabulary that can be used to discuss the financial arrangements associated with all types of housing in all types of tenure.

Figure 2.1 illustrates the idea that *housing finance is a system of money and credit that operates to enable all types of residential property to be produced, managed, acquired, maintained, repaired, renewed and exchanged.* In the diagram a key distinction is made between finance that is used for *capital purposes*, finance that is used for *revenue purposes* and finance that is used to *augment incomes*.

Capital expenditure. Capital expenditure is that incurred for the purpose of acquiring fixed capital formation. Fixed capital formation is composed of assets of a relatively permanent nature and, in a housing context, can be thought of as anything that increases the quantity or quality of the stock. It includes payments made to lawyers, surveyors and other professionals in connection with the purchase of land and existing buildings as well as all the material, labour and other costs incurred in connection with the erection of new buildings. Money spent on

Figure 2.1: Housing finance as a monetary system

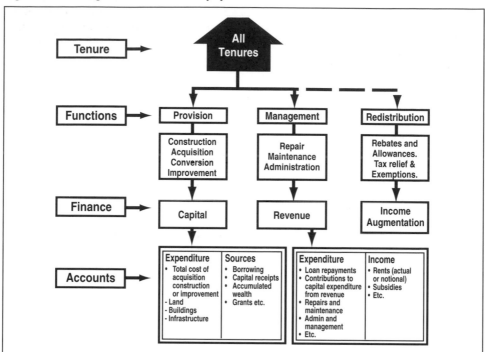

converting or improving, as against maintaining and repairing, the existing stock of dwellings results in more or better quality housing being available and is therefore regarded as capital expenditure in the same way as money spent on constructing new units is so regarded.

Sources of capital. Housing capital expenditure is typically financed by borrowing and/or by the use of accumulated savings, or reserves. It is often financed through the reinvestment of capital receipts from asset sales. Revenue income, grants, and gifts can supplement such sources.

Revenue expenditure. Revenue expenditure is that expenditure incurred in acquiring consumable and other non-permanent goods and services. This type of spending can be referred to as *current* or *consumption* expenditure and is sometimes termed 'running costs' or 'costs-in-use'. In a housing context, it refers to those recurring payments on general administration, loan interest and debt redemption together with those payments made for the purpose of maintaining, repairing and managing the housing stock. In other words, housing revenue expenditure comprises all outgoings incurred as part of the day-to-day provision of housing services together with that incurred in maintaining the real capital assets in a habitable state. Because the costs of servicing loans taken out to purchase capital items are regarded as part of revenue expenditure, capital expenditure decisions can have significant revenue consequences.

Revenue income. Revenue income pays for revenue expenditure. In a housing context, revenue income is derived from rents and/or other trading or employment earnings together with any available investment income or subsidy entitlement. In extreme cases, when a household or agency is unable to pay its recurring revenue costs, creditors may require them to generate the money by liquidating some of their assets.

The relationship between capital and revenue expenditure

The difference between capital and revenue is a theoretical one and, in practice, accounting procedures and conventions sometimes blur the distinction. What gets counted as capital or revenue may, for example, be determined by what funds are available. This has to be kept in mind when considering how various institutions actually classify their expenditure: for example, capital works may be financed from revenue. It is also worth re-emphasising the point made above that *capital expenditure decisions will carry with them future revenue commitments.*

Income augmentation. We have stressed the point that, for most households and agencies, housing is expensive relative to disposable income (i.e. income net of tax). This fact, coupled with society's desire to make it possible for everyone to be housed to some acceptable standard, has led governments at different times to introduce various subsidy arrangements that allow an increase in housing consumption by certain households. The idea is to provide financial help that will enable qualifying households to acquire and enjoy housing or housing-related services that they could not otherwise afford. Such financial help can take the form of rebates and allowances or tax relief and exemptions. There is some debate amongst practitioners and theorists about whether this type of support really is an element of housing finance or whether it should be classified as part of the social security system. It is in recognition of this debate that the diagram in Figure 2.1 ties income augmentation into the system of housing finance with a broken rather than a solid line.

Housing functions and housing finance

Having broadly categorised housing finance in terms of capital, revenue and income augmentation, we are in a position to look more closely at the various purposes to which money and credit is put.

Provision
The function of capital finance is to pay for new dwellings and for the acquisition, conversion and improvement of existing ones. It is needed to build and to buy: it pays for 'provision' in the widest sense of the word.

Dwellings may contain certain items of relatively expensive equipment such as central heating and double-glazing that are generally regarded as integral elements of the building. In new dwellings they are treated as part of the capital formation.

When such items are installed in existing dwellings they are, in practice, often paid for out of revenue income. Despite this, because they clearly add to, rather than simply maintain, the quality of the property, they are, in principle, real capital investment. This means that accounting practice does not always mirror the economists' theoretical distinction between capital and revenue used in this chapter.

Acquisition finance is required to purchase dwellings that are already in existence. Owner-occupiers and private landlords are the main purchasers of second-hand dwellings, although most local authorities and housing associations acquire properties that they usually improve or convert before letting on to their tenants. Private developers sometimes acquire blocks of dwellings or individual units that they convert or improve and then sell on to private buyers. Much conversion activity takes the form of altering large dwellings into a greater number of smaller units.

Management

Once the real capital formation has been built or acquired, capital expenditure ceases, with the exception of any later improvements, and the proprietor is then faced with all the recurring 'costs-in-use' that we have classified above as revenue expenditure. These costs stem from the need to manage the asset on a day-to-day basis.

Administration forms a major part of the management function, and revenue finance has to be provided to deliver the range of supervisory and support services landlords provide for their tenants and others. In a housing association or local authority housing department administration costs will include office consumables and expenses and the salaries of specialist staff. Some of the employees will operate at a professional level as housing officers and take responsibility for administering the procedures associated with allocations, rent collection, the management of maintenance and providing aid and advice to committees, tenants and the general public. Others will be employed to provide specialist services such as warden support for the elderly, while others will operate at a more technical level to provide such facilities as cleaning and caretaking.

Because over time dwellings and their fixtures and fittings deteriorate or become in some other way obsolete, the management function includes repair, maintenance and renewal services. Most private and social landlords operate a mixture of response and programmed maintenance and repairs.

Whether carried out in-house or contracted out to some other organisation, all housing management functions have to be paid for out of revenue flows. All dwellings have to be managed irrespective of tenure and, in this sense, private landlords and owner-occupiers are just as much housing managers as are the employees of housing associations and local housing authorities. Some day-to-day housing management functions, such as decorating or minor repairs, may be carried out by tenants. Indeed, some specific managerial responsibilities may be identified in a lease or tenancy agreement.

Income augmentation

Alongside the housing finance system, the social security system operates to alleviate poverty by redistributing real incomes. Broadly speaking, this works by the central government collecting taxation, part of which it then redistributes in the form of housing and social security benefits. In the case of housing benefits and allowances, local authorities act as agents of redistribution for the central authorities. Historically, owner-occupiers have received taxation concessions rather than direct payments or reduced charges.

Redistribution in the form of subsidies, payments, rebates and allowances occurs for two broad reasons. The historic reason has been to help low-income households meet their accommodation expenses. The subsidisation of housing can take many forms and these will be examined in subsequent chapters. At this point we will simply observe that, in recent years, there has been a shift towards fiscal welfare measures (income augmentation), and less reliance on supply-side ('bricks-and-mortar'), subsidies. The second reason that redistribution may occur is because the government of the day wishes to encourage a particular tenure. The Conservative administrations of the 1980s and 1990s, for example, wanted to encourage owner-occupation and accordingly maintained the system of mortgage interest tax relief.

Accounting and audit

The records of expenditure and income for a given period are kept in accounts. Periodic account can also be kept of the balance between an organisation's assets and liabilities. The production of audited accounts is an important aspect of the procedure by which those who manage an organisation are made accountable for their actions to some authority such as a body of shareholders, a management committee, councillors, a funding agency or local tax-payers.

Types and styles of accounts

As well as cash books and legers that record day-to-day financial transactions, most organisations produce annual accounts and some are legally required to do so. During the year, the organisation will record all of its financial transactions, and at the end of the year these records will be used to produce the final accounts that have to be 'signed off' at audit.

The final accounts consist of records that show the income and expenditure for the year and a balance sheet that lists the assets and liabilities held by the organisation at the year-end. The assets held will include such things as buildings and land, stocks of goods and debts owed to the organisation. The liabilities will include the amounts owed by the organisation to others in respect of capital (e.g. loans outstanding), and revenue commitments (sundry creditors).

Although all organisations produce accounts and balance sheets, this does not mean that these all look alike or contain the same sort of information: the style

of the accounts used will be determined by the needs of the organisation.
For example, the accounts of a company contain details of its trading activities,
profits made and distributions to shareholders. The accounts of a local authority
detail expenditure and income associated with the various services that it has a
duty or power to provide, together with local tax receipts and Exchequer
subsidies. Owner-occupiers are not required to keep accounts as they are not
responsible to others for their housing decisions, but they may choose to keep
records for their own information.

The nature and interpretation of accounts

While accountancy and account keeping demand professional skills and
qualifications, accounts are no more than the recording in financial terms of the
activities undertaken by the organisation over a given period, usually a year,
together with an end of period balance of that organisation's outstanding assets
and liabilities. From properly prepared annual accounts it should be possible, even
for the uninitiated, to comprehend the nature of an organisation's transactions
during the period covered and its financial worth as at the end of that period.

Accounts are prepared according to the *prudence principle*. This means that, as far
as possible, accountants work with facts rather than opinion, and with past events
rather than with future ones. Most accounts are prepared on an *historic* basis and
use market-related values. The period for which the accounts are prepared, usually
a year, is called *the accounting period.*[1] Because accounts do not deal with the
future directly, those wishing to make use of them for planning purposes can only
use them to identify trends from transactions that have taken place in previous
accounting periods.

Most people who use accounts are not so much interested in being able to do the
book-keeping involved in their preparation, as being able to understand and
interpret the information recorded in them. As well as allowing for the appraisal of
past results, accounts are a source of financial and statistical information that can
be used to provide guidance for policy. By careful analysis of accounting records
it may be possible to bring to light data that will assist in identifying waste and
inappropriate management decisions and help to suggest reforms and economies.
In order to use and make sense of accounts it is important to have an appreciation
of the organisation's aims.

There is currently much debate about how accounting procedures might be
reformed so that the records can be used more effectively as resource management
tools, rather than simply as book-keeping entries charting and dating cash-flows.
This shift in approach is called 'resource accounting' as against 'cash accounting'.

---

1   For internal management purposes, some accounts are monitored quarterly as well as
     annually.

Can 'cash' accounts measure success?

If the organisation's aims can be expressed simply in terms of money flows, then cash accounts can easily be designed to show whether these aims are being achieved. For example, they can show clearly whether the rent charged by a landlord is sufficient to cover the costs of providing the accommodation and earn profit. However, current accounting practice cannot give clear guidance about whether or not the stock is being managed in a business-like way, hence the shift to resource accounting. It is not possible to rely on the accounts alone to determine whether or not an organisation's more complex concerns are being adequately addressed. For example, it is not possible to find out from the accounts whether the rate of juvenile crime will be reduced as a result of the refurbishment of a run-down estate or whether homeless families will be better off in a hostel or in bed-and-breakfast accommodation. Because of their historic nature, cash accounts can only demonstrate in a limited way whether or not an organisation is making the 'best' use of its limited and valuable resources.

Resource budgeting and accruals accounting

In recent years, housing agencies have been expected to become more business-like and to demonstrate that their financial decisions are commercially as well as socially justifiable. This has opened up a debate about the nature of public sector accounting. Traditionally, public sector agencies have tended to record their financial transactions on a simple *cash-flow* basis, rather like a bank statement. Cash-flow accounting allows the organisation to track the periodic balances, the surpluses and deficits that exist in specific accounts. However, some critics argue that this approach provides a rather restricted form of accountability and public sector spending should be open to more rigorous scrutiny. In particular, they argue the need for an accounting system that provides the sort of information that allows us to judge whether or not the organisation is making the best use of scarce public resources. By the mid-1990s, the Treasury was arguing the need for government departments and public sector agencies to reform their accounting methods to allow for what is termed *resource accounting and budgeting* (RAB). By 2001 the government had introduced RAB fully into the administration of public spending as a way of reinforcing its fiscal strategy of clarifying the distinction between capital and current spending (discussed further in subsequent chapters). Resource budgeting enables the application of cost-benefit analysis to the appraisal of proposed public investments. The Treasury has said that such analysis can even be used to measure the benefit of relatively small-scale discrete investments such as refurbishing a block of housing or acquiring a school playing field.

The idea of RAB is that the accounting records should be kept in such a way that the information they contain helps organisations make decisions about how best to allocate scarce resources between competing ends. That is, resource accounting seeks to present information in a way that will enable managers to make optimal decisions about the use of the valuable and limited resources under their control. Optimal decision-making requires clarity about the objectives of the decision-makers. It cannot be understood simply by reference to the records of cash-flows that have been made in a given accounting period: it needs to consider the actual results of spending and investment decisions. In particular, it requires managers and auditors to be able to assess the *actual outcomes* of their decisions against the *planned-for outcomes*. RAB should seek to provide information that will help the organisation to judge the extent that its investment of funds has been effective. In this context the notion of 'effectiveness' has a particular meaning and this is discussed below (see also Figure 2.3 later in this chapter).

In a commercial setting 'profitability' is often used as the measure of successful resource budgeting. Housing agencies, however, are usually more concerned with managerial effectiveness than with crude commercial profitability. As we have said, in attempting to optimise the use of resources, we need to match inputs and outputs. The shift towards resource accounting practices involves *matching* costs and revenues to one another as far as their relationship can be established, and recording financial transactions on an *accruals* rather than on a *cash* basis.

To measure the commercial or social viability of a project or individual asset, accounts need to be kept in accordance with what is known as the *matching principle*. This states that, as far as possible, costs should be set against the revenue that they generate at the point in time when this arises. If they are not so matched then it becomes difficult to calculate the true return on the committed expenditure. The idea of the *matching principle* is that in order to determine the social or commercial return, revenue must be compared or 'matched' with all the costs that have been incurred in earning it. We are simply trying to answer the question, 'Did we make the best use of our limited and valuable resources?' In addressing this crucial question, we need to engage in resources accounting so that we can balance inputs with outputs, match effort with accomplishment, and compare what we planned for with what actually happened.

As well as embracing the *matching principle*, the effective measure of commercial or social profit and loss also requires accounts to be kept in accordance with the *accruals concept*. This states that to acquire a true profit and loss picture for a specific period (e.g. a financial year), we should recognise revenues and costs as they are earned or incurred, rather than as they are received or paid out, as occurs in the cash-flow approach. In accruals calculations, expenses are recognised, although not necessarily recorded, in the period in which they are incurred rather than in the period in which money happens to be paid for them. For example, if it costs £10,000 a year to rent a building then there is an expense of £10,000 to be recognised each year regardless of how or when the rent is paid. If, for example, it is paid bi-annually in advance, the accruals principle states that it would be inappropriate to charge £20,000 as an expense for year one. An *accrued charge* is an expense that has been incurred as at a particular date but not yet invoiced or paid. An *accrued revenue* is an income that has been earned but not yet recorded.

An important effect of the accruals approach is that capital expenditure is not all recorded as a cost in the year in which the asset is acquired. The front-loading of capital costs into the year of acquisition can act as an investment disincentive. Accruals accounting has the effect of reducing the recorded cost in the first year of investment and enables a longer-term rational view of the project's viability to be taken. Some argue that the change will remove a large part of the advantage that private landlords have over social landlords in accounting for investment, and thus will reduce the bias against investment in the public sector (England, M., 1997 p70).

Now that resource accounting procedures have been established in central and local government departments and public sector organisations, the Treasury is requiring agencies to move to the next logical step which is *resource budgeting*. Resource budgeting involves establishing techniques for appraising how to make the best use of available financial resources. In terms of the total sums involved, some of the most significant financial corporate decisions involve expenditures to acquire capital assets.

Accounting for the provision of capital assets

The process of planning and evaluating proposals for investment in fixed assets is called *capital budgeting*. Capital budgeting is about investing in the future and involves either committing the organisation's accumulated savings to the acquisition or improvement of an asset or the borrowing of funds so to do. The process of appraisal entails the use of *opportunity costing* techniques that are designed to ensure that the available money capital is being put to its best possible use. These techniques are necessary because *historic* accounts are designed to record the past rather than appraise the future. Before identifying the sort of techniques that might be used in capital budgeting, we need to be clear about the nature of the problem that they are seeking to overcome.

The problem: What we spend now on plant, buildings and equipment will have significant consequences for the long-run financial health of the organisation. Organisations can benefit from good capital budgeting decisions and suffer from bad ones for many years. Decisions are complicated by the fact that appraisals have to be made from estimates of future operating costs and returns which, by their nature, involve a considerable degree of uncertainty and cannot be deduced from accounts that have been produced on the *prudence principle*. It also has to be recognised that, compared with revenue spending, capital budgeting often commits relatively large amounts of money for relatively long periods of time. Furthermore, capital investment decisions tend to be difficult or impossible to reverse once the funds have been committed and the project begun.

In common with other welfare agencies, housing organisations need to take account of a wide range of non-financial factors when making capital budgeting decisions. Housing investment produces valued social returns that are reflected in the findings of tenant satisfaction surveys and in reduced levels of urban disutility such as crime and disease. However, restrictions on the growth in public expenditure, together with shifts in emphasis towards public/private partnership arrangements, mean that social housing investments are also expected to generate some quantifiable financial return. Without this return, investors will not be willing to make funds available to finance schemes and the agencies themselves will not be able to generate sufficient funds for their own future investment projects.

The techniques: There are a great number of sophisticated techniques for identifying and evaluating the financial and non-financial aspects of capital budgeting. These techniques are often used in combination. The choice of technique(s) will largely depend on the nature of the proposed investment and what it is that the organisation is seeking to achieve by the commitment of funds. Investment appraisal is a complex field and we will here simply point to four commonly used techniques by way of illustration.

1. *Cost-benefit analysis.* This technique seeks to value all the relevant gains and losses resulting from a proposed investment, including those of an intangible nature. A CBA operates within a specified time profile and discounting techniques are used to put a present value on future costs and benefits.

2. *Pay-back period.* This technique focuses on the length of time necessary to recover the entire cost of the investment from the resulting annual net cash-flow.

3. *Return on average investment.* This technique assesses viability by reference to an assessment of the expected average annual net income from an investment expressed as a percentage of the average amount invested.

4. *Discounting future cash-flows.* Discounting is the process by which we seek to determine the present value of future cash-flows. The present value of a future cash-flow is the amount that a knowledgeable investor would pay today for the right to receive that future amount. This will depend on the amount of the future payment, the length of time until the future payment will be received, and the rate of return required by the investor.

Accounting for the use of capital assets

The pursuit of 'Best Value' (and, before that compulsory competitive tendering) and the increasing tendency for public agencies to compete with the private sector, has made it necessary to know the true cost of a service, including the costs of managing and maintaining the stock of fixed assets. This, coupled with political pressure for public agencies to be more commercially orientated, has led a number of local authorities and other agencies to introduce a system of capital accounting that enables them to estimate the value of their fixed assets, make appropriate asset-use charges to revenue, and make allowances for depreciation.

Over time fixed assets can have their values eroded by wear and tear or obsolescence. The accruals principle states that this loss of value should be accounted for in the accounting period in which it occurred. This necessitates an adjustment to be made before calculating the profit or loss for the period in question. This adjustment is termed *depreciation*. Depreciation is a real cost of service provision and the matching principle requires a profit or loss calculation to compare revenue earned with *all of the costs* that have been incurred in earning it.

Audit and financial accountability

Investment appraisal decisions are the responsibility of management and because the returns are long-term, their effectiveness cannot be submitted to an annual audit. However, financial accountability does require the annual auditing of historic accounts. This means that external accountants specialising in audit work check the accounts and certify that they have been prepared in accordance with legislation and good accounting practice. The external auditors must be independent of the organisation whose accounts are being checked and they cannot be employees of that organisation. Large organisations also have internal auditors who are employees with responsibilities for ensuring that the financial systems of the organisation are properly designed and implemented.

Book-keepers and auditors record and check how money flows in and out of an organisation. Accountants rarely introduce evaluative goals into published accounts even when quantification of such goals would not be controversial. Their primary concern is to ensure clarity, transparency and probity with respect to financial transactions. It is for policy-makers and managers to determine criteria for measuring an organisation's success and to find evidence of achievement from a wide range of sources of which the published accounts will be just one. Many housing agencies set up an audit committee for this purpose.

Accountability and value-for-money

We will now turn to a different level of accountability by moving our attention from the records of financial flows (the accounts), to the operational results of financial employment (the functions) (see Figure 2.1). Finance is put to work with a view to generating some form of return or yield; so the question arises, 'How is that return measured and accounted for?'

If the financing of housing could be treated simply as a free-enterprise, commercial activity, questions of accountability and yield would be fairly straightforward. Where market ideology prevails, market forces are relied upon to establish accountability and returns are equated with trading profits and capital appreciation. Firms operating in the unsubsidised, free-enterprise sector of the economy are directly accountable to those proprietors who have a freehold, share or stock-holding interest in the company. Economic theory assumes that, under competitive conditions, the proprietary interests of the freeholder, sole trader, partners or shareholders automatically coincide with those of consumers.[2] Under such arrangements, profit, including capital appreciation of assets, is assumed to be the measure of success.

The notion that commercial competition is conducive to the generation of value-for-money led the Conservative administrations of the 1980s and 1990s to introduce a process of compulsory competitive tendering (CCT), into a range of local government services that included housing. Under CCT, authorities were not allowed to carry out work using their own employees unless the work had first been exposed to competition, and the in-house workforce met centrally determined specified financial objectives each year. In 1997 the in-coming Labour administration modified the process of CCT by introducing what they termed the 'Best Value' concept. This states that councils should not be forced to put their services out to tender, but will be required to obtain what they termed 'Best Value'. The idea of Best Value is that an authority that puts people first will seek to provide services that bear comparison with the best – not just the best that other authorities provide but the best that is on offer from both the private and public sectors.

In introducing the idea of Best Value, the Labour party manifesto stated that '*We reject the dogmatic view that services must be privatised to be of high quality, but equally we see no reason why a service should be delivered directly if other, more efficient means are available.*' This means that the notion of Best Value is an aspect of the government's partnership philosophy which argues that '*to maximise investment in the renewal of our infrastructure, public and private sectors must work together in a more modern and effective partnership.*' (*Chancellor's Statement on the EFSR*, HM Treasury News release 96/98, June 1998). The white paper, *Modern Local Government: In Touch with the People*, (1998) made it clear that Best Value is seen by the government as the key to making councils more efficient. Councils now have a legislative duty to deliver services such as housing to clear standards – covering cost and quality – by the most effective, economic and efficient means available. In addition, Best Value is seen as a vehicle to make councils more accountable to local people and to provide a framework within which to tackle difficult 'cross-cutting' issues that require co-ordinated action by a number of different services or agencies. The notion of Best Value is considered in more detail in Chapter 8 which looks at local government finance.

As we have seen in Chapter 1, housing cannot simply be treated as a commercial activity; because of its social and welfare outputs, criteria other than profit need to be taken into account in assessing returns on monies directed to its production and consumption. For this reason the question, 'How is the return to be measured and accounted for?' usually takes the form, 'How do we know whether we are getting value-for-money?' To answer this question we need to be clear about who constitutes the 'we' and what constitutes the 'value'.

---

2   In market theory this idea of the coincidence of interests is encapsulated by the phrase 'consumer sovereignty'.

We began to address these questions in the previous chapter by arguing that capital and revenue finance is employed to serve the interests of those with some form of proprietary stake in the dwelling or dwellings. We also pointed to the existence of non-proprietary interests in housing investment and consumption. Money spent on the provision and consumption of housing can enhance or damage the interests of a range of people and organisations including occupiers, landlords, neighbours, local and national tax-payers, and future generations. So any attempt to measure value-for-money has to begin by clarifying the issues, 'whose money?' and 'whose value?' By identifying the proprietary and non-proprietary interests involved in the employment of housing finance we automatically confront the question of what it is that constitutes value. In identifying who gains and who loses in the employment of housing finance, we necessarily have to differentiate between use value, investment value (both financial and social) and exchange value (see Figures 1.2 and 2.2).

Figure 2.2: Unpacking the notion of value-for-money

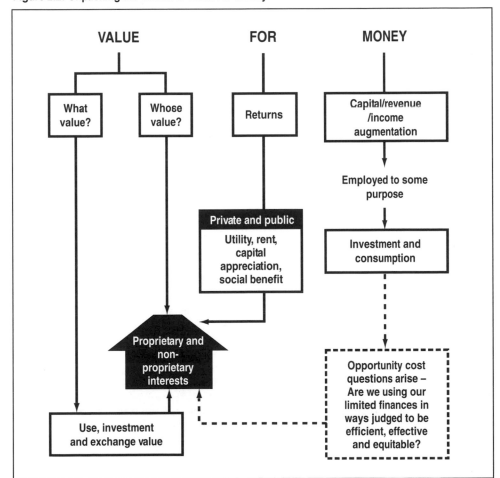

Figure 2.2 illustrates that it is proprietary interests that are at the heart of any analysis of value-for-money (VFM) in housing. That is, any VFM analysis must begin by clarifying who it is that pays the money and who it is that receives the value. Once this is established, the key question then arises, 'Given our concerns about these particular proprietary responsibilities and interests, are we making the optimum use of our limited funds?' In a specific context, this important question might be expressed as, 'Is the company's money being employed to the best advantage of the shareholders?' or perhaps, 'Is the housing association achieving its mission by spending this money in this way?' or, 'Would the local authority be better advised spending its capital receipts repairing its housing stock rather than repaying debt?' Such questions emphasise the importance of what economists refer to as *opportunity costs*. An opportunity cost is a cost conceived of in terms of the best alternative foregone. It is a concept used by economists to underline the fact that financial and other resources are limited and that once used up in one way they are no longer available to be used in some other way.

The notion of *opportunity cost* emphasises the point that achieving value-for-money involves making the 'best' use of what we have. However, because so many interests are associated with housing, the determination of what counts as the best use of financial resources in this field is far from straightforward. One way of dealing with the issue that is advocated by bodies such as the Audit Commission and the Chartered Institute of Housing is to assess the extent to which the proprietary and/or non-proprietary objectives are being achieved in ways that can be judged to be efficient, effective and fair.

Figure 2.3: Efficiency, effectiveness, equity and experience

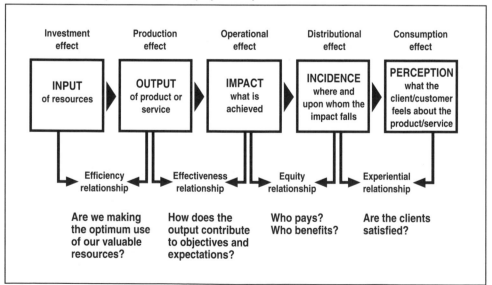

Measuring VFM

Because it is a relative notion, within an organisation, VFM is usually assessed against a set of agreed benchmarks. Publicly announced performance indicators will inevitably influence what employees do and how they do it – what you say you are going to measure is what you tend to get. For this reason, it is important for the organisation to select its indicators with care and to be clear about the relative importance that is attached to each. There is now an expectation that all social landlords who receive public subsidy must establish procedures that set quality and performance standards against which it is possible to measure the extent to which they are delivering their services in a way that delivers VFM. Public sector service providers that have tax raising or precepting powers have a duty to provide *Best Value* (see above).

Efficiency and VFM

Figure 2.3 indicates that efficiency is determined by considering the relationship between inputs and outputs. The idea of efficiency has its roots in engineering where the efficiency of an engine is calculated in terms of how much energy input is needed to generate a unit of power output.[3] Like an engine, an organisation is deemed to be operating below its optimum level of efficiency if either it could produce the same output with fewer resources or if, with the same resources, it could produce a greater output. It must be remembered that in the context of providing goods and services, quality as well as quantity is an aspect of output. This means that a better quality service or product would constitute an increase in output just as much as would a service expansion or an increase in the number of units produced.

Figure 2.4: The concept of 'efficiency'

Ways of viewing efficiency				
Business management	Economic theory		Business accountancy	Public sector planning
Output / Input	Goods and services / Resources	Marginal social benefit / Marginal social cost	Yield / Investment	Social return / Public investment

---

3   Indeed, some contemporary management theorists use the word 're-engineering' when referring to the process of restructuring corporate arrangements with a view to enhancing an organisation's efficiency.

Given its concern with opportunity costs, economic theory equates output with the results of economic activity, such as goods and services, and inputs with the factors of production, the limited resources. An assumption is made that, if measured in terms of market values, any additional employment of resources (the marginal costs), produces a more than proportional increase in goods and services (a marginal benefit), then some improvement in efficiency has taken place. In the public sector the marginal benefit might be seen as some form of social return (e.g. better health or less crime), and the marginal cost is invariably seen as public expenditure.

It is sometimes argued that, in the context of public and welfare services, current debates about the need for greater efficiency has a hidden political dimension. The contention is that as a justifying notion, 'efficiency' is intellectually sympathetic to free-enterprise market attitudes and many of those who are calling for 'more efficiency' in the running of public services are seeking to ally themselves with the core values of the private sector. In this way the notion of efficiency has been used to impose business management and budgetary arrangements on public sector and other welfare agencies. The concerns here are twofold. Firstly, when welfare organisations are reformed with efficiency 'savings' in mind, this occurs in a *managed* rather than a *free-enterprise* market, and when detached from the discipline of real market forces, the application of business management ideas can become procedural and unresponsive. A managed market is insulated from the warning bells of falling profits and other market signals that exist under proper free-enterprise arrangements and, as a result, there is a danger that, swept forward on an unconstrained wave of management ideology, the reforms may go too far. The second concern is that efficiency criteria tend to measure success in a relatively short-term time frame, giving undue weight to current cost savings and under-valuing longer-term effectiveness.

Effectiveness and VFM

Concerns like those mentioned above mean that the achievement of VFM involves more than making an efficient use of scarce resources. Most organisations are concerned to assess the output against its impact as well as against the quantity of resources used up in its production. The effectiveness of an output is assessed in terms of how well it contributes to the key objectives and expectations of those with some interest in the organisation's operations (see Figure 2.3). We can say that, to a large extent, what counts as 'value-for-money' depends on what we are trying to achieve. To make an obvious point, what counts as value-for-money to a commercial developer, will be somewhat different to that which counts as such to a social landlord. (This point is expanded in Chapter 14 – see section 'The distinction between commercial and social development').

Increasingly, effectiveness criteria are prescribed by society in the form of explicit expectations, regulations, laws and externally imposed performance targets. In the case of permanent organisations, like local authorities and housing associations, that utilise durable assets, effective performance has to be put into some time profile. We need to assess the future consequences as well as the current outcomes of putting money into housing.

Effective financial management of any organisation involves *meeting* proprietary plans and prevailing societal expectations (non-proprietary interests), in the near future, *adapting and developing* to accommodate changing needs and demands in the intermediate future, and *surviving* into the distant future. (This idea is developed in Chapter 17).

Equity and VFM

Any consideration of effectiveness is likely to bring to the fore questions of equity. In cases where public money or the public interest is involved there is likely to be a particular concern about the distribution of costs and benefits that result from an employment of resources. Most major decisions made by social housing agencies have to be demonstrably fair as well as effective and efficient.

Economic and financial decisions change situations – they have an impact. As a result, some people are made better off and some people are made worse off. The positive and negative outcomes of such decisions, the marginal social costs and benefits, are distributed differentially to different interest groups. So when we change things by spending money we should be clear about who is going to gain and who is going to pay or in some other way lose out.

Assessing the impact of financial decisions again brings up questions of time and inter-generational justice. Costs and benefits associated with housing decisions often come on stream at different times so it is possible for one generation of tenants or occupiers to enjoy or pay for the spending decisions made at some other time. This can be illustrated by reference to the issue of paying for major repairs. If future repairs are paid for by means of a sinking fund, then the burden will fall on current rent payers. If, on the other hand, they are paid for by a loan taken out at the time of the works, then future loan charges will displace the cost burden onto the rents of future tenants.

Experience and VFM

There is an old Swiss proverb that says, 'Don't ask the doctor, ask the patient'. We should never lose sight of the fact that consumption is the ultimate purpose of all economic activity. What the customer or client feels about the service or product is of prime importance. In the free-enterprise sector of the economy, market forces operate to reward those firms whose output is in demand and commercially punish those whose products are not in demand. In recent years public sector and other welfare organisations have made a conscious effort to monitor user satisfaction and feed the results into their policy-making processes.

The argument here is that if users are unsatisfied there must be doubts about whether the organisation is achieving value-for-money. In recent years a number of sophisticated but easy-to-use computer packages have been developed to help social landlords collect, organise and evaluate tenant priorities.

Economy and VFM

In discussing value-for-money, some commentators make reference to the need for 'economy'. In so doing, they are referring to the act of acquiring resources and are making the point that raw materials and other factors of production should be bought as cheaply as possible so long as they are commensurate with minimum specifications. As economy is concerned with the price of inputs, it is more sensible to treat it as an aspect of 'efficiency' than as a separate category.

Summary

This chapter has defined housing finance as a system of money and credit that operates to enable all types of residential property to be built, acquired, improved, maintained, repaired, renewed, and exchanged. It has categorised the elements of the system in terms of the functions to which the money is put. It has made the point that the application of finance to housing brings to the fore important issues about accountability and value-for-money and it offers a way of thinking and talking about these issues.

The real life system of housing finance is sometimes referred to as *the housing finance regime*. The current regime has evolved over a long period and within this evolution has come a wide range of financial practices and procedures that give the appearance of great complexity. The best way of dealing with this apparent complexity is to hold to models of the overall system that are clear and coherent. In this way, and only in this way, will it be appreciated that, in essence, housing finance is a straightforward subject.

In subsequent chapters the models we have built here will be used as conceptual frameworks to describe and discuss how housing finance currently operates in the different tenures. In so doing, we will find that accountability and value-for-money are constant themes.

CHAPTER 3:
The need-price dilemma and the affordability gap

In Chapter 5 we will consider the wider political, social and economic reasons lying behind the arguments for state involvement in the housing finance system. This chapter will focus on reasons for intervention that are associated with proprietary interests. In particular, we will consider the argument that one key reason for state intervention is to provide appropriate accommodation for those households who are unable to pay for it out of their disposable incomes.

The 'need-price' dilemma

The 'need-price dilemma' arises because everyone requires some minimum standard of residential accommodation in order to enjoy a dignified and healthy life, but for many low-income households access to such accommodation is not possible under free market arrangements. The 'need-price dilemma' can be summarised thus:

> *Dwellings are primary consumption goods but are expensive relative to disposable incomes.*

It is said that housing, along with such things as food, clothing and health care, is no ordinary consumer commodity. It is of primary importance because a home is central to a decent human existence. This idea was clearly expressed by the Royal Institution of Chartered Surveyors in its evidence to the Inquiry into British Housing in the 1980s.

> *'The principal objective of national housing policies should be to ensure that, as far as possible, every household shall be able to occupy a dwelling of a size, type, standard and location suitable to its needs, free from nuisance, harassment or arbitrary eviction.'* (NFHA, 1986, p151).

A broad statement of this kind is no more than a hope statement indicating a general policy direction. As the Inquiry itself pointed out, it raises more questions than it answers (NFHA, 1985, p7). In particular, it raises the following fundamental questions.

- What is housing need?
- What is an affordable rent or price?
- Are rent structures equitable?
- To what extent can market forces be relied upon to achieve society's housing objectives?

- If market forces fail to achieve the objective of a decent home for everyone at a price they can afford, what should the state do about it?

The first four questions will be considered in this chapter. The last question provides a focus for much of the rest of the book.

What is housing need?

Although in the second half of the nineteenth century there was a good deal of official and parliamentary concern shown about the living conditions of the poorer working classes, there was no meaningful intervention in the housing market until the outbreak of war in 1914. Even then, the rent control measures that were introduced in 1915 were seen as a temporary wartime expediency rather than a fundamental policy shift towards a social service approach to housing provision.

After 1919, the Liberal Party's election campaign to build 'homes fit for heroes', opened up the debate about whether market forces alone could be relied upon to meet the housing objectives of post-war society. Once the idea of housing as a social service had been mooted, it brought to the fore the question of what distinguishes the social policy concept of *need* from the market economic concept of *housing demand*.[1] The twentieth and now the twenty-first century concept of *housing need* has gradually emerged as a result of this questioning. By the end of the First World War the idea was established that the basic housing requirements of the 'working classes' were, in some degree, a concern of central government and should not be left to the vagaries of market forces and the charitable instincts of individual benefactors and parish officials. By requiring all local authorities to prepare plans to meet 'local housing needs', the Town and Country Planning Act 1919 set in place a statutory framework that would allow the provision of basic housing to be treated as a social service.

Today, the primary responsibility for assessing housing needs still resides with the local authority (under section 8 of the Housing Act 1985). As we will see later in the book, each local authority is currently required to demonstrate patterns of housing need within its area in order to support and justify its housing investment programme and any bids for resources to other funding agencies. It is expected to act as an 'enabler' that identifies needs and establishes plans to close any gap in provision. This no longer means that the authority necessarily has to provide housing and housing-related services itself. Local housing associations and other registered social landlords are expected to work with the local authority to help it define its enabling role and to produce solutions to any local needs problem.

The notion of *housing need* can apply to an individual household or to a geographical area.

---

1   Jonathan Bradshaw has pointed out (McLachlan, 1972), that the concept of social need is inherent in the idea of social service. Indeed, the history of the social services is, in large part, the story of how society came to recognise the existence of social needs and then organise itself to meet them.

Defining the needs of a household

The efficient, effective and equitable provision of any social service is dependent upon an understanding of what constitutes the needs of those who qualify to receive it. '*Social need*' is a contested concept insofar as it can mean somewhat different things in different contexts. Jonathan Bradshaw has usefully distinguished between four contrasting categories of social need as used by administrators, politicians and researchers (McLachlan, 1972).

1. *Normative need* is what some expert or authority defines as need in a given situation. It specifies some acceptable norm of provision to which everyone should have access, so that if an individual's or group's consumption falls short of this standard they become identified as being in need. This category is sometimes referred to as 'postulated need' because it defines the taken-for-granted minimum standard that the authority or expert declares should be available to all.

    Normative definitions underline the fact that the issue of needs assessment is really an aspect of society's desire to establish minimum standards. Such definitions are specific to time and place and are tied to the values and attitudes of those who set the norms. These norms might be postulated by an Act of Parliament, by a local authority, a management committee, an administrator, a professional body, a research group, or some other agency claiming authority or expertise. Building regulations, Parker Morris space standards, fitness standards, the current Decent Homes Standard, and point assessment systems all provide housing norm reference points for assessing housing need.

2. *Felt need* refers to an individual's own assessment of their requirements. This category of need is assessed by survey techniques involving questionnaires and interviews. In the private housing sector, for example, the volume builders sometimes employ market researchers to carry out consumer preference surveys to find out what type or style of housing is likely to sell well in a particular area. In the social housing sectors, felt need surveys have been employed to guide those producing design briefs for special needs housing such as sheltered schemes for the elderly. Many social landlords use the returns of tenant satisfaction surveys to provide service performance measures that help to check whether the agency is giving value-for-money (refer to the notion of a *consumption effect* in Figure 2.3).

    The highly subjective nature of felt need means that although it can be used to inform both the strategic planning and the day-to-day operational decisions of social landlords, it cannot be used to establish allocation eligibility criteria.

3. *Expressed need* is manifested when a felt need is acted upon. The way the majority of us express our felt needs most of the time is by purchasing goods and services. Effective demand is thus a form of expressed need: it is a felt

need, or a 'want', expressed in a market by spending money. In the social rented sectors, where a limited supply of dwellings and tenancies are allocated rather than sold, would-be occupiers express their felt housing needs by filling in application forms and registering their names on waiting lists and in an increasing number of cases expressing their views through choice-based lettings systems.

4. *Comparative need* is defined in terms of the characteristics of those who are already in receipt of the service. If other people in similar circumstances and with the same need characteristics are not in receipt of the service then they are defined as being in comparative need. This measure underlines the requirement for open and even-handed treatment in the distribution of services to applicants. That is, a housing agency should establish value-for-money indicators that assess the distributional effects of service provision (refer to Figure 2.3).

Defining the needs of a geographical area

A local housing needs assessment should be the starting point for devising a housing strategy. Comprehensive and up-to-date information on the nature and scale of current and future housing needs across all tenures is necessary as a basis for identifying priorities, evaluating options, developing programmes, and targeting investment.

The cheapest and easiest way of assessing the social housing needs of an area is to refer to the registers of *expressed need*. Although local waiting lists offer a readily accessible source of information, they provide an inadequate measure of need for a number of reasons. They are seldom up-to-date because when applicants move to some other district or solve their housing problems through the offices of other agencies, they may not bother to withdraw their applications. On the other hand, lists will fail to recognise the needs of those who are excluded from registering because they do not possess the appropriate qualifying characteristics. They fail to register those who are judged to be in need by some normative or comparative standard but who nevertheless do not feel in need. They also fail to account for those who feel in need of re-housing but who do not bother, or who mistakenly believe that they do not qualify to register.

As well as being out-of-date and incomplete, waiting lists are time-specific. Because they only register current expressions of need they cannot be used to assess future requirements. In assessing the future needs for social rented housing we have to employ a more dynamic methodology that allows us to project trends in household formation, tenure moves and private sector provision so that some crude figure for social demand can be estimated. This estimate can then be compared with current supply projections, planned new social output plus expected relets, to determine whether there is likely to be a crude surplus or deficit for the period under review. A more refined estimate of future need can then be sought by adjusting this crude residual to take account of such factors as stock condition and location, household fit, and affordability.[2]

A needs assessment typically involves:

- the collation and analysis of existing internal and external data on housing needs;
- a household survey to gather data on socio-economic circumstances and both normative and felt measures of need;
- an analysis of the local housing market and, in particular, its capacity to provide accommodation for private renting and owner-occupation.

This information is then used to produce:

- a household/stock balance;
- a measure of stock/needs mismatches (e.g. in terms of suitability, condition, and location);
- an assessment of the affordability of available accommodation;
- an assessment of the shortfall between market provision and overall need over the period covered by the strategy.

The *comparative concept* can be applied to the assessment of the needs of geographical areas. Part of the government's annual allocation of public funds to housing is distributed into the regions on the basis of an assessment of comparative local needs. The central authorities have a good deal of political discretion over which region gets what and, until recently, their allocation decisions have been strongly informed by indices of housing need that aim to ensure that limited resources are distributed in a way that is felt to be objectively fair. In this way, an element of funding has been distributed to the local authority regions by procedures that make reference to indices of need.[3] The central authorities seek to measure and weigh the need for local housing expenditure by reference to these indices as well as to broader regional investment strategies. The indices include statistical series and survey data relating to local house conditions and demographic characteristics that are deemed to reflect housing need. In recent years such formulaic mechanisms for distribution have become less influential.

---

2   A review and critique of needs assessment methods can be found in Whitehead, C. and Kleinman, M.A., *Review of Housing Needs Assessment*, The Housing Corporation, 1992. Guidance and examples of good practice are also given in the CIH *Good Practice Briefing, Issue 7*, April 1997. See also National Housing Federation, *Reinvestment Strategies: A Good Practice Guide*, 1997, Chapter 3.

3   In England, for example, The Generalised Needs Index (GNI) has been used until recently to distribute grants and permissions to borrow to local authorities. Parallel allocations have been distributed to the regional offices of the Housing Corporation by referencing the Housing Needs Index (HNI). For a discussion of current policy thinking see the ODPM, *Lessons from the Past, Challenges for the Future of Housing Policy: An Evaluation of English Housing Policy 1975-2000, Theme 1: Supply, Need and Access*, February 2005.

As we will see later in the book, the government has shifted the emphasis towards more flexible 'strategic' approaches to allocating resources and spending approvals.

Contemporary needs assessment exercises are also expected to take account of how housing investment will impact on the government's efficiency and social inclusion agendas.

The 'affordability' debate

Although the pricing question has long been at the forefront of the housing policy debate, there is no universally accepted definition of *affordability*. Without such a definition it is not possible to produce any officially accepted statistics measuring the number of households living in *unaffordable* housing.

The question of affordability arises from the fact that, for most people, good quality housing is expensive relative to their incomes.[4] Affordability only becomes an issue when the state normatively defines some minimum level of housing provision as a *merit need*. If the state was prepared to allow the poor to live in mean, insanitary and over-crowded hovels, the affordability question would not arise.

The problem of defining affordability

There are three broad ways of analysing affordability. These are: 1. the ratio approach, 2. the benchmark approach, and 3. the residual approach.

The ratio approach considers the percentage of income that is expended on housing. This was an established way of thinking about affordability by the end of the nineteenth century. At that time people often quoted a rule of thumb that said *one week's wages equals one month's rent*. In this way there was a popular belief that to be affordable, rents should not be more than 25 per cent of a household's income.

In the late nineteenth century, Hermann Schwarbe pointed to a significant statistical relationship between the income growth of households and their housing-related outgoings. Schwarbe was the Director of the Berlin Statistical Bureau and in that capacity brought together various statistical series that illustrated that the burden of housing expenditure was proportionally heavier for the poor than it was for the rich. The point he made was that, although the rich

---

4   The production of housing involves the use of land, a wide range of materials and much craft and professional expertise. For these reasons most dwellings cannot be regarded as being expensive *per se*. That is, although they are expensive relative to income, they are not expensive relative to the resources that get used up in their design, manufacture, assembly, marketing and exchange.

tended to spend more on their housing in *absolute* terms, the poor tended to spend more *relative* to their total disposable incomes. In 1867 he published his findings and presented them in a form that has become known as Schwarbe's Law of Rent. The 'law' states that: *a household's proportion of disposable income devoted to housing falls as total disposable income rises.*[5]

Schwarbe's Law points to a policy approach to the question of affordability that seeks to determine an 'appropriate' income-to-rent ratio. Taking this approach, Schwarbe himself argued that, in principle, no household should be expected to pay more than 20 per cent of their net disposable income on occupation costs.

Until recently the income-to-rent ratio approach dominated the debate about what constitutes an affordable rent for social housing. In particular, the National Housing Federation has commented at different times in terms of such a ratio (see below).

The benchmark approach considers what is affordable by reference to some fixed level of expenditure that is assumed to be reasonable.[6] Much of the twentieth century debate has focused on the benchmark idea. The 1919 Act required council house rents to be comparable with controlled rents in the private sector and, since that time, market theorists have consistently argued that the rents charged for social housing should be related to, albeit less than, what the market would charge. Welfare theorists, on the other hand, have tended to look to some measure of subsistence income as a benchmark guide to affordable rent levels, by arguing that rents should be within the reach of those on benefit or those in low-paid employment.

The residual approach takes into account that in recent years some people have argued that both the ratio and the benchmark approaches are inadequate and that a more appropriate approach would be to consider residual income. The argument here is that affordability is better assessed by reference to the financial resources that remain available to a household once the rent and other housing costs have been met. They argue the need to consider the overall financial predicament of the household so that the following key question can be posed: *'Is the residual income left over after meeting housing outgoings adequate to cover the other necessities of living?'*

Defining affordability for a particular household

It should be recognised that, when applied to a specific household, each of the approaches mentioned above has limitations as an instrument of needs analysis. A low ratio may be the result of living in poor standard housing. Similarly, a

---

5   In economic theory this situation would represent an income elasticity of housing demand of less than one.

6   The notion of a 'benchmark' is taken from surveying and refers to a fixed reference point on a stone or post against which other elevations can be measured.

---

benchmark or residual measure will tell us little or nothing about the actual living conditions of those who are above the mark or seeking to survive on the residual. As well as price and income, issues of 'quality' need to be considered. In this context, quality may include more than the physical condition of the dwelling. It could include such factors as overcrowding, security of tenure, accessibility to neighbourhood facilities, and travel-to-work costs.

In any particular case, the determination of what should count as an affordable payment will turn on our view of what is reasonable bearing in mind the household's circumstances and financial resources. Although the general notion of *affordability* is easy enough to grasp, over the years there has been much discussion and little agreement about how to define precisely what should count as affordable for a particular household at a particular point in their housing career.

Whether they are defining affordability by reference to a ratio, a benchmark, or a residual, there is little consensus amongst academic and practitioner commentators about what costs of occupation should be included in the calculation. Any workable definition will involve making judgements about whether or not to include such items as heating, maintenance, depreciation, insurance, etc. Affordability calculations could, but seldom do, take account of the fact that occupation costs interact. For example, money spent servicing a loan, or in higher rental charges, taken out or imposed to improve the dwelling's energy efficiency, will add to direct housing costs, but will enhance the property's value and reduce fuel bills. Similarly, over a given period, the higher rental charges of a centrally located dwelling may be more than offset by travel cost savings. It is interesting that travel-to-work costs are usually seen as significant in housing location theory but are usually excluded from affordability studies.

Because a particular household's needs can vary over time and needs vary as between households, an effective affordability policy must establish not one, but a range of normative standards. Such a policy will seek to give every household access to housing appropriate to its needs at a price that does not impose an unreasonable burden on its disposable income. Personal and official attitudes to affordability are, to some extent tenure-dependent.

Owner-occupation and affordability

A crude house price-to-earnings ratio is sometimes used as a general measure of affordability in this sector. Reference to such a measure helps to emphasise the cyclical nature of house price inflation and shows that the point at which the household gained access to the tenure in part determines the costs of home-ownership. The point needs to be made, however, that because most owners acquire their first homes by taking out a variable interest mortgage loan, interest rates, as well as purchase prices, affect the month-by-month costs of occupation. Indeed, to make meaningful cross-tenure or inter-household comparisons, we need to conceive of the costs of owner-occupation not so much in terms of the purchase price but rather in terms of the week-by-week outgoings that the household has to pay in order to maintain its occupancy. In addition to loan interest payments these outgoings will include building insurance premiums. The costs of owner-occupation might also be considered to include the opportunity costs of any capital invested in the property and some actual or notional annual sum that is assumed to be set aside for repairs and maintenance.

Interest rate fluctuations mean that in the medium term, affordability tends to be a more unpredictable and volatile factor for owners than it does for renters. In the last quarter of 1993, for example, the TSB Affordability Index indicated that a typical first-time buyer would need to spend 26 per cent of net income on mortgage payments compared with 67 per cent in the first quarter of 1990. It should be noted that a relatively small change in mortgage interest rates could have a significant *real income effect* for the household. This means that for people with modest incomes and relatively large mortgages, even a change in interest rates of less than one per cent will make a noticeable difference to the affordability of their mortgages.

When people first enter owner-occupation there is often an expectation that they will pay more in mortgage and other housing-related outgoings than they would to rent an equivalent unit of accommodation. This reflects the fact that an owner household has an investment, as well as a consumption interest in the property they occupy. People may also be willing to pay more for home-ownership in order to avoid certain perceived consumption disadvantages associated with the imposition of tenancy agreement restrictions.

Renting in general and affordability

Although in more recent times both ministers and the various funding bodies have staunchly refused to give a clear definition of an affordable rent, in 1988 the then Minister of Housing, William Waldegrave set out broad criteria relating to a somewhat imprecise benchmark that later became enshrined in the Tenants' Guarantee for affordable rents. He said that rents should be *'set and maintained at levels within the reach of those in lower paid employment'* (Cope, 1990, p106). As with changes in mortgage interest rates for the owner-occupier, changes in rent will have a *real income effect* on the household. It is this *real income effect* that needs to be considered when determining whether or not the rent increase is affordable.

Local authority renting and affordability

Although local councils have some discretion when setting rents, this has become circumscribed by the introduction in England of the government's policy of rent restructuring and convergence (see Chapter 12). The current financial regime is founded on the Local Government and Housing Act 1989 and this legislation makes no direct reference to the question of affordability.[7] However, the consultation paper that preceded the act, *A New Financial Regime for Local Authority Housing in England and Wales* (1988), identified the following objectives of the regime: (a) to strike a fair balance between the interests of tenants and charge payers and (b) to be fair as between tenants in different areas. To accommodate charge payer interests, the legislation imposed a duty on local authorities broadly to structure their rents in a way that both takes account of local market rent levels and also the capital values of the properties, calculated with reference to right to buy prices. Such considerations had the intention of raising average rents while still keeping them at levels that could be regarded as affordable.

> *'Rents generally should not exceed levels within the reach of people in low pay employment, and in practice they will frequently be below market levels. They should, however, be set by reference to these two parameters: what people can pay and what the property is worth, rather than by reference to historic cost accounting figures.'* (DoE Consultation Paper, 1988).

With the introduction of rent restructuring in England, these objectives have become somewhat academic.

Other social renting and affordability

Until recently, each housing association enjoyed a degree of freedom to develop its own rental policy, establishing the level of rent that should be charged and how that rent should be levied across its stock.[8] This freedom is now severely inhibited by the government's convergence policy (rent restructuring) that imposes a formulaic approach to setting rents and rent increases. This is discussed more fully in Chapter 15.

The Housing Corporation, in England, still expects the rent to be set and maintained at a level within the reach of those in low-paid employment. Landlords should not discriminate in their rent-setting between those who are eligible for housing benefit and others.

Private renting and affordability

In England and Wales, the commonest forms of renting arrangements for private houses and flats are assured and shorthold tenancies and these are explained and discussed more fully in Chapter 18. In the private sector rents are negotiated and set as part of a contractual agreement. Under these arrangements rent levels are really a matter of 'comparability' rather than 'affordability'. The landlord can

---

7   Although Section 162 refers to the notion of 'proportionality' which is an expression denoting an intention that local authority rents should bear a relationship to assured tenancy rents in the other rented sectors.

8   Although it was required to do so within a complex framework of guidance.

charge a full market rent for an assured or a shorthold tenancy. The timing of any rent increase is normally determined by the nature of the contract, and disputes over rent increases can be referred to a rent assessment committee who will decide what rent the landlord could reasonably expect for the property if he was letting it on the open market under a new tenancy on the same terms.

In this sector questions of affordability are addressed entirely by the housing benefit scheme that provides means-tested *rent allowances* to private tenants on low incomes (see Chapters 18 and 19 for more details).

Affordability and equity

The issue of affordability highlights the question of equity within the housing system. If regional rent variations are more pronounced than regional income variations an unregulated housing system may create locational horizontal inequities. That is, it may create different financial outcomes to people on similar incomes resulting from renting similar properties but in different parts of the country. Insofar as people on relatively lower earnings commit a higher proportion of their disposable incomes to housing expenses than people on relatively higher earnings, vertical inequities may exist. That is, there may be a lack of fairness as between different income groups. The fact that different tenures are taxed and subsidised in different ways can also lead to vertical inequities. *Horizontal equity* involves the similar treatment of people in similar circumstances. *Vertical equity* involves treating people in different circumstances differently in order to reduce the negative consequences that stem from these differences.

The social housing system attempts to address the question of locational horizontal equity through the operation of needs indices (see earlier in this chapter), that guide the distribution of finite national funds into local authority and housing association housing projects in accordance with a formulaic assessment of differentiated normative need. These days central funds are increasingly being distributed by referencing strategic outcomes, relating to regional economic and social policies, rather than to need calculations.

The question of vertical inequity is constantly discussed by social policy theorists and is an issue that has led to calls for the system of housing finance to be reformed in line with the principles of tenure neutrality and proportionality.

Affordability and the economy

There is some evidence that higher rents charged by local authorities and other social landlords damage the economy by increasing inflation and public spending. Rent rises will lead to losses for the public purse when tenants claim back a proportion of such increases through housing benefit. It should also be noted that in recent years rents have been used in calculating the retail price index which is then, in turn, used to increase government payments for pensions, certain social security benefits, index-linked gilts, and National Savings. It is also probable that rent inflation has fed into the wider economy by depressing demand for consumer purchases thereby adding both to unemployment and a fall in tax revenues.[9]

The recognition of housing market failure

If unfettered free-enterprise market arrangements were seen to achieve the housing policy objectives pointed to at the start of this chapter, there would be no calls for government intervention in the housing finance system. In large part, it is the failure of market forces to deliver these objectives that has brought about state involvement in this field. This 'failure' of the market has been recognised by historians, market theorists, and social policy analysts.

The historian's view of housing market failure. In the nineteenth century, particularly in times of trade recession and falling wages, many tenants would take in lodgers to help cover the rent charges. In other cases, the market reacted to low wage levels by depressing rents, which in turn, reduced the normal profits received by landlords. Under such conditions many landlords protected their investment returns by cutting back on repairs and maintenance. In this way, the unregulated market adjusted to low incomes by creating overcrowded, poor quality accommodation. Eventually these conditions were judged to be unacceptable and the state intervened to establish minimum standards for both existing and newly-built dwellings.

The economist's view of housing market failure. Economists point out that for markets to work efficiently there must be a high degree of competition. Competition depends on the existence of large numbers of producers and consumers so that no group of market participants can influence the market price through their actions. Competition also depends on the participants being knowledgeable about the nature of the product and the workings of the market. Furthermore, if for some reason it is difficult for new producers to set up in the market or for consumers to compare prices, this will also have the effect of diminishing competition. In a sense everything in the market-place is competing with everything else. However, the more alike two products are, the stronger will be their competitive relationship. On the supermarket shelf, a bar of chocolate is in a competitive relationship with a packet of sweets, but it has a much stronger competitive relationship with a similarly sized bar of chocolate produced by a rival chocolate manufacturer. We might say that it has a *perfectly competitive relationship* with an identical bar in identical wrappings, produced by the same chocolate company and stacked right alongside it. In other words, the more

---

9   This argument is based on the Joseph Rowntree Foundation report, *The Impact of Higher Rents*, Housing Research 109, 1994. The Rowntree research indicated that a 10 per cent rise in social rents would reduce GDP by up to 0.2 per cent and increase unemployment by more than 25,000. It would also raise retail prices 0.3 per cent and cost the Treasury around £100 million a year.

compact and coherent the market is and the less the products can be differentiated from each other, the stronger will be the degree of competition.

Many of these characteristics of competition only have a weak presence in the housing system.

Professional bodies, trade unions, employers' organisations, large and influential construction companies, multinational development companies, planning authorities, etc., all exercise a degree of monopoly power or influence and in so doing inhibit competition.

For all sorts of reasons it is difficult for participants in the housing system to possess complete knowledge of the product and its market. Housing is technically complex. For example, recognition of building defects or awareness of any future planning proposals likely to affect the property, or the existence of legal constraints on the way in which the property can be used, all require a degree of skill and information that most buyers and sellers do not possess. Furthermore, it takes time and effort to get a feel for a particular local housing market. In these various ways the market participants have an *imperfect knowledge* both of the product and its market and this clearly inhibits competition. It is because of this lack of knowledge that many people employ exchange professionals such as surveyors, lawyers and estate agents to help them with their buying and selling arrangements. We might say that the very existence of these exchange professionals is witness to the imperfectly competitive nature of the housing market.

The market's competitiveness is also weakened by the fact that house building is a highly capital intensive activity that also requires very specific skills of a craft, technical and professional nature. These factors act as barriers that make it difficult for new suppliers to enter the market to compete.

Competition is also inhibited by the fact that dwelling units are immobile and spatially separated. Because buildings are geographically fixed, a surplus in one area cannot be used to alleviate a shortage in some other area.

Finally, competition is inhibited by the way in which the housing system is fragmented in terms of tenure and dwelling type. Two geographically close and identically designed dwellings in similar states of repair will nevertheless have a weak competitive relationship with each other if they are being marketed under different tenure arrangements. Similarly, two very different types of dwelling in the same area and tenure sector are not likely to be in serious competition with each other. A surplus of large detached family houses in an area cannot be readily used to alleviate a shortage of bed-sits for students in the same district.

For all these reasons, economists argue that the housing market is *imperfectly competitive* and thus it cannot be relied upon to work automatically in the interests of consumers.

In addition to the housing market's technical failure to approximate to the conditions of *perfect competition*, it can be said to fail to meet society's housing objectives in another important respect. Namely, it has too restrictive a view of what counts as 'housing need'.

The social policy analyst's view of housing market failure. Social theorists argue that market arrangements fail to take proper account of the housing needs of low-income and other vulnerable households. Market theory equates need with the notion of *effective demand*. In so doing, it is said to recognise only those needs that are expressed in the market-place. *Effective demand* is defined as a want or need backed by cash. This means that under market arrangements needs can only be made 'effective' by purchasing the required goods or services from a market provider at a price set by the forces of supply and demand. Under such arrangements those without sufficient purchasing power are unable to make their wants and needs effective. The much-lauded freedom of choice denoted by the market notion of *consumer sovereignty* is restricted to those with sufficient income to pay the market price. Thus, in a free market economy everybody is free to sleep under a railway arch but only those with sufficient money can purchase a warm, dry room for the night.

Over time, to any one household, a particular type of housing can become more-or-less affordable. This will depend on *comparative* changes between the price of occupation of the dwelling in question (e.g. rent or mortgage repayment), and the disposable income of the household in question. Social analysts point out that we can only rely on the operation of market forces to accommodate the interests of low-income households if it can be demonstrated that the comparative price and income changes are such that good quality housing is becoming more rather than less affordable to this group.

Some market apologists argue that the market will provide for low-income groups through a process of *filtering*. This argument says that over time dwellings tend to decline in value and thus become accessible to people on lower incomes. Social analysts, however, point out that the effectiveness of 'trading up' or *filtering* as a means of raising housing standards hinges on the speed of value-decline relative to quality-decline.

> *'If the value of the standing stock depreciates so rapidly that even low-income households can afford units which are still above the quality standards of social adequacy, the private market is a satisfactory instrument of public policy.'* (Lowry, 1960, p364).

Because a coherent definition of social need has to be a prerequisite to the establishment of a social service, twentieth century policy makers have sought to identify broader definitions of housing need than that provided by the concept of *effective demand*. In subsequent chapters we will see that these normative definitions have tended to be tied to tenures and are constantly modified over time.

Summary

In this chapter we have made the point that housing policy seeks to resolve the dilemma that, although some minimum standard of accommodation is a necessity for all, housing is expensive relative to the disposable incomes of certain households. We have argued that both historical experience and economic theory indicate that an unregulated housing market would fail to achieve society's objective of providing all households with a decent and affordable home.

In the next chapter we will look at how subsidy arrangements have sought to bridge the gap between people's housing needs and their abilities to pay. In subsequent chapters we will make the point that housing subsidies and other interventionist measures are a response, not only to the market's failure to support the consumption interests of low-income households, but also its failure to support the broader non-proprietary interests that are vested in housing. In Chapter 5 we will draw particular attention to the question of public expenditure control and its effects on housing finance.

Further reading

Brown, T. and Passmore, J., (1998), *Housing and Anti-Poverty Strategies*, CIH/Joseph Rowntree Foundation: Coventry.

Freeman, A., Holmans, A. and Whitehead, C., (1999), *Evaluating Housing Affordability – Policy Options and New Directions*, LGA for CIH, LGA, NHF: London.

CHAPTER 4:
Rent-setting principles and the concept of subsidy

In the context of rent-setting policy, the 'need-price dilemma' (Chapter 3), manifests itself as a concern to balance affordability with sufficiency. In other words, the problem facing the social landlord is to set a rent that is sufficiently high to cover the costs of provision yet low enough to be affordable by those deemed to be in housing need.

Figure 4.1: Principles of rent-setting

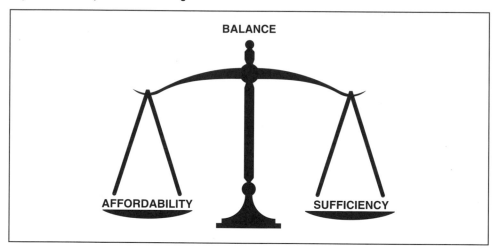

Rental sufficiency

Rent is a stipulated sum paid periodically by a tenant to a landlord in return for specified occupancy rights associated with the use and enjoyment of land or landed property. The rent may also pay for specified services provided by the landlord. From the tenant's point of view the rent is a *price* that is paid in order to acquire these rights of occupancy and associated services. From the landlord's point of view the rent is an *income* received in return for making these rights available and providing the services. Whereas the question confronting the tenant is, 'Given my income can I afford this rent?', the landlord has to consider the question, 'Given my outgoings is this rent sufficient?'

In any particular case, what will count as a sufficient rent will depend in large part on the landlord's motives for being in business. A social landlord, such as a local authority, a housing association or a charitable housing trust, may consciously seek to set a rent that is less than would be charged for the same property by a profit-seeking commercial landlord. Any particular social housing rent level will also be affected by the existence or otherwise of supply-side grants and subsidies. This of course means that, if existing financial support is reduced or withdrawn, this will automatically put an upward pressure on rents.

The total sufficiency rent

The following constitutes a list of items that a landlord conceivably could, although in practice may not, regard as legitimate financial costs to be covered by the rent charge.

- Loan service charges (LSC).
  These are paid on loans taken out to acquire, construct, improve or repair the dwelling. They would include an element to cover the repayment of the principal and an element to cover interest charges. They could include an element for mortgage insurance cover.

- Major repairs (MR).
  Major repairs might be paid for by taking out additional loans, in which case the costs will be added to LSC. An alternative approach is for an element of rent to be paid into a sinking fund and invested so that over time it accumulates into a balance that can be used to pay for or reduce (i.e. 'sink') the costs of such works. Calculated over the life of the dwelling, sinking funds are likely to be more cost-effective than loans. The choice between sinking funds or loans brings up questions of equity as well as financial efficiency as sinking fund charges will increase the rents of current occupiers while future loans will have to be serviced out of future rents.

- Other reserves (R).
  In addition to accumulating funds for future major repairs, an organisation may wish to set aside part of its income flow for other purposes. Contingency reserves may be established to cover any unexpected future expenses. Special reserve accounts may be set up to accumulate funds to cover future taxation liabilities. Reserve accounts may be set up to accumulate future investment capital. Investment reserves may distinguish between *replacement capital,* needed to cover the depreciation in the value of fixed assets due to wear and tear or obsolescence, and *expansion capital*, needed to increase or improve, rather than repair, the stock.

- Management (Mgmt).
  The rent might be expected to pay for the wages and associated administrative costs of running the range of housing functions and services offered by the agency.

- Maintenance (Mtnc).
  As defined by BS 3811, maintenance comprises all of the technical and associated administrative actions intended to retain a building and its facilities in a state that will allow it to perform its required functions.[1]

- Asset returns (AR).
  As items of fixed capital formation, dwellings have locked into them an investment value. The landlords may expect a financial return on this investment representing the *opportunity cost* of their money capital. In other words, if a dwelling is worth, say, £80,000, the landlord agency may require the rental income to generate a financial yield on that sum just as they would if they had invested it on the stock market or in some other commercial venture.

- Building insurance (BI).
  Some risks are insurable and some are not. Insurable risks are those that are associated with probabilities and include such misfortunes as fire, theft, vandalism and premature component failure. Non-insurable risks are associated with unquantifiable uncertainties such as changed market conditions, fluctuating interest rates, new restrictive legislation, and 'acts of God'.

- Profit (P).
  In a commercial business, profit represents the reward accruing to the successful entrepreneur and is held to be the motivating factor behind commercial, non-insurable, risk-taking. This means that in the case of the commercial landlord, some measure of profit is regarded as a normal cost of production and, as such, has to be provided for by the rental income.

- Bad debts (BD).
  In a housing context, the bulk of bad debts are in the form of rent arrears. If income from some properties is not being received then the consequential fall in the flow of income may have to be recovered in the form of higher rents in general. The profile of rent arrears over a period is often used as a performance indicator on the assumption that a well managed housing agency will have in place procedures for maintaining its flow of rental income.

- Voids (V).
  When a dwelling is unoccupied it is not generating an income and thus the costs of managing and maintaining the void stock have to be covered by other sources of income including the rents levied on other properties. At any one time it is inevitable that part of the stock will be unoccupied to allow post-occupancy surveys and checks, major repairs and so on. It might also be

---

[1] Maintenance work is usually classified as 'reactive' and 'planned'. Reactive maintenance is characterised by low value and high volume with an emphasis being placed on relatively fast response times. Planned maintenance can be divided into 'condition-dependent', prompted by condition surveys, and 'condition-independent', prompted by schedules based on lifecycle data.

argued that a certain level of voids has to be maintained if new tenants are to be offered a degree of choice in the allocation of their homes. As with rent arrears, the level of voids is usually looked to as a performance indicator on the assumption that a well managed agency will not have an unnecessarily high number of empty properties at any one time.

- Service charges (SC).
  These are charges that are made for services to tenants that are in excess of normal housing management functions for such activities as caretaking, landscape and garden maintenance, warden services, etc. Strictly speaking, service charges are additions to, rather than part of, the rent. However, from the tenants' point of view they are experienced as part of the rent and we will, therefore, include them in the full sufficiency rent formula. The Housing Corporation's concept of *housing plus* (1995), points to a growing awareness that many social housing tenants need a wide range of services to support their tenancies and in the future the social landlord's core functions may be more widely viewed than they are at present.

A completely unsubsidised *total sufficiency rent* (TSR), would need to cover all of the above, viz:

$$TSR = LSC + MR + R + Mgmt + Mtnc + AR + BI + P + BD + V + SC$$

In any real life situation, the actual rent charged may be less than the TSR because of the receipt of subsidies. Actual rents will also deviate from the TSR because particular landlords may set their rents in accordance with principles that do not require them to pursue a policy of total rent sufficiency.

Rent-setting principles provide the rationale for rental policies. Different tenures tend to look to different principles when determining rents, and within a particular tenure, the underlying logical principles guiding rent-setting can change over time. At any one time in any particular tenure, rents can be set with reference to one or more of the logical principles discussed below.

Rent-setting principles

Historically rents have been set on a variety of bases, of which the most common have been:

- capital value related;
- points based; or
- formula based.

Capital value systems provide a clear link with location and other market factors. This may be seen as an advantage because tenants often put a high value on location. However, if this is the only basis for determining rent, it might produce excessive variability where market values vary widely. *Points systems* are more complex and can accommodate more refinements that may allow the landlord to take on board a wider range of tenant preferences. However, they may fail to provide sufficient regard to market values, unless these are consciously included in the weighting. Points systems can also be difficult and costly to administer. Rent differentials can be more easily controlled with *formula based systems*. However, formulaic approaches tend to be rather inflexible and run the danger of incorporating excessive subjectivity. On their own, they may also fail to pay due regard to market values, which social landlords are now obliged to take into account.

The following constitute a more detailed set of contrasting rent-setting principles that could be used to guide the pricing policies of providers of rented accommodation. They are each grounded in a different socio-economic logic.

1. *Marginal cost pricing* is the principle that stipulates that rents should be closely related to the costs of production at the margin in order to promote the efficient use of scarce resources. This means that if we produce an extra (i.e. marginal) unit of housing output we should charge a price that covers the extra (i.e. marginal) costs of producing it.

   It is the price that economic theory says will be charged in an unregulated, perfectly competitive market.[2] The marginal cost price is thus the *perfectly competitive economic price*. The theoretical argument runs as follows. We should charge rents that cover the costs of production including 'normal' (i.e. competitive) profit.[3] If consumers are not prepared to pay this price this indicates a lack of demand and we should not waste resources in producing goods and services that are not in demand.

   Of course, in reality, a lack of effective demand may be due to a lack of disposable income rather than to people not wanting, needing, or valuing the accommodation. For this reason, if marginal cost pricing is used as the guiding principle for setting rents in the social housing sectors, it may have to be accompanied by some form of income augmentation in order to make such rents affordable.[4]

---

2   See Chapter 3 for a discussion on the conditions of perfect competition.
3   Normal profit is that level of profit that is just sufficient to persuade the supplier of a good or service to stay in the competitive market. It is treated as one of the costs of production, along with wages, interest payments, and the costs of raw materials, etc. Profits above this level are called 'excess'. In a perfectly competitive market excess profits cannot be maintained in the long-run. This is because the opportunity to receive excess profits will encourage competitors to increase their outputs and this, in turn, will force prices back down to a point where, once again, only normal profits are made.
4   Indeed this was the case in 1972 when the government extended the concept of 'fair rents' to the residential sector. Fair rents were set by a rent officer who sought to establish what the rent would be if the conditions of perfect competition existed (i.e. no shortages). It was recognised that such market-related rents would not be affordable by all those in housing need and therefore a parallel system of rent rebates and allowances was introduced at the same time.

2. *Market pricing* is the principle that stipulates that rents should be freely negotiated and determined by market forces. All real markets are more or less imperfectly competitive so that, in contrast with the marginal cost rent, the real market rent may be inflated by such things as scarcity and consumer ignorance of alternatives. In the real world landlords are often in a position to exercise a degree of monopoly power that enables them to charge more than the marginal cost price for a particular property.

3. *Historic cost accounting* is the principle that stipulates that rents should be set at levels that generate an income that is just sufficient to meet the historic costs of providing the service. Under this principle rents are simply set to recover actual costs and no account is taken of what the market would charge. In the extreme version of this principle no account is taken of either the property's current use or investment values.

Because the burden of debt diminishes over time, under a system of historic cost accounting older dwellings will tend to have lower loan service charges attached to them than equivalent properties that have been built or acquired more recently. Eventually the mortgage debt will be amortised so that the LSC element in the total sufficiency rent will disappear altogether. The reduced or liquidated debt burden associated with certain properties can provide an opportunity to let them at less than market rents and still cover the historic costs of provision.

The existence of differential historic costs has in the past allowed social landlords to allocate low-cost housing to low-income households thereby moving some way towards reconciling the claims of *sufficiency* and *affordability*. Where the stock was built or acquired over a long period, the differential costs between individual dwelling units can be significant. This means that if historic cost rents were to be set in a way that tied each dwelling's rent to its particular historic costs, the standard deviation within the overall rent structure could be unacceptably high. For this reason, where historic cost accounting principles have been adopted, they have been used to spread the cost savings across the stock as a whole by a process of *rent-pooling*.

Rent-pooling focuses on the relationship between the aggregated historic costs of providing the whole stock of dwellings and the aggregated flow of rental income generated by that stock. The idea is that, rather than charging rents that cover the historic costs of providing individual dwellings, the authority seeks to collect rents that cover its costs in total. Having determined the required income flow, the authority then has to devise a method of setting the rents of individual dwellings in a way that the unit price charged is felt to be reasonable when compared with others. Over the years social landlords who adopted historic cost accounting, have used three main methods of differentiating the rents of individual properties. Under the old rating system, individual dwellings were periodically valued for rating purposes. This value was termed the *gross value* and was assumed to represent the annual rent that the dwelling would generate when let. Councils used to refer to these values when deciding how to differentiate between the rents of individual dwellings. Point and formula systems have also been used to guide what constitutes a 'reasonable' rent (see below).

Rent-pooling has been commonly used to even out historic costs over the total housing stock where older properties are cheaper to service than newer ones. It is recognised that the differentials that emerge as a result of historic cost accounting are in large part the result of not taking account of the current values of the properties. Since 1972, council house rents that have traditionally benefited from historical cost savings, have been set in a way that also makes some reference to the property's capital value.

4. *Capital value pricing* is the principle that stipulates that rents should be set in such a way that they provide a specified return on the capital values. The operation of capital value rents requires two figures: an estimate of the capital value with vacant possession, and an agreed rate of return. The former might be set by reference to private markets and the latter either to private markets or to the official government discount rate.[5] The capital value might be arrived at by reference to the owner-occupied property market. The rate of return can be set by reference to current yields in the finance market.

It would, of course, be possible to discount the market figures to reflect the welfare nature of social housing. Because of its mission to house the poor, a social landlord may, for example, be prepared to accept a lower rate of return than it could get on other investments. This has tended to be the case when this principle is applied to social housing: even in the nineteenth century the 'five per cent philanthropy' movement sought a reasonable rather than a commercial return on its 'charitable' investments. The idea of social housing rents reflecting capital values is not so much about maximising investment returns as using financial disciplines to encourage the efficient financial management of public or charitable funds. It is more about accountability than profitability. In this way, achieving a target rate of return might be thought of as a sort of performance indicator for the social landlord.

Those who advocate using capital values as the basis for setting rents argue that affordability concerns can be addressed through some separate administrative mechanism.

---

5   Most advocates of capital value pricing argue the need to determine a rent that will produce a rental income stream that is sufficient to provide landlords with a return on the capital invested comparable to other investments in the economy. The current government discount rate on new investment might apply in this case.

5. *Consumption expenditure pricing* is the principle that stipulates that tenants should only pay for what they receive. As a principle it is grounded in the philosophy of the welfare state. It is based on the argument that the capital costs of providing a service should be paid by the tax-payers who then become the long-run owners of the school buildings, hospital equipment, council housing stock, or whatever. Under this principle, the receivers of a social service might legitimately be asked to pay towards the provision of consumables they enjoy, such as school meals, prescribed medicines, housing maintenance, etc., but would not be expected to pay for the servicing of debt associated with the acquisition of fixed assets that remain in the ownership of the education authority, hospital board, local authority housing department, etc.

This principle has never been fully applied to the British social housing system and the principle's welfare-statist logic is unlikely to be accepted by contemporary social commentators and politicians who are increasingly sympathetic to establishing rent regimes that reflect market prices and capital values.

Although consumption pricing is not normally used as the over-riding principle for setting rents, it is used by social landlords to differentiate the 'price' of one unit of accommodation from another. Social landlords do for example, use points systems to value the different utilities generated by different types of dwelling. The aggregated points for a particular dwelling are then used to fix its 'appropriate' rent. This is looked at in more detail in Chapters 12 and 15.

All rents are normally rationalised and legitimated by reference to one or more of the above principles. Rents tend to be rationalised differently in different tenures, and in any particular tenure the balance of rationalisations can change over time.

Rent-setting in practice

Over the years there has been much talk amongst policy-makers and academics about the desirability of harmonising the rents of council houses and those of housing associations, and relating them both to local private sector rents. With all its faults, the old *fair rent* regime established in the early 1970s did point to a common approach to price setting across the whole rented sector. The shift away from *fair rents* in the late 1980s resulted in the abandonment of a common approach, and in the 1990s rent levels tended to be rationalised differently in different tenures. Deregulation in the unregistered private sector allowed private landlords to charge assured and assured shorthold rents that were more or less in line with market pricing. Housing associations with assured tenancies were expected to take the incomes of their tenants into account so that the rents they charged could be seen to be affordable. Their ability to do this was helped by the receipt of Social Housing Grant and other fiscal aid. It has also been aided by their ability to incorporate historic cost accounting into their projected business costs. In local authorities pressure on rent levels has also been eased by the dampening effect of historic costs: indeed, because of the generally older age profile of their stocks, the historic cost effect tends to be more significant in this sector. However, the 1990 finance regime for local authorities established the principle of aggregate guideline rents and required councils to take some account of both property values and how rents are set by the private sector locally when formulating their rent policies. More recently rent-setting decisions in England have had to take into account the government's rent restructuring policy that seeks to achieve a degree of equivalence between the rents charged for similar properties by different landlords.

How rents have actually been determined in the different tenures is described and discussed in detail in subsequent chapters.

Rent restructuring in England

By the time of the 2000 green paper (*Quality and Choice: A Decent Home for All*), significant differentials had been established between the rents charged by the various types of landlord. This was judged to be unsatisfactory as it inhibited the government's dual policy objectives of fairness and choice. It is clearly unfair that people living in similar homes in the same locality should be paying different rents simply because they are each renting from a different form of social landlord. Rational choices are also being distorted by the fact that some tenants are making choices based on the characteristics of the landlord rather than the characteristics of the dwelling. Subsequent to the green paper, the government announced its rent restructuring policy for harmonising rents for similar properties in similar locations by 2012. From 2001 onwards, when social landlords reviewed their rent charges, they were required to use a *formula* that took account of the average rent for the sector (RSL or council), relative earnings (regional), number of bedrooms, individual property values, and average sector property values (RSL or council). Within certain limits, a social landlord could alter its rents to take account of inflation and the needs of its business plan, but it could only do so within the context of the formula. In this way, the government sought to harmonise rents over a 10-12 year period.

In the summer of 2004, the government reviewed its rent restructuring policy and proposed some changes to the calculation formula and the way in which the subsidy system should support this for local authorities. It became clear that because the formula for RSL and council rents had been using different inputs, there was little chance that rents, even for identical properties, would convert within the timescale. The average rent and valuations for RSL and council properties varies and this resulted in the same property having a higher rent if it is an RSL home than a council home. The RSL formula is now used as a guide for all properties. In addition, higher bedroom weights have been introduced for larger properties. This effectively increases rents for three-bedroom dwellings. Under the original formula there existed a 'cap' on the amount that actual rents can go up or down in moving towards the end target rent (i.e. the converged rent to be achieved by 2012). Recent changes have removed the limit on how much rents can be reduced. This is largely of concern to some high rent housing associations whose rents are required to fall by the formula.

The government has recognised that the effect of these changes (particularly the harmonising of the formula) is to put an additional upward pressure on council rents. This on its own would simply increase the amount of negative subsidy councils would be paying back.[6]

Ways of subsidising

All of the following have been used as *mechanisms* for subsidising housing:

- Price control and regulation.
- Tax relief and exemptions.
- The provision of grants to the providers of housing.
- Rent rebates and allowances (income augmentation).
- Right to buy discounts.
- Rent-pooling.

The precise operational form of a subsidy will largely be determined by its intended function(s). This means that in seeking to assess the effectiveness of a subsidy we have to start by determining its function.

The function of a subsidy

We can identify the following possible functions of a subsidy:

1. *To overcome demand deficiency*. This centres on the affordability debate discussed in Chapter 3. Housing's characteristics as primary consumption constitute a necessary but not sufficient reason for providing subsidy. The issue is not simply that basic housing is a necessity but that it is a necessity that not everyone can afford. In short, some minimum level of housing consumption is regarded as a *merit need*. Subsidy is the mechanism by which

---

6   However, the government is now recycling some of the extra income through increased Management and Maintenance Allowances in the subsidy calculations. This effectively means that councils are able to keep more of the extra income raised than previously would have been the case. The original introduction of rent restructuring was accompanied by a 2 per cent increase Management and Maintenance Allowances. The government is now proposing a 4 per cent increase. This is rather a technical point. What it adds up to is that from 2005, more generous revenue allowances are providing an increased income stream for some councils which has helped to make their business plans more viable.

society has sought to bridge the gap between a sufficient and an affordable rent so that this *merit need* can be met. The concepts of *merit need* and *demand deficiency* are discussed fully in Chapter 19.

2. *To redistribute the benefits of good housing to all*, so that areas of poverty are not further worsened by poor housing standards. The argument here is that society as a whole has an interest in ameliorating the social and economic costs associated with bad housing. Where the issues of acceptability and affordability are brought together in housing policy, the question of 'subsidy' is bound to arise.

3. *To influence proprietary behaviour* (as an aspect of 2 above). In particular, to encourage individual investment in housing that would not otherwise take place. That is, to help pay for private investment that generates *positive externalities*. A *positive externality* is a benefit from economic activity for which no compensation is paid. The argument here is that non-proprietary interests may result from encouraging owners and tenants to renovate, or in some other way improve, their properties. These non-proprietary interests, or positive externalities, may include such factors as environmental enhancement, safer communities, and economic growth.

4. *To establish a degree of vertical and horizontal equity with the housing finance system.* A policy commitment to tenure neutrality may be associated with this objective.

5. *To foster the development of a particular form of tenure.* A policy commitment to influence tenure preference may be associated with this objective.

6. *To offset market failure* – e.g. the failure of historical markets to provide for today's needs; the inability of the market to react quickly enough to changes in demand; the inflexibility of the market due to its fixed locational nature in relation to demand; and problems of financing (Refer to Chapter 3 and Hills, 1991).

It has to be recognised that a subsidy may have consequences beyond those that have been planned for. In particular, subsidies in one tenure are likely to have implications for other tenures. The ultimate beneficiary of a subsidy may turn out to be other than that for whom it was intended, or it may produce an unintended undesirable effect in another sector of the economy.[7]

---

7   The possibility of creating undesirable knock-on effects by subsidising housing has been discussed for many years. *'No thoughtful man will advocate the letting of houses below their economic rent, by means of subsidies...because...wages follow rents, and therefore that policy would only result in providing capitalists with cheap labour at the expense of the general body of ratepayers.'* (Nettlefold, 1908, p55).

Defining 'subsidy'

Originally the word subsidy simply meant a 'payment'.[8] In English history the term became used specifically to describe financial grants made by parliament to the Crown to pay for wars or other special needs. From this it was extended to apply to any parliamentary grant in aid including those made to commercial agencies, public bodies and individual citizens. The term was then applied to any financial support to suppliers or consumers of goods and services, whether from parliament or from other sources. In contemporary financial parlance the word has come to have a more focused technical meaning that is derived from economic theory.

Economic subsidy

In market theory a subsidy is said to exist if a good or service is sold below its market price. Thus the term 'subsidy' is used to describe a deficit between the price that is *actually charged* for a good or service and the higher price that *would have been charged* by the market. The idea here is that if a good or service is sold at a price that fails to cover its costs of production, including profit, the consumer is said to be enjoying an 'economic subsidy'. This is a rather theoretical view of subsidy and, in practice, it is difficult to determine the extent of economic subsidy when goods and services are provided outside of competitive markets. The social housing system has evolved out of welfare rather than market arrangements and, for this reason, it is often more sensible to conceive of subsidy in this sector as a money transfer.

Money transfer or cash-flow definition

The cash-flow approach to defining subsidy seeks to measure and track money transfers between people and organisations. This is the way subsidy is measured and traced in official statistics and accounts. The most common transfers take the form of public sector grants or allowances to certain qualifying housing providers or consumers. We must recognise, however, that some important housing subsidies do not involve a tangible transfer of funds; the old mortgage interest tax relief and current rent-pooling are two notable examples of economic subsidies that do not involve direct cash payments.

---

8   The etymology of the word 'subsidy' shows it to be linked to the word 'subside'. Subside comes from the latin *subsidere* – *sub* meaning below/under and *sidere* meaning to sit down or settle. The word 'subsidy' comes from the latin *subsidium*, a word that originally referred to troops stationed in reserve in the third line of battle. The front-line troops would be at the battle front; the second-line troops would be the reserves that could be quickly called upon to support the front-line; and well behind the front-line, settled down and waiting, would be the third-line troops – the auxiliaries or *subsidium* (from *subsidere* – in waiting/to settle down). From this application it came to be applied to a sum of money paid by one prince or nation to another to purchase the services of auxiliary troops. It was then used more generally to mean extraordinary aid in money rendered by subjects to a sovereign, usually to pay for wars.

Ways of categorising housing subsidies

Subsidies that are derived from the state and are an aspect of government policy we can term *fiscal subsidies*.[9] Subsidies that arise as a result of one private citizen or organisation aiding the production or consumption of some other private citizen or organisation and are not directly derived from government policy, we can term *'non-fiscal subsidies'*. In the field of housing, examples of non-fiscal subsidies are rent-pooling (tenant-to-tenant subsidies), and grants from charities to help provide or manage dwellings for special needs groups such as the elderly or the disabled.

Subsidy as an aspect of fiscal policy

Fiscal policy embraces both taxes and subsidies. It must be understood that fiscal policy is not simply concerned with raising funds to pay for public activities and to support the worthy and the needy. Throughout history governments have used taxes and subsidies to achieve wider economic and social objectives by deterring certain activities through taxation and encouraging other activities through subsidisation.

Subsidies may be used to influence market behaviour. That is, where the market fails to promote society's politically determined objectives subsidies may be used to promote greater *social efficiency*, by altering patterns of production or consumption, and/or *social justice*, by altering the distribution of real income. In this way, politicians see subsidisation as a policy instrument for altering what gets produced and consumed and by whom.

Because housing finance policy has developed in the context of political and administrative concerns that are tenure-specific (e.g. concerns to encourage owner-occupation, concerns to make social rented housing more affordable, etc.), most subsidies are tied to specific tenures. Although understandable, this tenure-specificity has inhibited rational discussion about how the subsidy system might be reformed with a view to enhancing cross-tenure efficiency, effectiveness and equity. To liberate our thought and understanding from this limitation we will end this chapter by briefly considering ways of classifying housing subsidies that are not tenure-specific. In subsequent chapters subsidies will be described and analysed on a tenure by tenure basis.

Classification by financial category

In Chapter 2 (Figure 2.1), we drew a key distinction between finance that is used for capital purposes, finance that is used for revenue purposes, and finance that is used to augment incomes. Within the context of any particular tenure it is possible to provide subsidy to support any or all of these functions. Social Housing Grant is

---

9   Fiscal means 'of or relating to the finances of the state', from the latin *fiscus*, meaning public money.

an example of a capital subsidy going to housing associations and other social landlords. The Management and Maintenance Allowance is an example of revenue support to local authorities, if entitled. The housing benefit system provides income augmentation to tenants who qualify to receive it[10] and mortgage interest tax relief used to be used to provide income augmentation to owner-occupiers purchasing their homes by means of a loan.[11]

The incidence of a subsidy

Gibb and Munro (1991), distinguish between the *formal* and the *effective* incidence of a subsidy. The distinction enables us to make the point that those who formally receive the benefit can pass its financial impact or 'effect' on to others. A social landlord, for example, may receive a capital grant that reduces the total scheme costs of a housing development (formal incidence) and, as a result, the tenants enjoy lower rental charges (effective incidence).

In the owner-occupied sector, the formal receipt of mortgage interest tax relief used to enable some house purchasers to bid higher prices for the homes they purchase thereby effectively passing on the financial benefit to house builders and land owners. Where subsidies get transformed into higher house prices we say that the subsidy has been 'capitalised'.

Cross-subsidy

Cross-subsidy occurs when administrative arrangements require one housing account, activity or group to aid some other housing account, activity or group.

Before 1990 local authorities could make transfers from the General Fund to the Housing Revenue Account (HRA), and vice-versa. Many councils used this power to lower rent levels without the HRA being forced into deficit. This ability to cross-subsidise one account with another was made illegal by the Local Government and Housing Act 1989.

The old municipal principle of *rent-pooling* is an example of cross-subsidisation of one group of tenants by another. Under rent-pooling arrangements tenants living in established dwellings with small or no debt charges attached to them have their rents increased beyond the historic costs of provision so that tenants occupying newer properties with relatively high historic costs (debt charges) can have their rents reduced to more affordable levels.

Planning gain is another example of cross-subsidy. Under a development proposal requiring planning permission, it is possible for a local authority to grant permission, subject to an agreement with the developer that part of the profits

---

10   See Chapter 19.
11   MITR was abolished in April 2000 – see Chapter 7.

from the sale of the properties on the open market will be used to subsidise the provision or improvement of a number of social housing units that are associated with the primary development. Such compacts are termed 'section 106 agreements' after the section in the Town and Country Planning 1990 that gives them legislative force. Section 106 agreements are often made in partnership with housing associations who, subsequent to the development, manage the low-cost dwellings that are let or part sold to households deemed to be in housing need.

Visible and hidden subsidies

A subsidy can be said to be 'visible' if its existence and nature are widely known and understood. All direct grants and benefits, or money transfers, are openly publicised, reported on and accounted for in expenditure statistics that are in the public domain (see Chapter 5). Not all subsidies are so clearly perceived and understood. If a subsidy's existence is obscured by administrative arrangements or its cost to the Exchequer is not openly discussed, it is said to be 'hidden'. It is sometimes said that subsidy received through tax exemption is less obvious than subsidy provided through the receipt of grant or benefit. It may be that the 'hidden' nature of mortgage interest tax relief and capital gains tax exemptions protected the main subsidies going to owner-occupation from the scrutiny and criticism to which more 'visible' subsidies have been subjected.

By controlling or regulating prices at the point of consumption the old Rent Acts effectively required landlords to provide a hidden economic subsidy to their tenants.

Universal and targeted subsidies

A subsidy is said to be 'universal' if it is available to a whole class of people (e.g. a tenure group), irrespective of their individual incomes or normative needs. As the term implies, 'targeted' subsidies are aimed at specific households on the basis of some assessment of need and/or income and savings.

When the Exchequer provides a development grant to help pay for the capital costs of a social housing scheme, the formal incidence of that subsidy is universal. By reducing the need for a residual loan, the grant lowers the historic costs associated with the scheme and as a result the rents are universally lower than they otherwise would have been. The exemption from capital gains tax enjoyed by owner-occupiers is an example of an economic subsidy that is universally available to all owner-occupiers irrespective of their circumstances.

The means-testing involved in the distribution of targeted subsidies makes them relatively more complex to administer than universal subsidies. However, by concentrating limited funds on those in most need, they are usually regarded as being more rather than less socially efficient. Although housing benefit is the most prominent targeted aid available to help with housing costs, the social efficiency argument has led to a whole range of other subsidies being means-tested. Home improvement grants, for example, are distributed by local authorities in accordance with a means-test formula.

As well as targeting financial support at individual households through the application of means-tests, it is also possible to target state resources at specific geographical areas through the application of needs indices. (See discussion on comparative need in Chapter 3.)

Supply-side and demand-side subsidies

Throughout the twentieth century there has been a continuous debate about the most appropriate way of subsidising the housing needs of low-income tenants. In essence this is a debate about whether it is better to subsidise supply or demand. Any support measure that has the effect of influencing production and provision can be termed a *supply-side subsidy* and any measure that influences consumption can be termed a *demand-side subsidy*.

Financial aid to providers is sometimes referred to as a *supply-side subsidy* and financial support to consumers is referred to as a *demand-side subsidy*.

Supply-side subsidies

Provider (supply-side) subsidies are formally directed at landlords or developers with the intention of aiding them to provide quality accommodation at less than market rents. Where the grants in aid are provided to help cover the capital development, or redevelopment costs, they are sometimes referred to as 'bricks-and-mortar' subsidies. Provider subsidies can take the form of either capital or revenue aid. Such subsidies invariably take the operational form of a *money transfer*. Such financial support arrangements are described in subsequent chapters.

The supply-side arguments. Market economists tend to argue that supply subsidies to housing are only really justifiable in times of national emergency such as periods of war or post-war reconstruction. This is because, at such times, national priorities are such that the free market economy is abandoned or severely disrupted by a shift towards command economics. If housing is needed at these times, then the state may have to intervene directly and help pay for its production. In contrast, advocates of the welfare state tend to argue that, at all times, the housing needs of some vulnerable groups have to be guaranteed by the state and, consequently, suppliers should be aided to ensure that such needs are met.[12] Proponents of this approach point out that the universal nature of supply

12   This is the merit need argument – see Chapter 19.

subsidies makes them less complex to administer than means-tested personal assistance. It is also argued that they are less socially divisive because, as a general subsidy, they are less inclined to stigmatise the recipients.

Consumption (demand-side) subsidies

These are directed at the users of housing with the intention of giving qualifying recipients additional income with which to pay for a standard of accommodation that would otherwise be beyond their means. They are sometimes referred to as 'personal' subsidies. By far the largest amount of personal subsidy is channelled through a form of assistance called *housing benefit* which is a government sponsored scheme designed to help people on low incomes with their rents (see Chapter 19 for details). Some home-owners also received consumption support in the form of mortgage income tax relief (see Chapter 19).

The demand-side arguments. Critics of supply-side subsidies argue that they are inefficient and distort the market. They are deemed to be wasteful of public money because their universal nature gives help to people whether they are in need or not. They distort the market by producing rents that are not related to either the true costs of provision or to the current value of the property. By contrast, means-tested demand-side assistance (e.g. rebates) can be tightly targeted at those in most need and also allow the authorities and associations to set rents that are more in line with provision costs or current values. In this way, the flow of rental income into the housing system is not diminished as a result of policies designed to aid low-income households.

Some commentators argue that by not directly distorting opportunity costs or market prices, income support measures are not, strictly speaking, housing subsidies at all but part of the social security system. However, because such measures as housing benefit and mortgage interest tax relief have the same income effect as a subsidy and, in any case, indirectly *do* affect costs and prices, we will classify them as 'housing subsidies'.

The shifting balance of assistance

Since 1980 there has been a gradual but emphatic change in policy emphasis towards the demand-side arguments that has resulted in a shift from supply-side, particularly 'bricks-and-mortar', subsidies to demand-side, or 'personal' subsidies. As a consequence of this shift in emphasis rents have risen and the housing benefit budget has expanded. Between 1980 and the mid-1990s social housing rent levels increased at a rate greater than inflation while during the same period the number of people claiming housing benefit in the form of rebates and allowances more than doubled.

Summary and conclusion

In this chapter we have made the point that a rent has to be *sufficient* as well as *affordable* and that any deficit between these two primary objectives may have to be made up by the provision of *subsidy*. In economic theory a subsidy is thought of as the difference between what is actually charged for a good and what would have been charged. In practice, many subsidies take the form of a cash payment or a tax concession. Subsidies tend to take different forms in different tenures. We have made the further point that a gap between affordability and sufficiency may not be the only reason for subsidising the provision or consumption of housing.

We will end by making the point that the current systems of rents and subsidies were not so much designed as that they evolved. This has produced a number of irrationalities and inequities that can be identified and analysed by reference to the ideas in this chapter. One barrier to reforming and rationalising the system is the *subsidy ratchet effect*. By this we mean that there is usually only limited resistance to the introduction or extension of subsidies because they tend to create identifiable beneficiaries. Once these beneficiaries have been created, however, they have a vested interest in seeing the measures retained and this creates a political resistance to reforms that require the reduction or abolition of subsidies.

Further reading

Chartered Institute of Housing (1997), *Good Practice Briefing No.11 – Rents and Service Charges*, December 1997, CIH: Coventry.

King, P., (2001), *Understanding Housing Finance*, Routledge.

PART TWO

Housing finance: the regime

Introduction to Part Two

Part One of this book sought to establish a way of conceptualising the policy issues that surround what might be termed the 'housing finance debate'. Part Two seeks to provide the reader with an up-to-date description and critical analysis of the 'housing finance regime'. It also considers some aspects of financial management. It begins by considering the role of the state in the housing system and, in particular, why and how the central authorities seek to support and control housing spending. It then turns to an analysis of the capital and revenue funding arrangements as they operate in the various tenures. Chapters 16 and 17 describe and discuss how regulated social businesses seek to plan their finances and control the management of their resources. Chapter 18 considers the role of the private landlord. The final chapter considers the fiscal arrangements that exist to support those households that have difficulty in meeting their basic housing costs.

Although largely descriptive, this part of the book makes constant reference back to the theories and cross-tenure ideas and issues that were outlined in Part One.

CHAPTER 5:
The state and housing finance

We have stressed the point that housing is a commodity of central importance both to the social and economic well-being of individuals and the wider community. Recognition of this importance underpins much of the state's involvement over the years in the housing system and its associated financial arrangements. This involvement has a political, social and economic context. Although politics, economics and social concerns are fundamentally entwined, for the purpose of analysis we will consider them separately.

Political context

Much state activity is straightforwardly pragmatic and takes the form of responses to social and economic factors that are not directly under the control or influence of the government. For example, the nature of state involvement in the provision of housing, health, and education will, to some extent, be affected by such things as the changing structure of the population, divorce rates, world commodity prices, and international treaty obligations. However, despite this, much of what governments say and do is consciously planned for in the sense that it stems from political aims and manifesto pledges.

It should be recognised that government welfare policies are not arbitrarily plucked out of the air but are derived from the values and attitudes of policy-makers. It is possible to detect two broadly distinct and competing approaches underlying the various housing policy changes that have occurred since the beginning of the twentieth century. Simply put, some policy enactments have been derived from what might be termed a *market ideology* and others from what might be termed a *welfare ideology*.

Two historical agendas

Although it is beyond the scope of this book to describe the detailed history of housing policy, it is useful for the student of housing finance to be aware that, broadly speaking, legislative changes have been driven by two competing political views about society's social and economic objectives.

Market ideology is grounded in the belief that free-enterprise tends to be naturally efficient and fair and that the activities associated with the provision, consumption and exchange of housing should, as far as possible, be conducted by private individuals or firms rather than by the agents of central and local government. Market ideology tends to favour rent policies related to market prices and replacement costs rather than to people's ability to pay or to historic costs. It also tends to advocate subsidy arrangements that put purchasing power into people's pockets rather than those that are designed to lower or suppress market prices. That is, it tends to favour welfare arrangements that augment the incomes of poor households so as to give them more effective market power, rather than promoting policies that subsidise production or impose price controls. This is because both production subsidies and price controls are seen as distorting the market and keeping prices 'artificially' low by inhibiting or preventing them from rising to their 'true' market levels. Because it embraces the notion of 'self-reliance', market ideology is sympathetic to the idea that owner-occupation is deemed to be the 'natural' and 'normal' tenure arrangement for most people.

Welfare ideology is grounded in the belief that certain commodities have a social importance that is so great that the state should guarantee some minimum standard of provision for everyone. It emphasises the notion of *need* rather than that of *demand*, and it represents the value system that underlies what is popularly referred to as 'the welfare state'. It has been instrumental in developing the concept of *welfare rights* and, in the housing field, is associated with the proposition that every household should have a decent home at a price they can afford. It tends to be sympathetic both to price control (or regulation) arrangements and to the provision of production subsidies designed to reduce the price of housing for people on low incomes. In general it sees an active role for central and local government in the housing system. The welfare approach to housing provision and consumption is often reinforced by the argument that the housing market is so imperfectly competitive that it cannot be relied upon to achieve society's objectives.[1]

The following schema, Figure 5.1, illustrates how the two ideologies lead to different housing finance practices depending on the policy adopted. As a generalisation, market ideology tends to lead to demand-side income augmentation measures while welfare ideology tends to be more sympathetic to the provision of supply-side 'bricks-and-mortar' subsidies.

Figure 5.1: Market and welfare ideologies

MARKET	THEORY PRACTICE	WELFARE
Ideology Notion of 'self-reliance' within an enterprise culture		*Ideology* Notion of 'entitlement' and 'welfare rights'
Policy Emphasis on 'effective demand' and market mechanisms		*Policy* Emphasis on 'social need' and ability to pay (administrative mechanisms)
Delivery Market-related tenancies and rents Income support in the form of tax relief, rebates, allowances, etc. Measures to encourage owner-occupation		*Delivery* Regulated tenancies and rents Production subsidies (e.g. Exchequer grants to local authorities and SHG) Measures to support public provision of housing

---

1   See Chapter 3 for a discussion on *Housing market failure*.

Although market ideology is generally associated with the political 'right' and welfare ideology with the political 'left', it would be an over-simplification to say that these two worldviews have exactly mirrored the party political divide in Britain over the years. For example, the Conservative administrations of the 1950s directed large-scale financial support in the form of production grants towards the provision of council housing while at the same time pursuing a market approach by relaxing controls on private sector rents. In recent years, despite its general commitment to welfare ideology, the Labour party has developed the notion of 'sustainable home-ownership'. For such reasons it is more useful to think of two *ideological* rather than two strictly *party political* agendas competing for prominence in the housing policies of the last hundred years.

The market agenda of recent Conservative administrations has resulted in the gradual shrinking of the amount of economic activity carried out by local government and public corporations. Between the elections of Margaret Thatcher in 1979 and Tony Blair in 1997, General Government Expenditure on housing fell in real terms by some 71 per cent (see Table 5.2, p90). Although this represents a dramatic cut in capital spending on housing, it over-states the amount by which housing expenditure in total was reduced in this period. This is because the expenditure category 'housing' does not include the rising costs of housing benefit – nor does it include the costs of a number of other measures designed to support home-ownership (e.g. discounts on right to buy sales).

The current political agenda: a 'third way'?

In May 1997 a 'New' Labour government was returned to office with a policy agenda that stemmed from the work of the Commission on Social Justice. The Commission was based at the Institute for Public Policy Research, the left-of-centre think tank. It was set up in 1992 while the Labour party was in opposition. It was established on a date that coincided with the fiftieth anniversary of the publication of the immensely influential Beveridge Report, *Social Insurance and Allied Services*, which became the foundation of the post-war welfare state in the UK. The final report was published in 1994 (Commission on Social Justice, 1994) and it set out a broad policy agenda that centred on the following four propositions.

- There is a need to transform the welfare state from a safety net in times of trouble to a springboard for economic opportunity.
- There is a need to invest in people and radically improve access to education and training.
- There is a need to promote real choices in the balance of employment, family, education, leisure and retirement.
- There is a need to reconstruct the nation's social wealth and reform its social institutions so as to provide a dependable social environment in which people can lead their lives.

The 'New Labour' group of opposition politicians led by Tony Blair and Gordon Brown were also influenced by the early Clinton thinking in the US about the so-called 'third way' that embraced policy programmes relating to welfare to work and social inclusion.

In office, the new government's commitment to the ideals of the commission and the 'third way' found early expression in the form of declarations to enhance education spending and, where appropriate, to move people from welfare dependency to employment and economic independence. The new prime minister also established a Social Exclusion Unit to help co-ordinate the policies of government departments, local authorities and other agencies around the notion of 'Best Value', and to recommend changes in spending priorities.

To ensure that the priority reassessments were considered in a thorough and systematic way the government set up a *Comprehensive Spending Review* that was informed by the over-riding principle that public spending should produce '*stability and investment for the long term*'. The review covered all aspects of public expenditure and, in all, there were 43 separate departmental reviews carried out within Whitehall. Bi-annual spending reviews are now an established feature of the government's approach to expenditure planning and control and we will say more about them later in the chapter.

Together with the 'fiscal code' from which they stem, spending reviews have altered the old control climate in one important respect. They have shifted the measurement emphasis away from *costs* and *inputs* towards the auditing of *quality* and *outputs* (e.g. more emphasis on improving school reading levels, reducing crime and illness, up-grading housing conditions, etc.). The idea is that the output targets should be achieved in ways that are judged to be cost-effective. To this end a policy commitment emerged to replace traditional cash accounting with a system of *resource accounting* in the year 2001. Widely used in the private sector, resource accounting requires departments and public bodies to know what assets they hold and to acknowledge that they are not 'cost free' simply because they are paid for, but that they cost money to keep running. The intention of resource accounting is to encourage public bodies to manage their assets in a more business-like fashion by making sure that the accounts record how much the asset is costing in the current period. This contrasts with cash accounting that records when the capital is *paid for* rather than when it is *used*.[2]

Although it may be an exaggeration to refer to these changes as a new ideology or 'third way', they clearly do help to explain the political values that lie behind the

---

2   The idea of resource accounting predates the Labour government. The idea was introduced (for Whitehall departments) in the Treasury white paper of July 1995. At that time, the then chancellor, Kenneth Clarke, explained the basic idea of resource accounting by saying that it would allow auditors finally to get to grips with the quality of service provided, instead of '*measuring our performance by the rate at which we burn £10 notes*'. (Reported by Michael White in *The Guardian* April 1998).

present government's reshaping of the old historical divide between the ideals of Beveridge's welfare state and the principles of the market. As we will see later in the book, these postulations clearly inform the Labour government's views about how best to finance housing consumption and production.

Implementing central government housing policy

Central government operates mainly through legislation and regulations and by controlling the allocation of resources. To implement its policies it works with and through the following:

(i) Government departments and national agencies, sometimes referred to collectively as 'regulators'. These regulatory authorities include the following. In England, the Office of the Deputy Prime Minister (ODPM) and the Housing Corporation. In Wales, the Welsh Assembly Government (WAG), formerly the Welsh Office. In Scotland, the Scottish Executive and Communities Scotland. In Northern Ireland, the Northern Ireland Housing Executive (NIHE) and the Department for Social Development. As well as having a regulatory function, these also administer the allocation and distribution of capital grants and revenue subsidies to local authorities and registered social landlords such as housing associations.

(ii) Local authorities that are responsible for preparing local housing strategies, have important statutory duties and still own a significant proportion of the stock of social homes (except in Northern Ireland).

(iii) The private sector, in the form of housing associations, house builders, private landlords and lending institutions.

(iv) Voluntary bodies and agencies that engage in partnering arrangements with the above.

The governing agencies

In England, central-local relations centre on the Office of the Deputy Prime Minister (ODPM). The ODPM has ultimate responsibility for developing and administering local government's structure, powers, conduct and finances. In this capacity, it has overall responsibility for the development and administration of the government's housing policy. The ODPM also supervises the government's neighbourhood renewal programmes and measures to tackle social exclusion.

In Wales, in the period between the mid-1960s and devolution, it was the Welsh Office and the Secretary of State for Wales that had general responsibility for housing and local government matters. Significant changes resulted from the creation of the Welsh Assembly. Under the Government of Wales Act, the assembly has established a Partnership Council to ensure that the role of local government is safeguarded and that the assembly and the 22 unitary Welsh local authorities work together in an effective way. The powers and responsibilities held by the Secretary of State have been transferred to the assembly (although primary legislation remains a Westminster responsibility).

A new co-ordinating housing agency originally called the Welsh Office Housing Department came into existence in November 1998 by merging Housing for Wales (Tai Cymru) with the Welsh Office Housing Division. This integrated department brought the policy, financial, operational and regulatory arrangements of all social landlords together into one supervisory organisation. This is intended to facilitate a more strategic approach to social housing provision. This reconstructed department now has its policy objectives set by the ministers and the National Assembly for Wales. As well as policy and finance and operational sections, it has a performance unit that has, amongst other things, taken on the regulatory functions. Under the auspices of the National Assembly for Wales, this new body assesses local authorities' housing strategies and operational plans, allocates funding to housing associations on the basis of Best Value for money in meeting needs, and allocates development funding.

Prior to devolution in 1999, the Scottish Office Development Department (SODD) was responsible for developing and administering policy on housing and local government in Scotland. With the advent of the Scottish Parliament, its functions have been incorporated in the Scottish Executive, which reports to the parliament through the minister responsible for housing.

The Scottish Executive's primary housing aims are to ensure an adequate supply of housing in Scotland, enhance consumer choice and bring about an effective use of resources, which will involve, among other things, the encouragement of private finance. The Scottish Executive sponsors Communities Scotland (previously Scottish Homes), the national housing and regeneration agency whose purpose is to assist owner-occupation and to promote the development of a diverse rented sector by funding and supervising housing associations and other landlords who provide new and modernised housing to rent. The executive provides advice and guidance to local authorities and other agencies on securing an adequate supply of housing for community care groups as part of the government's policy for Care in the Community, and for homeless people in priority need.

In Northern Ireland, housing policy is the responsibility of the Department for Social Development (DSD), which reports to Northern Ireland ministers or, when devolution is operating, to the Northern Ireland Assembly. In practice, much detailed policy and practical implementation is devolved to a centralised authority called the Northern Ireland Housing Executive. The executive is a 'quango' supervised by the DSD and is also the owner of what was originally local authority housing in the province. The structure and functions of this agency are described briefly in an annex to Chapter 8.

The establishment of a Scottish Parliament, Welsh Assembly and Northern Ireland Assembly are all part of New Labour's blueprint for devolving power. English regional government is continually discussed but, as of yet, not fully acted upon. Until recently, the government's argument appears to be that what the English regions need is economic rather than political regeneration, through effective, streamlined, co-ordinating agencies in the form of non-departmental public bodies such as Regional Development Agencies and their associated regional housing boards (since 2003). These are now charged with the responsibility of devising housing strategies that underpin, and thereby aid, the social and economic development of their regions. Elected regional assemblies were later advocated, but with a 'no' vote on a referendum for the first of these (in the north-east) it seems likely that only the administrative apparatus a regional level will be strengthened (for example, by combining the regional housing and planning functions into one board).

Co-ordination versus devolution

Under New Labour it is possible to detect two somewhat contradictory tendencies. The government has established multi-departmental arrangements co-ordinated by the Cabinet Office with a view to establishing what the civil servants refer to as 'cross-cutting' policies to tackle issues of high political priority. The Social Exclusion Unit was the highest profile example of this approach. The idea of the unit was to bring ministers together from across Whitehall, together with representatives from business and the voluntary sector, to deal with the multiple chronic deprivation that disfigures the poorest parts of Britain.

However, this cross-cutting approach stands in sharp contrast to the devolution philosophy of the government. Since the Scottish Parliament, Welsh and Northern Ireland Assemblies and the English Regional Development Agencies were established, an increasing number of administrative issues have been devolved to these national or regional institutions. It is inevitable that the devolved powers will embrace matters of finance. This is bound to work against the 'joined-up' approach to policy formation and implementation being looked for by the Cabinet Office. One of the most effective ways of achieving 'joined-up' policy is to provide parcels of public money that are ring-fenced and accounted for by reference to specific cross-cutting activities that focus on special areas of concern. This is difficult to achieve if the accountability patterns are complex and multi-faceted and purse-holders are independent of Whitehall.

It can also be argued that devolution to English regions has weakened the position of local authorities at a time when, in other respects, the government appears to want to strengthen them. For example, while local councils now have prudential borrowing powers (see Chapter 9) and their obligation to prepare local housing strategies is now enshrined in law, they have lost influence (to regional authorities) over housing association investment and other investment decisions that are a key part of their strategic role.

Social context

The emergence of social concern

Nineteenth century *laissez-faire* market attitudes remained largely unchallenged until a coherent and systematic welfare agenda began to emerge in the last quarter of the century. By that time there was much official and journalistic comment linking overcrowded and squalid living conditions with such social and moral evils as incest, prostitution and petty crime. But government intervention was most of all stimulated by the growing contemporary awareness of the relationship between insanitary housing and the incidence of communicable diseases such as cholera and typhoid.

The question of housing subsidies became an issue once the state began to intervene to establish minimum standards of housing provision as part of its drive to improve public health. The law prevented free market forces from adjusting housing standards downwards in line with the limited incomes of working-class people. As a result, a more obvious gap emerged between the rent paying capacity of many households and the rent levels that needed to be charged by the market to provide less over-crowded and better quality dwellings. Simply put, once the state had intervened to improve housing standards, it brought to the fore the question of how the improved conditions should be paid for. It became clear that to realise fully the government's health and housing policy objectives would require additional interventionist measures in the area of housing finance.

After 1914 three broad strategies were adopted: rent control and regulation, the public provision of subsidised housing for the 'working classes', and the encouragement of area-based slum-clearance schemes. In addition, later in the century, financial assistance was also directed to the housing association movement and tax concessions and income augmentation measures were introduced to help people meet their housing-related expenses. In this way it can be argued that the social rationale for intervention was tied to society's desire to increase both the quantity and quality of the nation's housing stock and to help low-income households gain access to decent homes that are necessary for them to live healthy and active lives.

The qualified achievements of intervention

In many respects the interventionist measures have been successful and some recent commentators have argued that a prominent feature of Britain's recent housing history has been the closing of the post-Second World War gap that existed between the number of households and the number of dwellings. Between 1951 and 1980 the rate of growth of housing units was faster than the rate of growth of households, thereby creating an officially recorded crude national surplus of stock. Figures based on census and other official data indicate that a deficit of some 800,000 dwellings in 1951 had been transformed into an apparent surplus of 200,000 by 1971, and that this small crude surplus had been increased to about one million by 1980. The figures suggest that since 1980 the rates of growth of the housing stock and of households have remained more or less equal. By the late 1990s there were some 25 million dwellings in the UK (Wilcox, S., 1999, Table 17C, p112) which more or less matched the officially recorded number of households (*Social Trends* 28, 1998 edition).

Although the apparent balancing of supply and demand has led some commentators to argue that, in general terms, housing need in Britain has been satisfied, such a crude comparison between the size of the total stock and the total number of households does not by itself show whether there are sufficient dwellings, and it certainly tells us nothing about the adequacy of the stock in terms of quality. Although recent investment is turning around the massive backlog of disrepair in the social housing stock (estimated by CIH in 1998 to be more than £20 billion across Britain), there is concern that private housing is deteriorating at a faster rate than it is being maintained.

Apart from crucial questions about the fitness of the stock, the apparent balance masks the existence of severe local and regional shortages and takes no account of the thousands of 'concealed households' made up of young adults, couples and one-parent families who live as part of someone else's (often a parent's) household. It does not tell us anything about the relationship between housing costs and the ability to meet them, nor does it take account of the fact that not all of the dwellings are available for occupation (e.g. second homes, temporary voids and unlet properties held vacant with a view to sale). Current concerns are of a more local or regional nature. In particular, the government is now seeking to address the lack of affordable housing in the south-east of England and certain 'hot spot' urban and rural districts throughout the UK. All of these qualifications mean that housing problems persist and that many households remain in housing need. We will consider the implications of this later in the chapter.

Despite these important qualifications, the global figures do indicate that, as an historical trend, over the last one hundred years general housing conditions for the mass of the British people have greatly improved. Much of this achievement has been the result of the financial provisions associated with the various forms of government intervention into the housing system.

These provisions constitute an important part of the mechanisms by which money and credit pass through the housing system so as to enable all types of residential property to be built, improved, bought, rented, maintained, renewed and redeveloped. The arrangements operate within a legal and administrative framework established by acts of parliament and ministerial directives, and since the end of the First World War this framework has been subjected to a continuous stream of reforms and modifications that have stemmed from changes and shifts in government policy.

Throughout this period government policy has been concerned to utilise the housing finance regime to provide systems of support that are judged to be productive, efficient and equitable. In addition, there has been an over-riding concern that the state should maintain a degree of control over the housing finance system to ensure that housing is regulated in the interests of the government's wider social concerns and its macro-economic policy objectives.

Economic context

The government's declared central economic objective is '*to achieve high and stable levels of economic growth and employment, which will promote greater fairness and social cohesion, while also respecting the environment*' (*Economic and Fiscal Strategy Report*, 1998). The pursuit of this objective gives central government a legitimate interest in influencing the nature and scope of public expenditure. A number of significant reforms to the UK's public spending, planning and control regime were implemented in the highly influential 1998 Comprehensive Spending Review. These have been refined and extended in a series of bi-annual spending reviews that have taken place subsequently. Central to any understanding of the current approach to public spending is the Chancellor of the Exchequer's Fiscal Code and the 'fiscal rules' that flow from it. Before we examine the Code and its associated 'rules', we need to say something about the nature and scope of public expenditure.

The extent of public expenditure

Total public spending currently amounts to approximately £460 billion (2004). This represents more than 40 per cent of national income and is equivalent to nearly £8,000 for every man, woman and child in Britain. Some of this spending is used to provide a wide range of services such as housing, health care, defence, education, law and order, and some takes the form of transfer payments (for example the government spent over £51.5 billion on state pensions and over £12.5 billion on housing benefit payments in 2003/4).

Categorising public expenditure
There are various ways in which public expenditure might be classified. For the purposes of analysis it is useful to distinguish between the following categories: spending authority; function or programme; capital and revenue; economic activity and transfers.

Spending authority. The annual fiscal reports that set out the government's spending plans identify three broad spending authorities: central government, local authorities and public corporations. Central government is by far the largest spender, followed by local authorities.

Function and programme area. Social Protection, which includes housing benefits, is the largest programme area (almost exactly a third of the total in 2003/4), followed by Health and Social Services (about 17 per cent), and

Education (about 13 per cent). In recent years the share taken by Housing and Community Amenities has fallen from 6.7 per cent (of GGE) in 1978/79 to 1.6 per cent (of TME) in 2003/4.[3]

Capital and current spending. The broad definition of *capital spending* used in the fiscal reports covers payments by the public sector either to renew or increase the nation's stock of physical assets. It covers expenditure on fixed assets (net of certain asset sales), stockbuilding, capital grants and net lending to the private sector (for capital projects). The wages and salaries of certain people in planning and supervising capital projects are included, and for local authorities it also includes the capital value of assets acquired under financial leases, property leased for more than 20 years and all vehicles leased for more than one year. The broad definition of *current spending* used in the fiscal reports covers payments made by the public sector on providing services, and largely consists of the wages and salaries of central and local government employees and the purchases of consumable goods and services by public sector organisations. In this context the notion of 'consumable' normally signifies that the purchase will be used up in the current financial year. It includes local authority payments of such things as mandatory student awards and rent rebates and allowances as part of housing benefit. Both local authority and central government spending is measured net of VAT. In 2003/4, as a percentage of total planned public spending, current spending constituted 93 per cent.

Economic activity versus transfers. The aggregate figure for public expenditure falls into two distinct economic categories:

   (a) expenditure to generate economic activity; and,
   (b) expenditure on transfer disbursements.

Expenditure on economic activity produces real wealth and consists of all current and capital spending by central and local government and public corporations that directly contributes to the output of goods and services. Such expenditure absorbs real economic resources to produce housing, health, defence, education, and transport services, etc. In other words, it represents a measure of the state's direct financial engagement in economic activity.

By contrast, transfer disbursements involve a redistribution of money wealth from one set of private hands to another set of private hands and, as such, they are not directly used to finance public sector economic activity. They include such items as housing benefit payments, subsidies to the private sector, state pensions and other social security payments.

---

3   GGE and TME are somewhat different ways of officially measuring public spending. They
    are explained and discussed later in this chapter (refer to section '*Defining public
    expenditure*').

If we make the assumption that those who pay the most taxes and contributions do not receive the most disbursements, then we can say that such payments *redistribute* rather than *absorb* resources. Transfer expenditure has a direct *income redistribution effect* but only an indirect *economic effect*. The indirect economic effect results from the fact that the less well off receivers of transfers will have a tendency to spend a higher proportion of their income than the better off givers. This means that the transfers will affect the nature and scope of consumer spending and savings in the economy.

This way of categorising public expenditure allows for a more penetrating analysis of the global figures. It underlines the point that figures that show a growth in total expenditure may be masking a number of interesting social, economic and political issues. For example, it is sometimes argued that increases in public expenditure result in a redistribution of resources away from the private towards the public sector of the economy. This is not necessarily true: transfers, which in recent years have been a fast growing element of public expenditure, may simply have the effect of redistributing resources between individuals within the private sector.

The argument for controlling public expenditure

Given the sums involved, central government has a legitimate interest in seeking to obtain value-for-money in its spending. Furthermore, the quality of public sector spending is bound to have an impact on the overall performance of the economy.[4]

In the post-war period, British governments have instigated fiscal and monetary measures designed to establish an economic climate that will stimulate growth in output, employment and trade. Controlling the rate of inflation has been a central theme in the economic policies of all recent governments. Stable prices are seen to be a prerequisite to the maintenance of both long-run business confidence and international competitiveness. Inflation is also seen as being particularly damaging to the interests of vulnerable groups living on low and fixed incomes. Contemporary economic orthodoxy identifies a strong link between public expenditure and inflation and it is for this reason that controlling the level of public expenditure has become a key aspect of macro-economic policy. Simply put, the argument runs as follows. Public expenditure has to be paid for either by public sector borrowing or out of taxation. Increased borrowing involves an expansion of credit, and thereby, effectively an increase in the money supply. If the increased money/credit base is not matched by an equivalent increase in national output, additional money demand will bid for roughly the same volume of output and prices will rise as a result. If, instead of borrowing, the public expenditure is paid for by raising indirect taxes (VAT, etc.), this additional financial burden to suppliers is likely to be passed on to consumers in the form of higher prices.

---

4   Both the Bank of England and the Treasury constantly make the point that the health of the economy depends in part on the existence of an orderly and stable housing market. Consequently, ministers often draw attention to the relationship between economic performance and the availability of decent, affordable homes.

If, on the other hand, the increased expenditure is paid for by means of direct taxation (income tax, etc.), this may lead to compensatory wage claims that will add to both consumer demand and production costs and this would also put upward pressure on prices.

When political arguments in favour of small government and low taxation are added to the economic reasoning outlined above, it can be understood why recent administrations have made the control of public expenditure such a prominent part of their strategies for regulating the economy.

Cash-limiting public expenditure on housing as an expressed part of government economic regulation began with measures introduced in 1976 by the Labour chancellor Denis Healey, and then became firmly embedded in the policies of the Conservative administrations that followed the general election of 1979. In comparison with other welfare programmes such as education and health, housing expenditure is capital intensive. This means that, unlike these other programmes, significant short-term savings in housing expenditure can be made by cancelling or postponing proposed building, improvement and repair works. In more labour intensive programme areas substantial savings can only be made by laying-off personnel. Of course, reducing the level of building activity creates unemployment in the construction industry and its related professions, but it does so in a less specific and obvious way than by sacking identifiable teachers, social workers, nurses, doctors and administrators. Furthermore, unlike much other welfare provision, social housing is used by a minority of the electorate thereby limiting the political impact of any cutbacks. For all these reasons it has proved to be politically easier to cut housing expenditure than most other big spending programme areas.[5]

Sources of public finance and the borrowing requirement

To pay for public expenditure central and local government collects revenue, sells assets and borrows money. Currently just over a third of revenue receipts are taken by the Inland Revenue in the form of income tax, corporation tax, petroleum revenue tax, capital gains tax, inheritance tax and stamp duties. About a third is collected by Customs and Excise in the form of VAT, fuel and tobacco duties, etc. Almost a third is raised by the combination of social security contributions, business rates, council tax, oil royalties and vehicle excise duties. Interest, dividends, rent, etc. contribute about six per cent of total receipts. In the recent past, privatisation receipts brought in about one per cent of the total general government receipts (HM Treasury, 1996 and Wilcox, 1995 Table 11b). Asset sales are largely derived from the sale of land and existing buildings (about £5 billion in 2003/4). The shortfall gap between total public spending and collected revenues creates a requirement for the public sector to borrow from other sectors of the economy and from overseas.

---

5   In 2003/4, the total expenditure on housing and community amenities totalled just over £7.5 billion.

European Structural Funds

Some housing projects are part funded from the European Regional Development Fund (ERDF). The ERDF is one of three European Union Structural Funds, the others being the European Social Fund and the European Agricultural Guidance and Guarantee Fund. While ERDF grants are additional to national expenditure, in the UK they are treated as public expenditure because the UK is a net contributor to the European Union budget. Provision for this is included in the public expenditure programmes of the departments co-ordinating funded projects.

Measures of public sector debt

The gap between what the government collects (in taxes and other revenue receipts) and what it spends sets the public sector's net cash/credit requirement. In the published finance tables this requirement is referred to as *Public Sector Net Borrowing* (PSNB). PSNB is an accruals-based measure[6] that is calculated net of privatisation receipts and excludes certain other financial transactions that would be included in a 'cash-flow' but not in an 'accruals' calculation. It embraces the market and overseas borrowings of UK public corporations as well as the deficit spending of central and local government. The PSNB is the primary measure of the government's budget deficit

The cash/credit gap always used to be measured in terms of a broader cash-flow financial indicator known as the *Public Sector Borrowing Requirement* (PSBR) which, despite its title, does not exactly match what the government has to borrow. The PSBR (still used) measures the public sector's net cash requirement rather than its actual borrowing requirement. The shift from the PSBR to PSNB was made in 1998 to give greater accuracy (and prominence) to the recording of public sector debt. (*HM Treasury News Release 101/98*, 11 June 1998). The change was based on the assumption that this stricter measure of public sector indebtedness gives a better indication of the underlying budgetary position. By being an accruals-based measure, PSNB excludes privatisations and other financial transactions that affect cash measures of borrowing such as the PSBR. This means it is more consistent with the national accounts and internationally agreed measures of the deficit and is not distorted by year to year cash movements.

In recent years the Chartered Institute of Housing and some other organisations have advocated the use of a different measure of public sector indebtedness called the *General Government Financial Deficit* (GGFD). This is the measure that has been adopted by the EU to establish the economic convergence criteria for European Monetary Union.[7] The key feature of GGFD is that, unlike the PSNB and the PSBR, it does not include borrowing by *public corporations*. The CIH

---

6   The distinction between an accruals-based and a cash-based approach to recording financial transactions is discussed in Chapter 2 (refer to section *Making good use of scarce resources*).

7   The government has to use the GGFD to show it has met the Maastricht Treaty criteria. The requirement is that a participating member state's GGFD must be less than three per cent of its GDP.

argument in favour of using the GGFD as the main measure centres on the fact that it would allow borrowing to be undertaken by local authority-owned companies that would not count against the main measure of public borrowing, thus giving them similar freedoms to those enjoyed by housing associations. This might be relevant to the future of arms length management organisations (ALMOs – see Chapter 10).

The principles and rules governing public finances

The presentational framework for analysing, planning and controlling the nation's public spending is broadly structured in line with national and international accounting conventions. The precise nature of the current format was introduced by the chancellor, Gordon Brown, in the first *Economic and Fiscal Strategy Report* in June 1998. The current fiscal procedures are based on an over-arching commitment to a financial management framework that will support long-term planning; focus on outputs rather than inputs; recognise the essential difference between current and capital spending; and promote prudence, stability and investment for the long term (*HM Treasury New Release*, 97/98 11 June 1998). This commitment has produced public expenditure planning and management arrangements that are grounded in a five-point fiscal code and three key fiscal rules. In line with the code's principles, public expenditure planning and management now operates in line with revised accounting rules known as *resource accounting and budgeting* (RAB).

The five-point fiscal code[8]
1. *Transparency* in the setting of fiscal policy objectives, the implementation of fiscal policy and in the publication of the public accounts.
2. *Stability* in the fiscal policy-making process and in the way fiscal policy impacts on the economy.
3. *Responsibility* in the management of the public finances.
4. *Fairness*, including fairness between generations.
5. *Efficiency* in the design and implementation of fiscal policy and in managing both sides of the public sector balance sheet.

---

8   In the 1998 Finance Act the government legislated for a *Code for Fiscal Stability* which requires more open and comprehensive reporting of the public accounts. Among other things, the fiscal strategy's key assumptions are examined and tested by the independent National Audit Office. Under the *Code for Fiscal Stability*, that was given the force of law in the 1998 Finance Act, an *Economic and Fiscal Strategy Report* (EFSR) has to be prepared and laid before parliament each financial year. This sets out the government's fiscal strategy and planned spending totals and explains how the government's new fiscal approach seeks to achieve the central economic objective of '*high and stable levels of growth and employment*' (EFSR, 1998, Chapter 1). The EFSR is accompanied by a series of Treasury press releases designed communicate the government's spending intentions to a wider public and amplify the thinking behind its fiscal strategy.

Three key fiscal rules

The present chancellor has established two key operational rules, one applying to current spending and the other to capital spending. He has also confirmed the continued operation (for the time being) of a third long-established Treasury dictate known as the 'financing rule'.

1. Current spending (cyclical and non-cyclical) is subject to a fiscal edict called *the golden rule* which states that departments must meet all current expenditure out of current revenue over the economic cycle. Put another way, this means that, in the medium term, the government will borrow only to invest and not to fund current spending. This is part of the government's commitment to see that debt is normally only generated to cover capital investment (that can generate long-run returns to help service that debt). The surplus on current budget (current receipts minus current spending) is called the 'current balance' and is used to determine whether the golden rule is met over the economic cycle. The golden rule promotes *fairness* between generations by ensuring that the bill for today's current spending (which mainly benefits today's tax-payers) will not be passed on to future generations. It promotes *responsibility* by highlighting the distinction between the nature of current and capital spending – thus pointing to a duty to maintain the level of investment required to meet the economy's needs and to ensure that the public capital stock is kept in good condition. The golden rule is monitored through the 'public sector current surplus'.

2. Borrowing to fund capital expenditure is constrained by the second of the chancellor's key fiscal rules. The *sustainable investment rule* states that net public debt as a proportion of national income (GDP) should be held over the economic cycle at a 'stable and prudent level' (currently set at around 40 per cent). The rule was introduced to help contain the level of interest payments on the public debt (by bearing down on the debt to GDP ratio). The 'public sector net borrowing' figure[9] shows performance against the sustainable investment rule.

3. The third fiscal rule is a long-standing Treasury edict called *the financing rule*. This is a simple Treasury regulation that states that *for an organisation to borrow outside of the PSNB (previously the PSBR) it must be under private ownership and control*. How this rule affects the ways in which housing is funded is discussed in some detail later in this chapter.

Delivering the five-point fiscal code: the Budget, spending reviews and public service agreements

The golden rule is being implemented using a definition of the current balance that is in line with the concept used in the national accounts (that are themselves

---

9   See earlier section *'Measures of public sector debt'* for explanation of PSNB.

published according to the definitions set out in the *European System of Accounts 1995* – ESA95). In terms of this definition, depreciation is counted as current rather than capital spending. This ensures that current tax-payers meet the costs of maintaining the capital stock. Using agreed and recognised definitions helps to make performance against the golden rule more *transparent*. The new code requires governments to report regularly on progress in meeting their fiscal objectives. Since 1998 the familiar *Financial Statement and Budget Report* has been supplemented each year by an *Economic and Fiscal Strategy Report* that sets out the government's long-term strategy and objectives. The code now also requires a *Pre-Budget Report* to be published that will allow the skills and expertise of others to be drawn upon when formulating policy. Together, these reports are intended to allow parliament (in particular the Treasury Select Committee) and the public, to scrutinise the government's fiscal plans. A key feature of the new system is the introduction of bi-annual *spending reviews*. These set firm and fixed three-year departmental spending limits and, through public service agreements (PSAs), identify the key improvements that the public can expect from these resources. Successive spending reviews have targeted resources at the government's priorities, have matched these resources with administrative reforms, and have set targets for improvements in key public services, including housing and community renewal.

The spending reviews include 'New Spending Plans' for Scotland, Wales and Northern Ireland. These provide the limits of devolved fiscal freedom for these areas. Within these limits of growth or constraint, the ODPM, the Scottish Executive, the National Assembly for Wales, and the Northern Ireland Assembly, work with the various Secretaries of State and the Treasury to make subsequent announcements about detailed spending plans for the devolved governments.

The introduction of pre-Budget reports and periodic spending reviews is intended to add *transparency* to the system of public expenditure management. The introduction of public service agreements[10] underlines the code's commitment to *responsibility*, *stability*, and *efficiency*.

The principle of *responsibility* is also manifested in the government's commitment to keep debt at levels that are judged to be 'prudent'. A *responsible* approach involves holding public debt to a 'sustainable' proportion of GDP.[11] In this context, 'sustainability' exists if, on the basis of reasonable assumptions, the government can be expected to maintain its current spending and taxation policies indefinitely while continuing to meet its debt interest obligations. The *responsibility principle* is based on the assumption that 'excessive' borrowing has

---

10 See glossary at the end of the chapter and also refer to Chapter 8.
11 To a large extent the 'prudent' level of debt depends on the size of the economy since it becomes possible to sustain a higher money level of debt as national income grows. This is why the fiscal rule is specified in terms of the ratio of public debt to GDP.

detrimental economic effects. This assumption produces the intention that borrowing should be used only to fund value-for-money investment.[12] *Spending reviews* are the mechanism chosen by the current government as the key method of determining what counts as a value-for-money investment.

This *responsibility* approach is consistent with the principle of *fairness*. By funding current spending from current revenue over the economic cycle, today's tax-payers bear the full cost of the public sector current spending from which they benefit.

By design, the fiscal rules are intended to lead to greater economic and fiscal *stability*. The new strategic approach is meant to allow decision-makers to plan and invest for the longer term, confident in the knowledge that the public finances will not be managed in a 'profligate' fashion that might necessitate a sudden adjustment at some point in the future.

In pursuit of resource *efficiency*, the National Assets Register has been established to provide an indication of the extent and location of public sector assets. Departments are encouraged to dispose of assets that are not contributing to service objectives. The principle of *focusing on outputs* rather than inputs is exemplified by the current rationalisation of the private sector's role in public service provision. With increasing use of Public/Private Partnerships (PPP), and especially the private finance initiative (PFI), the public sector is moving more to being a sponsor (as against a direct provider) of investment where this offers a more effective way of delivering public services. In the new fiscal framework, the benefits of PFI, and other forms of PPP, are now seen in terms of securing the best value for money, rather than producing a temporary reduction in the PSNB (or PSBR). The argument here is that a simplistic focusing on the PSNB does not give a true indication of investment *efficiency*. In order to evaluate the true economic consequences of public investment we need to consider how that investment affects both sides of the public sector balance sheet. This in turn requires a shift to resource accounting and budgeting.

Resource accounting and budgeting (RAB)

RAB now underpins the operation of the *golden rule* and the drive towards better stewardship of public assets. Based on accruals accounting and making a clear structural distinction between current and capital spending, RAB captures the full cost of resources consumed in the production of outputs in each reporting period. It is also expected that the introduction of *capital charging* for government departments will provide strong incentives to use capital productively. (See also Glossary at the end of the chapter).

---

12 Prudential borrowing for local authorities is discussed in Chapter 9.

The public sector balance sheet

The PSNB and PSBR focus on the public sector's net financial liabilities. The government is now beginning to pay more attention to movements in the public sector balance sheet, which includes tangible assets as well as net financial liabilities. There are, however, data and conceptual difficulties that need to be addressed before the balance sheet can be given a more formal role in the fiscal framework. In particular, the shift to resource accounting and budgeting will provide more accurate balance sheet data as well as underpinning the golden rule.

By recognising that certain forms of public expenditure constitute capital investment, resource accounting establishes a public sector 'balance sheet' that allows policy-makers to consider properly the long-run economic and financial consequences of investing or not investing in capital projects. It makes clear for example, that if taxes were raised and invested in more or improved council housing, then the public sector's asset base would have increased without any additional debt being incurred. It would make clear that if council houses were built with borrowed funds then both local government debts and assets would have increased. Such an approach would also show that if council houses were sold and the receipts used to pay off public sector debts, it would have the effect of reducing the stock of built assets and thus the ability of local authorities to generate future rental income flows. The implications for local government finance of such a shift are discussed more fully in subsequent chapters.

Public expenditure planning and control

The government's task can be thought of as comprising two broad activities:

(a) making a political decision as to what total should be planned for and how that total should be allocated between different programmes; and

(b) controlling and accounting for the actual spending outturns so that the outcomes match the plan and the constitutional requirements of parliamentary control over spending of public money are fulfilled.

As we have seen, the planning process now includes the publication of periodic spending reviews and an annual autumn pre-Budget statement by the Chancellor of the Exchequer that sets out his early thinking for the year ahead. The process culminates in the *Financial Statement and Budget Report* that the chancellor presents to parliament in the spring prior to the passage of the Finance Bill. Once enacted the Finance Bill gives statutory force to the provisions of the annual unified Budget.

Reliance on cash limits

For their plans to be realised governments need to establish procedures that influence the behaviour of those institutions and organisations that do the front-line spending. Cash limits are the main control mechanism. Cash limits quite simply set a ceiling on the amount of cash the government proposes to spend or authorise on specific services or blocks of services during a particular financial planning period.

The majority of cash limits are based on the Supply Estimates (see below and in the Glossary) and cover direct expenditure by central government and its voted grants and lending to other public sector bodies. In this way, the bulk of public expenditure is cash limited, including the amount of money the government contributes towards local government finance (called Aggregate External Finance) and capital expenditure financed by borrowing.

The emphasis on cash-limiting as a control mechanism has focused attention on cash-flow management in the public sector and sharpened up procedures for controlling costs. However, it has been criticised for under-valuing long-term investment. It is also regarded by some as a 'surrogate pay policy' for the public sector because in setting a limit, the government seems to be taking a view about the appropriate level of salaries and wages in the coming year.

Defining public expenditure

There is no single definitive meaning of the term 'public expenditure'. Indeed, there is potential for confusion arising from the fact that a number of terms are used by journalists and commentators. These include, for example, 'state spending', 'government spending', and 'public spending', and it is not always clear from the context what the term being used precisely means.

The definitions of public expenditure used in official British publications that reference the Public Expenditure Statistical Analyses and the various fiscal reports all stem from accepted national accounting concepts that, in turn, broadly follow international guidelines. These official definitions can be rather confusing because of their technical nature and because they are periodically redefined or re-labelled. Until 1999, the aggregate often referred to in official tables was 'GGE' which stands for General Government Expenditure. GGE measures public expenditure for the government sector as a whole and is composed of three broad elements:

1. Central government spending.
2. Local government spending.
3. Subsidies to nationalised industries and public corporations.

Since 1999, the official total of public spending has been known as *Total Managed Expenditure (TME)*. TME is split into two categories: cyclical and non-cyclical. Cyclical spending, called Annually Managed Expenditure (AME), is assumed to be subject to changeable forces and events outside the control of the various spending departments, and is therefore subject to annual reviews rather than to longer-term plans. AME includes much of the social security spending. Non-cyclical expenditure is sometimes called 'The Control Total' and is planned three years in advance under a procedure that sets Departmental Expenditure Limits (DELs).

Housing expenditure is seen to be non-cyclical and thus capable of being planned for; it is therefore part of The Control Total. The relationship between these three categories of public spending can be expressed by the formula: DEL + AME = TME. The move to a three-year planning period is part of the government's general commitment to get away from procedures that emphasise 'short-termism'. In this way, it seeks to reinforce a commitment to the fiscal code's objective of *stability*.

That part of TME that is subjected to parliamentary scrutiny is called *supply expenditure*. The term *supply expenditure* refers to that expenditure that is directly financed by money voted by parliament in the Supply Estimates. Voted expenditure covers most of central government's own expenditure and central government support for the expenditure of local authorities. The main category of expenditure within the TME that is not covered by the Supply Estimates is expenditure related to the National Insurance Fund which provides over half the spending on social protection (previously called 'social security').

Within TME, capital and current expenditures are planned and managed separately to ensure that the fiscal rules are met and to prevent capital investment being cut back to meet short-term pressures on current expenditure. This is part of the government's general commitment to draw a distinction between the need to manage day-to-day spending prudently and the need to invest wisely in the future. As we made clear earlier in this chapter, the distinction between capital and current expenditure is seen to be of some economic significance. Capital investment in industry, commerce and the social fabric is regarded as an essential element in the maintenance of long-term economic prosperity and social well-being.

Departmental planning and control: spending inside the DEL

The public spending round has been a feature of British economic life since the early sixties. It has established an annual cycle of year-on-year incremental bids by spending departments.[13] The planned spending totals are arrived at by a process of negotiation between the Treasury and the various spending departments and are discussed in parliament as part of the Budget debate before being enacted via the provisions of the Finance Act. These arrangements were substantially

---

13 Since 1978 the allocation of increases or decreases in public expenditure in Scotland has focused on a population-based mechanism rather than relying on the conventional approach of political bargaining between departments and the Treasury over their totals. This mechanism is known as the 'Barnett Formula'.

revised in line with the recommendations of the 1998 *Economic and Fiscal Strategy Report* (see above discussion). The present government's criticism of the established public spending round (i.e. pre 1997) is that settlements were reached by bargaining over inputs rather than by an analysis of outputs and efficiency. This, it is argued, led to excessive departmentalism; an unrealistic and unhelpful split between private and public provision; and a bias towards consumption today rather than investment in the future.

Through the process of spending reviews (established in 1998), non-cyclical programmes (including housing) are set 'firm and realistic' plans and fixed capital budgets for three years at a time. (Where possible, similar agreements are made for the associated current running costs). The planned for limits reference performance targets and are set in cash terms to provide a clear incentive for departments to control their costs. They are reviewed only if inflation varies substantially from forecast. In this way, the new system moves from an annual cycle to multi-year plans. To ensure that the chancellor's fiscal rules are met, and to make possible long-term investment in the nation's infrastructure, departments are given distinct current and capital budgets and are expected to manage them separately. The idea is that investment plans are not squeezed out by pressure of current spending. As well as a clearer distinction between current and capital spending, service expenditures have to be justified by 'proper analysis' of their effectiveness rather than bargaining over inputs. For this reason, cost-benefit analysis has become a strong feature of resource budgeting in the public sector.

These multi-year plans are now drawn together in the aggregate *Departmental Expenditure Limits* (DEL).[14] These arrangements put an emphasis on the co-ordination and integration of services rather than departmentalism and a piecemeal approach to spending. The idea of this planned approach is to move away from a procedure of *incremental budgeting* (in which a department is given a bit more or a bit less than before) to the laying down of departmental targets for efficiency and performance (i.e. *resource budgeting*). Under the old arrangements the Treasury and individual spending departments engaged in 'bilateral' bargaining meetings. Under current arrangements inter-departmental consequences of spending (or not spending) have to be analysed. The new system is also based on a 'proper understanding' of the role and limits of government: '...*a shift from the state only as owner, manager and employer to the state as also facilitator and partner*' (*Economic and Fiscal Strategy Approach*, 1998, Introduction).

To bring a degree of flexibility into the planning approach, since 1999 departments have been given extended powers to carry budgets over from year to year. Departmental agents, such as local authorities, are given the same flexibility to carry over year-end under-spends. Resources are consciously allocated and monitored on the basis of agreed outcomes, and departments and their spending

---

14 DEL includes spending funded by some inter-departmental budgets that are subject to special control arrangements.

agents are set clear quality standards. In local government this takes the form of a duty to provide *Best Value*. As part of the Best Value regime, an inspectorate of housing has been established to help improve the management of council housing, set standards for performance and guarantee high quality of investment. It operates under the Audit Commission and carries out regular inspections of housing departments. (This is discussed fully in subsequent chapters.).

About 60 per cent of TME is within DEL. The remaining 40 per cent is largely made up of Annually Managed Expenditure (AME).

Annually Managed Expenditure: spending outside the DEL

Firm multi-year limits are not seen to be appropriate for the large demand-led (i.e. cyclical) programmes that are brought together in Annually Managed Expenditure (AME). AME expenditure can be volatile, difficult or impossible for the spending department concerned to control (i.e. is demand led), of no burden to the central purse (i.e. self-financing), or large in relation to the overall size of the department concerned. For these reasons this category of expenditure is subject to annual scrutiny as part of the Budget process and taken into account when the government sets its plan for TME and DEL. The main elements in AME are social security benefits, tax credits for individuals, local authority self-financed expenditure (LASFE), self-financing by public corporations, Scottish Expenditure financed by the Scottish variable rate of income tax and non-domestic rates, payments under the Common Agricultural Policy, net payments to EU institutions, expenditure finance by the National Lottery, net public service pensions, and central government gross debt interest.

Social security benefits include payments both of social security and national insurance benefits by the Department for Work and Pensions (DWP) and the DSS (Northern Ireland). It includes central government support for certain benefits paid by local authorities, e.g. housing benefit and council tax benefit. It now also includes central support for local authorities' payments of rent rebates that is the responsibility of the DWP.

The relative position of housing in total public spending

Public expenditure by function

The main programme areas identified in the white papers and fiscal reports are shown in Table 5.1.

If shares of public expenditure are measured against the total value of national output (Gross Domestic Product) rather than against total expenditure, the order of public spending priorities is not altered. Public sector spending on housing and

Table 5.1: Percentage shares of total government spending[15]

Year	1978-79	1989-90	1994-95	1998-99	2003-4
Social security	26.0	30.3	34.5	34.9	33.2
Health and social services	14.2	16.8	17.7	19.6	16.5
Education and science	14.5	14.2	13.4	13.5	13.3
Defence	11.5	11.6	8.5	7.8	6.0
Law and order	3.9	5.0	5.9	6.1	6.0
Transport	4.6	3.9	3.9	3.0	3.5
HOUSING	**6.7**	**2.1**	**2.1**	**1.3**	**1.6**
Agriculture, fish and food	1.6	1.3	1.5	1.7	1.1

(Sources: based on *Government Expenditure Plans 1990-91 to 1992-93*, HM Treasury; Wilcox 1995, 1996 and 1999, and *Public Expenditure Statistical Analysis 2004*, Cm 6201, HM Treasury)

community amenities as a proportion of GDP in 2003/4 was 0.7 per cent (HM Treasury, 2004). The relative national decline of the programme area is illustrated by the fact that in 1981/82 its share of GDP was as high as 1.6 per cent (HM Treasury, 1996). Measured in absolute terms, some seven billion pounds was set aside for social housing in 1975. To have kept up with inflation, this figure would have had to have risen to something like £30 billion, but is in fact only £7.3 billion (2003/4).

Current national investment in housing

The level of housing investment can be measured in a number of ways – gross fixed housing capital formation as a percentage of GDP, dwellings constructed compared to population size, or net additions to the stock. Whichever measure is used, research indicates that housing investment in the UK is low by the standards of other developed economies.[16] In recent years the UK devoted, on average, 3.2 per cent of GDP to gross fixed capital formation in housing which is similar to Sweden but less than countries such as France, Belgium and the USA, who invested over 4 per cent, and significantly less than Germany, the Netherlands, Canada and Ireland who invested more than 5.5 per cent in house building and improvements (Wilcox, 2004).

Between 1980 and 1997 General Government Expenditure on housing fell by nearly 68 per cent in real terms – the most severe drop in expenditure for any

---

15   This is a composite table drawn from a number of sources. The figures for total spending up to 1999 are based on GGE but those for 2003/4 are based on TME. Over the years, the spending classifications have altered slightly and statistical measures have been adjusted. This means that comparisons over time are approximate only.

16   Research funded by Avebury International, Michael Oxley and Jacqueline Smith, *A European Perspective of Housing Investment in the UK*, Avebury, 1996. See also Wilcox, 1997, p70, Table 7.

government service during that period. Whereas household numbers increased by 280,000 per annum in the period 1981-93, the number of dwellings increased only by about 200,000. Social housing completions fell from an average of 134,000 per annum in the 1970s to about 34,000 in the early 1990s. In recent years, the rate of house building has increased. In 2002/3 completions for the UK totalled some 184,000. Of these, about 164,000 were in the private sector, about 20,000 were in the housing association sector, and less than 400 were in the local authority sector (ODPM, National Assembly for Wales, Scottish Executive, the Department for Social Development, Northern Ireland). The recent Barker Report on housing supply, *Delivering Stability: Securing Our Future Housing Needs* (HM Treasury, 2004), suggests the need for a significant increase in the rate of house building over the next few years if property is to be affordable to first time buyers and those on low incomes.[17]

The dramatic decline in housing's share of public expenditure during the 1980s and 1990s is illustrated by the following table of comparisons. (Wilcox, 1999, p106, Table 15b.).

Table 5.2: Real growth in percentage share of GGE 1980/81 to 1998/99

Law and order	88.3
Social security	79.0
Agriculture, fish and food	35.7
Health and social services	73.7
Education	31.2
Culture, media and sport	86.1
Overseas aid	15.9
Environmental services	11.9
Transport	-13.5
Trade and industry	-23.4
Defence	-15.3
HOUSING	**-71.5**
Misc. expenditure	21.1
Total expenditure on services	39.4

The cuts in the housing programme in the last two decades of the twentieth century were particularly heavy in the local government sector. By 2000, housing investment allocations to councils had dropped to a quarter in real terms of what they were in 1979. Although dramatic, these cutbacks in the housing programme area have to be seen against wider commitments in public spending in this period on housing benefit, mortgage interest tax relief, capital gains concessions, discounts on *right to buy* sales, and other financial aid given to support home-ownership and urban renewal. Financial support for these housing-related measures either did not appear in the public accounts or were counted as elements

---

17   The Barker Report is discussed more fully in Chapter 6.

of other programme areas. Taking these measures into consideration we can argue that Table 5.2 somewhat over-states the real cuts in government support to housing in this period and that there was not so much a huge cut in housing expenditure as a redistribution of support away from bricks-and-mortar subsidies towards housing benefit and support to home-ownership.[18] The nature and scope of this redistribution is discussed in subsequent chapters.

Figure 5.2: The changing balance of subsidy

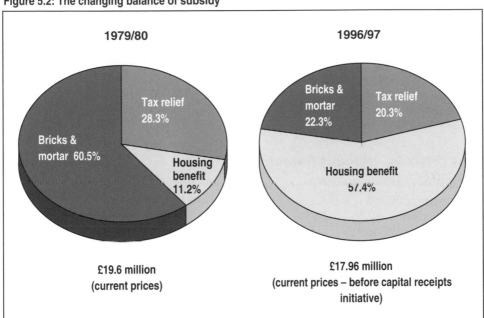

The need for future investment in housing
===

Between the budgets of 1993 and 1996 the government cut its commitment to housing development and renewal programmes by some £1.3 billion: the CIH estimate that these cuts alone represented a loss of 220,000 social rented homes (Wild, 1996, p14). The government itself is now concerned that there has been an under investment in housing development in recent years and that this is creating instability in the housing market as well as inhibiting other aspects of its social and economic policy agenda – particularly those associated with health, educational performance, inclusion and employment.

Of equal concern is the state of the existing stock. The physical state of the nation's dwellings is officially measured by reference to the findings of periodic

18 The 1995 white paper *Our Future Homes* indicated that total housing expenditure on all rented housing in real terms was about the same in 1994/95 as it had been in 1979/80.

condition surveys that examine a cross section of the national stock by referencing an official 'housing, health and safety rating' (currently replacing the old 'fitness standard'). This new rating system (HHSRS) assesses health and safety hazards in the home and designates them to a category according to their severity.[19] The fitness/HHSR standard applies in England, Wales and Northern Ireland. The statutory measure of housing quality in Scotland is whether a dwelling is Below Tolerable Standard (BTS).

These house condition surveys are carried out separately in the various national regions under the auspices of the ODPM (England), the Northern Ireland Housing Executive, The Scottish Executive (via Communities Scotland), and the National Assembly for Wales. Traditionally, house conditions surveys have taken place on a five year rolling basis. There are now moves to operate them on a continuous basis to enable progress towards the government's targets relating to decent social housing (that are monitored annually). The continuous approach for the English House Condition Survey was introduced in 2002.

The drive for 'decent homes'

Tables 5.1 and 5.2 indicate how badly housing has fared in recent years in comparison with other programmes. The most obvious practical effects of these substantial cuts have been rising rent levels, a reduction in public sector house building, and a reduction in the frequency of repairs and maintenance of the existing public stock. Despite this, the various house condition surveys have demonstrated significant improvements in recent years where 'condition' is assessed by reference to such factors as disrepair, poor insulation and other measures of fitness for purpose. As we will see in subsequent chapters, the government is now utilising the mechanism of Public Service Agreements to set higher standards of 'decency' for all public and private sector landlords.

In England, the government's key housing target is to make all housing from social providers (councils and housing associations registered with the Housing Corporation) 'decent' by 2010 and to reduce progressively the proportion of vulnerable households in the private sector living in non-decent homes. The *Communities Plan* also places decent homes within the broader framework of raising the quality of life for all communities – a concern not only for decent homes but also with decent places. English local authorities are required to engage in an options appraisal exercise to determine the appropriate form of ownership and management for their stock. Central to these exercises (discussed in detail in Chapter 10), is a concern to ensure that the option selected provides adequate scope to deliver the Decent Homes Standard by the target date. In 2004, the Scottish Minister for Communities announced a cross-tenure Scottish Housing Quality Standard in line with the Partnership Agreement to introduce a Scottish Decent Homes Standard (see Chapter 10).

---

19   The change to HHSRS is unlikely to come into force before 2005/06.

The new Decent Homes Standard and its equivalents in Scotland and Wales extend the fitness levels to include additional requirements for state of repair, modern kitchen and bathroom facilities, adequate levels of insulation and an effective heating system to ensure the home can be kept warm. They are discussed more fully in subsequent chapters.

There is a general consensus that Britain needs to invest more in both private sector and social housing. More than 1.5 million homes in Britain are classified as unfit and many more provide inadequate living conditions when compared to the new decent homes standards. There is a shortfall in provision and much of the stock in all tenures is under-maintained. In the late 1990s the Commons Environment Committee estimated that an extra 90,000 affordable rented homes would be needed each year for 20 years and the Environment Secretary stated that 4.4 million homes would be needed by the year 2016. However, on current trends, this overall target will not be met, and even if it were, it is clear that regional and local shortages would still exist and problems of affordability would still persist well into the twenty first century.

These problems have been discussed in a number of recent official and unofficial reports, most notably in the Barker Review of housing supply, *Delivering Stability: Securing Our Future Housing Needs*, HM Treasury, 2004). This study was commissioned by the Treasury and it points to the need to provide a further 146,000 new homes a year (in England) in order to make property as affordable to first-time buyers as it was it the late 1980s. Among other things, Barker makes the case for higher spending on social housing to help address the imbalances in the supply of affordable accommodation. The report indicates that additional investment of well over a billion pounds per annum will be required to deliver additional social housing to meet projected future needs.[20]

Although estimates of the size of the investment backlog vary, the Chartered Institute of Housing and others have called for a building programme of some 100,000 affordable rented houses per year to satisfy unmet need, and originally estimated the backlog of disrepair and improvement work in British council housing to be £20 billion (see Moody, 1998). Government has responded by increasing investment levels in the existing stock of council housing, either directly through greater public expenditure or by encouraging stock transfer. More recently, it has responded to the need for additional rented housing by increasing the Housing Corporation's resources in England, and especially by its plans for significant new development in the south-east.

Controlling housing expenditure

The precise mechanisms for cash-limiting public expenditure on the provision and consumption of housing will be discussed in subsequent chapters. We will see that

---

20   The Barker Report is discussed more fully in Chapter 6.

they involve a wide variety of mechanisms that are constantly under review. They include the use of legal constraints on borrowing, fund capping and establishing eligibility criteria for subsidies and benefits. They also involve indirect 'accounting' controls that operate by establishing notional rather than actual money flows. By these mechanisms public funds are allocated against notional rather than actual expenditures. These notional figures are set by the central funding authority and this allows them to manipulate the level of support they give. The detailed ways in which expenditure is controlled varies from sector to sector and, to some extent at least, from one national region to another. It is a topic that we will return to again.

Treasury rules and the differences between local authorities and housing associations

As we shall see in Chapter 10, in many ways stock transfer was a means of putting in place for the council housing stock the financial freedoms already enjoyed by housing associations. This debate about the respective freedoms of the two sectors has been revived regularly, in different forms, over the last two decades. For example, in 1995 the CIH advocated 'local housing corporations' which would be owned by councils but not subject to the same borrowing rules as local authorities.[21] The case for 'local housing companies', now the established structure for stock transfers, was also based on creating a body with housing association rules but more accountable than a conventional association to the local authority and tenants.[22]

Most recently, there have been renewed calls for a so-called 'level playing field' between local authorities and associations in terms of finance, government support and ability to develop new homes. These have been fuelled by demands for a 'fourth way' for council housing, beyond the options of stock transfer, ALMOs and PFI which are discussed in Chapter 10.

It is therefore pertinent to ask the question: what are the financial differences between housing associations and local authorities? Or to put the question more narrowly and precisely, what financial and business freedoms do associations have, which local authorities would like to have without giving up ownership of their stock (as happens with transfer)? Here are some of them:[23]

1. make their own judgements about their borrowing;
2. be able to borrow outside narrow public sector limits;

---

21 Hawksworth, J. and Wilcox, S. (1995) *Challenging the Conventions: Public Borrowing Rules and Housing Investment*. CIH, Coventry.

22 See Wilcox, S. *et al.* (1993) *Local Housing Companies: New opportunities for council housing*. JRF/CIH, York.

23 Based on John Perry's presentation to HouseMark ALMO chief executive's symposium, April 2004.

3. borrow against the value of their assets or future revenue streams;
4. be free of the constraints of old debt;
5. be in charge of all the sources of revenue available to them;
6. be free of the constraints of a revenue subsidy system;
7. be able to obtain project-specific grants for new projects;
8. have full control over existing assets;
9. be able to add to the stock if there is new demand;
10. refinance so as to generate surpluses to reinvest in the stock or in the community.

These freedoms give associations considerable freedom over their revenues and over their investment in both existing and new housing stock; they also enable them to make realistic 30-year business plans. Of course, established associations have old debt (item 4), but new ones created through stock transfer are effectively given a 'clean sheet' to create new debt for the new investment they want to undertake.

Some progress is being made towards reducing or removing some of these differences. For example (item 1), local authorities have (from April, 2004) enjoyed a 'prudential' borrowing regime which has replaced the previous system of credit approvals or borrowing consents (see Chapter 9). The ODPM has discussed (but not yet taken forward) reforms such as restructuring debt (item 4), removing some of the constraints of the housing subsidy system (item 6) and introducing capital grants in place of revenue subsidy for new projects (item 7). By being largely free of revenue subsidy, council housing in Scotland could already be said to enjoy more freedom than the sector in England (see Chapter 9).

Arms length management organisations (ALMOs – see Chapter 10) in England are currently (in 2005) arguing for more of the freedoms listed here. Some progress has been achieved: the ODPM has announced that they will be eligible, like housing associations, to bid for Social Housing Grant for new housing development.

The arguments of those who want the so-called 'level playing field' tend to focus on councils being able to borrow against their asset base or against future revenue streams (item 3), or more especially to be free of the constraints of the public spending rules (item 2). However, the government has already ruled out the first of these in the Local Government Act 2003. On borrowing constraints generally, apart from its own strictness about these rules, the government is constrained by international accounting conventions as to how it classifies borrowing – as government debt or as non-government, private debt. Expenditure directly by a central or local government body will inevitably be judged as creating or potentially creating government debt, and is therefore always going to be more tightly controlled according to the fiscal rules set out earlier in this chapter.

Summary

In this chapter we have made the point that the workings of the housing system help to determine the nature and scope of the 'welfare state' and because of this, the ways in which housing is produced and consumed are of political interest to the government of the day. The state has also intervened in the housing finance system because it recognises that the economic and social well-being of the nation is influenced by how we deliver and manage housing and housing-related services. A third broad reason for intervention is that the financial arrangements associated with the housing system have a significant impact on the ability of a government to fulfil its macro-economic policy objectives.

A tension exists between the need to invest public money in maintaining and improving the nation's stock of dwellings and the government's need to control public expenditure in order to pursue its economic objectives. This tension has led to a call from housing practitioners and academics to make a sharper distinction between capital and revenue expenditure. In June 1998 fiscal arrangements were reshaped around the chancellor's two new fiscal rules – to finance current spending from taxation and to keep net public debt below a fixed percentage of GDP. The 1998 reforms reflect the government's belief that *'Britain must have sustainable public finances, not just for the odd year or two, but throughout the economic cycle'*. (Chancellor's Statement on the EFSR, *HM Treasury News Release 96/98*, 11 June 1998).

In the chapters that follow we will see that the government's desire to control public expenditure plays a crucially important part in determining the nature and scope of the various housing finance regimes that operate in the different tenures.

Glossary

Total Managed Expenditure (TME)
A measure of total public spending drawn from national accounts – the expenditure side of the government's fiscal framework. It represents public sector current expenditure plus net investment plus depreciation.

Departmental Expenditure Limits (DELs)
That part of TME (about 60 per cent) that the government seeks to control. DELs identify those departmental financial resources that are subjected to three-year spending limits.

Annually Managed Expenditure (AME)
That part of TME that cannot reasonably be subject to firm multi-year limits. It includes most social security spending.

Supply Expenditure

That part of TME that is voted for by parliament (about two-thirds of the total).

The Comprehensive Spending Review (CSR)

A highly influential comprehensive review of the aims, objectives and achievements of all spending in each department that took place in 1997/98. It provided a zero-based analysis of each spending programme to determine the 'best' way of delivering the government's objectives. It allocated substantial additional resources (for a fixed term) to key priorities such as education and health and established the notions of 'Best Value' and 'resource accounting and budgeting' for central government activities. As part of this process it introduced the notion of public service agreements (PSAs).

Public Service Agreements (PSAs)

An innovation introduced in the 1998 CSR. They are part of the mechanism for delivering 'Best Value' from central government spending. They establish agreed output targets detailing the outcomes departments are expected to deliver with the resources allocated to them. The government monitors progress against these PSA targets, and report in detail in annual departmental reports, giving parliament and the public the opportunity to monitor the effectiveness of departmental spending. Departments are also required to publish progress against their PSA targets in an autumn performance report. In the field of housing, the highest profile PSA is currently the Decent Homes Standard.

Spending Reviews

Periodic reviews (currently bi-annual) of the government's overall spending programme to ensure that it is appropriately coherent ('joined-up') and consistent with the fiscal code and its associated 'rules' It covers a three-year planning period. The Budget preceding a Spending Review sets the parameters or 'envelope' for the exercise. In the Review, the Budget AME forecast for year one of the Spending Review period is updated and AME forecasts are made for years two and three of the Spending Review period.

Resource Budget

Measures the total resources consumed by a central government department. A department's resource budget is divided into 'resource DEL' and 'resource departmental AME'.

Resource Account

Measures expenditure when it accrues rather than when the cash is spent. Resource budgets include non-cash costs such as depreciation and charges for bad debts. They include resources consumed but paid for later.

Further reading

http://www.hm-treasury.gov.uk: *Public Expenditure Planning and Control in the UK – A Brief Introduction.*

Coopers and Lybrand, (1996), *Consensus for Change – Public Borrowing Rules, Housing Investment and the City*, CIH: Coventry.

HM Treasury, *Public Expenditure: Statistical Analysis 2004* (or current year) Cm 6201.

Timmins, N., (2001) *The Five Giants – A biography of the welfare state,* Harper Collins: London.

Wilcox, S., *UK Housing Review* (latest edition), CIH/CML: Coventry/London.

CHAPTER 6:
The nature of owner-occupation

Its growth and significance

During the twentieth century, owner-occupation developed from being a restricted way of holding residential property that catered largely for the housing needs of the upper echelons of society into the nation's predominant tenure arrangement.[1] This growth has been particularly prominent over the last 25 years. During the 1980s the proportion of households that owned their own homes rose from about a half to two-thirds. By the end of the 1990s the proportion had risen to about 68 per cent. Between 1997 and 2003, 1.1 million new home-owners came into existence. In the early years of the twenty first century, the growth in this sector has been supported and fuelled by mortgage interest rates that have been at the lowest level for almost forty years.

The value of the nation's housing stock is now equivalent to 57 per cent of the nation's total wealth and housing equity[2] now represents a significant proportion of all personal wealth held in the UK. Figures from the Office of National Statistics indicate that at the start of 2004 the total net worth of the UK, including financial assets, was £5,344 billion. The most valuable asset was the housing stock with a total value of £3,045 billion. The value of housing assets belonging to households and non-profit organisations is worth more than £2,000 billion (2004).[3] The dominant place of private housing in the nation's wealth has important implications for the economy and society. It has implications for the wider economy because house price movements can have a significant impact on household confidence and hence spending and saving decisions. It also has important implications for the distribution of wealth among households and for the transfer of wealth between generations.

The concept of ownership

Proprietary analysis, referred to in Chapter 1, makes the point that a house is not 'owned' in the same way that consumer durables such as cameras and refrigerators are 'owned'. In purchasing a dwelling the owner-occupier does not

---

1   One of the reasons that conveyancing is such a convoluted business involving the employment of legal advisers is that until the twentieth century, property transactions were largely restricted to the landed classes and involved the transfer or break-up of complex estates.

2   Housing equity is that part of the asset's value that is unencumbered by mortgage debt. This is discussed more fully in Chapter 7.

3   By contrast, UK individuals' holdings in stocks and shares were worth £204 billion at 31 December 2003, according to the Office for National Statistics.

so much gain absolute possession of the building and the land, as acquire a bundle of legally enforceable *freehold* or *leasehold* rights relating to their use and disposal. This is an important point because it underlines the fact that others may also 'own' legal rights or interests in the same property, such as tenancy rights or rights of easement. Such legal interests have a market value of their own and their existence can therefore affect the exchange value of the freehold or leasehold.

Figure 6.1: Ownership rights

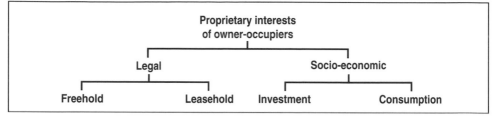

The fullest individual, legal ownership of real property is called 'fee simple'. *Fee simple* is associated with freehold rights and it is the form of ownership that most of us think of in relation to owner-occupation. It is the strongest form of legal ownership and, subject to any underlying rights of the Crown and any mortgage encumbrances, planning laws and health codes, the fee simple holder has absolute ownership of the property. These rights can be left to the owner's heirs for ever or until such time as they dispose of the property.

Leasehold is an agreement whereby a 'buyer', sometimes called a 'tenant', 'leaseholder' or 'lessee' acquires the right to use the landed property for a specific period in return for a land rent to the fee simple owner, the 'lessor'. At the end of the period, which can be up to 999 years, all the property rights revert to the party that holds title in fee simple. Leaseholders can be thought of as a class of owner-occupier. The term owner-occupier carries no legal weight and 'long' leaseholders usually consider themselves to be owners; indeed, they are considered as such by virtually everyone else, including the government.[4] They are, however, subject to regulation by third parties, the lessors, who can influence their expenditure, their ability to sell the house or flat, and its market value. Ultimately, these third parties can also influence the right of the occupier to remain in the home they have bought. The issue of leasehold reform is discussed later in the chapter.

The imagery and culture of ownership

During the second half of the twentieth century, the aspiration to own one's own home and thereby become part of the 'property-owning democracy', was actively encouraged both by the rhetoric that accompanied government housing policy and by the commercial advertising that was part of the rapidly expanding property and

---

4   See for example, Discussion Paper – Leasehold Reform: Joint submission by LEASE and the British Property Federation (November, 1999).

mortgage markets. In addition, as home-ownership became more and more accessible to a wider section of society, the advantages of owning one's own home were increasingly pointed to in the organs of the popular media.

The case for expanding owner-occupation is grounded in the presuppositions of market ideology (refer to Chapter 5). Insofar as it embraces voluntaristic, demand-led market mechanisms that operate to fulfil 'natural' domestic desires in ways that enhance life chances, the tenure can be said to encapsulate the values of a free-enterprise culture. In the minds of those who are ideologically predisposed towards owner-occupation, its growth is also seen to foster individuality and personal responsibility.[5] In terms of this view, home-ownership is assumed to be 'good' for the individual, enhancing self-fulfilment, personal independence, financial security, etc., and also 'good' for the wider community, by spreading capital wealth and thereby cultivating 'responsible' attitudes towards property in particular and society's socio-economic structures in general.

By the 1980s the popular discourse on home-ownership was characterised by pronouncements that carried a distinct cultural symbolism of responsibility and self-fulfilment. This helped to create a political climate in which the government could argue that it almost had 'moral' duty to make home-ownership more widely available. That as many people as possible should be encouraged to own their own homes was presented as a common sense proposition.[6] Although attitudes to home-ownership were modified by the sharp downturn in the property market that occurred after 1989, in Britain today there still exists a powerful ideological advocacy of owner-occupation. Politicians, mortgage providers and the press still commonly employ such housing imagery as 'castles' (of security), and 'ladders' (of mobility), and many commentators still point to the moral imperative of most people becoming home owners in line with their 'natural' desires and interests.

The popularity of owner-occupation

Recent attitude surveys indicate that aspirations for owner-occupation continue to be strong.[7] The shifting aspirations in favour of home-ownership can be explained in part by government policies favouring this tenure. In particular, the right to buy initiative opened up new opportunities for lower-income groups to enter the sector during the 1980s and 1990s. However, the desire to own one's own home in the

---

5   See Appendix 1 for fuller discussion of this point.

6   This compares with what we might term 'rational' or 'uncommon sense' explanation of the growth of the tenure. This non-ideological explanation accepts that the advantages of home-ownership can be tangible but argues that they are not intrinsic in the tenure. That is, it argues that they do not naturally occur in all places when a certain stage of socio-economic development is reached, but rather that they are largely the consequence of financial, fiscal, legal and other arrangements that are specific in terms of time and space.

7   In a 1996 Gallup poll survey, owner-occupation was shown to be by far the most popular form of housing tenure across all sectors of society. More recently, results from the Council of Mortgage Lenders Annual Market Research (2004) also showed that the majority of GB households wished to be home-owners, with 72 per cent stating they would like to be owners within two years and 81 per cent in ten years' time. (CML *Housing Finance*, Summer 2004 p10).

---

short term stabilised during the late 1990s (Smith, 2004). The slight preference shift towards renting can be in large part be explained by the downturn in the housing market that occurred between 1989 and 1995. As well as resulting in thousands of repossessions, the changed conditions after 1989 left many households with problems of negative equity and burdensome mortgage debts. However, the continuing popularity of home-ownership is illustrated most effectively by the continuing rise in house prices. Although house price inflation has a clear regional dimension, in general it has stubbornly persisted into the early years of the current century.

The size and structure of the tenure

As a tenure arrangement, owner-occupation has expanded continuously since the end of the First World War. Some 70 per cent of Britain's housing stock is now owner-occupied, compared with about 55 per cent in 1979 and less than 10 per cent in 1914. The trend of increasing home-ownership was significantly accelerated by the policies of the post-1979 Conservative administrations. During their terms in office, from 1979 to 1997, an additional 3.8 million households gained access to the tenure, an increase of some 38 per cent. The rate of increase has now slowed down and there is much current debate about the extent to which there is scope to expand owner-occupation in the future.[8] Future growth is likely to depend largely on economic factors. Given the current demographic structure in the UK, there is probably scope for further growth particularly if the current period of low general inflation and stable interest rates is sustained.

Fig. 6.2. The dominance of owner-occupation

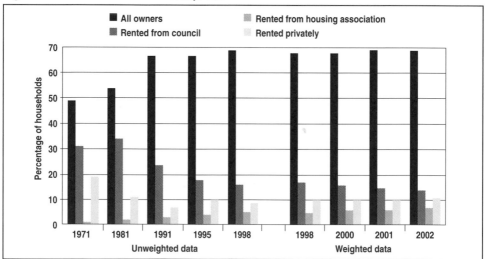

(Source: *Living in Britain 2002*, Office for National Statistics, 2004)

---

8   See, for example, Alan Holmans' article 'Owner-occupier households: recent trends in England and the USA, Australia, Canada and New Zealand', in *Housing Finance* No.45, February 2000, pp30-35.

About 30 per cent of all households in the UK own their homes outright and some 40 per cent own with a mortgage liability. The current figure of 70 per cent total home-ownership conceals a marked social stratification and significant national, regional and local variations. Over 90 per cent of the professional/managerial class are now home-owners compared with about 30 per cent of unskilled manual workers. Home-ownership is more prominent in Wales and the south-east and south-west of England than it is in Scotland and the north of England. Within particular towns and cities, significant variations can also exist at the district level.

Less traditional forms of home-ownership: park homes

Park homes are mobile homes that are used for residential purposes. Some 100,000 British households live in park homes. Their construction and their tenure distinguish these homes from other types of owner-occupied property. Although generally owned by their occupiers, these dwellings are usually sited on land that is owned by someone else. The relationship between the home-owner and the park owner is governed by the Mobile Homes Act 1983 (as amended by subsequent legislation). This legislation gives the occupier the right to a written statement setting out both the 'implied' and the 'expressed' terms of the agreement. Most importantly, the statutory rights implied by the act include matters relating to security of tenure. The legislation also establishes the principle that the park owner has a right to take a commission when a park home is sold on site, by means of a transfer agreement. The expressed terms outline the local details of the relationship between the parties. They cover such things as the rules about pitch fees and their review. They also cover any other rules relating to the specific responsibilities and rights of the parties, such as the right of potential park home occupiers to be made aware in writing of the terms under which they will occupy the site prior to sale.

In January 2005 the ODPM published a consultation paper outlining proposals to give park home owners new rights and a degree of added protection in their dealings with site owners.[9] These aim to raise minimum standards on sites, make it easier for local authorities to rectify site license breaches, deter 'bad' site owners from running down sites, and generally support the long-term reputation of the industry.

The dual nature of the owner-occupier's proprietary economic interests

As indicated in Figure 6.1, owners have both consumption and investment interests vested in the dwellings they occupy. To the owner-occupier the dwelling possesses both the characteristics of a home and an asset. As we will see, the dual

---

9   ODPM/Welsh Assembly Government (Jan 2005) *Park Homes Site Licensing: Proposals For Reform.*

nature of the occupier's economic interests in the property has, over the years, led to much debate about how this tenure should be treated with respect to taxation liability and subsidy support. This dual interest (consumption and investment) also has to be borne in mind when analysing questions relating to the affordability and sustainability of the tenure.

The affordability and sustainability of owner-occupation

Throughout most of the 1980s the market for owner-occupied housing was sustained by a combination of factors. These included: a growth in real incomes, an expanding mortgage market, and continued fiscal support in the form of mortgage interest tax relief (abolished 1999)[10] and exemptions from both capital gains tax and Schedule A income tax.[11] We will look at the nature and scope of the mortgage market in some detail in Chapter 7, and the various tax arrangements covering this sector are also discussed in Chapter 7.

As the dominant tenure, it is clear that the government expects owner-occupation to play a significant part in the nation's overall housing strategy. Early in 1998 the government outlined a series of plans for dealing with Britain's housing needs for the early part of the following century. At that time it was estimated that a further 4.4 million homes would be needed by 2016. This projection has since been modified and later ODPM releases suggest a 3.8 million household growth over the twenty-five years to 2021. The recent Treasury-sponsored Barker Report (2004) suggested that a further 146,000 new homes a year would have to built in England to make property reasonably affordable to first-time buyers. Whichever statistical projection is used, one thing is clear – the meeting of national supply targets will involve a continued expansion of owner-occupation.

Supply-side constraints: stock adjustment models

There is much debate about the extent to which this tenure can or should be relied upon to close the gap between future housing needs and probable supply outturns. Some commentators make the point that there are severe supply-side constraints on private house building.[12] By deducting demolitions from completions, we can calculate the net additions to the private housing stock. By projecting recent net additions up to the year 2021, it would appear that the required increase in

---

10 The rise and fall of mortgage income tax relief is discussed in the next chapter.

11 Before 1963 the Inland Revenue treated owner-occupied dwellings as assets that had the potential to generate an income. This potential income was calculated as an 'imputed rent' and taxed under Schedule A of the income tax schedules. The collection of Schedule A income tax on the main residences of owner-occupiers was abandoned after 1963. This is discussed more fully later in the chapter.

12 See in particular the Barker Review, *Delivering Stability: Securing Our Future Housing Needs*, Review of Housing Supply, Final report published March 2004. See also the earlier commentary, *Supply and sustainability: home-ownership in Britain*, by Geoffrey Meen, Duncan Maclennan and Mark Stephens in Wilcox, 1997, pp17-22.

building is well beyond the capacity of the construction industry at the current time, based on existing policies. The ability and willingness of the building industry to respond to the challenge will depend, to a large extent, on the general long-run performance of the economy. New house sales depend on transaction rates in the housing market and, in turn, these tend to increase in times of economic growth and decrease in times of economic slow-down.

Even if there is continued economic growth and a consequential general sustained demand for owner-occupied housing, the construction industry's response to any such increase may be inhibited by a variety of specific factors that reduce what economists refer to as the *price elasticity of housing supply*. The price elasticity of supply measures the responsiveness of producers to a given increase in price. If prices rise by a certain percentage, and supply adjusts more than proportionately, we say that the response is 'elastic'. Conversely, if the output response is less than proportionate to the increase in price, we say that it is 'inelastic'. In 2003, Kate Barker, a member of the Bank of England Monetary Policy Committee which sets interest rates, was commissioned to produce a report identifying the main barriers to the production of more new housing. This investigated, among other things, why the supply of new housing is price inelastic. The report indicated that, in the future, the price elasticity of supply may be inhibited by the following variables.

- The capacity of the construction industry.
- Shortages of land.
- The slow and unwieldy nature of the planning consent system.
- The planning restrictions themselves, including political constraints on the use of greenfield sites.

Demand-side constraints: inflation, affordability and other proprietary perceptions

House prices, which in the UK have tended to spearhead general inflation for sustained periods, have tended to exert a powerful influence on general consumption and in so doing have contributed a degree of volatility to the economy as a whole. The Barker Report suggested that UK house price inflation averaged 2.4 per cent between 1971 and 2001, compared with 0 per cent for Germany and 0.8 per cent for France. For short periods house price inflation in the UK has proved to be particularly volatile thereby causing a degree of economic uncertainty that has proved to be an impediment to labour market flexibility, made public service planning difficult, led to added travel congestion costs in some 'hot-spot' areas, and created negative equity problems for households that purchased at the top of the price cycle boom.

Any demand-side analysis has to recognise the interrelated nature of housing tenures. Attitudes towards owner-occupation will be affected, to some extent, by the government's policies towards other housing tenures. If a household acts rationally, it will seek that form of tenure that gives it the greatest utility in return for the money it spends on housing. If owner-occupation is taxed and subsidised generously in comparison with other tenures this will add to its popularity and vice-versa.

Individual perceptions of the desirability of owner-occupation are particularly influenced by the question of *affordability*. In the owner-occupied sector, the question of affordability is made more complex by the dualistic nature of the occupier's proprietary interests, as discussed above. Unlike a tenant, an owner-occupier has an investment as well as a consumption interest in the property. This means that an owner-occupier household may be prepared to pay a premium over and above what they would expect to pay in rent for the dwelling because they appreciate the fact that they will eventually acquire a valuable asset.

Housing analysts point to two key ratio measures of owner-occupier housing affordability (e.g. Wilcox, 1996). Because of the dualistic nature of the owner-occupier's proprietary interest, it is possible to consider affordability in this sector both in terms of the real cost of capital, relating to the proprietary investment interest, and in terms of a cost-to-income ratio, relating to the proprietary consumption interest.

The real cost of capital. Because owners have a long-run investment interest in their dwellings, affordability in this sector is sometimes discussed in terms of the ratio between the *nominal* and the *real* costs of borrowing and investing. This approach enables analysts to make the point that capital appreciation and house-price inflation can work to the long-term financial advantage of owners so that, over time, the acquisition costs can become more and more affordable. If, over a given period, interest rates are, say, six per cent, and over the same period, the asset's exchange value has appreciated by the same amount of six per cent, then, although the nominal cost of the loan, or the opportunity cost of the money capital withdrawn from savings to purchase the property, is six per cent, the real capital cost is zero.[13] By focusing on the *real cost* of capital, it is possible to argue that, over the longer period (e.g. since the 1930s) the cost of acquiring owner-occupied housing assets has fallen.

The cost-to-income ratio. Because owners have a continuing consumption interest in their dwellings, affordability in this sector is sometimes discussed in terms of the ratio between the household's disposable income and its occupancy costs. For new entrants to the tenure, mortgage repayment costs often constitute a high proportion of these outgoings. This means that existing owners experience a *real income effect* when mortgage interest rates go up or down. The real income effect measures how much the household's disposable monthly income changes as a result of an alteration in interest charges. An apparently 'small' change in interest

---

13 Up to the year 2000, the real cost of borrowing was further reduced by the ability of home-owners to offset some of the interest charges on their mortgage debts against their income tax liabilities.

rates, say one per cent, can bring about a significant *real income effect* on some households. In other words, it can alter the household's disposable income by a greater proportion than the interest rate change.

Although interest rates can fluctuate over time the mortgage debt itself is fixed. That is, loan service charges are governed by the principles of historical cost accounting.[14] The original debt is gradually repaid, either directly or via an endowment arrangement. This means that for most households the mortgage burden tends to diminish over time. For those who remain in the tenure long term, the debt is eventually extinguished (amortised) when the mortgage is paid off.

The continuing commitment to sustainable home-ownership

Chapter 4 of the 2000 DETR green paper is entitled 'Encouraging sustainable home-ownership' and makes the point that in the future the government will continue to support the tenure through its general economic policies and by providing specific financial support in the following forms.

- By helping the less well off and those who live in areas where house prices are high relative to earnings, to gain access through shared ownership and low-cost home-ownership initiatives.
- By helping existing owners who encounter unforeseen difficulties through benefit assistance with payments of mortgage interest.
- By helping poorer owners to meet the costs of repairing, adapting and maintaining their homes through renovation grants, disabled facilities grants and related assistance.

Given that the sector now houses more than two-thirds of the population it clearly plays an important role in the country's prosperity. This brings up questions about how the state should engage with the housing market. Should the government simply pursue a policy of allowing the housing market to create and allocate private homes within a macro-economy of low inflation and interest rate stability? Or should it have an active policy of intervention that allows it to influence housing market operations?

The Chartered Institute of Housing believes that an active policy towards home-ownership is essential. In particular, they believe the government has a duty to evaluate carefully how public money used to subsidise home-ownership should be best spent. The Institute's concern stems partly from the size and importance of the sector and partly from the consequential social and economic impact of market weakness or failure (things going wrong – e.g. homelessness, negative equity, key worker shortages, social exclusion, property disrepair, urban decline, etc.).

---

14   See Chapter 4 for an explanation of historic cost accounting.

People have to live somewhere, and if significant numbers of would-be home-owners fall out of the market, this will increase the demand for public investment in rented housing and welfare benefits. A housing stock that is fairly fixed (can only be added to or replaced slowly) has to be kept in good condition to prevent further demands for public subsidy. Furthermore, growing public expectations about the environment also require an active policy of intervention to control where and how dwellings are to be built and renewed.

These questions and issues point to the need for home-ownership to be 'sustainable'. So what does 'sustainable' mean in this context? The Institute points to FIVE key features of a sustainable market for owner-occupation. (*Sustainable Home Ownership: New Policies for a New Government*, CIH, 1997).

1. *Affordability*. Those in the sector must be able to meet the continuing costs of occupation.
2. *Asset management*. The condition of the stock must be maintained and where necessary improved.
3. *Economic significance*. The sector must contribute to local strategies for employment and economic growth.
4. *Environmental concerns*. The sector's development should be in sympathy with wider environmental and land-use policies.
5. *Fiscal rationality*. Public subsidy for home owners must be economically, socially and politically justifiable.

As in other tenures, the affordability of owner-occupied housing has been, and will continue to be, affected by a variety of financial support measures. Some of these measures have been designed to ease the financial burden of *being* an owner-occupier whilst others have been designed to ease the financial costs of *becoming* an owner-occupier. Before looking at how the tax and subsidy system affects existing owners we will look at the range of measures that have, in recent years, been put in place to encourage access to the tenure.

One important feature of recent policy in the UK has been a declared intention to assist those on the affordability margins of owner-occupation to gain access to the tenure through a variety of 'low-cost home-ownership' initiatives.[15]

Within the Conservative party there has been a long-standing political commitment to expand home-ownership. (See Appendix). The present government continuously affirms its commitment to affordable and sustainable home-ownership. The Home Ownership Task Force was established by the deputy prime minister in March 2003 following the *Sustainable Communities Plan*. The Task Force's remit was to look at the whole range of programmes

---

15 For an outline and analysis of these initiatives see Bramley, G. and Morgan, J., (1998). See also ODPM, *Housing Signpost: A Guide to Research and Statistics*, Issue 14, 2002. See also the appendices at the end of this chapter.

aimed at helping people into home-ownership. It examined who has been helped through current initiatives, to what extent these initiatives freed up social tenancies for other occupants, and it discussed the scope for better targeting and design.[16]

The Task Force recommended that reform be taken forward on six interrelated fronts:

1. Increasing the supply of affordable housing.
2. Making the market work better.
3. Developing a new framework of simplified low-cost home-ownership products.
4. Making the existing sustainable home-ownership programme more effective.
5. Providing more information and advice to would-be home-owners.
6. Developing new measures designed to sustain existing home-ownership.

This programme can be thought of as embracing two broad commitments. Firstly, to make it easier to gain access to the tenure (*becoming* an owner-occupier). Secondly to help sustain the tenure for those who have gained access (*being* an owner-occupier). The former of these commitments is better established than the latter.

Measures designed to encourage the expansion of owner-occupation

Many researchers and commentators are now pointing to a growing wealth gap between owner-occupiers, who own housing assets, and tenants, who do not. In this respect, we might argue that extending the scope of home-ownership is a worthwhile objective for a government committed to reducing inequalities and enhancing social inclusion. With this in mind, the government has been under pressure to extend the established right to buy policy that was originally introduced in 1980. In 2005, the Deputy Prime Minister launched a five year programme to address this issue. The programme entitled *Homes for All* seeks to help people on low or middle incomes onto the property ladder. The plan is to enable some 80,000 people to enter home-ownership by utilising publicly owned land to build new homes as part of a new First Time Buyers' initiative. This initiative focuses on England and the government plans to work with its regeneration agency, English Partnerships, to spend tens of millions of pounds

---

16 The Task Force was chaired by Baroness Dean, former Chairman of the Housing Corporation, and comprised of 20 members drawn from a wide range of private and public sector agencies. It also considered evidence from other organisations and individuals. The Task Force report, *A home of my own*, was published on 13 November 2003 and copies of the report and executive summary are available on the Housing Corporation's website at www.housingcorp.gov.uk.

buying former hospital sites from NHS trusts and government departments such as the Ministry of Defence to build more low-cost homes to buy. The idea of this initiative is to separate the cost of land from the cost of construction so that well-designed affordable homes can be provided in 'hot-spot' areas such as London and the south-east.

The 'Homes for All' programme also includes the following key points.

- A commitment to maintain a strong social housing sector.
- A public competition to build a home for £60,000 (2005 prices).
- Changes to the planning system to encourage the building of affordable homes in rural areas.
- A continuation of the right to buy and right to acquire schemes (see below).
- A new scheme called 'Social Homebuy' to enable tenants from local authorities and housing associations to buy an equity stake in their own homes at a discount.

A key element of the programme will be the commitment to give more tenants the opportunity to get a foothold on the ownership ladder by allowing them to participate in the Social Homebuy scheme. This scheme can be thought of as the latest of a stream of measures over the years designed to meet the aspirations of those who wish to become home owners. Before looking at the latest proposals, we need to say something about the earlier policies.

The right to buy (RTB)

This initiative has enabled many occupiers to purchase their rented homes with discounts. Councils have always had the right to sell their dwellings to their tenants. The 1979 Conservative manifesto pledged to convert this 'right to sell' into a 'right to buy' that would give council tenants the opportunity to purchase their homes with generous discounts. The RTB has been by far the largest home-ownership initiative.

The right to buy policy was included in the Housing Act 1980 and the Tenants' Rights etc. (Scotland) Act 1980. The statutory right to buy (RTB) formed the centrepiece of the 1980 legislation. Although previous legislation had granted local authorities discretionary powers to sell, in practice few transfers occurred so the statutory obligation to offer for sale was an important change in emphasis. The new legislation established the principle that a secure tenant opting to purchase is entitled to a discount on the market value of the property, and that this discount should be dependent on the previous length of the tenancy. The idea is that those who have been paying rent over many years should be able to purchase their homes more cheaply than short-standing tenants. The regulations require a minimum residency period and they put a ceiling on the total amount of discount that can be granted to any one purchaser. RTB discounts can be thought of as *purchase grants* to those who enter owner-occupation by this route.[17] The right to a discount is like having a gifted cash deposit; it gives automatic equity in the property, something that takes years to accrue in the private sector.

The RTB eligibility requirements are constantly under review. The current situation is outlined in Appendix 2 to this chapter.

Recent changes in Scotland

On 30 September 2002 the Scottish secure tenancy came into force. It replaced the previous secure tenancy held by local authority tenants and the secure and assured tenancies that applied in the housing association sector. The Scottish secure tenancy provides a single, common tenancy for virtually all tenants of local authorities and registered social landlords in Scotland and brought with it quite significant changes to the right to buy.

A Scottish secure tenant with a council or a registered social landlord (such as a housing association), may have the legal right to buy their home at a discount. However, the precise details of their RTB will be determined by the particular circumstances of their tenancy including when it started and the eligibility rules applying at the time.

The effect of RTB on capital receipts

The RTB is acknowledged to have been the greatest and most far-reaching act of privatisation in the UK. Nearly two million sales have taken place under the legislation, generating many billions of pounds worth of receipts, more than the combined sales of British Gas, Electricity and British Telecom.[18] Since the introduction of RTB, in excess of £25 billion has been generated as a result of the sales of local authority dwellings. The bulk of these receipts has gone to pay off debt, or was clawed back by the Treasury. However, several billions of pounds have been held by local authorities as 'housing capital receipts' and are therefore available to aid future capital investment. Although the discounted sales produced a substantial flow of capital receipts the government's commitment to reducing the public sector borrowing requirement prevented all of these financial resources being reinvested in the council stock. Indeed, the legislation setting up the 1990 capital finance regime specifically required authorities to hold the bulk of the receipts in reserve or to redeem debt.[19] The implications that follow from this

---

17 When a unit of social housing is purchased at a discount by the occupying household, we can regard the discount received as an implicit subsidy to owner-occupation. However, this subsidy may be partly offset by future housing benefit foregone.

18 By the end of March 2000 around 1.4 million dwellings had been sold in England (about 1.8 million in Great Britain) under this scheme. Sales peaked at over 100,000 a year in early 1980s, and again in 1988-9 following a rise in the housing market. Sales have since declined and are now around 60,000 a year, earning £2.2 billion in capital receipts.

19 It is estimated that by 1997 local authorities had accumulated some £7.5 billion in 'set-aside' receipts (KPMG, 1996).

---

will be discussed more fully in subsequent chapters when we look at local government finance.

The rent to mortgage scheme

The rent to mortgage scheme led on from the right to buy scheme. Not everyone could afford to buy their home outright, even with a discount and the Rent to Mortgage scheme was introduced in 1993 to help tenants buy their homes by paying just part of the RTB price to begin with. They were expected to do this by to taking out a mortgage from a bank or building society. The scheme was not popular and is being phased out under the provisions of the Housing Act 2004.[20]

The future of RTB

A number of measures affecting the right to buy were included in the Housing Act 2004. These include:

- Extending from two years to five years the period that a tenant must spend qualifying for the right to buy.
- Extending from three years to five years the period during which owners must repay their discount if they resell their home.
- Exempting dwellings scheduled for demolition from the RTB.
- Requiring owners who wish to resell within 10 years of exercising their RTB to offer their homes back to a local social landlord.
- Ending the 'deferred re-sale' deals whereby inducements are offered to tenants by private companies who obtain possession of properties and let them out at market rents.
- Ending the little used rent to mortgage scheme.

The government has stated its commitment to maintain the current features of the RTB scheme. However, it is constantly criticised by some academic commentators who see it as an irrational way of achieving sustainable home-ownership. These critics argue that we should break the link between the residency term and the level of granted discount.[21] They point to a need to scrap the idea of discounts related to years of tenancy and move to a straightforward purchase grant. Such a grant could be allocated against other, arguably more sensible criteria, so as to encourage the sale of specific property types or to stimulate sales in specific localities. By such methods it might be possible to use public funds to encourage mixed tenures on those estates and in those neighbourhoods where such a result might help to achieve other policies related to the government's broader urban regeneration and social exclusion objectives.

Right to acquire (RTA)

This scheme was introduced in the Housing Act 1996, and gives eligible tenants of housing associations and other RSLs a statutory right to buy their home at a

---

20 Between 1997 and 2004 it is estimated (Council of Mortgage Lenders) that the RTM scheme only resulted in 590 sales in England.

21 We might argue that this link is being weakened anyway by the introduction of maximum levels of discount in certain regions (see above).

discount,[22] depending on the local authority area in which the property is located. The discount is funded by a grant from the Housing Corporation. Tenants are always required to contribute 50 per cent of the purchase price. The scheme only applies to RSL properties built or purchased with public funds or transferred from a local authority after 1 April 1997. Some properties are exempt from RTA including sheltered housing and those in small rural settlements. Eligible tenants must have spent a minimum time as a public sector tenant and RSLs should be able to advise them whether their home qualifies for the RTA scheme.

The voluntary purchase grant (VPGs)

The voluntary purchase grant scheme (VPG) was introduced in England in 1996. It is designed to enable housing association tenants who, on the whole, are excluded from RTB, to acquire their existing homes at a discounted price that varies according to the local authority area in which it is located. It is important to note that the scheme does not apply to all tenants as it is up to the RSL whether it takes part in the scheme and some properties may be excluded. Any tenant interested in this scheme would need to ask their RSL if they participate.

Unlike RTB, these grants are discretionary and cash-limited. English associations have to apply, or bid, to take part in the scheme. Under the arrangements, a participating RSL that sells a home is able to claim a grant equivalent to the amount of discount from the central funding body (the Housing Corporation).[23] It is a condition of the grant that all the proceeds from the sale must be placed in a separate Disposal Proceeds Fund. This fund can only be drawn upon to provide replacement social housing assets. Some landlords are concerned about the financial implications and difficulty of replacing properties 'like with like'. Social landlords are generally more at ease with helping tenants to acquire homes in the private sector than purchasing their existing homes. They are generally concerned not to dispose of units that were specifically designed as social housing. More particularly, they are concerned about the possibility of losing good quality units that are in popular locations.

The original 'Homebuy' grant scheme

In recent years a number of cash and loan incentive schemes have been in operation.[24] They have all been devised to encourage tenants in the social rented

---

22 Generally between £9,000 – £16,000.
23 The work of the Housing Corporation and nature and scope of RSL activity is described and discussed in Chapter 12.
24 A whole raft of low-cost home-ownership measures have been tried and tested in recent years. The Tenants' Incentive Scheme (TIS) was introduced by the Housing Act 1988. It empowered local authorities, under certain conditions, to give cash grants to their tenants to help them obtain accommodation in the private sector and thereby relieve pressure on the waiting list. Do-It-Yourself-Shared-Ownership scheme (DIYSO) allowed people who rent their homes from a housing association or a council, or who are on the local authority waiting list, to find a property on the open market and buy it jointly with an association. Homebuy is replacing both these schemes.

sector with higher incomes to move into the owner-occupied private sector thereby freeing up social tenancies for someone else who is deemed to be in greater need. In recent years in England and Wales the main scheme has been 'Homebuy'. This was designed to help tenants of RSLs and local authorities and people on the waiting list in priority housing need, to purchase a home. In England the scheme arranged for a housing association to administer an interest free loan covering 25 per cent of the market value. The remaining 75 per cent was funded by the applicant through a conventional mortgage and savings. The loan is repaid when the dwelling is sold. The Welsh Homebuy scheme has been rather more flexible than the English model in that there is provision to vary the size of the equity loan.[25]

The amount paid back is 25 per cent (30 per cent in Wales) of the value of the property at the time of re-sale. Although no interest is charged on the loan, because house prices tend to be increasing, the amount repayable is generally greater than the value of the original loan. Funding for the scheme is cash-limited and provided by the regulator (e.g. the Housing Corporation). This means that housing associations are allocated funds through a process of bidding. From April 2004, associations have been able to offer a new build Homebuy scheme under which Homebuy purchasers can buy a home from an RSL rather than one on the open market.

One of the key objectives of the original Homebuy scheme was to release existing social lettings that can then be re-let to people in housing need. The scheme is therefore targeted at areas where there is a shortage of social housing. Applicants have no statutory right to help and not everyone who is eligible is accepted. Acceptance depends on RSL funds being available in a particular area and the suitability of the home being vacated for those in housing need, as identified by participating RSLs in consultation with local authorities. As part of its 'five year plan', in 2005 the government announced its intention expand the scheme to give tenants a greater opportunity to acquire a part share, called an 'equity stake', in their homes.

Equity stakes: the development of 'Social Homebuy'

In January 2005, as part of its 'Homes for All' initiative, the government announced its intention to introduce a new Homebuy scheme to allow thousands of people currently priced out of the housing market to acquire home-ownership status. The intention is for the government to work in partnership with the mortgage lenders to establish a new fund worth about £1 billion that can give first-time buyers an opportunity to own up to a 75 per cent stake in either a housing association property or a home on the open market. This scheme will enable (potentially) some 300,000 tenants to acquire a share in the value of their homes. A key feature of the new arrangement is that residents will be given the

---

25   In Wales, the equity loan will normally be for 30 per cent of the approved purchase price but it can be increased to a maximum of 50 per cent in certain circumstances (but only where the applicant is unable to afford 70 per cent).

opportunity to 'staircase' to full ownership. It is expected that in order to maintain the viability of the social sector, if a Social Homebuy property is subsequently offered for sale on the open market, the former housing association owners will be given first refusal. At the time of writing, the operational arrangements of the scheme have still to be published. It is expected that the scheme will be voluntary in the first place, but that housing associations and local authorities will eventually be expected to apply it as widely as possible. There are concerns, however, that associations will experience a reduced funding stream because they will be required to sell to tenants at a discount, but when they buy back they will have to pay the full market price. This will prevent them replacing like with like and this may over time degrade the overall provision of social housing.

Advocates of equity stakes argue that such a measure has the potential to improve the image of social housing and improve the wealth and asset ownership of social tenants. They also argue that equity stakes might enable tenants to take advantage of life-changing opportunities and give them a greater sense of pride, responsibility and involvement in their housing. It will also have the positive effect of blurring the lines between the sometimes stigmatised social housing sector and other forms of housing tenure.

Local authority cash incentive scheme

The objectives of the cash incentive scheme (CIS) are to release local authority accommodation for letting to those in housing need and to encourage owner-occupation. The scheme works by the payment of grants to tenants to assist them to buy properties in the private sector. It is up to each local authority to decide whether to run a CIS scheme and tenants have no mandatory right to a grant. A Regulatory Reform Order which allows local authorities to run schemes without the Secretary of State's consent, came into force in April 2003. The Regulatory Reform Order allows local authorities to set the size of grant payable to take into account the local housing market.[26] All grants must be means-tested.

Local authorities can target the scheme to free up accommodation in areas where there is a shortage of social housing; or to release types of property for which there is a high demand, e.g. family sized accommodation. Currently there is no central funding for CIS and so local authorities must fund schemes from their own capital resources.

Scottish initiatives

In Scotland GRO grants have been available to stimulate new-build homes for owner-occupation.[27] These are given to private developers to help fund the cost of

---

26 But they must be set within parameters set by the ODPM that requires them to be a percentage of average RTB discounts.

27 The post-war growth in owner-occupation was less marked in Scotland than elsewhere in Britain. In response, GRO grant was introduced in 1990 with a view to contributing to Scottish urban regeneration in a way that also stimulates the growth of owner-occupation. By 1996 GRO constituted 16 per cent of new provision.

new or improved homes, particularly for first-time owners. Grants of up to 40 per cent of total project costs have been available, although the average grant (1999) has been about 25 per cent. Rural home-ownership grants are available to individuals in rural areas of Scotland towards the costs of building or buying their own home. These are available to people on low incomes who would otherwise find it impossible to own their own home in a rural part of Scotland because of high building costs, lack of utility services, or inflated home prices. These grants are designed to facilitate the general policy of Communities Scotland to develop more homes for sale. In Scottish rural areas, Rural Home Ownership Grant (RHOG) has been available to assist people into the tenure in locations where there is a lack of suitably priced accommodation.

Northern Ireland initiatives

In recent years, the main low-cost home-ownership initiative in Northern Ireland has been an equity sharing scheme called 'co-ownership'. The arrangements operate through a housing association on a DIYSO basis.[28] By 1997 'co-ownership' purchases had surpassed 14,000, with nearly 10,000 of these having subsequently staircased to full ownership (Bramley and Morgan, 1998).

Collective ownership

Collective ownership is different from shared ownership. Whilst shared ownership schemes are designed to give individuals a 'personal' stake in their homes, housing co-ops are designed to give groups of people a 'collective' interest in the homes they occupy. Housing co-operatives can take two tenure forms:

1. *Tenant management co-ops (TMCs)*. These are currently favoured by the Housing Corporation. Under these arrangements the occupiers do not have a stake in the equity of their estates but are delegated management responsibilities by their landlords who typically will be a council or housing association. Strictly speaking, this form of co-op should not be classified as a form of owner-occupation as no equity is transferred.
2. *Ownership co-ops*. These contrast with TMCs in that the occupiers collectively own the equity in the properties. This gives them a form of collective proprietary interest in the properties that make it appropriate to classify them as 'owners'. The housing association manages the co-op on behalf of the owners. They collect rents, carry out repairs and maintenance, allocate homes which become vacant, deal with disputes and generally run the co-op's affairs in the interests of the collective membership.

Starter Home Intiative

This was one of a number of proposals included in the Housing green paper in recognition of the difficulties faced by key workers on low income when purchasing a house in high demand, high price areas. The Starter Home Initiative

---

28 This scheme replaced a NIHE equity sharing scheme in the early 1980s.

has helped around 10,000 key workers, particularly nurses, teachers and the police to buy homes in urban and rural areas where high prices would otherwise prevent them from living in or near to the communities they serve. This initiative has now been developed into the key workers' initiative.

Key workers' initiative

The 2000 green paper signalled the government's intention to provide further support for people on the threshold of home-ownership. They proposed to introduce a new *Starter Home Initiative* that would operate on a competitive basis, with innovative proposals invited from housing associations and other RSLs. The initiative was planned to be flexible and capable of adapting to local circumstances and needs. It aimed to be of assistance to people on low incomes who live in areas where house prices are relatively high. The proposal focused particular attention on the plight of 'key' workers such as schoolteachers, nurses, and firefighters.

In response to the green paper proposal, the government has now introduced the new key worker housing programme, 'Key Worker Living'. Under the first round of this programme covering a three-year period, some £690 million has been earmarked to be spent to support recruitment and retention in key public services. The new programme builds on the foundations of the Starter Home Initiative discussed above.

Key Worker Living (KWL) is targeted at public services in London, the south-east and east of England where the high cost of housing is contributing to serious recruitment and retention problems. It will help key workers employed in the public sector delivering front-line services that are vital to the education, health and safety of local communities. Key workers being helped include nurses and other NHS staff, teachers in schools and in further education and sixth form colleges, police officers and some civilian staff, prison and probation service staff, social workers, occupational therapists and, in London, local authority planners.[29]

Developing owner-occupation through leasehold reform

One other way in which owner-occupation has been developed is through leasehold reform. A lease is a contract by which property is conveyed to a person for a specified period for a stated consideration, a rent. The contract creates a 'leasehold estate' that can be thought of as a personal property interest. In addition to a purchase price, the terms usually require the leaseholder to pay a periodic ground rent to the freehold landlord. A 'lease option' is an arrangement whereby the lessee has the right to purchase the freehold either during the lease term or at its end.

---

29 See Appendix 5 for details of KWL.

In the UK some houses and many flatted units are let under leasehold contracts and for many years there has been some concern about the financial predicament of those people whose leases come up for renewal or who want to sell at a time when the lease is close to its expiry date. The transfer or renewal price depends on a controversial calculation that involves taking account of what is called the 'marriage value'. The *marriage value* is based on a calculation that links together the freehold and the leasehold interests. It is a complicated calculation made up of the rise in property prices and the declining value of the lease. Over time the marriage value will tend to increase thereby generating an element of 'profit'. In some cases this value increase, or 'profit', can be considerable, amounting to tens, or even hundreds, of thousands of pounds. Surveyors often disagree about the valuation and tenants can challenge the landlord's claim at a tribunal. Some argue that the complicated nature of the calculation and difficulties of challenging the landlord's figure, gives the freeholder an unfair advantage in the negotiation.

Leasehold relationships are grounded in ancient laws that many now regard to be anachronistic. In particular, it is felt to be inappropriate in modern times for a landlord, who only has a limited equity stake in a property, to be in a position to manipulate the law in ways that restricts the proprietary interests that owner-occupiers have vested in their homes. In opposition the Labour party pledged itself to reform this arrangement which they saw as a relic of the feudal age. The recent debate has centred on how the marriage value 'profit' should be split between the two proprietary interests, the freeholder and the leaseholder. In the past, the landlord has been able to claim up to 100 per cent of the marriage value and to be guaranteed a minimum of 50 per cent. In November 1998, the government acted on its manifesto pledge and produced a consultation paper in which it restated its intention to reform the system. It then sought to alter the arrangements so that any value increase will be shared equally between the two parties or according to a 'fair' formula that relates to the length of the lease.

The Labour government's commitment to more fundamental reform was given clear expression in the 2000 green paper (para.4.17). The intention was to alter the law to allow householders to enjoy the same degree of security and control over their homes that other owner-occupiers expect. They therefore signaled their intention to introduce a new form of tenure called 'commonhold'. The provisions of Commonhold and Leasehold Reform Act (2002) came into force in September 2004. They created a new way of owning property in England and Wales. *Commonhold* can be thought of as a new kind of freehold ownership. The legislation allows leaseholders to dispense with their landlord and obtain a share of the property's freehold. Similar tenure arrangements have long existed elsewhere in the world[30] and the reform brings us into line with most other developed countries.

---

30 Commonhold is similar to Strata Title, a type of home ownership which has been in use in Australia for 50 years. It also has much in common with condominiums in the U.S.

The advantage of commonhold is that it gets rid of the concept of the 'wasting asset' so that sellers and purchasers of commonhold properties (called 'units') will no longer have to worry about how many years are left on the lease. Commonhold also gets rid of the problem of dual interests (e.g. absent landlords, who only own the freehold for the money they can make out of it from the tenants). Owners, known as 'unit-holders', become members of a commonhold association (a private company limited by guarantee and registered at Companies House)[31] that owns and manages the common parts of the development. This means that it should be easier to run the building strictly for the benefit of the unit owners. Commonhold is available for new schemes and leaseholders in existing developments can convert to commonhold if all parties agree (including the freehold landlord). The new arrangements give the owner of each home in a block a proprietary interest similar to freehold, in that it will not be time limited.

Once the commonhold is in place, the new law removes the need for a governing lease. The association will be founded on a corporate constitution that provides a legal framework of rights and obligations between the owners of each flat (who are referred to as unit-holders) and between each unit-holder and the commonhold association. The framework is relatively simple. It creates a freehold estate in commonhold land that is divided into units (e.g. flats) and common parts. Each unit-holder owns the freehold, not a lease, of a unit. The common parts are all those parts of the building that are not contained in a unit, for example, the physical structure, the walls and roof, the lift and the stairs etc, and common areas such as the corridors and entrance hall, the carpark, garden, etc.

Although the association sets the legal parameters of rights and duties, it is recognised that commonhold arrangements could lead to tensions and potential conflicts between neighbours. To alleviate any possible problems, members will have to sign up to a 'commonhold community statement' that can be thought of as a non-corporate constitution. This will set out all the management rules and regulations that would have been found in a standard leasehold contract, relating to such things as subletting, the management of maintenance activities, pet ownership, noise and use of gardens. The key point however is that, as a form of community ownership, it will be up to the commonhold members to enforce these rules and regulations.

The Commonhold Community Statement provides for an association to set a *commonhold assessment*. This provides an estimate of the overall costs of the general operation of the building, its maintenance, repair and insurance. This is like the service charge provisions in a lease but instead of it being set by a third party landlord it is set by the Commonhold Association. There may also be one or more reserve funds held for the mutual benefit of the association. The community association will request payment from each unit-holder in accordance with the percentage allocated to each unit in the Commonhold Community Statement.

---

31 It is run according to its Memorandum and Articles that are available for inspection at both Companies House and the Land Registry.

Although the new system was devised to get rid of the leasehold system that has traditionally been the most common form of ownership for properties such as blocks of flats, conversion to commonhold is not compulsory and this means that both systems will exist side by side for years to come.[32]

So far our discussion has focused on measures designed to ease access to owner-occupation. Before concluding will be briefly consider some of the issues surrounding the financial problems of *being* a home-owner. There are particular concerns about the predicament of those who find themselves on the margins of owner-occupation.

Sustaining the 'marginal' owner-occupier

Whilst rents will generally continue to increase over the life of a tenancy, it is expected that mortgage repayments will account for a progressively smaller percentage of income over the life-time of the mortgage. Research indicates that, in the recent past, tenants paid about twice as much as owner-occupiers in cash terms over a twenty-five year occupancy period. (NFHA, 1990, p12). However, it is still possible for individual owners to experience life changes that can suddenly make it difficult for them to fulfil their mortgage obligations. Some owners who have difficulty meeting their mortgage obligations may be entitled to receive help in the form of Income Support for Mortgage Interest. This, together with mortgage payment protection insurance, is described and discussed in Chapter 19.

Some 12 million people in the UK now have mortgages. In recent years there has been much debate amongst economists, social theorists, housing practitioners and mortgage lenders about how the radically changing nature of the labour market is affecting the long-term security of marginal home owners. The shift towards short-term contracts and part-time employment for a wider range of occupational groups brings to the fore important questions about how the mortgage and insurance markets need to be restructured to allow for more flexible personal repayment plans.

Owner-occupiers are currently denied access to housing benefit that is operated through the social security system. By operating through the tax system, the *working families' tax credit*, introduced in 1999, had a significant impact on the financial position of some low-income home-buying households. Not only is the scheme more generous, but it has also led to an improvement over the earlier take-up rate of family credit by home-buyers (which was about 50 per cent).

Added value and the idea of a 'valuations gap'

Because of its primary function as a home, most decisions to improve an owner-occupied dwelling are designed to add utility, that is, comfort and convenience.

---

32   The process of conversion can be costly and existing leaseholders have to gain the agreement of the freeholder to proceed.

However, an improvement is also likely to add to the property's exchange value. Precisely how much is added to the exchange value will depend on the nature of the improvement and the location of the property. Estate agents often make the point that it is possible for an owner to 'over invest' in their homes. In making this point they are considering the improvement expenditure from a strictly investment point of view. The argument centres on the notion of what land economists refer to as the *neighbourhood effect value* (NEV). The NEV is defined as that part of a property's total value that is determined by its location. Because location is such a powerful determinant of property value, it may turn out that an investment in improvement will not be fully capitalised into the dwelling's exchange value. This means that if the purpose of the improvement is to increase the market value of the property, account has to be taken of the neighbourhood in which the dwelling is located. For instance, a £50,000 annex on a house worth £120,000 in a district where the maximum selling price is £130,000 is unlikely to up-grade the property's value to £170,000. The extent to which improvement expenditure gets capitalised into the exchange value depends on the nature of the expenditure, as well as the location of the property. Some property experts suggest that central heating is the principal improvement that is likely to guarantee recoupment of outlay and the modernisation of a kitchen or bathroom is also likely to add value, although with these types of improvement, the owner is unlikely to get back all the expended costs.

Support through specialist agencies

Finance is arguably the single largest barrier to owners repairing their properties and in the next chapter we will say something about low-start mortgages that are specifically aimed at the lower-income home-owner. However, in addition to financial problems, many marginal owner-occupiers also need technical help and advice if they are to cope with the problems of managing their property assets. In recent years government sponsored agencies have been set up with a brief to help sustain vulnerable home-owners.

Home Improvement Agencies (HIAs) are small, locally-based not-for-profit organisations.[33] They help home-owners and private sector tenants who are older, disabled or on low income to repair, improve, maintain or adapt their homes. They provide people-centred, cost-effective assistance, and help to tackle poor or unsuitable housing, enabling residents to remain in their own home, safe, secure, warm and independent. HIAs currently operate in 247 local authority areas. They are sometimes referred to as 'Care & Repair' agencies or 'Staying Put' schemes. They are usually managed by housing associations, local authorities, or some form charitable organisation. A major scheme of expansion and restructuring began in 2004. This will establish HIA services in a further 78 local authority areas.

---

33   The Office of the Deputy Prime Minister (ODPM) currently supports the running costs of about 230 HIAs in England.

A number of challenges are on the horizon. The *Supporting People* programme is introducing new arrangements for commissioning and funding housing-related support services from 2003/04, bringing new responsibilities and ways of working.

Energy saving agencies exist to give advice and channel grant funding to households seeking to improve their homes in ways that reduce fuel bills. It is estimated that the average British home wastes several hundred pounds a year in running costs because of insufficient insulation or inappropriate heating and lighting arrangements. Local energy efficiency advice centres exists to give owners information about the availability of grant aid to improve the efficiency of their homes. They can also arrange for home inspections to give on-the-spot advice about how to save on energy emitions. General advice can also be obtained from local authorities and specialist agencies such as the Building Research Establishment.

Fiscal reform

It might be argued that other strategies such as government guaranteed fixed rate loans, changes in inheritance tax and capital gains tax may provide some added incentive for repairs and home improvements. Some environmentalists[34] suggest using the fiscal system more imaginatively to aid existing home-owners manage their properties. Such measures as reducing council tax or stamp duty on homes that pass energy efficiency tests has been postulated.

Leaseholders

In the leasehold sector, repairs and improvements are normally managed through a third party. It is usual for there to be a repairing covenant under the terms of the lease that places a duty on the lessor to keep the dwellings in a good state of repair. Service charges can be made to cover future repairs and maintenance costs. These have to be held in a sinking fund that, under Section 42 of the 1987 Act, have the status of a trust fund. Lessees have a statutory right to inspect the management accounts and any supporting documentation. It is intended that future reforms will give the leaseholders the right to appoint their own managing agents, thereby giving them more direct control of the administration, maintenance, and improvement of their homes.

Summary

The primary forms of ownership are freehold and leasehold. Within these broad categories others may 'own' certain legally enforceable rights relating to tenancy agreements and easement.

---

34   E.g. The government funded Energy Saving Trust and the Energy Saving Trust Scotland.

An owner-occupier has both a consumption interest and an investment interest vested in his or her dwelling. It is both a home (consumption interest) and an asset (investment interest).

In thinking about affordability in this sector we need to take account of this dual proprietary interest. The two key ratio measures of owner-occupier housing affordability are the cost-to-income ratio and the real cost of capital.

The price elasticity of housing supply is a way of analysing the supply-side constraints affecting the sustainability and continued growth of the sector.

Recent governments have introduced a variety of measures designed to encourage the growth of the tenure. Foremost amongst these have been right to buy discounts and other 'purchase grants'. Shared ownership schemes are aimed at low-income households who cannot afford outright purchase even with the help of a discount or a grant.

The Leasehold Reform Act has given leaseholders enhanced rights and introduced a new form of property ownership called 'commonhold'. It allows freehold ownership of individual flats, houses and non-residential units within a building or an estate. Possession is not limited by time as with a lease.

Current government policy is concerned to ensure that home-ownership is 'sustainable'. This involves both helping would-be home-owners gain access to the tenure and also helping those on the margins of home-ownership to look after their properties and pay their housing-related bills.

Appendix 1

The political and cultural significance of home-ownership

A generation ago the basic philosophy underlying the advocacy of extended home-ownership was summarised by the chairman of the Building Societies Association when he claimed that home-ownership *'satisfies a basic human need to surround oneself with something that is absolutely personal and private'*. (Quoted by Saunders 1990, p59). In 1980 this sentiment was reiterated by the minister piloting through the legislation giving council tenants the right to buy their homes. In commending the new legislation to parliament he stated that there is *'a deeply ingrained desire for home-ownership'*. (Michael Heseltine, quoted by Saunders, 1990, p59). Several years later Margaret Thatcher is reported as having declared that *'the desire to have and to hold something of one's own is basic to the spirit of man'*. (Quoted by Saunders, 1990, p59). Some commentators have argued that in post-war Britain the political and popular debates about the benefits of home-ownership brought about a somewhat uncritical acceptance of the desirability of pursuing policies to stimulate the growth of this tenure.

The notion of a 'property-owning democracy' was given early expression in 1951 by Harold Macmillan, the then Housing Minister, when he stated the following: *'We wish to see the widest possible distribution of property. We think that, of all forms of property suitable for such distribution, house property is one of the best ... we mean to see that as many as possible get a chance to own their own house.'* (*House of Commons, Parliamentary Debates, 5th series, vol. 494*, session 1951-2, Cm2251.) Two years later this position was given formal and official expression in the 1953 green paper on Housing: *'One object of future housing policy will be to continue to promote by all possible means, the building of new houses for owner-occupation. Of all forms of ownership this is one of the most satisfying to the individual and the most beneficial to the nation.'* (Ministry of Housing and Local Government, *Houses: The Next Step*, Cm8996, HMSO, November 1953, para 7, pp3-4).

By 1971 the Conservative government related home-ownership to *'a deep and natural desire'* on the part of households to have independent control over their living spaces (White paper, July 1971, *Fair Deal for Housing*). In the years that followed, the Conservative party continued to espouse this ideal in all its election manifestos. Its 1979 manifesto devoted more space to this topic than to social security, education or health.

Prior to the election (1977) the official commitment to owner-occupation was expressed in highly propositional terms: *'A preference for home-ownership is sometimes explained on the grounds that potential home owners believe that it will bring them financial advantage. A far more likely reason for the secular trend towards home-ownership is the sense of greater personal independence that it brings. For most people owning one's home is a basic and natural desire, which for more and more people is becoming attainable.'* (1977 green paper, *Housing policy: A Consultative Document*, Cm6851, HMSO, 1977).

A similar view was reiterated in the 1987 white paper. *'Clearly, the majority of people wish to own their own homes. This wish should in the government's view be supported. Home-ownership gives people independence; it gives them a sense of greater personal responsibility; and it helps to spread the Nation's wealth more widely. These are important factors in the creation of a more stable and prosperous society ...'* (*Housing: The Government's Proposals*, Cm214, HMSO September 1987).

Appendix 2

Right to buy provisions: eligibility: key features

Although since September 2002 Scottish regulations are somewhat different, the system operates on similar principles across the UK. The current arrangements have the following key features.

- The RTB scheme is open to virtually any secure tenant who can afford to buy with the exception of those occupying dwellings in connection with their employment (e.g. some police houses) and housing specially provided for the elderly and (in certain cases) the disabled.
- The applicant must have been a public sector tenant for a minimum continuous period. This period is five years in Scotland[35] and until recently two years in England and Wales. The Housing Act 2004 lengthened the qualification period and the discount repayment period in England and Wales to five years to bring it in line with Scottish regulations.
- If they live in a house in England or Wales, the discount will be between 32 per cent and 60 per cent. If they live in a flat, the discount will be between 44 per cent and 70 per cent. However, there is a ceiling on all discounts. This varies according to where the applicant lives.[36] The current regional discount ceilings are published by the ODPM. In December 1998 the government announced a cut in the maximum cash-limit on RTB discount from £50,000 per sale to £38,000 in London and the south-east, and to £22,000 in the north-east. The government is concerned that sales are affecting the availability of affordable housing in some areas, and that the rules are being exploited by commercial companies. So in March 2003 it reduced the maximum discount available to tenants in 41 high demand areas in London and the south-east. In these districts the maximum discount was further reduced to £16,000.

  In Scotland, the level of discount has been reduced under the provisions of the Housing (Scotland) Act 2001. For those tenants who qualify for the 'modernised' RTB (i.e. those gaining the right to buy on or after 30 September 2002), they can buy (after the 5 year qualifying period) with a discount that will start at 20 per cent after 5 years and rise by 1 per cent a year for all house types, up to a maximum of 35 per cent of the market value or £15,000, whichever is the lower.
- A special rule called the 'cost floor' may apply. The discount will be reduced to reflect what the landlord has spent on building, buying, repairing or improving the home during the last 10-11 years before the application to buy.
- If the applicant has previously bought another council property, any discount that they received then will usually be deducted from the discount that they get when they buy again.
- The new owner can sell the property whenever they like. But if they sell within three years of buying it, they will have to repay some or all of the

---

35 As a result of the Housing (Scotland) Act 2001, changes were made to the RTB. These changes came into force on 30 September 2002. For tenancies that had the RTB and which date from before this date, the qualifying period remains at 2 years.

36 For example, if you buy in the west midlands, the maximum discount is £26,000. In the south-east of England it is £38,000, and in Wales it is currently £16,000.

discount that they received.[37] After three years, they can sell without repaying any discount. But if they live in a rural district, they may only be able to resell to the council or to a person who lives or works locally.

- In Scotland, RTB restrictions may apply for a fixed period in specific local authority districts in which there is a shortage of social housing. These are called 'pressured areas' and their declaration by the local authority requires approval from Scottish ministers.[38]

- The landlord is not bound to complete the sale if the applicant owes rent arrears. Furthermore, the tenant may lose the secure tenancy and no longer have the right to buy if the landlord has obtained a suspended possession order against the property as a result of rent arrears (which they have subsequently breached).

- Assured tenants of a housing association do not normally have the RTB. However, where the home of a local authority secure tenant is transferred to an RSL, the tenant may keep the RTB, although on slightly different terms. This feature is called a 'preserved right to buy'.

- A RTB house will be acquired freehold. A RTB flat will acquired on a long leasehold basis (usually 125 years). Normally, this means that the owner will be responsible for the interior of the home whilst the landlord will be responsible for looking after the structure and the exterior of the block. Service charges may be imposed on leaseholders to pay for major repair and improvement works.

- Landlords have to deal with right to buy applications within certain time limits.

- In March 1999 the government announced an incentive to help councils buy back ex-council flats and houses from people in financial difficulty.

Appendix 3

The history of tenants' incentive schemes (TIS)

TIS developed out of the notion of 'portable discounts'. It was originally intended that the RTB should include tenants of charitable associations. This provision in the 1980 Bill was vigorously opposed by the associations who argued that it would undermine the very essence of their charitable status: the provision was withdrawn after a defeat in the House of Lords. In 1984 the Housing and Building Control Bill again attempted to extend the RTB to tenants of charitable associations, and again the draft provision was not enacted after a defeat in the House of Lords. However, the 1984 legislation did introduce a 'portable' discount scheme known as 'HOTCHA' (Home Ownership for Tenants of Charitable Housing Associations). This was designed to give certain tenants of charitable associations in England and Wales, but not Scotland, an equivalent benefit to the

---

37 If they sell during the first year, all of the discount will have to be repaid; during the second year, two-thirds must be repaid; or during the third year, one-third must be repaid.

38 These restrictions only apply to tenancies that gained the RTB on or after 30 September 2002.

RTB. Under these arrangements several thousand tenants were given cash equivalents to the eligible discounts to help them buy dwellings on the open market either as an outright purchase or by a process of shared ownership. It worked by the association purchasing properties on the tenants' behalf. The cost of the discount was claimed from the Housing Corporation via the mechanism of Housing Association Grant. In this way, the Housing and Building Control Act gave tenants of charitable associations an opportunity to become owner-occupiers on much the same basis as RTB tenants in other agencies while, at the same time, preserving the rented stock of such associations for the purpose of social renting. The HOTCHA arrangements were replaced in 1990 by a similar, albeit more restrictive, procedure known as the Tenants' Incentive Scheme (TIS). This scheme aimed to provide home-ownership opportunities to tenants who do not qualify for RTB: this included assured tenants and tenants of charitable associations. The TIS arrangements involve associations bidding for funds to operate an approved scheme of tenant transfer and therefore the portable discount is only available to tenants of associations with such an allocation. In 1994 new rules were introduced to prevent housing association tenants using the scheme's resources to buy homes outside the UK. The argument here is that the original idea behind the scheme was, in part, to stimulate the UK housing market.

Appendix 4

The history of shared ownership

The idea of shared ownership was pioneered in the 1970s by the Notting Hill Housing Trust and Birmingham City Council. These early schemes were based on what was termed a 'community leasehold' arrangement in which the occupier acquired a fixed equity share in the dwelling. This meant purchasing a fixed 50 per cent share and paying rent on the remaining 50 per cent. Under such a community leasehold arrangement, the occupier never owned the property outright, since it remained a 'community asset', and when they wanted to move, the occupiers were obliged to sell their fixed share (that may well have appreciated in value) to a nominee from the local community.

In the 1980s the Conservative government sought to underpin their RTB initiative by developing the idea of shared ownership so that it could be used to help people become full and outright owners of their homes. The 1980 legislation provided clear terms governing how local authorities and housing associations might provide this more radical form of shared ownership agreement. Initially, shared ownership was restricted to local authority and non-charitable housing association new-build schemes, but was eventually also offered to existing tenants under the provisions of the Housing and Building Control Act 1984. Shared ownership is defined in England, Wales and Northern Ireland as housing schemes where the social landlord has granted a shared ownership lease as defined in Section 622 of the Housing Act 1985. In Scotland shared ownership schemes have to be approved in accordance with guidance notes published by Communities Scotland.

By the mid-1980s procedures existed that allowed occupiers to acquire up to 100 per cent of the equity in their properties by a process of gradual purchase called 'staircasing'. Under these arrangements, the householder typically begins by purchasing between 25 and 75 per cent of the total equity. They then pay rent on the unpurchased share. Unsold equity normally remains with the organisation that built or previously owned the dwelling, e.g. the council or housing association. Occupiers can subsequently purchase additional shares up to a level determined by the particular agreement. The total cost of rent plus mortgage is normally less than the total cost of outright ownership and this fact means that the arrangement can open up access to owner-occupation to people on moderate incomes. When the 'owner-occupier' wants to sell they have to contact the 'owner-landlord' who will then match the property with people on their waiting list. If at the end of three months they have been unable to find a purchaser, a private sale (e.g. through an estate agent) can be sought.

As well as helping tenants to acquire their existing homes, in recent years social landlords have helped tenants and others in housing need to buy homes on the private market (see discussion in main text).

Appendix 5

Details of the key workers' initiative

The key workers' living initiative (KWL) will provide help for those at different life stages – home-ownership for first-time buyers, larger properties to meet the household needs of existing home-owners (e.g. family sized homes), shared ownership schemes and properties for rent at affordable prices. Four products will be available:

- 'Equity loans' of up to £50,000 to buy a home on the open market or a new property by a registered social landlord (some London schoolteachers will be eligible for a higher limit). With an equity loan the mortgagor does not make monthly repayments as they do not repay the loan until they sell the property or stop being a key worker. The loan terms are similar to those operating in the Homebuy scheme.
- Higher-value equity loans of up to £100,000 for a small group of London schoolteachers with the potential to become leaders in their field.
- Shared ownership of newly-built properties.
- 'Intermediate renting' at subsidised levels.

In addition to meeting the sector eligibility criteria, the key workers' household income must not exceed £60,000 (£80,000 for the higher-value equity loans) and they must be unable to buy a home suitable for their household needs within a reasonable travel-to-work area of their employment.

KWL aims to keep key workers in the jobs they have trained for thereby retaining the skills needed in local public services. If a key worker leaves the qualifying employment they will have to repay the assistance within a reasonable timescale. This will be recycled to assist further key workers.

Zone agents will market and administer the programme providing a one-stop-shop for applicants. A zone agent is a registered social landlord that markets housing schemes for key workers across an area.

For the purposes of this scheme, a key worker is someone (a) employed by the public sector, (b) in a front-line role delivering an essential public service, (c) in a sector where there are serious recruitment and retention problems.

Further reading

Dwelly, T., (Ed), (1997), *Sustainable Home ownership – The Debate*, CIH/JRF: Coventry and York.

HM Treasury, *Delivering Stability: Securing or Future Housing Needs*. The Barker Review of Housing Supply, HMSO, 2004.

Smith, J., (2004), 'Understanding demand for home-ownership: aspirations, risks and rewards', in Council of Mortgage Lenders' journal, *Housing Finance,* No. 62, summer 2004.

CHAPTER 7:
Owner-occupation:
capital and revenue finance

Having considered the nature and scope of owner-occupation and the various measures designed to encourage its growth and development, we will now discuss the basic financial and fiscal arrangements that surround its acquisition, exchange and consumption. In this analysis we will make a clear distinction between capital and revenue finance.

Acquisition, exchange and capital finance

Sources of capital finance

Money capital is used to purchase new and second-hand homes and to make improvements to such dwellings. Money capital is the key to both gaining access to owner-occupation and to increasing the quality of such housing once access has been achieved. Initial access usually involves either having sufficient funds for outright purchase or the taking out of a loan. The gaining of a loan usually depends upon a combination of factors including the borrower's income and prospects of income and the capacity of the property to act as a sound security against the advance.

The changing nature of the mortgage market

Since 1980 it is possible to detect three broad categories of change affecting the mortgage market. All three are the consequence of increased competition. First, the institutional framework has been restructured with the emergence of new providers and by the transformation of many building societies into banks. Second, the industry has developed a wider product range. Third, criticisms of past practices have resulted in greater regulation.

In the 1970s the market was dominated by the building societies that regularly provided up to 90 per cent of lending in any one year. In the early 1980s the commercial banks, together with a number of specialised mortgage institutions entered the market and for a time, annexed over 40 per cent of the market. By the late 1980s the market stabilised with the societies providing about 60 per cent and the banks a little over 35 per cent of total lending. In the 1990s a number of significant 'mutual' building societies converted into 'commercial' banking institutions.

An aspect of the new competitive environment has been an increasing tendency to respond in a more flexible way to the particular needs of borrowers. In the 1970s the institutions tended to see themselves as providing a fairly standard product to a fairly typical group of borrowers. This typification can be characterised as *a twenty-five year repayment or endowment loan to young or middle-aged couples in secure employment wishing to acquire a not-too-dilapidated detached or semi-detached house in a not-too-run-down neighbourhood*. The institutions now see themselves as providing a fuller service and a broader range of products to a wider group of people. They have become aware that they are operating in a complex market where single people form a substantial group of borrowers, lower-income households have expectations to become owners, divorced and separated couples need to form new households, and retired people wish to take out new mortgages for specialised housing. Before examining the various types of mortgage finance that are currently available, we will need to say something about the institutions that supply such finance.

The institutional framework

New entrants into the owner-occupied market acquire their dwellings by means of inheritances, savings, gifts or loans. The lump sum necessary to acquire the asset and cover the transaction and relocation costs may, of course, be assembled from more than one source. Banks and building societies are by far the most important source of mortgage finance. Over the years other providers have included local authorities and insurance companies.[1] After 1981 the banks began to make a significant contribution to the total provision of home loans and have, since that date, been an important but volatile influence in the mortgage market.

The traditional distinction between building societies and banks

The commercial banks are public limited companies operating under the auspices of the Registrar of Companies. They are owned by shareholders whose shares are quoted on the Stock Exchange. Traditionally, building societies have operated in a separate financial sector.[2] Since the first comprehensive Building Societies Act in 1874,[3] they have been treated as mutual co-operative organisations and, until recently, they have been set apart from the controls and regulations of the banks

---

1   A number of insurance companies have traditionally engaged in the mortgage market and they have also been a source of top-up loans when a first mortgage offer is insufficient to meet a purchaser's needs. Local authority mortgages played a significant part for a short period after the return of a Labour government in 1974. They were usually given for older properties for which traditional mortgage finance was not so readily available.

2   There are 63 building societies in the UK with total assets of over £230 billion. About 15 million adults have building society saving accounts and over two and a half million adults are currently buying their own homes with the help of building society loans

3   The first building society was formed in the UK in 1775 when workers formed a co-operative to pool their savings.

and other finance institutions. Their special legal powers were derived from a succession of statutes that were eventually consolidated into the Building Societies Act 1962 and the Building Societies (Northern Ireland) Act 1967, which recognised their mutual, non-profit-making nature by requiring their overall supervision to be administered by the Registrar of Friendly Societies. Eventually, new legislation in 1986 and 1997 gave the societies greater powers to act commercially.

The societies have traditionally secured the bulk of their funds in the 'small savers' market, sometimes referred to as the 'retail savings market', by issuing shares to investors. Although shares confer membership of the society, they are not transferable and are therefore not comparable with shares in a public company. Normally the investor is issued with a passbook in which is recorded the share value standing of their credit. This can be added to and withdrawn from with little fuss and at immediate or short notice. Some societies also offer 'bond' or 'term' shares that have to be held for a fixed period in order to obtain a higher rate of interest. Members have voting rights in relation to elections to its board of directors. As well as receiving money from investing members, societies may, subject to the provisions of the statutes, receive deposits and borrow money from other sources. Depositors who are not members do not have voting rights but do have a prior claim on the assets should the society be wound up.

Concern about the financial instability resulting from the unwise use of funds for property speculation by a few societies after the Second World War led to the imposition of various restraints on building society activities. Legislation in the 1960s required building societies to concentrate their lending in the form of mortgages and it prevented them from offering the range of financial services provided by the clearing banks. Because mortgages involved them lending over relatively long periods while taking deposits which could be withdrawn at short notice, care was taken to underpin both their general financial stability and their short-run liquidity.[4] They were required to hold a proportion of their total assets, prescribed by the Registrar, in the form of cash and gilt-edged or local authority securities. They were also obliged to hold a proportion of securities with a fairly short maturity date so that, if necessary, liquid funds could be realised to cover any abnormal level of withdrawals with a minimum risk of capital loss.

The common features of building societies and banks

In a housing context building societies and banks can be thought of as playing a similar role: namely, they act as financial intermediaries bridging the savings and mortgage markets. In recent years, the distinction between building societies and

---

4   The practice of borrowing 'short' and lending 'long' contravenes one of the basic principles of sound financial management. It allows for the possibility of a liquidity crisis if ever there is a loss of confidence in the society and savings are withdrawn at short notice. Because of this, building societies have tended to be conservative in their lending and investment policies. It also helps to explain why their investment policies have been supervised by external agencies.

banks has become increasingly blurred. Under powers given them by major legislation in 1986, the societies now offer a range of financial services formally the province of banking institutions. As deposit-takers, building societies have traditionally been regarded as savings institutions and their share and deposit accounts have been regarded as safe and accessible refuges for money balances which depositors wish to accumulate and keep for some future use such as the deposit on a dwelling or on a holiday. However, nowadays societies offer a range of banking-type facilities that have led to deposits with them being increasingly used as transactions rather than savings balances. The most significant developments have been the linking of building society deposits to instant access accounts with chequebook and cheque guarantee card facilities and the provision of high street cash points. In parallel with these developments, the banks have greatly expanded, and aggressively marketed, their mortgage lending facilities.

It can be argued that banks and building societies are now competing in the same markets both as lenders and deposit-takers. Because of their growing functional similarities, since 1984 the Inland Revenue has treated building societies and banks on a more or less equal basis.[5]

The growth of competition and the changing structure and role of building societies

As we have seen, the institutions playing the most dominant part in the mortgage market have traditionally been the building societies. Essentially they have acted as financial intermediaries standing between the retail savings market and the housing system. In this position they have channelled funds from savers to borrowers and in so doing have played a crucial part in the striking increase in owner-occupation that has taken place since the end of the war.

By 1981 the societies were experiencing serious competition from the clearing banks in the field of mortgage provision.[6] The societies tended to charge higher rates of interest on their more substantial loans, whilst the banks tended to offer flat-rate mortgages whatever the size of the advance. Because of this, the banks made significant inroads into the more expensive end of the housing market and

---

5   From April 1991 basic rate tax is deducted at source but non-tax-payers are able to arrange to obtain gross interest on their accounts. In addition, savers can claim back from the Inland Revenue any tax deducted by the bank or building society that is in excess of their total tax liability for the year.

6   There had already been a significant shift towards more competition between the societies themselves. The most prominent manifestation of this shift was the breaking up of the so-called *building societies' cartel*. The cartel arrangements, which operated throughout the 1970s, involved the trade body for the movement, the Building Societies Association, setting recommended rates of interest for both savers and borrowers. The arrangement was 'official' in that it operated with government approval and thereby became exempted from the provisions of the Monopolies and Mergers Act 1976, which is legislation designed to prevent restrictive trade practices. Over time the cartel was criticised from within and without the movement, and in any event, by the end of the decade, market pressures were undermining the arrangements. The cartel was gradually dismantled in the early 1980s.

---

this in turn encouraged the societies to liberalise their attitudes to lending on 'down market' properties.

The Building Societies Acts 1986 and 1997
Despite their attempts to respond to external competition, the 1962/67 legislation prevented the building societies from competing effectively with rival institutions in the banking and insurance sectors. They were, for example, prohibited from offering overdraft facilities and cheque guarantee cards on their newly-introduced cheque book accounts; in addition they were only permitted to offer insurance services in conjunction with a mortgage loan. Both the 1984 green paper *Building Societies: A New Framework* (Cm9316), and the Building Societies Association's own discussion paper published a year earlier[7] were critical of this situation. They argued that, whilst societies should remain mutual finance organisations, they should be allowed a wider range of powers in order to meet the growing competition from the banks and other institutions. The consultation process eventually led to a major piece of reforming legislation in the form of the Building Societies Act 1986. This Act repealed all previous legislation regulating building societies.

Under current legislation (the Building Societies Act 1986 as modified by the Building Societies Act 1997), building societies have the choice of two distinct courses of development. They can convert to, or be taken over by, a public limited company, and so become a bank, or they can remain as a mutual society with additional operating powers.

The new acts of parliament and their related measures have expanded building society powers. Whilst their prime activity remains the provision of first mortgages, the legislation has gone some way towards removing the distinctions between societies and other banking-type institutions. By easing the restrictions on the provision of unsecured loans and on investment in land and property development, the reforms also allow societies to become directly involved in partnership schemes to provide low-cost housing to purchase, rent or make available on a shared equity basis. The legislative reforms have encouraged the building society movement to undergo significant structural changes. By 1998, a number of its largest members, including its flagship society, the Halifax, had followed the lead of the Abbey National, and merged with, or converted to, banks. These changes have transferred more than 75 per cent of the total assets previously held by the building societies sector into banking.

Mortgages

Houses that are not inherited or bought outright are usually acquired by means of a loan. Where the property itself is used as a security for the repayment, the loan is referred to as a mortgage. A mortgage is a form of loan that is secured by pledging

---

7   The John Spalding Report, *The Future Constitution and Powers of Building Societies*, Building Societies' Association, January 1983.

a piece of real estate as collateral. The word 'mortgage' is made up of the two French words – *mort* meaning dead and *gage* meaning pledge. This is because all existing rights associated with the pledged estate die and are passed over to the lender if the borrower defaults on the agreed terms.

Some people get confused about the use of the terms *mortgagor* and *mortgagee*. What has to be remembered is that it is the householder who makes over the title to the house as security for the loan and is therefore classed as a 'mortgagor', just as someone who makes available employment is an employer. Conversely, it is the lender who receives the title and is therefore classed as a 'mortgagee', just as someone who receives employment from someone else is an employee. Because with mortgage arrangements the property is pledged as security, the mortgagee retains the title deeds until the loan is repaid. Mortgages are made up of two basic elements: the outstanding debt or 'principal' and the 'interest charges'. How these two elements are treated depends on the type of mortgage agreement entered into.

Types of mortgage

Repayment mortgage

The most straightforward type of house purchase loan is the *repayment* or *annuity* mortgage. This is sometimes referred to as a 'capital and interest mortgage'. These arrangements involve the borrower making periodic payments, usually monthly, to the lender, partly of interest on the outstanding loan and partly of capital to repay the loan. In the early years, most of the monthly payment goes toward paying off the interest, but as the outstanding loan is gradually repaid the interest element reduces and eventually the major part of the payment is used to repay the principal. The actual monthly payment will depend on the size of the loan, the length of the repayment period, known as the 'term', and the prevailing rate of interest. The typical arrangement involves a *level payment mortgage* that requires the repayment of a fixed monthly sum that only varies with changes in the rate of interest. In Britain the mortgage term is usually no longer than 30 years.[8]

Some lenders offer *low-start repayment mortgages* that are technically known as 'gross profile mortgages'. With such an arrangement the monthly payments are lower in the early years of the term but gradually increase each year so that during the later years they are higher than they would otherwise have been with an ordinary repayment mortgage. These loans are designed for people who, at the time of taking out the loan, are on a tight budget but have expectations of a rising income. Over the full term of the loan such arrangements are usually more expensive than conventional repayment mortgages. Low-start mortgages should be distinguished from 'discounted' mortgages. Some lenders promoted these heavily in the late 1990s as a way of attracting new business. They involve the mortgagor paying a reduced rate of interest for an initial period, typically a year or so, without the penalty of having to pay higher rates later in the term. We will say more about the different ways in which interest can be charged later.

---

8   Although some pension mortgages can be longer – see below.

With straightforward repayment mortgages it is possible to make an arrangement to pay a monthly *voluntary excess payment* and thereby shorten the loan term. Whether or not such a decision is worthwhile is sometimes difficult to determine and will depend on individual circumstances. A financial advisor, for example, may suggest that the mortgagor would be better advised to invest the voluntary payment in some form of 'tax-efficient' pension top-up or an Individual Savings Account (ISA).[9]

Interest only mortgages

The principle of an interest only mortgage is that the mortgagor makes monthly payments to cover the interest on the loan and is then responsible for arranging alternative means to pay off the capital amount of the loan at the end of the term. This is often achieved by using the proceeds of a life assurance policy, but some other savings and investment scheme could be taken out in parallel to the mortgage. These days the scheme can be associated with an ISA or pensions plan (see below).

A well-established approach is to take out an *endowment policy* that is arranged by the mortgage lender. This involves the borrower paying two separate payments each month. They pay interest directly to the lender together with a premium to an insurance/investment company. These premiums generate a fund that is designed to repay the principal on maturity. In this way, the capital is repaid at the end of the term using the proceeds of the matured policy. The endowment policy is deposited with the lending institution throughout the duration of the mortgage term. As well as providing an investment element, an endowment also generates life assurance protection for the purchaser. There are various types of endowment mortgage, all with built-in life cover but with somewhat differing arrangements and potential benefits and risks.

Low-cost endowment mortgage

A low-cost endowment mortgage is designed to keep the monthly payments to a minimum. It brings together a term assurance policy that will repay the loan should the mortgagor die prematurely and an investment-type endowment insurance policy to produce a sum of money on maturity which should be enough to pay off the debt at that time. It may, in addition, provide a lump sum over and above the debt liability. In cases where the investments turn out to perform less well than was anticipated, mortgagors may be required to increase their premiums part way through the term. Under a normal low-cost endowment mortgage the premiums payable are the same each month. Some companies offer low-start, low-cost endowments that allow the premium payments to be reduced in the early years.

Full endowment mortgage with profits

A full endowment mortgage operates in a similar way to the low-cost model, but the life cover is provided entirely by an endowment policy rather than partly by a

---

9   Individual Savings Accounts were launched in 1998 to replace Personal Equity Plans.

term assurance. As well as guaranteeing a sum to pay off the loan, the policy incorporates a planned savings scheme that seeks to produce a sum of money at the end of the term that may be significantly greater than that needed to cover the debt. This is done by bonuses being added to the initial sum so that at the end of the term, the policyholder should receive a lump sum over and above the mortgage loan repayment.

The way it works is that the company regularly credits the policy with 'reversionary' bonuses and on maturity with a 'terminal' bonus. The size of these is determined by the profits that the insurance company makes by investing the premium payments. Once declared and added, the bonuses cannot be removed; they will add to the value of the policy and revert to the policyholder at the end of the term. The company will only take into account the reversionary bonuses when calculating the amount needed to cover and repay the mortgage; the terminal bonus acts as a sort of 'safety buffer' that guarantees that the loan will be more than repaid.

Compared with repayment mortgages, endowment policies are less flexible. In the case of a repayment mortgage the borrower can normally lengthen or shorten the term of the loan to suit changing circumstances. By contrast, an endowment mortgage is a long-term contract, including automatic life assurance, and once the agreement is made, the parties are normally committed to it for the full term. If the policy is cashed in early the mortgagor may not get back all the premiums they have paid. All endowment policies are 'portable' and the policyholders are able to take them with them when they move house. How endowment mortgages perform crucially depend on movements in the stock market. In recent years poor stock market performances have resulted in many endowment policies failing to cover the long-run debt repayment.

Pension-linked mortgages

Pension-linked mortgages are a form of interest only mortgage. With this type of scheme, the borrower pays contributions into a pension fund and also pays premiums to a life assurance scheme. This provides for a lump sum and pension at retirement age, which becomes the maturity date. These schemes are usually aimed at the self-employed or people who do not belong to a company pension scheme.

The principle involves building up a fund that will repay the loan as well as provide the policyholder with a retirement pension. They work in a way that is similar to that of *with profits endowments*, but instead of an endowment policy, the mortgagor takes out a retirement annuity which, as well as providing a pension, pays a lump sum on retirement, or thereabouts, which is intended to pay off the mortgage. There are no guarantees and final benefits are related to the market performance and the skills of those responsible for the investment. These plans can be tax efficient, but pension rules can be complicated and difficult to understand without guidance from an expert in the field.

Pension mortgages may be tax efficient but can be restricting: they rely on the mortgagor having a personal pension throughout the life of the mortgage and as many people move in and out of company schemes, such personal pensions may be difficult to manage efficiently. The rules do not allow people to hold a personal and a company pension at the same time; nor do they allow them to use their occupational pensions to fund their mortgages. This means that pension mortgages are inflexible for people moving in and out of self-employment. By tying together these two financial assets, the mortgagor/policyholder may create a financial conflict of interest and at some future date, the interests of one may have to compromise the other. In an uncertain world, in which people increasingly have complex career patterns, it is often sensible to separate mortgage management from retirement planning. Despite the above argument, because of the tax advantages, pension mortgages have been popular with high earning executives and self-employed groups who have considerable control over their own pension arrangements.[10]

Unit-linked mortgages

Compared with ordinary with profits policies, these schemes have a greater element of risk associated with them; their values will tend to fluctuate with the stock market. They operate in a similar way to endowment assurances in that the cash sum produced by the policy at maturity is credited to the mortgage account and any surplus is then paid to the policyholder. The savings element of the policy is channelled into an investment fund by the purchase of 'units'. The fund may deal in British or overseas property and stocks and shares, and the value of the units will fluctuate in line with how the fund prospers. The cash amount at maturity will be dependent on the value of all of the units held at that time. The company may sometimes review the value of the units to ensure that they are increasing at a rate sufficient to repay the mortgage and, if they are not, they may request additional premiums in order to acquire further units. If the value of the policy matches the mortgage debt at a time prior to the maturity date, the policyholder may choose to repay the mortgage at that time; in this way, unit-linked schemes provide an additional element of flexibility over other endowment schemes.

Specialist savings arrangements

Some mortgage lenders offer a range of other vehicles for tying savings into a mortgage deal. Some of these will seek to utilise government sponsored Individual Savings Accounts (ISAs) that are designed to provide a degree of tax efficiency to the 'saver'. These tax-efficient 'savings mortgages' are now quite popular and are increasingly being offered as an alternative to the more traditional repayment and endowment arrangements. Like an endowment they involve taking out an interest only loan and at the same time paying a monthly premium. The premiums are paid

---

10 Pension managers have tended to have a rather paternalistic attitude and argue that it is not in an employee's interest to reduce a pension entitlement to pay off a mortgage. However, with the introduction of radical new pension arrangements in 1988 and the consequential intensification of competition in the pension plans market, attitudes are changing.

into an *Individual Savings Account*. That cash will then be invested, probably in bonds and shares. The principle is that this will create a fund that will be big enough to pay off the mortgage at the end of the term. One drawback does exist however: anyone with such a mortgage is likely to be disqualified from receiving income support if the fund is valued at more than the qualifying capital allowance when they claim (Benefit entitlements are discussed more fully in Chapter 19).

Varying interest rates

Interest rate 'deals' are wide-ranging. The following represent the main options that are currently available.

Standard variable rate. With this option the monthly repayments will fluctuate as lenders periodically alter their loan interest charges.

Fixed rate. A fixed interest is normally negotiated for a specified period, typically two years, rather than for the full term. Although a fixed interest charge gives the mortgagor a degree of certainty with respect to future housing costs, whether or not it is cheaper in the long-run will depend on how interest rates fluctuate over the fixed period. Fixed interest mortgages often include a 'lock-in' clause in the small print. This means that at the end of the fixed period the mortgagor may be required either to transfer to a variable rate mortgage, or pay a penalty surcharge to transfer to some other fixed mortgage scheme. Fixed interest schemes have tended to be more popular in America and Europe and there is currently a good deal of debate about whether they might be used more extensively in the UK (see discussion on the Miles Report below).

Capped rate. This guarantees the borrower that the interest will not rise above a pre-set rate, the 'cap', for a specified period.

Tracker rate. This provides the option to pay an interest rate that will rise and fall in line with rates set by the Bank of England for a specified period.

Discounted rate. This offers the borrower a reduced rate for a short initial period. It is really a marketing ploy (see discussion above on repayment mortgages).

Annual review schemes
The real income effect of a relatively small change in interest rates can be significant (see index for further discussion on 'real income effect'). If mortgagors wish to plan their outgoings on an annual basis they may opt for an *annual review scheme*. Under these arrangements the interest rate is fixed for a year so that if there is a change in rates during the year it will be ignored until the following review period, that is, the following year. If during the current review period interest rates are raised, there will then be a 'postponed' under-payment owing at the end of the period. In the following review period the repayments are adjusted to take account of this under-payment.

The Miles Report

In his 2003 Budget Statement, the chancellor voiced his concern over the way mortgages have been taken out in the UK. Approximately 65 per cent have been taken out on variable interest terms, with those that are on fixed terms being for relatively short periods of up to five years. This is different from the USA and the rest of Europe. It is the latter that is of particular concern to the government as there is pressure from the European Commission to establish a greater degree of conformity. Concern was expressed that in Britain borrowers fail to appreciate the security advantages of fixed interest borrowing and often prefer to go for short-term discounts instead.

Professor David Miles was asked to produce a report on how long-term fixed finance could be made more available to private borrowers. This report was published prior to the 2004 Budget. The Miles Report concluded that a wider availability of long-term fixed interest finance would bring greater stability to the economy as a whole and to the housing market in particular. However, from the lenders' point of view, long-term fixed mortgages are problematic. Building societies and banks cannot themselves borrow (from retail savers) for a 25 year term. This means that, in order to provide long-term fixed mortgages, they will need to make expensive arrangements with other money market institutions. This requires a premium charge on the fixed rate mortgage that may well make the product unattractive to borrowers. It is worth noting that this form of liberalising the mortgage market could lead to a surge in demand for 'right to buy' sales because potential purchasers are often concerned about their ability to cope with the uncertainties associated with flexible interest rate arrangements.

Mortgage protection and indemnity insurance

In recent years, both the government and lenders have placed more emphasis on *mortgage payment protection insurance* (MPPI). Indeed, there is now an explicit expectation that all home-owners should take more responsibility for protecting themselves through private insurance and the industry is aiming to achieve a higher take-up of MPPI by new home-buyers. The reasons for this pressure partly stems from the changing socio-economic profile of mortgagors, more of whom are now on temporary contracts of employment or are in jobs that do not provide the sort of stable, secure incomes that have historically underpinned owner-occupation. The pressure to take out MPPI also stems from the general shift in government policy away from sole reliance on the state for safety net provision[11] to forms of partnership provision with the private sector. Under MPPI policies, if mortgagors lose their jobs through ill health or redundancy and cannot make the payments, the policy will normally cover them.[12]

---

11 The key difference between Income Support for Mortgage Interest (discussed in Chapter 19) and MPPI is that the former is largely tax funded whilst MPPI is funded by premiums paid by mortgagors themselves.
12 However, experience shows that some of these policies fail to cover self-employed work, jobs with fixed contracts or contracts that run for a shorter period than the term of the loan, so that when borrowers' circumstances change they are no longer covered.

This policy expectation has proved to be problematic for all sorts of reasons. A particular problem relates to how the benefits system treats the payout income derived from such policies.[13] If mortgage protection policies pay out so that money is transferred to the lender this has never been regarded as 'income' in the calculation of entitlement to state benefits. Some policies pay out direct to claimants rather than to lenders and, until recently, there had been some confusion about whether such payments should be treated as 'income' in benefit calculations. After much lobbying, the situation has been clarified and payments to claimants are, since June 1998, now also disregarded when assessing benefits. For a fuller discussion of mortgage interest protection see Chapter 19.[14]

A mortgagor may be asked to pay a mortgage indemnity premium that safeguards the lender against the value of the property not covering the value of the outstanding debt in the event of default. Although these are being phased out by a number of the larger lenders, they are still quite common. They are normally required when a borrower is unable to put down a deposit of more than a specified percentage. Indemnity insurance plans should be distinguished from mortgage protection policies. Although both are charged to the mortgagor, the former are primarily designed to benefit the lender and the latter are primarily designed to protect the borrower.

The changing nature of employment, negative equity and repossessions

Many feel that the mortgage industry and the social security system have been slow to respond to the changing nature of employment and that this has added to the problem of insecure owner-occupation. The 1980s and 1990s saw a restructuring of the labour market so that by the end of the 1990s some ten million Britons relied on part-time work, fixed-term contracts, low pay or self-employment. Job security is also an important factor in determining the risk of repossession. During the 1990s, a significant number of heads of repossessed households were not in work when they lost their homes, either because of

---

13 Confusion has also surrounded the question of capital calculation for benefit purposes. Endowment policies have been classified differently from strict 'saving-related' schemes because of the way the benefit authorities regard the nature of the cover. If the surrender value of the endowment is over a certain amount (the current saving limit for income support), it has not disqualified claimants from receiving benefit. This is because the DSS regards endowments as life insurance-related rather than income-related and the value of life insurance policies has always been disregarded in calculating income-related benefits. This has meant that endowment policies have been disregarded whether or not they were linked to mortgages. PEPs and ISAs have no life insurance content, and are taken into account in the usual way as capital. So a PEP or ISA without built-in life insurance cover is seen as an investment rather than as part of the mortgage and will therefore count as capital. The whole question of benefit entitlement to owner-occupiers is discussed fully in Chapter 19.

14 See also article by Deborah Quilgars, 'High and dry down Acacia Avenue', *Roof* March/April 1999, pp22-23, Chapter 16. Refer also to Janet Ford, 'MPPI take-up and retention: the current evidence', in *Housing Finance* No.45, February 2000, pp45-51.

---

redundancy or because they were looking after a family full-time.[15] People in full-time employment headed only a third of repossessed households. Two out of ten heads of repossessed households were self-employed.

Suggestions have been made for restructuring the mortgage industry and the fiscal support system so that they are more in tune with the current realities of the contemporary employment market and the needs of those owners who are finding it financially difficult to remain in the tenure. The most persistent policy suggestion has been the call for a unified housing benefit scheme covering low-income owners as well as tenants (see Chapter 19). Other proposals are aimed at the industry rather than the government. They include the following:[16]

- More flexible mortgages in which repayment periods, payment schedules and interest rates can be varied according to the mortgagor's ability to pay. This would involve encouraging mortgage deals in which people pay more in prosperous periods and less when earnings fall.
- To reduce the impact of falling income, introduce a system of 'staircasing-down' from home-ownership on a similar basis as part-owners can gain access to the tenure by 'staircasing-up'. This would produce a more flexible tenure in which those leaving home-ownership can retain occupation of their homes instead of having them sold over their heads (often at a fraction of their market values) while they become homeless.
- The introduction of a statutory code of practice for any lending that is based on the security of someone's home. The code would be designed to ensure that, so long as mortgagors paid a debt servicing figure that was in line with the market rent, they could not be forced out of their home.
- Mortgage advisors should make more effort to demonstrate the different risk characteristics of variable and fixed mortgages, e.g. by demonstrating what would happen to their payments if interest rates were to rise.
- Lenders should offer their full range of mortgages to all customers (including existing borrowers) rather than restricting the best deals to new customers or those remortgaging.

Some of these reforms have now been introduced (see discussion later in this chapter in 'The question of regulation').

Positive equity and equity release schemes

Equity represents the value of a mortgaged property after the deduction of any charges against it. In other words, it is that part of the property's value that is 'owned' by the occupier, as against the mortgage provider. Over the years, there

---

15 See also article by Deborah Quilgars, 'High and dry down Acacia Avenue', *Roof*, ibid.
16 Data produced from *Roof* magazine – derived from 57 lenders who between them account for 73 per cent of all mortgagors.

has been much debate about the extent to which equity growth in the owner-occupied sector leaks out into the wider economy, thereby causing increases in money demand. The question is important because increases in money demand will induce inflationary pressures that could cause damage to the government's broad macro-economic policy objectives (refer to Chapter 5).

There are a number of ways in which residential property equity can be unlocked and spent on general consumption. As the market value of an occupier's dwelling increases over time it may be possible to borrow against the equity growth. If the mortgagor borrows from the institution with which he or she has a mortgage, the interest charged will usually be the same as the standard variable mortgage rate. This means that the new loan will cost significantly less than taking out an ordinary personal loan. If the mortgagor borrows from a different lender, there is likely to be an arranging fee and the rate of interest is likely to be slightly higher than the standard variable mortgage rate. Nevertheless, over the term of the loan, total charges will normally still be less than they would be for a personal loan. Equity release loans tend to be for a minimum amount, £10,000, and the total amount that can be borrowed will depend on the mortgagor's income, the value of the property, and the level of outstanding debt. Equity release loans are often used to finance home improvements. Many households unlock part of their accumulated housing equity later in life by 'trading down'. This typically involves selling the family home and then purchasing a smaller and less valuable retirement property. Equity can also be unlocked when the occupier dies and their estate is inherited by people who then sell the fixed assets with a view to acquiring liquid assets.

The current debate on equity release

Equity release schemes became particularly popular in the early 1980s when house prices were rising rapidly. The buoyant nature of the housing market in the late 1990s and early 2000s also encouraged many people to unlock the liquid wealth tied up in their homes. More than £1 billion has now been unlocked in this way. The various equity release schemes take two broad forms. They can be used to generate an income flow and/or provide a lump sum payment. The company that loans the money recovers it from the householder's estate after death or when they sell the property (e.g. to move into a care home).

Generating an income

A few years ago 'Home Income Plans' became a popular way of generating an additional monthly income. At that time the most common form of plan involved taking out a secure fixed 'interest only' loan that was then used to purchase a life-time annuity providing fixed periodic payments until death. The cost of the annuity and the income which flowed from it were based on life expectancy. The income from the annuity was used to pay the interest repayments on the loan and the balance remaining was then available to the borrower. The annuity was typically linked to an investment bond. The principle involved people remortgaging their houses and investing the borrowed funds on the stock market in the expectation that stock market gains would both cover the costs of the extra mortgage and also provide extra cash. This specialist equity release product worked well in periods when house prices were rising and the stock market was buoyant. But when, in the 1990s, share prices collapsed and interest rates rose, the schemes failed and participating home-owners found themselves owing more than the value of their homes. As a result of the fuss that this caused, these schemes were eventually banned and a new organisation (SHIP) was set up to try and re-establish confidence in 'safer' forms of income generating equity release.

Safe Home Income Plans (SHIP). SHIP participants provide a code of practice that guarantees that their products possess the following four safety features:

- no negative equity liability – the accumulated debt will never exceed the value of the property;
- independent legal advice is incorporated into the agreement;
- guaranteed tenure for life;
- freedom to move without financial penalty.

Generating a lump sum

There are three broad ways of releasing equity capital by means of a scheme. The first, called 'home reversion', involves selling part of the dwelling. The second, called the 'roll-up mortgage', involves taking out a loan against its value. In both cases the money received is not repaid until the occupier dies or goes into long-term care. A third approach is the 'shared appreciation mortgage'.

Home Reversion Plans. These arrangements are well-established and typically involve an older home-owner selling all or part of their property to an investor for a discounted cash sum (or an annuity income for life) while retaining life occupancy rights in the form of a life-time lease. The return to the investor, that is the effective cost to the occupier, is equivalent to the difference between the discounted purchase price and the final sale price when vacant possession is obtained. The level of discount on market value is mainly determined by the life expectancy of the client. Older occupiers will normally receive more as the institution anticipates a shorter period of 'rent-free' occupancy before acquiring its claim on the equity. The down-side for the occupier is that as house prices rise they (or their heirs) will lose the financial benefit that results from any equity growth.

Life-time mortgages (sometimes called 'roll-up mortgages'). Under these arrangements the occupier receives a loan that does not require any repayment of interest or principal until the occupier dies or redeems the mortgage. The interest charges simply get rolled up through time and are added to the original loan figure (the principal). As the interest is rolled up into the debt, interest gets charged on the interest. Interest tends to be charged at a premium rate on roll-up mortgages. All this means that, by the end of the term, the outstanding debt may be significantly higher than the original sum borrowed. In most cases the final debt turns out to be a multiple of the original loan figure. This makes such products 'high risk'. Because of this level of risk the Financial Services Agency has been given the task of introducing a regulatory system (see below). The danger of debt appreciation has also stimulated the development of more flexible products based on the 'draw-down' principle.

The draw-down principle allows some occupiers to negotiate a more flexible form of roll-up mortgage that allows them to negotiate a maximum loan figure but only draw as much of that figure as they currently need – with an option to draw down more as and when it is needed. In this way the home-owner only pays interest on that part of the agreed figure that has been actually borrowed (the drawn-down amount).

Shared appreciation mortgages, These were piloted by the Bank of Scotland in the late 1990s and are gradually becoming available through other banks.[17] They were initially targeted at older people (established owner-occupiers) who want to release some of the equity tied up in their properties. They involve the owner-occupier agreeing to give up a certain increase in the value of the property in exchange for releasing some of that cash, thus any equity growth is shared with the mortgagee. Consideration is being given to extending the principle of shared appreciation mortgages so that new, younger buyers can take out smaller, and therefore cheaper, mortgages in return for sharing any future capital appreciation with the mortgagee.

It is possible that income supplements or capital sums received through equity release schemes will affect the entitlement to pension credits (introduced October 2003) or other social security benefits to which the home-owner is entitled.

We will now turn to the question of regulation. In so doing we will say more about the issue of equity accumulation and equity release.

The question of regulation

In recent years the home loans industry regulated itself by a voluntary code of practice. This mortgage code set out minimum standards that lenders and intermediaries had to meet in order to provide protection for borrowers. The code embraced a list of commitments that sought to give protection with respect to:

(a) how the mortgage should be arranged,
(b) what information should be presented by the mortgagee prior to agreement, and
(c) how the loan will be managed once it is in place.

---

17 At the time of writing, this type of mortgage is not available. They are in abeyance but could well be introduced in the near future.

Despite the existence of the code, the Office of Fair Trading continued to publish concerns about the level of customer complaints to trading standards officers and citizens' advice bureaux about mortgages. MPs' post bags and items in the press also highlighted complaints against a small number of 'rogue' mortgage providers. In 1999, as a result of such stories, the influential committee of MPs and peers who were scrutinising the legislation for the new Financial Services Authority (FSA) called on the government to bring home loans and long-term care insurance within the scope of the regulating Authority's terms of reference. The drive to integrate the regulation of all financial services has meant that the FSA has now taken over the regulatory roles previously exercised by the Building Societies Commission, the Friendly Societies Commission and, in relation to credit unions, the Chief Registrar of Friendly Societies.[18]

The idea of formalising the code of practice is to promote the integration of financial regulation and help achieve the benefit of a single regulatory culture. The new system seeks to create arrangements that bring consistency and coherence to the regulation of all financial sectors, including banking, insurance, mutual societies, and other financial services.

The Treasury announced the outcome of its review of mortgage regulation in January 2000.[19] Briefly the government decided the following:[20]

- Not to regulate mortgage advice along the lines of the approach taken for investment advice under the Financial Services Act.
- The FSA will require lenders to disclose all the main features of loans clearly and openly. In effect this means that lenders, but not mortgage intermediaries, will need to be authorised by the FSA, whose remit will cover mortgage advertising, a standard disclosure regime, commission disclosure, and compensation arrangements.
- A new CAT standard for mortgages should be introduced, covering Charges, Access and Terms. This seeks to create a format for providing a straightforward, easy-to-understand mortgage that would appeal to borrowers who want a 'transparent' deal with no complex 'strings' attached.

---

18 It also acts on behalf of the Treasury in the conduct of insurance supervision under the Insurance Companies Act.
19 Circular No 1233, dated 26 January 2000.
20 The green paper also considered encouraging the development of a more active secondary market in mortgages through a process of securitisation. The securitisation of home loans is common practice in the USA. It involves lenders selling on mortgages by issuing bonds. Because the market judges the bonds to be a relatively low risk investment, they can generate funds at relatively low rates of interest. It is argued that the securitisation process also increases competition by breaking up the mortgage process into its component parts (marketing, processing applications, raising finance, and servicing mortgages) and allows mortgage providers to out-source those components that can be provided more effectively or cheaply by others.

At the end of October 2004, the Financial Services Authority (FSA) began regulating the mortgage industry in an effort to simplify the 'regulation landscape' and offer greater protection for consumers. The Authority now oversees both the selling of residential mortgages and the advice associated with the sales process.

Increasing regulation

New regulatory rules were introduced in October 2004. Under these rules, firms conducting a regulated activity (see below) will require a license from their 'designated' professional body or authorisation from the Financial Services Agency. It should be noted that the new rules govern mortgage advice rather than mortgage products. The new rules set in place regulated mortgage contracts where:

- the borrower is an individual or trustee;
- the lender takes a first charge over property in the UK;
- the property is at least 40 per cent occupied by the borrower or an immediate family member.

Second charges, unsecured lending, home reversion schemes, buy to let mortgages, and loans to limited companies remain unregulated.

Regulating equity release schemes

The operation of equity release schemes are discussed above. Since October 2004 the FSA has been charged with the responsibility to regulate life-time ('roll-up') mortgage schemes. The financial watchdog regulates how the products are marketed and requires a degree of standardised information so that potential purchasers can more easily compare the costs and benefits of competing products. They also put a duty on the selling agency to offer the product that is judged to be 'most suitable' for the purchaser, given their needs and circumstances. In addition the Financial Ombudsman has been given authority to make binding agreements on firms when a complaint is upheld. In extreme cases a complainant may have access the FAS's compensation scheme.

At the time of writing there are no plans for home reversion schemes to be incorporated into the FSA's regulatory system. This is because they are not technically mortgages. In effect, a home reversion agreement involves a full or part sale of the property to a third party in exchange for financial benefit and leasehold rights. There is pressure from the Consumers' Association and others to bring these sorts of schemes into the regulatory framework to prevent a confusing dual system of equity release arrangements becoming established.

The exchange process

It often takes several months to complete the sale of a property. A number of exchange professionals can be involved. These typically include an estate agent, a solicitor, a surveyor, and a mortgage institution. Because a contractual agreement is at the heart of the process, solicitors, or commercial conveyancers, usually play a key role in driving the arrangements towards completion. Most solicitors use the Law Society conveyancing code as a reference for appropriate practice and this, to some extent, has the effect of standardising the process. Special forms are used that include an information questionnaire that the seller completes. This sets out details about the property and acts as a checklist of what is being sold. The seller's solicitor then provides a pre-contract package for the prospective buyer, which is essentially a draft contract with documents relating to the client's title to the property. The buyer's solicitor obtains *searches*. These investigate public records to check whether the property is subject to any legal liabilities or encumbrances. Once the searches have taken place, the conveyancer will formalise any necessary amendments to the draft contract. Meanwhile, the buyer will normally arrange a survey and, if necessary, a mortgage loan. Once these transactions have been dealt with, a completion date is set and contracts can be exchanged. Between exchange and completion, the purchaser's solicitor arranges for the mortgage funds to be released and prepares a transfer document so the contract's financial consideration can be passed over.

For years the home-buying process has been criticised for being unnecessarily lengthy and cumbersome. Outside Scotland, where legal obligations are established on the exchange of contracts, the process has also been criticised for allowing the would-be purchaser to be 'gazumped', or the seller to be confronted with a withdrawn or reduced offer weeks into the negotiations. New measures are currently being considered that are intended to reduce the time lag between offer, acceptance and exchange of contracts. By 2007, the government hopes to have changed the way homes are bought and sold in England and Wales. Their aim is to make the home-buying and selling process faster, more transparent and more consumer friendly. By shifting more of the responsibility and cost of the exchange process on to the vendor it is planned to reduce the risk of last minute renegotiations. After testing in a number of pilot areas, it is expected that sellers will be required to prepare an information pack for prospective purchasers. It is proposed that the pack will include draft contracts, title deeds, an independent surveyor's report on the condition of the property and its energy efficiency, warranties and guarantees for any work carried out, the results of searches and answers to commonly asked questions. Under these arrangements, the survey will be to a standard format prescribed by the government, and the surveyor would be liable to both the seller and the buyer for its contents. Although developers will not be required to include a survey report in their packs, they will have to include copies of planning consents, warranties and guarantees.

The above proposals will have implications for social landlords who are involved with property sales. As an extension of existing 'Best Value' principles, social landlords involved in sales will be expected to adopt performance targets ensuring that those with whom they deal receive a fast and efficient service.

Exchange costs

The following constitute the main exchange costs associated with residential property transactions. They do not all apply in all cases.

- *Estate agents' fees.* Most agent's tariffs differentiate between a 'sole' and a 'multiple' agency. A higher fee is usually charged if there is more than one agent commissioned to sell the property. Some agents charge a flat fee and then additional charges for the erection of a board and placing advertisements in the press, whilst others have an overall marketing agreement with no additional charges.
- *Legal fees.* Legal fees are paid for the services of a solicitor or conveyancer. The final bill will be broken down into various charge categories. The contract administration charge is normally calculated as a percentage of the purchase price plus VAT. In addition to a charge covering contract administration and legal advice, the following might also be included in the final account:
  - *A Land Registry fee.* This is a charge to check the nature and scope of the seller's title to the land and buildings.
  - *A local authority search fee.* This is charged to check the existence of any current or proposed planning restrictions or other factors that might affect the occupier's consumption or investment interests.
  - *Stamp duty.* Stamp duty is a sales tax that is charged to higher priced real estate transactions (see below).
  - *Property survey fees.* When a mortgage loan is involved, the lender will normally require a surveyor's report and mortgage valuation. This is usually a simple visual inspection that is designed to confirm that the property's value is sufficient to cover the debt liabilities. This survey report is not designed to provide a detailed condition survey and therefore a purchaser may choose to commission a fuller structural survey before making a final offer.

Taxation and capital finance

Stamp duty[21]

Stamp duty is a transactions tax that is levied every time a dwelling is sold. The tax is criticised by some housing economists because it is assumed to distort the workings of the housing market and discourages the mobility of labour. Because the rate is applied to the full value of the property, rather than to the marginal element of value above each threshold[22], it tends to lead to an artificial bunching

---

21 Stamp duty also applies to documents transferring other types of property such as shares and other securities.

22 The stamp duty rates currently stand at one per cent on properties sold for more than £120,000 but for less than £250,000; three per cent where the sale price is above £250,000 and less than £500,000; and four per cent where the price is more than £500,000. From 30th November 2001, stamp duty exemption has been available for the purchase of property in certain designated disadvantaged areas of the UK, and where the consideration, or premium for a lease, does not exceed £150,000.

of prices just below each threshold level. It also encourages avoidance measures such as inflated payments for 'fixtures and fittings' as a way of allowing the official selling price to remain in the lower tax category. It discourages mobility because it is paid on the full value on each move. If the duty was levied only on that part of the exchange value above the margin (as in the case of capital gains tax – see below), rather than on full value, the tax burden would not be determined by the number of times the household moved.

It is also criticised as a fiscal anomaly with no clear social or economic purpose. It is simply a revenue raising measure. It might be argued that recent stamp duty rises were introduced (2000) in an attempt to dampen down house price inflation, particularly in the south-east of England. However, because of the continuing rise in house prices, there is now a campaign to abolish stamp duty on homes up to the value of £150,000. Organisations such as the Royal Institution of Chartered Surveyors and the National Association of Estate Agents argue that house price rises mean that, in recent years, stamp duty has been transformed from a levy on high value homes to a general tax that hits the majority of purchasers including first-time buyers.

Capital gains tax

Britain, like many other countries, does not tax capital gains on an owner-occupied dwelling where it is classified as the 'only or main residence' of the occupier. If two or more main residences are held simultaneously, the individual may select which property they wish to qualify for exemption. In strict economic terms this concession may be criticised as bringing a distortion into the wider capital market. The argument here is that dwellings are capital assets and the tax privilege will attract funds away from other, more productive, classes of asset, thereby inhibiting investment efficiency and general economic growth in the economy. Despite this economic argument, it is possible to justify the tax concession in social policy terms. The case here is that private residences should be treated as 'domestic' rather than 'commercial' assets. It is argued that the tax system should not penalise the acquisition of those forms of real property that most owners regard as 'capitalised savings' to be inherited by their children or used to fund their own declining years.

With some exceptions,[23] if someone owns a second home the Inland Revenue treats this as a taxable investment. This is true even if it is not let out on a commercial basis, but it is held as a holiday home. In its first Budget, the New Labour government altered the capital gains tax rules as they apply to second homes. The old rules were based on the idea that the tax was levied on sale on the basis of 'proceeds less costs'. This provided an indexation allowance, or inflation protection, in the calculation of the 'gain' and the seller was then allowed an

---

23 For example, if an individual disposes of a residence previously occupied by a dependent relative, rent-free and without other consideration, capital gains tax exemption will normally be granted.

annual exemption before the tax was levied. Under the new rules there is still an annual exemption, but other aspects of the computation have changed significantly. Indexation has ceased so there is now no inflation protection built into the system, and the new regime tapers away the gain, depending on how long the asset has been held.[24]

Over the last few years, as house prices have risen, the estimated notional value of this relief is in excess of £10 billion (2004).[25] It should be recognised that, some at least, of this 'lost' Exchequer revenue is eventually recouped through inheritance tax.

Inheritance taxation

To introduce a capital gains tax charge on ordinary housing transactions would be politically difficult. It would also be inconvenient and expensive to administer, given the volume of transactions. It is more convenient to tax capital appreciation on domestic assets through the mechanism of inheritance tax. Inheritance tax is payable on death and is charged as a flat-rate percentage of the value of the estate over an exempted figure.[26] The tax is not payable if the deceased's spouse inherits the estate and other exemptions are possible if the estate is willed to a charitable foundation. The 'estate' upon which the tax is charged covers all cash and assets including residences, cars, any life assurance benefits and investments, and valuables such as antiques and jewellery, minus any outstanding debts.

Occupancy and revenue finance

The idea of housing expenditure and revenue

As managers of their homes, owner-occupiers are responsible for meeting all the associated costs-in-use. They are responsible for all the recurring revenue charges with respect to interest and debt redemption on mortgage or other loans taken out to acquire their properties, together with all the payments made for the purpose of maintaining and repairing the fabric of the dwellings once they have been acquired.

In practice, the day-to-day revenue expenses of owner-occupation are met out of the household's total disposable income, which is generally derived from employment earnings or any welfare benefits to which they are entitled. However, in its strictest sense, the housing revenue of an owner-occupier stems from his or

---

24 The taper works over a ten-year period. Under current regulations, the capital gains taxed are initially charged at the tax-payer's marginal rate, so that, for instance, a 40 per cent marginal tax-payer would go in at the 40 per cent band for a three-year holding period. It then steadily tapers away so that after ten years it has fallen to 24 per cent.
25 Wilcox, S. *UK Housing Review 2004/2005*, CIH/CML, p24
26 At the time of writing (2004/5) this tax is chargeable at 40 per cent on that part of the estate's value in excess of £263,000.

her ownership of the dwelling as an economic asset. This means that, in theory, it is conceived of as the revenue benefit that is generated by the asset and then enjoyed by the owner. This benefit takes the form of a stream of housing services and can be thought of as an *income in kind*. This income in kind is referred to as 'imputed rent' or 'imputed income'.

Revenue income

As with the case of landlords, owner-occupiers can be said to receive 'incomes' that are directly derived from the dwellings they own. Also, like housing organisations, owner-occupiers can be said to receive these incomes in the form of 'rents' and 'subsidies'. However, the difference between the housing income of an owner-occupier and that of a landlord is that in the case of the former, the 'rent' is not paid by a tenant but is conceived of as an *imputed rent*. Because no cash is actually received, the idea that owners pay themselves 'rent' is counter-intuitive and rather difficult to grasp. However, it is important to understand the notion of imputed rent because it features strongly in the general debate about the nature and scope of owner-occupier subsidies.

The non-taxation of imputed rental income

An owner of a dwelling may either let it out to another person or occupy it as a home. If they let it out, the rental income they receive after allowances will be taxed as part of their income. It will be taxed under Schedule 'A' of the income tax schedules, which deals with income from land and landed property. If, on the other hand, the owner chooses to occupy the dwelling, they receive a benefit that can be thought of as an income in kind, and this benefit is not now subject to income taxation, although it was prior to 1963 – see below. In this way, an owner-occupied residence might be thought of as a durable asset that yields a flow of untaxed housing services that are consumed by the owner-occupant. The term 'imputed income' is used to describe the monetary value that is attributed to these services.[27]

The abolition of Schedule 'A' income tax and the changing nature of mortgage interest tax relief

As a general taxation principle, if tax-payers take out loans to acquire consumption items, such as family cars, holidays, jewellery, etc., they cannot offset the cost of servicing such loans against their income tax liabilities. By contrast, if tax-payers take out loans to acquire investment items (e.g. fleet cars, plant, machinery, etc.), they may, under certain conditions, be entitled to claim income tax relief for interest paid. In this way, the Inland Revenue treats consumption and investment expenditure differently when it comes to allowing tax relief in loan interest charges. One of the long-standing debates in housing

---

27 It is possible, of course, for an owner-occupier to take in a lodger or let out part of the dwelling. In such circumstances, that owner would receive actual revenue income in addition to the imputed rental income.

finance is whether owner-occupied housing should be treated, for tax purposes, as consumption or investment.

Prior to 1963, owner-occupied dwellings were treated for tax purposes as though they were investments. The imputed income benefit received was taxed, but certain costs, including that of servicing the mortgage loan were granted as allowances. This means that, at that time, mortgage income tax relief (MITR), was not technically a 'subsidy', but rather a legitimate tax allowance set against investment earnings. As such, MITR was on a par with similar allowances in the business world.

The reason that the main residences of owner-occupiers were exempted from Schedule 'A' income taxation after 1963 was largely political and was the result of the rating revaluation that took place in that year. The tax was assessed on the assumed letting value of the property, net of repairs and maintenance, and rateable values were used as the basis of the assessment. However, residential properties were only periodically revalued for rating purposes and at the time it was the 1936/37 rating valuations that were being used to calculate the imputed incomes. A long overdue rating revaluation was to take place in 1963/64 and, if the Schedule 'A' tax had been retained, it would have meant that, in many areas, the tax burden would have trebled or quadrupled. This would have had damaging political consequences for the government at a time when more and more of the electorate were becoming owner-occupiers.[28]

When Schedule 'A' income tax was abolished, a political decision was made to allow owners to continue to set their mortgage interest costs against their income tax liabilities. The changes had the effect of converting MITR from a legitimate allowance on a tax charge that was actually paid, into an effective housing subsidy. Many commentators argued that once the tax was scrapped, MITR became an anomalous, tenure-specific, fiscal benefit.

Mortgage income tax relief (MITR) and the introduction of MIRAS

In more recent times, the Treasury did not treat mortgage income tax relief (MITR) as a 'subsidy', preferring to regard it as a 'tax forgone'. This failure explicitly to recognise the real income effect of the tax privilege produced what might be termed a 'hidden subsidy' for the tenure. After 1983 the process of administering the subsidy was simplified with the introduction of MIRAS. Mortgage Interest Relief At Source involved the mortgage providers working with

---

28 As well as exempting owner-occupation, the Finance Act 1963 altered the whole way in which Schedule 'A' tax was assessed. Before the 1963 Budget the tax had been charged on an annual value related to the rateable value. After the 1963 Budget the taxation of income from land and buildings (Schedule 'A'), was based on the actual profit arising, i.e. receipts less allowable expenditure.

the Inland Revenue to calculate the relief entitlements of individual borrowers.[29]
The concession, and therefore the 'subsidy', was gradually phased out and was
eventually abolished in 2000 (see appendix to chapter).

Maintenance costs

Debt servicing charges are not the only recurring housing costs confronting home-
owners. Indeed, many owner-occupied dwellings are owned outright.[30] Owners
have to spend money to maintain their properties in a state of good repair whether
or not they are buying with the help of a loan.

The distinction between 'primary maintenance' and 'improvement'

Primary maintenance work is undertaken to prevent or arrest the building's
structure and fabric from deteriorating and is therefore concerned with maintaining
the building envelope. In other words, primary maintenance is carried out to ensure
that the building is 'safe and sound'. This type of maintenance might occur in
response to some form of unexpected structural failure or it might be planned and
budgeted for in advance. Improvement work is undertaken to add to the building's
size or quality rather than to maintain it in working order. This may involve
building some kind of extension to the property or converting it to a different use
(perhaps from a large house into flats), installing some feature or facility it
previously lacked, or refurbishing it to bring it up to some higher standard of
accommodation. In this way, improvement works can be said to be adding to the
capital value of the dwelling rather than simply maintaining its value.

In Chapter 2 a theoretical distinction was made between 'capital' and 'revenue'
finance. It was made clear that, in theory, capital finance is used to add to the
quantity or quality of the housing stock and revenue finance is used to maintain the
stock in a reasonable state of repair. On this basis, 'maintenance' can be thought of
as requiring revenue finance and 'improvement' can be thought of as requiring

---

29 Before 1983 the relief was granted by means of the Inland Revenue adjusting the borrower's
    tax coding and assessment. This system was changed in 1983 with the introduction of
    MIRAS. Under the MIRAS scheme, borrowers paid the monthly interest on their mortgage
    loans net of tax relief. MIRAS cost the Exchequer some £2.7 billion in lost revenue in
    1997/98 and £1.9 billion in 1998/99 and £2 billion in 1999/2000 (estimated) – from a peak
    of £7.6 billion in 1990/91. The reader needs to be clear that MIRAS was the allowance
    'process', and MITR was the 'concept'. Under the MIRAS process, the lender had to
    calculate the borrower's periodic repayments and then work out the tax relief at the
    qualifying rate on the interest element. This saved a great deal of work for the Inland
    Revenue because, for standard rate tax-payers, there was no longer a need to deal directly
    with the local tax office.
30 Census figures indicate that about 69 per cent of dwellings are owner-occupied (England
    and Wales). This breaks down to 43 per cent owned with mortgage debt attached and 26 per
    cent owned outright.

capital finance. In financial practice, however, the distinction between 'primary maintenance' and 'improvement' can be blurred. Some primary maintenance work, such as a major roof repair or the reinforcing of foundations to arrest subsidence, may require as much or more money than some improvement work such as installing central heating. Furthermore, like much improvement work, some primary maintenance jobs may qualify for grant aid or require loan finance. In other words, improvements and primary maintenance works may be financed in similar ways and from similar sources.

The distinction between 'primary' and 'secondary' maintenance

In contrast to 'primary' maintenance, 'secondary' maintenance tends to be paid for more on a month-by-month basis and includes repairs of non-structural building elements and components. It includes non-essential external redecoration and nearly all internal redecoration, as well as the various minor jobs around the house. Most do-it-yourself (DIY) activity falls into this category of secondary maintenance. Whether carried out by a contractor or on a DIY basis, these activities are typically paid for out of current income or savings rather than by means of a grant or loan.

Factors affecting the level of maintenance

The amount of money an owner-occupier spends on maintenance over a period will be affected by: (a) their financial resources and priorities; (b) the age and condition of the building; (c) the level of wear and tear to which it is subjected; (d) the owner's ability and inclination to do work on the property themselves; (e) the quality of the building and the nature and quality of previous improvement and maintenance work; and (f) the way the market values maintenance work. We will say something briefly about each of these.

(a)   The primary element of a household's financial resources is its disposable income. Because dwellings are costly to repair, low-income households are likely to suffer relatively poor housing conditions in the absence of government aid. In this way, it has long been argued that 'housing decay is one manifestation of poverty'.[31]

As we saw in Chapter 6, recent governments have done much to encourage the growth of owner-occupation. In particular, since 1979 there has been a series of measures aimed principally at those who, before that date, would not have considered owning their own homes. In addition to specific policies aimed at low-income households, the decline in expenditure on public sector rented housing (see Chapter 5), combined with the continual shrinkage in the availability of private rented housing (see Chapter 18), has served to

---

31   Building Economic Development Committee, *Ways to Better Housing*, NEDO, 1986, p19.

persuade large numbers of people to become owner-occupiers. Many of these will have been relatively poor households that have competing demands on their limited resources and who, as a result, will have chosen to 'under-maintain' their homes, that is, maintain them to a level that is below the minimum standard deemed desirable by government policy and established professional practice.

In higher income households, maintenance also has had to compete with other budget items. In any household, what actually gets spent on maintenance will, to a large extent, depend upon the priority it is given over the other claims on the household's savings and disposable income. In other words, money spent on the dwelling will have an *opportunity cost* (see Chapter 2) in the form of the sacrifices of some other household need or demand. In the case of a relatively wealthy family, living in a well-maintained house, the sacrifice may have only a limited effect on their collective lifestyle; it might, for example, involve saving less for a short period or taking less expensive holidays for a year or two. However, in the case of a low-income family, living in a poorly maintained house, the sacrifice needed to repair it to a satisfactory standard may involve a considerable reduction in their general standard of living over an extended period.

With the reduction in grant expenditure and the curtailing of the area-based improvement programmes (see Chapter 11), owner-occupiers have been increasingly placed in the position of having to rely more and more on their own resources. There are considerable difficulties in obtaining meaningful information on how much home-owners spend on repairs and maintenance. This is partly because only a limited amount of research has been done on the topic and partly because researchers have found that owners do not usually keep records of such expenditure. Furthermore, much of the maintenance work is done on a DIY basis or by someone else working within the informal economy. Researchers in this field find that the problem is further compounded by the fact that most owners find it difficult to cost work done by themselves or by friends or relatives (Mackintosh *et al.*, 1988).

(b/c) It is self-evidently true that buildings decay through time and use: accordingly, the annual maintenance costs tend to increase as the building ages. In this respect, it is of general interest that in most regions of Britain over 20 per cent of the housing stock was built before 1919 (Wilcox, 1997, p105).

(d) Other factors affecting the level of maintenance in this sector are the knowledge, skill and energy of owners together with their inclination to do or organise maintenance work themselves. In other words, resources other than finance will be available to some households. Where it exists, household expertise and energy can be combined with finance to carry out certain maintenance tasks. However, it is difficult for most home-owners to acquire substantial experience in maintenance; few will ever undertake a major job, like a roof replacement, and of those who do, very few indeed will re-use the expertise gained, (Mackintosh *et al.*, 1988). This contrasts with professional housing agencies, such as local authorities or housing associations, that continually accumulate or re-use such knowledge.

One form of direct help is the support of agency services. Home Improvement Agencies (HIAs) provide independent advice and help to elderly and disabled people and people on low incomes to undertake building repairs, improvements and adaptations to their properties. They help vulnerable people to stay put in their homes rather than be forced to move into an institutional setting. HIAs are usually small schemes, staffed by three or four people, operating within a particular district. They are managed by a variety of organisations, often housing associations, but also local authorities and independent bodies such as Age Concern. Grants, of up to 50 per cent of revenue costs of HIAs, are channelled through local authorities who are responsible for assessing the need for HIA services in their areas and for bidding on their behalf.

(e) Decisions aimed at determining best financial practice in the field of building maintenance and renewal centre on what might be termed the time-cost dilemma.[32] This poses the following decision question: *Is it better to spend more on the works now and thereby achieve relatively low future costs-in-use; or is it better to spend less now and instead pay for relatively higher costs-in-use sometime in the future?*

The time-cost dilemma highlights the point that the nature and quality of previous renewal and maintenance works can affect current and future maintenance costs. This relates to the points made in (a) and (d) above. That is, some owners may 'under-maintain' through choice, ignorance or lack of income. From the point of view of a professional builder, surveyor or housing manager, some private owners may decide to carry out building work in the 'wrong' way. It may be that some owners create future maintenance problems by doing jobs in an inappropriate sequence, with inappropriate techniques, with inappropriate materials or by employing an inappropriate contractor. The use of the word 'inappropriate' here is intended to indicate a situation in which conventionally accepted 'good practices' by a local authority or registered social landlord would have resulted in things being done differently.

(f) The way the housing market operates tends to militate against providing owners with an incentive to maintain the structure of their properties in accordance with conventionally accepted 'good practice'. More precisely, it tends to discourage owners from undertaking primary maintenance. The housing market seems to operate in a way that emphasises the value of decorative work (such as painting, kitchen fittings, etc.) more highly than less

---

32 The time-cost dilemma arises because buildings are durable assets and money has a 'time value'. This poses a dilemma for those making decisions about how much to invest in any building project. For a full discussion and explanation of the dilemma see Garnett, 1996.

visible primary maintenance work to the building's fabric and structure. In other words, market weaknesses in the form of imperfect buyer knowledge, may affect the rational maintenance behaviour of owners so as to emphasise short-term consumption goals relating to the appearance of the dwelling, rather than the longer-term investment goals relating to the physical life of the building.

Furthermore, where property prices are depressed, maintenance may be neglected as the costs may not be recouped in the re-sale value of the property. Where prices are rising, more owners may be encouraged to maintain or improve their dwellings but, on the other hand, it may also make economic sense for them to downgrade maintenance in order to increase their 'yield' as property prices reflect location factors rather than house conditions. This market phenomenon is referred to as the 'valuation gap' and it offers an economic explanation for 'under-maintenance'.

Management and insurance costs

In the case of owner-occupation, most supervision and administration costs are counted in time rather than in money terms. Insurance is, however, a financial cost that most private households have to meet. Although there is no legal obligation for an owner-occupied dwelling to be insured against damage or destruction, a prudent owner will take out appropriate cover and all lending institutions insist on such cover before approving a mortgage loan. Insurance policies vary in terms of cover provided and premiums charged, but all will be based on a calculation of value that relates to the costs of replacement rather than to the purchase price. Because the re-building costs of a dwelling can be in excess of its market value, the owner may have to insure the property for a larger amount than its potential sales price. Most insurance companies provide index-linked policies in which the sum insured and premiums automatically rise in line with re-building cost inflation.

New building insurance and warranties

The National House Building Council (NHBC) offers a ten-year warranty on newly-built dwellings to cover defects after hand-over. If the dwelling is covered by the warranty and defects appear within the first few years, the NHBC will arrange for an inspection of the property and, if defects are found, it will set a deadline within which the repair work has to be started. It also offers what it terms 'catastrophe insurance' to cover serious structural faults that appear between years three and ten. Cover can also be provided for the roof coverings, rendering and internal floors.

Summary

Most owner-occupied dwellings are acquired with the aid of a mortgage loan.

The occupier's *equity* is represented by that part of the property's value that is unencumbered by debt.

Banks and building societies are the primary providers of house-purchase finance. In recent years the interplay between competition and legislation has reduced the distinctions between 'mutual' building societies and 'commercial' banks.

In the climate of enhanced competition, a wide range of mortgage 'products' are now available. However, an important distinction still remains between 'interest-and-capital' mortgages and 'interest only' mortgages.

The government has recently introduced statutory regulation by giving the FSA responsibility for regulating key aspects of mortgage selling. We are moving towards a unified system of regulation for all financial services.

When sold, the main residences of owner-occupiers are not subject to capital gains taxation. But they may be subject to inheritance taxation.

Prior to 1963 MITR was classified as a *tax allowance* rather than a *subsidy* because the Inland Revenue treated the main residence of a tax-payer as an investment asset that generated a flow of 'income' that could be legitimately taxed. After 1963 MITR should be classified as a subsidy because Schedule 'A' income tax was abolished. MITR has now been phased out.

In analysing the broad management costs confronting the owner-occupier we should distinguish between the following: debt service charges, primary maintenance, secondary maintenance, improvement expenditure, and insurance premiums.

Appendix

The rise and fall of mortgage interest tax relief

Income tax was first introduced in 1799 and the idea of giving income tax relief on the interest element of personal debt dates back to the early nineteenth century. Under the provisions of the Income Tax Act 1803, borrowers received relief on the interest portion of all personal loans including charges on house purchase mortgages. Initially, the extent of the relief was calculated by multiplying the mortgage interest charge by the borrower's marginal tax rate. This meant that the original MITR system was distinctly regressive insofar as the relief granted was relatively higher for those with big loans living in big dwellings and for those earning larger incomes and paying relatively higher marginal tax rates. After 1974 tax relief on interest paid by individuals was restricted to loans for the purchase or improvement of property.[33] From that date it was not possible to set the interest on non-property personal loans against income tax liabilities.

1974 saw a further rule change that marked the beginning of the long, slow death of MITR. Up to 1974 the relief was available for the full cost of the mortgage loan. In that year, however, a debt ceiling was fixed at £25,000. In practice, this had no

---

33 The concession was abolished in 1969 except for interest paid on mortgages, although it was reintroduced briefly between 1972 and 1973.

effect on the tax position of the overwhelming majority of home-owners as, at that time, the average mortgage, at about £6,500, was well below the ceiling.[34] By the time MIRAS was introduced in 1983 (see footnote 29), the tax concession had played its part in spurring on house price inflation. During the thirty-year period prior to the introduction of MIRAS house prices rose at twice the rate of inflation. Partly in response to this rise, in 1983 the debt ceiling was raised to £30,000, a level at which it remained fixed thereafter. In the early 1980s, the interaction between continuing rapid house price inflation and the fixed ceiling meant that eventually the real income effect of the relief was systematically diminished.

Concerns about the need to establish tenure neutrality led the mid-decade Inquiry into British Housing, chaired by the Duke of Edinburgh (NFHA, 1985), to advocate the replacement of MIRAS and housing benefit with a single needs-related allowance. But royal patronage was not enough to overturn the Conservative party's commitment to use the fiscal system to expand home-ownership and, for the time being, MIRAS lived on.

Up to 1989 unmarried couples living in the same dwelling and sharing the burden of the mortgage charge could each claim personal relief up to the ceiling of £30,000 against their income tax liabilities. This was seen as discriminating against married couples, or as even a fiscal incentive to 'live in sin'. The dual tax relief was abolished in 1989. Because the change was signalled several months beforehand in the chancellor's Budget speech, this reform led to a sudden surge in demand in the housing market. People advanced their purchasing plans so as to avoid the in-coming restriction. This helped to spin house prices upwards and, in so doing, helped to burst the 1980s housing boom.

Successive Finance Acts systematically reduced the impact of MIRAS. With politicians finding it increasingly difficult to justify the concession in social and economic terms, it was phased out as the principal subsidy to owner-occupation. In the 1990s the real income effect of the tax concession was significantly diminished by a sequence of Budget changes that reduced the rate of tax against which the allowance could be claimed. After 1990 it was no longer possible to claim the relief at the borrower's marginal tax rate and relief was limited to the standard rate of income tax no matter how much the mortgagor earned. In 1994 allowances were restricted to a 20 per cent rate (i.e. less than the standard rate of income tax). In 1995 the rate of relief on payments of mortgage interest was reduced to 15 per cent and after April 1998 they were reduced to 10 per cent. The death of MITR was finally announced in the 1999 Budget in which the chancellor declared that relief on mortgage interest payments was to be removed altogether from 6 April 2000. MITR for those aged 65 and over who take out a loan to buy a life annuity (a mortgage home income plan) ended in March 1999. Existing loans of this kind continue to qualify for relief for the remainder of the loan period.

---

34   Average house prices at that time were in the region of £11,500.

CHAPTER 8:
Local government and housing finance: an introduction

Introduction

Local government has been an important provider of housing services since the early twentieth century and has had powers of intervention to deal with poor housing conditions and set basic standards for new housing for much longer. More recently, its role in setting a housing strategy for all tenures at local level has become more prominent, whilst its direct role as a landlord has been in decline.

Nevertheless, the relationship between local government and housing finance is an important and complex one, and five chapters of the book are devoted to it. This chapter sets the scene and describes some overall aspects of local government that are relevant to understanding housing finance issues. The next four chapters then deal, respectively, with housing capital finance, housing investment, wider strategy and housing revenue. Cross-references are made between chapters to help readers understand the relationship of the parts to the whole.

This chapter begins with an overview of local government (including its relations with central government), then provides an overview of local authority finance in relation to housing. It then includes a substantial section on local authority performance and how central government seeks to influence it. Finally, we consider some of the issues in the debate about the future of local government.

An annex to this chapter deals with Northern Ireland, as its remaining local government has no housing responsibilities.

An overview of local government

Local government is seen to matter because it is the one public institution that, through its democratic mandate, can empower citizens locally. It provides a range of major services to local residents and firms either alone or in partnership with central government, the private sector, or voluntary groups. Currently in Great Britain there are 442 local authorities responsible for spending around £80 billion each year from taxes and charges. This represents a quarter of all government expenditure.[1] The government meets a large part of this cost through grants and

---

1   Expenditure on local government in the UK is approximately 10 per cent of GDP; in Scotland almost half the funds allocated each year to the Scottish Executive are automatically reallocated to local authorities. Local government spending in Northern Ireland is relatively less significant as many local responsibilities are dealt with by central government departments (or the Northern Ireland Assembly under devolution).

business rates. The rest comes from the council tax that is levied on local residents.

The structure of local government

In many parts of England the responsibility for providing major local authority services is divided between county councils and district councils. Where this two-tier model applies, the counties, often referred to as the 'shire counties' because they broadly correspond to the historic county boundaries, are responsible for the wide-scale services such as education, highways, police, social services, libraries, waste disposal, and trading standards. The district councils administer the more local-scale services such as housing, environmental health, building control, waste collection, cemeteries, parking, parks, leisure and recreation, roads and footpaths. In this two-tier model, some responsibilities, such as planning, traffic management, tourism, architecture, galleries and museums, may involve both tiers.

The other model for local government is the unitary council in which a single authority has responsibility for providing and delivering the full range of local government services to a designated area. The whole of local government in Scotland and Wales is organised on a unitary basis. In England, all the London boroughs are unitary authorities, as are the metropolitan districts. Many more unitary authorities were established after 1995, mostly, but not always, based on large or medium-sized cities such as York, Bristol, Hull, Portsmouth, Southampton and Plymouth. However, they also include areas such as South Gloucestershire, North Somerset, Rutland, and the Isle of Wight. Details of the structure of local government are given in Figure 8.1 in the box.

Delivery, responsibility and accountability: the pillars of local government

The system of local government finance has its roots in the seventeenth century Poor Law. This legislation, which dates from 1601, established two basic principles of local government finance: (1) that a monetary amount or 'rate' should be levied from local residents to help pay for local services, and (2) that those who administer such services should be accountable to the elected representatives of those who have to pay these rates. Contemporary local government functions, including housing, are administered by authorities that are popularly referred to as 'councils'. The term 'council' reflects the fact that an assembly of locally elected 'members' or 'councillors' is the embodiment of local government's democratic authority.

The periodic reforms of local government that have taken place in response to the changing range and volume of municipal services have transformed the old arrangements designed to deal with seventeenth century pauperism into a large-scale modern complex business. Throughout these structural transformations,

Figure 8.1: The structure of local government in Great Britain

The basic structure before 1995

Until the mid-1990s, in most of Britain there was a two-tier local government structure. Outside London, England and Wales were divided into counties (the first tier) and districts (the second tier). Mainland Scotland was divided into regions (first tier) and districts (second tier). The London boroughs and the Scottish Islands were single-tier 'unitary' authorities.

In the non-metropolitan parts of England and Wales the upper tier authorities were county councils. In Scotland, regional councils constituted the upper tier. These 'first tier' authorities were responsible for providing wide-scale services such as education, strategic planning, social services, traffic management and highways.

The second tier authorities were designated as 'districts', although some had the title 'city' or 'borough' for historic reasons. England and Wales contained thirty or so metropolitan district or borough councils and over three hundred non-metropolitan district councils. In Scotland there were 53 district councils operating beneath the nine regional councils. These second tier authorities provided more local services such as housing.

Some areas also had parish councils that had limited powers and acted as 'sounding boards' on local issues. These third tier authorities continue to exist. They have particular responsibilities for providing and maintaining such parochial facilities as playgrounds, footpaths and village halls. In Scotland the third tier comprises community councils.

The shift towards regionalism and single-tier authorities after 1995

The structure of local government has been regularly subjected to reorganisation. For example, the two-tier system described above, was the result of a major restructuring that took place in 1974, and 1975 in Scotland. In March 1991, the Secretary of State for the Environment announced further restructuring with the preferred option being a system of unitary authorities in England. This restructuring is now complete and has resulted in some remapping of boundaries and, in many areas, to a shift from two-tier to unitary provision.

A similar reorganisation resulted in the wholesale restructuring of the Scottish local government system. Since April 1996 it has operated as a system of unitary authorities that are responsible for the provision of all local government services, while the three island councils of Orkney, Shetland and Western Isles already had unitary status.

Since April 1997 a number of district councils in England, along with the counties of which they were part, were converted into unitary authorities. In 2000, the Labour government created the Greater London Authority (GLA), although this is best seen as a regional authority and the precursor of regional assemblies, rather than a local authority.

Current Structure

Country	Single-tier authorities	Two-tier authorities
England	33 London boroughs 36 metropolitan authorities 47 shire unitary authorities	34 county councils 238 district councils
Scotland	32 unitary authorities	–
Wales	22 unitary authorities	–

however, the traditional principles of *local responsibility* and *local accountability* have been maintained. Indeed, the present government was first elected on a manifesto which said that local decision-making should be less constrained by central government and more accountable to local people.

Of growing importance, however, has been a third, more recently-established principle, of '*delivery*'. By this is meant that local government should provide high quality services in its area and always strive to improve them. This was first expressed by the present government in the principles of 'Best Value' and more recently in their requirements on councils to comprehensively assess their performance. The Local Government Act 1999 requires councils to deliver services that are:

- responsive to the needs of citizens;
- of high quality and cost-effective; and,
- fair and accessible to all who need them.

The three principles of delivery, responsibility and accountability are repeated in the government's comprehensive white paper on local government, *Strong Local Leadership – Quality Public Services*[2] which will be referred to during this chapter.

Local government's constitutional position and powers

An important feature of local government in the UK compared with, say, many other European countries, is that it has no constitutional standing and its existence, powers and financing are entirely decided by the central state. The most notable example of the power of central over local government was the abolition by the Thatcher government of the Greater London Council in the mid-1980s. But it is continuously reflected in the controls and sanctions imposed on local government, and the dependence of local councils on centrally-determined sources of funding.

One practical aspect of this dependence is the illegality of any act of local government unless it can be attributed to a specific power which it has in statute. If an authority does something that it does not have the power to do it is said to be 'ultra vires'.[3] To some extent the present government has removed – or at least loosened – this straightjacket by creating a general power in the Local Government Act 2000 (s2) enabling councils to do anything to promote the economic, social or environmental well-being of their areas, providing that it does not require raising new finance and does not conflict with other statutes. A similar power was included in part 3 of the Local Government in Scotland Act 2003. The '*well-being*' power has already been used in the housing field – for example, it is

---

2   DTLR (2001), Cm 5327, HMSO, London.
3   Meaning 'beyond its authority' (literal Latin, 'beyond strength').

the power under which councils can set up arms length management organisations (ALMOs – see Chapter 10).

A further loosening of the constraints was made by the Local Government Act 2003, which gave local authorities in certain circumstances the power to trade and the power to charge (for discretionary services). Along with the freedom to borrow on a prudential basis (described in Chapters 5 and 9), and the freedom to invest, local authorities have now accumulated a range of discretionary powers which significantly increases the scope for initiative at local level and the ability to do things without permission from central government. Nevertheless, these flexibilities are always constrained, and the statute gives fall back powers to central government to decide in what circumstances they can be used or to withdraw them if they are judged to be subject to abuse.

The Whitehall government retains the power to decide the functions of and financial arrangements for local authorities in England, Wales and Northern Ireland, but under devolution the Scottish Parliament now determines the powers and duties of local councils where these fall within its own powers (as in most housing matters).

The provision of local authority housing services

As we have seen, the power or responsibility to provide a service is given by act of parliament (or 'statute') or by instruction from the central government department responsible for the national planning of that service, acting under statute. Such powers and responsibilities are usually given to a particular class of local authority. Where there is no unitary authority, housing services are provided by the second tier of local government. Legislation establishes these authorities as 'local housing authorities' with powers both to provide housing and to intervene in other ways. In England and Wales this is the Housing Act 1985 and in Scotland the Housing (Scotland) Act 1987.

In addition to the power to provide housing services, local authorities have been given a range of other housing duties and powers. For example, the law requires housing authorities to help the unintentionally homeless find suitable accommodation. As well as being landlords themselves, councils provide grants for the improvement of privately owned dwellings and they support other landlords, such as housing associations, in the provision of accommodation for people on low incomes or with special needs. Local authorities also administer the distribution of housing benefit.

Central government has often called on housing authorities to separate their role as 'landlords' from their role as strategic housing authorities which consider all the housing needs and housing provision in their area, not just council housing. An updated responsibility to have a housing strategy (in England and Wales) was included in the Local Government Act 2003. This issue and the wider powers of housing authorities are dealt with Chapter 11.

Central-local relations

The present government has said that it expects the local government finance system to reflect *'the nature of modern councils' relationship with their communities and with central government'*.[4] This means that they should be accountable and responsive to their local tax-payers, be increasingly responsible for raising expenditure locally, have an open and soundly-based system of business rates, and receive a fair distribution of government grant.

Yet by international standards, British local authorities are heavily dependent on central government financial support. The bulk of local spending is financed by the national tax-payer and this in itself establishes a high degree of interconnection between central and local decisions on councils' finances. Central government seeks to ensure that public spending is carried out in ways that are supportive to macro-economic policy objectives such as the control of inflation and minimising public sector debt. It is also responsible for managing total public expenditure in a way that is judged to be financially 'prudent'.

Because local authority spending makes up around a quarter of total public expenditure it has to be subject to the same constraints. Central government also has a political interest in ensuring value-for-money and the efficient use of resources in the delivery of local services, while keeping the overall burden of taxation as low as possible. For all these reasons, it has a strong interest in local government's taxation and spending decisions. In recent years, central control over local finances has focused on the government's powers to cap revenue charges, to allocate grants to local authorities, and to influence or restrict their ability to borrow and to utilise their capital receipts. Financial decisions have also, as we shall see, become inextricably linked to central government's concern with 'delivery' and local government's performance.

One issue which has dogged relations between central and local government for decades is the balance of funding of local services between central and local government. Because this balance is so skewed towards central funding of local services, it places an obstacle in the path of central government attempting to create a greater sense of accountability at local level. If, for example, councils decide they want to increase spending on local services by one per cent, this will create a four per cent rise in local council tax, unless central government support is also increased. The unpopularity of local tax increases combined with the scale of the increases needed to have any impact on services is a considerable source of tension. At the same time, governments have generally backed away from the logical response to this situation, to create stronger local sources of revenue such as a local income tax, also because of the likely political impact. The outcome is that, despite the rhetoric, central government still retains considerable

---

4   DETR (1998) *Modernising local government: Local democracy and community leadership,* Cm6646, HMSO, p7.

responsibility for local services. The issue of revenue support for local authorities is considered in more detail in Chapter 12.

Local government finance and housing: an overview

Local government finance is a complex area and it is not necessary to consider all aspects of it in detail in order to understand housing finance. Some issues, such as the fiscal regime in which local authorities operate, are dealt with elsewhere. The following four chapters deal with detailed aspects of local authority housing finance. In this section we will therefore set out some of the general features of the local government finance system and how it relates to housing.

Main types of local authority spending

As with most other organisations, councils have to be accountable for both their day-to-day revenue spending and their longer-term investment spending (see Chapter 2). A local authority's budget is therefore divided into *current* and *capital expenditure*. Current expenditure mainly pays for the day-to-day running costs on such items as salaries, fuel bills, office consumables, etc. Although strictly speaking, such revenue spending does not provide long-term physical assets, in practice some revenue monies can be used for this purpose and redesignated as 'capital spending'. Capital expenditure produces assets that have an extended physical life. Examples include the acquisition of land and buildings and the construction and improvement of housing (for more detail on the definition of capital spending see Chapter 9). About eight times as much is spent annually by local government on current running costs as on capital investment. This gap has widened in recent years as central governments have actively sought to restrict the capital spending of local authorities. Nevertheless, housing remains their biggest single item of capital spending.

Financial accountability

Financial accountability is achieved by a process of audited accounting. Accounts receive money from various sources, such as grants, tax levies, rents, charges, fees, and transfers, and make outward payments to cover the costs of providing a service or acquiring an asset. Some transaction accounts may not actually 'hold' funds but they will record financial in and out flows that are associated with particular activities. Unlike other services, some housing transactions are ring-fenced within special transaction accounts.

Until the 1990s local authority accounting was based on what accountants refer to as the 'fund and entity approach'.[5] This approach treated the authority as an entity

---

5   CIPFA (1995) *Financial Reporting in Local Government: Capital*, CIPFA, London.

comprising separate service departments, like housing, education, etc., each with its own funds and accounting records. The costs of providing each service were recorded in the departmental fund accounts. The separate revenue accounts paid the running costs of the services including the debt charges, the interest and repayment of principal. In this way, each service could be seen to be bearing the costs of the debt associated with the fixed assets owned by that fund. All borrowed money was normally pooled into a consolidated loans fund so that service accounts in surplus could 'lend' funds internally to service accounts in deficit. This system of internal borrowing, called 'loans pooling', allowed the authority to make the best use of its cash. Under loans pooling most authorities tied the loan costs to services and projects. Typically, individual capital projects were amortised internally over a sixty-year period, although the external borrowing period could be flexible. This means, for example, that large-scale housing projects were typically financed from the consolidated loans fund over a sixty-year period, but the fund itself borrowed from external sources over a variety of shorter periods. This system of loans pooling allowed the authority to develop a balanced portfolio of loans and to take advantage of borrowing opportunities as and when they arose.

The 'fund and entity' approach to local authority accounting in England and Wales was radically changed by the Local Government and Housing Act 1989.[6] After 1990 Housing Revenue Accounts were universally 'ring-fenced' so that the costs of providing council housing always had to be recorded separately from all the other local authority services. The other, non-council housing services, ceased to have separate revenue accounts; these were replaced by a combined revenue account referred to as the 'General Fund'.

More recently, further changes have occurred. Starting in 1994, a system of *resource accounting* has gradually been introduced into local authorities. This relatively new development has altered the way in which the costs of acquiring and managing assets are accounted for. Resource accounting simply seeks to lay out the accounts in a way that allows managers, members and the audit authorities to assess the full and proper costs of providing an aspect of services provision, so that a judgement can be made about the extent to which value-for-money is being achieved. (Resource accounting is discussed further in Chapters 2, 5, 12 and 16).

The shift to resource accounting means that authorities no longer keep consolidated loans funds. However, the treasurer[7] is still expected to manage the authority's overall finances in a way that is prudent and efficient. This means that, in practice, much of the authority's borrowing will still be consolidated and managed at the corporate level. This will normally be achieved by having some form of loans and investment unit that is chaired by, and answerable to, the treasurer.

---

6   This act did not have the same effect in Scotland where Housing Revenue Accounts (HRAs), were already partially ring-fenced.
7   Often known as the Director of Finance or Controller of Finance.

Housing Accounts

The most important accounts used by a housing authority are:

- *The Housing Revenue Account (HRA)* records the income from council house rents and any housing subsidies designed to pay for the running costs of council housing provision. These include management and maintenance costs, and capital financing charges on HRA capital schemes. HRA capital schemes are projects that contribute to the quantity or quality of the council's housing stock. They would include any investments in new house building and all the major repairs and improvements that are made to the existing stock. The HRA is 'ring-fenced' which means that the account cannot be subsidised by transfers from the General Fund. The ring-fence has been tightened so that normally surpluses stay within the HRA (previously, in England and Wales, they had to be paid into the General Fund).
- *The Consolidated Revenue Account (CRA)* is a fund account that makes and receives payments with respect to all of the authority's revenue income and expenditure. It includes a recorded summary of the financial transactions of the Housing Revenue Account. This means that the HRA is not a separate 'fund' but a ring-fenced 'transaction account' recording the financial transactions associated with provision of the council housing service.
- *The General Fund (GF) Account* is normally referred to as the 'General Fund'. It collects local taxes and central government grants to pay for services. Revenue payments are made from this account to meet the costs of providing services other than council housing. It thus records payments made for housing matters that affect the wider community – such as the assessment of local housing needs and some services for the homeless, advice to private tenants and landlords, the administration of housing benefit, and capital financing charges on GF capital schemes (i.e. non-HRA investments). GF capital schemes encompass housing projects other than those that are related to the council's own housing stock, including such things as advice centres, hostels for the homeless, purchase of land for the purpose of building for sale or disposal for housing development, slum-clearance, and grants and other forms of assistance to improve private sector housing.
- *The Capital Receipts Accounts* collect the sales proceeds of liquidated assets. Capital receipts are kept separately because they can only be used for capital purposes, either to pay for capital works or to repay debt. This means that these funds can be used to help finance capital housing projects, but only within certain restrictions (see Chapter 9).

Details of how these financial arrangements work are found in the next four chapters. Capital finance is mainly dealt with in Chapter 9 and revenue finance in Chapter 12.

Local authority performance and the role of central government

Earlier in the chapter we pointed to delivery, responsibility and accountability as being the three principles of local government services. Much of the relationship between central and local government, including the financial relationship, is concerned with central government's attempts to ensure adherence to these principles. In particular, the present government has placed strong emphasis on delivery of better public services and the mechanisms to achieve this. Because of their influence on finance (not least, on the levels of central government financial support which individual authorities receive), we now describe these mechanisms in some detail.

First, we deal with the overall approach to local services which can be summarised under the heading 'Best Value' and the associated mechanisms for judging performance. Second, we look specifically at how performance is measured. Third, we consider the standards and targets which central government sets for itself and for local authorities. Forth, we describe the enforcement mechanisms and specifically the role of the audit and regulatory authorities. Fifth, we look at the wider arrangements for the local authority to influence its environment, apart from direct service provision.

Improving service delivery and achieving 'Best Value'

'Best Value' constituted a major change in the way local authorities provide local services and supersedes the previous government's system of *compulsory competitive tendering (CCT)*, the rigid and restrictive nature of which sometimes failed to guarantee value-for-money. In its far-reaching 1998 white paper on local government reform[8], the Labour government made it clear that it would allow councils to decide how most effectively to provide services so long as they give 'Best Value' to the public they serve. These provisions were contained in the Local Government Act 1999. There is now a requirement on local authorities to *'deliver the quality of service that people expect at a price they are willing to pay'*.

The original aim of Best Value was to ensure that within five years individual council services achieved performance levels that were only achieved by the top 25 per cent of councils at the start of the five years. Inspection reports, published by the Audit Commission, give each council a star rating based on performance, ranging from no stars for poor performance to three stars for excellent performance. The reports also provide an assessment of whether performance is likely to improve. If performance does not improve the government has the power to switch control of a service away from the council. The emphasis of the initiative is on continuous improvement. If a council has improved its performance from 'poor' to 'fair' it will get a better inspection report from the Audit Commission than a council whose performance has stayed at 'fair'.

---

8   Cm 4014.

Under Best Value councils were required to apply the so-called 'four Cs' to all of their services: challenge, consult, compare, and compete:

- *Challenge*
  This involves challenging the way that councils traditionally approached their services. Councils have to ask themselves whether they really need certain services and identify customer needs for each activity. The Audit Commission checks whether councils have been genuinely self-critical by checking that challenges have not just been raised, but acted upon with evidence of appropriate changes.

- *Consult*
  Councils have to show that they have consulted local people and key local stakeholders as part of their Best Value reviews, and they need to monitor customer satisfaction with services. But council staff also need to be involved in the consultation process. Again the Audit Commission checks that this consultation has been acted on.

- *Compare*
  Under this heading councils have to benchmark their services against other councils, and private and non-profit service providers. They also have to show how they are doing against national Best Value performance indicators and, no matter how well they are currently performing, they must introduce an improvement plan.

- *Compete*
  This is the aspect of Best Value that most resembles the previous CCT regime. Councils have to show that in-house services are the most cost-effective by subjecting them to external competition. If in-house services are more expensive councils may have to switch control of that activity to a private firm or the voluntary sector unless they can demonstrate that the additional expense produces more than proportionate benefits to service users.

The local government white paper, *Strong Local Leadership – Quality Public Services*,[9] built on the Best Value approach and set out a new performance framework within which the government is committed to working in partnership with local government to secure a progressive improvement in authorities' performance. It sets out four main drivers of public service reform:

- *National standards*
  A framework of clear and exacting performance standards, with performance independently monitored so that people can see how local services compare;

---

9   DTLR (2001) *op cit.*

- *Devolution*
  This gives successful councils more freedom to deliver these standards;

- *Flexibility*
  Artificial bureaucratic barriers are removed which prevent staff and authorities from improving local services; and

- *Choice and contestability*
  Expanding choice so that users of public services are given the kind of options that they take for granted in other walks of life, and taking full advantage of alternative means of provision where these would offer Best Value.

The 'clear and exacting performance standards' are part of a new instrument called *Comprehensive Performance Assessment (CPA)*. Unlike the service-by-service Best Value approach, CPA is a 'whole council' inspection that will eventually rank every authority in England in one of five categories, ranging from 'poor' to 'excellent'. These rankings create a league table of local government performance, with those in the highest categories receiving more control over their budgets and more freedom to sell services, and those in the lowest categories being forced to accept an intensive package of government help.

The new assessments have brought some changes to the Best Value regime. Most significantly, councils are no longer required to review all their services as a matter of course. They will focus instead on the services that are highlighted by the CPA as being in need of review. But Best Value is still the underlying principle that governs the way that local government strives to improve its services. While CPA is a profound modification, it is not a new service improvement regime in itself.

In Scotland, the Best Value regime is less prescriptive, consisting of a general duty (in the Local Government in Scotland Act 2003) which is about securing continuous improvements in performance, breaking even in trading activities, observing proper accounting practices, and reporting to the public. The elements of Best Value are:

- balancing quality service provision against costs;
- achieving sustainable development;
- ensuring equal opportunities;
- continuously improving the outcomes of the services they provide; and,
- being accountable and transparent, by engaging with the local community.

This last characteristic requires local authorities to demonstrate responsiveness to the needs of its communities, citizens, customers, employees, and other stakeholders through on-going dialogue with other public sector partners, local business, voluntary and community sectors and open, fair and inclusive consultation arrangements.

How performance is measured

Under the Best Value regime, performance is measured by *performance indicators* (often referred to as PIs or BVPIs). These aim to incorporate challenging, clear, and realistic targets for service improvements that relate to an overall plan for quality enhancement within the local authority. The indicators might be based upon some or all of the following.

- User satisfaction surveys and consultation exercises. These can be used to gather information and to monitor year by year trends in user satisfaction.
- Complaint monitoring and the establishment of mechanisms that record what action has been taken to deal with complaints.
- Comparative cost analysis. This would involve comparing costs against those of other private or public sector providers, including other authorities, who are offering services of a similar type and quality and on a similar scale. Comparative cost analysis focuses on the question of the *efficiency relationship* discussed in Chapter 2.
- Cost-benefit analysis. This is a technique designed to measure Best Value in a way that takes a wider and longer-term view of what counts as the relevant costs and benefits associated with a proposed investment of resources. A shift away from a cash-flow towards an accruals approach to accounting will make CBA more practicable (see Chapters 2 and 5 for discussion on accruals accounting, and Chapter 16 for discussion on CBA).
- Voluntary competitive tendering, in contrast to the old CCT method favoured by previous Conservative administrations.
- Process benchmarking. This involves setting target standards of performance and measuring outcomes against those targets. Process benchmarking focuses on what in Chapter 2 we referred to as the *effectiveness relationship* (see Figure 2.3, see also Chapter 15).
- The balanced scorecard approach. This is a methodology developed by the Harvard Business School that seeks to take account of the fact that running a large, complex organisation requires the managers to keep in view four important 'perspectives' relating to: (1) how customers see the establishment – client perspective; (2) decisions about priorities and how best to operate – internal business perspective; (3) decisions about how to improve and create value – innovation and learning perspective; and (4) how the organisation is viewed by those who have a proprietary financial interests in the organisation – financial perspective.

Local authorities can establish their own PIs[10] but in England and Wales there are nationally established BVPIs against which councils must measure their performance. The number and definition of the BVPIs changes from time to time.

---

10 The organisation HouseMark encourages the comparison of local performance information across the UK; for example, its ALMO performance improvement club pools performance information from English ALMO authorities.

Some examples of current (English) ones are as follows:

- rent collection and arrears: proportion of rent collected;
- average length of stay in bed & breakfast accommodation and in hostel accommodation, for homeless families;
- number of private sector dwellings returned to use or demolished, as a result of direct action by the authority; and,
- satisfaction of tenants with the overall service (result of a tenant satisfaction survey, disaggregated between BME and non-BME tenants).

As can be seen, some BVPIs are financial and relate to the authority's own stock, others are more wide-ranging. Measuring performance against BVPIs is only one part of Comprehensive Performance Assessment (see below).

Standards and targets

The approach to Best Value in Scotland does not involve centrally-decided BVPIs but instead relies on housing authorities (and housing associations) striving to achieving a range of standards agreed with COSLA and the SFHA (the trade bodies for councils and housing associations respectively). There are more than fifty of these standards, and some examples are:

- *Access to housing*
  We ensure that people have fair and open access to our housing list and assessment process. We work with others to maximise and simplify access routes into our housing.

- *Lettings*
  We let houses in a way that gives reasonable preference to those in greatest housing need; makes best use of available stock; maximises choice; and helps to sustain communities.

- *Tenancies*
  We offer the most secure form of tenancy compatible with the purpose of the housing. The agreement makes clear the rights and duties of the tenant and landlord. We act to uphold these rights and duties in a fair and responsible manner.

The standards are intended to encourage any landlord, organisation or function to assess itself against four key, Best Value questions:

- How do we know we are doing the right things?
- How do we know we are doing them well?
- How do we plan to improve?
- How do we account for our performance?

As in England, the Scottish arrangements depend upon an inspection regime (see below).

The UK government sets out a range of targets for its services, and for agencies that it funds such as local authorities. These targets are called *Public Service Agreements (PSAs)*. Some operate at UK level (for example, on benefits issues) whereas others on housing, for example, apply only in England. Setting PSAs, and assessing performance against them, is an intrinsic part of the bi-annual Spending Review (see Chapter 5). The ODPM has seven PSAs within its remit, of which just two relate directly to housing, PSA 5 and PSA 7:

- *PSA 5*
  Achieve a better balance between housing availability and the demand for housing, including improving affordability, in all English regions while protecting valuable countryside around our towns, cities and in the green belt and the sustainability of towns and cities.

- *PSA 7*
  By 2010, bring all social housing into a decent condition with most of this improvement taking place in deprived areas, and for vulnerable households in the private sector, including families with children, increase the proportion who live in homes that are in decent condition.

Each PSA has interim targets (or 'milestones') by which progress towards the main target can be assessed. They also spawn their own PIs, so that for example one PI for PSA 7 is that returns from local authorities and housing associations in 2004 show no more than 1.1 million non-decent homes remaining to be tackled.

Other PSAs within ODPM relate to issues such as local government and regeneration. The PSA system holds central departments to account, but they are also taken strongly into account in judgements made about relevant local authority services.

The inspection regime

The essence of Best Value is that authorities should be making their own judgements about their performance and where it needs to be improved, but a key part of the government's drive to improve public services has been its reliance on an external inspection regime. Thus bodies such as Ofsted judge performance against education standards and targets, and the Benefits Fraud Inspectorate examines performance in delivering benefits (including councils' delivery of housing benefit). These bodies issue public reports on the individual judgements they make as well as making more general reports on performance nationally. The over-riding purpose of inspection is to '*act as a catalyst for improvement*'.[11]

As part of this approach, the government announced in June 1998 its intention to set up an inspectorate for housing within the Audit Commission to report on the

11 Audit Commission (2004) *A Modern Approach to Inspecting Services* (see www.audit-commission.gov.uk).

work of local authorities in England. The inspectorate draws up and carries out a programme of cyclical inspections covering each local authority. It assesses performance on all requirements of the Best Value framework and undertakes out-of-cycle inspections to deal with specific initiatives, such as ALMOs (see Chapter 10). In cases of performance failure, it undertakes follow-up inspections to ensure that its directives have been acted upon. It also promotes the dissemination of best practice across local authorities. In terms of process, inspection examines whether target setting and performance plans are sufficiently exacting; whether the authority's comparative analysis with other public and private providers is convincing; whether they have properly assessed the possibility of competition; and to what extent and in what ways community involvement has been secured. In terms of outcomes, the inspectorate assesses how the needs of service users are met.

Reports from the housing inspectorate form one part of the *Comprehensive Performance Assessment (CPA)* framework that applies to all English local authorities. The overall assessment of an authority's performance combines the assessments of individual services. Each service is weighted, with education and social services having the highest ratings and housing a medium weighting – which means that an authority with a poor housing service could still have a 'good' overall rating under CPA, but could not be rated as 'excellent'.

In Wales, the National Assembly for Wales used to direct the work of the Audit Commission in relation to Best Value inspections, but from April 2005 there is now a separate Wales Audit Office.

Best Value in Scotland has followed a similar but not entirely parallel route to that of England and Wales. The legislation for the establishment of unitary authorities in Scotland in April 1996 had already placed on local authorities the statutory duty to seek efficiency, effectiveness and economy in the use of resources. The Local Government in Scotland Act 2003 gives councils new duties to improve service delivery and report to the public on their performance, and for the first time puts Best Value on a statutory basis. Its equivalent of the English CPA will be Best Value audits, carried out by Audit Scotland, on a three-year basis in each authority. The first of the 32 councils was inspected in 2004.

Monitoring Best Value in housing is now the specific responsibility of Communities Scotland, which was charged under part 3 of the Housing (Scotland) Act 2001 with creating and operating a single regulatory regime covering both local housing authorities and housing associations. Its inspections are similar to those of the English housing inspectorate, with a similar grading system. It has an agreement with Audit Scotland intended to co-ordinate their respective functions in relation to local authorities.[12]

---

12 See Communities Scotland (2001) *Memorandum of Understanding* (available at www.communitiesscotland.gov.uk).

The Northern Ireland Housing Executive (NIHE) is applying the principles of Best Value to its activities on a voluntary basis. Delivering a high quality housing service in accordance with the government's principles of Best Value is one of the Executive's key strategic objectives for the future. The Executive sets its own key performance indicators by reference to the objectives in its corporate plan, and monitors these and publishes the results. Examples of its PIs include re-letting 95 per cent of properties within two weeks, and ensuring that voids do not exceed two per cent of the stock.

Sanctions for poor performance

The government has powers to intervene where there are serious failures in the delivery of local government services. The Best Value legislation gives the relevant Secretary of State a range of intervention powers. The Audit Commission's roles in referrals are:

- to consider and respond to recommendations from appointed auditors that the Commission should carry out an inspection;
- to comply with any direction from the Secretary of State to carry out an inspection of an organisation's compliance with the legislation; and,
- to exercise its power, if needed, to make recommendations in its inspection reports that the Secretary of State considers using his or her intervention powers.

There are three broad sets of circumstances that may lead to referral to the Secretary of State by the Commission:

- serious service failures that could result in danger or harm to the public;
- persistent failure by an organisation to address recommendations made by inspectors; and,
- serious failures in a number of services in an organisation, which reveal fundamental weaknesses in an organisation's corporate capacity to manage services and make improvements.

Audit Scotland has similar powers to those of the Audit Commission, but Communities Scotland also has 'lower key' powers of intervention, including requiring authorities to prepare a remedial plan to tackle poor performance, or appointing an external manager for a service.

Other ways in which local authorities can improve local services

One of the premises of Best Value is that an authority should not seek simply to improve its own performance but also to achieve a wider improvement in services available in its area or in the quality of the local environment. The main instrument for doing this is the *Local Strategic Partnership (LSP)*, which involves not just the authority but other services such as health and police, and representatives of the wider community such as local businesses and the voluntary sector. LSPs generally focus efforts on tackling deprivation or achieving neighbourhood regeneration. They can enable authorities in England and Wales to meet the requirement in the Local Government Act 2000 to prepare 'community strategies' showing how they will improve the economic, social and environmental well-being of their inhabitants. A similar arrangement exists in Scotland where authorities have to prepare 'community plans' for their areas and the equivalent to LSPs are *Community Planning Partnerships (CPPs)*.

One of the criticisms of the Best Value regime and the range of targets and different inspection methods is that it makes local co-ordination of services more difficult, because managers are so focused on the targets for their particular service and may be less interested in cross-cutting issues such facilities for disabled people. One way in which this has been tackled is through *Local Public Service Agreements*, which if agreed with central government command extra resources for tackling particular issues such as reducing welfare dependency and getting people into work.

Another mechanism is *Local Area Agreements*, which are being piloted in some authorities. In these, agencies come together to agree joint priorities and targets that may differ from those set by central government. They agree to pool resources between services to achieve these new priorities. The pilots are focusing on three cross-cutting issues – children and young people, safer and stronger communities and health and older people.

Local authorities are therefore no longer simply concerned about the quality of their own services, but are engaged in wider improvements to public services and to the environment of their areas. This wider focus is also taken into account in the Comprehensive Performance Assessments (in England) mentioned earlier. It also links to the debate about the nature of local government with which we conclude this chapter.

The changing role of local government

Throughout the 1980s and 1990s changing views developed about the role of local government that led to the emergence of a 'new orthodoxy'[13] about how best to run public services. This reformed view places a strong emphasis on a 'partnership' approach to service provision in which elected local authorities work through and with a range of other local agencies. The changes that have stemmed from this revised view have tended to produce a more organisationally fragmented system of responsibilities that is sometimes described as 'new public

---

13   Stewart, J and Stoker, G (1995) *Local Government in the 1990s*, Macmillan, London. See p199.

management' (NPM), and which some commentators suggest has features that are more in line with the notion of local *'governance'* than that of local government.[14]

NPM embraces the following interrelated features.

- An increased emphasis on the notions of efficiency and effectiveness (refer to Chapter 2).
- The introduction of competition and the pursuit of Best Value.
- The development of partnerships with private sector firms, voluntary bodies and other agencies.
- A greater use of private finance.
- A greater internal use of business methods such as *total quality management* and *performance monitoring*.
- A commitment to cultivate user satisfaction (see Chapter 2).

In the specific field of housing, the shift in emphasis away from government towards governance has produced a move away from direct service provision to 'enabling'. The role of local authorities as direct providers of social housing has been systematically diminished by such measures as 'right to buy' and stock transfers. Although in many areas local authorities still own relatively large stocks of residential property, their landlord role is gradually being superseded by their strategic role as assessors of housing need and 'enablers' (see Chapter 11).

A different and in some ways conflicting reform movement is often described as 'new localism'. This is championed by the New Local Government Network[15] and centres on the devolution of responsibility to local level, possibly even to neighbourhoods, with maximum freedom to decide priorities and ability to create local level partnerships to deliver them. To some extent new localism is a reaction against the centralising tendencies of present and past governments, arguing for local authorities to be given more power, resources and discretion. Examples of new localism in housing would be the community gateway approach to stock transfer and ALMOs (see Chapter 10) and also the moves towards neighbourhood management as part of local regeneration initiatives (Chapter 11).

The extent to which central government has been willing to devolve power has largely depended on an authority's ability to demonstrate the attainment of what is called 'earned autonomy'. This means greater freedom, possibly even financial freedom, for high performing local authorities. An example of this in housing is the discussion which is taking place at the time of writing about granting ALMOs which are ranked as 'excellent' some of the greater business freedoms available to housing associations (see Chapter 10).

---

14 Lowndes, V. (1997) 'Change in Public Service Management' in *Local Government Studies*, vol 23, no 2, Summer 1997.
15 www.nlgn.org.uk

A final element in this brief summary of elements of local government reform is the promotion of greater choice, which is a theme being pursued vigorously by all political parties. This may mean choice between different service providers, or it may mean choice within services such as having different ways of paying council house rents. Central government has specifically promoted choice-based lettings as an alternative to administratively-determined 'allocation' of council lettings to prospective tenants. Promoting choice between landlords is also an aim of the new pathfinder experiments in housing benefit (see Chapter 19).

It is evident from this chapter that the local-central relationship is still in a state of flux. In 2004, the government issued a wide-ranging discussion paper[16] on its vision for the future of local government, calling for a more coherent and stable relationship, a fairer finance system and greater community leadership and citizen participation. This may well lead to further developments in the areas described in this chapter.

Summary

Every part of Britain is covered by one, and sometimes two, local authorities. In recent years the structure of local government has been reformed in a way that has created a greater number of unitary authorities. This has helped local government to take a more strategic approach to the provision of local services. This approach has been enhanced by an expectation that local authorities will work in partnership with other local agencies to provide local services. This has brought about a somewhat changed view about the nature and scope of local government that increasingly sees local authorities acting as assessors of need and enablers rather than as direct service providers. Their role is increasingly seen to be strategic: assessing local housing needs, planning how these needs are to be met (often by others), participating in the funding of projects to meet those needs, and monitoring the effectiveness of implementation.

Housing finance in local authorities is split between the Housing Revenue Account, the net costs of which are met by council tenants through their housing rents, and those transactions in the General Fund where the net costs are met by council tax payers. The requirement to ring-fence the HRA produces an important distinction between two classes of social housing spending. These are sometimes referred to as 'HRA housing' and 'non-HRA housing'. In this way a clear administrative distinction is made between the financial management of the council's own housing stock and monies spent on other types of housing project.

The present government has established and driven forward a 'modernising' agenda for local government, particularly through the Best Value framework within which all local authorities are encouraged to meet needs in ways that take

---

16   ODPM (2004) *The Future of Local Government – Developing a 10-year vision.*

account of local opinion and are judged to be efficient and effective. There is a tension between the government's desire to remain in charge of its modernising agenda and the argument that 'what works' is best decided locally rather than centrally. We have seen that the drive to modernise local government has many different elements, and a frequent criticism is that so many measures, targets and initiatives confuse rather than concentrate the efforts to improve public services. In any event, the debate about the balance of power between central and local government is far from resolved.

Annex

The special case of Northern Ireland

There are no local housing authorities in Northern Ireland because the Northern Ireland Housing Executive operates as an all-powerful housing authority throughout the province. In the late 1960s there were concerns that the allocation and management of public sector housing were being influenced by sectarian factors. In response to these concerns, the 1969 Joint Declaration of Principles called for a complete restructuring of the province's housing administration. This restructuring took place in 1971 with the creation of the Northern Ireland Housing Executive (NIHE), set up to operate as a single regional authority. The establishment of the NIHE distanced housing administration from the hothouse politics of local government. The new body took over all of the province's 150,000 local authority homes and then operated as a non-sectarian builder and manager of affordable social housing. In addition, it was charged with responsibility to develop a strategic view of housing development in the province by undertaking research and providing housing advice to others including private sector providers.

The Executive operates as a quango with devolved powers from the Department for Social Development. Under devolution, the DSD is responsible to the Northern Ireland Assembly, but if the assembly is suspended it is accountable to ministers in the UK Parliament.

The NIHE is headed by a chief executive with ten board members, all of whom have to be approved by the DSD. The Executive has a professional management team. A degree of local democratic accountability is established through the Northern Ireland Housing Council that has one representative from each of the province's 26 local government bodies or district councils. The Council has regular meetings with the Executive and nominates three members of the Executive board. The Executive is organised into 37 district offices with its headquarters in Belfast.

From the late 1980s pressure was mounting to bring Northern Ireland's broad housing policy more into line with that in the rest of the UK. In particular, consideration was given to shifting the Executive's role away from direct provider towards that of enabler. This meant that responsibility for the new-build programme was transferred to a number of developing associations with the NIHE's role becoming more regulatory and strategic. More recent discussions of the future of the NIHE have been based on the lessons from stock transfer and ALMOs in England, and whether they have any lessons for Northern Ireland (see page 240).

Currently (2004), the NIHE has a stock of just over 100,000 units, although this is declining by some 5,000 annually through sales to tenants. It spends about £260 million annually in maintaining the service and the housing stock.

CHAPTER 9:
Local government: the capital finance regime

The capital finance system governs local authorities' spending on the construction, improvement and major repairs of such social assets as council housing, schools, roads, community and leisure centres, and on regenerating local areas. Although some of this spending is funded from the authorities' own resources, including the proceeds of asset sales, much is supported directly by central government in the form of subsidy towards the costs of borrowing.

The main purpose of this chapter is to describe the capital finance regime as it applies to housing authorities generally from April 2004, although it will make references to the regimes operating before 2004 where this helps in understanding the current arrangements. Previous chapters set the context for this by describing overall relationships between central government and local housing authorities in Great Britain and the differences between housing authorities and housing associations in financial terms. The next chapter will describe the financing of capital investment in an authority's own housing stock, which involves considering radical options such as the transfer of a council's stock to a housing association or (in England) setting up an arms length management organisation (ALMO) to manage its housing and thus benefit from special subsidy towards investment. It will also cover the current debate about the future of local authority housing finance, which in many respects is about reducing the differences between councils and housing associations.

Defining capital finance

We have discussed the concept of capital in Chapter 2 (in particular Figure 2.1). In the local government sphere what counts as capital finance has traditionally been defined in legislation, as in part IV of the Local Government and Housing Act 1989. To prevent authorities from avoiding revenue controls by designating revenue expenditure as capital (other parts of the legislation prevent authorities from running deficits on their revenue accounts) the legislation required all expenditure to be charged to revenue unless it is used for:

> *'the acquisition, construction, preparation, enhancement or replacement of roads, buildings and other structures; where enhancement means the carrying out of works which are intended:*
> * *to lengthen substantially the useful life of the asset; or*
> * *to increase substantially the open market value of the asset; or*

- *to increase substantially the extent to which the asset can be used for the purposes of or in connection with the functions of the local authority concerned'* (i.e. adapt the asset to make it more useful).

Some examples of the interpretation of this definition that apply particularly in housing services are these:

- construction, improvement, and major repair of dwellings;
- making grants or loans to third parties for capital purposes;
- increasing substantially the thermal insulation of a building or the extent that it can be used by elderly or disabled people; and,
- reducing substantially the fire risk in a building.

The Local Government Act 2003 takes a different approach by referring to expenditure which *'falls to be capitalised in accordance with proper practices'*. The Secretary of State can define this more fully by regulations. These have so far been used to extend the definition to include:

- acquiring computer software;
- repaying previous grants or assistance made to the authority for capital purposes;
- buying share or loan capital; and,
- carrying out capital works on land which the authority does not own or rent.

As before, it has been made clear that the new definition also includes grants and loans to third parties for capital purposes.

The new, somewhat simpler definition is part of a government move away from crude statutory, sector-specific accounting rules towards more reliance on established accounting conventions that are used in other sectors of the economy. This shift in emphasis, as explained later, is gradually transforming the way in which the government monitors and controls the capital spending of local authorities, and is slowly leading to more local autonomy.

Capital spending and control

Central government capital support to local authorities

The government may support local authority borrowing in different ways and allocate it to authorities in accordance with a variety of different principles:

- Sharing out support according to 'needs' formulae. For example, social services funding is partly given according to numbers of elderly people in the area and a Generalised Needs Index (GNI) is used in the initial distribution of housing resources in England.

- Assessments of social efficiency and managerial effectiveness, so that support for housing has often been dependent on the quality of an authority's strategic programmes.
- Through a process of competitive bidding that emphasises commercial and economic efficiency and effectiveness, as in much regeneration funding and the major Community Ownership Programme in Scotland.
- Providing a national dimension to resource allocation in Scotland, Wales and Northern Ireland and a regional dimension in England.

Under devolution, the devolved bodies (such as the Scottish Parliament) are able to decide how their 'block' of spending is allocated between different services. In England, as we shall see, the regional housing boards have significant discretion as to the distribution of resources within their regions.

These general allocation methods seek to embrace the principles of equity, efficiency and effectiveness discussed in Chapter 2. In the context of these general principles, the current government is particularly concerned to improve the ability of the capital finance system to influence strategic and corporate planning within local authorities and to give them the incentive to develop local performance plans that focus on cross-cutting issues such as social exclusion/inclusion, employment, and youth crime as well as producing 'Best Value' approaches to service provision and asset management. In relation to housing, the reforms to local authority capital finance are also driven by the overwhelming importance which the government has attached to achieving the standards it has set for council housing, by a target date (in England, 2010).

Aims for the capital finance system

The following objectives have been put forward as those of an 'ideal' system governing local authority capital expenditure.[1] Such a system should seek to:

- maximise the value of local government investment within public spending constraints;
- tackle needs and resource inequalities between authorities;
- strike the right balance between local discretion and the government's priorities;
- encourage authorities to take an integrated, corporate approach;
- be inherently stable;
- be simple, open and accountable;
- encourage prudent financial behaviour; and
- be economical to administer.

In describing the current arrangements, we will make reference back to these aims as a way of highlighting criticisms of the present system and of pointing to possible reforms and future shifts in emphasis.

---

1   Based on research carried out by the Audit Commission, set out in DETR Cm7257, para 2.7.

The capital finance regime and government support for capital spending

The capital finance regime – Introduction

The capital finance system for England, Wales and Scotland has been substantially changed by the introduction in April 2004 of the concept of *prudential borrowing*. In England and Wales, the capital regime was redesigned and simplified according to 'prudential' principles in the Local Government Act 2003, although the system still partly reflects the rules established by the Local Government and Housing Act 1989. In Scotland, the prudential regime was established through the Local Government in Scotland Act 2003, but apart from the prudential borrowing element the rules remain essentially the same as under the Local Government (Scotland) Act 1973.

We refer in this chapter to the system established in England and Wales by the Local Government Act 2003, and the regulations which followed it, as the '2003 Act regime' or the 'new regime'. (Where appropriate, we also refer to the 'prudential borrowing regime', meaning the special rules and principles on which the new regime is based). The regime established by the Local Government and Housing Act 1989, which came to an end in April 2004, is referred to as the '1989 Act regime' or 'previous regime'. A similar distinction is made in relation to the Scottish 'regimes' although, as we make clear, the differences are less marked.

These systems govern local authorities' capital spending on council dwellings, other community assets, and on regenerating local areas. The basic principle is now one of 'financial prudence', which means that borrowing and credit may be freely used provided that they are affordable. As we shall see, 'affordability' is carefully defined. Prudential principles also ensure financing options are chosen on value-for-money grounds and discourage the use of speculative forms of investment.

Under the different regimes, the essential ways of financing capital spending are:

- borrowing, now within the prudential framework;
- central government support for borrowing, through grants and subsidies; and
- usable capital receipts from sales of land and other assets.

Other sources of capital finance include the following:

- revenue used to finance capital projects – usually referred to as revenue contributions to capital outlay (RCCO), or in Scotland as 'capital from current revenue' (CFCR); and,
- contributions from other public bodies and the private sector.

These five elements can be thought of as the 'types' of capital finance available to local authorities.

Figure 9.1 shows the main elements of the housing capital finance regime, as they apply from April 2004 to a typical local authority in England, and how they link to the local authority's revenue resources. The next part of this chapter aims to explain the five main elements of the capital finance regime by reference to this diagram, with consideration of the differences applying in Wales and Scotland.

Figure 9.1: The new local authority housing capital regime in England, from April 2004

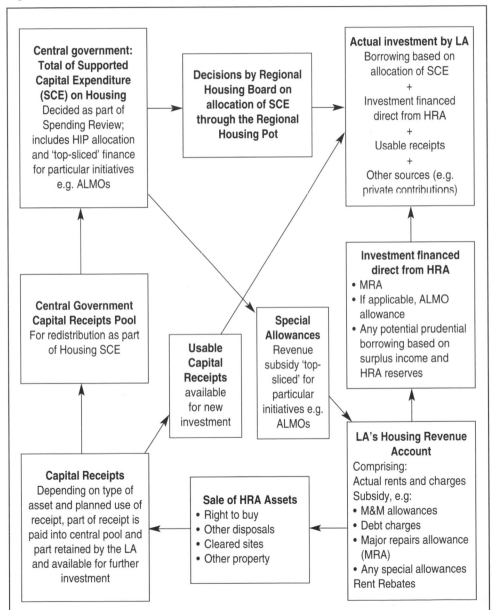

Borrowing within the prudential regime

Borrowing is, and always has been, the most important way of financing local authority spending. Borrowing allows projects to go ahead for which there would otherwise be no funding. It also spreads the capital costs of provision over future years in a way that more or less matches the benefits received. Unlike private sector borrowing, local authority loans are not secured against individual assets or groups of assets. Consequently, the amount borrowed for expenditure on a stock of council housing is not directly attributable to any one advance or loan. The debt relating to each property, or group of properties, is therefore a notional calculation based on an apportionment of the total debt across the whole stock.

Local authorities have the power (for example from section 1 of the Local Government Act 2003) to borrow funds for any purpose relevant to their functions, and also for the prudent management of their finances. The previous capital finance regime ensured that each local authority's annual level of borrowing for capital purposes required government approval. This meant that the total amount of a local authority's long-term borrowing was effectively limited to the value of 'credit approvals' (in Scotland, 'borrowing consents') issued by the central authorities.

An important purpose of the Local Government Act 2003 was to establish the principle of a 'prudential' borrowing regime for local government that mirrors the prudential regime (see Chapter 5) governing overall public finances. The radical element of this change was moving responsibility for decisions on borrowing back to local government: the first time for many decades that there has been a retreat from the creeping centralisation of decision-making, epitomised strongly by the 1989 Act regime. Government has now recognised that extensive and detailed control over borrowing '*has effectively shifted control from local to central government, blurring accountability, limiting local freedom and introducing an obstacle to capital investment*'.[2]

The regime established by the Local Government Act 2003 (and the Local Government in Scotland Act 2003) overturns one of the fundamental principles of earlier capital finance regimes – that local authorities require *permission* from central government to borrow money for capital projects. But this does not mean that capital spending is no longer controlled, or indeed that the overall effect is to create a liberal regime for capital spending in place of a rigid one. The changes can be best described as a shift of responsibility from central to local level for borrowing decisions, but within a framework designed to ensure that locally-taken decisions are both consistent with it and do not lead to any significant growth in capital spending beyond levels set by the chancellor (see Chapter 5). These three characteristics of the new regime can be described in turn.

---

2   Quoted from *Local Authority Housing Finance - A Guide to the New Arrangements* (ODPM, 2003).

The *shift of responsibility* occurs because central government no longer sets an approved level of borrowing through permissions issued to authorities, either generally or for specific projects. The concept of credit approvals, or borrowing consents, no longer exists. Instead, authorities regulate their own borrowing in accordance with a professional code drawn up by the Chartered Institute of Public Finance and Accountancy (CIPFA) (see Figure 9.2 in the box).[3]

The new legislation attaches great importance to affordability as the ultimate constraint on the amount that a local authority can spend or borrow. The legislation for England and Wales requires simply that authorities keep under review how much money they can afford to borrow, while in Scotland they must review the amount they can afford to allocate to capital expenditure. In practice, when making a decision to invest in a capital asset, each authority must do more than simply determine whether it can afford the immediate cost: in order to ensure long-term affordability, decisions also have to be prudent and any borrowing must be sustainable.

Figure 9.2: Principles of the CIPFA Prudential Code for local authority borrowing

Local authorities are free to invest so long as their capital spending plans are affordable, prudent and sustainable. The CIPFA *Prudential Code* sets out the indicators that local authorities must use, and the factors that they must take into account, to demonstrate that they have fulfilled this objective.

Local authorities now have a statutory duty to keep the scale of their capital investment under review and ensure that their borrowing is affordable. While the government, the Scottish Executive and the Welsh Assembly Government have the power to issue detailed regulations, it is intended that this will be achieved instead by requiring local authorities to have regard to the *Prudential Code*. As a consequence, while the Code does not itself constitute statute, local authorities have a strong obligation to follow its requirements.

In the new system the decision to invest is constrained by a local responsibility to determine whether it is affordable and represents a prudent and sustainable level of capital investment. The *Prudential Code* is the means by which local authorities demonstrate that they have satisfied this obligation.

Each local authority has to set prudential indicators specified in the Code. This will be done for the forthcoming financial year and at least the two subsequent financial years. The determination of prudential indicators, and any subsequent revisions, must be done using the same decision-making process as is used for setting the budget.

The purpose of the indicators is not to make comparisons between authorities. They are used by each authority to make judgements about the affordability of its borrowing; each authority decides what limits on its borrowing it should apply in using the indicators.

This system of self regulation imposes duties on as well as giving freedoms to local authorities. The chief financial officer is responsible for ensuring that the council has taken the Code into account and for monitoring compliance with the limits it has established. →

---

3   *The Prudential Code for Capital Finance in Local Authorities* (CIPFA, 2003).

The fundamental constraint on capital investment by a local authority is whether it can afford it. Affordability is ultimately determined by a judgement about acceptable council tax levels or, in the case of the Housing Revenue Account, rent levels. The Code includes specific indicators of affordability. These use as their starting point the financing costs for the local authority, including all interest payable, net of interest and investment income.

Each authority will need to form a judgement about whether it is committing an excessive proportion of its revenue to capital financing costs. In the Code, authorities are required to calculate a range of indicators that measure the impact of their plans on the revenue stream and on council tax or rents.

The investment will also have broader implications for running costs and income. The Code therefore requires that the authority not only considers its anticipated capital resources but also its overall revenue forecast for the following three years.

In the Code there are several technical indicators that trace the link between the decision to make capital investment and the decision to borrow. Indicators of 'prudence' are also included in the Code to help determine the prudent level of external borrowing. A key indicator is that, over the medium term, net borrowing is only for capital purposes.

The *framework* set by the CIPFA code allows councils to decide how much they can borrow within prudential limits, based on such considerations as their commitments to finance past borrowing, the support they expect to receive from central government, their long-term revenue resources and reserves, usable receipts, and the costs of new borrowing. Each local authority follows a set of prudential indicators which guide its borrowing levels, and there are separate indicators for its landlord function (funded through its Housing Revenue Account) compared with those for the rest of its capital spending. The separate indicators also ensure that tenants' rents are only used to support capital spending on the housing stock, not on other services. Authorities have to determine their own affordable borrowing limits, based on these indicators.

The *levels set by the chancellor* are, as under the previous financial regime, the totals for local government borrowing set as part of each Spending Review, which themselves contribute to the totals of Public Sector Net Borrowing and of overall public sector debt (see Chapter 5). Whereas until 2004 these totals were effectively translated by the Treasury and ODPM into individual decisions about how much each council could borrow, the control mechanism is now less direct. The main element of control is the level of borrowing support which each council receives from central government, which itself will be a strong influence on the amount of actual borrowing that takes place. Another element is the framework itself, and particularly the prudential code, which puts close limits on the extent to which authorities can use their new discretion to indulge in further borrowing. Finally, ministers retain reserved powers to intervene with local authorities which would undoubtedly be used if the combined actions of individual councils were to lead to an overall borrowing level which, though within the prudential framework, nevertheless significantly exceeded the levels set in the spending reviews or prejudiced the chancellor's policies about government borrowing and debt.

In practice the impact of the prudential borrowing arrangements will be felt more strongly and more quickly in non-HRA areas of a council's spending, for three reasons. First, council housing (unlike many other council activities) is partially dependent on subsidy, so that any growth in investment will depend more on whether extra subsidy is available than on any 'spending freedoms' which the new regime allows. Second, whilst in other areas of a council's spending (e.g. leisure centres, markets, municipal bus companies) any increase in charges can be used for new investment in the service, because of the operation of the HRA subsidy system and the associated rent regime, this does not apply in council housing where in general any rent increase is reflected in a loss of subsidy. Third, the government has specifically ruled out the possibility of councils borrowing against the value of actual assets (such as their housing stock, or the rental income from their housing) as opposed to the overall income stream of the authority. This effectively prevents authorities raising a 'mortgage' on the value of their stock in order, for example, to improve it. These limitations on the abilities of local authorities to manage their finances contrast with the relative freedoms available to housing associations, a point developed earlier in Chapter 5.

The government has maintained in the 2003 Act similar arrangements to those introduced in the previous capital finance regime, to ensure that councils cannot 'get round' the prudential requirements by creative deals such as leasing buildings instead of building them directly or buying them. Deals which create a liability which is similar to a loan are called 'credit arrangements' and the act makes clear that such liabilities are to be treated as if they were debts of an equivalent value.

The effect of the introduction of the prudential regime in Scotland is in one sense more radical than in England and Wales. Because several Scottish authorities already invest considerably from revenue in capital projects (explained further below), and the subsidy system does not apply in the same way as it does south of the border, the potential for extra investment through a prudential regime in Scotland is significantly greater. The cost of the extra borrowing will, however, have to be borne from rental income.[4]

Central government support for borrowing

Support for borrowing in England and Wales
Whereas under the 1989 Act regime the key government decisions influencing local authority capital spending were the credit approvals it gave, the key decisions now relate to the level of *supported borrowing*. The amount of

---

4   See Wilcox, S., 'Border Tensions – Devolution, rents and housing benefit' in Wilcox, S.
    UK Housing Review 2002/2003 (CIH/CML, 2002).

supported borrowing is known as the authority's Supported Capital Expenditure (SCE), and this (as happened with credit approvals) is initially determined service by service. So as well as an overall SCE for housing established nationally, each authority is allocated a housing SCE as well as SCEs for other services.

SCEs constitute estimates of what central government thinks an authority needs to spend on capital projects in the next financial year relative to the needs of other authorities. The department of state responsible for each service area sets its own criteria for arriving at an authority's individual SCE figure. As well as a comparative needs element, these criteria tend to include competitive elements to reward efficient performance, and elements that give recognition for particularly persuasive bids. SCEs are issued for housing, transport and a range of other services. This means that an authority may receive several SCEs covering the various services where the government supports capital investment.

The housing SCE is determined as part of an annual allocation process, often still referred to as the 'HIP allocation' (in England) and discussed in more detail below. Because the majority of government support for borrowing for housing purposes is through revenue (i.e. through the Housing Revenue Account, or through Revenue Support Grant in the case of spending on private sector housing renewal – see Chapter 12), the amount allocated to an authority is known as its Supported Capital Expenditure (Revenue), or SCE(R), for housing. Current practice is to allocate a firm amount for the coming financial year (announced towards the end of the previous calendar year), together with a provisional amount for the subsequent financial year. Although this is expressed in terms of the level of borrowing that will be supported, what the authority actually receives is the appropriate revenue subsidy, spread over a period of years, to help finance that borrowing.

The overall level of supported borrowing is determined as part of the bi-annual Spending Review (see Chapter 5). When the housing SCEs are added to the support for housing association capital investment (known as the Approved Development Programme), a considerable proportion will be offset by the total of pooled capital receipts (see below). This has the effect of reducing significantly the call of housing investment on new public borrowing. As an illustration, in 2001/02 in England the total of new investment through the HIP and the ADP was almost £1.6 billion, but of this total more than £1.2 billion was financed not by new borrowing but from the proceeds of capital receipts, mainly from right to buy sales.[5]

In Wales, the new regime operates essentially as it does in England with the exception that there is no 'pooling' of capital receipts (this aspect is explained later).

---

5   Figures from *The Way Forward for Housing Capital Finance* (ODPM, August 2002), p9.

Support for borrowing in Scotland

A similar move to a prudential borrowing regime has taken place in Scotland, and borrowing consents (equivalent to the previous credit approvals in England) are no longer issued annually to local authorities. There is still a fundamental distinction between HRA capital finance and capital allocated to General Fund investment. HRA capital finance is effectively unsubsidised for most authorities, because very few are eligible for Housing Support Grant. At the same time, there has been no central constraint on the growth of rents. Revenue-funded capital investment (CFCR – see below) is consequently more important than in England. Housing investment outside the HRA, mainly on private sector renewal, is supported by a specified capital grant, Private Sector Housing Grant (see below).

Support for special initiatives

Under the 1989 Act regime the government operated a dual system of credit approvals. In addition to its Basic Credit Approval, a council may have been given a Supplementary Credit Approval (SCA) for specific, government-approved projects and initiatives or if government considered the original borrowing consent needed to be supplemented during the year. A similar arrangement existed in Scotland.

With the disappearance of credit approvals from 2004, the government now relies entirely on additional capital grants or revenue subsidies to support special initiatives. In 2003/04, immediately before the start of the new regime, government departments awarded about £2 billion to authorities in England in the form of capital grants for such items as school repairs, transport and – in housing – disabled facilities grants. At the same time, some £3.5 billion was awarded in the form of credit approvals with appropriate revenue support. The housing 'HIP allocation' was, at £834 million, among the biggest items to receive such revenue support, others being transport revenue support and new pupil places in schools. Some of these grants or revenue support items are either for recent new initiatives or for past ones where additional support is still required. In housing, for example, about £100 million is awarded annually (in England) for disabled facilities grants which fund adaptations to private sector properties (see below).

Where extra support is to be provided for special initiatives relating to council housing, there is now a tendency to award this as additional revenue subsidy (see Chapter 12). Thus the capital funding of ALMOs (see Chapter 10), for example, is now a separate allowance within HRA revenue subsidy.

In 2003 the government consulted[6] on the general principle of whether support for capital expenditure, both generally and for special initiatives, should be through capital grants rather than revenue subsidy. A move towards capital grants for HRA investment would both bring local authorities slightly closer in their funding arrangements to those of housing associations (who receive capital grant) and help

---

6   *Support for Local Authority Capital Investment - A Consultation Document* (ODPM, 2003).

keep down local authority debt (by making it unnecessary to borrow for that part of the investment for which capital grant is paid). At the time of writing there have been no specific developments in this direction, however.

To obtain extra borrowing support whether as a grant or through revenue subsidy, an authority normally has to bid within the context of a particular initiative. Currently the largest such initiative in relation to English council housing is the ALMO programme (see Chapter 10) which up to 2005/06 has provided support for additional borrowing totalling almost £2 billion, so far benefiting 49 ALMOs. An example in Scotland was the New Housing Partnerships Fund, which financed a range of new initiatives, many involving partial or whole stock transfer. This has now been replaced by the Executive's Community Ownership Programme, to which only councils developing stock transfer proposals can apply. These English and Scottish programmes have annual bidding rounds in which councils make their case for extra funding. Those bids which are approved receive extra borrowing support in the following year and normally for several years thereafter.

These extra grants or revenue subsidy should be thought of as mechanisms by which central government exercises additional influence over local government spending patterns. During the 1990s there was a shift in emphasis towards supplementary approvals and grants, which meant that the central authorities exercised more and more control over local authority spending patterns. The supplementary approvals are funded by a process called 'top-slicing'. This involves, prior to distribution, setting to one side a proportion of the total allocation of credit approvals or supported borrowing. These 'top-sliced' approvals are then distributed, directly or through competitive bidding, in a way that reflects government priorities.

The term 'specified capital grant' is reserved for a particular type of Exchequer transfer. Specified capital grants (SCGs) contribute to particular types of capital spending that all authorities are likely to have to confront, of which the main one in England is now the provision of disabled facilities grants to disabled people living in private sector housing. Such grants are mandatory, and the SCG contributes 60 per cent of the cost of each one. However, the total level of such grants in any one year is limited nationally and for each authority, so in practice despite their mandatory nature councils have to 'manage' the demand for and approval of such grants so as not to exceed the annual grant limits, otherwise they face paying 100 per cent of the costs for grants above those levels.

In Chapter 11 we will see that local authorities often provide a good deal of help to up-grade sub-standard dwellings in the private sector. Except for the adaptation work for disabled people just mentioned, this expenditure is now all discretionary in England and Wales. Government supports 60 per cent of the costs of any expenditure incurred, and this is paid as part of Revenue Support Grant.

In Scotland, spending on assisting the repair, improvement and (for disabled people) adaptation of private sector property is assisted by Private Sector Housing Grant, which totals £60 million in both 2004/05 and 2005/06. Amounts of grant are partly allocated according to past spending patterns and partly through a bidding process.

Capital receipts

What are capital receipts?

Capital receipts are an important source of funding for capital finance, both for the local authorities receiving them and, as we have seen, for housing investment as a whole. A capital receipt is essentially a sum of money received from the disposal of land or some other capital asset such as a council house. The 2003 Act and regulations extend this definition to include repayments by third parties of grants or loans made to enable them to invest in capital assets, and also the proceeds of any sale by a local authority of its mortgage portfolio. However, sums of less than £10,000 are not treated as receipts, and neither are grants received from central government or other bodies.

Capital receipts need not be cash amounts. If, for example, instead of selling a property for cash an authority receives another property in exchange, it must work out what the receipt would have been in cash. This is the 'notional receipt' from the disposal and is counted in the arrangements for pooling (or, previously, 'set aside') of receipts.

Under the Local Government and Housing Act 1989, local authorities were required to set aside a specified proportion of most types of capital receipts. As part of its expenditure control mechanism in England and Wales, the government did not allow the whole of a receipt to be spent on new projects. Each receipt was deemed to comprise a 'usable' and a 'reserved' element and only the usable element could be employed to fund new capital spending. The remaining (reserved) percentage had to be set aside as provision for future credit liabilities and/or used to repay current debt.

In Scotland, authorities moved from a position where all their receipts were fully reusable until 1996, to one where controls were in place that were similar to those that applied in England under the 1989 regime, i.e. councils had to set aside 75 per cent of their receipts from house sales (e.g. through RTB), and transfer receipts were also treated in a broadly similar way to those in England. These controls led to a significant reduction in council housing debt, but were widely criticised by Scottish local authorities and the new regime has reverted to the practice of leaving the use of receipts at the discretion of each authority.

Similar local discretion now applies in Wales. However, where a Welsh authority still has debt (as they all currently do), any support for debt charges assumes that a proportion of receipts (for right to buy receipts, 75 per cent) is being used to repay the debt. There is no pooling of receipts, although this will be introduced should any Welsh authorities become debt-free. The following sub-section, on the pooling of receipts, therefore only applies to England.

Pooling of capital receipts in England

The 1989 Act set aside system was ended by the 2003 Act. However, as pointed out above, the cash from receipts plays a major role in financing housing capital investment. The Local Government Act 2003 recognised the continued importance of capturing the value of housing receipts by introducing new 'pooling' arrangements that replaced, but have much the same effect as, the old set aside rules. Instead of setting aside a proportion of receipts (notably, 75 per cent of RTB receipts), councils now have to make an actual payment to government of the equivalent amount, at the end of each quarter of the financial year. This cash is recycled as part of the future funding for councils and housing associations.[7]

A secondary purpose of pooling is to redistribute spending power between 'receipts rich' authorities (often those with higher-value housing stocks) to 'receipts poor' authorities which often have greater investment needs but (perhaps because they have a lot of unpopular housing) have lower levels of receipts. The government argues that where receipts 'fall' is relatively arbitrary and therefore it is right that much of the spending power associated with them is pooled and redistributed according to housing need.

There are exemptions to the pooling system for non-RTB receipts (for example from land sales) where the proceeds are recycled into affordable housing or regeneration projects. Stock transfer receipts are also exempt, because of the continued expectation that the transfer receipt will pay off the debt on the stock transferred. There are also provisions to encourage re-sale of RTB properties that the authority repurchases. Figure 9.3 summarises the way that pooling applies to particular types of receipt, and the exemptions and allowances that apply. A further reduction in the overall amount to be pooled (not shown in the figure) can be made by taking account of a proportion of any spending in the previous year on buying back RTB properties where the former tenant was in financial difficulty.

An important effect of the new pooling system is that it captures the receipts of those authorities that had become free of debt, and thereby escaped the old 'set aside' system. This normally occurs on stock transfer, but some authorities have achieved 'debt-free' status without transfer, usually as part of a strategy to have more control of their financial resources. Like 'in debt' authorities, they will now have to contribute new receipts to the pool, although there are transitional arrangements to ease their position in the first few years of the new system.

---

7   See letter from ODPM to local authorities in England, 10 December 2003, containing a commentary on regulations following the Local Government Act 2003. The letter says that the available funding is 'higher than it would otherwise be without this pooling' (of receipts).

Figure 9.3: Use of capital receipts in England, from April 2004

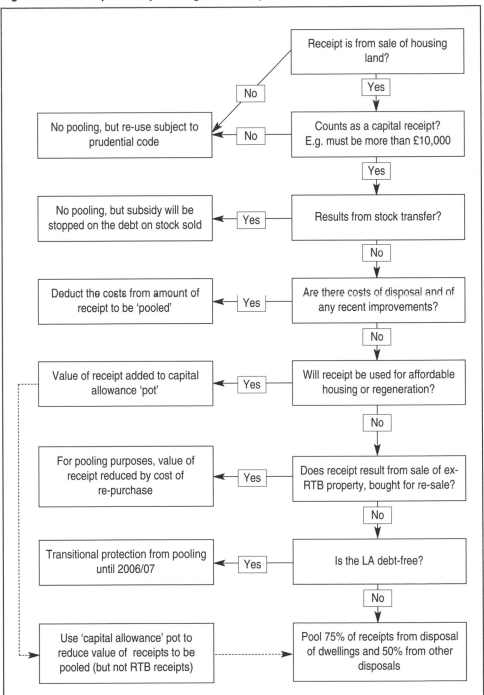

Based on a diagram by Trowers & Hamlins (Sceptre Court, 40 Tower Hill, London EC3N 4DX). The diagram is only a summary of the provisions and is not a substitute for specific legal advice.

The new arrangements also replace the unpopular 'RTIA' (usually referred to as 'Rita') mechanism where government assumed that a certain level of receipts was available to fund capital spending by each authority, and reduced its capital allocation accordingly. This mechanism was no longer used from 2003/04 onwards.

Revenue used to finance capital projects

Although we earlier showed how capital expenditure is distinct from revenue expenditure because it leads to the creation of fixed assets, in recent years there has been a growing tendency for *revenue funds* to be spent directly on projects such as planned maintenance programmes, and this has blurred the capital/revenue distinction. As we shall see, this has been exacerbated by the government's tendency to make available funding for new initiatives or new allowances as revenue subsidy rather than capital grant.

In theory, a council can invest as much as it likes of its council house rent income on building and improving its housing stock (HRA schemes). Similarly, it is theoretically free to build what it likes in the way of community projects (General Fund schemes), from its council tax revenues. Although local authorities are technically free to finance capital spending directly from their revenue flows, their ability to do so in England and Wales is limited by the prudential framework and, in the case of housing, by the subsidy system. It is further inhibited by any negative political impact that such a decision would have on council tax and rent levels. In any event, because of the 'ring-fence' around the HRA, authorities are not allowed to take resources from the General Fund to finance council housing projects or to systematically finance General Fund projects out of the HRA.

Apart from the impact on rents and hence on tenants, in England there have been other controls on rent levels which have been partly designed to deter councils from putting rents up in order to fund investment. One of these is the rent rebate subsidy limitation, which curtails subsidy on rent rebates above certain levels, making it more difficult for councils to raise rents. More recently, rent restructuring and associated subsidy changes have also made it more difficult for authorities to increase income by raising rents. These mechanisms are described in Chapter 12.

Revenue resources used directly to fund capital projects, without borrowing, are called *revenue contributions to capital outlay* (RCCOs), or in Scotland *capital from current revenue* (CFCRs). Such spending was particularly high in England in the 1980s because (until the rules were changed) it was a way of reinvesting the cash from right to buy sales. More recently in Scotland, CFCRs have accounted for about one-third of total investment, because most Scottish authorities no longer receive subsidy for new borrowing. As pointed out earlier, there is now the potential in Scotland for this spending from revenue to be converted into additional borrowing under the prudential regime.

In England two important developments have added to the importance of revenue resources in financing capital projects. First, in 2001 the government introduced the major repairs allowance (MRA) as an extra item of HRA subsidy, which represents the estimated long-term average amount of capital spending required to maintain a local authority's housing stock in its current condition. It is specifically designed to be spent for capital purposes (and is described in more detail in Chapter 12). (A version of the MRA has been made available to Welsh authorities, starting in April 2004, but it is not available in Scotland.)

Second, from 2002/03 a number of English authorities have set up arms length management organisations (ALMOs) to manage their stock, and have benefited from special ALMO allowances towards the investment needed to achieve the Decent Homes Standard. From April 2004, these allowances have also formed part of HRA subsidy, and may be spent either directly or to finance the extra borrowing required. ALMOs are described in more detail in the next chapter.

Grants and contributions from other public sector bodies and from the private sector

As well as receiving support from government departments, local authorities can receive capital grants or contributions from non-departmental government bodies – such as the National Lottery distributors or English Partnerships – the private sector, and the European Community.

A 'capital contribution' is a financial contribution to capital spending from a third party that has the same effect as a grant without technically being a grant. Planning gain agreements, for example, can direct financial resources from developers into local authority housing projects but are not classified as 'grants'. Under current ministerial guidelines, local authorities may require developers seeking planning permission for housing developments above a certain size to reserve a proportion of homes for social housing. Developers may avoid this requirement by offering councils a commuted payment which can then be used to develop social housing on a different site. There is no limitation at all on the use of non-departmental grants to finance capital expenditure: they provide welcome additional funds to those generated by normal government funding allocations, usable receipts and revenue transfers.

Local authority debt

What determines the level of local authority debt?

At any one time, an authority's actual level of external debt will depend on three broad factors: internal Treasury policies; the structure of the authority's historic costs (refer to Chapter 4); and the authority's ability to attract grants and contributions. To become debt-free an authority must (1) have no long-term borrowing, and (2) have set aside reserves sufficient to meet its outstanding liabilities.

As statutory authorities, council debts are automatically underwritten as local authorities cannot be declared bankrupt. However, council treasurers must seek to balance financial efficiency with prudence. They will try to manage the authority's profile of debt in a way that balances the need for flexible access to funds with the need to minimise service charges, while at the same time ensuring that the authority is not taking on unnecessary risks. The level of outstanding debt will vary at different times. This is because at certain times, even if the funds are available, it will be inappropriate to repay loans if they have been secured at low interest and/or where early repayment would incur a penalty charge.

Under the 1989 Act in England, authorities with debt had to set aside an amount from their revenue resources every year (known as 'minimum revenue provision' or MRP) to ensure some progress towards debt repayment. A broadly similar requirement continues under the new system, but only for non-housing debt (however, in Wales the arrangements still continue for HRA debt).

From 2004/05, the mandatory requirement to make payments against debt disappeared in England for HRA housing. The reason for this is part of the major change towards putting the HRA on a resource accounting basis (see Chapter 12). Within the HRA, councils must now make provision for a depreciation charge which can be used either to pay the debt on assets or maintain them so that their useful life is extended. The major repairs allowance (which is part of HRA subsidy – see Chapter 12) funds this charge. The extent to which local authorities repay debt is now very much a local decision, but they must abide by the requirement in the 2003 Act to set an Affordable Borrowing Limit and to manage their debt according to the CIPFA code (see Figure 9.2). There are thus strong incentives to continue to repay debt so as to maintain what is called 'headroom' for further borrowing under the code.

For reasons mentioned above, not every authority with the potential to become debt-free will choose to do so. Under the previous English capital finance regime, there was an incentive to becoming debt-free because of the flexibility it gave in using future capital receipts (e.g. from right to buy sales). However, this advantage is being withdrawn so that from 2007 all receipts will be subject to the 'pooling' arrangements described earlier in this chapter, whether or not the authority is debt-free. From then on being debt-free will have few immediate advantages other than the obvious one of having no on-going debt charges.

In Scotland, growing HRA debt (in contrast to falling debt levels in England) was an important factor in the debates about whether stock transfer should take place (see Chapter 10). In Glasgow, for example, before the recent transfer of its housing stock to the newly-formed Glasgow Housing Association, about half of tenants' rents were being spent directly on debt charges. Transfer enabled the old debt to be written off and the rental income made available for better housing services and improvements to the stock that, it was argued, would have been impossible without transfer. However, with the introduction of the prudential regime, both Scotland and Wales have reverted to the policy that debt management is a local responsibility, within the CIPFA Code, as it now is in England.

The actual amount of HRA-related debt varies considerably from authority to authority, depending on the amount that has been borrowed historically and the amount of capital receipts that have been set aside since the debt was incurred. For some urban authorities, the HRA debt is many thousands of pounds per unit, whereas for some other authorities, mainly district councils, the HRA debt is already nil or close to nil.

Much local authority borrowing is through the Public Works Loans Board (PWLB), now integrated with the Debt Management Office, a Treasury agency. Since the government is able to borrow cheaply, the PWLB can make loans to authorities at rates which are lower than those normally available in the market. However, authorities remain free to borrow from the private sector. The PWLB also underpins the financial stability of local government by acting as the 'lender of last resort' to local authorities.

Allocation of government support for borrowing to local authorities

In England, the methods used to allocate Supported Capital Expenditure (SCE) to local authorities are complex and vary significantly from service to service. The bulk of this support, some two-thirds, goes to three service areas: housing, transport and education.

Supported Capital Expenditure for housing is distributed to local authorities on a basis that is partly formulaic, and partly based on decisions now made through regional housing boards (for background on the boards, see Chapter 5). Figure 9.4 describes the allocation process. The housing SCE covers both HRA and non-HRA investment and the form that the actual support to a local authority takes depends on the split of its spending between the two.

In both England and Wales, at local level the allocated government support for housing forms part of the 'single capital pot'. The discretion which in practice has always existed at local level to use capital allocations flexibly between services was formalised from 1999 onwards by the creation of this 'pot'. Into the pot is 'put' the allocation for each service at local level and the authority is able to decide its own distribution of capital spending given the level of borrowing support it is going to receive. In practice, most authorities tend to follow the pattern of spending implied by the calculations made for each service, judging (in many cases) that to depart significantly from these might adversely affect future allocations.

The idea of allowing a degree of discretion about how an authority's allocations should be committed stems from the principles of local government identified in Chapter 8. These say that local knowledge and accountability should play the dominant part in determining how the money is spent. The principles of local democracy indicate that the central authorities should be more concerned with controlling overall spending levels than with dictating local priorities. It is felt that local flexibility underpins the ability of the capital finance system to influence strategic and corporate planning within authorities and gives them the incentive to focus on cross-cutting issues such as social exclusion and youth crime.

In Wales, a version of the major repairs allowance was introduced from 2004/05. This requires much of the funding that previously was allocated as credit approvals to be used instead as revenue subsidy. Any remaining support for local authority investment is now in the form of special initiatives.

In Scotland, as we have seen, there is no general support for local authority capital investment in HRA housing and the available funds are principally directed towards special initiatives (e.g. a central heating programme). The Scottish Executive does support non-HRA investment and part of these funds is allocated competitively (as mentioned earlier).

Figure 9.4: Allocation of Supported Capital Expenditure in England

Investment allocations in England currently have two components: a general purpose housing SCE allocation, and a guideline allocation of SCG to help pay for the awarding of disabled facilities grants. Until 2004/05, the allocation process was largely the responsibility of the appropriate Government Office for the Region (GOR), and was based on an assessment of need and of each authority's housing strategy and other performance indicators.

In England, the process of allocation now begins with the national total of SCE being divided amongst the nine administrative regions. In determining this division the government makes reference to estimates of relative regional need based on a formula known as the Generalised Needs Index (GNI).

This formula is subject to discussion with the local authority associations and depends, for example, on the profile of the housing stock within each region and on measures of overcrowding. Even quite small changes in the formula can produce relatively large sums of capital being moved between regions. The GNI weights factors to do with the local authority stock condition (about 60 per cent) the private sector stock condition (about 10 per cent) and the need for new provision (about 30 per cent). In this last category measures of concealed and overcrowded households are included, as are measures of the need for affordable, sheltered and special needs accommodation.

Following the regional distribution, the GOR used to make individual allocations to each local authority in its area. This was only partly informed by the GNI formula, and partly based on the GOR's assessment of each council's efficiency and effectiveness.

→

In 2004/05 a major change took place with the introduction of regional housing boards (RHBs), whose role is to prepare a Regional Housing Strategy and, based on this, advise ODPM on the distribution of resources in their region. The boards consist largely of representatives of government or government agencies (such as the Housing Corporation and English Partnerships) in the region. In future it is intended that they give way to elected Regional Assemblies, and in the interim they are already likely to be combined with regional planning bodies. As well as the board, there is a Regional Housing Forum with representatives of local authorities and other interest groups which advises the board.

RHBs have responsibility for both local authority housing investment (traditionally known as the HIP) and the regional ADP for the Housing Corporation. The two together constitute the 'regional housing pot'. For the first two years of the system, they are expected to recommend allocations which result in authorities having at least 70 per cent of the funding they would have had under the old distribution mechanism. But from 2006/07 they will have much more unfettered discretion over the allocations to individual authorities, albeit subject to annual guidance published by ODPM.

Following the RHB decisions, each authority now receives an allocation (often still referred to as a 'HIP' allocation) of SCE for housing for the coming year, with a provisional one for the year after. ODPM has said it will move towards three-year allocations in future.

This description in Figure 9.4 of the allocation of supported borrowing by central government seems to leave little room for local discretion. We now need to make the point that, although the central authorities exercise considerable power, the system does allow for a degree of influence to be exercised by the local authorities themselves. The system seeks to reconcile local perceptions of local needs with the wider national concerns of central government. Although for many years central government extended its control over local government spending, the twin principles of local government finance pointed to at the start of Chapter 8 (local responsibility and accountability) always required the system to take some account of local views about local needs. The new prudential borrowing regime should, at least in theory, represent a move towards more local discretion and flexibility, albeit still within fairly narrow parameters.

Summary

Capital investment is in many respects the most visible aspect of local authority housing finance because it determines the 'bricks-and-mortar' of meeting housing need. Currently it is of major importance because whether an authority has sufficient ability to invest will determine whether, within available resources, it can meet the government's targets for bringing its housing stock up to a decent standard.

During the 1980s and 1990s local authorities saw a general decline in their potential to invest, combined with increasing restrictions on the use they could make of their resources. The pattern has now changed with some increases in resources and, across England, Scotland and Wales, a new prudential borrowing regime which to some extent shifts responsibility for borrowing decisions to local level and creates more flexibility for authorities to decide the level of investment they can afford.

As before, however, the main determinant of local authorities' ability to invest is the amount of government support available for that borrowing. This continues to be decided by central government, although there is now a regional level of decision-making on resource allocation in England, as well as flexibility at local level to decide how the available support should actually be used. There is also a strong redistributive element to resource allocation in England, with the 'pooling' of the receipts from sales – especially right to buy sales – making a major contribution to each year's investment resources.

In Wales and Scotland, general support for local authority housing capital investment is much less significant, and more central funds are directed through particular initiatives. In Scotland, however, the prudential borrowing regime does give councils more real discretion than it does in England and Wales to decide to increase investment levels and bear the cost from rents.

This chapter's focus has been on the mechanics of 'normal' capital investment by local authorities. In the next chapter we will see what options councils have – particularly in the context of improving their housing stock – for raising investment resources through other means.

Further reading

The best source of up-to-date detailed guidance on the system in England is the latest version of the government's HRA Manual (currently ODPM, 2004) which describes the capital as well as revenue control systems.

For Wales and Scotland, information can be found on the Welsh Assembly Government (www.wales.gov.uk) and Scottish Executive (www.scotland.gov.uk) websites.

CHAPTER 10:
Investing in local authority housing

Introduction

The previous chapter described the way that the capital finance system enables investment in housing to take place, but was principally about the mechanics of the system rather than what the system is for. This chapter focuses on the 'why?' and 'what?' questions about capital investment in council housing. It is particularly concerned with investment in the existing stock of homes built by councils, and how government has recently prioritised this work, obliging councils to pursue it vigorously and providing different options for how it might be done.

The outcome in most cases is intended to be a radical change in the way council housing is run and may often result in it no longer being managed directly- nor even owned by – by the council concerned. Many commentators have argued that the government's real purpose is not investment but what might be called 'regime change' – getting council housing out of the direct control of councillors, and into a more 'business-like' environment (which relates back to the discussion about the nature of local government in Chapter 8). This chapter, however, deals mainly with the mechanics of change rather than the broader arguments about the government's motives.

Background – the state of council housing

To understand the importance of the state of the existing council stock when considering investment issues, it is necessary to review briefly what happened to council housing over the period from the mid-1970s until just before the turn of the new century. First, there was a massive reduction in the *level of investment* in existing housing and a virtual halt in new building by councils. Capital spending by councils fell in real terms by the late 1990s to less than one-third of what it had been in the late 1970s.[1] New building by councils fell from levels of more than 100,000 per year in the 1970s to just a few hundred by the late 1990s. Second, there was a big reduction in the *size of the council housing stock*, because of the success of the right to buy from 1980 onwards and later of large scale voluntary transfer, so that by 1999 councils owned less than 4 million dwellings compared to more than 6 million 25 years earlier. Third, councils tended to *lose their best housing stock* through right to buy, leaving more flats and less popular properties,

---

1   See Wilcox, S. (2004), Table 57b.

often in less attractive areas. Fourth, housing built by non-traditional construction methods, especially during the 1960s and early 1970s, began to show signs of *serious defects* that would require either demolition or extensive modernisation.

The outcome from these developments was that council housing became older and fell into poorer condition as the investment that it needed was not carried out. In 1998, CIH published an estimate[2] that the *backlog of repair and improvement* work needed across Great Britain had reached between £21 billion and £23 billion. In the late 1990s the phenomenon of *low demand* for council housing gained attention for the first time, in part reflecting its poor condition. The wider problem of *social exclusion* (see Chapter 11) was also recognised as applying particularly to council housing estates that were increasingly lived in by people on low incomes, with little choice as to where they lived, a process known as *residualisation*. The state of the housing stock, whilst by no means the only reason for this, was certainly a contributory factor.

The same CIH report called for the government to set a standard that it felt council housing should be restored to, a target for achieving that standard – it proposed ten years – and a range of alternative ways in which councils might go about securing the investment their housing stock required.

The government responded to this and similar demands in the April 2000 housing green paper and in that year's Spending Review:

- by *increasing investment*, and initially directing the increases mainly into the existing council housing stock;
- by *setting a new standard* called the Decent Homes Standard, and a *target date* (2010) by which all council homes should reach the standard;
- by requiring councils to produce *business plans* based on resource accounting principles for their housing stock and their Housing Revenue Accounts; and
- by offering a clear *set of options* by which councils could achieve the required investment, either by using public funds directly or through the use of private finance, and
- by requiring councils to carry out *option appraisals* that would state clearly the course(s) of action they were following to secure decent homes.

In Wales and Scotland there were similar responses prior to and after devolution, although (as we shall see) there were crucial differences compared with England.

This chapter uses these five sets of government actions as its structure for describing how greater investment is now being directed into council housing and the implications that this has for the whole shape and future of the sector. It concludes by looking at further options for the future of council housing, beyond the ones currently available.

---

2   Moody, G. (1998) *Council Housing – Financing the Future*, CIH, Coventry.

Increasing investment in council housing

As mentioned above, in 1997 the present government inherited an investment programme for housing that had been in decline for more than 20 years (see Figure 10.1). Furthermore, within this programme new building by housing associations had been prioritised at the expense of investing in the existing – mainly council-owned – social housing stock.

Figure 10.1: Gross social housing in Great Britain at constant prices

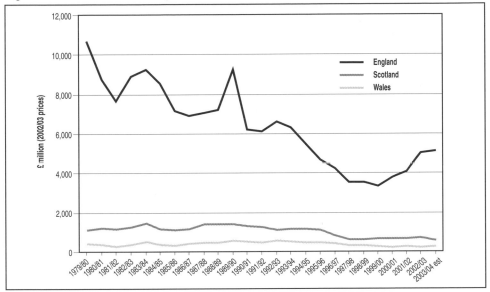

Source: Wilcox, S., (2004) *UK Housing Review 2004/2005*, Table 57b.

At the same time the new government imposed its own constraint on public spending once it took power, namely that it would follow for the first two years the spending plans left by its immediate predecessor. This brought about a further decline in public investment generally and in housing investment in particular. Fortunately certain exceptions were allowed. In the period before the election the shadow Labour ministers had been lobbied to 'recycle' the money that the outgoing government had required, since 1989, to be set aside from capital receipts. Local authorities had had to use this money, mainly from the proceeds of council house sales (see previous chapter), to offset or actually repay old housing debt. The CIH estimated that[3] some £5 billion was potentially available to be recycled. In the event, a similar sum was made available under the 'capital receipts initiative' in England. Proportionate amounts were also made available under the 'Barnett formula' for Scotland, Wales and Northern Ireland, but only in Scotland was this extra money channelled into housing. But, as Figure 10.1 shows, the initial effect on overall investment was to stem decline rather than reverse it.

---

3   Moody, G. (1996) *Boosting Housing Investment through Capital Receipts*, CIH, Coventry.

Significant real increases in investment have only come about since the second of chancellor Gordon Brown's Spending Reviews, which was published in 2000 and took effect from the financial year 2001/02 onwards. It was in this year that housing investment (in England) began to exceed the levels that Labour had inherited from the Conservatives. Having said that, the year-on-year increases in investment after 2000 were impressive. In cash terms, more than £2 billion extra was allocated to housing in England in the Spending Review 2000. As a result, the average growth in overall spending on housing was 13 per cent annually over the three years 2001/02 to 2003/04. Since then actual and planned growth has been more modest, but the trend has still been upwards.

Another significant development is that much of the funding directed to local authority housing is now specifically aimed at tackling poor conditions in the existing stock. The first significant development in this respect was the introduction of the major repairs allowance in 2001/02 (dealt with in detail in Chapter 12), that earmarked £1.6 billion of what previously had been general housing investment monies specifically for major repair works. The second major development was the introduction of funding for arms length management organisations (ALMOs) from 2002/03 (dealt with later in this chapter). ALMO funding is aimed at addressing the Decent Homes Standard and meeting the 2010 target (see below).

Together with existing or new financial arrangements for stock transfer and for PFI projects (also dealt with later in this chapter), the Spending Reviews in 2000 and 2002 both ensured that extra resources were directed into council housing, and more especially that this was done in a way that encouraged or required them to be used in dealing with the backlog of disrepair and failure to modernise that was the legacy of the previous 20 years.

As we have noted, there was no equivalent response to these changed priorities in Scotland and Wales, at least initially. In Scotland, the additional funding from the 'capital receipts initiative' enabled the Scottish Office prior to devolution to create the New Housing Partnership Fund, which was used principally to facilitate stock transfer and was maintained by the Scottish Executive after devolution took place in 1999. This fund is now known as the Community Ownership Programme. However, there was no direct increase in central government resources available to councils that retained their stock.

In Wales, there has been a similar emphasis on stock transfer as the route to tackling the improvement/repair backlog, without any initial increase in resources. In fact, for two years after Labour took office local authority housing investment continued to fall, only then to level out rather than actually increase significantly.[4] Unlike Scotland, however, the Welsh Assembly Government has recently introduced a major repairs allowance on English lines, albeit three years later and funded from the existing allocation for housing. The provision for the MRA in

---

4   Williams, P. (2002) 'Stand and Deliver! – Tackling the housing challenges in post-devolution Wales' in Wilcox, S. *UK Housing Review 2002/03*, CIH/CML, Coventry.

2004/05 is £108 million and overall investment in Wales is now increasing. As in England, the introduction of the MRA on a formulaic basis gives local authorities more certainty about future resource levels.

In Northern Ireland, much of the previous analysis in this chapter does not apply as in many respects the pattern of government intervention and investment is the mirror image of the rest of the UK. As Chris Paris has shown,[5] spending on housing in the province was proportionally much higher than in England during the 1980s and 90s (see Figure 10.2). It enabled the Northern Ireland Housing Executive (which took over housing responsibilities from local councils) both to maintain its stock and build significant numbers of new houses, often replacing poor condition property that in the rest of the UK might still have been in use. Only recently, as spending has fallen, have repair backlogs begun to emerge, but not on the same scale. Nevertheless there is a debate about the future shape of social housing provision in the province, to which we will return later in this chapter.

Figure 10.2: Housing spending per head in Northern Ireland and Great Britain

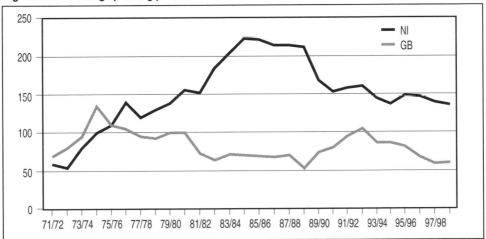

Source: Paris, C. *Housing in Northern Ireland.*

Setting standards and targets for council housing

We noted above that with the change of government in 1979, there were calls from the CIH and other lobby groups for the backlog of disrepair in council housing to be acknowledged, an estimate to be made of the cost of tackling it, and standards and targets to be set, as the basis for the use of the increased resources which it was hoped would be forthcoming.[6] In England, the response to these demands was the April 2000 green paper *Quality and Choice: A Decent Home for All.*[7]

---

5   Paris, C. (2001) *Housing in Northern Ireland*, CIH, Coventry.
6   Moody, G. (1998) *Council Housing – Financing the Future*, CIH, Coventry.
7   DETR (2000).

The green paper estimated the backlog of work needed to English council housing to be £19 billion. It set a new standard to be met, the Decent Homes Standard (DHS) (see Figure 10.3), and a target of bringing all local authority (and housing association) properties up to this standard by 2010. It also set an interim target that the number of non-decent homes should be reduced by one-third by 2004. By setting the new standard and the targets the government paved the way for the increased resources just described, but also put local authorities on notice that they would be expected to deliver the standard and targets even if, in most cases, this would require a radical change in the management or ownership of their housing stock.

The standard and targets are part of a wider government strategy for delivering improved public sector performance (see Chapter 8). They represent one of about 130 Public Service Agreements across the public sector, that are monitored regularly by the service departments and by the Treasury to ensure that extra resources lead to real service improvements. PSA 7, the one relating to decent homes in both the social and private sectors, actually reads:

> 'By 2010, bring all social housing into a decent condition with most of this improvement taking place in deprived areas, and for vulnerable households in the private sector, including families with children, increase the proportion who live in homes that are in decent condition.'

Although considerable progress has been made towards meeting the PSA 7 target, there are still some doubts about its feasibility. The ODPM announced in May 2004[8] that the first one million non-decent homes (owned by both councils and housing associations) had been made decent since 1997, leaving slightly more than one million still to be tackled. It has now set a new 'milestone' of cutting the number by half by 2006. Meanwhile, a report by the relevant House of Commons Select Committee has called into question whether the 2010 target will be met.[9] Others have questioned the narrow basis of the DHS and pointed out that wider regeneration of poor estates may be as important as physical improvements.[10]

Scotland and Wales have also set targets of similar kinds. Scotland's standard, set in 2004, is called the Scottish Housing Quality Standard (SHQS). It applies to all housing but the target for achieving the standard in the social rented sector has been set at 2015, with individual social landlords being responsible for setting their own 'milestones' towards achieving this target. The summary version of the standard[11] is that housing must be:

- compliant with the tolerable standard;[12]
- free from serious disrepair;
- energy efficient;
- provided with modern facilities and services;
- healthy, safe and secure.

---

8   ODPM press release 2004/0115, 5 May 2004.
9   *Decent Homes: Fifth Report of the ODPM Housing, Planning, Local Government and the Regions Committee*, United Kingdom Parliament, 7 May 2004.
10 See for example the joint submission to the Spending Review 2004 by CIH, LGA and NHF (available at www.cih.org/policy).
11 Letter from Scottish Executive to local authorities, 4 February 2004.
12 The tolerable standard is roughly equivalent to the fitness standard that applies in England and Wales.

Figure 10.3: The Decent Homes Standard in England

The standard requires that each home must:
a) meet the current statutory minimum standard for housing (the fitness standard);
b) be in a reasonable state of repair;
c) have reasonably modern facilities and services;
d) provide a reasonable degree of thermal comfort.

In more detail:

Criterion A: meeting the current statutory minimum standard for housing
- The fitness standard is the current minimum standard for housing.
- A home will be unfit (and therefore fail the Decent Homes Standard) if, in the opinion of the local authority, it fails to meet one of a range of requirements, and is therefore not considered reasonably suitable for occupation. They include criteria such being free from serious disrepair and having the basic amenities such a WC, bath or shower, etc.
- The fitness standard will be replaced soon with the new Housing Health & Safety Rating System. Councils are therefore recommended to apply this rating system to their properties, as well as applying the fitness standard.
- The Housing Health & Safety Rating System is designed to ensure that a home (including its structure, means of access, any associated outbuildings and garden, yard and/or amenity space), provides a safe and healthy environment for the people who live there and those who visit.

Criterion B: be in a reasonable state of repair
A home will meet this criterion unless:
- *one or more key building components* are old and because of their condition need replacing or major repair, or
- *two or more other building components* are old and because of their condition need replacing or major repair.
Key building components are those which, if in poor condition, could have an immediate detrimental effect on the building and lead to damage to other parts of the home, e.g. a leaking roof could lead to damp, ceilings collapsing and faulty electrics, etc.

Criterion C: have reasonably modern facilities and services
A home will not meet the Decent Homes Standard if it lacks three or more of the following facilities:
- a kitchen which is 20 years old or less;
- a kitchen with adequate space and layout;
- a bathroom which is 30 years old or less;
- an appropriately located bathroom and WC;
- adequate noise insulation;
- adequate size and layout of common entrance areas for blocks of flats.

Criterion D: provides a reasonable degree of thermal comfort
The definition requires a decent home to have both efficient heating and effective insulation:

Efficient heating	Effective insulation
Any gas or oil programmable central heating	Cavity wall insulation (where there are cavity walls that can be insulated effectively) or at least 50mm loft insulation (if there is loft space).
Electric storage heaters / LPG / solid fuel	Cavity wall insulation (where there are cavity walls that can be insulated effectively) and at least 200mm loft insulation (if there is loft space).
Similar efficient heating systems, e.g. based on renewable resources	The extent of insulation will depend on whether the form of heating is similar to gas and oil heating systems or to the electric, LPG or solid fuel heating systems.

It therefore goes further than the Decent Homes Standard in, for example, its energy efficiency requirements.

In Wales, the equivalent standard is the Welsh Housing Quality Standard, to be achieved by 2012. It goes further than the English or Scottish standards, requiring that houses be:

- in a good state of repair;
- safe and secure;
- adequately heated, fuel efficient and well insulated;
- contain up-to-date kitchens and bathrooms;
- well managed (for rented housing);
- located in attractive and safe environments; and
- as far as possible suit the specific requirements of the household (e.g. specific physical impairments).

As yet there is no strategic standard or target in Northern Ireland (although, as we have noted, it does not have equivalent problems). The Housing Executive uses the Decent Homes Standard to assess stock condition, and while there is no target of achieving full 'decency' by 2010 it has indicated that it expects to achieve this.[13]

Preparing business plans for council housing

Another element in the drive to improve the quality of council housing is the requirement that each authority in England that has a housing stock and a Housing Revenue Account (HRA) must have a business plan. The first business plans were produced in 2001/02 and they are updated annually. (In Figure 10.4 we describe the aspects of the plans that relate specifically to investment in council housing; general material on social housing business plans appears in Chapter 16.)

The main purpose in requiring business plans to be prepared, in the context of the DHS, is to oblige councils to take a long-term view of the tangible assets represented by their housing stock and of the resources available for investing in it. The plans must be prepared on resource accounting principles. In many cases the early results from business plans indicated that councils could not achieve the DHS with the levels of resources they expected to have available over the ten years to 2010, when the DHS had to be achieved. In this situation, councils had no alternative but to consider the further options available to them apart from conventional ownership and management of their stock and reliance on traditional sources of income such as rents and subsidy. These options are considered in the next section of this chapter.

---

13   NIHE (2004) *The Northern Ireland Housing Market – Review and Prospects 2004-2007.*

Figure 10.4: The HRA business plan

The HRA business plan is a long-term plan for managing the authority's housing assets and financing the necessary investment. It should show how the authority intends to manage its housing assets in the context of:

- its housing strategy;
- stock condition;
- demand for social housing; and
- likely availability of resources.

The plan must show how the authority will tackle the major issues that affect the delivery of the authority's landlord function, including achievement of the Decent Homes Standard, balancing supply and demand for housing, improving performance (responding to repairs, collecting rents) and addressing particular housing needs such as those of BME people and the elderly. The business plan will also need to set out how the authority will monitor the delivery of the service and improvements to it, and achievement of its targets.

It should establish a medium/long-term framework for delivering improvements to the council housing stock, including its performance on housing management and options for improving quality of services and/or efficiency with which they are provided.

It must include sound information on:

- the current condition of the authority's stock and its performance on service delivery;
- detailed financial forecasts, including the need for resources, funding sources, output targets and sensitivity analysis;
- a clear statement of priorities for action, based on the analysis of the current and likely future position;
- a full description and analysis of the options for making progress in the priority areas;
- progress to date.

The business plan should then set out the authority's action plan. This will contain the medium and long-term strategy to implement the preferred option, and to maintain and improve the condition of its stock and the service offered to tenants.

Business plans should be the product of full consultation with residents and other stakeholders as well as of a properly joined-up decision-taking process within the council that ensures that informed decisions are taken on relative priorities and due account is taken of the links and potential synergies between different service areas.

Source: adapted from *Business Plans for Council Housing: Guidance*, available at www.odpm.gov.uk

The requirement to produce business plans applies differently in Scotland and Wales. In Scotland, authorities must prepare a 'delivery plan' by April 2005 showing how they will achieve the SHQS target by 2015. In Wales, local authorities were required to assess the resources needed to achieve the WHQS in their own stock in 2002 and have business plans in place by 2004; not all authorities achieved this, however. (The approaches in Scotland and Wales effectively incorporate the 'option appraisal' process described later in this chapter.)

actice the first business plans in England were of variable quality, and further
rk has been needed to update them and make them 'fit for purpose'. The first
lans were considered as part of the 2003 'PSA Plus Review' of progress towards
achieving the DHS. It expressed three main concerns about them:[14]

- *The need for robust business plans:* the assumptions in the business plans
  form the basis of delivery by 2010 and they need to be firm and realistic;
  there is a tendency towards excessive optimism in the public sector about
  the ability to deliver against planned deadlines at estimated costs – local
  authority delivery of decent homes is unlikely to be an exception.
- *The need to deliver against plans:* central government must have
  confidence in the capacity of the local authority to deliver decent homes
  on the basis of a robust plan.
- *Local authorities needs ownership of plans:* some authorities still consider
  they are producing business plans because they are required by central
  government and they do not see the need for them as a key tool in
  managing their business.

In June 2003, just over 100 English authorities (out of 270 with housing stock)
were thought to be at risk of failing to meet the DHS target,[15] either for the
reasons just mentioned or because they were not yet pursuing rigorously one of
the available options.

Options for bringing investment into council housing

As we have seen, the main focus of business plans for council housing is on
remedying the backlog of disrepair, and on meeting the standards set by
government by the target date. The business plan process requires councils to
assess the investment needed to achieve the standard, and then consider the
options for bringing in this investment within the required period of time. This
one-off 'option appraisal' element of business planning is described later in this
chapter. To enable readers to understand the process, we deal first in some detail
with the range of options open to councils.

The range of options available

Chapter 9 described the process by which local authorities raise investment funds
for housing, making use of the subsidy available from central government,
together with capital receipts, and whatever resources can be made available from
their revenue accounts after day-to-day service costs and other charges have been

---

14   ODPM (2003) *Report of the PSA Plus Review.*
15   ODPM (2003) *The Decent Homes Target Implementation Plan.*

met. Before the mid-1980s, using the capital and revenue subsidy system, and hoping for sufficient 'credit approvals' from central government to allow more borrowing, was essentially the only means by which councils could pay for new investment in their housing stock.

This option does of course still exist, and is often referred to as 'stock retention'. Stock retention is the basic option for all councils with housing stock who are considering how to meet government standards, and is the option against which other options must always be compared. In addition, there are three further options (in England) for bringing the necessary investment into the housing stock:

- transferring the stock to a new landlord – a housing association or specially-created local housing company – that can raise investment funds on the private market;
- setting up an arms length management organisation (ALMO) to manage the stock, and bidding for funds under the government's ALMO programme;
- using the private finance initiative (PFI) to improve the stock whilst keeping in it council ownership.

There has often been discussion of further options beyond those listed here. Confusingly, these are frequently called a 'fourth way', involving stock retention but with additional freedoms or subsidies that would provide the necessary investment without having to pursue any of the other three options just listed. This debate, and some of the possibilities, are considered at the end of this chapter. For the moment, however, the government has firmly ruled out a 'fourth way'.[16]

In Scotland and Wales, essentially the only option apart from stock retention is stock transfer – neither ALMOs nor PFI schemes are currently available.[17] However, as we saw in Chapter 9, stock retention in Scotland does offer greater scope than is the case in England, because prudential borrowing in Scotland is not restricted by rent restructuring and a tight redistributive subsidy system. It may prove to be sufficient in some authorities to deliver the required levels of investment.

Stock transfer

Stock transfer is quite simply the process of transferring (or selling) housing stock to a different landlord. For tenanted stock in the social sector, this essentially means transfer to a registered social landlord. The landlord may be an existing housing association, or a new one (often following the form of a 'local housing

---

16 Letter from deputy prime minister to local authorities, 28 October 2004.
17 In theory the ALMO option is available in Wales but without extra subsidy; at the time of writing no Welsh councils have pursed this option.

company') created for the purpose. 'Large scale voluntary transfer' or LSVT typically refers to transfers of more than 500 homes. A council may transfer the whole or only part of its stock ('whole stock' or 'partial' transfer). Partial transfer can form part of a mixed strategy, involving retention or one of the other options for other parts of the stock.

Transfer is attractive principally for investment reasons. Once the stock has been transferred, any borrowing needed to improve it no longer counts as public borrowing, and is therefore not subject to government constraints. Although the new landlord, rather than the local authority, is responsible for the new borrowing, transfer only goes ahead once a deal is 'signed and sealed' that enables sufficient borrowing to take place to meet the stock's investment needs and satisfy promises given to tenants prior to transfer. This usually means modernising properties to higher standards than are actually required by government, and can involve extensive 'remodelling' of estates (demolition and possibly new building) to ensure the marketability of the stock. In Figure 10.5 we provide a brief history of housing stock transfer.

In this section we consider in turn government policy towards transfer, the investment it generates, the transfer process, the involvement of tenants, and the financial and performance aspects of transfer.

Stock transfer and government policy

Although transfer has come to form such an important part of housing policy, it was not originally a central government innovation but a solution devised at local level to tackle investment problems and also address the loss of stock through right to buy (see Figure 10.5). However, previous Conservative governments actively encouraged transfers during the early 1990s as a complementary policy to right to buy in reducing the municipal housing stock. When Labour took power in 1997 it decided to maintain the impetus towards transfer and, in the April 2000 green paper, allowed for transfers totalling 200,000 units each year in England. *'We won't be forcing anyone to transfer, but we will expect everyone to consider it as one of their options'* said Hilary Armstrong, then English housing minister.[18] In Scotland, the government and then (since 1999) the Scottish Executive vigorously promoted transfer through the New Housing Partnerships programme (now Community Ownership Programme), leading notably to the 2002 transfer of Glasgow's council housing.

In addition to promoting transfer in principle, governments have also sought to influence the nature of the landlord chosen or created to accept the transfer property. Earlier transfers led to the creation of what were effectively new versions of old-style housing associations, that in some cases have been little different from 'traditional' associations in the ways they have operated, for example they may have expanded well outside the original local authority area.

---

18   Reported in *Inside Housing*, 19 September 1997.

Figure 10.5: A brief history of stock transfer

Transfer of former publicly-owned housing into the hands of non-state, not-for-profit landlords has been taking place in Britain for more than 15 years. Across Britain it has resulted in the ownership transfer of nearly one million homes to housing associations. It has eliminated state housing from around a third of England and from Scotland's largest city as well as levering in well over £7 billion of private investment in repairs and modernisation of stock formerly owned by local authorities. Partly as a result of transfers, the ratio of council housing to housing association property has fallen from 13:1 in 1986 to 2:1 in 2003, and landlords set up specifically to take on transferred housing are poised to overtake the stock-holdings of conventional associations.

Whilst the stock transfer dynamic suffered a major shock with the tenant rejection of the proposed Birmingham transfer in 2002, government commitment to the policy remains undiminished (in Wales and Scotland, as well as in England).

Stock transfer is usually seen as having begun with the December 1988 hand-over of Chiltern DC's stock to Chiltern Hundreds HA. Initially, transfer in England was largely restricted to southern shire district councils working in relatively unproblematic areas, but by the end of the 1990s it had changed in character. Transfers involving cities and industrial areas in the Midlands and the north suddenly took off after 1997 and by 2003 covered large urban authorities such as Bradford, Coventry, Sunderland and Walsall.

Partial transfers in urban areas have generally involved specific estates or groups of estates, typically run-down inner city neighbourhoods with deeply ingrained social and economic problems. As yet, transfers of this sort are the only ones which have taken place in inner London. By the end of 2003 partial transfers had come to account for 100,000 of the 970,000 homes transferred since 1988 (see the pie chart below). Another 50,000 were the result of the Scottish Homes divestment programme. Only around five per cent of transferred stock has been inherited by existing housing associations, mainly in the context of smaller partial transfers.

Stock transfers in Britain 1988-2003 by transfer type

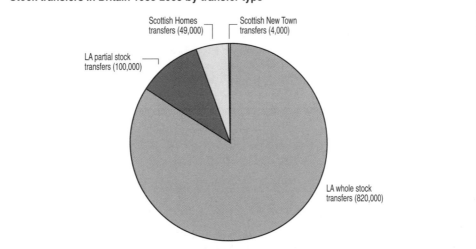

Source: Text and diagram in this box adapted from Pawson, H., 'Reviewing Stock Transfer' in Wilcox, S. (2004) *UK Housing Review 2004/05*, CIH/CML, Coventry.

Following work by CIH and the Joseph Rowntree Foundation,[19] the Housing Act 1996 allowed local housing companies to be registered with the Housing Corporation, and this paved the way for a different style of transfer landlord – that was to become the norm – involving a higher proportion of tenants as board members, with a strong local focus, and often involving neighbourhood regeneration work alongside house improvement.[20]

Governments have also favoured the 'breaking up' of the council stock, so that one large landlord does not replace another. For some time there was, for example, a fairly strict size limit of 12,000 on the number of properties that could be transferred to each new landlord (in England) and the transfer of Glasgow's stock to Glasgow Housing Association has been on the basis that it will devolve management or ownership to smaller local bodies. It is still policy in England to encourage competition between potential landlords in the run up to transfer. Even so, in practice more than nine out of ten transfers are to new landlord bodies specially created by the councils concerned, and in several cases (Sunderland, Bradford, Coventry) to ones with more than 20,000 properties.

Stock transfer and investment

The financial principle behind stock transfer is that of equity release. The objective is to improve the housing stock by reinvesting the capital receipt generated by the sale in new building and in improving the existing stock. It becomes possible because the stock's asset transfer value is greater than its historic cost value (refer to Chapter 4). Put simply, because the outstanding debt associated with the stock is often significantly less than its exchange value, the new landlord is able to borrow on the strength of the difference (i.e. the unencumbered equity) and then invest the funds raised in improving the houses. Interest in LSVT was originally confined to those councils where the transfer valuation exceeded loan debt and allowed for the necessary 'catch up' repairs.[21] LSVT brought to the fore the question of how private lenders assess the value of social housing. How to value council housing assets is an important issue and is discussed in Chapter 12. Transfer values are based on the principle of the social housing being a 'going concern'.

The transfer deal will need to take account of any shortfall between the value of the stock and the costs of improvement and of outstanding debt on the properties. The government now allows the transfer of council housing that does not generate a capital receipt or where the receipt does not fully meet outstanding debt. Until the principle of residual debt funding had been accepted, transfers were restricted to authorities where the price received cleared the outstanding debt.

19 Wilcox, S. *et al.* (1993) *Local Housing Companies – New Opportunities for Council Housing*, JRF/CIH, York.
20 See for example Nevin, B. (1999) *Local Housing Companies – Progress and Problems*, CIH for JRF, Coventry, and HACAS Chapman Hendy (2002) *Beyond Bricks and Mortar – Bringing Regeneration into Stock Transfer*, CIH, Coventry.
21 DoE (1995) *Evaluating Large Scale Transfers of Local Authority Housing*, HMSO, London.

Current provisions for assisting high debt/high-cost transfers are:

- meeting the costs of outstanding debt on whole stock transfers, to the extent that it is not covered by the receipt;
- meeting the revenue costs of outstanding debt on partial transfers (rather than this having to be borne by the remaining housing stock); and,
- considering 'gap funding' of transfers that need a central government payment as well as debt relief in order to cover the cost of modernising the stock (the 'gap' is that between the value of the stock and the finance needed to modernise it).

High-cost (or 'negative value') transfers that receive gap funding will involve a payment to the transfer body by the local authority, rather than the other way round. Such payments are often called 'dowries' and can also be looked at as the opposite of a capital receipt. Even where a dowry is paid, however, the case for transfer is that a substantial part of the capital cost of modernisation is raised through private finance.

For low-cost transfers, the investment advantage applies to the transferring council as well as to the transfer body. Whereas the latter has new resources through new borrowing, the former has a usable capital receipt. Because the receipt can be quite sizeable, the government imposes two constraints on its use. First, the housing debt relating to the stock must be paid off. Then, since 1993 (except for a short period) a 'levy' has been imposed on any remaining receipt, currently set at 20 per cent. This payment to government is a one-off reflection of the fact that – in most cases – these low-cost transfer authorities would have been in receipt of 'negative' housing subsidy (paying money to government from their HRA, rather than receiving it – see below), that the government will no longer receive. Despite these constraints, in 2002/03 for example transfers created £132 million of usable receipts for the councils making them.

A final point about investment is that the advantages of transfer do not occur only at the point when the transfer takes place. Because the funders insist on a relatively cautious approach to the borrowing required, although some transfer bodies have hit unexpected problems the majority have managed to 'out perform' their business plans and create surpluses in later years.[22] These surpluses accrue to the transfer body and it is up to it to decide how they are used. As Hal Pawson (amongst others) has pointed out,[23]

> *'Stock transfer has created social landlords which, whilst subject to state regulation, cannot be directly controlled by central government. This is an important issue given transfer HAs' capacity to generate future revenue*

22 See the assessment by HACAS Consulting (1999) in *Housing Associations – A Viable Financial Future?* CIH, Coventry.
23 Pawson, H., 'Reviewing Stock Transfer' in Wilcox, S. (2004) *UK Housing Review 2004/05*, CIH/CML, Coventry.

surpluses beyond Whitehall's reach, and therefore not susceptible to redistribution according to centrally-defined priorities.'

The transfer process and tenant involvement

Transfer takes place under powers largely contained in the Housing Act 1985, the Housing and Planning Act 1986, the Leasehold Reform, Housing and Urban Development Act 1993, and the Housing Act 1996. In Scotland recent measures are contained in the Housing (Scotland) Act 2001. Legislation and policy statements by bodies such as the Housing Corporation effectively require transfers to be to registered social landlords and impose various conditions on the transfer, only the most important of which are set out here.

Transfers in England, Scotland and Wales require a ballot of tenants in which the majority of those voting support the transfer. In England, about three out of four full stock transfer votes have resulted in such a majority; the proportion of 'successful' ballots for partial transfers is even higher. In Scotland the three whole stock ballots to have taken place since devolution have already produced a majority of 'yes' votes in each case, but in Wales out of two ballots, one – in Wrexham – produced a 'no' result. Whereas in the earliest transfers there was often little tenant involvement other than the formal ballot, it is now normal to begin tenant consultations at a much earlier stage and to involve them in the process. Indeed, one model for transfer (and for developing other options such as ALMOs) is called a 'community gateway' model because it embodies much greater tenant involvement and control.[24]

In England, the ODPM draws up an annual transfer programme. Authorities wishing to be in the programme submit applications towards the end of the calendar year, along with a detailed financial appraisal of the public expenditure implications of the proposed transfer. Scottish authorities apply to the Scottish Executive and transfer consent is granted by Scotland's First Minister. In Wales the consent procedure operates in a similar way through the National Assembly. In each case there are guidelines – reviewed annually in England – that contain both requirements and advice to transferring authorities.

The main purpose of a transfer is to benefit tenants, but it should be remembered that leaseholders also have a proprietary interest in the proposed deal. Many estates have a number of leaseholders or owner-occupiers who bought their homes under the right to buy. Although there is no statutory duty to consult leaseholders or owners before a transfer can progress, good practice requires that they be informed and be given information about how the proposals will affect their

---

24   See HACAS Chapman Hendy (2003) *Empowering Communities – the Community Gateway Model*, CIH, Coventry. In Wales, the Welsh Assembly Government has developed a community mutual model for stock transfer that has elements in common with the community gateway model. A WAG research report (available at http://www.housing.wales.gov.uk/rreports.asp?a=23) looks at the model and includes recommendations for its future development/implementation.

financial interests, for example, through the expected effects on future service charge levels.

The stock transfer process is a lengthy one, often taking two years from start to finish even in relatively straightforward cases, and it can take longer if, for example, negotiations are required to secure extra government support such as 'gap funding' (see above). Various decisions are required in the course of this process, for example as to whether the stock is being transferred to a new body set up for the purpose or to an existing housing association. Especially if it is to be to a new body, well before transfer there will be a 'shadow' board established and senior staff who are to be transferred at the same time as the stock will cease to act on behalf of the council. Consultants will invariably be required – usually of several different kinds and at different stages. One of these is specifically appointed to give impartial advice to tenants and their organisations.

Financial aspects of transfer

Both the policy of stock transfer and the increasing use of fixed assets as collateral for private sector loans, have brought to the fore the tricky question of how to put an appropriate value on units of social housing. (This question is addressed more fully in Chapter 17) Transfer valuations are particularly sensitive to the cost of dealing with any catch up repairs and future repairs. This is especially true of ageing estates in which the units were built at the same time and where building elements, such as windows, roofs, etc., may need renewing or repairing en bloc or over a short period. Valuing non-traditional buildings can be particularly problematic because some necessary works might not be regarded as repairs in the usual sense (putting the building back to its original condition), but rather as correcting basic design flaws.

One of the most sensitive issues that has arisen in considering stock transfer has been that of rent. There are two main questions – what difference it makes to rents generally, and what differences will occur between different groups of tenants. The first question was typically dealt with by a 'rent guarantee' built into the transfer agreement, which said that rents for existing tenants would not increase by more than a certain amount (the limit often being one per cent above inflation, or 'RPI+ 1%') for a period (normally five years) after the transfer. Nevertheless, opponents of transfer often argued that rents would go up faster as a result of transfer than would otherwise be the case. The second issue, rents for new tenants, came about because transfer bodies often aimed to charge new tenants higher rents and not observe the same rent guarantee as for existing tenants.

The rent issue has been largely neutralised (in England) by the government's policy of restructuring council and housing association rents, introduced in 2002 (see Chapter 12). This limits rent increases to 0.5 per cent above inflation, plus the amount required to achieve convergence of council with housing association rents over ten years. This caused problems for some stock transfer bodies that had expected to be able to raise rents at one or even two per cent above inflation once outside the rent guarantee period. However, it means that, essentially, the only differences in rents arising from the transfer should largely be those that result from the capital value of the houses being increased through improvement work. These increases would eventually occur anyway if the houses stayed in council ownership and were improved.

In Wales, while there is no rent restructuring plan, the assembly requires stock transfer bodies to adhere to its policy about rent increases and affordability, set out in its transfer guidance. In Scotland there are no overall policies on rents and each case is decided individually. For example, in the Glasgow transfer tenants were promised that rents would go up no faster than inflation for five years. This was possible because about half of the pre-transfer rent was needed to pay the costs of old debt, which were taken over by the Scottish Executive on transfer, freeing up considerable resources to fund improvement of the stock.

Another financial aspect of transfer has been the different treatment of housing benefit costs before and after transfer. Local authority tenants receive rent rebates that until 2004 in England and Wales were partially funded from the rents paid by other tenants who did not receive rebates. But after transfer to a registered social landlord, the same tenants would instead receive rent allowances whose costs are funded (largely) from central government. This anomaly was partly dealt with after April, 2004 when rent rebates were taken out of the Housing Revenue Account and paid on a similar basis to rent allowances. This had always been the case in Scotland.

However, there is still a difference pre- and post-transfer in England because most local authorities contribute to the housing subsidy system from the notional surpluses they are judged to make on their revenue accounts. Once transfer takes place, the new landlord has stand alone accounts and it no longer has to transfer money into (nor can it receive payments from) any subsidy 'pool'. The removal of these payments from the housing subsidy 'pool' is reflected in the imposition of the transfer levy (see above), although this is a one-off capital payment rather than an on-going payment of annual surpluses.

Stock transfer and service to tenants

The case for housing transfer does not rest solely on financial advantage. It provides an opportunity to create new types of provider and to engage smaller bodies that are based in, or are closer to, the communities where the homes are transferred. Transfer can help to improve the diversity of housing management. It may result in greater tenant involvement, particularly their direct involvement as members of the board of the transfer body. The government argues that it also helps to separate out local authorities' strategic responsibilities from their landlord functions. The transfer body may have, or may develop, the resources to take on wider community development and neighbourhood regeneration that improve conditions more generally.[25]

---

25   Examples of this are contained in the report by HACAS Chapman Hendy (2002) *Beyond Bricks and Mortar – Bringing Regeneration into Stock Transfer*, CIH, Coventry.

In addition to promises about rents, mentioned above, transfer is normally based on promises to deliver improvements to the housing stock and housing services within certain timescales. A study by the National Audit Office has shown that the majority of transfer bodies set up before 1998 have now met these promises.[26] In terms of the performance of transfer bodies compared either with local authority landlords or with traditional housing associations, there seems to be little evidence of significantly better tenant services. However, it has been argued[27] that the new bodies are distinct in various ways, such as:

- their single-minded focus on housing service objectives;
- their more managerialist and entrepreneurial tendencies;
- their less hierarchical, more inclusive and more egalitarian working regimes.

Many also improve the level of tenant involvement compared to their predecessor organisations.

As Pawson has pointed out:[28]

> 'These kinds of changes are generally fairly consistent with the tenets of New Public Management and it is true that NPM-style reforms have been widely attempted by local authority landlords over the past decade. Nevertheless, there seems little doubt that, freed of some of the constraints which limit the application of such reforms in the LA context, they have been implemented much more fully by transfer HAs.'

Stock transfer therefore creates new bodies that fit into a wider approach to delivery of public services that goes well beyond housing (see Chapter 8).

Arms length management organisations

Arms length management organisations (ALMOs) have a relatively recent history (see Figure 10.6) yet they are already beginning to rival stock transfer in terms of the amount of council housing stock they cover. By April 2005, there were 49 ALMOs operating or being set up, covering 740,000 homes. Subsequent ALMO 'rounds' are expected to take the total above that for stock transfer.

The principle behind an ALMO is fundamentally different from that of stock transfer. The essence is that an authority setting up a successful ALMO receives extra government subsidy, enabling it to make the investment needed to bring its homes up to the Decent Homes Standard. There is no transfer of ownership, only the 'separating out' of the management of the stock to a company that consists largely of the council's former housing management staff. Most ALMOs cover the whole of a council's stock, but there are some exceptions.

---

26 National Audit Office (2003) *Improving Social Housing Through Transfer*: Report by the Comptroller and Auditor General, The Stationery Office, London.
27 Pawson, H., 'Reviewing Stock Transfer' in Wilcox, S. (2004) *UK Housing Review* 2004/05, CIH/CML, Coventry.
28 ibid.

Figure 10.6: How the ALMO model developed

The 1997 Labour government was interested in an alternative to stock transfer and the then housing minister Hilary Armstrong was keen on separating councils' landlord role from their other housing functions. CIH and the Local Government Association decided to look again at the options that might be pursued.

CIH had already tried and failed to sell the idea of what it called 'local housing corporations' to Labour in opposition. This involved setting up arms length companies, owned by the council, to which the stock would be transferred. They would operate under what would now be called a prudential borrowing regime, but would also – like housing associations – be able to raise funds privately.

It was clear that Hilary Armstrong couldn't go that far. So the 1999 report *New structures for council housing*, jointly published by CIH and LGA, looked at a range of options for separating out the landlord role and increasing investment, of which only the last went as far as stock transfer. The fourth option was called a 'local management company', and it turned out to be a concise description of what later became the ALMO.

The key features were the setting up of a council-owned company to manage the housing stock, with councillors and tenants on the board. There would be a contract between it and the council and the company would manage the capital programme as well as dealing with housing management. Subsidy would be received on a long-term basis rather than through yearly decisions. Where the 'local management company' idea differed from what were to become ALMOs was in the extent of financial autonomy that the CIH/LGA report envisaged.

There was already one model for a local management company in existence, the Kensington & Chelsea Tenant Management Organisation, which was to become one of the first ALMOs. But there were no precedents for any housing company having all the powers which ALMOs were to enjoy. Further work would be needed to develop the ALMO model into a live option that councils could adopt.

Eventually the government began to take interest and then the April 2000 green paper said that arms length companies with greater borrowing freedoms would be permitted as a further option for high-performing councils. The government set up an implementation group with the LGA, CIH and practitioners to work out the details. Later in 2000 the ALMO model was born, complete with company rules and the basic documentation needed for councils to get started.

However, the key step was to establish how ALMOs would be financed. The Treasury had refused to budge from its strict rules about what is and isn't counted as public spending, but seemed to be persuaded that more public subsidy should be available if it was going to be well spent. The spending review in July 2000 finally confirmed that this extra subsidy would be in place from 2002 onwards.

Source: adapted from an article in *Inside Housing*, 14 May 2004.

In this section we consider the requirements and process for establishing an ALMO and gaining access to additional investment, the relationship between the ALMO and the council, tenant involvement and the financial and performance aspects of the ALMO's operations. Prospects for further development of the ALMO 'model' in future government policy are considered later in the chapter.

Requirements and process for establishing an ALMO

As with stock transfer, a council wishing to set up an ALMO must apply for consent to assign the management of its stock, under s27 of the Housing Act 1985. But additionally it must 'bid' for the investment funding it requires from government. In practice the two steps are combined in an application to one of the government's bidding rounds, announced periodically.

In order to make a bid, a council must already have carried out an option appraisal process (described later in this chapter) that identifies an ALMO as the preferred option. The bid must also demonstrate:[29]

- how the setting up of the ALMO will separate the council's strategic housing role from its 'landlord' role, give the ALMO genuine management freedom, involve tenants and lead to a better housing service;
- how the council expects to be able to improve its performance so as to meet the government's performance tests (see below);
- how the extra resources for which the council is bidding will enable the Decent Homes Standard to be achieved by the 2010 target; and,
- how the plans for the ALMO fit in with demand for the housing stock and help to deliver sustainable communities in the local authority area (up to 5 per cent of the funds can be earmarked for works aimed at improving sustainability).

The bid must include an assessment of the investment needed to achieve the DHS, and this will depend on the authority having carried out a rigorous stock condition survey. Originally, ALMOs were able to bid for up to £5,000 extra capital per property, but this limit has been replaced by an assessment method using an ALMO 'building costs model'. The model requires stock condition information for a range of housing archetypes and allows estimates to be made of the expenditure needed on various categories of repair and improvement over thirty years. As well as demonstrating ALMOs' progress in meeting the Decent Homes Standard, the model looks at wider aspects such as value-for-money and the general viability of the scheme. The model also requires the recording of all relevant sources of funding available to the local authority in order to check that the bid for ALMO funding is sufficient – but no more than needed – to achieve the decent homes target.

Approval of its bid under one of the ALMO rounds is the first step in the process of securing extra resources. The authority must then get tenants' approval (see below), obtain the formal ODPM consent and then set up the ALMO and assign management of the stock to it.

---

29 These and other steps in the process are set out more fully in government guidance – see, for example, ODPM (2004) *Guidance on Arms Length Management of Local Authority Housing*, ODPM, London.

The next crucial test, and one that marks out ALMOs from the other options, is that the ALMO must secure a 'good' (2 star) or 'excellent' (3 star) rating for services that it provides, in a Best Value inspection by the Audit Commission's housing inspectorate. Getting one of the two highest ratings on inspection is the trigger to release of the additional government subsidy required if the ALMO is to make the investment required in the stock. Up to mid-2004, four out of five ALMOs that had been subject to inspections had achieved the required performance level. An ALMO that fails the test can re-apply, although this may of course mean some delay in its investment plans.

The relationship between an ALMO and the local authority

An ALMO is a company that is owned by the local authority. It is possible for an ALMO to be formed from a tenant management organisation (TMO), as happened in Kensington and Chelsea, but the vast majority of ALMOs are newly-formed bodies. The formal relationship between the two is structured by the constitution of the ALMO and the agreement or contract between the ALMO and the authority.

The ALMO's constitution is likely to be based on a model devised in the process of developing the new ALMO arrangements (see Figure 10.6). It will be governed by a board of directors that will have council nominated directors, tenant directors and independently-appointed directors.

Whereas the constitution is permanent (although with provisions for making changes) the agreement between the authority and the ALMO will run for a fixed period, typically five years or ten years. It sets out the functions that will be carried out by the ALMO (as against those that will be retained by the authority), the authority's expectations about performance and on issues such as tenant involvement, and arrangements for monitoring them. It also covers the financial arrangements and the obligations of each party.

Quite apart from the formal arrangements, the relationship between the housing management service and the remainder of the council's functions will be radically changed by the creation of the ALMO. For example, most ALMOs have chosen names that are distinct from the council's (e.g. Salford's is called 'New Prospect'), and many have established new offices or changed their identity in other ways. In this way council housing is re-labelled (or 'reinvented') while still remaining in council ownership. At the same time, ALMOs necessarily have a closer relationship with the authority than is the case with transfer.

The housing functions left with the authority itself include those non-landlord operations that are carried out by authorities which have transferred their stock, including the strategic housing role and services such as dealing with homelessness or private sector renewal (although the actual division of functions varies from one ALMO authority to another). The authority normally retains and administers its Housing Revenue Account and must establish an effective 'client side' relationship with the ALMO, neither of which is the case with stock transfer. Although investment funding is based on borrowing by the council, the programme of carrying out the works is invariably delegated to the ALMO.

Relationship between an ALMO and tenants

Tenants are expected to be involved from the outset in developing the ALMO, and there must be a positive test of tenant opinion – usually a ballot – before the ALMO is approved by ODPM. In practice, ALMOs have attracted more support in such ballots than have stock transfers, although in one well-known instance – Camden – tenants rejected the ALMO even though the high performance of the authority would have guaranteed it the extra investment funds. This has fuelled demands for a so-called 'fourth option' (see below).

Tenant board members have a particularly important role, and in many cases have already become an important element of the ALMO, in some ways replacing the traditional role of the councillor on a local authority housing committee. As board members, tenants have more power than they would as tenant representatives on a council committee, where their role is only advisory.

Most ALMOs have taken other steps to strengthen their relationship with tenants, often in similar ways to stock transfer bodies. A crucial difference, however, and one which is often important in debates about establishing an ALMO, is that tenants remain 'secure' tenants of the local authority, whereas under transfer they become 'assured' tenants of the new landlord. (This distinction will disappear if proposals for a single form of tenancy are proceeded with in England and Wales, as has already happened in Scotland.)

Financial aspects of the ALMO's operations

The funding available to ALMOs amounted (in capital terms) to £2 billion additional investment over the first three years since ALMO funding began in 2001/02. This capital sum is not however paid to local authorities. Instead, the authorities bid for additional HRA subsidy based on the extra borrowing they expect to require, once they have considered the other resources available to achieve the DHS, such as the major repairs allowance (see Chapter 12). The extra subsidy is paid annually and is based on the actual costs of the extra borrowing. Under the prudential regime, supplementary credit approvals (that used to be required for the borrowing) are no longer needed.

The agreement between the ALMO and the authority specifies the resources that the ALMO is able to use. It will normally include all the investment resources mentioned above, together with the use of any HRA reserves. In terms of revenue resources, the ALMO will normally collect rents on behalf of the authority, and receive a management fee based on the rents, subsidy and other income to the HRA. In most cases (but not all) responsibility for managing the HRA remains with the council.

Both capital and revenue resources will be covered by the ALMO's business plan. This is usually, but not invariably, a distinct document from the authority's HRA business plan, but obviously there has to be a close relationship between the two. Despite the closeness of the ALMO's financial relationship with the council, it is not free of risk to the ALMO. It has to manage its costs in relation to its income. So, for example, many ALMOs have met or expect to meet difficulties caused by sale of properties through the right to buy, because their management fee from the council is reduced but their day-to-day costs may not fall by an equivalent amount.

Performance aspects of the ALMO's operations

The most important aspect of an ALMOs performance is that it meets and retains the standard needed to secure at least a 'two star' rating from the Audit Commission and is therefore eligible for and continues to receive the ALMO allowance towards its investment costs. After the initial inspection there are further inspections to monitor performance.

Other ways in which ALMOs' performance is monitored are:

- Monitoring and publishing performance indicators, through the HouseMark ALMO performance improvement club.[30]
- Establishing performance targets in its business plan and reviewing progress against them as the plan is reviewed annually.
- Monitoring of and research into ALMO performance, particularly the achievement of the decent homes target, by the ODPM.
- Reporting to its board and to tenants through newsletters and other means.
- Undertaking tenant satisfaction surveys.

Early assessments based on results from HouseMark's ALMO performance improvement club indicate that ALMOs are performing well and are on target to achieve the decent homes target.[31] Tenant satisfaction levels are also reportedly higher than for council housing generally.

In many ways the ultimate test of an ALMO's performance is its acceptability to its customers and to the local authority. Unlike transfer, the ALMO depends on a renewable contract, that can be terminated or that the authority can refuse to renew if performance is inadequate. Whereas the stock transfer body needs to retain the confidence of its funders, the ALMO needs to retain the confidence of the parent authority if it is to have a continued existence.

The private finance initiative

PFI schemes to refurbish council housing might be regarded as the 'Cinderella' option of those available, because only a few schemes have been initiated and

---

30 See www.housemark.co.uk
31 See Perry, J. 'Full Speed Ahead' in *Inside Housing*, 14 May 2004.

those that are now being implemented were in preparation for a long time. Like an ALMO, PFI is a way of funding housing improvement without transferring ownership of the stock. Unlike ALMOs, the investment funds are borrowed privately although extra subsidy is required in the form of 'PFI credits', that in the case of HRA housing are an additional form of HRA subsidy. The private finance initiative generally is described in Chapter 5. Here we deal solely with PFI as an option for refurbishment of council housing, describing the way it works, its advantages and disadvantages, and progress to date.

The PFI option for council housing

A PFI refurbishment project normally relates to an estate or neighbourhood, not to the whole of a local authority's stock. It is therefore an option that is likely to be combined with others as part of a strategy for achieving the DHS. The local authority retains ownership of the stock and the tenants retain their secure tenancies. A consortium of private sector firms (typically a lender, a housing association and a building contractor) raise capital to refurbish homes under a contract negotiated with the local authority. The contract may typically last 30 years. The consortium provides repairs, maintenance and possibly housing management services to the stock over this period.

Resources to support the capital element of the projects are provided by central government in the form of PFI credits. The revenue element of projects is supported by the normal Management and Maintenance Allowance (see Chapter 12). The private consortium is paid a performance-based fee by the local authority. Performance is measured against the local authority's output specification for the stock, which describes the desired level of service. The private consortium is only paid in full if the agreed standards are met.

Establishing a PFI project

As we shall see, one of the difficulties in establishing PFI successfully has been the complexity of the issues, financial obstacles and the sheer length of time that projects have required. Any description of the process is therefore bound to be a simplification. As with the other options, PFI must proceed from an options appraisal. There must also be a test of its acceptability to tenants but, as with ALMOs, this need not be a ballot.

Once the government announces a 'round' of bids for PFI refurbishment schemes (which, as with ALMOs, it does periodically but not to a regular annual timetable), the steps are these:

1. Submit an 'expression of interest' in the PFI round, complying with any criteria for bids in that round.
2. Complete a standard spreadsheet that examines the financial impact of the scheme and the likely requirement for PFI credits.
3. Scan the market for potential contractors (so-called 'soft market testing').

4. Once the scheme is accepted for entry into the round, complete an outline business case (OBC) for the project and submit it to the ODPM.
5. Prepare an outline specification, which begins to describe the expected outcomes of the project and the performance required of the contractor.
6. For bids approved by the Project Review Group (which reviews all local government PFI bids), the next stage is – advertise the contract in the Official Journal of the European Communities (OJEC) and begin the procurement process.
7. Produce invitations to tender that go to short-listed contractors.
8. Produce the output specification, typically saying what outputs are expected but not how they are to be achieved.
9. Devise the payment mechanism, which sets out how payments are made and the rules for matters such as the circumstances in which payments can be reduced and by how much.
10. Set out the contract terms, that must comply with the published criteria, known as the Standardisation of PFI Contracts.
11. Receive and evaluate bids, select the preferred contractor and negotiate the final terms of the contract.
12. Submit the final business case (FBC) to the ODPM for approval of PFI credits.
13. Sign and initiate the contract.

The output specification, payment mechanism and contract terms are the three key elements of the PFI contract. They are described in more detail in Figure 10.7.

Experience to date
By mid-2004, three authorities (Manchester, Islington and Reading) had established PFI refurbishment contracts, and a number of others were in the pipeline. Following the Spending Review 2004 the government announced a further round of PFI schemes for refurbishment of council housing, with £360 million allocated annually from 2005/06 for three years for further rounds.

Advantages and disadvantages of PFI
PFI's biggest advantage is that, because there is no transfer of property, the issue of valuation does not arise. This means that PFI may be more appropriate than stock transfer in situations where low values or uncertain housing markets might make transfer problematic. PFI can also sit comfortably with regeneration initiatives that might be needed in such estates. One possibility therefore is to combine use of PFI for particularly difficult estates with another option such as transfer for the remainder of the authority's stock.

PFI shares with the ALMO option the advantage that the stock remains council owned, and the tenants remain secure tenants of the authority. Like an ALMO, the PFI governance arrangements can provide opportunities for tenants to take part in the management of the contract and hence of the service they receive.

Figure 10.7: Elements of a PFI contract to refurbish council housing

---

1. The output specification

This sets out what the council and tenants expect of the contractor or 'operator'. It is written in terms of outputs or outcomes. This means specifying what the local authority wants to see as a result of the project, rather than how they expect the operator to achieve that result. This allows the private sector to bring innovative ways of thinking and working into the project.

Example
   'Ensure that the estate is safe for residents and visitors at all times' is an output.
   'Provide 24 hour security patrol' is an input.

The first example allows the operator to choose the most appropriate method of making the estate safe, which may or may not be a 24 hour patrol.

The second ties them into something which could be inappropriate, ineffective, unpopular or poor value-for-money. The authority will assess bidders' proposals as part of the overall evaluation of bids.

2. The payment mechanism

The output specification has two elements to it, both of which are linked to the payment received by the operator:

- *Availability standards*, which relate to the physical condition of the dwellings. An availability standard could be *'homes should be watertight at all times'*. This might mean that a home with a leaking roof did not meet the availability standard and was therefore 'unavailable'. Available homes are the basic unit of payment. For example, if 450 out of 500 homes on an estate are available, and the council pays £10 per day for each available unit, the contractor would receive £4,500 out of a possible £5,000 for that day.
- *Performance standards*, which relate to how well the operator carries out the services it is responsible for. A performance standard could be: *'98 per cent of requests for emergency repairs must be answered within 12 hours to receive full payment'*. If the contractor only answers 96 per cent of emergency requests within 12 hours during a given month a certain percentage of its payment for that month would be deducted.

The impact on payment of not meeting the standards is formally set out in the 'payment mechanism'.

3. The contract terms

This contains the legal framework for the contract between the operator and the council.

Source: adapted from *Housing Private Finance – A Tenant's Guide* available at www.odpm.gov.uk

PFI is distinct from both ALMOs and stock transfer in that the contractor is deriving an income from the contract and the level of the income relates to performance – in other words there is a direct financial incentive for good performance or disincentive for poor performance. Contracts are long-term, so payments will depend on the quality of day-to-day services such as repairs or estate security in addition to performance in delivering the initial refurbishment work. Tenants can be actively involved both in preparing the specification (including the performance standards expected) and in monitoring the contract over the longer term.

The main disadvantage of PFI has been its complexity and the long time period needed to set up contracts. For this reason many authorities are sceptical as to the value of PFI in delivering the Decent Homes Standard within the ten-year target period. Because PFI is only really appropriate for use in single estates or neighbourhoods, other options are likely to be needed for the rest of an authority's stock. Unless expertise in PFI projects is already available, there will be a need to establish an expert 'client side' for the PFI contract to secure its effective implementation and management.

For these reasons the use of PFI is likely to remain limited, and it will take time for the relatively few contracts now underway to prove whether PFI has something to offer in refurbishing council stock that cannot be achieved by other options. PFI has both enthusiastic proponents and detractors – but the reality is that the case for PFI must be considered 'not proven' until there is more evidence of the outcomes in those places where projects have started.

Appraising the options for investment in council housing

As we have seen, in addition to stock retention, there are other options by which councils can seek to meet the standards required of them in the time available. As we have also seen, good practice (and government policy) requires that councils do not simply choose a particular option for (say) ideological reasons, but that the choice results from a vigorous appraisal of the options and comparison with the 'status quo' of stock retention. All councils in England, Scotland and Wales are required to go through this process, but the terminology, requirements and timescales all differ. Figure 10.8 summarises the position.

Figure 10.8: Summary of option appraisal requirements in England, Scotland and Wales

Term used	Required by (date)	Standard to be met	Target date (to meet standard)
England Option appraisal	July 2005	Decent Homes Standard (DHS)	2010
Scotland Option appraisal; Standard Delivery Plan (SDP) where stock retention	April 2005	Scottish Housing Quality Standard (SHQS)	2015
Wales Business plan	Initial versions, September 2002 Final versions, 2004	Welsh Housing Quality Standard (WHQS)	2012

In one sense options appraisal is an intrinsic part of business planning and cannot be separated from it. The special circumstances that apply in social housing, however, require an identifiable options appraisal stage. This is because of the link between securing the investment and a decision on the future management and ownership of the stock. Delivery of the investment may well require a new organisation such as a stock transfer body or ALMO, which will then develop its own business plan showing (amongst other things) how it will achieve that. Option appraisal is therefore normally a one-off process, whereas business planning is continuous.

This section of the chapter outlines the process of appraising and choosing options, based on the guidance applying in England, Scotland and Wales.

The objectives of option appraisal

The essential objectives in making the appraisal are:

- establishing the present condition of the housing stock and where and how far it falls short of the desired standard;
- identifying the investment requirements to meet the desired standard within the target time period;
- appraising the options for delivering the investment and achieving the target; and,
- selecting the most effective option for the circumstances of the particular local authority.

In addition, the authority may want to add further objectives, for example about improving the housing service more generally or putting it in a better position to meet housing demand.

Steps in the option appraisal process

The stages in the option appraisal process are likely to be these:[32]

1. *Identifying key stakeholders.* This will clearly involve the tenants, future tenants, councillors and staff, together with local community interests, and outside bodies such as government agencies.

2. *Defining objectives.* The over-arching objective is to ensure that housing complies with the defined standard by the target date and will continue to comply with it thereafter. As already mentioned, authorities may want to add other objectives, such as ones to improve the quality of the housing service generally or reconfigure the stock to meet demand.

---

32   Adapted from Communities Scotland (2004) *Option Appraisal – Guidance for Local Authorities* (see www.communitiesscotland.gov.uk)

3. *Establishing information requirements.* Obvious information requirements for an appraisal will include:
    - assessment of future demand for housing;
    - audit of current stock condition and likely life of key components, what remedial work is needed to bring housing up to the required standard and to keep the housing at or above the standard in the future;
    - forecasts of all future revenue streams, capital income, expenditure profiles;
    - performance on key aspects such as re-let times, rent collection, ad hoc repair times, delivery of investment through the capital programme;
    - a review of demolition and re-build programmes and costs.

4. *Managing the process.* A steering group with clear, timed and specific objectives will need to oversee the whole process and ensure the involvement of stakeholders at key stages.

5. *Resourcing the option appraisal.* Carrying out a comprehensive option appraisal will require a range of resources over the appraisal process. Some will be found in-house, other more specialist services may need to be brought in.

6. *Property information and condition.* It is essential that the business plan has current, robust data on stock condition, composition and the costs of management, renovation and improvement. This will involve both an initial stock condition survey and the setting up of a property database that is flexible enough to adapt to changing circumstances, include new factors as they become apparent and produce reports for questions liable to be asked of the database. Such a database will also assist in the monitoring, planning, costing and undertaking of cyclical maintenance. Consideration will need to be given to how the relevant data are collected and updated and that the lifecycles of building components are taken into account.

7. *Housing demand.* In addition to the physical condition of the housing stock there will need to be consideration of likely future demand for housing. This assessment should look at needs against the type of housing stock available, and ensure that the long-term planning delivers appropriate housing.

8. *Housing service improvements.* Consideration should be given to current service levels and the expected ability of the authority to improve/maintain them. For example, in relation to the ALMO option (in England), an authority will need to establish whether and how it can meet the required performance requirements.

9. *Financial analysis: resource and expenditure needs.* It is essential that there is a good understanding of all cost and revenue streams of the current

organisation, and an analysis of the funding streams of the different options, over a 30-year term. The key variables underpinning the profile should be explicitly identified and sensitivity analysis carried out on the central assumptions to assess the likelihood of any variation affecting the delivery of the required standard. Resources available will be influenced by factors including:

- inflation – general and building costs and movements in interest rates;
- rental income;
- central government subsidy;
- right to buy receipts;
- other income.

10. *Financial analysis: comparisons.* The likely resource levels should then be compared with cost forecasts. By comparing different options it will be possible to identify the most cost-efficient way to deliver the required standard. Care needs to be taken to ensure that appraisals avoid being over optimistic about what can be delivered for a given cost.

11. *Establishing the 'stock retention ' option.* Probably the most important part of the appraisal process is assessment of the outcome from a continuation of the current policy with the current level of resources. This will indicate whether it will deliver the required standard within the target period and provides the benchmark against which to assess the further options under consideration. It is important to note that the requirement is to meet and then *maintain* the housing at or above the required standard.

12. *Identifying and evaluating each of the alternatives.* The appraisal needs to assess each of the options to discover whether they deliver the objectives, and the costs of doing so. The appraisal will need to consider whether a 'whole stock' approach is appropriate or a mixed strategy involving various options. The evaluation should also consider aspects such as:

- tenancy terms under the different options;
- opportunities for greater tenant involvement in management of their housing in future;
- future governance and accountability for housing;
- the authority's corporate and wider strategic housing objectives;
- impact of options on the rest of the authority's finances (capital and revenue);
- impacts on staffing arrangements.

13. *Agreeing a decision and the way forward.* There is the possibility that the most appropriate option may be only marginally better than a second (or third) option from a first review. As the process proceeds these options will need to be kept under review because as additional information comes available there is the possibility that the appropriate order of options may

change. There may also be a degree of subjectivity in the analysis over which parties may disagree, however at some point a final decision will need to be made as to the most appropriate option, recognising that this decision has been taken based on the available information. Once the decision has been taken then the plans need to be implemented on the basis of that decision.

14. *Tenant and leaseholder involvement.* For all option appraisals it will be a requirement that tenants are consulted, meaningfully involved in the process and as a result have a significant input into the conclusions and the final option chosen.

15. *Approval by government agencies.* On completion the appraisal will be formally sent to the appropriate government agency for approval or 'signing off'. Each agency has established criteria for judging the appraisals covering issues such as the robustness of the data and the financial appraisal, and the involvement of tenants.

Steps following the option appraisal

If the outcome of the appraisal is that the authority should proceed to stock transfer or (in England) an ALMO or PFI project, then the procedures involved are as described earlier in this chapter. One possible outcome is that the chosen option is subsequently rejected by tenants, for example through a stock transfer ballot. This would require the appraisal to be redone, attempting to identify another option more likely to be accepted by tenants.

If the outcome of the appraisal is that the authority should retain all or part of its housing stock and can meet the required standard from expected resources, its business plan will need to show robustly how this is to be achieved and will need continuous monitoring against the standard and the target timetable. In Scotland, authorities that retain their stock have to prepare and obtain approval of a 'delivery plan' (essentially a business plan) showing how this will be done.

In the event of the government agency rejecting the options appraisal the authority will of course be unable to pursue any option other than stock retention, and may well be open to the sanctions available to government through the resource allocation process or otherwise.

There are already some examples of authorities reaching a 'stalemate' position where tenants have rejected one or more options and it is not clear how the authority can proceed. In 2004, the London Borough of Camden reached this position, having considered the various options and having had the ALMO option rejected by tenants in a ballot. This has fuelled demands for a so-called 'fourth option', which we now consider in the final section of this chapter.

Further possible options for council housing

The debate about the future financing and institutional arrangements for council housing dates back at least to the time of the first stock transfers. Some of the present possibilities open to councils – transfer to local housing companies, management of housing by ALMOs, and the prudential borrowing regime (see Chapter 9) – are themselves responses by government at different times to this debate. Nevertheless, there is a view that the current options are insufficient and require too great a departure from the present ways of running council housing, and are therefore branded as 'privatisation'.[33] Proponents of council housing in its present form may simply argue for more resources through the present system of housing subsidy.

Others argue for financial or institutional change, beyond or instead of the changes that have already taken place. Their objectives are varied, but often include:

- allowing councils the same financial freedoms as housing associations;
- changes in the rules about public borrowing and the way they limit borrowing for investment in council housing;
- addressing the structural weaknesses of the present system of financing council housing, for example its dependence on cross-subsidy of one council by another, and putting the system on a more sustainable basis.

Some of these issues have already been considered in Chapter 5, and it would be impossible to give here a full presentation of all the wider possibilities that have been suggested at various times. This final section therefore outlines briefly four of the main proposals, and readers are referred to the source material for fuller information on each. We also include a note on possible developments in Northern Ireland.

Further development of the ALMO model

Given that the ALMO model is relatively new and that it already combines the principle of retaining council ownership of the stock with the availability of additional investment, it obviously offers promising prospects for further development. Indeed, in the Communities Plan the government offered further 'financial freedoms' based on an earlier consultation paper.[34] ALMO authorities have argued vigorously for further freedoms, as the current funding regime effectively means that after delivering the decent homes target they will return to present levels of resources, with all their limitations.

---

33 Term used frequently by Austin Mitchell MP in a Westminster Hall parliamentary debate, 30 June 2004.
34 ODPM (2002) *The Way Forward for Housing Capital Finance*; see also Chapter 5.

Amongst the possibilities that have been put forward for ALMOs are:[35]

- restructuring their debt, so that more of their resources (e.g. rental income) are available to finance investment or activities such as wider community regeneration;
- allowing them to retain a higher proportion of capital receipts;
- allowing them to retain the income from increased rents, rather than having this lead to reductions in subsidy.

All of these would be feasible without further institutional change, but would require government either to find extra resources or to forego resources that it obtains from the pooling of receipts or rental incomes. In 2005, an ODPM review group was considering options for the future of ALMOs, and a joint project between CIH, HouseMark and the National Federation of ALMOs put forward proposals similar to those above.

Local housing corporations

The original model for local housing corporations pre-dates ALMOs and can be seen as one of its antecedents (see Figure 10.6).[36] Now that ALMOs exist, one possibility is that they be allowed to develop into local housing corporations, with greater financial freedoms. This would however require two fundamental changes. One is that the government permits (and the authorities and tenants concur with) transfer of the stock to a council-owned company, derived from the ALMO. The other is that this company – the local housing corporation – is not subject to the same constraints on its financial operations as a local authority. In particular, the government would have to take advantage of international accounting conventions that would enable its borrowing to be considered outside the government sector (see Chapter 5). Currently, neither of these fundamental changes seems likely to take place.

Prudential borrowing with additional resources

Prudential borrowing, introduced across British local government in April 2004, was originally said to offer new possibilities to councils to bring in investment for council housing whilst retaining the stock. However, as we pointed out in Chapter 9, whilst there are increased opportunities in other services as a result of the prudential borrowing regime, they are severely limited in the case of council housing in England and Wales by the operation of the subsidy system. However, interest in a further option that would take advantage of the new regime has been fuelled both by the fact that it does offer a further option in Scotland (effectively because most Scottish councils do not have to pool notional 'surpluses' as do English councils) and by one of the possibilities considered in the government's

---

35 See for example Perry, J. 'Full Speed Ahead' in *Inside Housing*, 14 May 2004.
36 The case for local housing corporations is set out in Hawksworth, J. and Wilcox, S. (1995) *Challenging the Conventions – Public borrowing rules and housing investment*, CIH, Coventry.

consultation paper *The Way Forward for Housing Capital Finance*.[37] This suggested the idea of creating an 'investment allowance' as part of the HRA subsidy system that would create 'headroom' for additional borrowing under the prudential regime.

A range of Labour MPs has put forward this proposal as a possible 'fourth option'.[38] The difficulty is that the government has not yet pursued the investment allowance idea and that it would inevitably require extra resources that would (under present rules) form part of government expenditure.

Securitisation

A final possibility, originally put forward by the Local Government Association, is called securitisation. Although publicised as a retention option, securitisation would involve transfer of the housing stock to a local authority-owned company for at least 35 years.[39]

To ensure that the finance raised is not local authority borrowing (that by statute cannot be earmarked to specific projects) the proposal requires:

- transfer of the housing stock to a wholly-owned local authority company (LACO);
- the LACO to set up a private sector special purpose vehicle (SPV) to issue bonds in the capital markets;
- management of the housing to be by contract with the LACO, but with payments made to the contractors by the SPV;
- monitoring and control of management performance by the SPV;
- tenants to have assured tenancies, as with large scale voluntary transfer (LSVT);
- tenant consultation and a positive ballot before transfer, as with LSVT.

A change in government policy is required if this option is to proceed, to allow transfer to a council-owned company.

Securitisation is the sale of an asset that provides finance, similar to borrowing. In this case, the securitisation relies on the LACO selling its rental income for 35 years to the SPV. In exchange, the SPV provides finance for:

- the purchase price for the transferred housing to be paid to the local authority;
- the payment of the LACO's management and maintenance costs;
- the capital expenditure programme.

---

37 ODPM, August 2002.
38 See *Inside Housing* 18 June 2004 ('ODPM facing broad coalition of MPs still calling for fourth option') and Sillett, J. (2004) *Housing: The Right to Choose*, LGIU, London.
39 This description is based on a note by Colin Woods of Tribal HCH, dated 30 April 2001.

The SPV raises this finance by issuing highly-rated bonds. The private sector SPV will have effective control of the LACO's management arrangements.

The LGA put forward two principal advantages compared with LSVT:

- the local authority owns the LACO so any surpluses in the future will belong to the local authority rather than to an RSL;
- the cheaper borrowing by the SPV, the longer period of borrowing and the fact that the LACO is local authority owned, rather than an RSL, will enable the valuation (and hence the finance raised) to be significantly higher than with stock transfer.

There are currently no proposals to take this option forward, but one authority (Bolton) did originally put forward a proposal for stock transfer based on a lease rather than a sale, and this has similarities to the securitisation proposal.

Possible developments in Northern Ireland

As we have pointed out, the equivalent of council housing in Northern Ireland is provided by a government agency, the Northern Ireland Housing Executive (NIHE). The debate about the future of council housing in the rest of the UK has prompted some debate about NIHE's future.[40] One option, given that it already operates at arms length from government, might be for it to be given more financial freedom and independence. Another might be to re-establish it as a large housing association able to borrow privately. But also, given its sizeable stock of around 100,000 units, other options might include transfers on an area basis or a version of ALMOs. Mixed approaches, with elements of competition from existing housing associations, might also be feasible. Some of the possibilities being considered in England for restructuring debt could also be appropriate.

It is unlikely that any of these developments will be pursued in the near future, but they have been investigated by the Northern Ireland Department for Social Development and at some stage proposals may be brought forward.

Summary

Levels of investment in council housing have been a pre-occupation of housing policy-makers for many years. The setting of standards that council housing should meet, and target dates for achieving them, have been key developments in policy-making across Great Britain. More direct investment is now taking place in council housing in England, but resources available directly to councils in Scotland and Wales have not increased to the same extent. Further options are available to bring in the investment in the form of private finance, principally through stock transfer.

---

40 See the CIH discussion paper (2001) *Large Scale Voluntary Transfer and the NIHE* (available at www.cih.org/home_ni).

Councils across Britain are now expected both to be more systematic in their planning for the use of resources – by producing business plans – and also specifically to decide which option or package of options they will pursue in order to secure the investment and achieve government standards and targets.

Despite the fact that in England a wider range of options is available to councils, it is here where there have been greatest demands for a further option in which both ownership and management of the stock stays with the local authority, but the required investment can still be made. Until now, government has resisted moves of this kind.

CHAPTER 11:
Local government: housing strategies and the wider housing role

Introduction

Both present and previous governments have encouraged local authorities to develop their strategic housing role, and to separate this role from the one of managing their own housing stock. Where an authority transfers its stock to another landlord, the strategic role becomes its main housing function together with 'non-landlord' services such as homelessness and housing advice. The strategic housing role embraces both public and private housing, and both delivery of new housing and intervention in existing housing. There are also wider housing services which the authority operates, including wider neighbourhood renewal programmes, approving renovation and disabled facilities grants, facilitating borrowing by owners for improvement, organising area renewal programmes, providing services to private landlords and tenants, and promoting affordable housing development.

The aim of this chapter is not to give a full description of all of these activities but to outline them and to consider the financial arrangements for them. The chapter does not repeat the material on housing investment strategies in Chapter 9, and Chapter 12 will cover local authority revenue finance in general, including General Fund revenue spending which is the relevant source of finance for most strategic activities and wider services. Part of the context for the strategic housing role is provided by wider strategies and partnerships at local level (community planning, local strategic partnerships, etc.) which are dealt with in Chapter 8.

The chapter begins by considering the local strategic housing role in England, Wales and Scotland, and then deals with specific operational areas that are separate from council housing and constitute the wider housing service. Readers wishing fuller up-to-date information on specific topics (such as homelessness law and practice, the regulations concerning houses in multiple occupation, or the legislative framework for private housing renewal), should consult the latest guidance on government websites.

The national policy context
Overall policy on local housing strategies

The broad strategic framework within which local authorities develop their individual local housing strategies is set by central government. The present government's priorities in England were set out in December 2000 with the publication of the policy statement *The Way Forward for Housing*.[1] It calls for authorities to have 'a stronger strategic role in housing, meeting needs across all types of housing and integrating housing policy with wider social, economic and environmental policies'. Four specific measures highlighted were:

- increasing local authorities' resources and giving them greater flexibility to adopt policies that meet the needs of their communities across all types of housing;
- providing guidance to enable local authorities to carry out proper needs assessments and stock condition surveys to underpin their housing strategies;
- developing closer partnership working between the Housing Corporation and local authorities, in particular ensuring that investment in new social housing meets local priorities; and
- encouraging collaboration between neighbouring local authorities to ensure that problems are tackled effectively and not shifted from place to place, including the problems of low-demand housing.

Policy was strengthened by the Local Government Act 2003 which included a specific power for the Secretary of State (and his Welsh equivalent) to require authorities to have a housing strategy and to be able to specify what the strategy should contain.[2]

The Housing (Scotland) Act 2001 requires Scottish local authorities to undertake a comprehensive assessment of housing needs and conditions, and to produce strategies to tackle the housing problems in their areas. These strategies should include plans to eradicate fuel poverty. In addition, authorities must have regard to the long-term supply of appropriately trained construction management and labour within their areas. Authorities must also ensure that their strategies encourage equal opportunities.

Despite these recent changes the current policy framework should be seen as a development of an approach to local housing planning and management that has been in place for a number of years. From 1987, ministers have made it clear that they expect the primary role of a local housing authority to be a strategic one. In particular, they expect authorities to focus on the identification of housing needs and demands, to encourage innovative methods of provision by other bodies to meet such needs, to utilise private finance, and to encourage participation by the private sector. None of these objectives have been abandoned by the present government. In particular, it is clear that the government expects each authority to improve its performance by showing a greater ability to plan strategically, take an

---

1   ODPM, December 2000.
2   This was the result of joint lobbying by CIH and the LGA, see the paper *Modernising The Legal Basis For Local Authorities' Strategic Housing Role* (CIH/LGA, January 2001, available at http://www.cih.org/policy/paper005.htm).

integrated 'corporate' approach, and deliver high quality services with clear and meaningful involvement of tenants, residents and other local 'stakeholders'.

Recent development of the strategic role

The recent development of the strategic housing role has been influenced by:

- The need to understand housing strategy as an essential element of wider strategies to tackle social exclusion and promote economic, social and environmental well-being, linking it to wider community and corporate strategies (see Chapter 8).
- The increasing diversity of service providers and the need to co-ordinate and guide their activities. This is particularly the case where authorities have transferred their own housing stock or put it into arms length management. Some larger authorities such as Glasgow, Liverpool and Manchester have made transfers to different local bodies, and in these circumstances overall strategic co-ordination becomes particularly important.
- The increased focus on housing markets has provided the driving factor in planning for new housing. This has fundamentally changed the way new market and affordable housing is planned for, making it necessary for local housing and planning departments to work together on housing market assessments and draw on their combined expertise to deliver sustainable housing developments.
- The Planning and Compulsory Purchase Act 2004 that introduced the system of Local Development Schemes to replace local plans in England (and regional spatial strategies at regional level). Local authorities now have to decide themselves on the suite of planning documents they have to produce. It has become good practice for planning and housing departments to work together to prepare a 'housing development and investment document', bringing together and co-ordinating the spatial and investment elements within the statutory planning system. This includes the direction of investment to existing private and public housing and plans for strategic demolition, as well as where new housing is to be located.
- Regional housing strategies (closely linked to regional spatial strategies) as the basis for investment within the English regions. This, together with the rechannelling of Local Authority Social Housing Grant through regional programmes has effectively shifted the focus of investment decision-making to the regional level. It has not interfered with councils' ability to make their own decisions for spending the money they receive. However, it has had the positive effect that local authorities are now working more collaboratively with each other (in sub-regional groups) to draw up strategies to co-ordinate their investment in relation to wider market trends, rather than competing with each other for resources.
- The Housing Corporation's investment partnering programme. The decision to rationalise the ADP programme by choosing a limited number

of housing associations or partnerships for new development and investing in large programmes (£10 million over two years minimum) has reduced the influence of local authorities in commissioning new schemes. They have a growing role though, in determining the mix and location of this and market housing on sites to deliver sustainable communities.

- In Scotland, recognition of the need to take account of wider housing markets in directing new investment, and reconsideration of plans to devolve more power to individual local authorities.[3]

- The strengthened powers which the government is likely to provide whereby planning authorities can determine the mix of market and affordable housing in their areas through planning agreements (see later in this chapter).

- A more strategic approach to investing in private housing in England and Wales following the regulatory reform order in 2002. This ended the previous renovation grant regime and requires local authorities to publish policies setting out how they intend to invest in poor quality housing in their areas.

Housing strategy can now be broadly divided into two types of strategic activity – those that are directly related to the housing market (i.e. planning for new housing, investing in existing housing and clearance of obsolete housing) and those that are less market-oriented such as letting policies, Supporting People policies, homelessness policies and anti-social behaviour strategies.

The new regional strategic housing level has made it even more important to recognise that there are different levels of decision-making (local, sub-regional, regional and national) and it is important that the right decisions are made by the right people at the right level, and that it all fits together into one cohesive strategy.

The strategic housing role of local authorities

Requirements on local authorities

A successful housing strategy should seek to use scarce public resources in a way that is judged to be efficient, effective, equitable and in line with the needs and reasonable expectations of local people (refer to Figure 2.3 in Chapter 2 for a summary of this philosophy). The ODPM, Welsh Assembly Government and Scottish Executive publish guidance on their expectations for local housing strategies. In the past, these (usually annual) submissions were part of the regular timetable by which councils bid for central resource allocations (in England, 'HIP allocations', see Chapter 9). This is no longer the case, for three reasons:

- government has recognised that housing strategy needs to be set over a longer time frame since requiring annual submissions encouraged both short-term thinking and a superficial approach to strategy development;

3   See the paper from Communities Scotland (2004) *Strategic Housing Investment in Scotland.*

- annual allocations of capital resources have become less significant as funding has shifted to revenue support (in England and Wales), and since the introduction of the prudential borrowing regime across Great Britain (see Chapter 9) and the ending of credit approvals; and,
- in England, government policy has changed towards emphasising the regional strategic housing role and to some extent this can be seen as reducing the importance of local housing strategies.

Each government agency has slightly different requirements and the terminology used also varies slightly. In England the ODPM now expects authorities to produce a housing strategy looking at least three years ahead. Guidance is no longer produced annually but is set out on the ODPM website.[4] The Welsh Assembly Government calls for a locally agreed, long-term 'housing vision' with clear objectives and target outcomes consistent with the authority's community strategy, produced on a five-year cycle. It also requires an operational plan setting out interim targets and actions.[5] The Scottish Executive requires authorities to produce five-year local housing strategies.[6] All authorities have now done so.

The elements of a successful housing strategy

Strategy should be seen as an on-going, iterative process with the housing strategy document being a key output which gives a 'snap-shot' of the overall process and interprets it for its users – such as other government agencies, housing associations, private developers, specialist providers and community organisations.

The strategy document should be concise. It should seek to set out the following in a focused way, and compress them into a limited number of interrelated objectives.

1. How the housing authority assesses the state of local housing markets, addresses issues of housing 'affordability' and tackles unmet housing needs.
2. How housing strategy forms a coherent element of the authority's wider corporate strategy. In particular, how intervention in housing will underpin other local strategies designed to expand employment and economic growth, encourage inclusiveness, enhance environmental quality, reduce crime and the fear of crime and regenerate deprived neighbourhoods.
3. The time profile within which the overall strategy is expected to operate.
4. The resources required to deliver it.

---

4   See www.odpm.gov.uk, the section on Effective Housing Strategies and Plans. This guidance was produced by CIH for the ODPM, and the material is drawn on in the text of this chapter.
5   For current guidance see www.wales.gov.uk/subihousing/index.htm
6   For detailed guidance see www.lhs.scot-homes.gov.uk; the guidance draws extensively from the CIH guide *Designing Local Housing Strategies* (CIH, 1998).

5. How the authority has taken account of local views, including tenants' opinions.
6. How the authority will dispatch its mandatory and inferred duties to house the homeless, those living in sub-standard accommodation, and disabled people, and how it will identify and respond to the needs of minority ethnic groups.
7. How housing plans can be seen to fit in to the authority's land-use planning priorities.
8. How the investment in housing will contribute to the improvement of private dwellings in its area.
9. How the authority intends to develop its 'enabling' role through wider partnerships within the public sector, and with the private sector and voluntary organisations.
10. The relationship between the overall housing strategy and other key housing-related strategies or programmes.

All these strategic objectives clearly interrelate and reinforce each other in all sorts of ways. Bearing this in mind, we will now say something about each.

The authority as 'enabler' and 'assessor of need'

The strategic role of local authorities has developed in recent years as their role as enablers has become more prominent. In particular, good authorities now see their role extending to the understanding of the wider housing market in their area, and the part that they might play in it. A housing strategy provides a framework for bringing together the various housing market participants. It should provide a co-ordinated, cross-tenure approach to dealing with local housing problems and issues. In partnership schemes, the local authority will often be expected to play the lead role and co-ordinate the work of the various contributing agencies, firms and voluntary bodies.

There are various players in the local housing market, including councils, private house builders, mortgage lenders, private landlords and housing associations. Each of them will have different reasons for needing to understand how it works. Whether the strategy and the assessment on which it is based will meet their needs, so they can input into it and help deliver it, depends on whether the strategy:

- *covers* both the private housing market as well as the social housing sector;
- *considers* the interaction between tenures;
- *examines* the scope for using the private market to meet housing need;
- *considers* deficiencies in the market and potential measures to improve its efficiency and effectiveness; and,
- *involves* private sector agencies in the assessment process.

Some authorities are bringing together these elements in overall *housing market assessments*, which aim to understand the operation of the whole housing market in their area and how their strategy should respond to it. For example, one authority has built up a picture of 'mover' households (both in-migrants and out-migrants), 'emerger' households (which come from households already living there) and homelessness. This enables them to identify gaps in private sector provision which the social sector should aim to fill.

Understanding local market conditions will enable the strategy to identify and plan to meet the various needs which the market alone is unable or unlikely to address. Most needs fall within one of five categories:

1. needs for works to be done on the existing housing stock;
2. needs for more dwellings or different dwellings (e.g. more large family houses);
3. problems of affordability;
4. problems of management of the stock, e.g. in the private rented sector or low demand or abandonment; and
5. needs for housing-related care and support.

The wider corporate strategy
An effective housing strategy should be treated as part of the authority's wider corporate plans rather than a self-contained arrangement belonging to the housing department. The housing strategy must be consistent with the authority's corporate objectives and overall financial strategy. It should embrace the aims and activities of every department insofar as these affect housing. Current guidelines from all the three government agencies make it clear that 'housing needs' should be seen as part of a wider corporate approach to service delivery that should be developed as part of the government's Best Value philosophy and wider community planning. Authorities are expected to be explicit about how housing investment impacts on other issues such as social and physical regeneration, community safety and welfare to work. The wider frameworks for local authority community planning are dealt with in Chapter 8.

The strategic time profile
Government policy requires local housing strategies to distinguish between their longer-term 'strategic', and their shorter-term 'management', operations. The authority must show that it is planning for the longer term, usually at least five years, by presenting a focused strategy and delivering a Best Value service. Underpinning the overall strategy will be more detailed objectives and targets that will normally be set out in an annual plan. In Wales, authorities actually have to produce two related documents, a longer-term strategy and a shorter-term operational plan. In Chapter 16 we will make the point that financial planners need to distinguish between different planning time profiles (see Figure 16.1) and that a coherent strategy needs to distinguish between current and future costs and revenue streams.

Planning the use of resources
Authorities need to identify all the resources available to them. This does not simply mean the likely levels of finance: resources include land, partnerships,

legal powers and the tenants and residents themselves. The resource assessment should be realistic and take into account the economic climate, known public expenditure programmes, and the degree to which the private sector will be able to contribute.

The extent to which the local housing strategy will direct the use of the authority's own housing resources will vary from place to place, because some authorities will be using almost all their resources on their own housing stock (directed by their council housing business plan). There may be an allocation of funds for private sector renewal (see later in this chapter) and possibly for new facilities, such as hostels, for the homeless. Local authority owned land may be an important resource in providing for new housing development by housing associations or the private sector. Promotion of new affordable housing is dealt with later in this chapter; more information on the use of capital resources is in Chapter 9 and on revenue resources in Chapter 12.

Consultation

As part of its objective of making local authorities more accountable for the services they deliver, they should engage tenants and other stakeholders in the development of local strategies. Tenants' groups and other interested parties must be involved as the strategy is developed – it is not good enough to pass a completed strategy statement out for comment and observation.

It is important that appropriate approaches and methods are used to find out what people and communities are concerned about. Local forums, focus groups, citizens' juries and community conferences are given as examples in the Scottish guidance and the CIH Good Practice Guide.[7]

Best Value principles make it clear that consultation has to embrace more than just the service users. Effective links between housing and other departments will enable the local authority to achieve much more. Liaison with neighbouring authorities also needs to be demonstrated. Outside the local authority, there are numerous bodies and interested parties that need to be involved, including housing associations, police and health authorities, and voluntary bodies, together with local builders, landlords, estate agents and mortgage lenders, and employers.

Specific housing needs

We have already made the point that over the years authorities have been mandated to provide various housing services and this fact establishes a degree of priority spending within their housing plans. In recent years, the two main areas of statutory responsibility have been for homelessness and the renovation of sub-standard private sector housing. Renovation grants and wider renewal of older private housing are discussed later in this chapter.

---

7   Goss, S. and Blackaby, B. (1998) *Designing Local Housing Strategies*, CIH, Coventry.

Because authorities are required to produce specific homelessness strategies we will deal these in the context of related strategies (see below). In this context we will also deal with minority ethnic needs, and needs for care and support.

There are other housing needs which the strategy may identify and address. Housing inequality is by no means limited to BME groups, and disabled people (for example) should have their needs considered in the strategy. In addition to adaptation of existing dwellings (dealt with later in the context of renovation grants), the strategy may want to promote 'Lifetime Homes' or (in Scotland) 'barrier free' housing in new developments.

Other areas of need will emerge from considering the age structure of those in different housing tenures and how this might change. With an ageing population, the needs of growing numbers of older people for smaller dwellings might be particularly important. On the other hand, there may be extended families with unsatisfied needs for larger properties.

The spatial planning dimension

The local housing strategy must recognise that addressing gaps in the local housing market has a spatial/planning as well as a financial/resource dimension. The Sustainable Communities Plan has focused attention on this issue in its proposals to address housing demands in the south-eastern part of England, saying that *'communities are more than just housing. They have many requirements. Investing in housing alone, paying no attention to the other needs of communities, risks wasting money – as past experience has shown.'*[8] It has therefore drawn attention to the need for close integration of housing strategies and development planning so that each complements the other.

For example, one weakness of housing market assessments is that they are sometimes done in isolation and do not clearly feed into an integrated statutory planning process and housing strategy. Assessments are only worth doing if they lead to action by the local authority and other actors in the market. This is more likely to happen if both planning and housing authorities in an area undertake the assessments and resources are deployed in ways which reflect the assessments and will lead to action to address the issues they bring out.

Another important aspect of the relationship is the potential for 'planning gain' from new developments, where the developer either agrees to incorporate affordable housing as part of the scheme or makes a payment which allows development elsewhere. These issues are covered later in the chapter in the context of promoting new affordable housing.[9]

---

8   *Sustainable Communities: Building for the Future* (ODPM, 2003) p5.
9   The whole issue of the relationship between planning and housing, in the context of community sustainability, is discussed in a policy paper by CIH and the Royal Town Planning Institute, *Planning for Housing – the Potential for Sustainable Communities* (CIH/RTPI, June 2003 – downloadable at www.cih.org/policy). On joint strategic working, see also the paper by CIH, LGA and RTPI (2004) *Intelligent Approaches to Housing – Achieving better integration in planning for housing* (available at www.cih.org).

Older private sector housing

Local authorities are expected to utilise their own resources and also to work in partnership with others to develop a strategy for housing renewal. Many larger authorities have specific housing renewal strategies, strategies for dealing with poor conditions in the private rented sector, or strategies for tackling empty properties. The focus of these strategies may be on physical conditions, management issues, or on wider neighbourhood renewal.

More detail on such programmes is given later in this chapter.

The enabling role and wider partnerships

Local authorities now engage in a wide range of partnerships at both strategic and practical levels, and housing strategy is an area where they are likely to be particularly important. This is partly because the authority has only limited powers and resources for intervening directly in the housing market, and will need instead to influence others who may be able to do so. So, for example, new affordable housing needs might be met by housing associations, but may also require partnerships with private developers and with funders such as banks and building societies. Provision for homeless families may involve partnerships with voluntary sector providers who create and run services such as night shelters, hostels for those suffering domestic violence, 'foyers' for young people and so on. Identifying and providing for the needs of BME communities may involve working with BME-led housing associations, faith groups, local community organisations and groups working with those in special need such as asylum seekers and refugees.

Partnerships can therefore be seen as one form of 'resource' or 'delivery mechanism' available to the authority to put its housing strategy into effect, along with its directly-available resources such as its own legal powers, financial resources and staff.

Housing strategies and other related strategies

The local housing strategy, as we have seen, is not the only housing-related strategy which the authority is likely to have. Especially in larger authorities, there are likely to be complementary strategies to which the housing strategy must relate, and special strategies dealing with particular issues or particular aspects of housing need. Below are just some examples of these related strategies.

Homelessness strategies

Authorities across Britain are now expected to have 'homelessness strategies' which set out how they will both deal with and prevent homelessness, and there have been government initiatives focused on aspects of homelessness such as rough sleeping, begging, and the use by authorities of bed-and-breakfast accommodation for families. Clearly the homelessness strategy has to fit within and be an integral part of the wider local housing strategy if it is to be meaningful.

Neighbourhood renewal strategies

Neighbourhood renewal strategies are aimed at the comprehensive improvement of community facilities and quality of life in run-down areas of an authority where only a 'holistic' approach will achieve the required results. Housing is likely to be an important component of neighbourhood renewal, but not necessarily the lead agency. Such programmes may also result in neighbourhood management initiatives,[10] or (in Scotland) be part of wider Social Inclusion Partnerships. More detail on funding for neighbourhood renewal is given later in the chapter.

Strategies for the authority's own housing stock

Quite apart from its overall housing strategy, if the authority has its own stock it will need a business plan and quite possibly an options appraisal for the future of that stock, in particular setting out how it intends to achieve the required standard of improvement and repair. These are discussed in Chapter 10. Their significance for the overall housing strategy is that the stock is itself an important resource for meeting housing need, and the resources it requires for its improvement are a major call on the authority's overall capital investment resources.

BME housing strategies

All public authorities have a duty to promote equality of opportunity and good race relations under the Race Relations (Amendment) Act 2000. Local authorities must therefore ensure that their strategies address equalities issues. Many authorities will want to develop special black and minority ethnic housing strategies, and to carry out surveys of the housing needs and aspirations of BME people.[11] A particular needs group is new migrants, such as asylum seekers and refugees. In addition, many authorities are now addressing wider issues of community cohesion, following the disturbances in 2001 in several northern cities.[12] Specific housing strategies for black and minority ethnic communities are not a statutory requirement but they help to implement the authority's race equality obligations and ensure that the particular and varied needs of BME people are not overlooked or just subsumed into the wider housing strategy.[13]

Energy conservation policies

The Home Energy Conservation Act 1995 (HECA) designated all councils as energy conservation authorities and placed a duty on them to devise strategies that would result in significant improvements of the energy efficiency of the housing stock over 10-15 years. Progress is to be reported on periodically, including the local authority policy (if any) for tackling fuel poverty.

Supporting People

Plans and partnerships for implementing the Supporting People regime (see Chapter 19) have to take account of the availability of and need for housing

---

10   See *Neighbourhood Management: A good practice guide* (CIH, 2001).
11   For an example of this in Bradford, see *Breaking Down the Barriers: Improving Asian Access to Social Rented Housing* (CIH, 2001).
12   See *Community Cohesion and Housing: A good practice guide* (CIH, 2004).
13   For guidance on these, see *Black and Minority Ethnic Housing Strategies* (CIH, 2000).

services. Given the importance of community-based support, and the growing needs of (for example) older people, it is especially important that the housing strategy addresses this link.

Are strategies 'fit for purpose'?

Both the English and Scottish guidance notes set out what a 'fit for purpose' local housing strategy requires. The Scottish guidance says that it must:

- have effective links with other plans and strategies;
- be based on a robust analysis of local housing markets;
- propose actions which are appropriate, prioritised and deliverable;
- make clear how resources will be sourced and used;
- be based on an effective process for developing and delivering the strategy;
- have a suitable monitoring and evaluation framework for measuring progress and outcomes; and,
- be well presented and communicated.

The ODPM says the strategy should:

- set priorities for action;
- ensure that nothing is overlooked (although action in lower priority areas may have to be delayed); and,
- choose the most effective way of making progress in priority areas; and deliver effective action on the ground.

The Audit Commission has set out much more comprehensive 'key lines of enquiry' on local strategies and the enabling role, which describe the characteristics which an excellent service in this area should demonstrate.[14] It has also carried out research into wider housing services in authorities that have transferred their housing stock; the research is often cited as challenging the government's argument that the separation of the strategic role from landlord responsibilities is advantageous.[15]

Local authorities' wider housing role

As we said at the beginning of this chapter, local authorities operate a range of housing services, some statutory and some discretionary, which go beyond their 'landlord' role and therefore exist irrespective of whether a council still has its own housing stock. These services are closely related to the strategic housing role,

---

14 Can be seen at www.audit-commission.gov.uk/housing.
15 The report by the Audit Commission (2002) *Housing after Transfer* concluded that in some cases transfer authorities had 'lost interest' in housing, doing only the minimum to satisfy statutory requirements.

---

partly because some of them are 'enabling' services themselves, such as promoting the voluntary sector or new affordable housing, but also because (like the strategic role) they are usually financed from the authority's General Fund, not its Housing Revenue Account. The pressures on these services therefore have more similarity to those on non-housing services which also depend on the General Fund and are subject to the annual vicissitudes of the Revenue Support Grant settlement and decisions on council tax levels (see Chapter 12).

The second half of this chapter briefly describes these wider services and, particularly, how they are financed.

Promotion of new affordable housing

Although in theory any local authority can use the capital resources available to it (and described in Chapter 9) to build new housing, in practice the level of new council house building is low and likely to remain so. The main way in which an authority seeks to meet new housing needs is by promoting affordable housing development by others.

Since the 1980s the main way of doing this is by securing new development by housing associations. However, local authorities' ability to influence new housing association development is changing. In England, authorities are no longer able to provide Local Authority Social Housing Grant (LASHG) which previously enabled them to recycle their capital receipts into new provision and, in some cases, fund significant development programmes. They have also lost some of their more general influence on housing association development to the new agencies at regional level. Yet in Scotland, authorities which transfer their housing stock are now able to able to receive a new *local housing budget* for their areas, from the Scottish Executive.[16] This can be used to direct funding to housing associations, significantly strengthening the authority's strategic role. Investment by housing associations is considered in detail in Chapter 14.

Local authorities can nevertheless influence housing association development in ways other than through control over investment. One important method is in using their own land. Associations may be encouraged to develop in particular locations and to meet particular needs by the provision of land, especially in places where land is in short supply. Making land available is an important 'bargaining counter' in securing the development which the authority wants.

Another way of securing affordable housing, whether from associations or from the private sector, is through the land-use planning system. Planning authorities are able to require developers either to allocate land for affordable housing as part

---

16 However this recent development is already under question, see the consultation paper by
    Communities Scotland (2004) *Strategic Housing Investment in Scotland*.

of a wider development scheme, or to make financial contributions, known as 'commuted sums', to facilitate either affordable housing development on the same site or on a different site. These so-called 'section 106' agreements (in England and Wales, 'section 75' in Scotland) enable planning authorities to require affordable housing, often built by a housing association, to be provided and to help towards creating 'mixed communities'.

A further way to provide affordable housing is to arrange for its construction by (say) a housing association but for the authority itself (or possibly an ALMO – see Chapter 10) to manage the housing. This may be particularly appropriate for a small development that is part of an existing council estate, and where the new housing is intended to meet a particular need, e.g. for large family accommodation, amongst the local population. Such housing will be outside the HRA and the tenancies will not be secure council tenancies. Only a few authorities have put together development packages of these kinds, and they have usually involved types of private finance initiative (see Chapter 10).

Dealing with homelessness

Since the late 1970s, local authorities have had the duty to provide accommodation for households who are unintentionally homeless. Most authorities have sought to exercise this duty by housing such households in permanent self-contained units within the council's own stock or that of some other social landlord. Where this is not possible, such households have to be housed in temporary (often 'bed-and-breakfast') accommodation until suitable permanent homes become available. (Statutory homelessness duties have been changed in recent years in England, Wales and Scotland, and the reader is referred to more specialist texts for current powers and duties.)

Homeless households accommodated in council dwellings become tenants and the costs of providing their homes and the income received by the authority from housing them is treated as revenue and recorded in the HRA. Temporary accommodation rents, services for the homeless (such as advice centres) and costs of hostel accommodation are charged to the General Fund. If the authority wishes to spend capital monies on providing accommodation for the homeless it has to do so within the capital funding constraints described in Chapter 9.

Many authorities also use General Fund monies to support specialist provision for homeless people and other related needs in the voluntary sector. Examples include emergency night shelters, resettlement services, units meeting special needs such as those suffering from domestic violence or substance abuse, etc. With the introduction of the Supporting People programme (see Chapter 19), another source of funding has opened up for these specialist services. This is also an area where there are often specific government funding initiatives, for example to deal with 'rough sleeping'.

Neighbourhood renewal and challenge funding

Since the 1970s, both central and local government have placed a great deal of emphasis on tackling inner city problems and the regeneration of run-down areas. Whilst not strictly a 'housing' service, this kind of community regeneration activity normally has a housing component and will involve either the housing authority or housing associations as partners.

Housing agencies are often the instigators of neighbourhood renewal, as part of their wider commitment to the 'sustainability' of their existing estates or new developments. If carried out by housing associations, these are sometimes known as 'housing plus' activities (see page 348). Some inner city associations now regard themselves as 'regeneration agencies' as much as they do as 'landlords'. One study of the regeneration activities of inner city stock transfer landlords defines the scope of community regeneration (or neighbourhood renewal, the terms are effectively synonymous) as being a range of actions to tackle social exclusion, including addressing:

- worklessness and poverty;
- crime and fear of crime;
- low standards of educational achievement;
- poor health;
- poor service and transport infrastructure, including lack of play and leisure facilities;
- poor housing and physical environment; and
- the needs of those likely to be disproportionately represented within deprived communities, including BME groups, lone parent households, children and older people.[17]

The existence of two different policy-making systems, local and national, has meant that, in many cases, local authority regeneration initiatives have been promoted through and underpinned by national funding, often in the form of 'challenge funding'. The basic idea behind challenge funding is that limited central government support should be distributed on the basis of competition. This involves 'top-slicing' the overall national allocation and then inviting authorities, and/or their partners, to bid for a share of the top-sliced element against specific project criteria established by ministers. These almost invariably require the bidders to demonstrate that they have fully embraced the partnership approach, involving not just other public agencies such as health or police services but also private sector partners.

The introduction of the Single Regeneration Budget (SRB) for England in 1994 emphasised the Conservative government's commitment to challenge funding as a

---

17 List taken from *Beyond Bricks and Mortar: Bringing regeneration into stock transfer* (CIH, 2002).

mechanism for distributing regeneration resources. In setting up the SRB, housing improvement was identified as a specific objective along with an increase in community safety, the enhancement of the environment, an expansion in community and tenant participation and an improvement in the industrial competitiveness of firms. The fund was set at £1.4 billion in its first year and these public resources were expected to act as a lever to encourage private sector investment.

As part of the Conservative government's commitment to stock transfer, it launched in 1995 the Estates Renewal Challenge Fund (ERCF), intended to facilitate inner city, high-cost transfers. In practice, the available funding was used in many cases to finance wider regeneration activities, notably in places like Poplar (Tower Hamlets) and Optima (Birmingham).[18] In addition, stock transfer bodies also found that they could either build an element of regeneration into their initial business plans, financed as part of the original loan which facilitated the transfer, or were later able to produce surpluses which could be used for regeneration activities.[19]

The Labour government which took power in 1997 placed strong emphasis on tackling social exclusion and on neighbourhood renewal. It established a Social Exclusion Unit in 10 Downing Street which launched a wide-ranging programme of consultation, research and policy development through 'policy action teams' (PATS) drawn from government and the voluntary and private sectors. Their recommendations formed the basis of the government's *National Strategy for Neighbourhood Renewal*.[20] This strategy is now the responsibility of the neighbourhood renewal unit within the ODPM.

There is insufficient space to describe fully the proliferation of renewal and regeneration programmes that have resulted, which may have a bearing on the activities of housing organisations. Here is a brief synopsis of some of the main funding sources in England available as a result of these programmes:[21]

Neighbourhood Renewal Fund
Set at £525 million annually, this fund is aimed at the 88 most deprived local authority areas and helps to 'shore up' mainstream services in poor neighbourhoods. It is aimed particularly at meeting the five main Public Service Agreements (PSAs – see Chapter 8) which describe the government's 'floor targets' for education, jobs, crime, health and housing in poor areas.

---

18 See *Bricks and Mortar* above.
19   The transfer in Partington, Manchester is one such case (also described in *Beyond Bricks and Mortar*).
20 Social Exclusion Unit (1998) *Bringing Britain Together: A national strategy for neighbourhood renewal*, and also Cabinet Office (2001) *A New Commitment to Neighbourhood Renewal*. Cabinet Office, London.
21 Based on NHF (2002) *Neighbourhood Renewal Funding Streams 2002 – At a glance guide* (to which the reader is referred for more detailed information).

Neighbourhood Management Pathfinders
This fund of £45 million over the period 2001-2004 is helping to establish the neighbourhood management initiatives foreseen in the report of PAT 4.[22]

New Deal for Communities (NDC)
The main challenge/partnership fund for neighbourhood renewal, which is directing about £2 billion over ten years into 39 local partnerships aimed at tackling multiple deprivation at neighbourhood level.

Regional Development Agencies' 'Single Pot'
These regionally-disbursed funds now include the SRB mentioned above, total more than £2 billion annually, and are used for a wide range of regional economic development initiatives such as providing sites and infrastructure, loans for small businesses, technology transfer, etc.

Neighbourhood wardens
Funding to promote warden schemes aimed at reducing crime and anti-social behaviour, and maintaining the environment.

In Wales, there is a similar range of programmes. The Communities First programme, worth £83 million over its first three years, is an area-based regeneration fund similar to the NDC, aimed at Wales' most deprived communities. The People First and Sustainable Communities programmes are much more limited funds focused on community-led initiatives.

Scotland also has a range of regeneration initiatives, now focused on Communities Scotland's role as the national housing and regeneration agency. Strategy is set out in the report, *Better Communities in Scotland: closing the gap*, published in 2002.[23] Communities Scotland took over responsibility for 48 Social Inclusion Partnerships (34 area-based, the rest thematic), and the £68 million funding (2004/05) is now being partly distributed through local Community Planning Partnerships (see Chapter 8). SIPs will be subsumed into a wider Community Regeneration Fund from 2005/06.

Addressing low demand for housing

In England, a particular focus for community regeneration and the drive for more sustainable communities has been on those areas suffering from low demand for housing, in both the private and social housing sectors. Low demand was recognised as part of the work of Social Exclusion Unit mentioned above, and this led to the creation of nine Housing Market Renewal Pathfinder projects in the

---

22 See Social Exclusion Unit (2000) Report of Policy Action Team 4: *Neighbourhood Management*. CIH (2001) publishes *Neighbourhood Management: A good practice guide* which explains the financial and other aspects of such initiatives.
23 Scottish Executive (2002).

north and Midlands. The activities to be carried out by the pathfinders are still
under development but they include:[24]

- demolition of obsolescent housing;
- refurbishment;
- building new homes of a kind that people want;
- promoting sustainable communities;
- wider use of compulsory purchase orders to deal with empty or under-used
  land and property;
- use of 'gap funding' to subsidise developments where the costs of
  development exceed estimates of sale values;
- community safety; and,
- encouraging economic development through Regional Development
  Agencies and other sources of funding.

Further funding for the pathfinders, and for work to begin in other low-demand
areas, was announced in the Spending Review 2004. Financial provision will
progressively increase to reach £450 million by 2007/08.

Improving older private housing

Local authority support for the private sector includes providing information and
advice to owner-occupiers, private landlords and tenants, and to a wide variety of
would-be investors and voluntary agencies. More specifically, authorities provide
financial help to improve private dwellings and to provide adaptations for disabled
people. They also work in partnership with others to renew older mixed-tenure
areas that include poor quality private housing.

An important part of a local housing strategy will be the council's plans to deal
with sub-standard private sector properties in its area. Dealing with areas of run-
down private housing has a considerable policy history which cannot be explained
in detail here.[25] After the discredited slum-clearance programmes of the 1960s and
1970s, successive governments encouraged area-based renewal programmes, in
which house renovation, environmental improvement and possibly selective
clearance were concentrated. Activity peaked in the 1980s as the government
directed resources into this policy area. Many large cities had significant 'renewal
strategies', where the local authority often worked in partnership with housing
associations, building societies, local building firms and residents' groups. To
accompany these programmes, grant aid to both home-owners and private
landlords became very generous, often covering a large proportion of the costs of
improvement work, which could run well into five figures. Not surprisingly given
the level of investment, renewal programmes often had a significant impact and in

---

24 List adapted from Harriott, S. and Matthews, L. (2004) *Introducing Social Housing*, CIH,
   Coventry.
25 The best history up to the early 1980s is Gibson, M. and Langstaff, M. (1982) *An
   Introduction to Urban Renewal*, Hutchinson, London.

some respects (e.g. the activities of the inner city community-based housing associations in Scotland) were the precursor to wider regeneration programmes and 'housing plus' activities. They also influenced later programmes such as Estates Action and New Life for Urban Scotland which sought to apply similar community-based methods to tackling run-down council estates.

In the late 1980s policy began to shift away from such heavy investment in privately-owned housing. In England, financial support for renovation of private housing began a period of rapid and fairly chaotic evolution, driven particularly by the desire to cut costs. First, grants were restricted to mandatory grants aimed at the worst properties and poorer householders. Then there was a shift back to discretionary grants, but of more limited scope than before. Finally, in 2002 a 'regulatory reform order' swept away most of the complex legislation applying to grants in England and Wales, and gave councils more general powers to assist private owners through loans as well as grants.

At the time of writing, many councils in England and Wales are still operating a much more limited renovation grant scheme, based on the previous legislation, and are only beginning to develop other options. These may include, for example, equity loans where the council takes a share of the house value in return for financing improvement works, or arranges such a loan through a bank or building society collaborating with the authority. Local authorities have powers to indemnify other lenders who make loans to low-income householders. To take advantage of these more flexible powers in the reform order, authorities must first have a published policy as to how financial assistance will be disbursed.

Area action now takes the shape of 'Renewal Areas' which councils can declare having carried out what are called Neighbourhood Renewal Assessments. Renewal Areas, the successor to earlier Housing Action Areas and General Improvement Areas, can cover several hundreds or even thousands of older properties, and are zones in which grant and loan facilities are concentrated, councils may undertake wider environmental improvements and local advice centres may be opened to promote house improvement. The powers which councils have to undertake 'group repair' schemes (earlier known as 'enveloping') may be particularly appropriate in Renewal Areas, to secure basic improvements (e.g. new roofs) for whole blocks of older property.

Local authorities can also declare 'clearance areas' to enable them to acquire and demolish private housing in poor condition. There are complex powers of compulsory purchase and compensation, which will not be dealt with here as these measures are now little used. However, it is likely that demolition will become a feature of the Housing Market Renewal Pathfinders mentioned above.

Except for specific grants for adapting houses occupied by disabled people, capital finance for private sector renewal depends on the amount available through the 'single pot', describe in Chapter 9. Now that (other than for disabled facilities grants) there is no longer specific subsidy for these activities, the scale of private sector renewal work in England and Wales has declined.

In Scotland, there have not been the same frequent changes to the grant system and the improvement and repair grants available have essentially been the same for the last 20 years. However, the Housing (Scotland) Act 2001 introduced measures to restrict grants to lower-income households, and authorities now have to apply a means-test. Scottish authorities receive annual allocations of Private Sector Housing Grant to support their renewal activities, for part of which they have to bid.

Northern Ireland also has a system of renovation, repair and disabled facilities grants, essentially based on those available in England in the 1980s, and administered by the Northern Ireland Housing Executive.

Support for private owners can also come from the voluntary sector in the form of 'Care and Repair' services or home improvement agencies, often aimed at older people or those with disabilities, and providing packages of grant and loan assistance combined with help in making applications and in supervising the works.

Tackling poor conditions in the private rented sector

The previous description of housing renewal policies applies equally to the private rented sector as to home-owners, but in addition there is a range of powers available to local authorities to require the repair, improvement and satisfactory management of private rented housing. These apply particularly to multi-occupied property which traditionally has exhibited some of the worst conditions, including disrepair, inadequate basic amenities and means of escape from fire. Furthermore, the living arrangements in houses in multiple occupation (HMOs) necessarily place special demands on the management of such properties. The Housing Act 1996 gave landlords in England and Wales clearer responsibilities, and local authorities stronger powers, to take action. This usually involves requiring works to take place to rectify substantial disrepair, to make the property fit for habitation, or works to make it fit for the number of occupants. The 1996 Act also provides for a revised HMO registration scheme that allows authorities to adopt one of two model schemes and to charge HMO landlords registration fees for re-registering after five years to help meet the costs of HMO enforcement activity. Similar powers applied in Scotland from 1991.

As Peter Kemp says,[26] *'what to do about the condition of HMOs is an unresolved and highly intractable problem'*. The Scottish Executive introduced a mandatory licensing scheme in 2000, and the Housing Act 2004 provides for one to be introduced in England and Wales (see Chapter 18). However, previous efforts to improve conditions in this sub-sector have been frustrated by lack of staff and

26   Kemp, P. (2004) *Private Renting in Transition*, CIH, Coventry, p90. This section of the chapter draws heavily on this text, which gives a full description of the financial and other aspects of private renting in Great Britain.

resources, and other problems, which as Kemp says *'are also likely to affect the success of mandatory licensing both north and south of the border'*.

The Housing Act 2004 includes a discretionary power for authorities to license private landlords more generally. This would add a further power to various earlier ones to tackle disrepair and other problems in private rented property. Despite these various powers, private rented housing remains in poorer condition than other sectors. For example in England in 2001, one in ten private rented dwellings were unfit. In Scotland in 2002, seven out of ten dwellings were in 'critical disrepair'. In England and Wales, the test of condition will change as a result of the current Housing Bill to become a wider Housing Health and Safety Rating system, and powers to intervene will then relate to this new standard.

Summary

Local authorities have a wider housing role that goes beyond the management and improvement of council housing. Even those that have transferred their stock should have developed a local housing strategy which looks across all aspects of housing and identifies the need for the local authority and other agencies to intervene, and sets the priorities and identifies the resources for doing so.

In addition to the strategic role, authorities have a range of wider housing duties and powers, many concerned with private sector housing. Government policies towards, and financial support for, this wider role have tended to change even more rapidly than is the case for the council housing service. This chapter has given readers an appreciation of the extent of this wider role and its financial implications, without describing in detail the considerable range of legislation and funding sources that relate to it.

Further reading

CIH, LGA, RTPI (2004) *Intelligent Approaches to Housing – Achieving better integration in planning for housing* (available at www.cih.org).

Goss S. and Blackaby, B. (1998) *Designing Local Housing Strategies – A Good Practice Guide*, CIH/LGA, Coventry.

Kemp, P. (2004) *Private Renting in Transition*, CIH, Coventry.

Sim, D. (ed) (2004) *Housing and Public Policy in Post-Devolution Scotland*, CIH, Coventry.

CHAPTER 12:
Local government revenue finance

Introduction

The previous three chapters have all concerned capital investment by local authorities. In this chapter we turn to revenue spending. There is of course a direct relationship between the two, as debts incurred in making investments have to be paid for, and buildings and services have running costs which must be financed. The relationship, as we shall see, is even more complex than that, because some aspects of housing subsidy and revenue expenditure lead directly to investment in bricks-and-mortar. This final chapter of the five on local government deals first with general issues about revenue finance, then with the General Fund and housing expenditure which is not related to council housing, and finally and most substantially with the Housing Revenue Account and rents, expenditure and subsidy relating to council housing.

Much of the system which applies in England applies similarly in Wales. However, Scotland has some very distinctive features (in relation to HRA finance) with significant implications for the possibilities open to local authorities there compared with those in England.

The concept of revenue

As explained elsewhere (Chapter 2), the conceptual distinction made by financiers between capital and revenue mirrors the distinction made by economists between production (development) and consumption (use). Once a capital asset has been acquired, constructed, or improved, capital expenditure ceases; but of course the need to expend money on it does not. As we move from the production to the consumption phase of the asset's life, we are confronted with the financial problem of meeting the 'costs-in-use'. These day-to-day running costs constitute *revenue expenditure*. Revenue expenditure has to be met out of *revenue income*. As we will see, revenue expenditure and income are accounted for separately from capital finance.

Revenue expenditure

Where the asset's acquisition or construction was financed by means of a loan, the subsequent need to service that loan (pay interest and repay the principal) creates an obvious cost-in-use.[1] The financing costs of borrowing are classed as 'revenue expenditure'. In most cases, this expenditure is supported by government revenue grants. Almost all such support comes from two grants: these are the *Housing Revenue Account* (HRA) subsidy for borrowing to finance spending on council housing (*Housing Support Grant – HSG* in Scotland), and the *Revenue Support Grant* (RSG) for other borrowing. Loan service charges are, however, just one of many revenue expenses that have to be paid by local authorities. In the local government setting, physical assets are acquired in order to provide some kind of service to local people. This provision imposes a wide range of costs-in-use that include such things as staff salaries, office stationery, fire insurance, and building maintenance. These revenue expenses have to be met to keep the services running efficiently and effectively.

In practice, the distinction between capital and revenue is fuzzier than it is in theory: in particular, as we saw in Chapter 9, local housing authorities often use 'revenue' funds on 'capital' projects. However, local authorities are not normally permitted to sell assets and use the capital receipts to finance revenue activities; nor are they allowed to pay for revenue spending by establishing long-term debt.

Gross and net revenue expenditure

Revenue expenditure can be expressed as a gross or as a net figure. Gross expenditure measures the running costs of the service without taking any account of inward flows from such sources as rental income, charges for the use of community facilities (such as swimming pools, function rooms, etc.), any fee income earned, and service specific grants received. Net expenditure is gross expenditure minus these receipts. When an authority sets its annual budget and the council tax, it will be concerned with the level of net expenditure because it is this that represents the financial gap that has to be filled by local taxation or by subsidy. Net expenditure is also the common yardstick for comparing spending on different services within an authority and for comparing spending on the same services by different authorities. However, it must be remembered that it is the gross level of spending that measures the total financial cost of providing the service. For the HRA the budgeted net expenditure must be no greater than zero, i.e. the account has to be at least in balance at the year-end.

Revenue income

Potentially, and depending on the type of expenditure, revenue costs can be financed by a mixture of the following:

---

1   Debt servicing creates a charge against revenue that is variously referred to as a 'debt charge', a 'loan charge', or a 'capital financing charge'. It can also be referred to as an 'item 8 debit'. These regular charge payments will include an element of interest and an element of principal repayment. Over the life or 'term' of the loan, these payments will gradually diminish and eventually write off or 'amortise' the debt.

- Local taxation (council tax, and the council's share of business rates – see below).
- Revenue support (RSG, HRA subsidy, service-specific revenue grants).
- Rents for council housing and charges for associated properties such as lock-up garages and estate shops (that go into the HRA).
- Rents from other properties (that go into the General Fund).
- Income received from council mortgages or loans (e.g. for RTB purchases).
- Interest earned from the investment of capital receipts.
- Fees and charges for council services.

General Revenue Finance

Before turning to the specific question of housing revenue finance, we need to say something about how the central authorities provide general revenue support to local authorities, and what local sources of funding councils have. What follows is a simplified overview. Although the detailed control and funding mechanisms vary slightly in different parts of Britain, particularly since devolution, the general principles are the same. References to the Secretary of State therefore mean the Scottish Executive or the Welsh Assembly Government where appropriate.

Revenue support represents central government's contribution to council finance and is designed to ensure that the whole cost of local services does not fall on local tax-payers. It also ensures that the level of tax does not vary across the country simply because of differences in the needs and resources of individual local authorities.

Local taxation

In line with the 'local responsibility' principle mentioned at the start of Chapter 8, a significant part of the income of local authorities is raised in the form of local taxation. Two distinct types of 'rate' are levied locally: the business rate and the domestic rate. The business rate is variously referred to as the 'uniform business rate', the 'national non-domestic rate' or the 'non-domestic rate'. We will refer to it as the *business rate*. The domestic rate is now called the *council tax*.

Although the picture varies from year to year, generally a little more than half of local government spending is met by central government, and of the remainder about half is funded by business rates and half by council tax.

The business rate
The business rate is the council's share of the money paid into the nation-wide business rating pool by shops, offices and factories. It constitutes a levy on local businesses based on a national rate in the pound set by the government multiplied by a notional value of the premises they occupy, referred to as the 'rateable value'.

These rates are the means by which local businesses contribute to the cost of providing local authority services.

The rate is a nationalised system that is intended to be fair to businesses by exposing them to even-handed treatment wherever they happen to operate nationally. Before the start of each financial year, the Secretary of State estimates the amount in the pool that will be available to distribute to local authorities. This is called the *distributable amount* and once fixed, is shared out amongst all local authorities according to the number of residents in each local authority area.

Along with the Revenue Support Grant arrangements (see below), the business rate provides a degree of resource equalisation. Given the uneven distribution of rateable assets across the country, without this equalisation, councils would have to set widely different local tax levels in order to provide a similar level of service.

Most business rates are collected by 'billing authorities'[2] in line with national criteria. The centrally pooled funds are then redistributed back to the local authorities and police authorities on what is deemed to be an equitable basis that takes particular account of population sizes (although recently there have been problems resulting from under-counting in some areas in the 2001 census).

Council tax

The council tax is levied on households within its area and, together with the business rate, constitutes the local taxation base. Council tax is the means by which local residents contribute to the cost of providing local authority services. The amount payable depends on the valuation band of the dwelling, the number of adults who have their main residence in it, and whether any discounts or exemptions apply. The tax is levied on the occupants of the house, whether tenants or owners, and only if the house is empty does the landlord begin to bear a responsibility for payment.

Council tax is levied on local households by the billing authority. The proceeds are paid into its collection fund for distribution to precepting authorities and to its own General Fund. Councils are free to fix the overall level of council tax collected but the Secretary of State has reserve powers to limit excessive increases. Until the Local Government Act 1999 came into force the government set these limits in advance, and 'capped' authorities which exceeded them. The 1999 Act made these into reserve powers which are now less frequently used, but the 'threat' of capping still deters councils from making what might be seen as unjustified increases.

---

2   These are London boroughs, metropolitan authorities, other unitary authorities and shire districts; other authorities are the 'precepting authorities' whose tax which is collected by the billing authorities. This distinction does not apply in Scotland and Wales.

Because it only pays for 25 per cent or so of the total costs of local services, council tax has a high 'gearing effect' on local tax levels. This means that to get a one per cent increase in council revenue the council tax would have to rise by four per cent. The *gearing effect* limits the ability of a local authority to raise revenue finance in this way. The implications of this for central-local relations were discussed in Chapter 8.

It is recognised that the strength of a property-based tax rests on the fairness of the valuation of property on which it is levied.[3] By using banded rather than individual property values, the council tax has proved to be more robust in the face of changing property prices than the earlier rates system. So long as the band differentials are judged to be fair, it makes it possible to extend the period between expensive and potentially disruptive revaluations. Nevertheless, as we make clear below, there is considerable pressure for further reform.

Revenue expenditure limitation or 'capping'

Expenditure limitation was first introduced by the Rates Act 1984. This legislation gave central government the power to impose direct controls on that part of local authority revenue expenditure that is financed from local taxation. This power works through a system of revenue expenditure limitation or 'capping'. The so-called 'capping powers' were revised by the Local Government Finance Act 1992 and during the 1990s capping, or the threat of capping, became a significant political tool.

The government's ability to control council expenditure in a direct way brings to the fore the whole question of local accountability discussed at the start of Chapter 8. With the introduction of Best Value and measures to improve local democracy, the government has ended 'crude and universal capping' so that councils are no longer told in advance what they may spend. Nevertheless, in 2004, for example six English local authorities had their budgets 'capped'. Similar powers exist in Scotland and Wales but have not yet been used.

Critics of capping argue that it undermines the basic local government principle of local accountability and that it mechanistically ignores local knowledge of local needs. Some argue that a fairer system would be to place all councils within a fixed spending band analogous to the exchange rate mechanism while others argue the need for a more fundamental overhaul of local government finance to make it more adequately reflect differences in local needs.

Capping applies to General Fund expenditure only; different mechanisms, based on the provisions of the Local Government and Housing Act 1989 and applying in England and Wales only, are used to control expenditure on council housing. These HRA account controls are discussed below.

---

3   DETR (1998) *Modern Local Government – In touch with the people*, Cm4014, para 5.23.

Controlling revenue spending in general: the Finance Settlement

Every summer the government decides how much it thinks local government should spend and how much it will receive in grants in the following year. In late November or early December, the Secretary of State announces a provisional Finance Settlement to parliament and to the local authorities. After this announcement, there is a period of consultation, leading to the House of Commons approving a final Local Government Finance Settlement in late January or early February, in time for the authorities to set their budgets for the following financial year. Similar mechanisms apply to the devolved bodies, one important difference being that in Scotland the Executive makes a three-year spending settlement, giving councils much greater certainty. This is now under consideration in England.

The process by which the Finance Settlement is made consists of a series of calculations; those for England in 2004/05 are set out in Figure 12.1. It begins with the government setting a level of revenue spending that it considers appropriate for local authorities to spend in aggregate; this is called *Total Assumed Spending* (TAS). This figure is determined as part of the Spending Review (see Chapter 5). TAS is meant to represent the total amount that local government as a whole needs to spend in that year in order to provide a 'standard' level of service.

Fig 12.1 Illustration of Local Government Finance Settlement
Figures relate to the settlement for 2004/05 for English local authorities

	£ millions	Per cent of TAS
Total Assumed Spending (TAS)	73,425	100.0
Revenue Support Grant (RSG) to local authorities	*26,956*	*36.7*
RSG to other bodies	*54*	*0.1*
Specific grants	*12,850*	*17.5*
Total government grants	39,850	54.3
Income from business rates	15,000	20.4
Aggregate external finance (AEF)	**54,860**	74.7
Assumed income from council tax	**18,619**	25.4

Source: LGA (2004) *Guide to the RSG Settlement.*

The amount of support authorities receive from the government in respect of TAS is known as *Aggregate External Finance (AEF)*. Some three-quarters of local government revenue finance comes from central government. Just over half comes through direct grants, of which the most significant is Revenue Support Grant

(RSG). The remainder is the amount assumed to be collected through the business rate (see above). We now consider the grant aspect of central government support in more detail.

Central government support through grants

Revenue Support Grant (RSG)

The bulk of central financial support comes in the form of RSG. The purpose of the RSG is to bring about a more or less equal local tax burden between areas that have different needs and taxable capacities. Its calculation is tied to a spending assessment called the *Formula Spending Share* (FSS – see below; the terminology and mechanism is slightly different in Scotland). It is important to understand, however, that RSG support is not channelled into the running of the council housing service whose finances are ring-fenced from the authorities' general funding arrangements and are helped through a different mechanism called *HRA subsidy* (discussed below).

RSG is simply that part of AEF that is not provided from business rates or specific and special grants. In line with the government's public expenditure control priorities, the allocation of RSG begins with the Spending Review process (discussed in Chapter 5). This determines how much money in total local authorities will be permitted to spend (TAS). The government then determines the proportion that will be financed by the Exchequer. This then determines the proportion that authorities collectively will have to find for themselves. Having fixed the Exchequer's total commitment to support general local authority revenue spending, the government then turns its attention to the question of how best to distribute that sum.

The allocation of RSG centres on a calculation methodology referred to as the Formula Spending Share (FSS). This has replaced, but is similar to, the previous Standard Spending Assessment. Using a number of formulae, the government assesses how much it is reasonable for each local council to spend in providing its range of General Fund services for a given period. Although the allocation process allows for an assessment of particular local needs, it is, nevertheless, fundamentally resource driven in that the FSS system is a statistical device for sharing out a fixed pot of public expenditure.

The amount of RSG an authority receives is determined by the following formula:

> RSG = its FSS *minus* its share of the business rate pool *minus* the amount it would get if it set its council tax at a national standard rate.

The FSS is built up from major service blocks such as education, police, fire, highways and social services; non-HRA housing is covered by an 'other services' block. Whether the assessments are judged to be fair depends crucially on what is included as an indicator and how they are weighted. The assessments are inevitably criticised for being too crude and failing to reflect the subtle social, economic and cultural needs of different local authority areas.

Specific grants

Whereas RSG is a general grant which each authority can use as it wishes, there is also a large number of other grants, often tied to specific government initiatives. These range from significant funds such as the school standards grant to much smaller grants for rural policing. In housing and related fields the grants include those for the housing benefit scheme and Supporting People (see Chapter 19), and also the Single Regeneration Budget and the Neighbourhood Renewal Fund (see Chapter 11).

Reform of local government finance

We described wider issues about the reform of local government in Chapter 8. Here we need to make reference to some possible reforms which could affect what has been said about the way councils finance their General Fund services. As we have seen, changes have already been made since the current government first took power in 1997, such as the review of the RSG system in 2002, and others such as a move to three-year spending settlements (already in place in Scotland) are now planned.

Further developments centre on the Balance of Funding Review[4] and the subsequent inquiry into local government finance, chaired by Sir Michael Lyons. The latter has not reported at the time of publication of this edition of *Housing Finance*, but some directions are clear. First, the Balance of Funding Review accepted that the problem of 'gearing' mentioned above is a serious one, because it limits local government flexibility and accountability. Second, it agrees that the only way to deal with this is by shifting the balance of funding from central to local level, but measures to do so must be looked at on their own merits. They must also preserve an element of equalisation of resources to ensure that poor local authority areas do not lose out. Third, the options appear to be (a) a reformed council tax system, (b) the so-called 're-localising' of business rates, or (c) a local income tax, or a combination of these.

The Lyons review, to report by the end of 2005, is charged with considering these possibilities. However, the government has already concluded that the council tax should be retained, albeit with reforms such as additional council tax bands to reflect rising house prices. It also wants to consider improvements to council tax benefit to improve take-up.

The announcement of the Lyons review was received with scepticism,[5] with the postponing of the conclusions of the Balance of Funding Review considered a 'wasted opportunity'. The government's political difficulty is that council tax

---

4   ODPM, July 2004.
5   See, for example, Travers, A., 'The Ex-Files' in *Public Finance*, 30 July 2004.

levels are a highly contentious issue, and a shift in the balance of funding implies either higher council taxes or a completely new tax at local level, both of which are likely to be unpopular.

Housing Revenue Finance and the General Fund

The distinction between HRA and non-HRA housing revenue finance

In any discussion on local authority housing spending, we must always make a clear distinction between monies spent on, and derived from, an authority's council housing service, and monies committed to providing housing services to people other than council tenants. Revenue expenditure and income on council housing are recorded in a separate account known as the Housing Revenue Account (HRA). Revenue transactions relating to all other council services appear in the General Fund. It is particularly important to note that it is not now normally possible to make a contribution to the HRA from the General Fund. There are also now only limited circumstances in which surpluses from the HRA can be paid into the General Fund.

It should be noted that while all local housing authorities have services that require General Fund finance, many no longer have a Housing Revenue Account because they no longer have council housing stock. After a full stock transfer, the HRA is normally wound up, with the only remaining properties (such as hostels for the homeless) being those financed from the General Fund.[6]

General Fund housing services

Expenditure not related to council housing and council tenants but which relates to wider housing services includes local authorities' wider strategic housing role and the services which they provide to private owners, private tenants, the homeless and people in special categories of need such as rough sleepers. It also includes councils' funding of the voluntary sector, providing facilities such as hostels for victims of domestic violence, supporting residents' associations and running advice services.

The funding of the running costs of these services is a small part of the wider General Fund described above. In other words, much of the funding will depend on RSG, some may be assisted by specific grants, and the rest will have to be financed from local resources. Hostels and other facilities may make charges to offset their costs. The General Fund does of course have to meet the debt charges arising from capital spending for these services, such as house renovation grants or construction of a homeless persons' hostel.

These non-HRA housing services are described in Chapter 11.

---

6   Permission to close the HRA is required from the Secretary of State; this is automatic if there are no HRA dwellings, but the HRA can also be closed if there are less than 50 dwellings – they are then administered through the General Fund.

The Housing Revenue Account

Keeping a Housing Revenue Account is a statutory requirement for local housing authorities in England, Wales and Scotland which have housing stock let to secure council tenants. It is therefore sometimes referred to as a 'landlord' account. However, the HRA is not actually a separate fund but a ring-fenced account, relating to the landlord functions, within the local authority's overall finances.

The form of the HRA is set in statutes and in the regulations which flow from them. The remainder of this chapter is concerned first with the overall basis of the HRA and then with the way that its constituent elements (rents, subsidy and expenditure) work and how they relate to each other. We deal finally with the way that resource accounting principles (see Chapter 2) relate to the HRA.

Reference will be made throughout to Figure 12.2, which represents the HRA subsidy system diagrammatically, and which is complementary to Figure 9.1 in Chapter 9. The diagram shows the workings of the HRA subsidy system for a typical English or Welsh local authority. We will make the clear the significant differences in the way that the HRA works in Scotland. Those requiring technical details beyond the scope of this chapter are referred to the official guidance available online and which is periodically updated.[7]

The basis of the present system (England and Wales)

The basis of the present system is provided by the Local Government and Housing Act 1989 ('the 1989 Act'). This prescribed the statutory framework for local authority housing finance, provided for the ring-fencing of the Housing Revenue Account, and introduced a new subsidy system and new controls on local authority borrowing to meet capital expenditure. This structure remains largely in place, although parts of it have been substantially altered by the Local Government Act 2003 ('the 2003 Act'). Following the conventions we established in Chapter 9, we refer to 'the 1989 Act regime' as the previous regime, and to the HRA as it stands after the 2003 Act as the 'new regime', although the recent changes in revenue finance are in reality less radical than those to the capital finance system and have been phased in since 2001.

The 1989 Act regime
The overhaul of the revenue regime which took place in the 1989 Act was a result of the then Conservative government's concerns that the previous system gave them limited ability to influence rent levels, and that councils were putting up

---

7   In England the ODPM publishes the *Housing Revenue Account Manual* (at http://www. odpm.gov.uk/stellent/groups/odpm_housing/documents/page/odpm_house_030081.pdf) and this also broadly applies to Wales. In Scotland the Executive publishes the *Scottish Public Finance Manual* (at http://www.scotland.gov.uk/library5/finance/spfm/spfm-64.asp) but this has only limited information on HRAs.

Figure 12.2: The new local authority housing revenue subsidy system in England and Wales, from April 2004

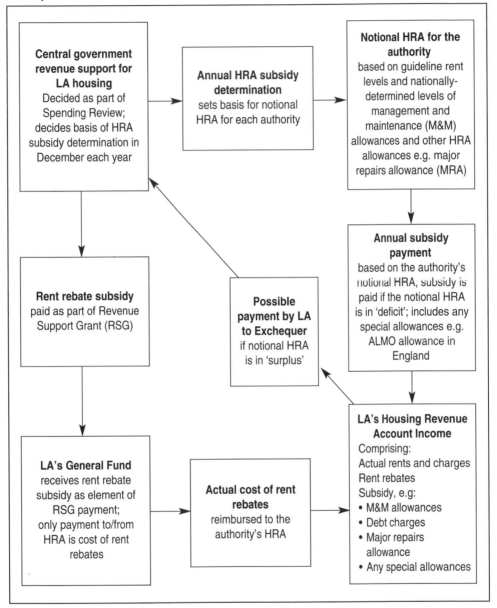

rents to create more revenue resources, at a time when capital resources were severely constrained. The costs were largely being passed back to the Exchequer through the increased bill for housing benefit (rent rebates) for council tenants. The rebate costs for an average tenant had grown fourfold in the previous decade.[8]

8   See Wilcox, S. (2004) Table 113.

The *official* aims of the 1989 Act changes[9] were that the HRA should:

- be simpler, so that subsidy provides authorities with consistent objectives;
- be fairer towards tenants and local tax-payers alike, and fairer between tenants in different areas;
- allow rents to be set at levels within the reach of people in low-paid employment and with regard to what people can pay and what the property is worth; and,
- direct subsidy to areas with the most need and provide an incentive for good management.

The 1989 Act introduced a single HRA subsidy consisting of two parts: the housing element and the rent rebate element. The housing element can become negative, and in most local authorities became a substantial negative amount. The rent rebate element was always a positive amount because it was simply the aggregate entitlement of all the council tenants to housing benefit. The net HRA subsidy that a local authority received was the sum of these two elements. So a large negative housing element had the effect of reducing the size of the rent rebate element. This meant that most authorities no longer received all of their potential central government support to pay their rebates, and indeed, some received very little or none at all. This led to the so-called 'Daylight Robbery' campaign by tenants' groups, arguing that the 'missing' subsidy should be reinstated. As we shall see, the scale of subsidy withdrawal or recycling was much reduced by subsequent reforms, so that this campaign no longer has the same force.

The second major change introduced by the 1989 Act was the ring-fencing of the HRA. The HRA should now only deal with finances that relate to the authority's role as a housing landlord, and funds in the account cannot normally be used to subsidise other council services, nor can other service funds be used to subsidise the HRA.[10]

In setting the boundaries of the ring-fence, there were certain gaps and grey areas. The costs of such functions as housing aid and advice and some homeless functions such as hostels have been treated differently by different authorities. A particular degree of confusion emerged with the passing of Section 127 of the Leasehold Reform, Housing and Urban Development Act 1993 which gave local authorities the power to charge certain welfare services to the HRA. It is now established that the costs of placing homeless families in temporary accommodation such as that leased from private landlords should not be charged to the HRA. The cost of employing staff to run the homeless service is typically split between the HRA and the General Fund. Any personal care costs associated with the running of sheltered housing for the elderly should not be charged to the HRA. Although the guidance allows road sweeping and children's play schemes on

---

9   See the ODPM's *Housing Revenue Account Manual* referred to above.
10 The limited circumstances in which money can move between the HRA and the General Fund are set out in the *HRA Manual*, para. 4.2.28 (2004 edition).

estates to be paid for from the HRA, the CIH argues that this should be resisted as it would mean that tenants are paying for these services twice: through their council tax and then again through their rents.

A more significant 'gap' in the ring-fence was that some councils in high value areas and with low spending needs generated sufficient rental income to pay the running costs of their council housing *and* the cost of rent rebates for their tenants, leaving a surplus in the HRA. Under the 1989 Act regime, this surplus had to be paid each year into the General Fund and in effect became a subsidy from better off council tenants towards council tax payers in the authority's area.

The *actual* effect of the regime introduced by the 1989 Act was to enable the government to reduce its subsidy payment overall, by requiring HRA surpluses to offset rent rebate costs. But it did not initially meet the government's aims of controlling the growth of HRA expenditure. Although, as we shall see, the government had a mechanism for setting the levels of rent that would be taken into account in deciding the level of housing element subsidy received by the authority, it had no means of preventing councils from setting higher, unsubsidised rent levels whose costs would be largely met from the rent rebates received by the majority of tenants. This was dealt with from 1996 onwards, when the government introduced 'rent rebate subsidy limitation'. This meant that a council setting a rent above guideline levels would not receive subsidy for the rent rebates paid out on the additional rent. This claw back of subsidy acts as a brake on rent increases, although some authorities do still set rents at levels which make them subject to the claw back.

The new regime following the 2003 Act

The basis of the HRA system operating after the implementation of the 2003 Act, from April 2004, is in fact the culmination of changes which began after Labour took power in 1997. Several major changes were made by altering the regulations or the subsidy system, without the need to alter statute. Nevertheless the 2003 Act and new regulations consolidated the changes and made crucial reforms in the shape of the subsidy system and the nature of the HRA ring-fence inherited from the 1989 Act. Some of these reforms we shall deal with later.

One major reform to the subsidy system at first sight appears to be a reversal of the change made in the 1989 Act, when subsidy for rent rebates was brought into the HRA subsidy system and negative housing element subsidy could then be used to offset the cost of rebates. The 2003 Act took rent rebate subsidy out of the HRA, making its subsidy arrangements broadly the same as those for rent allowances. In other words, from 2004 council tenants who receive housing benefit are subsidised through the same mechanism as private or housing association tenants who receive benefit.[11]

---

11 In Wales an anomaly in the devolution funding arrangements means that councils are still required to generate surpluses to cover the reductions to the Welsh Assembly budget resulting from the ending of the housing benefit link. See Wilcox, S., 'Another Fine Mess' in Wilcox, S. (2003) *UK Housing Review*, CIH/CML, Coventry.

The government argued[12] that the 'widespread belief' that better off council tenants had been subsidising their poorer neighbours' housing benefit was a 'misunderstanding', because under the system the cost of rebates was fully subsidised by central government but rent surpluses were being distributed from richer to poorer authorities. Its 2004 changes were designed to make the arrangements clear and transparent, with responsibility for rent rebate subsidy being passed to the Department of Work and Pensions and their accounting moved from the HRA to the General Fund.

From 2004, authorities with rental income in excess of the government's calculation of what they need to spend have to pay the excess to the government. This means that whether HRA subsidy in a particular case is positive or negative actually means (if positive) that a payment is made from the government to the local authority, whereas (if negative) the payment is from the local authority to the government. The pooling of what are judged to be surpluses offsets the costs of HRA subsidy to authorities with greater needs.

A related reform in the 2003 Act effectively tightens the HRA ring-fence by further closing the gap we identified earlier, by which HRA surpluses are paid across to the General Fund. This is now only normally allowed if there is an actual surplus and the authority does not receive HRA subsidy; except for minor amounts,[13] most surpluses are recouped by the subsidy system and have to be paid to the Exchequer, entering the subsidy pool we have just described. Transitional provisions protect from the full effect of the changes those authorities that were subsidising their General Funds, by phasing them in over a period.

You will have noted that in this discussion that we distinguish between the surplus which government *judges* an authority to have available, and *actual* cash surpluses which arise because income exceeds expenditure. A similar distinction can be made in relation to deficits. In the actual HRA, authorities have to budget to balance income and expenditure. In practice, there is inevitably some gap between the two. Normally an actual surplus is retained within the HRA; if there is a deficit the authority must budget to eliminate it in setting the following year's budget.

The new requirement that authorities in 'surplus' on their notional HRA actually have to pay it to central government is analogous to what happens in the capital account where debt-free authorities now have to pay part of their capital receipts from house sales into the capital receipts pool (see Chapter 9). Although the two mechanisms are different, they both affect 'better off' authorities and some experience the 'double whammy' of being subjected to both. One difference, however, is that the amount of surplus revenue paid into the 'pool' is known each year from HRA statistics. In 2003/04 it was expected to be £650 million in England,[14] reducing the cost to government of HRA subsidy by about two-thirds.

---

12 ODPM (2003) *Local Authority Housing Finance – A Guide to the New Arrangements*, p10.
13 And – as we shall see later – transfers to the major repairs reserve.
14 Wilcox, S. (2003) Table 161.

In summary, in England and Wales HRA subsidy is a deficit subsidy calculated by reference to a model of each authority's HRA. The model is called the 'notional' HRA. Rent guidelines and allowances for management and maintenance expenditure are calculated for each authority, reflecting variations in local circumstances such as property values and stock characteristics. Where the income from the guideline rent level is less than the amount judged to be needed for management and maintenance, together with the costs of debt, the HRA is judged to be in 'deficit'. Subsidy is payable to meet that deficit. Where assumed income is greater than the assumed costs, the HRA is in 'surplus' and the surplus is paid to the Exchequer as negative subsidy.

The current HRA subsidy system is shown diagrammatically in Figure 12.2 and Figure 12.3 below shows the income and expenditure for a simplified HRA of an English or Welsh local authority whose notional HRA is in 'surplus'.

Figure 12.3: Typical HRA in England or Wales

Income	(£m)	Expenditure	(£m)
Rents	55	Management, maintenance and administration	33
Major repairs allowance	12	Major repairs expenditure	12
Other	5	Revenue contribution to capital outlay *or* cost of prudential borrowing	1
HRA subsidy	–	Debt charges	15
		Negative subsidy (to pay to government)	11
Total income	**72**	**Total expenditure**	**72**

Source: based on the HRA for a mid-sized council in the English Midlands for 2004/05, with figures rounded and simplified by the authors.

As we shall see later in this chapter, there are other elements to the HRA which incorporate the principles of *resource accounting* (introduced in Chapter 2). As part of the Comprehensive Spending Review in July 1998, ministers made clear that they wanted to encourage local authorities to take a more business-like approach to managing their housing stock and move towards a form of resource accounting. In a statement on housing and regeneration policy, the deputy prime minister said:[15]

> *'The current system of local authority housing accounting does not encourage efficient investment. Introducing resource accounts will put local authority housing on a more business-like footing. This will enable authorities to make better decisions about the use and maintenance of their housing assets, by making transparent the costs of capital tied up in the assets and providing resources to maintain them.'*

15   Quoted in ODPM *Resource accounting in the HRA* (2004).

The government subsequently issued a consultation paper, *A New Financial Framework for Local Authority Housing: Resource Accounting in the Housing Revenue Account*, in December 1998. Since then a series of steps have been taken to incorporate resource accounting principles into the HRA in England and Wales, with the final elements being put in place by the 2003 Act. We return to this in detail at the end of this chapter.

The system in Scotland

Scottish local authorities are also required, by the Housing (Scotland) Act 1987, to maintain a Housing Revenue Account. However, the evolution of HRA subsidy which we have just described in relation to England and Wales did not take the same form in Scotland.

The first major difference relates to the subsidy system. HRA subsidy in Scotland is called Housing Support Grant (HSG). In theory, as in England, it is a deficit subsidy paid to those councils which, on the basis of certain assumptions, would not secure sufficient HRA income (mainly from rents) to meet their expenditure (loan charges and management and maintenance costs). The amounts of HSG payable are derived each year from a series of calculations which require assumptions to be made about rental incomes and management and maintenance expenditure. However, as these are standard assumptions used for all councils the main determinant for grant entitlement is the estimated level of debt servicing costs.

In the early 1980s most councils in Scotland qualified for grant. However, as government policy at the time was to reduce direct housing subsidy (HSG) in favour of indirect subsidy (housing benefit), over the years assumed rental income was increased ahead of inflation. This resulted in the gap between assumed HRA income and expenditure being reduced to the extent that in recent years only the two councils with the highest debt levels (Shetland and Western Isles) continue to qualify for subsidy at all. HSG remains a substantial proportion of total HRA income in Shetland and Western Isles, but for the other 30 Scottish councils it has ceased to be a consideration. In other words, most Scottish local authorities do not receive direct HRA subsidy, and meet their costs solely from their rental income (albeit with rents heavily subsidised through the rent rebate system).

The second crucial difference is that the recent change in England and Wales to take rent rebate subsidy out of the HRA was not needed in Scotland because the two have always been separate, with rebates being paid from the General Fund and financed by central government. A final difference is that Scottish local authorities have not yet been required to incorporate resource accounting principles into the management of the HRA and there is no major repairs allowance or other reflection of depreciation charges.

These differences have created a very different overall picture for council housing finance in Scotland, with authorities largely being unsubsidised, there being no mechanism for government to constrain or otherwise influence rent levels, and hence rents showing very marked variation according to whether councils have increased their spending and their debt.

Whereas in England there have been major reforms in the HRA first in 1989 and then those culminating in the 2003 Act, in Scotland there has simply been a steady evolution from the late 1980s onwards, away from dependence on direct subsidy and towards each authority largely determining its own HRA, free of central controls.

For most Scottish authorities, their HRA is therefore a straightforward balancing of their own income and expenditure. A typical HRA in 2003/04 is shown in Figure 12.4.

Figure 12.4: Typical HRA in Scotland

Income	(£m)	Expenditure	(£m)
Rents Other	52 3	Management, maintenance and administration Debt charges Capital funded from current revenue Other	31 7 11 3
Total income	**55**	**Total expenditure**	**52**
		Surplus carried forward	**3**

Source: based on the HRA for a mid-sized Scottish council for 2003/04, with figures rounded and summarised by the authors.

As we saw in Chapter 9, although Scottish councils generally have much more control over their own revenue finances, the lack of subsidy for capital spending (except for particular programmes) has also forced them to rely on funding investment from rental income (called CFCR – capital funded from current revenue), as seen in the example. This does, however, mean there is significantly more potential for Scottish councils to make use of the opportunities provided by the prudential borrowing regime (see Chapter 9).

The elements of the Housing Revenue Account

Figure 12.5 represents the main elements of an HRA. In a real set of accounts the elements would be split into sub-categories and other items of income and expenditure would be included. The precise content of an account clearly depends on an authority's debt profile and the nature and scope of its activities.

Figure 12.5: Main items of HRA income and expenditure

Income:
- rents and service charges paid by council tenants;
- HRA subsidy (HSG in Scotland) – if eligible;
- the major repairs allowance (MRA – in England and Wales only);
- any special subsidies (such as the ALMO allowance in England);
- other income such as rents from council-owned shops on estates; and
- interest received on council mortgages.

(Note: interest received from invested capital receipts from the sale of HRA assets has to be paid to the General Fund rather than the HRA.)

Expenditure:
- loan service charges;
- management costs;
- spending on repairs and maintenance;
- bought in services, including those from other council departments;
- other outgoings such as revenue contributions to capital outlay (RCCOs – called CFCRs – capital funded from current revenue, in Scotland);
- provision for bad debts;
- any 'negative subsidy' payment to the Exchequer (England and Wales only); and
- a contingency sum to cover any unforeseen expenses or shortfalls in income.

(Note: capital charges, depreciation charges and other items relating to resource accounting are not listed but are explained later in the chapter.)

We now have a picture of the overall 'shape' of the HRA, and how it has evolved in England and Wales, and separately in Scotland. The next stage is to describe the workings of the HRA, by reference to the main elements of its income and expenditure (see Figure 12.5; also refer back to Figure 12.2). We shall not in fact devote much space to the spending of HRA monies, as (unlike capital spending) this is largely straightforward, and it is not the purpose of this book to describe the details of managing housing stock. Most of the remaining description of the workings of the HRA will therefore deal with income, and most of *this* will be concerned with the two main kinds of income: rents and subsidy. We will however briefly cover the way expenditure on debt charges is dealt with and also explain the charges associated with resource accounting, because the last part of the chapter will describe the ways that the principles of resource accounting set out in Chapter 2 apply to the HRA.

In relation to rents and debt charges we will describe the situation in Scotland where it differs from England and Wales. The sections on subsidy and resource accounting apply only to England and Wales.

Housing Revenue Account income: Rents

Rent is the main form of income in their HRA over which councils have some control although, as we shall see, the extent of this control is increasingly limited.

In this section of the chapter we will consider the nature of rent, the principles of rent-setting, evolving national policy, and the setting of rents in practice.

The nature of rent

In Chapter 4 we made the general point that a conflict exists between the *social policy objective* of setting rents at levels that are *low enough* to be affordable to tenants, and the *commercial objective* of having *high enough* rents to cover the landlord's legitimate costs. What counts as 'legitimate costs' with respect to the provision of council housing lies at the heart of a long-standing debate. (Refer to the notion of *total sufficiency rent* in Chapter 4). In essence, the rent payment is the 'price' that the tenant pays in return for enjoying rights of occupancy together with the range of housing management services associated with the tenancy.

In the private market, a landlord's legitimate costs would include a return on the capital invested and a measure of normal profit (see Chapter 4). In other words, the private landlord will expect the rental income to cover the opportunity costs of being active in the housing market. Business people will expect a reasonable return on the money capital that is 'locked' into the asset, and to be rewarded for the energy, effort, time and risks associated with being a landlord. Private lenders to registered social landlords will also expect rent policies to be part of a viable business plan. In short, both private landlords and private lenders will expect the pricing system to be value-based and market-orientated.

In contrast, local authorities have traditionally been regarded as part of the 'welfare state' rather than as businesses. For this reason, historically, they have taken a cost/expenditure rather than a value/market approach to setting rents. In their role as agents for the welfare state they have traditionally sought to set rents on the basis of pooled historic cost pricing (see Chapter 4). This means that, traditionally, their rents have not aimed to make a profit or a return on capital, but rather have sought to provide affordable housing by ensuring that rental income plus subsidy covers the current outgoings, including the servicing of debt. The ability to 'pool' historic costs goes a long way to explain why council rents have tended to be lower than those of other tenures.

Therefore in principle the level of council rents is determined by the costs itemised in the HRA (see above). Although the rent constitutes a price to the tenant, from the council's point of view it constitutes the main HRA 'income'. Furthermore, as we have seen, if an authority in England and Wales is judged to be in 'surplus' for subsidy purposes, rents may well have to contribute to the payments made back to the government as 'negative subsidy'. In other words, tenants in that authority are not only paying for the cost of services they receive but also contributing to the national subsidy pool which assists other authorities.

One other general point needs to be made about rents, which is that they are intended to cover property-specific services which all tenants receive. Special services received only by some tenants, or communal services like a warden scheme or a community facility, should be paid for not through rent but as a separate service charge. As part of its rent restructuring policy in England (see below), the government is encouraging the separating out (or 'unpooling') of service charges, which is the practice followed by housing associations. Service charges are not covered by government rent policy although they may be eligible for Supporting People funding (see Chapter 19).

Council housing rents: principles

We can see the development of policy on rents over the last 30 years or so as a shift from a 'welfare' approach where rents were set at levels just sufficient to cover costs (or even less than that if they were originally being subsidised from the General Fund), to one in which under the 1989 Act and more recently there has been an increasing emphasis on relating them to market values. Over this period we can see the emergence of a general, cross-party consensus about the broad objectives of an appropriate public sector rent-setting policy. These objectives can be summarised as follows. Although there is substantial agreement about these objectives, how they should be balanced and linked is still a cause for considerable debate.

1. *Rents should partly reflect the asset value and condition of the dwelling.* A measure of capital value pricing would lead to greater comparability between different forms of renting and to rent levels that more accurately reflect consumer preferences. Many authorities have a relatively 'flat' structure for their rents that fails to reflect the different size and characteristics of their dwellings. It is argued that this objective also creates greater equity in rent levels as between one area and another. Also, now that resource accounting applies to council housing, its 'price' should relate more closely to its value as an asset. Rents that reflect asset value and condition are also less likely to show unjustified differences as between one sector and another – especially between council rents and housing association rents.

2. *Rents should be affordable.* The first objective is founded on economic rather than social principles, and therefore takes no systematic account of affordability. One common formulation of affordability[16] is that rents generally should not exceed levels within the reach of people in low-paid employment, and in practice will normally be below market levels (refer to Chapter 3). There can be no guarantee that rent levels determined by reference to proportionality and asset values will be within the means of low-income households. This problem was originally addressed by the introduction of rent rebates for those on low incomes (see Chapter 19). But this can create a problem as well as solving one, since if rent levels are simply pushed up in the knowledge that 'benefit will take the strain', it also makes it increasingly difficult for tenants to be able to stay in low-paid jobs and still afford their rent. One aspect of affordability is therefore avoiding the 'work disincentive' effect of rents being beyond the means of working households. For example, the Scottish Federation of Housing Associations has a policy that, for a rent to

---

16 For example, DoE (1988).

be affordable, households with one person working more than 16 hours per week should normally be able to pay it without needing housing benefit.[17]

3. *Rents should partly reflect current incomes and prices.* Implicit in this objective is the need to link rents to some kind of inflation or incomes index or housing market price index.[18] The argument here is that such indexing would produce greater equity of treatment between different forms of renting. Furthermore, by establishing a link between council rents and wider market forces, price distortions in the overall housing system would be reduced. We might also make the point that if future policies seek to attract private investment into the development of council housing, lenders will expect rents to bear some clear relationship to market forces. This was made a duty by the Housing Act 1985 which required rent-setting in local authorities in England and Wales *'to have regard to'* private sector rents. However, in England, this requirement has been repealed and overtaken by rent restructuring.

4. *Rents should not be unduly distorted by the relative wealth of one authority compared with another.* For example, authorities that have sold large numbers of dwellings and, as a result, have accumulated capital receipts are potentially in a position to spend more on their council housing service without having to increase rents proportionately. Conversely, authorities that do not have such accumulated reserves are, on the face of it, poorly positioned to invest in their stock unless they do so by hiking up rents. To prevent such inequitable rent differentials between authorities, resources are redistributed through the subsidy system and by mechanisms such as the pooling of capital receipts (see Chapter 9). The introduction of the needs-related major repairs allowance in England and Wales has also helped address these inequities (see below).

5. *Rents should not contribute to or be subsidised by the General Revenue Account.* Prior to April 1990 it was possible for authorities in England and Wales to make a contribution to the HRA from what were then rates, now council tax. It was also easier to transfer council house rental income into the General Fund to subsidise local tax-payers. Rent levels therefore depended to some degree on the extent of this cross-subsidy in a particular authority. The ring-fencing of the HRA in England and Wales was introduced partly to impose an accounting discipline on the management of council housing, and limit to particular circumstances the opportunities for one account to be subsidised by the other.

6. *Subsidy rather than rent should be treated as 'the residual'.* The implication of this is that general subsidies should be calculated on a deficit basis reflecting any shortfall in HRA income.[19] The argument here is that rents

---

17   SFHA (2002) *Developing Affordable Rents*, SFHA, Edinburgh.
18   See Malpass, P. (1990) *Reshaping Housing Policy: Subsidies, rents and residualisation*, Routledge, London & New York, p70.
19   Malpass, P., *ibid.*

should be set in line with rational principles and not simply be calculated as a residual to make up the 'cost/expenditure' shortfall that exists after the receipt of a standard subsidy.

Council house rents: From principles to practice

Although the principles described above are general, they apply differently in different parts of Britain. To establish a working system that is equitable, clear and coherent, these guiding principles have to be turned into detailed practice. These rules of practice are grounded in legislation and can be thought of as a regulatory 'regime'. Because any deficit subsidy system (principle 6 above) derives from the relationship between rents and expenditure, central government will have an interest in how both these amounts are determined. This interest is exercised via the regulatory regime. The current regime for England was established by the 1989 Act, but has been substantially changed by the policy of 'rent restructuring' which began in 2002.

Policy in Wales is still under development, and has not yet followed the 'restructuring' being carried out in England, partly because for reasons of past policy on housing association rents (see Chapter 14) there is a smaller gap between rents in the two sectors than is the case in England. The position in Wales is therefore essentially that established by the 1989 Act.

In Scotland there a broad consensus that social housing rents should be affordable,[20] but no stated government policy on rent levels or affordability beyond 'shared aspirations' between Communities Scotland as the regulator and the Convention of Scottish Local Authorities (CoSLA) and SFHA as the bodies representing social landlords. These state:[21]

> *'We set rents that take account of affordability, the costs of managing and maintaining our houses, comparability with other social landlords in the area, and that enable us to service existing loans and fulfil contractual obligations. We have a fair system for apportioning rents between individual properties.'*

Despite shared principles, there is wide disparity between the rents of different social landlords in Scotland, largely because of 'accidents of history'.[22] As we saw earlier in this chapter, the fact that almost all Scottish local authorities no longer receive subsidy through Housing Support Grant means that in effect they set their own rents so as to balance the HRA, with the rent level being determined by the costs of service delivery, and more especially the costs of either past or current investment. So high rent levels are associated with high debt levels in authorities

---

20 For discussion of rents and affordability in Scotland see Taylor, M. and Wilcox, S. (2004) 'The Funding and Affordability of Social Housing' in Sim, D., *Housing and Public Policy in Post-Devolution Scotland*, CIH, Coventry.

21 Communities Scotland (2001) *Performance Standards for Social Landlords and Homelessness Functions*, Communities Scotland, Edinburgh.

22 Taylor and Wilcox, *op. cit.*, p124.

such as Edinburgh and Shetland. Glasgow, prior to the transfer of its stock to Glasgow Housing Association in 2002, had one of the highest rent levels in Scotland and about half the rent was accounted for by debt charges.

Because only England has an explicit policy for local authority rents and this now largely determines the rent levels that are actually set, we will describe the policy in some detail.

Council house rents and rent restructuring in England

In 2000, rents of housing association properties in England were around 20 per cent higher, on average, than rents in local authorities. This general difference was made worse by wide local differences. For example, CIH pointed out that two adjoining London boroughs charged rents that were £15 different for similar houses, and that housing association rents in Southampton were on average £24 higher than council rents for similar properties.[23] This was seen to be both unfair and confusing to tenants. In the housing green paper, *Quality and Choice: A Decent Home for All*,[24] the government declared its intention that rents across the two social housing sectors should be put on the same basis. It therefore embarked on a policy of restructuring rents in the two sectors, based on the following principles:[25]

- social rents should remain affordable and well below those in the private sector;
- social rents should be fairer and less confusing for tenants;
- there should be a closer link between rents and the qualities which tenants value in properties; and,
- differences between the rents set by local authorities and housing associations should be removed.

Government has no control of rents, but it bases its subsidy decisions on rent restructuring which means that councils in practice have little alternative but to follow the policy.

Rents are being restructured over a ten year period from 2002-2012 so that they converge and that similar properties in the same area will have very similar rents regardless of ownership or how the home was financed. Under rent restructuring, rent levels are set according to a formula which takes account of the size, condition and location of the property, and local earnings (therefore reflecting particularly principles 1, 2 and 3 above).

By 2012, 30 per cent of rent should be based on relative property values and 70 per cent on relative local earnings. A 'bedroom factor' is applied so that

---

23 Quoted in the housing green paper, ODPM (2000) para. 10.13.
24 DETR (2000).
25 See ODPM (2002) *A Guide to Social Rent Reforms in the Local Authority Sector.*

smaller units have lower rents. This is expressed as a formula where weekly rent is:

70 per cent of average rent for the local authority sector
multiplied by relative county earnings
multiplied by bedroom weighting
plus
30 per cent of the average rent for the sector
multiplied by relative property value.

This is the 'formula rent' for an individual unit which will increase by RPI + 0.5% each year. (Service charges should only increase by RPI). Property values are based on Existing Use Value (i.e. the sale price on the open market). The base year for values is (January) 1999. Figure 12.6 shows a worked example.

Figure 12.6: Example of formula rent calculation under rent restructuring

A 3-bedroom council house in Gloucestershire, with a capital value estimated at £60,000 in January 1999.

average national LA rent in April 2000:	£45.60
average earnings in Gloucestershire:	£308.00
national average earnings:	£316.40
bedroom weight:	1.05
national average LA property value in January 1999:	£41,350

Putting these figures into the formula:
70% x sector-average rent x relative county earnings x bedroom weight
= 70% x £45.60 x £308.00/£316.40 x 1.05 = £32.63 subtotal
30% x sector-average rent x relative property value:
= 30% x £45.60 x £60,000/£41,350 = £19.85 subtotal
adding together the sub-totals, **April 2000 formula rent = £52.48 total**

This would be the **formula rent** for 2000/01. The real terms increases for 2001/02, 2002/03 and 2003/04 would lead to increases as follows:
Formula rent 2001/02 = £52.48 x 4.5% (2% increase + 2.5% inflation) = **£54.84**
Formula rent 2002/03 = £54.84 x 3.5% (1% increase + 2.5% inflation) = **£56.76**
Formula rent 2003/04 = £56.76 x 3.25% (1% increase + 2.25% inflation) = **£58.60**

Source: ODPM (2002) *A Guide to Social Rent Reforms in the Local Authority Sector.*

The new regime was introduced for both local authorities and housing associations in 2002/03 (with some differences in approach between the two sectors). For some landlords in the higher-value areas of London and the south-east it would have led to potentially large rent increases. To mitigate this government limited rent rises to a maximum of £2 per week on top of the RPI + 0.5% increase. Similarly in other areas formula rents were lower than those being charged and reductions were also limited to a maximum of £2 per week. In November 2001 it was further announced that there would be an absolute 'cap' on rents, depending on property size. For example, the maximum rent for a 3 bedroom property in 2003/04 was set at £97.57. These capped rents increase by RPI+1% each year.

The formula rent is used to derive the actual rent for the property, which is done by taking the actual rent for the previous year as the starting point. Figure 12.7 illustrates the procedure for the same property used in Figure 12.6.

Figure 12.7: Example of actual rent calculation under rent restructuring

---

Calculating the actual rent for 2002/03
First, the 2001/02 actual rent needs to be up-rated to 2002/03 levels by applying inflation (as measured by the GDP deflator) and the appropriate real terms increase.

Up-rated 2001/02 **actual rent** = £45 x 3.5% = £46.58

Next the authority calculates the difference between the 2002/03 **formula rent** and the **up-rated rent** above.

2002/03 **formula rent** – 2001/02 **up-rated rent** = £56.76 – £46.58 = £10.18.

Then the 2001/02 **up-rated rent** is moved 1/10th of this difference.

Rent 2002/03 = 2001/02 **up-rated rent** + (**formula rent** 02/03 – **up-rated rent** 01/02)/10
    = £46.58 + £10.18/10
    = £46.58 + £1.02
    = £47.60

In this case, the **formula rent** is below the cap, so the **rent caps** do not have an impact.

But, before setting the **actual rent** for 2002/03 as £47.60, the authority needs to check it has not exceeded the RPI + ½% +/– £2 limits. In setting 2002/03 rent, the September 2001 'all items' annual increase of 1.7% is used. Therefore 2001/02 rent x (RPI + ½%) = £45 x 1.022 = £45.99, and so the maximum rent for the property would be £47.99 while the minimum would be £43.99 per week.

The amount of £47.60 calculated above is within £2 of £45.99. Therefore, the authority would set its **actual rent** in 2002/03 for this property at £47.60.

Source: ODPM (2002) *A Guide to Social Rent Reforms in the Local Authority Sector.*

Local authorities do have some limited discretion within the restructuring policy. For example, there was some flexibility around the start date and there is a continuing discretion of plus or minus five per cent in the application of formula rents. Effectively, however, restructuring has ended what was often a very contentious decision about setting rent levels in a local authority, often taken at a 'rent-setting meeting' a short time before the start of the financial year. That said, it can also be seen as the logical culmination of a process which, from the 1989 Act onwards, has more and more tightly constrained councils' decision-making as to their rent levels.

The government was committed to reviewing rent restructuring after three years. Its review, published in 2004,[26] concluded that limited changes were needed. It judged that 'convergence' of rents with their restructured levels is in danger of taking longer than ten years in high value areas like London, but that the main aim of 'harmonisation' of council and association rents will be achieved. It recommended relatively minor adjustments to the rent increase formula and also higher 'weightings' for larger properties to prevent the differential between large and small properties being eroded. These changes have yet to be implemented.

Rents and their relationship to subsidy

As we have seen, the housing subsidy system is intended to fill the gap between a council's assumed income and its assumed need to spend. Most of this income is rent, so there is a direct relationship between rents and housing subsidy. In order to calculate how much subsidy an authority should receive, the government makes assumptions about the authority's rents. Of course, if subsidy were simply paid on the basis of *actual* rents, authorities could easily reduce them as the lost revenue would be met by increased government subsidy.

The assumption made about income from rent is based on the number of properties held, an allowance for properties that are vacant (2 per cent), and an assumed average rent for the authority: the guideline rent. Immediately prior to rent restructuring, guideline rents for subsidy purposes bore little relation to reality. On average actual local authority rents were some 16 per cent above guideline. Under restructuring, actual and guideline rents should converge (see Figure 12.8).

Currently about 60 per cent of tenants' rents is paid for through rent rebates. The government reimburses local authorities for the cost of rent rebates but only up to a *limit rent*. This is to discourage authorities from putting rent up excessively in the knowledge that most of the extra cost would be met through rent rebate subsidy rather than by local people. Authorities are free to go above the limit rent, but if they do so they must bear the cost of the extra rebates.

Starting in 2002/03, both *guideline rent* and *limit rent* are gradually moving towards the average *formula rent*. If an authority chooses to set a lower rent then it is foregoing rent that the government believes it could fairly charge, and it has to make economies elsewhere in its HRA. If an authority chooses to charge more than the formula rent it has to justify this to tenants and meet the extra cost of rent rebates.

Guideline rent and *limit rent* are moving in ten broadly equal annual steps towards the *formula rent*. The transition is taking place in a way which does not penalise those authorities which move *actual rent* towards the formula as envisaged in rent restructuring.

---

26 ODPM (2004) *Three Year Review of Rent Restructuring*, ODPM, London.

Trends in council rents

Rent restructuring imposes an upward pressure on council rents (and generally a downward pressure on housing association rents) as they move towards harmonisation. It therefore continues trends towards increases in real terms in council rent levels which have occurred across England, Scotland and Wales over many years. Trends in England, their relationship to policy, and how they are likely to develop are portrayed in Figure 12.8. The Audit Commission calculates that once rent restructuring is completed in England in 2012, rents will be about twice as much in real terms as they were in the 1980s.[27] Average rent by authority will then be between £50 and £110 per week.

Figure 12.8: Local authority rents and government policy in England – change in rents 1980 to 2012 at constant (2003) prices

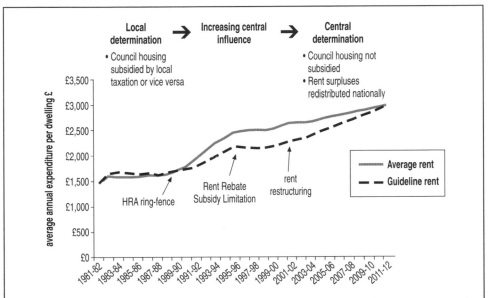

1980s
Local councils were allowed to transfer funds between the General Fund and the housing account, for example, to keep rents low or fund new council housing development.

1990s
The introduction of a ring-fenced HRA prevented councils from subsidising rents and new build, and encouraged councils to put rent up to cover the costs. Many councils increased rents above government guidelines and the government limited the amount of rent rebate subsidy it provided to deter them.

2000s
Council rents began to converge with housing association rents under the government's policy of rent restructuring. This effectively took direct control over rent-setting away from councils and will close the gap between guideline and actual rent.

Source: Audit Commission, 2004

---

27   Audit Commission (2004), in correspondence with John Perry.

Housing Revenue Account income: subsidy in England and Wales

We have seen that HRA subsidy is intended to meet the deficit between a council's judged income and expenditure. The judged income is its guideline rent. Judged expenditure is based on a set of allowances relating to housing services, together with an assessment of loan charges. The three elements together make up the notional HRA which determines whether the authority is judged to be in 'deficit' and how much subsidy is to be paid. Equally, it is used to decide if a council is in 'surplus' and is due to pay money back ('negative subsidy') to the Exchequer.

The relative importance of subsidy has changed according to government policy. After 1989, there was a trend towards cutting general housing subsidy because of the growth of rent rebate subsidy as rents rose. Many authorities ceased to be entitled to general subsidy. Then the pendulum swung back with the introduction of the major repairs allowance (MRA) in 2001/02, which brought many councils back into positive subsidy entitlement. In 2004, when rent rebate subsidy ceased to be part of the notional HRA, the amount of HRA subsidy again fell significantly.

Currently, HRA subsidy totals about £1 billion annually, about two-thirds of which is paid for by negative subsidy payments from councils with surpluses on their notional HRAs. More than half of English local authorities are net contributors to the subsidy pool.

The rest of this section deals with the way subsidy entitlement is established through the 'allowances' set nationally which enter each authority's notional HRA. The actual subsidy entitlement is decided nationally and for each local authority at the end of the calendar year. A draft determination announces the proposed national figures for guideline rents and the various allowances, and the calculations for each local authority. National bodies (including CIH) and individual authorities are consulted and a final determination for the following financial year is then usually made in December.

Management and Maintenance Allowances

Management and Maintenance (M&M) Allowances are the biggest element of HRA subsidy; by 2010 they will amount in each authority to between £20 and £40 per property per week. Even so, they are less than what councils actually spend on administering and looking after the stock. In 2003/04 M&M allowances totalled just over £3 billion in England, while spending on M&M was actually £4 billion. The real 'need to spend' was judged to be as high as £6.44 billion.[28] Recognising this, government has increased M&M allowances by six per cent in real terms in both 2004/05 and 2005/06.

---

28   See ODPM (2003) *The Allocation of Management and Maintenance Allowances with HRA Subsidy.*

M&M allowances are calculated by a complex formula which is summarised in Figure 12.9. This formula applied from 2004/05, and replaced the outdated and widely criticised formula introduced with the 1989 Act. It is being phased in gradually because the effect of the new formula is (broadly) to shift subsidy away from London and the south-east and towards northern authorities.

Figure 12.9: Main elements in calculating M&M allowances, 2005/06

Maintenance component

Thirteen building 'archetypes' are used to model the impact of built form, age and size of dwellings on maintenance costs. They relate to factors such as property type, form of construction and age. An authority's allowance depends on the proportion of each archetype in its stock.

Each archetype has certain 'base weights' associated with it – representing the differential costs of items such as responsive repairs, planned repairs and works to relets.

A 'backlog' factor is added to the responsive repairs base weight, representing the impact of the major repairs backlog on urgent, day-to-day repairs. The responsive repairs costs are also adjusted to reflect extra expenditure related to crime.

The allowance for planned repairs is simply represented by the number of archetypes in each council's stock, multiplied by the base weights.

A measure of the actual number of relets and tenancy terminations is used in assessing the relative cost of re-let works for each authority.

Relative crime levels are used in calculating the allowance relating to crime-related works to void properties.

There is an adjustment for geographical variations in costs.

Management component

The formula takes account of the proportion of flats, to cover the costs of managing communal and shared facilities, and because there is evidence of increased levels of rent arrears, neighbour disputes and racial harassment, particularly in medium and high-rise flats.

A separate deprivation factor is included, based on the government's Index of Deprivation.

Crime levels are used as a proxy for the costs of dealing with anti-social behaviour.

There is recognition that all authorities have a certain level of fixed costs, no matter how few dwellings they have.

A measure of the actual number of voids and relets is used, as there is evidence of the significant costs to all authorities of managing and re-letting void properties.

Major repairs allowance

The major repairs allowance (MRA) was introduced in 2001/02 in England and in 2004/05 in Wales as an intrinsic component of the new resource accounting approach to the HRA, and the principle of the allowance is discussed later in this chapter. It represents the estimated long-term capital cost of maintaining a property in its present condition. Currently it totals over £1 billion in England but is gradually declining as the stock declines. It is estimated that in 2012 average MRA by authority will be between £10 and £20 per property per week. The MRA in Wales was set at £108 million in its first year, 2004/05.

The calculation of the MRA is much simpler than M&M allowances. The same thirteen building archetypes are used as for the maintenance allowance, and each has a national MRA amount allocated each year, based on typical costs of replacing building components (e.g. windows, kitchen, bathroom, roof) for that building type. In 2005/06 the allowances ranged from £359 for older terrace houses to £854 for high-rise flats. An authority's total MRA is broadly decided by the numbers of each building archetype it has in its stock.

Other allowances

Government support for capital spending by authorities with arms length management organisations (ALMOs – see Chapter 10) is paid as a special ALMO allowance, in addition to other HRA subsidy.[29] The same applies to the 'credits' (subsidy) required to finance expenditure on PFI schemes (also see Chapter 10) that is not met by revenue. In 2004/05, there is also a special anti-social behaviour allowance, and in any one year the government may provide special allowances like this to finance particular policy initiatives.

Expenditure on and subsidy for debt charges

The final main element of subsidy is that relating to the costs of capital investment. It amounts to about £4 billion per year, but is the element of subsidy showing the greatest variation between authorities because some have high debts while others are debt-free. The existence of this element of subsidy means that the burden of past or current investment is shared across the council sector rather than falling on each individual authority that undertook it.[30]

While reference is often made to 'HRA debt' in practice all local authority debt is pooled and its costs met by the General Fund. The HRA pays a contribution to these costs based on the historic debt attributed to it, together with the costs of new borrowing undertaken during a particular financial year. The subsidy formula, though based on notional amounts, essentially subsidises all of the on-going loan costs of borrowing accepted for subsidy purposes in previous years, together with new borrowing which arises from that year's Supported Capital Expenditure (SCE) allocation, which we describe in Chapter 9. What is not eligible for subsidy is any unsupported borrowing which the authority undertakes under the prudential borrowing regime, or any revenue contribution to capital outlay (RCCO).

---

29 For later ALMO 'rounds' it is being added as an extra element in normal HRA subsidy, but the effect is the same.
30 Before April 2004 authorities were obliged to make annual payments towards reducing their HRA debt, called minimum revenue provision (MRP). This was abolished in England but continues in Wales.

As we saw earlier, this does not apply to Scotland except in the case of two heavily-indebted councils. The remaining Scottish authorities bear the costs of debt directly from rents.

Housing Revenue Account: expenditure

We are now able to summarise the main elements of HRA expenditure in England and Wales and show how they relate to the subsidy system. They are shown in Figure 12.10. It uses HRA technical terms, as each element is called item 1, item 2, etc. in the regulations relating to the HRA.

Figure 12.10: Summary of Debits to the HRA (England and Wales)

Item	Debit	Subsidy
Item 1	Expenditure on repairs, management and maintenance	Management and maintenance allowance
Item 2	Capital expenditure financed from revenue (RCCOs)	No subsidy
Item 3	Charges which the LA has to pay on HRA properties	Minor item – no subsidy
Item 4	[repealed]	n/a
Item 5	Negative subsidy payments to the Exchequer	n/a
Item 6	Contributions to the Housing Repairs Account (if kept)[31]	n/a
Item 7	Provision for bad debts	No subsidy
Item 8	Capital charges (mainly debt charges and depreciation – see next section of this chapter)	Notional interest costs are eligible for subsidy; depreciation costs are financed by the MRA
Item 9	Debit balance from previous year (if any)	n/a
Item 10	Any required transfers to the General Fund	Not usually permitted

Statute requires local authorities to set a HRA budget annually and make this available as a public document. In practice they have to do this immediately before the start of the financial year, usually in January of February, after the HRA subsidy determination and any other relevant government announcements and when they know approximately what surplus or deficit they will need to carry

---

31   Keeping a Housing Repairs Account is voluntary, and at the time of writing only 20 per cent of authorities do so; as it does not affect the workings of the HRA or of HRA subsidy it is not described here, but a description can be found in the *HRA Subsidy Manual*.

forward from the preceding year. In the past the main focus of decision-making on the HRA has been the setting of the new rent levels, but as we have seen in England this has lost some of its earlier significance.

Resource accounting and the HRA in England and Wales

The principles of resource accounting are described in Chapter 5. Here we explain how they apply to the HRA and what changes have been made to bring the HRA into line with resource accounting principles. Some of the changes that we have already mentioned facilitate this, such as taking rent rebates out of the HRA and making it more closely a 'landlord' account that reflects the actual costs of the housing service.

Why was resource accounting introduced?
Resource accounting is intended to enable local authorities to make better decisions about the use and maintenance of their housing assets, by making more transparent the cost of capital tied up in the assets and providing resources to maintain them. It will bring council house costing closer to the charging regime used in PFI deals thereby helping to open the way to the use of private finance to provide and improve council housing.

What is resource accounting?
Resource accounting is being applied across government. A key feature is that it assesses the cost of capital as the capital is 'used' rather than when it is 'paid for'. In this way, it is meant to record the 'true asset costs' of providing the service during the period covered by the accounts. By making the accounts more transparent, resource accounting should make it easier for managers to assess the extent to which the assets are providing value for money. Under these arrangements, the accounts include a charge for the capital, reflecting the fact that it is tied up (e.g. as in council housing) rather than free to invest and earn a return. Resource accounting encourages the organisation to think in a more business-like fashion by shifting the accounting focus away from its historic costs towards the current value of its assets. By making explicit the maintenance and repair costs associated with low-grade assets, it also draws attention to the consequences of a failure to invest and acts as a stimulus to longer-term planning. In council housing, this aspect was reinforced by the introduction of the major repairs allowance to help provide for future repairs.

Resource accounting aims to restructure public sector accounting rules so that they do not inhibit investment in worthwhile capital projects. Reformers argue the case for moving away from a 'cash-based' accounting model that focuses on cash-flows in a single year, towards an 'accruals' model that focuses on the balance of costs and benefits that accrue over time (e.g. over the physical life of an asset or the term of the loan taken out to build or acquire it). The argument is that cash-based accounting produces a bias in favour of short-term solutions that may prove to be more expensive in the long-run. Take the example of providing social housing for the homeless. Cash-based accounting shows that relatively large sums of public money will need to be committed in the development period causing a 'deficit' in the short-term 'cash' accounts. This may discourage the decision-makers from investing in such assets and instead choose what appears to be the 'cheaper' option of putting homeless households into bed-and-breakfast accommodation. However, accrual accounting, by taking a cost-benefit approach, may show that in the longer period, providing new social housing makes more financial sense than putting homeless people into bed-and-breakfast accommodation.

The new resource accounting arrangements

The object of the new arrangements was to enable authorities to take better decisions about the use of their housing assets by moving the HRA and the calculation of HRA subsidy to a resource accounting, or 'capital charging', basis. The changes make it easier to determine how much money a council has tied up in housing stock, how much it will cost to maintain it, and what level of subsidy is necessary to keep rents below market levels. This, it is claimed, makes the system more transparent for tenants and also highlights the true extent of the backlog in repairs. The key elements of the new approach were:

- making the HRA a true 'landlord' account (by accounting for rent rebates in the General Fund);
- establishing a value for the assets used (the housing stock) and assessing the backlog of work required to put it in good condition;
- making a capital charge to the HRA based on an assumed percentage return on the value of the stock;
- imposing an asset depreciation charge;
- providing a flexible allowance for major housing repairs;
- making rents relate to the value of the asset; and
- introducing HRA business plans and encouraging authorities to behave more commercially.

We now look at these developments (several of which have been discussed above) and how they facilitated resource accounting.

Rent rebates and the end of the cross-subsidy effect

As we have seen, the government has ended the cross-subsidy paid by council tenants in England and Wales to fund housing benefit. Having rent rebates in the HRA distorted its effectiveness as an operating (i.e. 'resource') account as such a charge was nothing to do with business efficiency and was unrelated to the costs of maintaining the assets. Also, because such a charge is not a feature of housing association accounts, it made it difficult to compare the two sectors. Removing rent rebates from the HRA turned it into a quasi-commercial landlord account, based on the value of its housing stock, rather than a welfare account relating to tenants' incomes. The new HRA more accurately reflects financial flows relating to the provision of housing assets.

Valuing the stock and surveying its condition

If councils are to prepare their own effective business plans, they must have 'proper' valuations and an assessment of the finance needed to put them in marketable condition. Similarly if the HRA is to reflect the use of the asset base, those assets must have a value attached to them. The question of stock valuations is discussed on pages 386-390.

Charging for the assets used by the HRA

The charge for assets has two elements. The first is the *capital charge* and relates to the opportunity cost of the capital tied up in the assets; the second is the *depreciation charge* and relates to the costs of depreciation and major repairs.

The capital charge is based on a percentage return (currently 3.5 per cent) on the asset value. Charging the account with the current opportunity cost of the tied up money capital rather than the historic debt cost encourages authorities to see their housing units as valuable economic assets that need to be managed in an optimal way. It underlines the fact that even properties that are out of debt (paid for) are not 'cost free'. In practice the capital charge is a 'signal' within the accounts of the amount of capital being used, it is not an actual charge that has to be met from rents.

The depreciation charge reflects the cost of consumption or 'depreciation' of HRA assets. Depreciation is the wearing out, using up, or other reduction in the remaining life of the asset through use, passage of time, or obsolescence. Depreciation can be measured in different ways, and the HRA rules allow authorities flexibility to decide how they will do it. However, given that the depreciation charge is effectively subsidised by the MRA, most authorities are in practice assessing depreciation on the basis of the MRA, which means that it is based on the annual cost of replacing the key building components that the MRA takes into account (see earlier MRA discussion).

The depreciation charge is intended to encourage authorities to produce stock condition profiles with realistic maintenance and replacement expenditure projections that will allow the production of more coherent asset management plans. The MRA provides greater certainty of future resources and thereby helps to underpin the drive for better asset management planning.

Providing a major repairs allowance

A major disadvantage faced by local authority housing managers compared with those in housing associations is that under the 1989 regime they effectively had available to them only the resources available in any one year for investment in the stock, with little certainty as to future years' allocations and very limited ability to build up reserves or carry money over one from one year to the next. The MRA changed that by providing a regular annual subsidy, calculated on a stable basis, which can be used either in the year in which it is paid or a later year, and enables a reserve (the major repairs reserve) to be established for investment in long-term maintenance of the stock. The MRA is aimed at being sufficient, once the backlog of disrepair has been tackled, to maintain homes in decent, marketable condition.

Making rents relate to asset values
As we have seen, this is an important objective of rent restructuring and is reflected in the fact that the property value is a key element in determining the rent. Where the principles of resource accounting are somewhat compromised is in the need for the rent also to reflect the objective of affordability, so actual rents are not (for example) based on obtaining a commercial return on capital but are significantly below that.

Introducing business plans and more freedom to behave commercially
HRA business plans are concerned with asset management and encouraging the authority to set out how it will maintain or enhance the value of its housing assets, and how its plans to invest in the stock will contribute to wider corporate objectives, such as the reduction in estate-based crime and the promotion of social cohesion. Previous accounting arrangements were felt not to encourage the production of business-like asset management decisions. Of course, a reformed accounting structure by itself cannot change behaviour. The government aims to reinforce these changes by other measures such as the Best Value regime. We discuss business planning fully in Chapter 16 and its relationship to the options for investment in council housing in Chapter 10.

Although resource accounting and related changes have been accompanied by government encouragement to housing authorities to behave more commercially, it has to be said that the scope for this remains limited and many decisions about the assets and their costs are still not made at local level (for example, enforced sales through the right to buy, and rents being effectively set by government through rent restructuring). Nevertheless, resource accounting and accompanying reforms have created greater stability for HRA managers, some increased flexibility, and the possibility of planning further ahead than simply the next year or two.

Summary

Revenue funds are used to pay for the day-to-day running of services rather than for the construction or acquisition of housing assets.

Local authority revenue transactions are recorded in two major ways. Day-to-day spending on services other than council housing is met from the General Fund. Spending on the provision of council housing, however, must be charged to a Housing Revenue Account (HRA). The distinction between HRA spending and non-HRA spending is key to an understanding of local government housing finance.

Central government supports the General Fund through the Revenue Support Grant and by redistributing the national pool of business rates. It supports the HRA by providing HRA subsidy. The HRA subsidy entitlement is calculated by reference to a notional account and its purpose is to cover the deficit on that notional account. The notional account provides a control mechanism through which the central authorities seek to administer the distribution of subsidy.

Apart from central government support, the main sources of income are council taxes (to the General Fund) and council housing rents (to the HRA).

Since 1990 in England and Wales, and for longer in Scotland, the HRA has been ring-fenced. This prevents transfer of money from the General Fund and restricts money transfers from council housing to support the council tax fund.

The HRA system in England and Wales, though still based on the 1989 Act, has undergone significant changes since 2001, culminating in the 2003 Act which introduced separate accounting arrangements for rent rebates. These changes have reinforced the character of the HRA as a 'landlord' account, and they have also introduced some of the principles of resource accounting to the HRA.

In Scotland there has been no such recent overhaul of the HRA, which in most authorities now receives little or no subsidy. This has created a different picture for spending on council housing in Scotland, with more flexibility to finance spending in the housing stock but also, in some cases, high levels of debt.

Further reading

ODPM (2004) *Housing Revenue Account Manual.* The current edition (it is revised annually) can be downloaded from the ODPM website (www.odpm.gov.uk).

CHAPTER 13:
Housing associations and registered social landlords: an introduction

The term 'housing association' is now commonly used to describe the various forms of registered social landlord (RSL) and is therefore used freely in the following chapters on this topic. This introductory chapter identifies the objectives of this housing sector and briefly describes its institutional framework of regulation and control. Chapter 14 considers development issues and describes and analyses the sector's capital finance regime. Chapter 15 describes the basic revenue finance regime for housing associations and says something about rents and the consumption interests of tenants. Chapters 16 and 17 consider some aspects of the financial management of such social landlords. How social landlords pay for the provision of support services for people with special needs is discussed both in an appendix to Chapter 15 and in Chapter 19.

What is the social rented sector?

Over the last forty years, governments have encouraged the development of the housing association movement as a 'third force' in housing provision. This encouragement has in part been motivated by a desire to prevent the housing system from becoming polarised between purely private provision on the one hand and municipal provision on the other. Although technically independent from central and local government, most housing associations have received funds from the public purse and have been held accountable for how this money has been spent. Along with other not-for-profit agencies, they are sometimes referred to as 'public interest companies' or 'community interest companies' – or more generally as 'social enterprises'.[1] Social enterprises are businesses with primarily social objectives whose surpluses are principally reinvested with a view to achieving those objectives. In this respect they contrast with commercial businesses that are driven by the need to maximise profit for shareholders and owners.

---

1   Housing associations are also included within the Neill Committee's definition of 'Local Public Spending Bodies'. These are conceived of as not-for-profit organisations that are rarely elected and whose members are not appointed by ministers, but which provide local public services that are wholly or part funded by the tax-payer. The concept of Local Public Spending Bodies was used by the Nolan Committee, now the Neill Committee. (*Second Report of the Committee on Standards in Public Life*,1996).

Housing associations can provide housing for rent, leasing, or part sale, and are established for the declared and limited purpose of giving housing advice or themselves acquiring, building, improving, maintaining, or managing dwellings (including hostels), or helping others so to do. In line with the present government's policy of developing housing and housing services in ways that promote social cohesion, well-being and self-dependence, associations have been given wider permitted purposes. The 2000 green paper *Quality and Choice: A Decent Home for All*, (DETR and Social Security), made it clear that the government now expects associations to contribute to housing-related manifestations of social exclusion (such as unemployment, relationship breakdown and drug dependency) and help address other factors that affect the quality of life (such as area regeneration and community safety). Since the late 1990s associations have also been able to develop group structures which allow sister organisations to be set up that can undertake activities that RSLs cannot, such as to develop units for outright sale.

There is no such thing as a typical housing association and the sector is becoming increasingly diverse. The legislative definition[2] embraces a variety of organisations variously constituted as 'societies' (founded on principles of self-help or mutuality), or 'trusts' (founded on principles of charity or the concern for the welfare of others), or 'companies' (founded on principles of business enterprise). More specifically, in England and Wales such landlords can be organisations previously registered (pre-1996), under part 1 of the Housing Associations Act 1985, industrial and provident societies (registered with the Registrar of Friendly Societies),[3] charitable trusts (registered with the Charities Commission), or companies limited by guarantee (registered at Companies House).[4] Social landlords can be charitable or non-charitable organisations. In this context, the notion of 'charity' involves the organisation defining and declaring specific benevolent objectives together with a commitment to use its financial surpluses solely for such purposes. A 'non-charitable' social landlord is allowed to operate without having to declare charitable objectives, but it is nevertheless debarred from trading for profit.

Most associations seeking charitable status do so under the 'relief of poverty' head of charity. To achieve this, they must demonstrate that a 'substantial majority' of beneficiaries are in 'necessitous circumstances'. Central government is currently considering 'modernising' the law relating to not-for-profit organisations and

---

2   Part 1, Chapter 1 of the Housing Act 1996. In the consultations that led up to the act, the government pushed for profit-seeking companies to be embraced by the legislation, but these proposals were not implemented and all social landlords must still operate on a not-for-profit basis.

3   An industrial and provident society is an organisation that conducts its business either as a co-operative or for the benefit of the community (rather than for its members) and which is registered under the 1965 Industrial and Provident Societies Act.

4   This form of company is similar to a conventional company limited by shares and its operations are governed by the Company Acts. However, instead of shareholders it has members, and instead of buying shares and receiving dividends, they offer a guarantee (usually nominal £1) as the limit of their liability.

charities and this means that in the near future there may be a widening of the definition of 'charitable purposes' that will make it possible for social landlords to apply for charitable status under a specific 'provision of social housing' heading.[5]

Many of the more recently formed social landlords have been created as a result of transferring local authority housing to the ownership and management of new landlords. The Housing Act 1996 extended eligibility for registration in England and Wales to not-for-profit, non-charitable companies including local housing companies set up by local authorities (refer to Chapter 10). It should be noted that large scale voluntary transfer (LSVT) of local authority stock to housing associations was already established before 1996 (allowed for under the Housing Act 1985). LSVT has helped to transform the balance of responsibility in providing social housing.[6] On current projections, housing associations will have become the biggest provider of social housing in England by 2005/6.

In Scotland LSVT (that began in local authorities with Berwickshire[7]) has been slow compared with England, although since 2003 first Glasgow then two smaller authorities have completed whole stock transfers. Since 1997, government policy has advocated stock transfer and the Scottish Executive has modified the registration and regulation regime to encourage the policy. In Wales, there is similar encouragement from the National Assembly but so far this has only resulted in fairly small-scale transfers. In Northern Ireland, the housing association sector is small (less than four per cent of the stock) and stock transfer has not yet been considered. In Northern Ireland there are 39 registered housing associations providing about 22,000 homes. These represent 16 per cent of the province's publicly-funded stock.[8]

What is a registered social landlord (RSL)?

Registered social landlord (RSL) is the technical or legal name for a social housing provider registered with the Housing Corporation in England or the Welsh Assembly Government. In Scotland the term 'registered social landlord'

---

5   Proposed changes stem from a report published by the Cabinet Office's Strategy Unit in September 2002 called *Private Action, Public Benefit*. Although not specifically analysed in the report, it has been suggested that a further purpose of '*the provision of social and affordable housing*' be created. The report recommends that charities should be allowed greater freedom to trade directly (without having to set up separate trading subsidiaries). This will allow them to exploit new revenue generating activities. On the other hand, it would clearly involve charitable organisations taking commercial risks and this would require a statutory redefinition of the role and responsibilities of trustees. They would have to accept a new duty of care with respect to these trading activities.

6   E.g. Since 1988 more than 800,000 homes have been transferred from 136 English local authorities to housing associations.

7   Transfer in Scotland during the 1990s was characterised by smaller-scale transfers in cities such as Glasgow, and larger scale transfers (often to housing associations) of new town and Scottish Homes stock.

8   The three largest associations, Belfast Improved Houses, Fold, and Oaklee, together provide about half of all association homes in Northern Ireland.

---

is also increasingly used by the Scottish regulator (Communities Scotland). The Northern Ireland Department for Social Development tends to use the term 'registered housing association' or 'social housing' when describing this sector. Most registered social landlords are technically housing associations, but trusts, co-operatives and companies may also come under the heading. To cut through the confusion the term 'housing association' is now commonly used to described all non-municipal providers of social housing.[9] The above mentioned 'regulators' seek to ensure that all these registered social landlords operate efficiently and meet specified minimum standards of housing quality and service to tenants.

Financing RSLs: an overview

Later we will look in detail at the sources of finance,[10] but for the time being we will simplify matters by saying that housing associations receive funding from three primary sources.

1. Rental income from *tenants*.
2. Grants from the *government*.
3. Loans from *private lenders*.

In addition to these primary resources, some social landlords receive financial support from associated charities and from private donations and bequests.

If registered with the appropriate regulator the organisation becomes eligible to take advantage of government subsidies. In recent years, about half of the capital finance for housing associations has come from the state in the form of grants and most of the remainder has taken the form of loans from banks, building societies or other institutions. By investing this mixture of public and private funds, housing associations have now become the main providers of new social housing in the UK. They have built about a quarter of a million new dwellings over the last ten years. By 2004 they were managing two million homes and each year re-housing over 120,000 households.

Within constraints, housing associations are allowed to generate surpluses, but unlike pure commercial enterprises, these cannot be distributed as dividends. Given their welfare objectives and level of public funding, commercial shareholding and trading for profit are not allowed and the unrestrained principles of business free-enterprise are deemed to be inappropriate. Having said this, associations are expected to operate in a business-like fashion and to use their financial resources in ways that are seen to be efficient and effective (see Chapter 2 for discussion on the notion of *value-for-money*).

---

9   Over the years there has been considerable debate about how to describe the sector (see Mullins, 'More Choice in Social Rented Housing' in Marsh and Mullins, 1998). To some extent this confusion persists.
10 Chapters 14 and 15 consider this topic in more detail.

Before looking in detail at how housing associations acquire and manage their capital and revenue funds, we need to assess their contribution to housing provision and say a little more about how their activities are managed and supervised.

The size and structure of the sector

By the end of the twentieth century, social housing had become recognised as being 'big business'[11] with associations owning around £50 billion worth of assets, managing an annual revenue turnover of several billion pounds, and receiving private finance in excess of £15 billion. UK housing associations now provide more than two million homes for more than four million people. About seven per cent of the stock of dwellings in Britain is rented from housing associations and other non-local authority social landlords (2002 *General Household Survey: Living in Britain* (2004, ONS)).

Individual housing associations vary in size from relatively small non-developing organisations managing a few dwellings and carrying out no new construction, to large active conglomerates managing 20,000 dwellings or more, operating a development programme, and employing hundreds of staff. Many associations are actively engaged in the process of building and refurbishing houses; the rest restrict their activities to managing existing properties. During the early 1990s the sector consolidated through a process of mergers so that by the middle of the decade the ten largest associations managed about a quarter of the movement's total stock and the largest 200 owned three-quarters of the stock. Although the larger associations are now prominent, the majority of associations are still relatively small in comparison with local authority housing departments. On average, associations in Scotland and Northern Ireland are smaller than those in England and Wales.

A concentration of development activity

Since 1989, as far as development is concerned, a sharper distinction has emerged between the relatively small and the relatively large associations, particularly in England. The emphasis on 'value for public money' (or 'grant stretch'), coupled with the need to raise a higher proportion of the capital funding from private institutions (called 'mixed funding'), has meant that development activity has increasingly centred on the relatively larger associations. These are better positioned to provide collateral for loans, enjoy financial and managerial economies of scale, and they can cross-subsidise more costly projects from surpluses. In contrast, smaller, specialist associations have less scope to demonstrate value-for-money in a development role.

---

11 This is reflected by the title of the 1997 conference of social housing finance executives and staff organised by the National Housing Federation in York: 'Housing Finance – Big Business'.

The aims and objectives of the sector

Despite the important structural and motivational differences that necessarily exist between organisations that have been set up at different times for different reasons, it is nevertheless possible to identify a number of general aspirations, activities, characteristics and objectives that are shared by housing associations as a whole. The common aim of the sector is to provide decent housing and related services for people on low incomes and in housing need. More particularly, the Housing Act 1996 sets as criteria for registration that RSLs (in England and Wales) must be non-profit bodies providing rented housing and with the following additional permitted purposes:

- providing land, amenities or services, or providing, constructing, repairing or improving buildings, for their residents;
- acquiring, or repairing and improving, or creating by the conversion of houses or other property, houses to be disposed of on sale, on lease or on shared ownership terms;
- constructing houses to be disposed of on shared ownership terms;
- managing houses held on leases or other lettings or blocks of flats;
- providing services of any description for owners or occupiers of houses in arranging or carrying out works of maintenance, repair or improvement, or encouraging or facilitating the carrying out of such works; and
- encouraging and giving advice to other voluntary organisations concerned with providing housing or services related to housing.

Although the primary function of a housing association is to be a social landlord, many have now moved into other areas of activity such as providing housing for sale, partnering renewal schemes, providing care activities, etc., and this has led to a wider use of group structures and unregistered subsidiaries. The government has now moved to recognise this growing diversity by widening the permitted purposes of RSLs to include regeneration activities, and by instigating various changes to the regulatory regime.

Accountability

Although, unlike local authority housing departments, housing associations are not controlled by directly-elected representatives of local tax-payers, they are subject to internal and external scrutiny and regulation.

Internal

Together this diverse group of non-profit-making organisations is sometimes referred to as 'the voluntary housing movement'. This is because until recently they were directed by unpaid committees or boards whose members are drawn from all parts of the local community, including their own tenants. (Although this is still largely the case, board member payments are now permitted in England,

and some, mainly larger, associations have begun to make them.). This group of 'volunteers' takes overall responsibility for the organisation's policy and work but is not usually involved in the day-to-day management. Typically, each association is managed by a paid chief executive who heads a team of officers, many of whom will be professionally and technically qualified. The financial effects of past activities are recorded in 'standard' accounts (see below and following chapters). End of period *financial statements* are produced which typically comprise the audited set of standard accounts together with a report by the board, legal and administrative details, and an auditors' report.

External

Housing associations are independent in the sense that they do not operate as direct agents of central or local government. However, they do receive significant sums of public money and because of this, their development and management activities are scrutinised and, to some considerable extent, controlled by the public bodies that have been vested with statutory powers of supervision (see below). They are also answerable to any external firms and agencies that have lent them money. Those associations that borrow a proportion of their development finance from private sources need to demonstrate to lenders that they are properly managed and have adequate collateral to cover their debts. The issue of financial planning and management is discussed more fully in Chapters 16 and 17.

Regulation and control

Housing associations across Britain originally had a common regulator but the picture is now more complicated because of devolved government in Scotland, Wales and Northern Ireland.

The role and duties of the regulators

Since their creation, the regulators have been charged with a general duty to encourage, scrutinise and control the activities of housing associations in their areas. They have five broad roles:

1. *To monitor the effectiveness* of governance and quality of services.
2. *To monitor and regulate* the sector's overall financial health, core performance indicators, risk management, rent levels, and non-core housing work (e.g. their work in areas such as community care).
3. *To channel public investment* to associations in a way that seeks to help meet local needs and achieve value-for-money.
4. *To promote improved performance* in service delivery by disseminating research findings, and publishing directives and guidance notes.
5. *To apply the principles of targeting and proportionality* that have been established by the government's Better Regulation Task Force.

Regulation principles

The Better Regulation Task Force has specified five key principles that good regulation should meet.

1. *Transparency:* regulation should be open, simple and user-friendly. Among other things, this means that rules should be unambiguous and unnecessary procedures should be avoided.
2. *Accountability:* the regulator should have clear lines of accountability to ministers, parliament, users and the public. Among other things this means that employees and service users should be able to report malpractice without fear of reprisals.
3. *Targeting:* regulation should be focused on key problems and minimise side effects. Among other things this means that regulation processes should focus on strategic issues and not be too prescriptive and process-orientated.
4. *Consistency:* regulatory judgements should be predicable. Among other things this means that officers in different regions should operate on a common basis (whilst allowing for differing regional needs).
5. *Proportionality:* regulators should only regulate when necessary and remedies should fit risks. Among other things this means that small, non-developing associations should not be subject to the same degree of regulation as larger associations that engage in development activities.

England

In England, the regulator is a non-departmental public body called the Housing Corporation. The Corporation is ultimately responsible to the Office of the Deputy Prime Minister (ODPM) for ensuring that associations provide value-for-money and operate in line with the requirements of the Regulatory Code and Guidance. Since April 2003 the Audit Commission has become involved in the process of inspection. Significant issues that result from the inspection are passed to the Housing Corporation that takes more of a regulatory perspective. The Commission and Corporation do, of course, work together so if, as part of the regulatory procedures, the Corporation comes across an operational problem, this may trigger an inspection by the Commission.

The Housing Corporation's headquarters are in London but for regulatory and investment purposes it operates through a network of five regional offices. Within each region a number of field offices deal with day-to-day administrative matters. The network of offices carries out the day-to-day liaison with the individual associations and plays a key part in managing the distribution of development resources (refer to Chapter 14). The Corporation is accountable to a board of management and a chief executive, all of whom are appointed by the deputy prime minister who also receives an annual written report from the Corporation.

The Corporation has a statutory duty to regulate the performance of over 2,000 English RSLs and to ensure that the homes they provide are efficiently and effectively managed. It channels public funds into the sector to help associations play a part in meeting the government's target for the supply of affordable homes for people in housing need. It is itself accountable to ministers and, through them, to parliament for how this public money is employed. Ministers expect to see that the grant aid is invested in ways that help to deliver the government's policies for the sector. Its regulatory activities are also expected to reinforce the government's broader policies relating to efficiency, decent homes, rent restructuring, urban regeneration, welfare to work, social exclusion, community safety, and energy conservation. As the sector's regulator, it seeks to ensure that associations provide their tenants with substantial rights and a good quality of service. As a catalyst of good practice, it commissions research and sponsors an Innovation and Good Practice Programme that supports practical projects that test new ideas for the benefit of social landlords, their tenants and the wider community.

The Housing Corporation's work is expected to take account of wider regional economic and planning strategies. In England eight Regional Development Agencies were launched in March 1999. Although their main role is currently seen to promote economic development and tackle the perceived imbalance in economic growth between the English regions, at some time in the future they could become included in the government's long-term plans for English devolution. Their responsible bodies, the regional chambers, could evolve into full-blown assemblies like those in Scotland, Wales and Northern Ireland if voters so decide. In any event, because housing is intrinsically linked to economic development, these new strategic bodies are bound to exert increasing influence over how housing provision is planned and financed in England.

As part of the drive to create a more strategic approach to housing development, *regional housing boards* were established in 2003 (following the publication of the *Sustainable Communities Plan*). Many aspects of housing need are now planned on a regional or sub-regional basis. This is in recognition of the fact that housing markets cross local authority boundaries and that a better use of resources is likely to be produced by using regional knowledge informed by a proper analysis of local housing needs. We will say more about their work in subsequent chapters (in particular see Chapter 14).

The Independent Housing Ombudsman
Tenants in England with a grievance against an RSL may seek support from the Ombudsman so long as they can demonstrate that all other avenues of redress have been explored.

Wales

In Wales, Tai Cymru, (Housing for Wales), used to regulate Welsh housing associations, having taken over responsibility from the Housing Corporation.[12] However, with the creation of the National Assembly for Wales, the Social Justice

---

12 Tai Cymru was set up by parliament in 1989. It invested more than £1.5 billion, and produced over 30,000 new and improved homes for people who could not afford to buy or rent on the open market. Like the Housing Corporation, it had a statutory responsibility to regulate RSLs.

and Regeneration Department of the Welsh Assembly Government took over both the regulatory and funding roles of Welsh housing associations.[13] Given that the department also regulates local authority housing, it became the first 'single regulator' in Great Britain, a role now also taken on by Communities Scotland (see below).

Wales has 77 housing associations owning about 60,000 properties, four per cent of the housing stock.

Scotland

Prior to devolution, regulation was the responsibility of an agency called Scottish Homes.[14] In Scotland, the regulatory function is now carried out by Communities Scotland, which was established by the Housing (Scotland) Act 2001 to have regulatory responsibility for both the housing association and local authority sectors. Communities Scotland is a Scottish Executive agency that aims to work with others to ensure decent housing and strong communities across Scotland. The Scottish Executive is the administrative arm of government in Scotland and it has responsibility for all public bodies whose functions and services have been devolved to it. It is accountable to the Scottish Parliament.

In pursuing its goals, Communities Scotland sponsors a wide-ranging research programme and works in partnership with local authorities, housing associations, the voluntary sector, private developers, economic development agencies, financial institutions and local communities. It is intimately involved with both housing development and refurbishment, and the sponsorship of partnership approaches to urban development and renewal.

In addition to its cross-tenure strategic role, Communities Scotland has a specific regulating role with respect to the activities of housing associations. Like the Housing Corporation in England, it regulates and channels funds into the sector (although there is provision in Scotland for the funding role to be delegated to authorities that have transferred their stock – see Chapter 11).

The profile of Scottish associations is rather different from those in England and Wales. Many were established in the 1970s as relatively small and locally-based associations, and a significant proportion were established to implement renewal programmes associated with the tenement housing so prominent in many Scottish

---

13   The Welsh Assembly Government develops and implements policy and is accountable to the National Assembly for Wales.

14   Scottish Homes was set up in April 1989 and, like the Housing Corporation in England, it received government funding and provided supervision of, and support for, housing associations. Scottish Homes was created by amalgamating the Scottish Housing Corporation and the Scottish Special Housing Association (SSHA). Its primary purposes was to help provide good quality, affordable housing for those in need and to contribute to the regeneration of local communities.

cities. Until recent large-scale transfers, there were just under 200 associations owning about six per cent of the housing stock; three-quarters of them had less than 1,000 properties each. Communities Scotland supports local authority stock transfers both to larger, specially-formed associations as in England, and to smaller tenant-orientated management co-operatives and associations.

The tradition of publicly-supported housing has been stronger in Scotland than elsewhere in the UK, and as a result, although development grant rates (still sometimes called 'Housing Association Grant' in Scotland) have fallen, they have remained significantly higher than those in England and Wales. As in England, the regulation activities operate through regional offices. The front-line support and monitoring work of the agency is carried out through five such offices, based on Scotland's local authority areas.

Northern Ireland

The Northern Ireland Department for Social Development, part of the Northern Ireland government, regulates and funds just 39 associations accounting for less than four per cent of the housing stock. The department is responsible to the Northern Ireland Assembly when devolution is operating, otherwise to Northern Ireland ministers in the UK government. There have been proposals, not yet implemented, to transfer the regulatory role to the Northern Ireland Housing Executive (NIHE – see Chapter 8). However, associations inevitably have a close relationship with the Executive which is often involved in facilitating new housing association development.

Policy in Northern Ireland has been to maintain firm central control of housing association capital funding. Fear of sectarian influence and discriminatory practices made Westminster slow to encourage a shift to mixed funding arrangements and the greater independence of action that would follow. By the 1990s, however, mixed funded schemes were being promoted in the province albeit with a greater degree of central government scrutiny than elsewhere in the UK. In the first eight years of mixed funding, it was estimated that associations raised just £125 million in private loans.[15]

As we explained in Chapter 8, since 1971 responsibility for the provision of public sector housing has been in the hands of the Northern Ireland Housing Executive, which was formed as a non-sectarian body to overcome the discriminatory allocation practices that had long been associated with local authority politics. The former local authority housing stock was transferred to the NIHE to manage and develop. In contrast to local authorities in other parts of the UK, the NIHE continued to have a significant house building programme in the 1990s and by the middle of the decade its new-build output constituted more than half of the UK's

---

15 Quoted in Mackay and Williamson 'Housing Associations in Ireland, North and South' in Paris, C. (Ed) (2001) *Housing in Northern Ireland*, CIH.

total public sector output. Direct housing provision by the Executive has now
been wound down and the development role has been passed to housing
associations. However, unlike other parts of the UK (such as with the former
Scottish Homes properties in Scotland), there is currently no proposal to end the
housing management role of the NIHE through stock transfer to other landlords.
A common waiting list and selection scheme is used by the Executive and the
housing associations.

Registration and its obligations

For administrative purposes, social landlords are divided into registered and non-
registered categories. Although we are primarily concerned with the contributions
of the registered sector, the reader should bear in mind that some social landlords
choose not to be registered.[16] By not being registered, such associations, trusts
and companies are not eligible to apply for a share of the grant aid that is
channelled through the non-departmental public bodies (see below and Chapter
14). They do, of course, avoid the duty to provide added information and the
other administrative requirements that come with regulation. One reason for
not registering is that it gives the organisation the freedom to operate on a
co-ownership basis.

The changing nature of regulation: the Regulatory Code and Guidance

Because strong regulation can have negative as well as positive consequences for
the ways in which housing associations operate, the various systems of central
regulation in England, Scotland, and Wales have recently been altered in ways
that encourage individual landlords to become more strategic and innovative. It
would seem that strong and detailed regulation was deemed necessary in the early
days of devolution as a way of enforcing quick and coherent culture changes. As
the government's modernising agenda becomes bedded down and Best Value
principles more fully accepted, the central control mechanisms are becoming more
flexible. Current regulations allow for a greater degree of local discretion and self-
assessment. We will illustrate this shift of emphasis by reference to the English
system and the Housing Corporation's new Regulatory Code and Guidance.[17]

In 2002, the regulatory system in England was modified. The new Regulatory
Code replaced the previous detailed 'performance standards' system. The new
regulatory requirements replace what was a rather routine 'tick box' approach
with a new system that is less prescriptive and more focused on outcomes.

---

16 Examples of non-registered associations include MHS Homes, which was the transfer body
    for Rochester's housing stock in Kent, and Waverley Homes in Scotland which has only
    recently (2003) become registered.
17 See also Chapter 14.

The code covers both management and development.[18] In Chapter 14 we will explore in more detail how the code impacts on development activities. In this introductory chapter we will simply outline the general principles that lie behind the code and consider some of the consequences that result from regulation.

The new code resulted from consultations throughout the sector and is designed to secure the continuous viability of housing associations by ensuring that they are properly managed with sound governance. By stressing self-assessment, backed up by 'proportionate' regulation, the Corporation seeks to establish a 'less intrusive' system that does not over-burden the administration of individual organisations. It seeks to encourage associations to be innovative and to improve services by being responsive to residents while, at the same time, paying careful attention to the overall management of resources and risks.

Registered associations are required to monitor their activities and seek to achieve value-for-money and 'continuous improvement' in line with the Regulatory Code and Guidance. This requires each association to operate a self-assessment exercise covering such factors as financial viability, risk management, effective leadership and governance, equal opportunities, performance of suppliers, contractors and consultants, rent-setting policy, management procedures and skills, customer care, the provision of decent homes, anti-social behaviour, and partnering arrangements.

The regulatory procedures focus on three broad areas of activity, namely:

- viability;
- governance;
- management.

For larger associations, three key features of the new 'lighter touch' arrangements are:

1. An annual compliance statement that will involve the board of management in considering their responsibilities with respect to the code; and
2. A regulatory plan, drawn up by the Corporation, which is a document specific to each association setting out the expected regulatory engagement and any concerns with details of how these will be tackled.
3. An annual viability review that focuses on the financial health of the organisation.

A wider range of information (such as business plans, risk management strategies and BME/diversity plans) also has to be made available to the Corporation, though associations have a degree of flexibility in how and when this information is produced. The Corporation retains its right to ask for other specific information,

---

18   See the Housing Corporation pamphlet, *The way forward: Our approach to regulation*, 2002, for a fuller summary.

but does not now intend to ask routinely for a mass of details. Broadly speaking, the code requires social landlords to *'develop and manage good quality homes that seek to meet people's needs now and in the future'*.

Since 2003 the Corporation has operated *Housing Corporation Assessments* (HCAs). These give a public statement of the Corporation's current view of each association under the three main headings of the Regulatory Code (viability, governance and management). It is expected that the HCA approach will be refined and developed over time as a means of enhancing the 'transparency principle' which is a key feature of both the Better Regulation Task Force (see above) and the Chancellor of the Exchequer's wider fiscal code (see Chapter 5).

When regulating the relatively larger associations (e.g. with more than 250 dwellings), the regulators pays particular attention to their financial capacity. A report is produced for each association that constitutes an annual assessment of its financial viability. These *annual viability reviews* (AVRs) are based on credit-rating methodology (see Chapter 17). The AVR report focuses on a rolling five-year assessment period. Although the details are treated as commercially confidential (i.e. are not published), the key findings of the AVRs are reflected in the viability section of the HCA.

The AVR report is structured to provide:

- An executive summary and a brief background description of the association and its activities.
- An analysis and commentary on:
    - its operating environment, strategy and turnover;
    - its operating margins and efficiency measures;
    - its cash-flows;
    - its capital structure and treasury management.

The approach to regulation is constantly under review. There is some concern amongst academics, practitioners and commentators that despite the 2002 changes, the sector is still 'over regulated' and there has been much debate about introducing an even softer approach to regulation that would be less bureaucratic in nature and allow for greater experimentation and diversity of practice. The argument is that overregulation leads to a 'compliant' management culture rather than a genuine 'performance' culture.

Housing associations and the efficiency agenda

Following the Sir Peter Gershon's review of public sector efficiency[19] and the subsequent Spending Review (2004), the government made it clear that it was committed to deliver significant efficiency gains across the social housing

---

19   HM Treasury (2004) *Releasing Resources to the Frontline: Independent Review of Public Sector Efficiency.*

sector.[20] By saving money through more efficient procurement and more effective management practices, social landlords are expected to release resources into front-line activities and thereby deliver better services to their tenants. In 2005, with this policy in mind, the ODPM announced it was piloting a series of initiatives to share best practice throughout the sector, including the increased use of procurement consortia. This drive for greater efficiency will be further addressed through changes in the bidding process for public funds.[21]

Accountability and financial management: an overview[22]

The need for professional financial management and the requirement to produce financial statements

The 1989 financial regime enhanced the financial profiles of housing associations and increased the risks attached to their financial management. This pointed to the need for associations to follow a clear professional code of practice for treasury management. (See Chapters 16 and 17 for discussion on financial planning and management and risk appraisal and management). Such a code was put forward in 1994 by the public sector accountants' professional body (CIPFA). The voluntary code is broadly based on that used in local authority housing departments but amended to take account of the views of the regulatory bodies in England, Scotland and Wales as well as of the appropriate UK federations. The code seeks to establish a framework that recognises the processes of control, reflects the decisions that have to be made, and concentrates on the policy issues that result. It is intended to ensure that there are appropriate reporting lines and procedures to enable landlords to implement their policies while, at the same time, making those who make these decisions properly accountable for their actions.

The code emphasises the point that the effective employment of money always involves a degree of risk and that treasury management decisions need to be explicit about the relationship between financial risks on the one hand and returns and benefits on the other. A Treasury policy statement is considered to be at the heart of sound and accountable financial management. Such a statement might be expected to give guidance on the following.

- The limits of approved treasury activity.
- How the financial management strategy is formulated.
- The approved methods of raising capital finance.
- The approved sources of finance.

---

20 The specific commitment is to achieve efficiency gains in the social housing sector worth at least £835 million a year by 2007-08.
21 For details see ODPM (2005) *Social Housing Efficiency: A Discussion Paper*.
22 This topic is discussed in detail in Chapters 16 and 17.

- Policy on interest rate exposure.
- Policy on external cash managers.
- Delegated powers.
- Review and reporting arrangements.

As well as clarifying and bounding financial responsibilities, a Treasury policy statement sets a clear and concrete structural framework within which financial policy can be developed. We will look at these issues in more detail in subsequent chapters.

The structure of RSL accounts

Since the early 1990s housing association accounts have had to be presented in 'plc format' in accordance with accounting policies detailed in the Statement of Recommended Practice (SORP), drawn up by the four national federations in England, Wales, Scotland and Northern Ireland. Prior to that date, housing association accounting practices were rather idiosyncratic reflecting their historical detachment from normal commercial business. With the development of mixed funding and the requirement to work more closely with private sector partners and funders, it became increasingly important to present their accounts in a format that matched that required by the various companies acts. In particular, it was felt that housing association accounts should have the following features. They should:

- reflect sound contemporary accounting practices and procedures;
- allow for the development of accounting policies that are relevant to the movement and which can be constantly applied to all social landlords; and,
- be clearly understood by other organisations who have an interest in, or financial relationship with, housing associations.

The main objective of the SORP is to provide guidance to associations on complying with the statutory instruments (first introduced in 1992) that require the accounts to conform to the relevant companies acts. Auditors and civil servants are also concerned that accounting practices in this sector do not diverge significantly from those used in local authority housing departments. In future, the demands of government policy mean that there will be an increasing need to compare efficiency and effectiveness criteria across the whole of social housing provision. This fact underlines the need for a degree of commonality in accounting practices across all social housing providers.

The need to take a cost-benefit approach to financial management

Given the fact that many housing associations are relatively small organisations, the drive to conform to the 'efficiency agenda' may put an upward pressure on costs. Because the sector's regulators place an emphasis on both cost reduction and Best Value, some social landlords will be confronted with a conflict of objectives. This means that any Best Value initiative involving the utilisation of additional resources should be analysed in ways that measure intangible, as well as tangible, costs and benefits. Best Value, resource accounting and resource budgeting all point to the need for social housing strategists and managers to develop cost-benefit assessment techniques that enable proper account to be taken of such relevant intangibles as tenant empowerment and staff morale.

Summary

Housing associations are non-profit-distributing organisations that, along with local authorities, provide and manage dwellings that are allocated principally on the basis of need rather than on ability to pay. Most are part publicly-funded, independent of local authorities and governed by boards of elected committee members (usually unpaid), drawn mainly from local communities. Housing associations are run as businesses, but any surpluses made are used to maintain existing homes and help fund new ones. Some associations provide 'general needs' rented accommodation, whilst others cater for specific groups such as the elderly or people requiring special support. Certain associations operate low-cost home-ownership schemes. They range in size from small, locally-based organisations to those with thousands of units across the country.

In recent years, housing associations have been the main providers of new social rented accommodation.

Although there is no such thing as a 'typical' association they share the following core values:

- a focus on need and affordability;
- a commitment to independence from local and central government;
- a concern to create and maintain 'sustainable' social housing;
- a commitment to obtain added value from housing management and investment;
- a commitment to build partnerships with stakeholders in communities;
- an increasing commitment to act as housing-centred regeneration agencies.

Registration places an obligation of external regulation and control, but also qualifies the association to bid for centrally provided resources.

The accounts and financial reports of housing associations are now in a common format which makes it easier to compare their performances and for private sector partners and funders to understand their affairs.

Further reading

Overall introduction to housing associations:
Harriott, S. and Matthews, L. (2004) *Introducing Social Housing*, CIH, Coventry

More detail on housing associations outside England:
Paris, C. (Ed) (2001) *Housing in Northern Ireland*, CIH, Coventry.

ODPM (2005) *Social Housing Efficiency: A Discussion Paper*, ODPM.

Sim, D. (Ed) (2004) *Housing and Public Policy in Post-Devolution Scotland*, CIH, Coventry.

Smith, R. *et al.* (2000) *Housing in Wales*, CIH, Coventry.

CHAPTER 14:
Housing associations, capital finance and development

Introduction

In this chapter we will examine the capital finance regime governing housing associations and the nature and scope of development activity in general. We will begin by identifying the differences and similarities between commercial and social housing development and outline the types of activity that are recognised by the Housing Corporation, Communities Scotland and the other regulators as constituting grant supportable capital works. As well as identifying the major sources of funding for social housing capital projects and describing the current policies for distributing social housing grant, we will discuss what is meant by '*a strategic approach to social housing investment*' and outline the regulators' current policies for encouraging and regulating investment in this sector.

The nature of investment spending
The distinction between commercial and social development

1. The commercial development model:
Most property development is carried out by private companies for profit. The typical commercial model involves the following economic sequence:

Acquire land and/or landed property
↓
Build, redevelop, refurbish or improve
↓
Create added exchange value
↓
Sell now or sometime in the future
↓
Realise profit or suffer a loss

Because property markets can be volatile, it is possible for a developer to make a loss on a project. This means that commercial development has to be regarded as a speculative activity.

2. The social development model:

Social housing development is not carried out for commercial speculative purposes (i.e. to make a profit), but in order to fulfil the landlord's mission and vision. The specific objectives of a particular development, and how they relate to the business plan, should be clearly understood by the project managers. The project's justification might be thought of in terms of the following sequence.

Acquire land and/or landed property

↓

Build, redevelop, refurbish or improve

↓

Create added use value

↓

Retain and maintain as a tangible asset

↓

Realise socio-economic returns over the life of the building

The socio-economic returns can take a variety of forms in that the development might result in a number of advantages to the landlord organisation and/or its tenants and residents, or to the wider community.

Social returns

In considering the intricacies of the capital finance regime we must never lose sight of the primary functions of investment spending in this sector. The social model indicates that development activity should generate 'utility' or 'use value' for the tenants or management savings for the landlord. It might also bring wider benefits to the locality. Major investment projects should be subjected to a cost-benefit option appraisal exercise to ensure that the money capital is being put to its highest and best use.

The most important result of any investment should be that the development will enhance the service to primary stakeholders, e.g. by housing people in need or by producing better quality homes for existing tenants. On the assumption that new buildings cost less to maintain than older ones, it might reduce maintenance costs.[1] The development scheme might result in a better use of the stock (e.g. an appropriate adaptation to a more needed use category). Improvements and major repairs are likely to prolong the useful life of the stock. Development can enhance the social reputation of the area and thereby help to attract employment and

---

1   Up-grading a property can increase maintenance if the up-grade involves technical improvements such as the installation of a sophisticated central heating system.

private investment. It can enhance the image of the organisation, the satisfaction of tenants and the morale of staff. On the assumption that there is a link between poor housing and social factors, it might have the effect of reducing crime, truancy rates, etc. All or some of these social returns might be taken into account in a development appraisal exercise in this sector.

The common features of commercial and social development

Although we have made some important distinctions between commercial and social housing development, the fundamental nature of development activity is the same in both sectors. Indeed, virtually all social housing development involves working in partnership with private sector contractors, land-use professionals, and funding agencies.

All effective development projects have the following common features:

1. The project has to represent value-for-money.
2. It will carry long-run and short-run risks that need to be identified at the outset.
3. All investment decisions carry long-term revenue consequences that have to planned for.

1. Value-for-money. New Labour's particular approach to the provision of value-for-money services is encapsulated in the requirements to provide continuous improvement through the principles of 'Best Value'. Since 1997, the government has sought to introduce the principles of resource accounting and budgeting (RAB) into central and local government. Resource accounting requires the public sector (and by inference social agencies such housing associations) to manage their existing assets in an open and business-like fashion. Resource budgeting requires agencies to carry out an option appraisal of any major proposed development project and to be clear about why this particular project was chosen over others that were considered.

Resource budgeting can be thought of as the option appraisal procedure that underlies the development decision. The argument is that to ensure we get value-for-money from a development, a full appraisal of the proposed project's costs and benefits has to be made (and compared with alternative uses for the money capital) before a decision to go ahead is made. Resource budgeting seeks to identify what economists refer to as the *opportunity cost* of the money capital committed to the project.

Money capital is the money resources we have available to acquire real capital assets. Money capital can be acquired from reserves, loan funds, the sale of assets, grants, bequests and income flows. We assume that our money capital resources are limited and valuable. Deciding how 'best' to use them, therefore, is the key to sound investment decision-making. Once they have been used up on project 'A' these scarce resources are no longer available to be used on any other project that we were also considering. Economists regard this 'lost opportunity' to use the resources on something else we need or want as the true resource cost of going with 'A'. This comparative way of thinking emphasises the importance of making the 'correct' choice about how to use limited resources such a money capital.

2. *Risk and uncertainty*. Development is a particularly risky business as the initial development assumptions can change and unforeseen problems can arise during the development period. We will say more about risk mapping and management later. For the time being, we will simply point to some of the more obvious problems that might arise as a result of development activity. Planning difficulties often occur. These can cause the project to be rescheduled, redesigned or even abandoned. Unanticipated physical difficulties with the site may arise causing the development period to be extended and/or additional costs to be imposed. Interest rates may alter thereby changing the original cost assumptions of the project. Similarly, building material costs may change significantly. The contract period may over-run for a variety of reasons and indeed, in extremis, the contractor may go bust. The development appraisal needs to incorporate plans to minimise or ameliorate these sorts of risk. For example, it may be possible to shift some of them on to the contractor. Risk assessment and management is a topic in its own right and is revisited in more detail in subsequent chapters.

3. *Revenue consequences*. One of the fundamental rules of finance is that *all capital investment decisions carry revenue consequences*. The point that has to be appreciated is that, no matter from where the money capital comes, its employment in a development project will inevitably carry revenue consequences in to the future. For example, if money is taken from corporate savings, reserves will be reduced. Because reserves are kept in interest bearing accounts, from the moment that the money is withdrawn, it stops earning interest. This loss of interest can be thought of as a revenue cost of the decision to invest in the development. If on the other hand, the money capital is acquired through borrowing, the resultant loan debt has to be serviced. The loan service charges constitute the long-run revenue consequences of the decision to borrow. Capital grants, such as Social Housing Grant, have the effect of reducing the need to borrow or use reserves to pay for the scheme. They therefore diminish the future revenue costs of the scheme and may, as a consequence, enable the social landlord to charge lower rents. Furthermore, when we convert money capital into real capital assets via the process of development, we inevitably establish other revenue consequences. For example, the new or improved assets have to be maintained and managed (new routine costs), and the new or improved assets earn rent (new income opportunities).

Capital expenditure and income

Capital expenditure is money spent on creating, acquiring or enhancing assets. As a general principle, to count as 'capital' the spending should produce a new asset, substantially increase the life or value of an existing asset, or add to the uses to which an existing asset can be put. Capital income is money received from the sale of assets.

Social landlords follow generally accepted accounting practice in deciding which items of spending are capitalised and which items are charged to income and expenditure. As a general principle, expenditure that relates to maintaining a building in its present state or restoring it to its original condition should be treated as revenue. Revenue spending thus helps maintain current property values and rent earning capacities. In contrast, acquisitions and works that result in real increases in the net rental streams are deemed to be 'productive' and thus counted as capital. An increase in the net rental stream may arise through any of the following, and they therefore all count as capital spending:

- Constructing or acquiring a new dwelling unit.
- Up-grading the rent category of an existing dwelling through improvement works.
- Reducing future maintenance costs through major repairs and renewals.
- Extending the economic life of a dwelling through major repairs and renewals.

In practice, social landlords have to interpret these accounting principles and produce a working list of which expenditures are to be capitalised and which are to count as revenue in the context of their own particular circumstances.

The nature of grant aid and the scope of regulation

Housing associations now provide the vast bulk of new social housing in the UK. They fund new development from a variety of sources including grants. Before examining the full range of funding sources, we need to say something about the nature of grant aid and the scope of regulation that accompanies its distribution. Social housing activities are regulated by central government through its funding and control agents. In England the regulator is the Housing Corporation; in Scotland regulation operates through an agency called Communities Scotland that is answerable to the Scottish Parliament; Welsh regulation operates through the Local Government and Housing Committee of the Welsh Assembly; and the Northern Ireland Housing Executive helps to carry out these functions in the province.

The main reason for regulation is that the Treasury provides significant financial support to the development of this sector and regulation can be thought of as the price that has to be paid for this financial backing. The main element in this support is an *Approved Development Programme* (ADP) that provides building grants called *Social Housing Grants* (SHGs). These have the effect of reducing the financial burden of development to the landlord. The reduced debt burden that results enables the social landlord to charge rents that are lower than those that would be charged by a private sector landlord developing the same scheme. In the final analysis, the grant aid comes from tax-payers and therefore the government is held to account by parliament for the ways in which this funding is spent.[2]

The changing nature of regulation

In Chapter 13 we made the point that, the various systems of central regulation in the UK have recently been altered in ways that encourage individual landlords to become more strategic and innovative. (Refer to section on the *Regulatory Code and Guidance*). Although the detailed processes of regulation differ somewhat between the regions of the UK, the underlying principles are common. To illustrate these principles we will make specific reference to the English system and the *Regulatory Code and Guidance* of the Housing Corporation.

How the Code affects development decisions

A key aspect of the Code is the expectation that development activities should be planned in ways that ensure that future as well as current needs are catered for. Social landlords need to take the longer view. Compared with private developers, they have to think about how current development decisions will impinge on their effectiveness as long-term providers of housing services. Private developers typically build and then sell the completed development on to a final user (see earlier in this chapter 'The commercial development model'). By contrast, housing associations typically build and then retain and manage the development as part of their tangible business assets (see earlier in this chapter, 'The social development model'). This means that housing associations have an interest in the whole life costs and benefits of the development rather than simply the short-run development costs and profits. The key development question is *'Does the proposed scheme provide 'Best Value' when considered over the full economic life of the scheme?'* In selecting a development, the developer landlord should seek to maximise the investment's long-run social returns in a cost-efficient fashion. Once again, this brings into focus the question of the opportunity cost of using the organisation's limited money capital on the proposed project. It also brings to the fore the so-called 'time-cost dilemma'.

In the field of social housing development, the *time-cost dilemma* is at the heart of the investor's opportunity costing exercise. Posed as a pair of linked questions, the dilemma asks, *'Is it better to spend more in the development period and thereby produce a 'better' scheme and reduce the long-run maintenance and repair costs?'* Or, *'Is it better to spend less on the development so that some of the scarce capital funds can be employed elsewhere on other projects?'* It is beyond the scope of this text to address these interesting but tricky questions. Suffice it to say that the Regulatory Code requires the investing agency to carry out an appraisal exercise to ensure that they are making the best use of their scarce resources.

---

2   Over and above this general point about accountability, the Treasury has a general interest in controlling the overall level public expenditure as part of its macro-economic planning strategy – see Chapter 5.

Code specifics as they relate to development

Under s36 of the Housing Act 1996, the Housing Corporation is empowered to issue guidance to the housing association movement. For ease of reference, those parts of the guidance that relate to a statutory duty are marked with an asterisk in the Code. Failure to meet these starred requirements can result in the association being charged with maladministration. Items without an asterisk are more advisory in nature, but are still expected to be taken seriously.

It is not always easy to make a clear distinction between development (investment) and post-development (management) issues. Indeed, the 'time-cost dilemma' points to a clear relationship between investment and management.

It is perhaps a self-evident fact that the nature of investment will impact on future management issues in all sorts of ways. In saying this we are making the obvious point that the quality of the day-to-day service will be influenced by past and present investment decisions. The Regulatory Code establishes the principle that housing associations must aim to deliver continuous improvements and value-for-money in their services and this implies investing in their stock of dwellings in ways that go beyond simple repairs and maintenance. The Code clearly identifies management objectives that are partially dependent on the quality of investment. Here are some examples.

Associations:

- Must seek and be responsive to residents' views and priorities.
- Must demonstrate a commitment to sustainable development and a better quality of life for residents by pursuing social, environmental and economic objectives across all their policies and activities.
- Must make necessary investment in the future of their stock a 'key priority' as a way of meeting people's needs and preferences now and in the future.
- Must demonstrate that their strategies and policies are responsive to their local economic and social environment and link into local housing strategies.

Each year, all associations with more than 250 dwellings are expected to provide five-year financial projections and these inform the Corporation's *annual viability reviews* that are based on credit-rating methodology (refer Chapters 13 and 17). These will continue to be used to help review those associations that have relatively modest development plans. However, where associations are seeking to commit to major development over a number of years, the Corporation can ask for longer-term projections. The *Re-inventing Investment* policy published in October 2003 (see below) extends the regulatory arrangements to ensure that development associations are giving value-for-money and providing appropriate development standards.

Development standards

Both the government and its regulators have expressed a commitment to enhance the image of social housing and to prevent it being seen as second-rate 'welfare' provision. That residents be happy with, and proud of, their homes is seen to be one of the planks in the government's wider policy of enhancing social inclusion. It is a clear objective of the regulators that the sector produces and manages 'good quality homes' that meet people's needs and reasonable expectations. In pursuing these high quality standards in England, the Corporation requires the following starred achievements:

- Condition must exceed statutory minimum requirements.
- The Decent Homes Standard must be actively pursued and monitored.
- All equipment and building components must meet required legislative and regulatory standards.

In addition, new development projects should comply with the recommendations of the Egan Report. Sir John Egan chaired the Construction Task Force that was set up to modernise the workings of the construction industry. The Task Force Report *Rethinking Construction* (1998) concluded that by adhering to certain principles, it was possible to reduce the construction costs of new social housing by about 10 per cent per annum. The Housing Corporation has taken forward the recommendations of the Egan Task Force by establishing the Housing Forum and by directing its investment to projects based on Egan principles. The concept of 'partnering' is central to the Egan approach to procurement. It advocates a greater use of partnering arrangements between contractors and suppliers and the commissioners of development, and consequently less reliance on the more traditional form of competitive tendering. The hope is that longer-term partnering arrangements will bring benefits to all in respect of costs, reduced defects, improved construction methods and shorter construction periods. In short, partnering is seen as integral to the government's attempts to modernise both the housing profession and the construction industry.[3]

The Decent Homes Standard

The most obvious requirement is that the Decent Homes Standard must now be actively pursued and monitored as part of the Code. In addition, we need to remember that the Code states that one of the fundamental obligations on housing associations is to:

'develop and manage good quality homes that seek to meet people's needs and preferences now and in the future, ensuring that the:
- *homes their residents live in are well maintained and in a lettable condition;*

---

3   At the time of writing, the government is engaged in a consultation exercise designed to help and encourage social landlords to adopt the Egan principles by creating a network of local procurement consortia to deliver improved efficiency in capital works. See ODPM, *Social Housing Efficiency: A Discussion Paper,* February 2005 and NAO, *Modernising Construction,* 2001.

- *maintenance is carried out effectively and responsively and in ways that reflect residents' preferences;*
- *necessary investment in the future of the stock is made a key priority.'*

A strategic approach to housing development

In recent years the government has made it clear that the funds that it provides to support the development of social housing in this sector (called the 'Approved Development Programme' or 'ADP') must be seen to be contributing to wider strategic objectives associated with regeneration, integration, efficiency and the establishment of 'sustainable communities'. These are common objectives across the UK. They will, however, be delivered by somewhat different administrative arrangements in different parts of the nation. Although the specific strategic targets will clearly relate to the perceived needs of the areas concerned,[4] there is now an over-arching policy commitment to strategic planning and effective outcomes across the nation.

In 2003 the deputy prime minister set out the government's vision for housing in England and the resources being made to deliver that vision. Similar objectives were identified in the Scottish Executive/Communities Scotland Investment Programme 2004/5 that was published in the same year. A common feature of the various strategic statements was an explicitly wider role for housing associations. In discussing the principles of this strategic approach we will illustrate our points by referencing current Housing Corporation policies and procedures.

The Corporation (in common with the other national funding bodies) has to make decisions about how and where to allocate its approved development programme (ADP). The Housing Corporation's current policy position is set out in its policy paper *Reinventing Investment* published in October 2003. This paper recognises the need for co-ordinating housing and planning in order to deal effectively with the different issues experienced in different parts of the country. With this in mind, regional housing boards have been set up to oversee the creation of regional housing strategies in each of the nine regions in England and to recommend to ministers how resources within single regional housing pots should be utilised.

Key features of the current investment strategy

Underpinning the drive to achieve a more strategic approach to investment decision-making, the new arrangements have the follow key features.

- Embrace a partnership philosophy.
- Deliver efficiency gains.

---

4   Communities Scotland, the Scottish Executive's housing and regeneration agency, for example, is committed to approving 18,000 new and improved homes for social rent and low-cost home ownership by 2006.

- Be flexible rather than formulaic.
- Be coherent.
- Be sustainable.

1. A greater emphasis on partnering

In 2002 the Corporation issued a discussion paper, *Partnering through the ADP* that built on the ideas of the Egan Report *Rethinking Construction* (see above). As a result of the discussions surrounding these reports, the Corporation has now established a policy of 'selective partnering' in the supply chain. This has three broad features that are intended to enhance supply-side efficiency. Firstly, there is now a policy of establishing a more collaborative relationship between the Corporation (as the provider of grant aid) and a selective number of 'development associations' that have track records of successful scheme completions.[5] As part of its efficiency drive, the Corporation is currently seeking legislative changes to allow it to pay Social Housing Grant to lead associations for onward payment to others. This would allow the Corporation to deal directly with even fewer associations and provide lead associations with greater scope for programme management.

The second idea is to cut out wasteful competition within the procurement process and allow the so-called 'partnering associations' to build effective relationships with certain developers and contractors with a view to delivering higher quality outputs.[6] The third aspect of partnering relates to the desirability of development associations working closely with the local authorities to ensure that proposed schemes meet local housing needs and can be developed without running into planning difficulties.

The Corporation now works with its partner associations through a series of *Partner Programme Agreements* (PPAs). These currently cover a two-year period of programme development activity[7] and specify the outputs and the grant level (both total and average) for the programme. PPAs are intended to provide a degree of certainty to the associations so that they can more readily devise a strategic approach to the provision of social housing in their areas, including setting up more effective partnering arrangements with contractors and others within the construction supply chain. The effect of this partnering approach is that an increasing proportion of grant funding is now allocated to relatively large schemes of work (e.g. £10 million or more). Within this arrangement it is possible for smaller associations to bid jointly with the larger, more experienced lead bidders.

---

5   This approach is already under way. In 2003 56 per cent of ADP allocations by value went to just 42 associations. (The remaining 44 per cent went to more than 300 associations).

6   In 2005 the government announced the establishment of a £33 million Efficiency Loan Fund to offer repayable financial assistance to help set up local procurement consortia to deliver improved efficiency in housing capital works. It will operate on a 'challenge fund' basis that involves bidding. See ODPM discussion paper, *Social Housing Efficiency*, February 2005.

7   Eventually they are expected to cover longer periods to encourage even more of a business planning approach to development.

The partnering associations are expected to develop effective working relationships with developers and house builders. This is hoped to bring about two effects that together are expected to impact in a positive way on quality and cost. Firstly, it is expected to allow for a relationship of trust and understanding to develop that will encourage innovation and effective communications. Secondly, it is expected to promote Modern Methods of Construction (MMC) and their associated cost savings. The idea behind MMC is that the building industry should actively seek to be innovative – where innovation is defined as exploiting existing and developing new technologies and ways of doing things.[8] This may involve the introduction a degree of standardisation of products and processes that can underpin the drive to establish acceptable design, layout, construction and site management standards. Some commentators have criticised this aspect of the new approach as they fear that it may encourage unimaginative, 'off-the-shelf' schemes and actually discourage innovation.

To strengthen the relationship between the regulator and the partnering associations, the Corporation will nominate senior Corporation officers as 'lead investors'. These will act as account managers and will be responsible (in conjunction with field officers) for managing and overseeing the association's overall programme.

To some extent, the partnership philosophy can also be seen to embrace relationships between the development associations and the local and regional authorities. The Corporation is likely to look more favourably on a proposed scheme if it fits in with the local authority's planning projections and requirements as this will enhance its viability as a project. The local authority is the local strategic housing enabler. This means that to qualify for grant, the scheme will need local authority support.[9] Although at project level, LAs are still seen to have an important planning role, the Housing Corporation's investment policy, and particularly the way in which it sets priorities for funding under the ADP, is going through a period of change, reflecting wider changes in public sector housing. In particular, the focus has now moved away from liaison at local authority level to liaison with regional housing boards (RHBs). The Housing Corporation's priorities are now set in line with the regional housing strategies developed by the RHBs.

The Housing Act 2004 extended the partnering principle by making provision for private contractors to bid for social housing grant (see below section *Extending grant aid into new partnerships*).

---

8   It includes the use of Modern Methods of Construction such as off-site manufacture, timber and light gauge steel frames, prefabrication and tunnel form of concrete casting. According to the Building Research Establishment, these offer some of the most important solutions to many of the housing and construction problems facing the UK.

9   Until recently, in addition to central government funding channelled directly through the Housing Corporation, English local authorities were allowed to sponsor RSL housing developments from resources they acquired through their Housing Investment Programme allocations. This facility was abolished in 2003 as part of the government's policy to fund social housing project more strategically out of a 'single pot'.

2. Enhanced efficiency

The Treasury is committed to delivering public expenditure efficiency gains worth over £20 billion by 2007/8 to feed front-line services (Gershon Report July 2004). This includes a commitment to deliver efficiency gains across the social housing sector of at least £835 million a year by that date. It is expected that a significant part of this gain will result from social landlords operating more effectively when procuring and producing capital works. The establishment of local housing procurement consortia have been identified as playing a particularly important part in securing such savings.[10] Through a process of validated self-assessment, social landlords are now expected to demonstrate that they are becoming more efficient both in the commissioning of new supply and the procurement of capital programmes involving major repairs and improvements.

3. Less formulaic and more flexible decision principles

Meeting local needs

In the past the Corporation's allocation of Social Housing Grant has relied heavily on formulae to guide decisions.[11] The Corporation has now changed this purely formulaic approach in favour of one that focuses more on those requirements for local housing investment that cannot be adequately measured simply by referencing standardised needs indicators. The earlier system tended to allocate resources to a local authority area on the basis of past and current needs. This worked well when all areas had a shortage of housing and similar problems. But it is now recognised that the issues and challenges faced both between and within districts vary considerably. For this reason the Corporation's new allocation system relies less on nationally devised formulae and takes more account of local and sub-regional needs.

Under the new arrangements the starting point for decisions about investment priorities are regional housing strategies. These are produced in partnership with the Government Office for the Region and, to ensure the fullest understanding and agreement on issues and priorities, they are subject to a high level of consultation with other regional stakeholders. The regional housing strategies will span several years (with annual updates) and are intended to provide an overview of priorities that takes account of the region's economic outlook and planning strategies as well as its demographic projections. This means that they will be expected to tie in with the work of the regional development agencies.

To help associations make appropriate proposals for funding that are relevant to local and regional circumstances, the Corporation's regional offices are to produce their own regional investment strategies highlighting the areas and types of

---

10 See ODPM (2005) *Social Housing Efficiency: A discussion paper.*
11 The two indices used to distribute resources to the English regions have been: (1) the Housing Needs Index (HNI) – a weighted basket of indices of housing needs constructed down to local authority level; and (2) the Housing Association Stock Condition Index (HASCI) – a measure of the relative condition of RSL stock in each region.

activity that they deem to be priorities for funding. These will be issued to RSLs at the same time as invitations are made to them to bid for funding. Where appropriate, they break the strategy down to reflect the needs of sub-regions (localities).

A more flexible operational framework

The move away from simplistic formulaic control is also reflected in changes that have been made to the operational framework. The traditional framework for determining the level of Corporation support for a development project comprises the primary elements of Total Cost Indicators, grant rates and quality standards.

For many years the Corporation has operated a system of benchmark costs to assess value-for-money. These nominal figures are called *Total Cost Indicators* (TCIs), and they represent the Corporation's estimate of the norm total cost of providing different types of housing in different parts of the country.[12] These officially determined indicative scheme costs are issued by the regulatory body in an annual circular. It is important to understand that they do not represent actual scheme costs – they are notional figures that are simply used to regulate the allocation process by setting a ceiling on what can qualify as an eligible bid. The indicative costs appear in 'look-up' tables that are regularly updated to take account of such things as changing building and borrowing costs.[13] As we will see, there is now less emphasis on this 'cost control' approach.

Grant rates

These represent, for each type of scheme in each area, the maximum percentage of total qualifying scheme costs that may be funded by SHG. The primary objective of the public capital subsidy has been to allow quality dwellings to be produced and let at rents below market levels so that they are affordable to those in low-paid employment. The link between grant rates and rents has to all intents and purposes been broken by the government's grant restructuring policy (refer to Chapter 15 and see below). Like base TCIs, headline grant rates are determined by reference to dwelling and scheme type and location.[14] In most cases, the actual grant paid is below this upper limit. For any particular scheme the actual grant has been negotiated by a bidding process. This means that there has been no standard rate

---

12 Broadly, the indicators assume that development costs will vary by: (a) location (local authority district); (b) the nature of the development (new build or rehab – high-rise or low-rise); (c) the type of need being met (general needs housing or supported housing); and (d) the size of dwelling (or numbers of people housed). TCIs relate to current construction and development costs and act as a check that an estimated scheme cost is providing value-for-money at the time a project is approved for grant. Projects on which costs exceed TCI are subject to technical scrutiny prior to approval and may, if justified, be approved.
13 Because sites and dwelling units vary, the tables incorporate cost modifiers that operate by adjusting the allowable TCI percentage or applying a multiplier to the calculation.
14 Thus, if for example the TCI calculation indicated an allowable total scheme cost of £1 million and the appropriate grant rate for such a scheme of these dwelling types in that area was currently set at 55 per cent, then the project would be eligible for grant aid of up to £550,000.

of grant contribution – it has varied significantly for different schemes, even if they are in the same local authority cost group area and involve the construction of similar types of dwelling. However, within particular periods, there has existed a general 'headline' level of grant that measures the overall average contribution of state funding committed to RSL projects.

This operational framework of TCIs and grant rates will remain in place for occasional and small-scale developing associations. However, for partner associations the system of approval has been altered as the Corporation now believes that the old framework is too constraining and discourages a truly strategic approach to development planning. Costs will no longer be taken into account when considering development proposals from partner associations as a cost ceiling approach is seen to be inappropriate. It is now up to the associations to incorporate costs into their business plans and then live with the consequences of the decisions they take. (Business planning and cost control are discussed more fully in Chapters 16 and 17). '*What matters to us is the grant take, rent levels and the quality of the housing to be provided.*' (Housing Corporation, *Reinventing Investment*, October 2003 p8).

The original idea of grant rates was to allow decent homes to be affordable to those in low-paid employment. However, the link between grant and affordability has been broken by the policy of rent restructuring and the setting of target rents that associations are expected to reach by 2012. Because of this, since 2004/5 the grant rate framework has not been used to determine the level of subsidy. Instead associations are now invited to put forward the level of subsidy they require in order to deliver the development programme as a whole. This then constitutes an element in the bidding and negotiating process. Grant allocation decisions are now more based on judgements about efficiency and effectiveness and the Corporation now looks to support schemes that embrace ways of working that will deliver both quality outputs and 'efficiency savings'.

Quality standards
There has always been an element of concern within the operational framework concerning quality standards. These have been checked by reference to a set of officially determined *Scheme Development Standards* designed to ensure that public money is only invested in schemes that reach a minimum quality threshold. Under the new arrangements the Corporation continue to treat the essential items within the Scheme Development Standards as a base threshold from which to consider associations' proposals. This means that housing quality indicators continue to constitute an element in the bidding and negotiation process.

4. Coherence: flexibility within a national framework

Although flexibility and the use of discretion are essential elements in any strategic approach to development, there still remains a concern to maintain a degree of coherence as between regions and localities. At the core of the regional investment strategies,[15] the Corporation maintains wider key objectives (currently three in number). By applying these key objectives to its allocation decisions, the Corporation seeks to ensure a consistent approach to its distribution of resources within and across sub-regions. The key objectives have been specifically chosen to ensure that housing investment cross-cuts with wider government policies. In England, the current key objectives are to:

1. Provide new affordable housing in areas of economic and demographic growth.
2. Aid the regeneration of deprived neighbourhoods by helping to fund the refurbishment or replacement of existing housing.
3. Contribute to the funding of new supported housing to meet the needs of a wide range of vulnerable groups.

These three key objectives are not fixed for all time. As pressures and needs change, the ADP will be directed to support other government priorities. At the time of writing, the following additional priority issues have emerged as candidates for ADP support.

- Homelessness.
- Key workers.
- Promoting community cohesion.

Within these broad objectives, other more detailed aims are set out such as supporting rural housing, contributing to low-cost home-ownership initiatives, encouraging community capacity building, supporting 'foyer' initiatives and promoting Modern Methods of Construction and using sustainable development principles.

Scottish priorities (set by Communities Scotland) are similar in nature and include a 'wider role fund' designed to allow housing associations to play a more dynamic part in community development by encouraging them to invest in a range of activities beyond their specific housing functions. These might involve initiatives in such fields as employment, training, health and community safety.

To ensure that the allocation decisions are understood and are 'transparent', they will be published, together with explanations of how and why they were taken, in the form of regional allocation statements. As mentioned in Chapter 13, the Corporation has introduced *Housing Corporation Assessments* (HCAs) that give the Corporation's view of each association under the three main headings of the regulatory code (viability, governance and management). Where relevant the HCA will include an assessment of investment performance.

The Corporation is also bringing in an all-year bidding system because it recognises that strategically important projects do not materialise at set bidding points in the year.

---

15 Formally known as 'regional policy statements'.

5. Sustainability: management competence and post-development viability

In funding a project, the Corporation is understandably concerned to ensure that an association has the capacity to deliver outputs on time and within budget. This means that backing is more likely to be given if the bid can demonstrate that financial planning has already taken place and that sites with outline planning permission have been assembled.

A strategic approach to development must necessarily consider the post-development period. Whether a development proposal can be regarded as 'sustainable' will depend in large part on the efficiency and effectiveness of the post-development housing management that is put in place. This means that housing management competence has to be considered alongside financial viability and development competence. This may involve making an assessment of the track record of managing partners, or on the subsidiaries of groups, at the bidding stage.

Extending grant aid into new partnerships

The Housing Act 2004 included provisions to extend the grant giving powers of the Housing Corporation and the National Assembly for Wales to support unregistered bodies.[16] This controversial break with past practices means that by 2006, in certain circumstances, private developers as well as housing associations will be able to bid for Social Housing Grant (SHG). By using grant aid to widen the pool of potential types of provider, the government is seeking both to drive efficiency and encourage innovation and creativity in the sector. As well as developing the 'partnering' principle, this reform should be seen as an aspect of the government's commitment to develop a more strategic approach to the provision of social housing. It can also be seen as an aspect of its wider 'efficiency agenda'.[17] The government has made it clear that the reform is not intended to bring about adversarial relationships between housing associations and unregistered bodies. Rather, the intention is to encourage a variety of partnerships, consortia and special purpose vehicles that can push forward the sustainable communities and efficiency agendas as well as help deliver wider regional priorities.

The new initiative brings to the fore a range of questions about standards and the role of regulation. The Housing Corporation will ultimately be responsible for

---

16 It did this by introducing a new section 27A into the Housing Act 1996. These powers were first used in February 2005 with the launch of a £200 million pilot investment programme. (Housing associations are supported with SHG under section 18 of the 1996 Act.)

17 At the time of writing, the initiative is being launched through a pilot project designed to assess the extent to which bodies other than registered social landlords might contribute to tackling local housing needs and support the efforts of local authorities to build sustainable communities.

ensuring that standards are maintained. In assessing bids the regulators will consider the capacity of the bidders to deliver as well as the appropriateness of the proposed schemes.[18] The Housing Corporation has made it clear that in the bidding process they will not be taking a 'level playing field' approach but will be looking for effective outcomes that produce decent affordable homes and high quality services to tenants.

The proposal has been generally welcomed by large commercial developers as well as traditional house builders, some of whom have indicated an interest in moving beyond the development process into the field of long-term management.[19] Despite this interest, the new initiative has generated some concerns on the part of the National Housing Federation and other commentators who point out that the shift to providing public funds for affordable housing to profit maximising firms is fraught with political, moral and practical difficulties.[20]

A key problem relates to the difficulties of subjecting private sector actors to the regulatory processes associated with RSL grant receipts (as discussed above). Private sector companies will have to be regulated through contractual rather than bureaucratic arrangements. Also, arrangements will need to be put in place to ensure that when non-RSL properties are sold the grant element is clawed back for reinvestment rather than distributed as profit to shareholders. Once the 2005 pilot scheme has been assessed it may be that new special purpose vehicle arrangements will emerge to prevent schemes being overly directed by developer influence. Such arrangements might allow new innovative forms of governance that incorporate private sector energy, funds and skills to be harnessed to housing association experience and to resident and community empowerment.

The debate surrounding the introduction of this initiative has also brought into focus the general question of regulation. Following the decision to open up development grant allocation, parts of the housing association movement are now lobbying to be given the freedom to drop out of Housing Corporation regulation so that they can operate under the same regime as non-housing association bidders.[21] It is early days to determine whether the new initiative will eventually lead to some streamlining of the regulatory regime for housing associations. As always, any change in capital funding arrangements will carry revenue consequences.[22] If associations do deregister then one consequence may be that private funders will not be prepared to lend at such preferential rates of interest.

---

18 An assessment panel chaired by the Corporation and including a range of technical, financial and legal expertise, has been set up to oversee all stages of the bidding process.
19 Some developers have mooted the possibility of setting up their own housing associations for this purpose.
20 The Chartered Institute of Housing has commissioned research to look at how standards can be maintained over the long term when private companies acquire grant aid.
21 At the moment, only associations that manage 100 or fewer homes can deregister.
22 Remember, throughout this text we have made the point that one fundamental principle of finance is that 'every capital decision carries revenue consequences'.

Sources of capital finance

Development funding can come from six main sources:

1. Government grants administered by the regulator.
2. Private loans.
3. Developers' contributions (planning gain).
4. Reserves.
5. The sale of assets.
6. Revenue income.

We will now say something about each of these funding sources.

1. Grants and the Approved Development/Investment Programmes

The capital grant supporting this sector is called Social Housing Grant, previously Housing Association Grant. In Scotland it is sometimes still called Housing Association Grant. Initially, the grant was calculated in such a way that it covered virtually all of the scheme costs. Since 1989 it has been distributed on the basis of directed competition, covers only a proportion of total scheme costs, and is set as a predetermined amount for each scheme. The remaining costs have to be met from private sector loans, accumulated reserves, or asset sales.

Activities that are eligible for grant support through the ADP (England and Wales) or the Investment Programme (Scotland) include constructing, acquiring, repairing, improving, adapting, or creating by conversion dwellings that are kept available for letting. Because of its political and administrative nature, grant allocation involves a number of conditions and complexities. We have already discussed the changing nature and scope of these regulatory requirements (see above).[23]

The post-1989 regime reversed the relationship between grant aid and rental income. Whereas, previously, rents were fixed at the outset and grant aid provided the deficit funding, from the 1990s onwards the grant contribution was predetermined with loans filling in any financial shortfall. Under the 'new' arrangements rents had to be mutable so that any increases on loan service charges could be covered.[24] This is the main reason why assured tenancies replaced the

---

23 In England, March 2004 saw the first allocations from the ADP under its new regime of *Reinventing Investment* which introduced a partnering route alongside the traditional development route. Similar changes in policy emphasis were also introduced by Communities Scotland as part of its 2004/5 Investment Programme.

24 The old Housing Association Grant (HAG) was initially a subsidy to cover the bulk of the development costs. The remaining costs were then largely paid for by taking out a serviceable loan. This meant that the grant covered the estimated costs of building a scheme minus an amount that the association was assumed to be able to afford to contribute without putting up rents beyond the 'fair rent' levels. These arrangements meant that rents bore little or no relationship to actual scheme costs. This was out of line with the Conservative government's general 'market' philosophy that prices should reflect, but not necessarily match, the marginal costs of production.

earlier 'fair rent' regime.[25] There was now an implied assumption that associations should operate in a more market-orientated business atmosphere and that their dependency on grant should be reduced. The so-called 'mixed funding' regime means that loan finance has become an important feature of the financing landscape.

2. Private loans

Loans can be short-term or long-term, carry fixed or variable rates of interest and be secured against various types of collateral, typically property or rental income flows. The types of loan currently taken out by associations and the issue of loan planning and management are discussed in Chapter 17.

The National Housing Federation estimate that over the period 1999-2002 the private borrowing requirements of associations was in excess of £6 billion. In recent years, banks and building societies have been the lead providers of committed funds (some 80 per cent of the total) with the bulk of the remainder coming from a variety of other institutional investors. Social landlords gradually reduced their reliance on variable rate funds so that by the end of the 1990s more than half of the private sector borrowing was based on fixed rates of interest. The sector has also shown a preference for long dated finance with nearly 80 per cent of committed funds having maturities of more than 14 years (NHF, *Private Finance Loans Monitoring Bulletin,* March 1999). Loan acquisition and management is a highly specialised area that is fraught with risk. It is therefore often arranged with the help of financial consultants who have specialist knowledge and experience and can help the association make informed decisions, or even negotiate the loan terms on the association's behalf.

Debt has to be managed and associations need to demonstrate to lenders that their finances are sound and that they have adequate collateral to cover their debts. The issue of financial management is an area of study in its own right and is covered in some detail in Chapter 17. Here we will simply emphasise the point that a development programme based on loan finance will establish a profile of debt that has to be incorporated into the business planning process (see Chapter 16). The key point is that the business plan must ensure that future revenue flows are capable of servicing the debt liabilities if the organisation is to stay in business.

3. Capital contributions through s106 agreements ('planning gain')

A 'capital contribution' is a financial contribution to capital spending from a third party that has the same effect as a grant without technically being a grant.

---

25 Chapter 15 describes how the 1989 reforms involved a shift from 'secure' to 'assured' tenancy agreements. The introduction of assured tenancies was seen to be a pre-condition for the required shift towards increased private funding. It was argued that social landlords must be freer to set rents on a more 'commercial' basis if they are to be expected to acquire funds from the private sector.

Planning gain agreements, for example, can direct financial resources from developers into local authority housing projects but are not classified as 'grants'. Under current ministerial guidelines, local authorities may require developers seeking planning permission for housing developments above a certain size to reserve a proportion of homes for social housing.[26]

In this way, local planning authorities may require that, as a condition of granting planning permission, a proportion of affordable housing is provided as part of a proposed housing development. In some circumstances local planning authorities and applicants may agree to an alternative arrangement for delivering an agreed element of affordable housing on a different site. Although grant would not normally be available to support a social housing development of this kind, the Housing Corporation has indicated that it may be possible to negotiate an element of support so long as it can be demonstrated that the result of grant aid would be that the s106 agreement (s75 in Scotland – see Chapter 11) would thereby deliver more social housing outputs or a more appropriate mix of dwelling units.

This is now an important source of 'affordable' housing units in both urban and rural areas. It can include housing for sale or shared ownership as well as for rent.

4. Accumulated reserves

Before 1989 the relatively generous grant regime provided major repair grants (MRGs) to help maintain housing association properties that were older than ten years and demonstrably in need of repair. When MRGs were abolished, associations were then expected to set up sinking funds. This means that after 1989 associations were generally expected to accumulate resources to pay for future major repairs out of current revenue streams. As well as seeking to control public expenditure, this change can also be seen to be a way of shifting the emphasis away from the principles of welfare provision towards the principles of commercial management.

Although limited grant assistance is still available if it is seen to be part of a wider strategy for social housing provision (see above), the costs of future major repairs are now normally planned for by setting up a sinking fund. By including an element in the rent charge, money can be set aside against future needs (such as major repairs). This money is normally invested in a fund in order to retain its value over time. We will return to the idea of sinking funds in Chapter 17 when we consider aspects of financial management.

A key regulatory distinction is made between 'designated' and 'restricted' reserves. Designated reserves are unrestricted but are earmarked by the management board for a particular purpose, such as major repairs. The designation

26   The 1999 Rogers Report, *Towards an Urban Renaissance*, the Report of the Urban Task Force, (DETR), advocated the levying of standardised impact fees as a substitute for planning gain agreements for smaller developments.

of reserves is an internal exercise and may be reversed by future board decisions. Restricted reserves are those reserves that are subject to external restrictions governing their use. Where an external body, typically a funder, requires that specific reserve funds be accounted for separately they are recorded as 'restricted'.

5. Asset sales (capital income)

For accounting purposes, social housing properties are regarded as 'tangible fixed assets' rather than 'investment assets'. As such, they are primarily valued for their economic usefulness rather than for their potential to appreciate in exchange value. Tangible assets are normally retained and maintained as they are required to run the business. They wear out of course and as we have seen, good accounting practice requires all tangible fixed assets to be depreciated year by year to reflect this fact. This requires the social landlord to charge a depreciable amount for their housing properties to the income and expenditure account on a systematic basis over their useful economic lives.[27]

Although social landlords are not in the business of acquiring properties to re-sell, there are times when it may be sensible or necessary to dispose of dwellings or other assets. The tenants' right to acquire, for example, will mean that property sales will occur over time (see Chapter 7). The sale of an asset generates a capital receipt that is then held in an interest bearing account as part of the organisation's reserves. These reserves constitute a potential source of funds for future development.

Capital income is derived from the sale of assets. Since 1996, RSLs in England and Wales have been given more control over how they can dispose of properties and reinvest the resources thus generated. There is also the possibility of grant recycling from the sale of assets.

6. Revenue income

Revenue income from rents, charges, fees, etc. can be directed to capital projects. However, the use of capital funds (loans, reserves, etc.) cannot be used to pay for the day-to-day costs of running the organisation.

Summary

The economic value of any capital asset is composed of three interrelated factors; namely, its potential selling price (its exchange value), its potential usefulness (its 'utility' or use value), and its potential to yield a return on money capital committed (its investment/social value). At any time, a building's exchange value

---

27   The useful economic life of an asset is defined as the period over which the organisation expects to derive economic benefits from that asset. A traditionally built new building is normally assumed to have an economic life of about 60 years.

will be determined by the perceptions of potential purchasers about its current use and/or future investment value. Whether in the commercial or social sector, the real, underlying, fundamental economic value of a building is determined by what it does – its usefulness, and in the final analysis, it is this that determines its investment value, its value as a social asset and its exchange value. In the end, all economic value is grounded in current or potential use value.

Development funding can come from six main sources:

1. Government grants administered by the regulator.
2. Private loans.
3. Developers' contributions (planning gain).
4. Reserves.
5. The sale of assets.
6. Revenue income.

The current capital funding regime is based on the following general principles:

- Because housing associations produce a social product that helps to satisfy a 'merit need', a percentage of the scheme cost might legitimately be covered by grant aid in the form of Social Housing Grant.
- Because of the duty to control total public expenditure, the level of grant should be predetermined and fixed before the works begin rather than be given as deficit funding on completion.
- It should contribute to the provision of high quality housing and the enhancement of end user satisfaction.
- It should help to achieve economies of scale and an efficient procurement process.
- It should create outcomes that reflect the housing needs of the region and its localities and districts. Although these needs should be objectively measured by reference to some index of housing need, the distribution of funds should not be purely mechanical. As well as referencing a needs formula, resources should be invested in ways that underpin a regional strategy for improving wider social and economic conditions.
- In addition to helping to provide good quality housing at affordable prices, the public funding is expected to aid housing associations to contribute to the government's wider policy objectives relating to sustainable communities, urban renewal and social inclusiveness.
- The strategic distribution should be consistent and coherent and key national objectives should be identified. These key objectives should be common across all regions.
- The allocation processes should be made in ways that are clear and transparent.

Since 2003, across the UK, the development grant system has been based on a 'single pot' approach that is meant to encourage a more strategic planning culture.

The allocation processes differ somewhat between the UK funding bodies and they are also subject to constant revision. Current moves towards regional devolution will inevitably alter how decisions will be made to approved development funds in the future. It is likely that they will be tied in more and more closely with other budgets to underpin the social and economic objectives of the various national/regional authorities and agencies.

All the regulators (The Housing Corporation, Communities Scotland, the Local Government and Housing Committee of the Welsh Assembly, and the Northern Ireland Housing Executive) now try to ensure that the investment of public funds into this sector is informed by strategic thinking.

The regulators have a duty to ensure that their development funds are used effectively and since 2002, the government has sought to ensure that these limited resources be focused on larger, more 'strategic' projects and targeted at a narrower range of RSLs (referred to 'preferred partners'). A 'preferred partner' is an association that can demonstrate a good development record.

Further reading

Barker, K., *Review of Housing Supply: Securing Our Future Housing Needs, Interim Report*, HM Treasury, 2003.

Barker, K., *Review of Housing Supply: Delivering Stability: Securing Our Future Housing Needs, Final Report*, HM Treasury, 2004.

DETR, *Quality and Choice – A Decent Home for All*, the Housing green paper, Chapter 8, April 2000.

Housing Corporation, *Reinventing Investment*, October 2003.

ODPM, *Social Housing Efficiency: A Discussion Paper*, February 2005.

CHAPTER 15:
Social landlords: income, expenditure and revenue finance

In Chapter 13 we looked at the nature and scope of housing associations and other registered social landlords (RSLs), and we also described the general framework of regulation within which they have to operate. In Chapter 14 we discussed the nature of development in this sector and how such activities are financed and regulated. In this chapter we turn to the question of income and expenditure in general and of rents and revenue finance in particular. Once we have looked at the contents of a typified general income and expenditure account, we will define revenue as a financial concept and consider how it is treated in the accounts. We will then turn our attention to the various consumption interests that are vested in the sector. We will conclude by examining the revenue finance regime and considering the theoretical and practical questions surrounding rent-setting policies.

Income and expenditure in general: the income and expenditure account

Day-to-day accounting

All businesses need to keep clear and accurate records of their day-to-day transactions, and current liabilities and assets. This involves setting up account books and ledgers, and keeping a variety of records, registers and statements. Typically these records will include cash and petty cash books, a purchase ledger and record of invoices, sales ledger, rent ledger, loans register, fixed asset register, bank statements, payroll records, and a record of stocks and stores. These records have to be kept in a way that complies with the requirements of the Inland Revenue and in a manner that is consistent with statutory accounting regulations and recognised good practice. These 'day books' provide the detailed information that is presented in the period accounts that are published for the dual purpose of ensuring transparency (external accountability) and informing business planning and management (internal analysis).

Period accounting

The income and expenditure account is one of the primary accounts that housing associations have to have audited every year.[1] The broad purpose of the account is

---

1   Under the Housing Act 2004 small associations have had their auditing requirements simplified.

fourfold. It charts what transactions have taken place and how much they cost. It shows how the net surplus/deficit for the year was arrived at. It charts any transfer to or from restricted and designated reserves. And it shows how the balance on the revenue reserve has changed from the previous accounting period. Figures 15.1 and 15.2 illustrate two versions of a typical income and expenditure account. Figure 15.1 shows how income and expenditure can be charted in a way that itemises where the income came from and how it was used in the current reporting period (e.g. a quarter year). In this format it can be thought of as a 'transactions account'. Figure 15.2 shows how transaction surpluses or deficits are accounted for at the end of the accounting period (e.g. end of financial year). In this format the income and expenditure account can be thought of as a 'summary account'.

A transactions account (e.g. Figure 15.1) provides a way of reporting to those who need to know what financial activities have occurred in a given period.

The basis of reporting in transactions format

1. The account must specify the period being covered (e.g. for 'second quarter 2006/7').
2. It records the movement of money into and out of the books of account (usually on an accruals basis).
3. In addition to the columns shown, best practice would be to show a forecast outturn for the year and a full year variance.
4. Unlike the financial accounts, it reflects 'actual' rather than 'book' transactions and therefore may not include financial charges such as depreciation.
5. Although a distinction is made between capital and revenue transactions, the cash-flow statement/forecast would be a mix of capital and revenue items.
6. Strictly, voids should be incorporated into the gross figure. For management purposes, however, it is useful to see them as a deduction.
7. The account is usually prepared on an 'accruals basis' which means that if some item of expenditure has been incurred in this reporting period but not yet paid (and the amount is known), it will be included. Similarly, any income item relating to this reporting period known but not yet received will be included. The purpose of the accruals approach is to give as true and realistic picture as possible of the financial position.
8. A 'prudent' approach is taken in drawing up the account. This means that only sums known with certainty are included. In particular, the account should not make any optimistic assumptions about possible financial flows that might over state the strength of the association's finances.

Figure 15.2 shows the end of year position in summary form.

The summary account is a financial account rather than a simple record of transactions and the basis of reporting is therefore somewhat different from the transactions account.

Figure 15.1: Income and expenditure account: transactions (indicative)

	Year to date Budget £	Year to date Actual £	Variance £	Annual Budget £
INCOME				
Gross rental income	X	X	X	X
Voids and bad debts	(X)	(X)	(X)	(X)
Service charges	X	X	(X)	X
Property sales	X	X	(X)	X
Other income	X	X	X	X
TOTAL INCOME	**X**	**X**	**(X)**	**X**
EXPENDITURE				
PROPERTY MANAGEMENT				
Property management expenses	(X)	(X)	X	(X)
Property insurance	(X)	(X)	X	(X)
Other property expenses	(X)	(X)	X	(X)
TOTAL PROPERTY MANAGEMENT	**(X)**	**(X)**	**X**	**(X)**
MAINTENANCE				
Responsive maintenance	(X)	(X)	(X)	(X)
Planned maintenance	(X)	(X)	X	(X)
Maintenance vehicle costs	(X)	(X)	X	(x)
TOTAL MAINTENANCE	**(X)**	**(X)**	**X**	**(X)**
STAFFING COSTS				
Direct staffing costs	(X)	(X)	X	(X)
Other staffing costs	(X)	(X)	X	(X)
TOTAL STAFFING COSTS	**(X)**	**(X)**	**X**	**(X)**
DEVELOPMENT COSTS (NET)	**(X)**	**(X)**	**X**	**(X)**
OTHER EXPENSES				
IT expenses	(X)	(X)	(X)	(X)
Other insurance	(X)	(X)	(X)	(X)
Professional fees	(X)	(X)	(X)	(X)
Committee expenses	(X)	(X)	X	(X)
Office building costs	(X)	(X)	X	(X)
Other office expenses	(X)	(X)	X	(X)
Write offs	(X)	(X)	(X)	(X)
TOTAL OTHER EXPENSES	**(X)**	**(X)**	**X**	**(X)**
BANKING & FUNDING				
Bank interest receivable	X	X	X	X
Banking & funding charges	(X)	(X)	(X)	(X)
TOTAL BANKING & FUNDING	**(X)**	**(X)**	**X**	**(X)**
Contingency	(X)	(X)	(X)	(X)
TOTAL EXPENDITURE	**(X)**	**(X)**	**X**	**(X)**
(SURPLUS)/DEFICIT	**(X)**	**(X)**	**X**	**(X)**

**Figure 15.2: Income and expenditure summary account for the year ended 31 March XXXX
(Presented in the format of SORP March 1999)**

	XXX1 '000	XXX0 £'000
Turnover	X	X
Less: Operating costs	(X)	(X)
Operating surplus	X	X
Profit/(loss) on sale of fixed assets	X	X
Interest receivable and other income	X	X
Interest payable and similar charges	X	X
	(X)	(X)
Surplus on ordinary activities before taxation	X	X
Tax on surplus on ordinary activities	(X)	(X)
Surplus for the year	X	X
Transfer from/(to) restricted reserves	(X)	(X)
Transfer from/(to) designated reserves	X	X
Revenue reserve brought forward	X	X
Revenue reserve carried forward	X	X

Notes on Figure 15.2 and the basis of reporting in summary format

Turnover represents the income received during the period and is therefore shown net of rent losses from voids. Rent losses from bad debts are included within operating costs. Turnover comprises rents receivable + service charges receivable + revenue grants receivable[2] + any other 'trading' income. The account can receive moncy in flows from rents, grants, interest earnings and private donations. In addition, in certain circumstances, some money can enter the account when assets are sold.

The operating costs record the running expenses of the housing and related services provided during the accounting period. They include depreciation, bad debts, cost of sales, staffing costs, overheads, property maintenance and repairs, management and other operating costs. Interest payable and similar charges are not classed as operating costs but appear as a separate item below the operating surplus. This is because interest is deemed to be part of the financing aspect of the business and as such, not tied to operations or turnover (even though a substantial part of the rental income is in fact used to meet loan interest charges).

Before calculating the surplus (or deficit) for the year, the effect of any corporation tax payable must be shown. Charitable organisations are not subject to corporation tax. Other taxation (e.g. VAT) is included with the related expenditure. The tax liabilities of housing associations are looked at in the Chapter 17.

---

2   If social housing grant was used to fund the costs of major repairs during the year and these were included in expenditure, then the grant would form part of the annual turnover.

Auditors, lenders and other readers of the account will pay particular attention to the figure representing the surplus for the year. It is important because it will determine whether or not the revenue reserves are being added to. Loan covenants (see Chapter 17) often stipulate minimum surplus levels.

Restricted reserves are set aside for specific purposes that are decided by outside parties (e.g. a donor or a lending institution). These will not normally be held as cash balances.

Designated reserves are financial resources that are held for specific purposes decided by the agency itself (e.g. a sinking fund for major repairs).

Rents and revenue finance

Revenue finance is concerned with the day-to-day income and expenditure of the organisation. Revenue income is needed to meet the running costs of being in business.

Income

The following constitute the primary sources of revenue income:

Rents. Rent charges are the prime source of income for all social landlords.[3] The rental flow represents the main business 'turnover' or 'trading income'. Housing associations can receive rents that are based on two distinctive types of tenancy contract. Contracts entered into before 1989 are typically based on 'secure' tenancy agreements. Under these agreements, the rent is determined by an independent rent officer and is calculated on a 'fair rent' basis. (The notion of fair rents is explained in Chapter 18). Contracts entered into after 1989 are typically based on 'assured' tenancy agreements and are determined by the association itself. (The notion of assured rents is explained in Chapter 18 and the issues surrounding rent-setting policy are discussed in Chapter 4 and at the end of this chapter). When secure tenancies are surrendered the relets convert to assured status. This means that over time, fair rent tenancies will be phased out. As we have seen, in calculating rental flows, allowance has to be made for voids and bad debts.

Revenue grants. These were significant before 1989 because the income from fair rents was insufficient to cover the normal running costs of associations and as a result many experienced a deficit in their revenue finances. For this reason, in certain circumstances, revenue deficit grants could be claimed to help finance the running of general needs schemes at that time.[4] These generalised grants were

---

3   In 2004, on average, a unit rent in this sector generated a cash flow income of £2,900.
4   The grant was reduced if the association was holding significant reserves and surpluses.

phased out because the central authorities argued that the need for them was diminishing as fair rent levels were rising and assured tenancies (with higher rents) were becoming the normal arrangement (see also Appendix 2 to this chapter).

Social Housing Grant (SHG). SHG is usually classified as capital support and, as such, is discussed fully in Chapter 14. However, if SHG was received to help finance major repair work, and these costs were treated as 'revenue', then the accountants' 'matching principle' requires the grant to be classified as revenue in such instances. The idea of the matching principle is discussed in Chapter 2.

Interest received. Those associations with invested cash surpluses are able to generate an additional income flow from these cash investments.

Donations. Some associations may also receive some financial support from associated charities and private contributions.

Asset sales. In addition to these primary sources of income, there can be an in-flow of money into the income and expenditure account when assets are sold. In cash-flow statements sale proceeds are a capital item, but would in general flow through into the revenue account. In this way, assets sales may produce financial resources that are counted as a contribution to income.

Current asset disposals. Properties developed for outright sale or on behalf of third parties should be treated as current assets rather than fixed assets. This means that such development activity is regarded as part of trading. Where there have been current asset property disposals in the period, for accounting purposes the disposal proceeds are included in turnover.

Surpluses on fixed asset values. Dwellings held as part of the landlord's stock of rentable properties count as fixed assets, as against current assets. They are represented in the books at a value called the 'carrying value'. If they are sold and the proceeds are greater than the carrying value then the surplus is treated as a contribution to income. This is a rather technical point and is really a book-keeping nicety. Any such surplus is simply the result of a valuation exercise; and of course, it is quite possible for sale proceeds to be less than the carrying value so that the sale has a negative income effect. For these reasons the surplus or deficit is shown as a separate item on the face of the income and expenditure account below operating surplus and above interest (refer to Figure15.2).

Expenditure

Revenue income is used to pay for the day-to-day running costs of the business. In social housing these so-called 'costs-in-use' include outgoings on the following.

Debt servicing. This has become an increasingly significant factor since the introduction of the 1989 finance regime. This regime requires associations to rely more heavily on private sources of finance to fund their development activities.

This produces loan debts that have to be serviced out of current income flows. Measured as unit costs (cost per tenancy provided) debt charges tend to be higher than those of local authority housing departments. This is because housing associations tend to have a relatively higher proportion of 'newer' dwellings that carry relatively higher debts.

Housing management. These are the direct and administrative costs of running the business. The main items of expenditure are staff salaries, and office expenses such as rent, heat, light, telephones, consumables, etc. Measured as unit costs, the administration costs of traditional housing associations tend to be higher than those of local authority housing departments. This is because most traditional associations tend to operate on a relatively small scale. Management economies of scale are more readily achievable in larger LSVT associations.

Property maintenance. An issue here is defining what building works should count as revenue and thereby be charged to the income and expenditure account, and which should be capitalised. Generally accepted accounting practice says that works that result in an enhancement of the productive capacity of the asset, that is, an increase to the net rental stream over the life of the property, should be deemed 'improvements' and capitalised. An increase in the net rental stream may arise through an increase in the rental income, a reduction in future maintenance costs, or a significant extension of the life of the property. An item that results in this kind of outcome should not normally be charged as revenue. (For further discussion on this point see section below on 'Accounting for income and expenditure').

Major repairs. Transfers to major repairs provisions are not counted as expenditure. The actual major repair spend clearly is counted as expenditure. Before 1989 capital grants, called major repair grants, could be applied for to help bring sub-standard dwellings back to an appropriate fitness standard. This support was largely withdrawn after 1989. Monies now have to be set aside in designated reserves for this purpose. The reserves are accumulated by making regular payments into some kind of sinking fund. The sinking fund payments are normally derived from an element in the rent charge. The statutory funding bodies used to make recommendations about the appropriate amounts that ought to be set aside in this way, but these days the association is expected to make its own decisions about how to deal with this in its business plan. (See Chapters 16 and 17 for discussion on business planning).

Accounting for income and expenditure

As we have seen, each social landlord is required to keep a record of its revenue finance transactions in an income and expenditure account. An indicative format for this is set out in Figures 15.1 and 15.2. You will recall that the income and expenditure account records the receipt of rental income. In commercial terms this represents the main item of business 'turnover' for the financial year. Operating costs are deducted from the turnover figure to display an 'operating surplus'. Other sources of income, such as any profit on the sales of fixed assets, net interest received and other income, is added to the operating surplus to produce a 'surplus on ordinary activities before taxation'. Tax adjustments are then made to give the 'surplus for the year'. This surplus, which of course cannot be distributed as a dividend, has to be transferred into reserves and these are valued in the balance sheet. (The layout of a typical balance sheet is shown in Chapter 17).

With the level and pattern of spending changing, and increasing pressures to demonstrate 'Best Value', social landlords need to ensure that they employ accounting practices that can be applied consistently to the expenditure incurred. They therefore follow generally accepted accounting practice in deciding which items of spending are capitalised and which items are charged to income and expenditure. As a general principle, expenditure that relates to maintaining a building in its present state or restoring it to its original condition should be treated as revenue. Revenue spending thus helps maintain current property values and rent earning capacities. In contrast, acquisitions and works that result in a real increase in the net rental stream over the life of the property are deemed to be 'productive' and thus counted as capital.

Rent Surplus Fund
One of the consequences of the 1989 revenue finance regime (discussed below) was that, in the early 1990s, social housing rent levels increased. This increase in rental income was an intentional outcome of the Housing Act 1988. In introducing the reforms the government intended that most associations would begin to make surpluses of income over expenditure. The legislation therefore required all housing associations that had been in receipt of capital grant aid to set up a special fund to receive such surpluses. The fund only applied to schemes built under the old finance regime (prior to 1989). This fund was called the Rent Surplus Fund (RSF). It no longer exists, having been abolished by the Housing Act 2004.

Tenants and the consumption interest

The percentage of British households renting from a housing association increased from one per cent in 1971 to seven per cent in 2002. By the turn of the millennium, not only had housing associations become the main provider of new homes to rent, but also they owned and managed as much as a quarter of the total stock of social housing. It is estimated that since 2005, the sector now manages more housing units than the local authorities.

The letting conventions of this sector are embedded in notions of beneficence and tenant support that stem from the historical values of the housing association movement (see Chapter 13). This means that landlords in this sector have a long tradition, going back to the establishment of almshouses in the twelfth century, of providing homes for those who are unable to afford market housing. This tradition recognises that access to a decent home is a prerequisite for people to live a dignified life and to participate socially and economically in the community. Today, these traditional housing association values continue in that most associations actively seek to play a part in tackling what has become known as 'social exclusion'.[5] In particular, they seek to deliver what the Housing Corporation once termed 'housing plus'. This term is meant to encapsulate the idea that investment in housing should have more than 'bricks-and-mortar' outcomes. It demonstrates a commitment to extra curricula consequences of housing investment such as providing tenants with better health and employment opportunities, reducing truancy rates amongst their children, and generally providing safer and more stable communities.[6]

Affordability and convergence

National Housing Federation figures (1997) indicate that by the late 1990s almost 70 per cent of rents charged in this sector breached its own definition of affordability. The Federation's definition utilised both a benchmark and a ratio measure of affordability (refer to Chapter 3). It stated that rents were affordable if the majority of working households were not caught in the poverty trap (because of dependency on housing benefit), or were paying more than 25 per cent of their net income on rent. In Scotland, the Scottish Federation of Housing Associations advocated a different measure of affordability[7] and there has been no formal measure in Wales. The idea of defining 'affordability' in some precise fashion has now become of academic interest because it has, to some extent, been superseded by the questions of 'comparability' and 'choice'. Current rent policy is largely driven by the commitment to rent restructuring and the drive for convergence by 2012. The key idea here is that rent disparities between different types of social landlord (for similar dwellings) should gradually disappear so that prospective tenants can make sensible housing choices based an assessment of their needs and preferences rather than on differential rents.

Although 'academic', affordability remains an important issue. By the early 1990s, nearly 75 per cent of housing association tenants were not in paid employment (i.e. they were retired, unemployed, or for some other reason 'at home'). Of the 25 per cent or so with jobs, most were in low-paid employment with an average income of under £10,000 (1992). It is worthy of note that today some 80 per cent of the working population earn more than the average new housing association tenant. This means that a relatively high proportion of tenants are in receipt of housing benefit. The incomes of tenants in social housing have been put on average at one-third of the incomes of home owners.[8]

---

5   'Social exclusion' is a declared political concern of the Labour government, and Tony Blair has highlighted housing as one of the 'seven pillars' of a decent society.
6   The nature and scope of housing association investment strategies is discussed in Chapter 14.
7   See SFHA Guidance Booklet No.5, *Developing Affordable Rents*, Jan. 2002.
8   Information on tenants' incomes and rents is recorded by continuous recording systems (CORE in England and Wales and SCORE in Scotland). These systems are operated by the NHF and SFHA.

Entering and exiting the sector

Many tenants are nominated to a housing association by their local authority housing departments. Some will be referred by a specialist referral agency or a housing charity. Individuals can always apply directly to a local association for a tenancy. The movement's welfare commitment means that consideration is given to methods of exit from, as well as entry to, the sector. In particular, if a tenant wishes to become an owner-occupier and can afford to do so, arrangements exist to help this to happen. In this way a renter with ownership aspirations is aided while, at the same time, a social tenancy is made available to someone else who is deemed to be in greater housing need. Under certain circumstances it may be possible for the tenant of a social landlord to purchase their home. (These exit methods are described in some detail in the chapters on owner-occupation).

The revenue finance regime

Both the capital and the revenue financial arrangements for this sector were radically reformed in 1989. The capital regime has been further revised and is described and discussed in the Chapter 14. The earlier revenue regime is briefly described in Appendix 2 to this chapter.

The 1989 revenue finance regime

The 1974 revenue regime (see Appendix 2) was reformed by the provisions of the Housing Acts 1988 and 1996 which laid down the structure of the current revenue finance arrangements. The new system introduced two key features.

1. The replacement of secure tenancies with assured tenancies
The driving idea behind the revised tenancy arrangements was to shift housing association practices on to a more commercially orientated footing. The key element was the replacement of fair rent tenancies with assured tenancies. Under the provisions of the act, existing secure tenancy agreements continued but new tenancies were to be 'assured'. In this way, over time, secure tenancies are being phased out. Rents for assured tenancies are derived from a contractual agreement between the landlord and the tenant. To all intents and purposes this means that they are set by the association. This provision means that associations can normally no longer look to rent officers to determine rent levels – they must have their own procedures for establishing and implementing rents. In setting rents they have to balance the requirements of affordability with those of sufficiency and accountability (see below, 'Rents and rent-setting policy' and also discussion in Chapter 4).

2. A shift away from the 'welfare' principle of revenue deficit funding towards the 'commercial' principle of self-financing from rental income
The shift towards assured tenancies and the freeing up of rents reduced the expectation of deficits. Although assured tenancy rents were not expected to be as high as rents for equivalent properties in the private sector, they were expected to rise to a point where deficits diminished or disappeared. After 1989 rents were

normally expected to cover all management costs. For this reason, under the new arrangements, the old Revenue Deficit Grant[9] was no longer payable to help cover the running costs of schemes that had been part funded by the private sector (called 'mixed funded' schemes). Such schemes are now expected to be largely self-financing from rents. Like the move from secure to assured tenancies, the move away from revenue deficit funding towards self-financing underlines the government's intention that associations should now operate less as welfare agencies and more as commercially viable organisations.

Rents and rent-setting policy

The key revenue in-flow for any landlord is rental income. Rents are set in accordance with the tenancy agreement and usually reflect the nature of the utility generated by the dwelling; that is, to some extent tenants pay for what they consume. Tenancy arrangements in this sector were reformed by the Housing Act 1988 in ways described above. In the years following the introduction of the 1989 regime, associations were allowed to set their own rents so long as they met their obligation to cover their costs. In recent years this freedom has been inhibited by the introduction of the government's rent convergence policy. (See below and Chapter 12, which also deals with rent-setting policy for local authorities and housing associations in Scotland).

In Chapter 4 we made the general point that a potential conflict exists between the social policy objective of setting rents at levels that are low enough to be affordable to tenants, and the commercial policy objective of setting rents at levels that are high enough to cover the landlord's legitimate business costs. In exploring the tensions generated by this conflict we identified a set of contrasting rent-setting principles that could be used to guide the pricing policies of landlords. Marginal cost pricing, market pricing, historic cost accounting, capital value pricing, and consumption pricing were all identified as basic principles that could be used individually or in combination to rationalise and legitimate charging a particular rent for a specific property.

New tenancy agreements are now based on the 'assured' principle. The Regulatory Code sets out the principles that associations currently have to follow in setting their rents. Broadly, they require rents and charges to be set at levels that:

- are below those that would be set by unrestrained market forces;
- are affordable to the low-paid employed in the locality;
- have some relationship to the asset's value as a dwelling;

---

9   The object of RDG was that it should make good revenue deficits where it is clear from the application and from the accounts that the association had done its best to manage its stock and its revenues efficiently. In cases where, despite good management, a deficit arose, RDG might be awarded. Although RDG was phased out after 1989, a new one-off up front grant could be paid to associations who experience setting up problems and are unable to cover outgoings from rents.

- allow the landlord to meet its current financial commitments;
- allow the landlord to cover its historic costs;
- allow the landlord to make appropriate provision for future repairs and other contingencies; and
- take account of rent restructuring requirements and the policy of convergence.

In the 1980s the government signalled to housing associations that their rents were 'too low'; in contrast, by the mid-1990s they were being urged to curb any proposed increases. By the late 1990s associations in England were confronted with a contentious policy that restricted rent increases based on the formula: retail price index + half a per cent + or − £2 per week. This policy has put particular pressure on LSVT landlords who had made pre-transfer pledges to their existing tenants to encourage them to vote in favour of transfer. These pledges often required the new landlord to carry out a repairs and maintenance 'catch up' programme within a certain timescale while at the same time holding current rent levels for a period after transfer. For such RSLs, the ability to meet these pledges rested on an assumption that annual rent increases for new tenancies would be significantly above the level of inflation.[10]

It might be argued that the RPI formula is rather a blunt control instrument as it takes no account of starting points and thus stands in the way of establishing rent changes that move towards fairer differentials – which is a key government policy. There might also be a danger that 'rent restraint' could act as a disincentive to the putting aside of adequate funds into designated reserves to cover anticipated future costs such as those associated with major repairs. It also has to be remembered that rents have to reflect long-term interest rates if the association is to cover its long-run costs. Furthermore, the limit on rent increases tends to reduce the value of the stock and this can affect the security available for underpinning private sector loans. All of these tensions are manifestations of the basic need-price dilemma discussed in Chapters 3 and 4.

In Wales in the 1990s, the regulator introduced 'rent bidding' on a local authority area basis. Any RSL charging more than ten per cent above the most competitive RSL in the area lost its development programme. This was later replaced by 'rent benchmarking'. Under this arrangement the Welsh Assembly Government set benchmark rents for different property types. Subject to limited exceptions, associations could not charge more than the benchmarks. Doing so would mean losing Social Housing Grant. Throughout the UK rent-setting policy is now largely driven and steered by the multiple requirements to charge affordable rents, achieve the Decent Homes Standard and to converge rents. The idea is to move the nation towards a more coherent social housing sector that provides quality homes that are affordable.

---

10 The Housing Corporation accepts that transfers have been predicated on rental assumptions that do not meet rent restructuring expectations. This means that new transfers should meet with rent restructuring expectations but can take account of rent guarantees.

The drive to convergence

At the time of the publication of the green paper it became clear that rents in the housing association sector were around 20 per cent higher, on average, than those for local authority housing. This differential was seen to be unfair and confusing to tenants. The 2000 green paper, *Quality and Choice: A Decent Home for All*, made it clear that reducing the gap between average rents in the two social housing sectors was to become a key objective of government policy. This commitment to developing a more coherent approach to rent-setting has put increased pressure on some RSL landlords to moderate rent increases, while allowing a greater degree of increase in parts of the local authority sector. Rent convergence is seen as a prerequisite to the goal of establishing a more unified and coherent social housing sector in which tenants can make choices about where to live based on an assessment of their needs and preferences rather than on the differential rents set by different kinds of social landlord.

Summary

Income and expenditure accounts have to be audited annually. They are presented in two formats: (1) as transaction accounts – usually quarterly and (2) as summary accounts – always annually. If they are part of the audited accounts, the format is as per the SORP.

As the tenants of social landlords are on relatively low incomes the question of 'affordability' is at the heart of the revenue regime's objectives. However, there is a tension between this objective and the recognised need for social landlords to set rents that enable them to remain financially viable.

In the 1980s the government put pressure on housing associations to raise their rents to be more in line with market levels. The pressure was formalised in the provisions of the Housing Acts 1988 and 1996 which brought in assured tenancy agreements. The shift to assured tenancy rents after 1989 resulted in the withdrawal of Revenue Support Grant for mixed funded schemes.

Since April 2003, a new fund – Supporting People – has been established to help cover the cost of providing financial aid to people in supported accommodation. This includes all funding streams that were previously available and is separate from the housing benefit system.

Currently rent-setting policies are driven by the combined needs to provide affordable, decent homes at affordable rents that will eventually be comparable as between different types of social landlord. This drive for convergence is called 'rent restructuring'.

The drive to rent convergence means that social landlords now only have limited discretion in setting rent increases.

Further reading

DETR, 'Moving to a fairer system of affordable rents', Chapter 10 of the 2000 green paper, *Quality and Choice: A Decent Home for All.*

Appendix 1: revenue grants and Supporting People

As we made clear in the text, the old deficit grant system was reformed with the introduction of assured tenancies. Although general deficit grants were phased out, supported housing (providing for special needs) continued to be given grant aid to help pay for the management costs that are necessarily more intensive than those associated with the provision of general needs accommodation.[11] After 1999 the ways in which public funds were directed into supporting the management of special needs housing were reviewed and this led to the introduction of radical new arrangements called 'Supporting People'.

Supported housing had traditionally set two or three elements of the overall rent charge: a basic rent; a service charge (housing benefit eligible); and where appropriate, a personal (non-HB eligible) charge. Under the rent restructuring guidelines, RSLs were given greater flexibility than was the case in general needs housing to allow them to take account of the higher management costs. In preparation for Supporting People, an additional support charge had to be separated out to cover the costs of support services only (as defined under the Transitional Housing Benefit Scheme (THB). In this way, in April 2000 (prior to its introduction), in charging for supported housing schemes, associations had to set two elements of rent/service charge. In setting the core accommodation element, they had to take account of rent levels for comparable general needs accommodation in the area. Higher management and support costs relating to the extra staff time required to work with vulnerable tenants had to be identified separately for the purposes of the transitional housing benefit scheme being introduced under the Supporting People policy.

The new Supporting People arrangements were eventually introduced in April 2003. The key idea behind the new arrangements is to give the local authorities a greater strategic role in the commissioning and development of supported housing in their areas. The co-ordinated Supporting People grant is paid to the administering authority to give financial support for the provision of housing-related services that were previously funded from a variety of funding streams including housing benefit. The first significant change on the introduction of Supporting People was the transfer of all revenue funding to a contract between

---

11   In England this support was called Supported Housing Management Grant (SHMG); in Wales it was called Supported Housing Revenue Grant (SHRG); and in Scotland it was called Special Needs Allowance Package (SNAP).

the administering authority and the RSL or support provider. This included THB support charges, Social Housing Management Grant (SHMG) and other grants such as Probation Accommodation Grant (PAG). The second significant change was the Supporting People grant each administering authority receives from the ODPM was capped. The administering authority is now responsible for reviewing all initial interim contracts and making decisions at a local level about with whom and for what services they wish to contract and at what price.

Providing support services: Supporting People

(NB. Supporting People is also discussed in Chapter 19).
Approximately ten per cent of RSL housing is targeted at people with special needs. There is a wide range of people who rely on such support. These include the frail elderly, people with learning disabilities, people with mental health problems, victims of domestic violence, people who suffer from alcohol or drug addiction, ex-offenders, and young people who are homeless or who are for some other reason at risk. The current provision of sheltered and supported housing seeks to help this wide range of vulnerable people to maintain stable and independent lives in the community by providing a range of specialist support services. Such services vary in scope and intensity and include general counselling and advice, assistance with administrative affairs, services provided by wardens, and liaison work with other agencies and individuals responsible for the person's welfare. The new system seeks to integrate arrangements to help fund these services under the auspices of a funding regime called 'Supporting People'.

Prior to 1989 special needs hostels were developed against specific design and staffing criteria and then received 100 per cent capital grant (HAG) funding. Once built, the costs-in-use that could not be met out of rental income were covered by a special revenue deficit grant.[12] This meant that so long as the costs-in-use met specific criteria and were approved by the funding agency, public money would ensure that these, like the capital costs, would be fully covered. Under the 1989 arrangements revenue support for this type of housing centred on a fixed bed space formula that allowed associations running hostel-type accommodation to apply for a revenue allowance that contributed towards the higher management costs of schemes for people needing specialist help. In contrast to the earlier arrangement, the management allowance did not provide full deficit funding and only paid a contribution towards the additional costs. By the late 1990s the expectation was that the running costs of supported housing should be met largely out of revenue income rather than through additional revenue grants. This meant that in the years immediately preceding the introduction of Supporting People, much of the revenue burden was carried by the housing benefit system (refer to Chapter 19).

---

12   Hostel Deficit Grant paid the difference between revenue and qualifying actual costs.

In these earlier years, social landlords had access to other sources of revenue funding for supported housing from a range of partner agencies. For example, Section 73 funding (1985 Housing Act) gave central or local government authority to help voluntary organisations concerned with the homeless or with matters relating to homelessness assistance by way of grant or loan. Home Office funding could be available to help with the running costs associated with the provision of housing for ex-offenders and people on probation. This normally involved the scheme setting aside an agreed quota of bed spaces – analogous to a local authority nomination agreement. Other resources could come from the Health Service and from charitable donations. Under the new arrangements these additional public funding streams have been pulled together into a unified support system, embracing housing benefit, in a way that is intended to allow local authorities to work with regional agencies and other service providers from the NHS, the housing association movement and elsewhere, to develop a more strategic approach to the funding of this kind of support activity.

The Supporting People programme was introduced by the government in April 2003 and it altered the way housing-related support is funded, commissioned and monitored across the UK.[13] The new funding regime replaced the previous arrangements for providing external funding to help pay for the costs of those parts of supported housing that are not related to housing management/repairs or to personal care. Before April 2003 this support was largely channelled through the housing benefit system. Since April 2003, housing benefit no longer meets the costs of service charges for support services. Instead, there now exists more general contractual arrangements administered by the local authorities. Separate grants like Special Needs Management Allowance and its equivalents have disappeared.

The Supporting People programme seeks to ensure that vulnerable people have the opportunity to live more independently. It promotes housing-related services that are cost-effective, reliable and which complement existing services and support independent living. It seeks to ensure that the funding of these services is co-ordinated and steered by local knowledge of needs.

To prevent disruption to existing arrangements, an effort was made to ensure that the initial aid (2003/04) was equivalent to previous funding flows. However, it is clear that the new arrangements do carry future funding risks to housing associations as once these interim contracts have been worked through, local authorities are expected review the use of Supporting People grants to ensure that vulnerable people are given the most appropriate service and support. In so doing they may decide to increase, decrease or remove it from a particular scheme. They may also decide to use it to fund new schemes or different projects.

---

13   The overall policy of Supporting People was the subject of a wide-ranging joint consultation exercise from all the government departments involved (in 1999). The policy is being implemented across England, Scotland and Wales, with national variations due to different local authority structures and other differences resulting from devolution.

Appendix 2: the revenue finance regime before 1989

To appreciate fully the nature and scope of the present revenue system, it helps to have an understanding of the pre-1989 arrangements and why and how they were reformed. The earlier revenue regime was established in 1974 and its main features can be summarised as follows.

- In line with the policy for most private sector rents, housing association rents were regulated 'fair rents'[14] set by independent agents of central government known as 'rent officers'[15]
- Management and Maintenance Allowances were granted. These were designed to give associations some security of income so that they could plan their budgets and cover their basic administrative costs, including the costs of development.
- A flexible Revenue Deficit Grant (RDG) could be applied for. This helped associations meet the additional current costs they faced as a result of expanding their development activities. This grant was put in place in recognition of the fact that rent levels were not negotiable but pre-set by rent officers. Because an association was unable to meet any legitimate additional revenue expenses by raising its rents it was felt necessary to provide this additional grant aid.
- The Housing Corporation was given enhanced powers so that it could impose an appropriate degree of regulation and control over the use of this public funding.

---

14 The 'fair rent' system was introduced by the Rent Act 1965 for the private sector and extended to public sector and housing association tenancies by the Housing Finance Act 1972. The provisions were consolidated in the Rent Act 1977 and subsequently amended by the Housing Act 1980. The provisions were again consolidated by the Housing Act 1985 and then further amended by the Housing Act 1988.
15 These officials are required to set rents that ignore the personal circumstances of both the tenants and the landlords. Furthermore, the rents they set must assume that the properties are not in short supply; this means that they must not include any price element that reflects the scarcity value that a particular tenancy may possess. They must, however, take into account other relevant circumstances including the property's age, location, character and state of repair. Fair rents are 'registered' and remain fixed for a period of two years. Either party can appeal to the Rent Assessment Committee and subsequently to the courts if they wish to challenge the rent officer's decision. A fair rent may consist of two elements; one relating to rights of occupancy and the other to service charges.

CHAPTER 16:
The purposes and principles of business planning

In our discussions on social landlordism up to now, we have tended to focus on the political and legal context within which financial management occurs. In other words, we have sought to describe and discuss the financial regimes governing how local authorities and RSLs manage their affairs. In this chapter and the one that follows, we will turn our attention to the question of financial management itself. In Chapter 17 we will look at the practices and procedures associated with the treasury management of individual organisations. In so doing we will examine some of the specific issues a social housing provider has to bear in mind when acquiring and using financial resources. Before doing this, we need to make the more general point that the use of limited resources has to be planned for if the landlord's business objectives are to be achieved in a cost-effective fashion. We will begin therefore by reflecting upon the wider objectives of financial management. In this chapter we will consider the reasons for social business planning and then discuss what is meant by the notion of 'social enterprise'. Having done this, we will outline the key processes associated with the production of a social business plan.

The reader should bear in mind that business plans vary in their nature and scope according to the type of organisation, its needs and objectives. What follows focuses on the purposes and principles of planning as an exercise and is intended as a starting point for those wishing to develop, manage and/or monitor the business activities of an organisation.

Why are social enterprises required to do business planning?

There is, of course, no one answer to this question. The most obvious reason is that any well-run organisation needs to think ahead if it is to be effective and efficient. It also needs to demonstrate that it is capable of learning from its own and other's experiences. In other words, the social enterprise should think strategically and consciously integrate best practice experiences into its own investment and management activities. Furthermore, social businesses are now expected to be answerable to their primary stakeholders (tenants, patients, students, parents, customers, clients, etc.). This accountability involves, among other things, explaining what they plan to do and then demonstrating the extent to which they have achieved these promised outcomes cost-effectively and on time. Other stakeholders (the government, regulators, local residents and businesses, community groups, etc.) may also have an interest in the organisation's plans and achievements. In particular, if the organisation wants to borrow money from a bank or some other financial institution, then the lender will require a workable business plan before venturing the funds. Similarly, grant providers want assurance that public or charitable funds will be put to good use.

Social enterprise and business planning

As part of its 'third way' and partnership philosophies, the government argues the case for instigating a 'social enterprise' approach to service investment and management.[1] There are two broad aspects to this way of thinking. First, it requires local authorities and public corporations to work with other socially orientated organisations in the community that are well placed to deliver good quality, cost-effective public services. Second, it points to the need for local authorities and public corporations themselves to become more 'business-like' in the way they run their affairs.

The drive for a social enterprise approach to public service provision and management goes beyond the housing sector. All departments of central and local government are now expected to incorporate business planning principles (such as resource accounting and budgeting) into their management practices and procedures. In addition, a whole range of social enterprises (sometimes referred to a 'public interest companies') now operate in many parts of the economy to help tackle a wide range of social and environmental issues. Social enterprises are businesses that have social objectives and whose surpluses are reinvested in the organisation or in the community, rather than distributed in the form of profits to shareholders or other owners.

Business planning is at the heart of effective social enterprise and this approach requires public services to be provided either by a central government or local authority department that has a credible business plan, or by an 'arms length management organisation' (ALMO) that is owned by the authority and has such a plan, or by some other public interest organisation that has such a plan.

Housing and social enterprise

In the social housing context, the pursuit of an enterprise culture means that, in future, the stock of dwellings has to be owned and managed under one of the following arrangements.

1. By a local authority that has a credible thirty-year financial plan for the Housing Revenue Account. This might incorporate private finance initiative (PFI) arrangements for part of the stock.

---

1 *Social Enterprise: a strategy for success* (DTI) was launched in July 2002. It set in place a three-year programme of how the government will work with partners to promote social enterprise activity.

2. By a housing ALMO that has a credible thirty-year business plan (that also might incorporate a PFI arrangement).
3. By a public interest company (typically an RSL) that has a credible thirty-year business plan.

Housing as a regulated social business

Throughout this book we have emphasised the point that all social housing has to be accountable to, and monitored by, regulators. This means that social landlords should be thought of as *regulated social businesses*. Lending institutions, grant providers and the regulators all expect social housing providers to operate in a 'business-like' fashion by providing evidence of performance-based objectives, results-orientated outputs, and financial viability. These three business markers are commonplace in the private sector which has developed a battery of tools and techniques to use in seeking to achieve them. The problem is that traditional business tools do not always sit comfortably in an externally regulated public interest setting in which the primary objectives and outputs are social rather than commercial. This means that private sector business planning techniques have to be adapted so that the housing enterprise can take proper account of the fact that it has wider community responsibilities as well as financial goals. In the social housing setting, this is currently achieved by embedding the principles of Best Value into the business planning process (see Figure 16.3).

The nature and scope of business planning

Business planning and value-for-money

The over-arching aim of a social housing business can be said to be the pursuit of value-for-money for its tenants and other stakeholders. Currently, value-for-money in the public service sector is defined by reference to the principles of Best Value. These principles have been referred to at various points throughout this text (see the index). The idea of value-for-money was introduced in Chapter 2 and the content of that chapter constitutes the starting point for the following discussion.

A plan is a 'thing' but planning is a 'process'

By focusing on activity we move our attention from product to process – from the idea of a static plan to the idea of a dynamic planning process. Business planning should not be founded on a product – a fixed historic document – but on a documented *process* that is systematic, open, and flexible.

Broadly speaking, we can think of a plan as a proposal for doing or achieving something. The business plan comprises a collection of documents that points to action – it sets out the over-arching strategy for the longer period. In order to progress the strategy, the organisation will need to translate it into a more detailed corporate or company plan that sets out operational objectives and tangible targets for the medium term. In turn, to achieve these corporate objectives and hit these targets, the various sections and departments within the organisation will need to devise fully detailed, action plans of their own to guide their immediate and short-term programmes of activity. This means that the overall business planning process involves a number of linked plans and other documents that cascade down from the strategic to the operation level. (See Figure 16.2).

The business plan is the highest level document and it sets and establishes the key business assumptions and earmarks the budgetary provisions of the organisation in the broadest terms. Business plans have to be financially viable. This is just as true of regulated social businesses as it is of free-enterprise commercial businesses. Typically, the business plan looks forwards for thirty years and it sets the overall prudential guidelines within which the business has to operate in order to demonstrate its ability to cover its long-run costs and repay any major long-term loan liabilities.

Strategic planning

At the very beginning of Chapter 1, we made the point that finance is not an end in itself but an instrument of action (i.e. a means to an end). This means that although financial planning and management are at the heart of every successful business plan, the documents should set out all the main political and social objectives of the long-term strategy for the business.

Long-term strategic goals are normally designed around mission statements. These tend to be written in language that is more aspirational than technical. They usually incorporate an analysis of the organisation's underlying values (that gives its activities a moral orientation), and a description of its operational culture (that gives its actions an ethical orientation). As well as providing a moral and ethical orientation for action, mission statements should succinctly summarise the business's over-riding purpose. The strategic plan is then grounded in this publicly declared mission. The strategic plan identifies four planning levels that can be represented by the acronym MOST.

Mission → Objectives → Strategy → Tactics

Objectives are specific goals that need to be achieved in order to fulfil the mission; they constitute the various priorities, projects and activities that naturally flow from the mission. The strategy describes how the objectives will be achieved and in so doing, it specifies key policy directions and identifies the real and financial resources needed. Usually there are a variety of approaches to delivering policies and acquiring and using resources. The organisation therefore also needs to consider its tactics. Tactics determine what the business does on a day-to-day basis to achieve its objectives. Tactics determine immediate actions.

The four key aspects of business planning

Inevitably, a business plan contains a lot of detail. However, we can summarise the general purpose of business planning by reference to four key activities: *assessing*, *determining*, *developing*, and *monitoring*.

1. Assessing the organisation's current position with regard to its performance, resources and business environment.
2. Determining its priorities and objectives for various planning periods (the long, intermediate and short-term).
3. Developing action plans and using its resources to achieve these time-specific aims.
4. Monitoring performance against the plan on a regular basis.

Figure 16.1: The classification of business planning functions

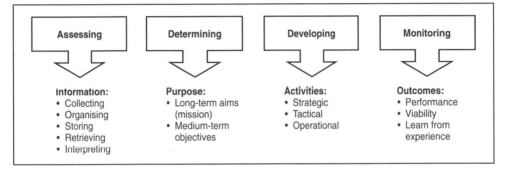

These four key of business planning functions permeate the overall planning process.

Figure 16.2: The overall business planning process

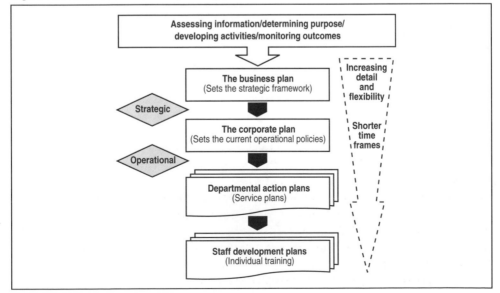

Below the strategic (or 'business') plan and the corporate (or 'company') plan sit the service plans for each service area, for example property services, supported housing services, financial services, and so on. These contain the relevant key tasks for each area. These are drawn down from the corporate plan but also include local performance indicators and additional key tasks where these are considered necessary. Progress against the tasks in these plans is reported by members of the management team to the executive (or a senior officer in the case of a local authority) on a regular basis (typically quarterly). They should then be reported to all staff. Any significant operational problems that emerge as a result of this process should be reported to the appropriate council committee (in the case of a local authority) or relevant committee of the board of management (in the case of an RSL or ALMO).

The scope of the planning process

Figure 16.3 outlines the scope of the business planning process. It indicates that the organisation should seek to attain its declared mission in a way that can be judged to be providing 'Best Value'. That is, it should plan and monitor its activities with a view to achieving all of the following: the efficient use of resources; performance-based objectives; and outcomes that are in line with the needs and interests of its stakeholders and valued by them (levels A and B in Figure 16.3).

Levels A and B in Figure 16.3 are derived from Figure 2.3 in Chapter 2. In our earlier discussion (Chapter 2) we made the point that the principles of Best Value embrace the whole process of housing provision and management – from the initial input of resources to the perceptions of the end users and others who have an interest in how the service is run. The point was made that the 'four Es' of efficiency, effectiveness, equity, and experience need to be monitored in any organisation pursuing Best Value. You should now reread Chapter 2 before proceeding.

The key relationships and central questions

The following discussion is based on Figures 2.3 (Chapter 2) and 16.3 (below). Level A in Figure 16.3 represents the four value-for-money (VFM) relationships that we identified in Chapter 2. The 'Best Value' social business has continuously to bear these four relationships in mind when developing and implementing its business plan. The identification of these VFM relationships points to the following questions that underlie the whole business planning process.

1. *Efficiency relationship*: Are we making the best use of our limited resources?
2. *Effectiveness relationship:* Are we achieving our declared objectives?

Figure16.3: The aims and tool of business planning

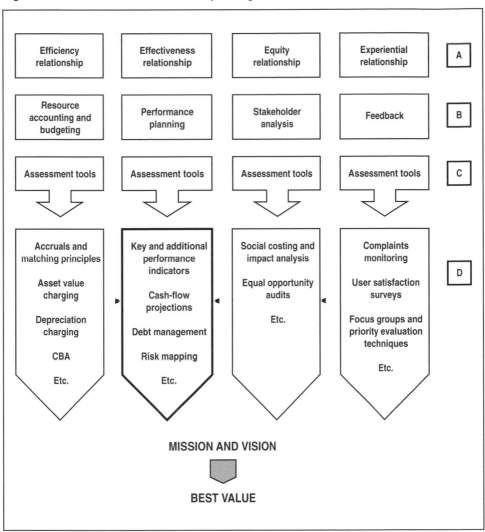

3. *Equity relationship:* Are the cost burdens and output benefits distributed fairly between the various stakeholders?
4. *Experiential relationship:* Are the service users and other stakeholders satisfied with what we do and how we do it?

These four *relationship* questions have to be addressed before the two key *delivery* questions can be considered.

1. Are we delivering our mission and vision?
2. Are delivering Best Value?

Delivering the mission and achieving Best Value

By addressing the four relationship questions, the social enterprise should be in a position to chart its progress towards its mission and assess the extent to which it is achieving Best Value. Each question has to be asked regularly and always answered in a way that is open, systematic and clear. This involves establishing robust management information systems and tools that are appropriate to the task of monitoring and assessment (refer level C in Figure 16.3).

The range of assessment tools used in social business planning is illustrated in Figure 16.3 (level D). You will notice that, in line with our conceptual model, the tools are grouped under the four VFM relationship concerns (the four Es). You will also notice that the three line arrows (level D) all point inwards towards the issues that relate to effectiveness. This emphasises the priority that Best Value gives to the establishment of a 'performance culture'.

Business planning is a complex subject and whole books have been written about how to go about it. We are here simply concerned to provide a conceptual overview of the topic and so we will conclude this chapter by outlining the nature and scope of the tools and procedures that need to be employed in managing the process. Some of the ideas and practices referred to have already been examined earlier in the book (notably resource accounting and budgeting). Later on, we will need to revisit some of the issues we are about mention. In particular, in the next chapter, we will say more about those aspects of the process that relate directly to questions of financial management.

Monitoring and measuring efficiency

Resource accounting and budgeting (RAB) provides the monitoring framework within which the social business pursues the efficient use of its tangible assets. Since 1997, the government has sought to introduce the principles of RAB into central and local government. Resource accounting requires the public sector (and by inference social agencies such RSLs) to manage their existing assets in an open and business-like fashion. Resource budgeting requires agencies to carry out an option appraisal of any major proposed development project and to be clear about why this particular project was chosen over others that were considered.

Resource accounting is sometimes referred to as 'management accounting' because it seeks to record the financial consequences (costs and revenues) of managing *existing* assets. The principles of resource accounting are discussed elsewhere (check the index).

Resource budgeting is sometimes referred to as 'investment accounting' and can be thought of as the option appraisal procedure that underlies a development decision. That is, it seeks to calculate the financial consequences of creating *new* assets (or renewing old ones). The argument is that to ensure we get value-for-money from a development, a full cost-benefit appraisal (CBA) of the proposal has to be made (and compared with alternative uses for the money capital) before a decision to go ahead is finalised. Resource budgeting seeks to identify what economists refer to as the *opportunity cost of the money capital* committed to the project. We will say something more about the CBA technique in Chapter 17 when we discuss the issue of intermediate term financial planning.

Monitoring and measuring effectiveness

In recent years performance indicators (PIs) and league tables have been published by the Audit Commission in England and Wales and by the Accounts Commission in Scotland. PIs should provide an information base to underpin performance review and quality management. Together with output specification, competition and benchmarking they should provide a basis for enhancing the spirit of Best Value.

Many argue that, in the past, performance figures, particularly when presented as a league table, have failed to take proper account of local circumstances and have therefore been difficult to interpret. For these reasons, their publication often carries 'health warnings' from practitioners, academic commentators, and even from the monitoring agencies themselves. However, despite these reservations, it is clear that the drive to achieve Best Value requires formal mechanisms of comparison between authorities and associations. It is of course important that in comparing one organisation's performance with others, we compare like with like. Furthermore, to be systematic, coherent and open, all the measurement and monitoring techniques need to be underpinned by a common accounting framework.

The establishment of a fair and effective system of performance review may require the creation of a tiered approach to measurement in which universal measures (key or 'headline' indicators) could be 'unpacked' to reveal performance and quality measures that are intended to take into account all local factors that affect a social business's performance in a particular area.

As the professional body of the public sector finance accountants (CIPFA) have made clear, the targets need to be supported by a series of performance standards that are specific, measurable, achievable, time-tabled, integrated into the organisation's overall plan, and brought clearly to the attention of managers and users.[2]

In social housing organisations, key PIs invariably include the following:

- Average weekly rents and service charge levels.
- Average weekly cost per dwelling on management.
- Average weekly cost per dwelling on repairs.
- Percentage of rent available that was collected.
- Current tenant rent arrears.

---

2   *Public Finance*, 20 June 1997 pp.10-11.

- Rent written off as not collectable (bad debts).
- Rent lost through dwellings being vacant (voids).
- Percentage of dwellings vacant and available for let.
- Percentage of dwellings vacant and not available for let.
- Average re-let times.
- Percentage of lettings to BME households.
- Average SAP rating (energy efficiency) of dwellings.
- Percentage of dwellings failing to meet the Decent Homes Standard.
- Percentage of emergency, urgent and routine repairs completed within target.
- Percentage of repairs where an appointment was made and kept.

Measures of tenant satisfaction are also treated as key PIs (see below).

Despite their unpopularity amongst many practitioners, published performance measures are now a permanent feature of the management landscape. They provide a mechanism for delivering the social sector's commitment to be accountable to service users, tax-payers, community interests, and the government.

The question of financial performance brings to the fore issues of cash-flow viability, debt management, and risk. Given their central importance to financial managers, we will discuss all of these issues in some detail in the next chapter.

Monitoring and measuring equity

Equity of treatment between individuals and groups is regarded as being particularly important in situations where public funds are employed. Public service providers should incorporate stakeholder analysis into their management procedures and include equity monitoring as part of their Best Value review processes. They need to analyse the distributional consequences of their more significant management or investment decisions and they should seek to ensure that they run their affairs in ways that embrace the principles of equal opportunities.

An important equity aspect of financial management relates to the issue of how the incidence of debt impacts through time. This is really a question of inter-generational justice. All social landlords are expected to follow the precepts of the Chancellor of the Exchequer's fiscal code and ensure that current revenue spending is not financed from loans that will project the costs of current consumption on future generations of tenants and other service users.

Monitoring and measuring experience

The introduction of Best Value has tended to shift the emphasis away from the cost of inputs to the quality of outputs. This shift in emphasis places a high value on the opinions of service users. Arguably the real experts on how a service is working are those people who use it. This means that the well-run social enterprise will seek to acquire regular feedback from its customers and other appropriate stakeholders. For many social housing landlords, this Best Value emphasis on incorporating user experiences into the monitoring procedures is reinforced by an explicit commitment in the mission statement to put the needs and concerns of residents at the top of their list of priorities.

Two key performance indicators that are used in this area are (a) percentage of tenants satisfied with the overall service, and (b) percentage of tenants satisfied with opportunities to participate in management decision-making. There are many techniques for gathering and analysing stakeholder feedback and the interested reader will have little difficulty finding an extensive academic and commercial literature on the subject. We will not follow it up here as our primary concern is with issues of financial management rather than general housing management. However, before concluding, we will point to one practical difficulty of assessing user feedback.

Experience from the regulators and the Ombudsman Service indicates that the level of user complaints sometimes increases as real service improvements are instigated. We might refer to this phenomenon as the 'User Satisfaction Paradox'. The paradox results from the fact that the very act of planning and implementing improvements will raise expectations so that user satisfaction can be thought of in terms of the following formula:

$$\text{User Satisfaction} = \frac{\text{Improvement in performance (divided by)}}{\text{Raised expectations}}$$

The monitoring problem here is that it may be possible to find appropriate ways of recording complaints, charting satisfaction scores, and quantifying improved performance, but it is extremely difficult to measure any changes in user expectations.

The relationship between business planning and financial planning

Financial management is a continuous process by which an organisation seeks to plan and control its income, expenditure, debts, and cash-flows. Planning describes the process by which an organisation decides (1) where it wants to be in the future and (2) how it intends to get there. Control describes the systems and procedures employed to ensure that the plans are (a) implemented appropriately, (b) monitored effectively, and (c) reviewed, refined and revised as necessary.

The politically astute have long recognised that *'When reason rules, money is a blessing.'* (Publilius Syrus, 1st century B.C. *Moral Sayings*). All plans need to be resourced. In the modern economy, just as much as in the ancient world, this means that our plans have to be financially viable. In the contemporary world of social housing, Best Value principles require us to demonstrate that our plans are cost-effective as well as viable. It is not good enough that they 'work' – they must be seen to work in ways that demonstrate both value-for-money and long-term financial viability. This means that financial planning and management are at the heart of modern business planning. We will now consider some of the more specific issues surrounding the important topic of financial management.

Summary

The purpose of business planning is to apply experience, judgement and reason to the information we have at our disposal with a view to making decisions that further the interests of the organisation and its stakeholders.

Best Value service providers, working in the public interest, must provide evidence of performance-based objectives, results-orientated outputs, and long-term financial viability. This means they must engage in business planning.

Business planning provides the strategic framework within which effective financial management can take place. Business planning should be thought of as a documented process that is systematic, flexible, and open to inspection and comment by all stakeholders.

In essence business planning allows the organisation to declare a statement of intent and then explain what it plans to do in pursuit of the long-term objectives that flow from this declaration of its mission and values. Over time it must demonstrate the extent to which it has achieved the promised outcomes cost-effectively and on time.

Reasons for business planning:

- Take a longer view.
- Integrate 'best practices'.
- Learn from your own and others' experiences.
- Communicate intentions to service users and the community (be accountable).
- Reassure those lending funds or awarding grant aid.
- Allow for external regulation and internal monitoring of progress and performance.

Further reading

Gray, D., *What's it all about? Registered social landlord accounts explained*, National Housing Federation, 1999.

HACAS Consulting, *Housing Associations – A Viable Financial Future?*, CIH, 1999.

National Federation of ALMOs, *ALMO Business Planning Guidance*, HouseMark, 2004.

CHAPTER 17:
Financial planning and management

Introduction

How an organisation goes about planning and managing its financial assets and liabilities will depend on a wide variety of factors. These factors will differ from one organisation to another and will, within any one organisation, vary over time. The reader needs to be aware that, although all social landlords are required to manage their finances effectively, financial needs, rules, regulations and protocols vary somewhat between the different types of social landlord. It also has to be recognised that, as with business planning in general, there is no one unchanging, definitively correct way of doing things. The reader will need to consider how, and to what extent, the various aspects of financial management discussed here apply to his or her own organisation and its current and future needs. In short, this chapter does not constitute a practice manual for a particular type of social landlord, but rather a contextual overview of the nature and scope of social business planning in general. Its purpose is to introduce the key issues and broad principles that surround this topic. It also seeks to demystify some of the technical terminology used by financiers and money managers.

The function of treasury management

Making the most of your resources

Before considering the practical elements of effective financial planning and management, we need to remind ourselves yet again that the key economic objective of the organisation is to make the 'best' use of its limited resources. You will recall that in Chapters 2 and 16 we stressed the point that the outcome of any financial transaction has to be judged in terms of its contribution to the declared corporate objectives. We can therefore say that the effective use of resources is the central purpose of financial management.

Focusing on resource (or 'opportunity') costs, rather than the more limited notion of monetary costs, helps to emphasise the point that financial management is not concerned with doing things as cheaply as possible; it is about getting value-for-money from limited resources. It also helps to explain why financial management is not simply the responsibility of the treasury or finance section of the organisation. Sound financial management has to be of concern to all those who make decisions that use up valuable resources. This means that it is also part of the remit of those operational managers who have responsibilities for managing departmental budgets.

The objectives of treasury management

Internal treasury management is concerned to:

- provide the financial resources necessary for the organisation to achieve its purposes;
- manage the associated risks (organisational and financial) that might threaten its ability to achieve these objectives;
- manage the financial assets in a way that ensures that they maintain their value;
- manage the financial liabilities in a way that ensures that they remain affordable.

Why is financial planning and control important?

Because social housing organisations are 'permanent' organisations with a responsibility to provide facilities to a succession of occupiers and service users, effective financial planning has to consider the future consequences as well as the current outcomes of putting money into the stock or the service. This means that effective financial management by social landlords involves:

- *adhering* to current regulations and meeting past promises *NOW*;
- *meeting* proprietary plans and prevailing societal expectations in the *NEAR FUTURE*;
- *adapting* and developing to accommodate changing needs and demands in the *INTERMEDIATE FUTURE*; and,
- *surviving* into the *DISTANT FUTURE*.

This idea of a series of interrelated time profiles lies at the heart of strategic financial management. Such a series of time profiles is sometimes conceived of as an *integrated planning and control cycle* that links the organisation's long-term aspirations to its immediate activities. These financial time frames mirror those of the business planning periods discussed in the previous chapter, i.e. longer-term 'strategic' and shorter-term 'operational' (see Figure 16.2).

Converting the idea of the cycle into a management process involves asking different types of policy question and creating a cascade of documents differentiated by time, scale and specific detail.

The scope of treasury management: the integrated planning and control cycle

Although all social landlords (LAs, ALMOs, RSLs,) are expected to run their affairs strategically, different providers can take distinctly different approaches to financial planning and control and Figure 17.1 should be regarded as a broad schema rather than a set framework that is appropriate to all organisations.

Figure 17.1: Financial planning integrated over time: the planning and control cycle

From
ASPIRATIONS

The distant future period (up to 40+/– years)
Embraces the sorts of questions asked by lenders of long-term capital, the chief executive and management board, e.g. 'What is our growth strategy?' and 'What is our corporate mission?' This period also poses the question of how to account for the long-term replacement of the organisation's fixed assets (depreciation).

Requires the production of a *strategic plan* covering the physical and economic lives of major assets, the period of long-term loans, and beyond. During this period the organisation might be expected to grow or amalgamate, and/or redefine its mission. The primary objective of this period is 'survival'.

The intermediate future period (up to 15 years+/–)
Embraces the sorts of questions asked by investment project managers, lending institutions, and the management board. Includes identifying objectives that need to be achieved to fulfil the mission and how best to acquire funds for development and renewal.

Requires the production of a *business plan* (strategic), a *corporate plan* (operational), *option appraisals* (project planning), and *risk registers* (risk appraisal and management). The primary objective of this period is 'adaptation'.

The near future period (up to 5 years +/–)
Embraces the sorts of questions asked by service users and/or front-line managers about imminent rent changes, proposed maintenance and minor works schedules, and sources of short-term finance.

Requires the publication of *budgets*, *cash-flow forecasts* and *work schedules* relating to specific projects, and *committee minutes* confirming policy decisions relating to the *business* and *corporate plans*. It also requires the periodic publication of performance indicators that measure trends and outcomes against the organisation's declared objectives. The primary objective of this period is 'meeting planned outcomes' and 'keeping promises'.

The present and recent past periods (annual)
Focuses on the immediate concerns of auditors, the regulator, front-line managers, and current stakeholders.

Requires the production of annual *accounts*, *financial statements*, and *annual performance measures*. The primary objective of this period is 'adherence to legal and good practice obligations'.

To
ACTIONS

In particular, the time periods are indicative only and they tend to merge into one another. However, in the discussion that follows the reader is encouraged to keep in mind this model of an integrated planning process. Sound financial management rests on an awareness of these different planning and control time horizons, and throughout the chapter reference will be made to the various questions, concerns, and forms of documentation mentioned above.

The idea of an integrated planning and control cycle (Figure 17.1) highlights the need to provide decision-makers with financial information that enables them to assess how current decisions will impact on future aspirations.

Financial profiling and long-term financial planning

The system of financial management must give a high priority to the presentation of relevant financial data to management committees in ways that allow informed decisions to be made about current management issues, prospective projects and longer-term strategic aspirations.

Financial profiling

The strategic approach to financial planning involves establishing a 'rolling' analysis of current and future revenues, costs and investment needs that is termed *financial profiling*. A financial profile is a projection. It is a projection of the near and distant future seen from the perspective of the present. It charts anticipated costs and revenues based on present knowledge and current assumptions about the future. It provides a present day 'snap-shot' of the anticipated financial future. The projection has to be based on a range of assumptions about such things as known and planned debt servicing charges, appropriate gearing ratios, building cost inflation, interest rates, expected maintenance, repairs and renewal needs (of the housing stock and other fixed assets), planned rental flows, and other anticipated sources of income. As the projection moves further into the future it moves away from a zone of relative certainty into zones of increasing uncertainty. We have to be more and more circumspect about our assumptions as we move away from a relatively certain present towards an increasingly uncertain future.

The profiling approach seeks to enable managers and decision-makers at a particular moment to:

- be certain about the immediate financial needs of the organisation, based on accurate information about the past, and firm assumptions about the current and near future accounting periods;
- be clear about the intermediate financial needs of the organisation, based on provisional estimates of incomes and costs relating to that period;
- have some conditional ideas about the long-term financial needs of the organisation, based on tentative assumptions about the distant future.

This static profile of the future, the 'snap-shot', is made dynamic by establishing procedures that periodically check the assumptions. In this way, as time passes and we roll towards the future, financial plans can gradually firm up and become more concrete. At any point in time, different futures can be anticipated through appraisal techniques such as discounting and sensitivity analysis. (More about these later).

Although they do not normally describe detailed financial arrangements, projected plans should make some reference to how current loans are to be serviced, when fixed capital assets will need renewing or replacing, and how general institutional growth and change are to be paid for. Although the strategic plan takes the long view (up to 40 years) it should be regularly revisited and revised in the light of operational experiences and changing circumstances. The act of reviewing creates a rolling process of change and modification (a moving film rather than a single snap-shot) that we can call 'profiling'. In this way a static projection becomes a dynamic process.

Long-term financial planning

The long-term strategic planning period is sometimes called the 'business planning period'. This is the time frame that a housing agency needs to bear in mind when planning how to look after its tangible assets and pay off its long-term debts. Tangible assets are those property and other real assets that the organisation needs in order to run its affairs. In a housing business, the main tangible assets will be the stock of dwellings. For accounting purposes, tangible assets have to be distinguished from investment assets. Investments assets comprise money reserves and any land bank that the enterprise might possess. Accounting conventions require tangible assets to be depreciated through time (unlike investment assets) to ensure that proper account is taken of their long-run refurbishment and replacement needs. (See below section, *Depreciation of the value of housing assets.*)

In local authorities and ALMOs the regulator tends to set the long-term planning period at thirty years because this is seen as an appropriate period for the authority to develop its services and manage its tangible assets effectively. In LSVT housing associations, the planning period is much the same because start-up loans tend to be negotiated over such a term (25-40 years). Clearly, any institution lending relatively large sums of money for such a period will want to see in place some form of business plan that covers the full length of this loan term. So we can say that long-term financial plans are largely concerned with questions of long-run viability, overall asset management and renewal, and long-term debt management.

Intermediate term financial planning

Intermediate-term decisions about specific projects and policy initiatives (such as a proposed stock transfer, major acquisitions or new building works) should be based on some form of financial planning that typically begins with the presentation of an option appraisal report and culminates with budgeting and cash-flow forecasting. An option appraisal report can be produced internally but is often commissioned from external consultants who will have had experience of working on similar projects with other organisations.

Option appraisals are usually presented in a cost-benefit format that identifies, and in some way quantifies, all the relevant advantages and disadvantages of following one course of action as against others. The 'costs' and 'benefits' should encompass everything that is judged to be relevant to the corporate mission and strategy. This may mean that some rather intangible costs and benefits have to be included, such as staff morale and tenant satisfaction. Because costs and benefits come on stream at different times, the report has to be put into a clear time profile that discounts the value of future costs and benefits back to a present value. There are many difficulties and problems associated with the production of a cost-benefit report and over the years a number of techniques and conventions have been developed to standardise their production.[1] When commissioning a cost-benefit analysis (CBA), the housing practitioner, or the management board, needs to be aware of the strengths and limitations of this kind of appraisal. They also have to be clear that they, and not their consultants, have to be responsible for making the final decision. This means that such reports should not 'make' the decision about which option to follow, but rather act as a guide and source of information and analysis. A CBA should be regarded as a management tool that guides those who carry the ultimate responsibility for taking the option decision. Once decided upon, the selected option has to be budgeted for and cash-flows have to be estimated.

Budgeting and planning for the near future

Budgets are intended to help the organisation ensure that, over a specified budgetary period, expenditure is met by income. The budgetary period may cover more than one financial year. Budgets are used to monitor and authorise expenditure and the collection of income. The budget process also enables the organisation to set and declare priority spending and to establish a rational sequence of spending events. More broadly, budgets can be used to co-ordinate different functions and activities, set targets, and provide a recorded basis for measuring performance and reviewing the organisation's strategy.

There are a number of recognised approaches to budgeting. These include incremental budgeting, planning programming budgeting systems (PPBS), and zero-based budgeting. The *incremental* approach is commonly used in the preparation of revenue budgets. It involves making incremental adjustments to the previous period's budget by focusing on those items that need to be altered because of changing circumstances, like inflation, new service agreements, salary increases, withdrawal of revenue grants. This is a largely conservative approach to budgeting as it assumes that, although circumstances will change, basic service provision will continue much as before. It concentrates on making provision for changes in the external environment.

---

1   For a fuller discussion of these see Garnett, D., 1994a and 1994b.

In contrast, *PPBS* focuses on the internal objectives of the organisation and identifies alternative ways of achieving these objectives. This approach is more relevant for capital budgeting where particular investment and reinvestment plans might be achieved by a variety of different spending programmes.

Zero-based budgeting takes a cost-benefit approach by comparing estimated outcomes with the costs of producing those outcomes. It extends the PPBS approach into a more overtly value-for-money analysis: as such, it is particularly appropriate where various levels of provision are possible for a variety of functions. It takes a strictly opportunity cost approach to spending by seeking to make explicit what would be gained or lost by spending 'more here' and 'less there'. By giving a priority to value-for-money outcomes, this approach may point to the need to make significant changes to previous spending patterns. Although in line with the philosophy of resource accounting and budgeting (RAB), zero-based budgeting can be relatively expensive and time-consuming to establish and operate. As with any CBA approach, it also involves making value judgements about the value of one course of action as against another, and is open to a degree of political manipulation.[2]

Budgets can be set at different levels (corporate, departmental, section). Experience shows that, once an organisation has reached a certain size, some resource use decisions are best made by those who have direct managerial responsibility for the spending outcomes. A cost centre is a sub-division of the organisation that is used for planning and accounting purposes. Typically the manager of the cost centre will be the budget holder and, as such, will be held responsible for controlling and justifying the devolved budget. The principle here is that devolved responsibility produces more informed decisions and a more intelligent and flexible use of limited resources, and is therefore less bureaucratic.[3]

Controlling budgets involves the management of cash-flows. Because cash management is such an important aspect of financial planning and control, we will discuss it in more detail when we analyse the key elements of effective treasury management (see below).

Managing the present and the immediate past: standard accounts and financial statements

Shorter-term financial information is presented in the audited accounts, appended notes, and accompanying financial statements. Two key accounts have to be kept by social housing businesses: these are an income and expenditure account and a balance sheet.

---

2   For a fuller discussion of types of budget and methods of budgeting refer to the National Housing Federation's *Financial Planning: a practical guide*, NHF, 1996, pp11-19.
3   For a fuller discussion on planning for cost centres refer to *Financial Planning: a practical guide*, NHF, 1996, pp8-10.

A standard *income and expenditure account* is set out and analysed in Chapter 15 (refer to Figure 15.1). This is a 'real' transactions account that records the movement of money into and out of the books. Unlike the financial accounts, it does not reflect 'book' transactions like depreciation, nor does it distinguish between capital and revenue transactions. The account is prepared on an 'accruals basis' which means that if some expenditure has been incurred and a bill is on its way, it will be included in the account. The same accruals approach is taken to income owed but not yet received. However, a prudent approach is taken and only sums known with certainty are included. The purpose of the accruals approach is to try and present as accurate a picture of the financial position as is possible.

A *balance sheet* is a statement featured in the annual accounts that indicates the value of the organisation's assets and liabilities at the end of the accounting period, and the ways in which these have been financed. The main purpose of the balance sheet is to show the state of affairs of the social landlord at the year-end date.

Figure 17.2 is in the format of a housing association account as dictated by the Housing Corporation and the Statement of Recommended Practice (SORP) that is issued by the National Housing Federation along with the Scottish and Welsh Federations. The example itself is an aggregate account which means that it represents the sum of housing association balance sheets whose financial year-ends fall within the corresponding period. As well as illustrating the general structure of a balance sheet, it therefore also provides the reader with some genuine and interesting information about the financial standing of the housing association movement as a whole. It provides a summary of all assets, liabilities (including loans), grants and reserves so as to reveal the global position of the sector. The information is taken from *2003 Global Accounts and Sector Analysis of Housing Association*, a report published jointly by the National Housing Federation and the Housing Corporation, 2004.

Figure 17.2 is just a simplified summary balance sheet as related to housing associations. Although other types of social landlord would produce an account with a somewhat different structure, the purpose of the balance sheet will be the same and the basic accounting principles will also be the same. In all cases, the standard accounts will reference other more detailed (or descriptive) information in the various financial statements.

Financial statements

In addition to the two main accounts, the business has to produce a set of *financial statements* that give an indication to the management committee, and other interested parties, of the year's transactions and how the organisation has fared financially over the accounting period. Among other things, these will explain how the current cash-flow was generated and spent and how surpluses or deficits were dealt with in the accounting period.

Figure 17.2: The format of housing association balance sheets

Line Ref.	All figures in £ million	2002/2003	2001/2002	2000/2001
	FIXED ASSETS			
A	Housing properties at cost or valuation	59,931	54,602	50,889
B	Capital grants	(27,719)	(26,235)	(25,454)
C	Depreciation	(812)	(664)	(425)
D	Net book value of housing properties	31,400	27,703	25,010
E	Other fixed assets	1,950	1,856	1,537
F	**Total fixed assets**	**33,350**	**29,559**	**26,547**
	CURRENT ASSETS			
G	Non-liquid current assets	434	263	255
H	Cash and short-term investments	1,787	1,988	1,905
I	Other current assets	2,168	1,488	1,330
J	**Total current assets**	**4,389**	**3,739**	**3,490**
	CURRENT LIABILITIES			
K	Short-term loans	373	284	350
L	Bank overdrafts	35	42	33
M	Other current liabilities	2,354	1,874	1,890
N	**Total current liabilities**	**2,762**	**2,200**	**2,273**
O	**Net current assets**	**1,627**	**1,539**	**1,217**
P	**Total assets less current liabilities**	**34,977**	**31,098**	**27,764**
	LONG-TERM CREDITORS AND PROVISIONS			
Q	Long-term loans	22,403	20,394	18,067
R	Other long-term creditors	917	558	371
S	Provisions	155	93	99
T	**Total long-term creditors and provisions**	**23,475**	**21,045**	**18,537**
	RESERVES			
U	Accumulated surplus	3,916	3,562	3,215
V	Designated reserves	1,432	1,374	1,471
W	Restricted reserves	462	495	490
X	Revaluation reserves	5,692	4,622	4,051
Y	**Total reserves**	**11,502**	**10,053**	**9,227**
Z	**Total loans, provisions and reserves**	**34,977**	**31,098**	**27,764**
	Number of housing associations included	**1,873**	**1,857**	**1,846**
	Number of homes	**1,945,249**	**1,765,980**	**1,616,857**

See notes overleaf

Notes to Figure 17.2

E/F   Fixed assets are investments that are held for a long-term purpose. 'Fixed' in this context means that the money capital is 'locked in' to the assets and cannot be easily realised. (See Chapters 1 and 2 for fuller discussion.)

G/H/I/J   Current assets are those investments that are held as part of short-term treasury management where the intention is to realise the investment in the short term without reinvestment of the sale proceeds (i.e. use the proceeds for some planned expenditure purpose in the immediate or near future.

A   The item 'housing properties' should distinguish between dwellings held for letting and shared ownership.[4] Anyone reading the full accounts should be able to distinguish between completed schemes and properties under construction. Properties developed for outright sale or on behalf of third parties should be treated as 'current assets' rather than as 'fixed assets'

Housing assets cannot be valued in market terms. They have to be valued either (a) at historic cost less SHG and depreciation; or (b) at existing use value less depreciation. In deciding whether to include housing properties at valuation, the association will need to consider the balance of costs and benefits. Although a valuation provides more meaningful information to the users of the accounts, periodic revaluation exercises cost time and money. The amount at which an item is included in the balance sheet is called the 'carrying value'.

Where valuations are used, the properties should be periodically revalued at least every five years. Where housing properties are revalued and the valuation exceeds the carrying amount, (net of capital grant and depreciation), the difference should be credited to the revaluation reserve (marked 'X' in the above account) and be reported in the statement of total recognised surpluses and deficits (see below). Where housing properties are revalued and the valuation is less than the carrying amount, the diminution should be recognised.

When housing properties carried at valuation are disposed of, any amounts in the revaluation reserve relating to those properties should be transferred to the revenue reserve. If conditions change causing a reduction in the recoverable amount of a fixed asset below its carrying value, this is called 'impairment'.[5]

E   Fixed asset investments other than housing properties should be stated at their market value. This is deemed to be the most appropriate basis of valuation because, unlike housing properties, there are no external restrictions attached to their disposal. Any upward or downward revaluations are accounted for in the statement of recognised surpluses and deficits.

F   For all investments included in a valuation, the historical cost should be disclosed in a note to the accounts.

V/W   The distinction between designated and restricted reserves is discussed in Chapter 14.

---

4   In shared ownership developments, the proportion of the development that is expected to be sold as the first tranche should be shown as a current asset. The remainder should be shown as a fixed asset from which SHG should be deducted.

5   Examples of events and changes in circumstances that indicate impairment may have occurred include: (a) social, demographic or environmental changes resulting in a fall in property prices locally; and (b) significant adverse changes in the statutory or regulatory environment.

The information presented in the accounts and their accompanying financial statements are necessarily detailed. The detailed requirements, published as the Statement of Recommended Practice (SORP)[6] change periodically. What the general reader needs to bear in mind is that the presentation of all this information is designed to guarantee accountability (transparency) and to allow informed decision-making to occur. Later in this chapter we will consider the important question of risk management. It is worth making the point straightaway that the production and presentation of deficient, misleading or inaccessible information is bound to add to the risks of running a business.

Having discussed the nature and scope of the integrated planning and control cycle and outlined the main financial accounts, we will now turn to the key issues that contemporary social landlords have to consider when planning and managing their finances. These issues straddle the different planning time profiles that we have been discussing.

Figure 17.3: The key elements of financial planning and control

Effective financial management depends on achieving each of the following:	1. Sound cash management.
	2. A balanced approach to borrowing.
	3. An appropriate way of valuing and depreciating tangible assets.
	4. Sound debt management.
	5. An appropriate policy for assessing and managing the financial risks.
	6. Clarity about how best to cover the costs of maintaining, repairing, improving and renewing the built assets over the longer as well as the shorter term.
	7. Effective tax planning.

The key elements of financial planning and control

1. Cash management

Cash management is about balancing the desire to earn interest (or avoid paying interest) with the need to ensure that monies are available to meet the known and reasonable requirements for liquidity. All businesses have to manage the month-by-month flow of cash in and out of the transaction accounts. This means that,

---

6   The Accounting Standards Board (ASB) has approved the National Housing Federation, the Welsh Federation of Housing Associations (WFHA), and the Scottish Federation of Housing Associations (SFHA) – the three Federations – collectively for the purpose of issuing recognised Statements of Recommended Practice (SORPs). This requires the three Federations to follow the ASB's code of practice for the production and issue of SORPs. The code provides the framework to be followed by the three Federations.

once set, internal budgets have to be monitored and managed. For each cost centre, adjustments may have to be made during the budgetary period to ensure that receipts can cover payments. At certain times, it may be necessary to delay certain payments until the cash-flow situation improves, or reschedule spending programmes, or abandon or increase planned spending, or acquire short-term finance to cover impending costs. The analysis and monitoring of cash-flow is particularly important with respect to capital budgets where the sums of money are likely to be relatively large.

When a housing organisation borrows it does so at a margin over a reference rate (e.g. London Inter-Bank Offer Rate, Bank Base Rate, mortgage rate, or a gilt yield). This margin between the reference rate and the rate charged to the borrower represents the lender's return on the loan. From the borrower's point of view, it represents a revenue charge. This charge is likely to be higher than any interest that could be earned from holding cash in a deposit account. This means that organisations with debts will generally want to pay them off rather than hold large cash reserves. Having said this there are two motives for holding some cash in a savings reserve.

1. *The transactions motive:* to maintain a degree of liquidity in order to transact its business and meet its regular financial obligations.
2. *The precautionary motive:* to maintain a degree of comfort over and above the transaction needs (a) in case of an unforeseen call for cash, or (b) an unanticipated opportunity arises that needs immediate access to cash.

Because social housing organisations are fairly 'risk averse' (see below), they will tend to hold any cash reserves in UK- or EU-based institutions that have been given a high security rating. Such ratings are provided by a specialist bank or ratings agency. For example, IBCA Ltd, Standard and Poor's, and Moody's Investor Services all provide such assessments of credit worthiness. Unfortunately, each agency has its own way of describing its ratings. For IBCA, for example, A1 represents the best, followed by A2, A3, B, with C being the worst. Standard and Poor's short-term ratings also badge the best as A1, but their scale describes the worst as D. Moody's ratings run from A1 Prime through to NP (not Prime) – the worst.

Risk averse organisations, like housing associations, will tend to deposit surplus cash reserves in banks with a rating of A2 or above. A support rating of A2 means a bank for which (in the opinion of the ratings agency) state support would be forthcoming even in the absence of a legal guarantee. This could be, for example, because of the bank's importance to the economy or its historical relationship with authorities and associations.

It is possible for local authorities and housing associations themselves to become credited rated. This would enhance their financial reputations and could become part of their borrowing strategies (see below). This would be particularly helpful if and when they seek overseas funding or become involved in large-scale, complex development activities that require sophisticated funding arrangements.[7]

In ending our short discussion on cash management, we need to stress the following point:

> because it determines short-run business viability, the constant monitoring of cash-flows constitutes an essential element in both performance review and risk management.

2. Borrowing strategies

Broadly speaking, social landlords need recourse to private loans for two reasons: (1) to counteract the effects of the reduced grant rates described in the earlier chapters, and (2) to help finance increased activity and provide decent homes. English and Scottish law both tend to interpret 'borrowing' very widely and the CIPFA Code of Practice suggests that the borrowing organisation defines the loan instruments it intends to use clearly in its business plan.

Most borrowing in this sector is in the form of loan facilities and overdrafts. Other instruments could include bond issues, leases, hire purchase, and credit agreements with suppliers.[8]

Before analysing how to develop a borrowing strategy we need to make the point that different types of landlord tend to have different borrowing needs (and powers). They also tend to borrow in different ways. LSVT housing associations, for example, usually need to establish a package of medium and long-term loan facilities in order to acquire the stock in the first place and then meet tenant promises relating to repairs and improvements. An ALMO on the other hand may rely mainly on a revolving overdraft facility guaranteed by the local authority. A very small traditional association or a new Black and Minority Ethnic organisation may tend to secure medium-term loans secured on individual projects. Having made this point, we will now consider some general aspects of borrowing and debt management that need to be understood by those with an interest in developing a strategic approach to financial planning and management.

Loan facilities

In devising a longer-term effective borrowing strategy, a clear distinction has to be made between two discretely different borrowing decisions:

- the decision to arrange a loan facility, and
- the decision to draw on that facility and actually borrow funds.

---

7   To date only two LAs and one HA have sought such a rating.
8   Credit agreements take the form of a deferred payment.

The arranged facility is an agreement that sets in place an entitlement to borrow up to a maximum and subject to any preconditions that were established prior to the agreement ('conditions precedent'). In many cases the landlord will only draw down part of this potential loan, keeping the rest as an 'insurance' against future needs. This approach is recommended by the regulators (e.g. the Housing Corporation) as it adds stability to the organisation's long-term finances. However, such a policy may incur a 'non-utilisation' fee on the undrawn part of the facility.

A loan facility can be arranged with any lending institution (bank, building society, etc.). Once established, money can be drawn down, so long as the period of availability has not expired and the 'conditions precedent' can be met. Drawings would normally be made in tranches of a minimum amount.

Although repayment would normally cancel that part of the facility, it is possible to negotiate what is called a 'revolving credit facility' that allows repaid amounts to be redrawn. This type of 'revolving' arrangement will normally be available only for a limited term (e.g. five years) and only for a fixed amount.

A number of social landlords have turned to specialist merchant banks to arrange highly flexible loan packages that cannot be provided directly by the more traditional clearing banks and building societies. These specialist institutions may be able to arrange 'designer loans' that include special features that allow the social business to operate more finely-tuned treasury management. These specialist loans can include facilities such as a 'reduction arrangement', whereby the business borrows an agreed sum for an agreed period but is given the facility to reduce the debt (and thereby lower the interest charges) for set periods within the term. This can prove useful if sometime in the future unexpected cash-flows emerge or cheaper sources of finance become available, such as a newly-introduced government subsidy. In such circumstances, part of the loan can be redeemed and then taken out again at some later date if the need arises. These specialist arrangements tend only to be available for longer-term loans (in excess of ten years) and will require more 'up front' time and money to arrange. However, they can prove to be cheaper in the long-run.

Overdrafts

Borrowing can operate in a more flexible fashion through the use of an overdraft facility. This will allow the organisation to borrower up to an agreed amount at short notice by creating a 'negative extension' on its current account. In this case, interest payable is calculated on a daily basis. Unlike a credit facility, an overdraft facility can be cancelled by the bank at any time and without giving a reason.

Other forms of borrowing

Social landlords have expanded the financial mechanisms for borrowing funds. Most of their private borrowing is still in the form of traditional mortgages from banks and building societies, but over time they have sought new ways of borrowing. Housing association bonds are now well-established. A bond is simply an IOU agreement under which a sum is repaid to an investor after a fixed period. Bonds can be issued by anyone but their issuing costs are relatively high for small amounts of money borrowed for short periods.[9] For this reason bonds are normally issued by public bodies or companies wishing to borrow relatively large sums for relatively long periods. They can be thought of as loans that repay a fixed rate of interest over a specified time and then also repay the original sum at par in full after an agreed period – when the bond 'matures'. Bond debt appears in the balance sheet as a liability. The debt should be stated at its current value (net amount) in 'long-term creditors'.[10]

Bonds can be traded (i.e. they are transferable instruments) so that the original investor can pass them on at a discount before the maturity date. The trading market for bonds is sometimes referred to as 'the debt capital market'. Bonds provide an appropriate form of finance for larger, more active landlords in that they produce long-term (i.e. 20–40 years) fixed rate funding that matches the economic life of the housing assets they help to fund. Where large sums are involved they can prove to be (incrementally) the cheapest form of secure funding. Local authorities have always sought to achieve financial economies of scale by financing major assets over a 60-year period. By accessing the large pool of institutional monies available from pension funds and life companies, the LSVT landlord in particular can, like the local authorities, acquire longer-term financing than is available in the bank market.[11]

Increasingly, specialist bankers are arranging sophisticated packages for LSVT landlords that can include a core funding element in the form of a bond issue with complementary funding in the form of a long-term (e.g. 25 year) banking facility. This sort of arrangement establishes opportunities for renewing and extending loan facilities into the future, thereby achieving one of the key borrowing objectives (see below).

The key borrowing objectives
Experience shows that success in raising private finance can often be traced back to sound planning long before approaches are made to lenders (Button, 1993,

---

9   For example, bond issues are sometimes guaranteed by what is called 'monoline enhancement'. This is a form of insurance policy that guarantees investors against any default on their interest payments.

10   The net amount is the gross redemption value less the discount net of amortisation. Immediately after issue, before any amortisation of the discount, the net amount will be equal to the net proceeds. Amortisation is charged to the income and expenditure account. Similarly, any significant early redemption costs (penalties for redeeming the debt) should be charged to the income and expenditure account.

11   Institutional investors (such as pension fund managers) and social landlords are both concerned with long-term cycles of lending and borrowing. The fund manager is concerned that the fund's invested resources keep up with long-run inflation, and the landlord's rents tend to rise with inflation.

p12). The objective of loan planning and management is to secure loan finance that balances in an appropriate way the following factors.

- Cheapness – low interest charges.
- Certainty – a degree of fixedness of interest rates.
- Coherence – matching cash-flow and debt service obligations.
- Renewability – an opportunity to extend the loan if this becomes necessary.
- Redeemability – an opportunity to cancel the loan if the needs arise.
- Security – a balanced loan portfolio in terms of loan type and term.

These features have to be negotiated with lenders whose priorities are somewhat different from those of borrowers. Lenders are primarily concerned with balancing the return on their investment with the risk of default. As a general rule, lenders tend to charge higher rates of interest for higher risk projects. This means that in negotiating a loan with manageable interest charges, the borrower has to under-write the debt in some way that satisfies the lender's desire for an appropriate 'risk-reward' relationship.

Negotiating loans

Loan negotiations involve making a contract that strikes an equilibrium between the borrower's and the lender's objectives. A key factor in this negotiation is the ability of the social housing organisation to persuade the potential investor that the loan is secure over its term. This involves establishing the following:

1. The legal and managerial competence of the borrower.
2. What collateral is being offered and what cover ratio is allowed.
3. How the value of the collateral is to be measured.

Status and legal and financial competence
Lenders require evidence of the corporate status of the borrower and its capacity to service the loan over its term.[12] The lender will want to inspect a current copy of the borrower's rules and constitution with evidence of its registered status. Having satisfied the lender that it has the power to take out the loan, the borrower must then show that it has carried out the necessary actions to exercise that power. The lender's solicitors are likely to require documentary evidence, such as minutes of an authorised committee of the borrower, that delegated powers are valid, comprehensive and relevant to the loan conditions. Audited accounts will have to be presented for inspection so that the lender can be satisfied that the borrower is in a position to service the debt. Supplementary statements may be required from the borrower's auditors confirming that there has been no material change in financial status since submission of the last audited accounts.

---

12   Since 1989, the movement as a whole has been successful in raising tens of billions of pounds from private sources.

Lenders will be interested in the borrower's overall debt profile and their ability to cover that debt if things go wrong. This means that they will wish to compare the loans outstanding with the total reserves. When expressed as a ratio this relation is called the *loan gearing*.

The lender will be concerned to monitor the borrower's continuing financial robustness. This is typically done by establishing an 'interest cover ratio' for each year of the business plan. This in effect, is a measure of the ease with which the organisation is able to meet its loan repayment responsibilities (see below – covenant conditions).

Lenders are always concerned with the managerial competence of those to whom they lend. For this reason the association should be able to demonstrate that it has in place mechanisms for maintaining the value of its built assets over the long term. For example, the financial planning of repairs and renewals is prudent in itself, but it is also necessary if the organisation wishes to borrow investment funds. Lenders will want to see projections of future costs (such as repair costs) to ensure that the agreed (covenanted) loan interest cover ratios and revenue break-even points are not likely to be breached.

Covenant conditions including collateral and effective loan cover ratio
Covenants stipulate the loan conditions. In particular, they specify how the loan is to be secured by collateral and effective cover ratio; penalties for default or for early redemption; and any penalties for changing the loan conditions. Covenants may also specify the financial performance borrowers are expected to achieve. For example, the lender may require the business to generate enough revenue to meet its interest charges one and a half or two times over. Covenants result from contractual negotiations and in practice they differ substantially.

Collateral constitutes the lender's security against default on the loan. It takes the form of an identified asset that is pledged as guarantee for repayment of money lent. Typically, property is put forward as the security, although in recent years some deals have been struck that pledge the organisation's rental income flow. The idea of pledging the rent flow, sometimes termed *securitisation of receivables* or *rental securitisation*, is an idea that was first developed in the USA. Under these arrangements, the rental income is paid direct to the lender via a financial intermediary. This gives the rental income a 'first charge' status (see below) thereby providing sound collateral for the loan. Once the debt service charges have been deducted, the surplus rent is then paid back to the landlord.[13]

As grant rates fall, the proportion of cost met by private loans has had to increase. This has meant that the value of the new units being developed are often insufficient to under-write fully the debt, and lenders have sought further security

---

13　For a clear explanation of the principles of rental securitisation see briefing by David Walker and Graham Brombley in *Inside Housing*, 17 February 1995, pp14-15.

from the existing stock (or the rental income flow). Where existing properties are pledged, security can be given by means of a 'fixed charge' or a 'floating charge'. If the loan is secured by a fixed charge, it is tied to specific, identifiable dwellings owned by the landlord. If the loan is secured by a floating charge, it may be covered by all or a range of the association's stock. A floating charge security may change over time as it can include any equity growth on properties already subject to fixed charges. Whether property or rents are put up as collateral, lenders to this sector typically look for fixed charge security to cover their loans. They will normally expect to have a fixed first charge. This means that they will want assurance that the asset is free from any existing prior claims so that they have first claim on the asset in the event of default. Because of lender aversion to floating charges, associations sometimes arrange consolidation of existing lenders' charges as a way of releasing the maximum amount of unencumbered asset cover.

The cover ratio stipulates what the lender is prepared to accept as a ratio between the value of the asset collateral and the agreed debt. So, for example, the lender may stipulate a 1.2 cover ratio meaning that a debt of £1 million will have to be covered by £1.2 million worth of assets. In the case of floating charge securities, lenders will normally require a greater effective cover ratio – something like 2.5. Clearly, much depends on how the properties are valued. How to value and depreciate units of social housing are now important questions in social housing management. These days, landlords need to put a value on their housing assets for a number of reasons. As well as the need to provide collateral for private borrowing, the whole principle of resource accounting is based on assumptions about the use of the financial resources that are locked into the fixed assets. For these reasons, the questions of valuation and depreciation will now be discussed as separate issues.

3. Valuing and depreciating tangible assets

Social housing valuations

There is no one definitive way of valuing a unit of social housing. Broadly, the value could be measured against its costs of production or acquisition (historic cost value); or it could be measured against its vacant exchange value (open market value); or it could be measured against its tenanted transfer value (existing use value). The type of valuation used will depend on the purpose for which it is being applied. The basis for rent restructuring for example, is simple open market value. Right to buy transactions are also based on open market values (reduced by a fixed discount). By contrast, a lender will not accept an open market valuation but will require the value to reflect the social nature of the asset.

So long as social landlords were deemed to be located in the welfare sector of the economy and were publicly funded, there was little or no pressure put upon them to value their housing assets in terms of current values. As welfare agencies, so long as they covered their costs over the long term, there was little concern about whether or not their assets had appreciated in value thereby generating equity.

This meant that housing units were simply valued by reference to their historic costs of provision. However, the principles of Best Value and the requirements of resource accounting now require social landlords to estimate and record the current value of their fixed assets. The introduction of mixed funding made it imperative that associations knew the exchange value of their assets. Many private sector loans are secured against the equity vested in the stock and, in any event, lenders will wish to measure the current overall financial standing of those to whom they advance loans.

There are a number of ways in which a unit of social housing might be valued. For accounting purposes (i.e. balance sheet valuations), properties are normally valued in terms of existing use. The accounting principle behind giving a book value to a housing property is that it should represent the lower of replacement cost (i.e. of an identical development today) or recoverable amount (its net realisable value or value in use). Under normal circumstances social tenanted properties will only be disposed of to another social landlord. Therefore, for all intents and purposes, the value of such properties is limited to Existing Use Value for Social Housing (EUV-SH). For social landlords the Royal Institution of Chartered Surveyors has introduced the EUV-SH into its Practice Statement within its Appraisal and Valuation Manual. EUV-SH seeks to estimate what another RSL would be prepared to pay to acquire the asset and keep it in existing use. This involves valuing the asset(s) on a 'going concern' basis.[14] EUV-SH has now also been adopted as the basis for resource accounting for local authority housing.

The basis of valuation for secured lending purposes can differ from that for accounting purposes. Whereas the landlord organisation regards the property as a 'tangible asset' (something that needs to be kept in order to run its business), the lender tends to be interested in the property as an 'investment asset'. Lenders are concerned with cover ratios (see above), and ease of acquisition and disposal in the case of default. Most lenders have private sector experience of securing loans against properties valued in terms of vacant possession open market prices. However, it has to be recognised that open market vacant possession is not a relevant basis of valuation for social landlords because the rights of the tenants have to be taken into account.

In the past, money has been lent to social landlords against housing assets that have been valued in rather rough and ready ways. Arguably the simple valuation would be 'discounted open market value' (OMV minus social discount). The discount is applied to reflect the continuing social nature of the asset. When this simple valuation has been used, the discount has tended to be fairly hefty (e.g. 50 per cent).

---

14 Although a logical way of recording the asset value, and recommended by SORP, work done by the NFHA in the early 1990s indicated that EUV-SH produced a relatively low valuation insofar as repossessed dwellings often raised higher sums on disposal through sales or re-renting than that represented by this 'going concern' valuation.

When an 'historic cost' approach to valuation is used, the question of how to represent any embedded capital grant (e.g. HAG/SHG), is brought to the fore. In such cases, associations have traditionally favoured the practice of deducting the grant element from the value but showing it in the balance sheet so as to record the extent to which government support contributed to an association's development.

In valuing a stock of dwellings for the purpose of large-scale transfer, a business planning approach is taken. This involves estimating a capitalised figure that represents the difference between the costs of managing, repairing and maintaining the assets and their potential to generate a rental income over the business planning period. This sort of calculation can result in the stock having a negative value. In such a case, for the transfer to occur, the transferring agency (typically a local authority) will need to provide a 'dowry' to allow the new landlord to achieve a viable business plan.

Depreciation of the value of housing assets

Depreciation measures the reduction in the value of an asset with the passage of time, due in particular to wear and tear. In the past, social landlords often argued that regular maintenance and periodic refurbishment of their housing properties have the effect of maintaining values thereby eliminating the need to provide for depreciation. With the shift in emphasis towards resource accounting, the Accounting Standards Board now questions the acceptability of this practice. For accounting purposes, social housing properties are regarded as 'tangible fixed assets' rather than 'investment assets'. As such, they are primarily valued for their economic usefulness rather than for their potential to appreciate in exchange value. Good accounting practice requires all tangible fixed assets to be depreciated to reflect the consumption of their economic benefit. This requires the social landlord to make a charge for the depreciation of their housing properties to the income and expenditure account on a systematic basis over their useful economic lives.[15]

Property valuers and accountants argue that few buildings can be regarded as having a limitless life, and that a point will eventually come at which redevelopment (full replacement) rather than maintenance, repair and refurbishment will be the most economic course. A depreciation charge puts an estimated value on the wearing out, consumption or other reduction in the useful economic life of a tangible fixed asset that has occurred during the accounting period.[16] Depreciation is concerned to take account of the declining use value that occurs with the effluxion of time (wear, tear and obsolescence). The principle here

---

15 The useful economic life of an asset is defined as the period over which the organisation expects to derive economic benefits from that asset. A traditionally built new building is assumed to have an economic life of 60 years.
16 The structure of a building and items within the structure, such as central heating boilers, lifts and general fittings, may have substantially different useful economic lives and, if material, may need to be depreciated separately.

is that an increase in the exchange value of a property does not justify ignoring depreciation. (Refer to Chapter 1 for a discussion on the distinction between use value and exchange value).

The depreciation charge is based on the balance sheet carrying value. Freehold land should not be depreciated and so the current value of the land should be deducted from the carrying value before assessing the need to depreciate. In different cases different methods of calculating depreciation may be deemed appropriate. There are several acceptable depreciation methodologies. The two most commonly used are:

- the straight line (annuity) method – where the asset is written off in equal instalments over its estimated economic useful life; and,
- the reducing balance method – where a standard percentage of depreciation is applied to the reducing depreciable amount of the asset.

The reducing balance method has more economic logic in that it assumes that the consumption benefits of the assets diminish at an increasing rate as they age. However, in order to prevent undue fluctuations and avoid the expense of continually having to value properties, the straight line method is often employed. We will return to the question of depreciation when we consider the issue of stock management (see below).

Impairment of the value of housing assets

The notion of depreciation has to be distinguished from that of impairment. With the passage of time, factors other than condition obsolescence (wear and tear) can come into play that 'impair' the utility of a tangible fixed asset such as a dwelling and thus reduces its value. In other words, events or changed circumstances may occur that cause the value of the assets to decline at a faster rate than that allowed for by the depreciation methodology. This is a problem because good accounting practice requires the landlord to ensure that properties are not shown in the books at an amount exceeding their exchange value, called the 'recoverable amount'.[17] For this reason social landlords are required to address the issue of impairment of housing properties in addition to depreciation.

The landlord should instigate an impairment review where there is an indication that carrying values may not be recoverable. The following are illustrative examples of events or changed circumstances that might prompt an impairment review.

- A change in demand for social housing in the area with consequential high void rates and transfer requests. There are many social, demographic, economic and environmental changes that might affect the demand in a particular area.

---

17 The recoverable amount is defined as the higher of their net realisable value and value in use.

- Significant adverse changes in the statutory or regulatory environment.
- A current or anticipated operating deficit or net cash out-flow.
- Where consumption standards have changed making a particular type of housing functionally obsolete. In other words, the buildings themselves might still have a long remaining economic life but fashions and attitudes have changed to bring about functional obsolescence, as against condition obsolescence. Examples might include houses without parking spaces, built at a time before the car was so dominant, and sheltered schemes with shared facilities, built at a time when large communal areas were favoured.

4. Debt management

In broad terms, the costs of servicing a loan will depend on how much is borrowed, when the loan was taken out, the nature of the investment product, the term of loan, what security is being offered to under-write the debt, and the status of the borrower (including the quality of its management procedures).

Long-term versus short-term borrowing

All businesses are financed by a mixture of long and short-term borrowing. Of the many issues that need to be considered when deciding the structure of the debt portfolio, the following are of central importance.

- *Coherence*. This involves matching the type of borrowing with the type of asset held, so that long-term debt is generally NOT taken out to pay for current assets or to pay for revenue spending.
- *Flexibility*. Short-term debt is easier to arrange and redeem.
- *Cost*. Because lenders will expect a higher reward for venturing funds for a longer period, long-term debt is normally more expensive to service.
- *Risk*. Much of the financial risk hinges on external factors such as inflation and interest rate fluctuations. In the case of longer-term debt, this brings up the key question about whether to opt for floating of fixed interest rates.

Variable versus fixed interest debt

The level of risk associated with debt will depend, to some degree, on how it was set up. The key distinction here is between variable and fixed interest rate agreements. The over-riding treasury objective is to ensure that debt liabilities do not become unaffordable and thus endanger the business plan. We can therefore think of debt management as an aspect of the wider issue of risk management. Floating rate debt carries an inherent interest rate risk while fixed interest debt carries an inherent inflation related risk.

The obvious risk of floating interest debt is that an unexpected fluctuation in the interest rate can affect the viability of the business plan in both the near future and intermediate future periods (see Figure.17.1). Because interest rates can change at short notice, this sort of debt brings with it a degree of cost uncertainty. The risk of fixed interest debt is that the borrower might become locked into relatively high debt charges if variable rates turn out to be lower than expected in the intermediate period. Fixed interest rates bring a degree of certainty but, depending on the rate of inflation, may turn out to be more expensive to service in the end. The key point is that both types of debt carry risks and the object of treasury management is to achieve an appropriately balanced portfolio of fixed and floating debt that provides the necessary funds without exposure to unwarranted risk.

Money market interest rates are defined by reference to specific measures such as the London Inter-Bank Bid Rate (LIBID) or the London Inter-Bank Offer Rate (LIBOR). These 'reference rates' can be thought of as the rates of interest at which the banks and building societies themselves borrow wholesale funds or lend to each other.

The uncertainties associated with floating rate debt can be modified by 'hedging'. A hedging arrangement seeks to reduce the risk associated with a particular action by taking some form of counteraction. This is done by taking out what is called a 'derivative contract'.[18] A derivative contract enables one party with exposure to unwanted risk to pass some or all of that risk to a second party in return for a fee.

Under such a contract the borrower in the original contract (from which this new contract is 'derived') purchases a 'hedging instrument' (or 'derivative') such as a 'cap' or a 'collar'. An interest rate cap will, in return for a premium, cover any difference between the so-called 'strike rate' and the reference rate (e.g. LIBOR). The strike rate is the rate at which the cap is evoked. If the reference rate (the rate of interest you have to pay) exceeds the cap strike rate (the nominal trigger rate set in the agreement), the seller will pay the buyer the difference. The payment will be made on the agreed 'strike date' (e.g. quarterly) and the agreement will run for a fixed term (the capping period). An interest rate floor is simply the opposite of a cap. It provides insurance for any organisation lending funds that its return will not fall below a certain level. By putting the two mechanisms together into a 'collar', it is possible to negotiate lower premiums for capping insurance.

Although fixed rate debt tends to be somewhat more expensive than floating rate debt, it brings a degree of certainty into the process of financial planning. For this reason, housing organisations typically operate loan facilities that build some periods of fixed rate security into their longer-term debt. For example, as part of a 30 year loan facility, they might negotiate set periods of fixed, or maximum ceiling, rates covering limited periods (typically 4-6 years).

Debt profiling
Towards the start of this chapter we discussed the strategic approach to financial planning and control in terms of a 'rolling' analysis that involves projecting

---

18   A derivative contract is one in which the value is derived from some other contractual
     arrangement – in this case from the obligation to pay the reference rate of interest.
     Derivatives are normally used to limit the exposure to risk.

current and future revenues and costs over the full business planning cycle (typically 30 years). The strategic approach to debt management needs to take a similar 'profiling' approach.

The management of long-term debt is of particular concern to LSVT landlords because in order to come into existence, they will have needed to have set up a substantial loan facility to acquire the transferred stock and then to deliver their business plan promises. Council-owned housing companies (ALMOs) can borrow a set sum once they gain two star status from inspectors but, at present, they have not been given the authority to borrow beyond this amount to fund further new developments and improvements. This is because, like local authorities, ALMO borrowing is part of the public expenditure control mechanism (see Chapter 5). This means that, at present, the management of long-term business debt is of primary concern to LSVT landlords and other RSLs that have development programmes embedded in their business plans. However, if in the future current restrictions are relaxed, then other social landlords may then be allowed to arrange long-term loan facilities. If this occurs, then they too will need to manage a debt profile that is modeled on the lines of Figure 17.4.[19]

Any housing organisation that has long-term debt must consider how that liability will be managed over the business planning cycle. To illustrate the principles, Figure 17.4 assumes the organisation operates on an LSVT basis. That is, at year 0 it sets up a loan facility that it plans to amortise (extinguish) over a 30 year business planning period.

Refinancing
Figure 17.4 represents a one-off 'snap-shot' of a debt profile associated with a single loan arrangement. In reality, as time passes and the business plan unfolds, it is likely that new loans will be continuously negotiated so that new initiatives can be progressed and the long-term financing of the business can roll on beyond the original 30 year planning period. In other words, the organisation will not finance its activities once and for all and for ever with a single one-off loan that it seeks to repay over 30 years. As time passes, new loan facilities will be arranged and come on stream sequentially so that the business can perpetually grow and develop into the distant future. However, in negotiating a loan facility at a particular moment, it will need to provide a 'snap-shot' analysis of its capacity to deliver the business plan at that point in order to reassure its stakeholders (particularly lenders) that it is able to meet its liabilities.

Figure 17.4 is, of course, an over-simple, highly stylised model. It nevertheless encapsulates many of the principles of debt management. It has to be understood, however, that such a profile is grounded in a set of assumptions about the future. Not only does it make assumptions about external factors such as future inflation

---

19   CIH argues that in order to deliver decent homes, all social landlords should be given
     similar business freedoms to those currently enjoyed by RSLs. See discussion in Chapter 5.

Figure 17.4: Profiling debt in relation to revenues and costs

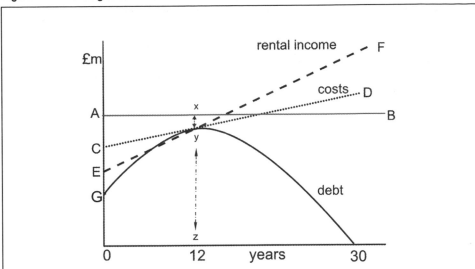

Assume that a loan facility has been arranged to help finance a 30 year business planning period.

Key to Figure 17.4
0-30 (horizontal axis) represents the business planning period. This sets the anticipated loan term.
0-A (vertical axis) represents the negotiated loan facility. This sets the maximum amount that can be borrowed.
A-B indicates that this ceiling on borrowing operates throughout the planning period.
E-F represents expected rental income projected over the planning period.
C-D represents projected costs over this period.
0-G represents initial debt at the start of the planning period.
G-y-30 represents the anticipated debt profile projected over the full term.

Commentary to Figure 17.4
All financial models are based on assumptions about costs and revenues. The cost line C-D, for example might assume an inflation rate of 2.5 per cent whilst the rental projection might assume annual rent increases based on inflation + 0.5 per cent + an increase of £2 a week (to bring rents in line with rent restructuring requirements). This would explain why E-F is steeper than C-D.

Note that at the start of the business planning period costs are assumed to be higher than revenues (C>E) which means that indebtedness increases. Eventually, however, the income flow outpaces the business costs and a surplus occurs that allows the debt to diminish. In this example, the break-even point (y) is expected to occur in year 12. In the period up to year 12, the organisation is making an accumulated loss (GEy). This pushes the debt profile up towards the ceiling allowed for in the loan facility. The debt peaks at the top of the curve (y), but remains below the negotiated ceiling (x). The gap between the ceiling and the peak (x-y) is called the 'headroom' and represents a sort of comfort or contingency zone in case things do not work out and the organisation needs to borrow a bit more.

After year 12 the plan assumes that revenues will exceed costs so that surpluses accumulate between years 12 and 30 (yFD). These are then used to pay off the debt so that after year 12 the curve begins to dip and eventually falls to zero in year 30 thereby amortising the debt.

and interest rates, but it also makes assumptions about a whole range of internal housing management issues that will affect cost and revenue levels. The revenue and cost curves, for example, are plotted on the basis of assumptions about future void levels, re-let times, bad debts, building costs, salary levels, etc. If these assumptions turn out to be pessimistic, the business plan may perform better than expected and the peak debt may be lower than anticipated and the loan itself may be extinguished before its term. On the other hand, if the assumptions turn out to be optimistic, then the peak debt may be higher than expected and it may take more than 30 years to amortise the loan. If things go badly wrong and the peak debt breaks through the ceiling (A-B), eliminating the headroom, it will be necessary to renegotiate the loan facility. By subjecting its underlying assumptions to sensitivity analysis, the model can help to highlight aspects of risk assessment and management. Sensitivity analysis is discussed below (see section headed 'Discounting and sensitivity analysis').

This brings us to the fifth of our seven key elements of financial planning and control (refer Figure 17.3).

5. Risk assessment and management

The relationship between risk, enterprise and sound management

The CIPFA code of practice for treasury management emphasises the point that the effective employment of money always involves a degree of risk and that treasury management decisions need to be explicit about the relationship between financial risks on the one hand and returns and benefits on the other. Enterprising organisations necessarily operate in a risk environment because risk is implicit in all areas of commercial activity. Well managed housing agencies will inevitably take risks both in pursuing their corporate plans and also in adapting their plans in response to changing external circumstances. An organisation pursuing a policy of total risk avoidance would soon experience corporate stagnation and decline – 'nothing ventured, nothing gained'. This means that the enterprising social business should not be seeking total risk avoidance so much as effective risk management.

Although, for reasons of analysis, we are here considering the question of risk as a distinct issue, in practice, risk management is an integral part of good general management. Everything we have said so far in this chapter about the presentation of financial information, borrowing strategies, and debt management, underlines the importance of an approach to management that minimises unwarranted risk and reduces uncertainty. Having said this, risk planning and management is increasingly seen as a subject in its own right. In recent years it is a topic that has come to the fore both in housing management practice and housing management training and education. In no small measure this has been a consequence of the 1989 reforms discussed in Chapters 13, 14 and 15. Since the introduction of the 1989 regime, there has been an explicit requirement that the financial risks associated with the provision and management of social housing should be taken by social landlords and their funders rather than by the Exchequer. With this relocation of the commercial risks has come the need to establish sound risk management principles and practices.

A strategic approach to risk management

A strategic approach to risk management emphasises the dual nature of business risk. In a business context, risks can be thought of as negative or positive. A negative risk refers to the danger of something going wrong and endangering the business plan. A positive risk refers to the danger of missing an opportunity that might enhance the business plan. In developing a coherent risk management strategy the organisation needs to be aware of the four broad approaches for dealing with specific negative risks (Baldry, 1998). These are risk transfer, risk retention, risk reduction, and risk avoidance.

Risk transfer. Insurance is the most obvious way of transferring a negative risk. Decisions have to be made about which risks should be moved to an insurance company in return for an annual premium. Some insurance companies specialise in providing defect insurance for housing agencies.[20] What insurance cover to purchase is very much a matter of judgement. It involves assessing the probability and impact of something going wrong and then weighing the insurance premium costs against the costs that would be incurred if the undesired event happened. The general principle is that the higher the probability the higher the premium. And the more catastrophic the event, the higher to premium. From the housing provider's point of view, if the impact is likely to be catastrophic (though improbable), serious consideration should still be given to taking out insurance cover.

In recent years, housing organisations have developed other ways of transferring risks. In attempting to minimise the additional commercial risks imposed by the 1989 financial regime, many associations have moved to contractual arrangements that specifically off-load some of the jeopardy to others. As a result, housing association developments in the 1990s were typically conducted under fixed price design-and-build contracts and/or involved purchasing 'off-the-shelf' designs. Such arrangements afford the association less detailed control over the nature of the scheme and inhibit the association from experimenting with designs and materials or from negotiating 'improvements' in detail once the scheme is underway. Interference from any in-house officials, such as the association's own architect, could undermine the shift in development risk to the builder that was the whole purpose of the chosen contractual arrangement. Extended product liability deals might also be struck with manufacturers and suppliers as a way of passing on the risk of early product failure.

Risk retention. The idea here is to make an informed decision about whether or not to tolerate the risk. A decision might be made to retain risks that could be insured

20 The National House-Building Council and Zurich are dominant in the market.

on the assumption that the organisation's reserves and control frameworks are so sound that the probability of problems arising is insignificant and the consequences of failure are in any event covered by resources. Some risks are difficult or impossible to transfer: significant amongst these are the disruption risks arising from postponement or cancellation of projects, a change in corporate policy, unexpected external changes in interest rates, the costs of production, or changes in the regulatory framework.

Risk reduction and avoidance. Risk avoidance is synonymous with a refusal to take risks. Certain risks can only be avoided by non-activity. However, we have already made the point that social housing agencies are obligated to deliver certain functions and that any activity necessarily involves risk-taking. The objective should be to achieve a defined outcome with minimum risk. There is no one technique for achieving this optimum position. It involves the cultivation of a general management culture that at all times and at all levels demonstrates an awareness of the need to (a) avoid exposure to unnecessary risks and (b) be clear about defensive procedures and contingencies. Risk reduction strategies can be particularly important at certain times. For example, they come to the fore when negotiating or renewing a contractual relationship.

Risk reduction and debt management

One way of reducing risk is to negotiate a degree of stability into contracts. Given its significance, this may be deemed particularly important in the field of loan management. Well over 60 per cent of the rent on new grant aided housing association schemes is typically spent on loan interest. This figure has increased as the capital grant element has been reduced. This is potentially the most variable element of the association's costs. Variability leads to uncertainty and uncertainty makes overall financial planning difficult. In particular, projecting future rent levels becomes difficult when future loan costs are uncertain. As we have seen, in order to bring a degree of stability into the cost structure, social landlords often develop 'hedging' strategies and seek to negotiate loans on a fixed interest basis (see above).

Putting the risk management strategy into operation

The total approach to risk management. Social landlords have to take a variety of decisions involving both negative and positive risks. Some major decisions associated with strategic and business planning carry self-evident risks. For example, major shifts in policy are inevitably embedded in uncertainties about the future. Similarly, decisions involving the raising of private finance are risk sensitive. Major contracts to develop land and buildings or to provide services are also seen to carry significant risks. However, we need to make the point that focusing on such major decisions can give a misleading impression about the nature and scope of risk management. Activities at all levels carry risks.

> 'Almost all activities can go wrong. Poor maintenance could result in an injury to a tenant or to a much more expensive repair at a later date.

Sloppy procedures could encourage a fraud. Under-insurance could lead to significant loss. A development opportunity might be missed because there is no cash reserve. Vulnerable residents could be mistreated by staff.' (Extract from the guidance notes to voluntary board members prepared by the NHF).

All of this points to the need for the organisation to take a total approach to risk management. A total approach requires the association's operations to be planned and managed effectively at all levels and across all planning time periods. It also requires them to give consideration to both negative and positive risk factors.

A balanced approach to risk management

It is argued (Garnett, 1995; Flynn, 1997; Baldry, 1998) that risk management in public service organisations has to take into account a wider range of considerations than is the case in private enterprise firms. This is because the values underlying the provision of public services are discretely different from those underpinning successful commercial businesses. Public service agencies are often required to consider broad questions of public policy that would be deemed to be irrelevant to most private businesses. They are also required to take more direct account of questions relating to distributional equity and social justice in their investment and management decisions (refer to Figures 2.3 and 16.3 and previous discussions on the topic of 'Best Value'). This means that risk management in public service agencies has to balance a broader range of factors than is often the case with private free-enterprise firms. Whether operating in a purely commercial or a public services environment, risk management should always begin with a systematic analysis of the risks and uncertainties confronting the organisation.

A systematic approach to risk analysis: risk mapping. Effective risk management requires the organisation to have a systematic approach to its analysis of total balanced risks. Registered social landlords in England are now required to undertake an annual risk appraisal or review exercise that involves the management team compiling a comprehensive list of risks to which it feels the association is exposed.[21] The exercise seeks to tackle the multi-faceted nature of risk by requiring the RSL to 'map' the areas of risk that they consider most pertinent to their organisation. It involves identifying the risks in relation to specific categories such as development, maintenance, finance, fraud, information technology, staffing, etc., and then allocating a 'risk ranking' to each one identified. Each broad category of risk can then usually be broken down into an extended sequence of sub-categories. For example, within the specific category 'maintenance', it should be possible to identify the sub-category 'gas servicing'. Within this sub-category we can then identify a sub-sub-category 'boilers': in turn this can be broken down further into 'specific model' and then 'component failure'. Decisions have to be made about the appropriate level of risk analysis.

---

21   Refer to the Housing Corporation's *Regulatory Code and Guidance* (2002).

Decisions about what to itemise should be informed by reference to probability, incidence and impact.

The probability factor (the chances of occurrence) can be analysed by reference to in-house data and published research by other landlords, manufacturers, insurance companies, the professional bodies and academic institutions. Incidence refers to the occurrence rate (probable frequency) of the risk event. The scale of the loss (the consequences of occurrence) is referred to as the risk impact. The impact should be analysed and quantified in some way. If possible, an attempt should be made to place an appropriate money value on the loss. Experience from the commercial world shows that the impact of the incidence of most risk events can be measured in financial terms – e.g. as the effect on turnover, market share and profitability (Baldry, 1998, p36). Given their more complex social objectives, providing a money value may be more problematic for public service agencies such as housing providers. Even if the effect of the risk event is on some intangible operational feature that is difficult to measure, such as reputation, staff morale, or landlord-tenant relations, if it is felt to be important, then its impact has to be measured and recorded in some way. In risk analysis there is always a temptation to measure what is easy to quantify rather than what is relevant to the organisation's mission. The principle has to be, however, that it is better to measure the right thing in a rough and ready way than to measure the wrong thing with impressive refinement. If it is not possible, or sensible, to put a money value on the relevant loss, then it should be recorded in terms of its effect on some non-monetary performance indicator target.

Avoiding 'perception bias'. Because, to some extent, risk is a perceived phenomenon, its real significance (probability plus impact) can be under or over-valued. Experience shows that this is particularly problematic when a 'bottom-up' approach to risk identification and appraisal is taken. Asking managers and their staff to appraise risks is always a sensible thing to do, but can lead to the following distortions.

- A tendency to focus on recent experiences.
- An over-confidence in established control mechanisms.
- A lack of critical analysis resulting from a desire to support colleagues.
- A tendency to focus on negative problems occurring rather than positive opportunities being lost.

We will say more about risk perception later (see below sections: 'Option generation, judgement and multiple criteria analysis' and 'Harnessing Stakeholder Perceptions'. Refer also to section 'The use of experts').

Classifying and quantifying the impact

The appraisal or review exercise should make clear the appropriate managerial responses to the actual or probable occurrence of such events. These responses must seek to mitigate the damaging effects upon the corporate finances or upon specific performance indicator targets. This means that potential losses have to be clearly associated with identifiable cost centres or departments (areas of specific managerial responsibility). Any linked consequences also have to be traced. For example, in the broad managerial area 'finance' we may wish to analyse the risk sub-category 'non-compliance with loan covenants'. The consequences here might be analysed as a default that will result in the withdrawal of the loan facility or a financial penalty. Within the broad management category 'staffing', the consequence of unanticipated sickness and absences might be measured in terms of increased workloads for other staff, service failures and/or increases in agency costs. Having identified, quantified, and ranked the risks the appraisal or review exercise should then consider the controls (policies, procedures and practices) that will reduce the probability of occurrence or the damage impact should they occur. Where they exist, controls should be tested for adequacy and, if necessary, improved. Where they do not exist, appropriate controls should be introduced.

The danger of producing a 'risk map' is that it may lead to complacency. Risk maps tend to be complex and need to be subjected to further analysis. The organisation should resist the belief that just because a number of potential problems have been identified, its risks have been managed. Risk mapping is only a starting point and it is the quality of the follow-up actions that determines its success as a management tool. It is only the first step in effective risk management. Any follow-up requires the application of appropriate and effective techniques.

Specific techniques for dealing with uncertainty and reducing risk

Risk appraisal and management involves the marshalling of evidence in order to make a judgement. The effectiveness of the exercise depends in large part on the quality and comprehensiveness of the data and the appropriateness of the marshalling and appraisal techniques employed. Risk appraisal and management is an expansive topic and it is not the intention of this text to provide a detailed and comprehensive description of the full range of techniques and approaches that have been developed in this field.[22] We will, however, point to some key tools and ideas that are commonly used by those seeking to analyse and manage risk and uncertainty.

Effective information and feedback systems

Risk analysis should be an automatic element in decision appraisal. Any decision to invest new resources or to realign existing resources carries financial risks: the object is to take a decision that proves to be 'sustainable' through the different planning time periods identified at the start of this chapter. A sustainable decision is one that the organisation does not live to regret. It is well understood that when decisions are informed by sufficient and relevant information they are more likely to turn out to be sustainable than if they are informed by insufficient or

---

22   For an overview of risk management issues and an extensive reading list see websites of the National Housing Federation and the Housing Corporation.

inappropriate information. This means that an organisation's information systems, and how they are utilised, should be regularly assessed to ensure that they are effectively contributing to the organisation's decision processes. Well-run agencies will inevitably make mistakes; the question is, 'Do we have in place identifiable mechanisms for learning from our mistakes and successes?' Of course, sound decision-making involves more than the acquisition of data and other types of information. An effective decision involves the application of judgement to information.

Option generation, judgement and multiple criteria analysis
It has to be recognised that housing investment and management decisions are multi-faceted in that they often seek to achieve a mix of financial, technical, social, legal, political, environmental and administrative outcomes. This means that appropriate options have to be generated that balance and reconcile different, and sometimes competing, proprietary and non-proprietary interests. Research shows that when there is a failure to generate appropriate options subsequent problems are likely to arise (Garnett, 1999). There is little point in using sophisticated option appraisal techniques on an inappropriate range of options. If we fail to present the most viable options for appraisal it is simply not possible to make a risk-efficient decision. Option generation involves ensuring that important development, reinvestment, or policy change decisions are justified at the outset by reference to a shared corporate understanding of the balance of interests being pursued, whether of tenants, other community interests, future generations, or whoever.

It is easy to say that option generation involves the application of judgement to information. The problem is that judgement is not an absolute quality; it is relative to the values and attitudes of the individual decision-makers. This means that project planning needs to make explicit the various personal or professional rationalities that lie behind different proposed courses of action. It may be the case that the treasurer will seek one course of action based on his or her understanding of the financial implications (budgetary rationality) while the estate managers are arguing for a different course of action based on their understanding of sound building practices (technical rationality). Other rationalities associated with housing management, administrative feasibility or political expediency may point to yet other ways forward. In the context of new projects or major policy changes, risk appraisal has to involve the reconciliation of these competing rationalities by some form of multiple criteria analysis.[23]

Harnessing stakeholder perceptions
It is well understood that public service organisations are subject to the influences and expectations of a diverse constituency of interested parties. Both academic research and Best Value philosophy indicate that the opinions and experiences of employees, clients and community stakeholders can be utilised in the appraisal and review exercise to identify and clarify the risk perception process. By widening the

---

23 For further discussion on multiple criteria analysis see Garnett, D., 1995 and 1999.

area of consultation we automatically widen the scope of risk identification. Conversely, a reliance on a limited range of internal managerial perceptions and professional interests may compromise the risk assessment exercise by limiting the range of objectives being considered.

Effective control frameworks
Control frameworks are essential weapons in any risk management armoury. They provide guidance, prescribe and proscribe certain actions, and set limits for a broad range of activities. These policies, standing orders and procedures typically require management processes to be monitored and appraised. They regulate the nature and scope of delegated authority, and declare the corporate view of what constitutes best practice.

To be effective, control frameworks have to be relevant to current circumstances, understood by those who are meant to use them, practical to operate, supported by training, constantly reviewed, and reinforced by a compliance culture (NHF, 1999c, p8). However, it must be understood that the emergence of unnecessary or inappropriate regulations and procedures itself constitutes a 'risk'. An organisation can be over regulated: when this occurs, the resultant compliance culture can inhibit initiative and have a deadening effect on staff morale, energy and confidence. All quality control managers should have pinned up on their walls the old West Country proverb, 'Worrying about the future can prevent it occurring'.

Analysing cumulative and linked risks
In analysing the incidence and impact of risk occurrence, consideration should be given to the possibility of cumulative and linked risks. A general distinction should be made between one-off, or infrequent, major events (e.g. a theft, fire, etc.), and cumulative risks. Cumulative risks are associated with smaller-scale events that may not be significant in themselves but which can have a damaging cumulative effect on the organisation's costs. These cumulative risks are sometimes referred to as 'aggregated risks' and are of particular concern to the managers of built assets.

A general distinction should also be made between isolated and linked risks. Some apparently small-scale risks can have significant knock-on effects that must be taken into account in risk assessment and management exercises. The connectedness of a linked risk might be technical: the failure of a small and cheap component might cause an entire system to fail causing expensive, inconvenient, or even life threatening consequences. The connectedness of a linked risk might be managerial: the failure of a light bulb might be regarded as a relatively insignificant event, but if the bulb is located in a dark stairwell, its failure might be highly dangerous. The connectedness of a linked risk might be environmental: we might develop a piece of land in a way that enhanced the organisation's productivity but which was damaging to local wildlife, or created some other third party or ecological problem. The connectedness of a linked risk might be political: we might instigate a policy change that increased the cost-effectiveness of our operations but which contravened central or local government guidelines thereby bringing into question our entitlement to public funds. All of this points to the need to assess risks in a way that makes explicit all the possible linked consequences.

Discounting and sensitivity analysis
Discounting is a technique that seeks to cost future money flows in terms of present values. When project appraisals and budgets cover an extended period, it may be necessary to put a present value on future costs/benefits or expenditures/incomes. This is because we are seeking to make rational decisions now, in the present, about impacts and monetary flows that will occur sometime in the future. Put most simply, the appraisal or the budget needs to take account of two issues resulting from the relationship between time and the value of money.

1. Different costs and benefits and expenditures and incomes come on stream or impact at different times.
2. A £1's worth of income or expenditure today will not have the same real value as a £1's worth of income or expenditure in the future.[24]

Sensitivity analysis is one technique that can be used to assess the impact of particular assumptions being proved wrong. Because planning involves looking to the future, and the future is uncertain, all plans have to incorporate assumptions about such things as interest and discount rates, building costs, rent projections, general levels of inflation, works completion dates, and the physical life of building components. Sensitivity analysis is a technique that seeks to test the plan's key incorporated assumptions about such variables. It asks the question, 'How sensitive is the planned or expected outcome to the assumptions being made?' Managers and risk analysts will need some idea of the consequences that might follow from variations in these assumptions that underpin the plan's projections, conclusions or recommendations. Sensitivity analysis plots a range of possible futures, each grounded in discretely different assumptions about such things as interest rates and the life spans of building components. With modern computer technology these futures can be presented to decision managers or committees in clear charted or graphical formats. These can then be used to help devise appropriate tactics. For example, with respect to a proposed building contract, the knowledge and understanding gained from a sensitivity analysis of building cost price projections might persuade the client to reduce the risk of price rises by insisting on a fixed price contract.

The use of 'experts'
Experts provide specialist knowledge that should inform, but not determine, a decision about what constitutes best action. Consultants and professional advisors do not have a legitimate authority to make final decisions; they should be used to advise those who do have such authority. Advisors should not relieve decision-makers of the task of determining how to respond to perceptions of risk but might

---

24   For a fuller explanation of discounting and the time value of money see Garnett, D., *The Theory and Practice of Cost-Benefit Analysis*, Faculty of the Built Environment Occasional Papers, UWE 1994, pp21-24.

be used to help generate unthought-of options, or to offer new perceptions of risk, or to test, challenge and reshape the organisation's existing perceptions. The best use of consultants is made when they understand what it is that the organisation is seeking to achieve. Research shows that in the field of social housing, where there has been little or no pre-planning before briefing consultants, the 'experts' may offer rational, but inappropriate, courses of action based on their own professional values and attitudes rather than on those of the client organisation (Garnett, 1996).

Experts may have information and experience that the client does not possess and they may be able to provide new insights that can be drawn upon in carrying out a risk assessment exercise. By interacting with the client they may also help to clarify the organisation's aims and objectives – but they cannot know better than the organisation itself what values and interests constitute the bedrock of its function. This means that any expert advice should reinforce or reshape, but not replace, the organisation's judgements about what to do. In selecting consultants we are choosing 'expert witnesses' to give informed opinions rather than appointing 'judges' to give definitive rulings.

Dealing with long-term structural uncertainties
There are a number of established techniques specifically designed to aggregate the knowledge and judgements of experts about possible future trends.[25] Although we cannot tell for certain what the future holds, it is possible to canvass informed opinion about external political and economic trends that may affect our long-term plans. These approaches to thinking about the longer-term are referred to as Delphi techniques – after the Greek oracle at Delphi who gave riddled answers to those seeking knowledge of what the future held in store.

A particular form of sensitivity analysis called 'stress testing' can be used to consider the impact implications of different possible futures. This involves asking a variety of 'what would we do if?' questions. For example, we might stress test our risk assumptions by asking 'What would we do if there was a change in government?' or, 'What would we do if an advantageous investment opportunity comes our way in two years time?' or, 'What would we do if we are suddenly required to freeze rents?'

We will now turn to the sixth of the key elements of effective financial management identified in Figure 17.3.

6. Stock management: resource accounting, depreciation and the planning and paying for repairs, renewals and reinvestments

We have already made the point that resource accounting and budgeting (RAB) are necessary techniques for effective business planning (refer to Chapter 16 section headed 'Monitoring and measuring efficiency'). For this reason, the shift

---

25   See, for example, Moore, C.M., 1987.

in local authority accounting practices towards resource accounting is being mirrored in the RSL sector. Under the current SORP, associations have to calculate the capital depreciation of their non-investment properties and charge this against income and expenditure in their accounts. As we have seen above, depreciation is a charge that reflects the loss in value resulting from wear and tear. Neither the grant funded element of a property's value nor the land is included in the depreciation calculation. The basic idea is that the published accounts should be in line with modern plc accounting conventions so as to make the 'true' costs of running the 'business' more transparent. This will involve accounting for the lifecycle costs of each asset as they occur so that their true costs-in-use can be estimated.

In Chapter 14 we explained that, since 1989, English RSLs have not been entitled to receive major repair grants to help cover the costs of repairing, renewing or improving their housing assets. This sort of work now has to be funded either by taking out a loan or by establishing a sinking fund for the purpose, or a combination of both.

The assessment of future major repair needs forms part of sensible financial planning and accounting policies should reflect the needs of the organisation. It is financially prudent to set aside amounts regularly to ensure that sufficient funds are available when the costs are due to be incurred. Until recently, the amount a landlord set aside into a sinking fund to cover future renewal and improvement costs tended to be a notional figure that was set formulaically. The Housing Corporation used to recommend that the annual contribution to such a fund should be between 0.8 and 1.0 per cent of scheme cost, depending on whether the scheme was a new-build or a refurbishing project. Research in the mid-1990s by Cambridge University's Department of Land Economy[26] indicated that when associations were under budgetary pressure, it is often the maintenance expenditure that suffered. This research looked at the behaviour of a sample of representative associations, and it showed that a majority underspent in this area in relation to the Housing Corporation allowances. The findings indicated that in the sector as a whole, there has been a lack of long-term planning for the provision of finance for future major repairs. Consultancy work carried out by the Building and Construction Research Centre based in the University of the West of England reinforces these findings and suggests that sinking funds established by many RSLs will not adequately deal with future repairs and refurbishments.[27] Social landlords concerned to establish good financial management practices should abandon the simple formulaic approach and seek to make provision that is in line with an informed estimate of real future requirements.

---

26 Chaplin, R. *et al.*, 'Rents and Risks', (1995), in *Investing in Housing Associations*, Joseph Rowntree Foundation.
27 Holmes, R. and Marshall, D., (1996), 'Property Profiling and Data Collection for Housing Repairs and Improvements: Part 2. Applications', Chartered Institute of Building, *CIOB Construction Papers No. 62*. Also, Marshall, (1996), 'Condition Surveys for Housing Associations: Some Potential Pitfalls and a Survey of Client Experience', *CIOB Construction Papers No. 68*. Editor: Harlow, P.

Exactly how provisions and reserves are designated and set aside is for each landlord to decide in accordance with its own policies, external regulatory requirements and legal/contractual commitments. The over-riding objective is to prevent undue fluctuations in costs that will damage long-run financial plans or drain free revenue reserves to a point where lenders' loan covenants are breached (see above section on 'Status and legal and financial competence').

Using component lifecycle cost data and techniques of property profiling, built asset managers can establish theoretical models of future repair and renewal costs for new-build schemes. For existing properties, cost models can be produced that are informed by condition surveys. Although there are many variables and uncertainties associated with lifecycle data, this form of rational planning is likely to lead to better stock management decisions than the mechanistic application of a standard formula. By using the 'stock management planning' approach clear forecasts of future requirements can be presented to decision-makers. To encourage strategic thinking, benchmarks can be produced that distinguish between the landlord's condition obligations and its condition aspirations. By the use of computer modelling, it is possible to build in assumptions about component life spans and future building costs so that decision committees can be presented with graphic representations of possible optimistic and pessimistic cost futures. This can help the manager or committee to clarify the risks of taking one financial decision as against another.

Reinvestment is an important financial aspect of long-term stock management. Until recently the principle of public financial accountability carried more weight than that of rational asset management. Regulations required the capital grant element to be repaid on disposal or demolition and this acted against associations developing strategic plans for the overall management of their housing stocks. The provisions of the Housing Act 1996 gave RSLs in England and Wales the ability to dispose of or demolish SHG funded properties without having to repay grant. Restrictions in Scotland were also eased where some disposals now do not lead to grant repayment and abatement of grant applies in demolition. This easing of the regulations allows landlords to sell or demolish properties and reinvest the proceeds without financial penalty so long as it can be shown that this is part of an active asset management plan that generates 'Best Value'.

7. Taxation and social landlords

As private sector organisations, housing associations are subject to corporation tax and VAT. These tax liabilities have to be allowed for in their financial management arrangements. This means that the financial planning of an RSL has to take account of any tax liabilities that will occur during the accounting period. The main taxes that affect RSLs are corporation tax and value added tax (VAT). The detailed regulations surrounding these taxes are rather complex and constantly being changed. However, as we are simply concerned to outline how tax liabilities impinge on the organisation's financial planning, we will focus on basic principles. The basic principles of corporation tax and VAT are fairly straightforward.

Corporation tax

Corporation tax can be thought of as a sort of companies' income tax. It is charged on the profits or other 'assessable gains' accruing to the organisation during the accounting period. In the accounts of a social business the assessable gain is recorded in the income and expenditure account and is usually referred to as the surplus on ordinary activities.[28] In determining the 'assessable gain' a deduction may be claimed for certain types of expenditure. Repairs, maintenance and replacement expenditure that restores a building to its original condition is an allowable expense for tax purposes and can be deducted from the turnover in the assessment of assessable gain. Improvement expenditure does not qualify for relief as this adds to, rather than maintains, the quality of the assets. This means that care should be taken to determine whether or not the works are an improvement. If works that are really repairs and replacements are capitalised in the books, it is unlikely that they will be allowed as a deduction from income, and this will result in an unnecessarily high tax bill. Any monies transferred to reserves do not qualify and, as the account shows, these are recorded after the tax has been deducted (refer to Figure 15.2 in Chapter 15). Relief may be given for bad debts, but only so long as a reasonable effort has been made to collect them.

Charitable organisations are not subject to corporation tax, which means that it is only non-charitable social landlords that are liable. Until recently, liable associations could receive grants to help meet the costs of paying the tax. However, these have now been phased out. This has resulted in a reduction of net surpluses for those landlords that do not have charitable status. This could, in turn, lead to increases in rents and/or cuts in general expenditure on the service.[29] In some associations this is leading to a debate about the possibility of changing to charitable status.

In recent years, corporation tax has been levied at two rates – the full rate and the small companies' rate. Where the assessable gains of a UK resident organisation do not exceed stated limits the full rate of tax is reduced. The application of the lower, small companies' rate is governed by the amount of profit or gain and not by the size of the organisation. The current rates are 30 per cent and 20 per cent (April 1999).

---

28 This surplus is calculated by taking the operating surplus net of deductible costs, and then adding in any profits resulting from the sale of fixed assets and any income received in the form of interest payments. The net operating surplus is effectively the rental income minus allowable property expenditure costs. These allowable deductions refer to expenditures that are deemed to be necessary to provide the housing service and keep the stock in a fit condition. They include certain expenditures on repairs and maintenance, insurance, and some management functions.

29 Particularly exposed in this regard are LSVT associations, whose business plans were often written on the assumption of continuing tax relief grant.

Value added tax (VAT)

In contrast to corporation tax, no VAT exemptions are granted to charitable organisations. This means that all registered social landlords are liable for VAT. VAT is a sort of purchase or trading tax that is charged on the value of supplies made by a registered trader. Organisations are required to register for VAT once their turnover reaches a specified threshold. The tax extends both to the supply of goods and also to the supply of services. Supplies of certain goods and services are exempt from the tax. These include the provision of finance, insurance and education and burial and cremation services. The granting of a lease or license to occupy land will usually be classified as exempt.

Non-exempt supplies are subject to tax at one of three rates.

- A zero or nil rate (e.g. most food products, water and sewerage services, books, newspapers and magazines, clothing, and transport).
- A standard rate of 17.5 per cent.
- A reduced rate of 5 per cent (e.g. domestic fuel). Since July 1998, the reduced rate also applies to the installation of energy saving material under certain government grant schemes.

In most commercial circumstances, the liability is calculated in a way that only taxes that element of value that has been contributed by that particular trader. In other words, the idea of the tax is to levy a charge on the additional value that has been added at each stage in the production process. This means that in most circumstances, a registered trader will both suffer tax (input tax) when acquiring goods and services for the purposes of a business, and charge that tax (output tax) when supplying goods and services to customers and clients. A normal commercial trader is required to calculate both the input and the output tax during the accounting period, and if the latter exceeds the former, the difference has to be paid over to Customs and Excise. In this way the tax liability is passed on 'along the line' and eventually comes to rest on individuals or organisations who are not VAT registered, or who do not themselves charge VAT on that particular good or service. When this end point is reached, it is assumed that the production process has ended and the purchaser has to pay their suppliers VAT on the full value of the goods and services without having an opportunity to pass the burden on as an output tax.

Because rents are not subject to VAT, we can say that the tax is not charged on the core outputs of social landlords. This means that as a general needs housing provider, the landlord, and not the tenant, is deemed to be at the end of the added value line (i.e. the taxable production process is assumed to have ended prior to the letting of the dwelling). Therefore, the landlord has to pay the full input tax on its supplies without being able to pass the burden on in the form of an output tax to its tenants.

Although social landlords do not charge VAT on their rents, they do have to charge output tax on specific services. For example, certain types of long-term hostel accommodation are subject to VAT at the standard rate[30] as are any management services it provides to other organisations. Heating and lighting services that it provides to a tenant's private area of occupation are subject to VAT at the reduced rate. Other charged-for personal services may also be subject to VAT.

VAT and building works
The current rates of VAT on building works are:

Zero per cent VAT on the cost of constructing new dwellings. The zero rating also applies to the following:

- Substantial alterations to listed buildings used as dwellings.
- New buildings used as children's homes, old people's homes and the provision of student accommodation – but not hotels and prisons.
- New buildings to be used by a charity for non-business purposes, e.g. a church.

5 per cent VAT on the cost of the following:

- Renovating dwellings that have been empty for three years or more.
- Converting properties into a different number of dwellings.
- Works necessary to convert a non-residential building into a dwelling(s).
- Converting a dwelling into a care home or other residential building.
- Installing energy saving materials in all homes.
- The grant funded installation, maintenance and repair of central heating systems and home security goods in the homes of qualifying pensioners, and the grant funded installation of heating systems for the less well off.

17.5 per cent VAT on all other building work including the following:

- Repair and maintenance of, or extension to, existing buildings.
- The costs of constructing commercial and industrial buildings such as shops, offices, and factories.

Many argue that it is irrational to tax housing renovation work at the standard rate while zero rating new house building. It is felt that this 'anomaly' positively discourages the process of housing repair and improvement.[31]

---

30 Where such accommodation is run by a charity and provides care and support in addition to accommodation, the total charge is exempt.
31 The 1999 Report of the Urban Task Force, *Towards an Urban Renaissance* (The Rogers Report), looked at the causes of urban decline in England. It proposed removing 'the anomaly' whereby renovation work on empty dwellings carries VAT at 'a punitive' 17.5 per cent, but house building and conversion of commercial premises for housing are exempt.

Summary

In this chapter we have stressed the point that social landlords operate in a regulated business environment that is characterised by political and social, as well as economic, uncertainty, and this means that financial planning and control are particularly important if the organisation wishes to make sustainable decisions and use its resources to the best advantage.

Internal treasury management is concerned to:

- provide the financial resources necessary for the organisation to achieve its purposes;
- manage the associated risks that might threaten its ability to achieve these objectives;
- manage the financial assets in a way that ensures that they maintain their value;
- manage the financial liabilities in a way that ensures that they remain affordable.

The well managed social landlord is, among other things, risk aware, performance orientated and a 'learning organisation'.

Treasury management is concerned with keeping the business plan financially viable. More specifically, it provides the basis upon which managers can make sound decisions and deliver the business plan's mission in ways that are judged to be efficient, fair and effective.

Financial planning and management have to operate through time. A series of interrelated time profiles lies at the heart of strategic financial management. Together this series of time profiles constitutes an integrated planning and control cycle. This cycle links the organisation's long-term aspirations to its immediate activities. Converting the idea of the cycle into a management process involves asking different types of policy question and creating a cascade of documents differentiated by time, scale and specific detail.

Further reading

Atrill, P., *Financial Management for Non-specialists*, Prentice Hall, 2003.

Baldry, D., 'The evaluation of risk management in public sector capital projects', in *International Journal of Project Management*, Vol.16 No.1 pp35-41, Pergamon, 1998.

Drury, C., *Management Accounting for Business Decisions*, Thompson, 2002.

Gray, D., *What's it all about? Registered social landlord accounts explained*, National Housing Federation, 1999.

HACAS Consulting, *Housing Associations – A Viable Financial Future?*, CIH, 1999.

CHAPTER 18:
Private renting

In recent years, there has been much debate in Britain about whether private landlords could or should play a more prominent role in the provision of dwellings. It is generally agreed that for much of the post-war era political, social and economic forces have operated to diminish the role of private landlordism. Following reforms in the 1980s and 1990s the sector has stabilised and a new political consensus has emerged as to both the role of the sector in meeting the nation's needs and the general direction of policy (Kemp, 2004). The main task of this chapter is to analyse critically recent attempts to support the development of this tenure and to consider what future financial measures might be needed to stimulate its further expansion.

Before setting out on this task, we will say something about the motive forces that drive consumption and investment in the tenure. To understand the part that private renting has played, does play and could play, in the provision of housing, we need to examine the proprietary interests involved.

The interests of tenants

The landlord-tenant relationship

The private rented housing sector embraces two distinctive sets of proprietary interests that are governed by contractual rights and duties. These contractual rights and obligations are set in a statutory framework that establishes such things as the broad nature of the tenancy agreement including the level of security enjoyed by the tenant (e.g. the Housing Act 1988), and minimum standards of health and safety (e.g. the Furniture Safety Regulations 1993 and regulations covering gas and electrical safety). It is generally recognised however, that both the investment interests of the landlord and the consumption interests of the tenant are best served by the cultivation of an informal working relationship that does not require recourse to law. A clear understanding of things like the inventory and the deposit as well as how and when the rent will be paid, especially if it involves a claim for housing benefit, can help prevent a breakdown in this crucial landlord-tenant relationship. Many people prefer to leave the letting arrangements in the hands of an agent as a way of depersonalising what is, after all, a business transaction.

Tenants and the consumption interest

Although, at the time of writing only about ten per cent of British households rent their homes from a private landlord[1] it is worth noting that for the greater part of

---

[1]   This percentage is significantly lower in Northern Ireland where as at March 2002 the private rented sector constitutes only 5.2 per cent of the total housing stock (around 34,000 dwellings), although the sector experienced rapid growth between 1996-2000 (up from only 3.8 per cent).

the industrial age the majority of the population have depended on private landlords for their accommodation needs. Private renting accounted for some 90 per cent of all tenure arrangements before the first world war and even at the end of the second world war more than 60 per cent of households rented their homes privately. Private renting was the largest tenure in Britain until the late 1950s.

Both the sector's historical dominance and its more recent decline can be explained in part by people's attitudes towards, and abilities to gain access to, other tenures. Arguably the most significant socio-economic characteristic of housing is that for most households it is expensive relative to disposable income. This has meant that historically even households with above average incomes have not been able to gain access to owner-occupation without inheriting or borrowing financial resources. This, together with the fact that social renting is a comparatively recent phenomenon, has meant that until the 1940s most people expected that their housing careers would begin and end in private rented accommodation. These expectations were eventually changed in the immediate post-war period by the large-scale council house building programme and the development of an increasingly sophisticated and aggressive mortgage finance market.

The result was that for the first four and a half decades of the post-war period the sector contracted both in terms of the absolute number of dwellings and as a proportion of the total stock[2] from 7.13 million dwellings (52 per cent) in 1951 to its low point at only 2.07 million dwellings (9 per cent) in 1989 when the sector was deregulated. For the first time in the post-war period the early 1990s saw a reversal in this trend, and from 1990-1995 the sector grew each year both in terms of the absolute number of dwellings and as proportion of the overall stock – rising to 2.44 million dwellings (10.3 per cent) in 1995. Since then the number of units has levelled off resulting in a gentle decline in the sector when measured as an overall proportion of the stock.[3] Nevertheless the relentless absolute decline of the sector that was a characteristic of the first four decades of the post-war period seems to have been reversed.

There is some debate as to whether the period of relatively rapid growth of the sector in the early 1990s was due to policies to stimulate private renting or more as a result of adverse economic conditions. The depression in the first half of the decade resulted in a slump in house prices in the owner-occupied sector. The resulting negative equity produced a class of 'reluctant landlords' who, in the case of owner-occupiers, rented out their homes in order to move on to new employment opportunities, whilst developers delayed selling their property and potential first-time buyers chose to defer buying in the short term until market conditions were more favourable (Kemp, 2004, p78). Thus it might be argued that the revival of the sector was not so much the result of successful policies to stimulate private renting and attract tenants, but more as a failure of policies to sustain owner-occupation and a buoyant housing market.

---

2   Figures for this paragraph are for Great Britain (i.e. England, Scotland and Wales only).
3   The proportion of the stock as at 2002 was down to 9.8 per cent but this still represents an overall expansion in the stock of around one-sixth since 1979, Kemp, 2004, p77.

Who are the tenants?

In this text we are primarily concerned to explore the part private landlords play in the satisfaction of general housing needs. However, we must make the point that private landlords provide dwellings in response to a diverse range of demands. A seminal paper on the sector identified four main roles for it in the housing market:[4]

- *The traditional role.* Tenants who have remained in the sector since the time when it was the main tenure – often retaining Rent Act rights to have their rent regulated as a result. This sub-sector has shrunk to only a small proportion and continues to decline. It is characterised by elderly tenants.
- *The tied housing role.* Tenants whose home comes with their business, such as a flat above a shop or people in licensed premises (public houses).
- *The easy access role.* This is the principal growth area of the sector. It exploits one of the potential advantages of the sector: moving home is relatively quick and easy. The sub-sector is characterised by newly-formed households, often young professionals who are not yet ready to commit to owner-occupation or students. House sharing is common within these groups and furnished lettings predominate.
- *The residual role.* Low-income households for whom private renting is the sector of last choice. It includes couples and families otherwise seen in social housing, who tend to rent unfurnished, often entering the sector from other tenures after relationship breakdown or eviction. Others are those who are a lower priority for social housing – principally single-person households or (childless) couples. Households in this sub-sector tend to have low incomes, either because of withdrawal from the labour market or being in low-paid work and so rely on housing benefit to help with their rent.

Research also indicates that in recent years the average age of private tenants has been declining, with the proportion under the age of 30 increasing and the proportion aged 60 and over falling.[5] Tenants in this sector are becoming more middle-class, with relatively more coming from the non-manual socio-economic groups and the proportion eligible for housing benefit falling.[6] Both these trends

---

4   Bovaird *et al.* (1985) 'Private Rented Housing its Current Role', *Journal of Social Policy*, 14; cited in Kemp 2004, p115.
5   In England in 1994-95 36 per cent of the heads of household in the private rented sector were aged under 30, 63 per cent under 45. By 2001-02, 52 per cent were aged under 35, 71 per cent under 45. The proportions for those aged 65 or over were 19 per cent and 11 per cent respectively. Down, D. *et al.* (1996), *Housing in England 1994-95*, Chapter 1, HMSO. Mew, H. *et al.* (2003) *Housing in England 2001/2002*, Chapter 1, TSO.
6   Rauta, I. and Pickering, A. (1992) *Private Renting in England in 1990*, HMSO. Although relative proportions in the non-manual socio-economic groups remained virtually static between 1994-95 and 2000-01 the average income of the head of household as a proportion of the average income in all tenures has risen from 72 per cent in 1994-95 to 85 per cent in 2000-01. Over the same period the proportion of those with incomes below £100 per week has fallen from 41 per cent to 17 per cent, although this does not take account of inflation (figures for England).

reflect the continued decline of the traditional role and the expansion of the easy access role as an increasing number of lettings are to young professionals (Kemp, 2004, pp116-118). It also reflects affordability problems for younger households aspiring to home ownership, whereby growth in house prices outstrips their earning capacity.

Assistance with rents

By the mid-1990s, it was estimated that, on average, private tenants spent over a quarter of their disposable income on rent, and that more than a quarter of tenants were spending a third or more of their income on rent.[7] The low or insecure earnings of many of the actual and potential households who rely on this sector mean that many cannot afford to secure private accommodation appropriate to their needs out of their incomes, and require help through housing benefit (which is discussed in detail in the next chapter). The significant rise in the national housing benefit bill in the 1990s was in part due to the growth in claims resulting from higher rents in the private rented sector. Rent allowances to private tenants rose from £800 million in 1988 to nearly £4 billion in 1995/96. They have since fallen somewhat to around £3 billion but still account for about one-quarter of housing benefit expenditure.

In January 1996, alarmed at the rapid growth in expenditure on rent allowances, the government introduced a 'cap' on the level of rent eligible for benefit[8] such that claimants are only entitled to assistance up to the mid-point of the range of market rents for similar sized properties in the locality.[9] The intention is to give tenants an incentive to negotiate their rents and encourage them to choose less expensive dwellings. The idea is to prevent landlords exploiting the system by increasing the rents of claimants safe in the knowledge that any increase would be fully covered by housing benefit. Significantly the introduction of these controls coincided with the end of the growth of the sector and the number of private tenants on housing benefit has declined from a peak of 1.16 million claimants in 1995 to around 0.71 million by 2003. This suggests that landlords are choosing to withdraw from the housing benefit sub-sector in favour of other markets.

From the government's (or rather Treasury's) perspective these rules have been so successful in controlling expenditure that this mechanism provides the basis for the trial run of housing benefit reforms whereby benefit is based on a locally determined flat-rate allowance (see Chapter 19). This reform is being tested in nine 'pathfinder' areas phased in during 2004 with a further nine starting between April and July 2005. In the pathfinder areas, housing benefit rent limits for the private sector are calculated on a similar basis to the existing controls, except that

7 *Department of Environment Housing Research Summary*, No.36, p3.
8 Announced in the 1995 Budget and introduced by regulations from January 1996.
9 The locality is not defined but is set by rent officers. In a moderate sized town such as Exeter it will roughly correspond to the urban area, larger cities may have a number of localities.

benefit is based on the flat-rate allowance even where the actual (contractual) rent is lower. The intention is that claimants have an incentive to choose between either accepting lower-priced accommodation and being able to pocket the saving; or to spend their allowance consuming additional (i.e. more expensive) housing.

At the time of writing it is unknown exactly how the market will respond in the pathfinder areas, although critics have suggested that it is doomed to failure as landlords will simply raise their rents to the level of the standard allowance. Once the evaluation has been made of the private sector pathfinders the reforms, subject to any modification, will be rolled out nationally, probably in 2006-07.[10] The government intends to pilot[11] a similar flat-rate allowance in the social sector albeit based on social sector rather than market rents. The social sector pilots are expected to be in place by April 2008.

If these reforms are eventually adopted in both the private and the social sectors (albeit with different methods for calculating the flat-rate allowance) it is expected that one of the effects will be to introduce a greater degree of competition for tenants. Under the current arrangements, where benefit for private tenants is based on the actual rent up to the rent cap, tenants will tend to favour the social sector where the benefit is rarely, if ever, subject to a rent cap. This preference may therefore disappear.

The nature and condition of the stock

In comparison with other European countries there is a lack of modern purpose-built private rented dwellings in the UK. In some other EU countries more private finance goes into the provision of apartments specifically designed as rented accommodation. This facilitates one of the potential benefits of private renting – namely, the ability to have access to the most recently built stock with all the advantages of the latest design features and modern conveniences but with just the right amount of space required at that time. The British private rented stock is dominated by relatively old dwellings many of which have been converted from family residences to accommodate the needs of single people or relatively small households. Such conversions are not always carried out to high standards and, as a result, tenants are required to share facilities.

The sector has the highest proportion of pre-1919 dwellings of all the tenures, although the proportion is declining (down from 54 per cent in 1996 to 43 per cent in 2001, Kemp, 2004, p81). Given the high proportion of older dwellings it is unsurprising that the proportion of its stock that fails to meet the government's

---

10 DWP (2004) *Housing Benefit Direct*, Issue 35.
11 The difference between a pilot and a pathfinder is significant. A pathfinder implies that the government is committed to introducing the reform and is merely trying to establish the best way it implement it. A pilot is a more fundamental appraisal in which the reform may be abandoned if after a trial it proves to be a failure or have unintended consequences. See for example, *HM Treasury Economic and Fiscal Strategy Report 2004*, paragraph 4.45.

Decent Homes Standard in England (see Chapter 10) is also the highest of all tenures (49 per cent in 2001, compared with 43 per cent in the local authority sector). But, as with other sectors, the condition of the stock has improved significantly in recent decades. In 1981, 13.5 per cent of the private rented sector was lacking at least one basic amenity, but this was down to 1.8 per cent by 1996 (Kemp, 2004, p83). The 2001 English House Condition Survey found about 10.5 per cent of the private rented stock to be unfit, compared with 20.5 per cent in 1991.

This figure is high when compared with other sectors. Just over three per cent of owner-occupied housing was judged to be unfit. The figures for local authority and housing association dwellings were 4.7 per cent and 3.4 per cent respectively. Unfitness and disrepair in Wales in 1997/98 for the private rented sector was estimated at 18.4 per cent (Welsh House Condition Survey). The Scottish House Condition Survey (2002), shows that the private rented sector accounts for 20 per cent of all homes below the Scottish 'tolerable standard' whereas the sector as a whole accounts for less than 10 per cent of the stock. However, since the total number of dwellings in all sectors which falls below the standard is only around one per cent this equates to only between two and three per cent of dwellings within the sector itself which fall below the standard. In Northern Ireland, where the private rented sector is proportionately much smaller, over half the dwellings fail the Decent Homes Standard.

In 1998 the housing minister announced the government's intention to introduce revised fitness standards and enhanced regulation for those parts of the sector with the poorest standards, notably houses in multiple occupation. These new measures are contained in the Housing Act 2004.[12] The enhanced regulation takes the form of a mandatory system of licensing for certain categories of multi-occupied houses. Local authorities will have responsibility for issuing licences and policing the system and will have discretion to extend the scheme to cover a wider range of multi-occupied properties. In areas of low demand local authorities will also have the power to introduce a general licensing scheme (i.e. not restricted to multi-occupied dwellings) if it will contribute towards the improvement of the area or there is a local problem with anti-social behaviour that wholly or partly emanates from private rented dwellings. The Housing Health and Safety Rating System (HHSRS) will replace the existing 'fitness standard'. The new standards will include measures of health and safety hazards and will be used to assess the relative risk to the occupant (the relative risk being higher when the occupant is vulnerable). It is intended that this system will provide a more appropriate measure of sub-standard housing and its consequences for the occupants and thus a better basis for targeting resources.

---

12 The Housing Act 2004 received royal assent on the 18 November 2004; however, most of the act's provisions will be brought into force by ministerial order. The Housing Act 2004 applies to England and Wales only. In contrast to this targeted approach regulation in Scotland the Anti-Social Behaviour etc. (Scotland) Act 2004, which is expected to be brought into force from November 2005, will require all landlords to register with the local authority. All landlords will be required to be a 'fit and proper person' to register and meet certain management standards. Further standards will apply to multi-occupied dwellings.

The interests of landlords

Landlords' investment interest

Despite the sector's long-term decline it would be wrong to describe the provision of market rented dwellings as a 'marginal' or 'insignificant' economic activity. Private landlords probably own something in excess of £150 billion worth of built assets: these generate an annual rental income of some £13 billion. The housing green paper (*Quality and Choice: A Decent Home for All*, April 2000) indicated that more than a quarter of all landlords only have one letting. In Britain as a whole only about one-quarter of the stock is owned by companies. Earlier studies have shown that, excluding those who share their home with their landlord, over 60 per cent rent from a private individual rather than a corporate body or business partnership.[13]

In deciding whether or not to invest in rented housing, rational landlords will consider the commercial opportunity costs involved. This means that they will take account of whether such an investment is the 'highest and best' utilisation of their limited money capital. In considering which to choose of a range of possible opportunities, the commercially motivated investor will assess, in the context of a given time frame, the price, risk and convenience of each potential investment against its expected rate of return.

The price is simply the amount of money paid to acquire the asset. Risks fall into two broad categories – commercial and insurable. Insurable risks are, to a degree, calculable and can be underwritten by an insurance company in return for regular premium payments. In this way, proprietors commonly insure against losses resulting from flood, vandalism, fire and theft. Premature failure of building components is another example of an insurable risk: to insure against such risks the underwriter might require the landlord to manage the dwellings in a prescribed way, e.g. carry out certain maintenance procedures on a regular basis. Commercial risks are normally non-insurable and refer to uncertainties associated with such things as the vagaries of the market or unforeseen changes in taxation or legislation that may affect the investment's profitability. The degree of convenience will be determined by the time, effort and worry involved in managing the investment.

The rate of return will be partly determined by the degree of capital appreciation in a given period (net of capital gains tax) and partly by the surplus of rental income over revenue costs in that period (net of Schedule A income tax). Rental returns are influenced by market conditions (e.g. demand and shortages), location, property type and condition, and whether the accommodation is furnished or unfurnished.

Deposits against loss and damage

The majority of tenants are required to pay an 'up front' deposit to the landlord to cover any loss or damage that may occur during the tenancy period. The *Survey of*

---

13 Siobhan Carey, *Private Renting in England 1993/94*, HMSO.

English Housing indicates that around seven out of ten tenants pay a deposit. The basic legal position is that the landlord must return the deposit at the end of the tenancy providing the tenant has met the terms. Evidence from Citizens' Advice Bureaux suggests that a minority of landlords exploit such arrangements by treating the deposits as automatic non-returnable charges or by claiming for non-existent damage.[14] In Britain these arrangements have traditionally been regulated solely by the terms of the contract and aggrieved tenants have the trouble and expense of going to law, usually the small claims court, if they wish to seek redress. In some states in Commonwealth countries, for example, New South Wales, Australia and parts of Canada deposit-taking is regulated. In these states the deposit is required to be held by an independent third party (the scheme regulator) who will adjudicate in the event of a dispute as to whether the deposit (or part of it) should be returned to the tenant when the tenancy ends – this type of regulated deposit holding is known as a custodial scheme. The interest earned on all the accounts held by the scheme regulator pays for the costs of administering the scheme.

Partly as a response to the bad publicity created by sharp practice and to improve the image of the sector, industry-run systems of self regulation have already operated in the UK for a number of years, such as the scheme run by the Association of Residential Letting Agents (ARLA). Unlike custodial schemes where the deposit is held by a third party these schemes operate by allowing the landlord to hold the deposit. At the end of the tenancy the landlord agrees to repay the whole of the deposit (or part of it) to the tenant if they can agree it should be repaid. In the event of any disagreement the amount in dispute is paid into a designated account held by the scheme administrator. The administrator will decide how much of the disputed amount (if any) should be repaid to the tenant and may also charge the landlord reasonable expenses. The administrator maintains insurance to cover the cost in the event that the landlord fails to pay the disputed amount plus any expenses into the scheme. For this reason these types of scheme are known as insured schemes. Landlords who fail to comply with the scheme's rules can be expelled. Despite this industry-led initiative, criticism of the sector continued as only a minority of landlords – usually those already committed to high standards – were prepared to commit to this form of self-regulation.

As a response, in March 2000 the government launched a pilot Tenancy Deposit Scheme (TDS) in five case study locations in England. The scheme was voluntary and managed by the Independent Housing Ombudsman (IHO) supported by government funding. TDS was set to run for four years to assess, amongst other

---

14 *Unsafe Deposit: CAB clients' experience of rental deposits*, National Association of Citizens Advice Bureaux, 1998. The *Survey of English Housing 2002/02* found that 70 per cent of landlords returned deposits in full, a further 15 per cent returned in part, and the remaining 13 per cent withheld in full. The most frequently cited reason for withholding was charges for cleaning and damage, an area that is highly subjective and therefore a likely source of dispute (Kemp, 2004, p139).

things, whether it could become self-financing. The TDS offered both a custodial and an insured option and in both cases the IHO adjudicated in the event of a dispute and their decision was binding. Research conducted for the Chartered Institute of Housing and the British Property Federation[15] found that there was industry support for the IHO as a regulator because he was viewed as fair and impartial by landlords and tenants alike.

In June 2003 the government announced that the pilots would be wound up and there were no plans to roll-out TDS on a national basis.[16] However, under pressure from backbench MPs and lobbying from organisations such as Citizens Advice, the government announced that it would introduce amendments to the housing bill which was already making its way through parliament. The amendments gave the government powers to introduce a mandatory dual scheme in which landlords could opt to join either an 'approved' insured scheme of their choice (such as the ARLA scheme) or otherwise join a custodial scheme. The minister has the power to approve reputable industry-run insured schemes for this purpose. The framework for a dual scheme is now contained in the Housing Act 2004[17] and is expected to be brought into force by ministerial order possibly in 2005 or 2006. The main sanction against landlords for failing to comply is that they will be unable to gain possession of the (shorthold) tenancy under the notice-only ground until such time as the deposit is lodged in an appropriate scheme (either insured or custodial).

The question of rent

Rent is the *price* paid by a tenant to a landlord for the temporary occupation or use of land, buildings or other property.[18] In commercial settings landlords acting rationally will seek to charge the highest rent that the market will bear. In a free-enterprise economy with no state intervention, the price a landlord can charge will be determined by market conditions. In particular, the level of rent will be affected by the degree of competition that exists.

Perfect competition and marginal cost pricing.
In the extreme case of a perfectly competitive market, rents would be determined by a process called marginal cost pricing. In these highly competitive conditions, the rents charged would be just sufficient to cover all the costs of providing the accommodation including what economists refer to as *normal profit*. In this way, normal profit is seen as a cost of production and is defined as that amount of profit just sufficient to make it worthwhile for the provider to stay trading in the market.

---

15 Rugg, J. and Rhodes, D., *Chains or Challenges?: the prospects for better regulation of the private rented sector*, CIH/BPF, 2001.
16 Tony McNulty MP, *Hansard*, 16 June 2003, col. 3WS
17 Housing Act 2004, sections 212-215 and schedule 10. The scheme applies to England and Wales only.
18 E.g. cars, telephones, televisions, etc. can be 'rented' for periods. When the use of something is acquired on an hourly or weekly basis, we normally talk of 'hire' rather than 'rent'.

Under perfectly competitive conditions, landlords will be able to raise their rents up to, but not beyond, the level of marginal costs. If they do attempt to put up their rents beyond the level that just covers marginal costs, then they would make higher than 'normal' profits and these 'excess' rewards would, in turn, attract extra provision of equivalent accommodation by competing landlords. This additional supply would then force rents back down to the level at which, once again, price just covered the marginal costs of provision. In this way it is argued that, in strongly competitive conditions, the power of a landlord to extract a higher rent is limited by market forces.

Imperfect competition and real market pricing.

In the real world there is no such thing as a 'perfectly' competitive housing market and for this reason landlords may be able to increase their rents to levels that enable them to make more than 'normal' profits. At a particular time and place the market for a specific type of accommodation will be more or less competitive. Perfect competition is a theoretical construct. It represents the extreme case in which there are no barriers to prevent new suppliers coming into the market to compete, and in which all the dwellings are of identical size, type and condition, and in which all the market participants have perfect knowledge of the market and the product, and none of them is large or powerful enough to do anything that will influence the price. The less the local market reflects these conditions the less competitive it will be.

In practice, within a specific market area, new landlords may be inhibited, or even prevented, from setting up in business because of planning restrictions, a scarcity of appropriate building land, or a shortage of capital finance. Within the area, dwellings will vary with respect to location, tenancy conditions, size, form, and state of repair. Landlords and tenants will only have an imperfect knowledge of what others are charging or offering, and may not have the professional expertise to assess the precise condition of a property. At any time there may be shortages or surpluses of particular types of accommodation and some of the market participants may have some influence through their size, professional affiliations or other connections that enable them to affect the negotiated price. For all these reasons the market will be *imperfectly*, rather than *perfectly*, competitive. This means that some landlords, at some times, in some locations, will be able to set rents for some types of property above the level of marginal costs without fear of these being forced down by competition. In charging what the imperfect market will bear the landlord will receive a rent that reflects the real market price for that accommodation, and at that price, more than normal profits might be generated. Of course, at that price, not every household deemed to be in 'need' of that kind of accommodation will be able to afford the rent.

Real market rents and housing policy

For some years there has been a consensus in Britain that the principal aim of housing policy is to ensure that every household is able to occupy a dwelling of a size, type, standard, and location suitable to its needs.[19] When landlords charge

---

19   Refer to the *NFHA Inquiry into British Housing: Report*, July 1985, p7.

what the market will bear, market forces will equate supply with effective demand which means that all the properties will be let. When this occurs the market is said to be 'in equilibrium' because demand is satisfied and the market is cleared. However, when a market is in equilibrium it does not mean that every household's housing needs have been met; it simply means that those who can afford to pay the going rent are satisfied and that landlords are satisfied.

Effective demand is defined as when a need or want is satisfied by spending money in the market. Clearly, some households have insufficient income to satisfy their housing needs. In the past there have been a number of policy responses to this problem. These have included augmenting the incomes of those who cannot afford to pay commercial rents (see above and Chapter 19), controlling or regulating market rents, and providing incentives to invest in private rented housing. This last approach, as well as providing tax breaks, has involved deregulation measures.[20]

Regulation and the private landlord

Throughout the twentieth century, governments periodically intervened in the market to restrict the activities of private landlords. These measures have had two aspects – to control or regulate rents and to establish a degree of security of tenure (see Kemp, 2004, chapters 2-4). The primary motives for intervention have been to keep rents within the means of low-income households and to protect tenants from the actions of unscrupulous landlords profiteering from shortages that exist in highly imperfect local housing markets.

The distinction between 'control' and 'regulation'

The notions of 'control' and 'regulation' are grounded in specific pieces of legislation. The former is the product of the various Rent Acts from 1915 onwards and is an aspect of the *controlled tenancy* arrangements they established; the latter is a feature of the 'fair rent' system of *regulated tenancies* that was introduced in Great Britain[21] with the Rent Act 1965 and developed by subsequent legislation. The fair rent legislation provided for disputed rents to be set by a rent officer.

---

20 Arguably the most significant response has been to invest public funds in the provision of 'social' housing which is then allocated to low-income households at less than real market rents. The financial arrangements associated with the provision and consumption of non-commercial ('social') housing are considered in other chapters.

21 The historical development of Rent Act intervention is somewhat different in Northern Ireland, which, although like the rest of the UK released a proportion of its stock from control in 1957, had no transitional phase of rent regulation. Further decontrol took place in 1978 whereby any controlled properties that were not let were released from control and no new controlled tenancies could be created. Rents in the controlled sector remain very low and cannot be increased unless the landlord makes improvements. The policy of partial decontrol led to a rapid decline of the whole sector (as in Great Britain during the period 1958-64) so that by the mid-1990s it accounted for around 3.5 per cent of the stock. However, by 2002 the number of controlled lettings had shrunk to around 6,400 (out of a sector total of 34,000) and more recently the (uncontrolled) sector has experienced a revival so that the total sector (controlled and uncontrolled) now accounts for around 5.1 per cent of the stock.

If either party disputed the officer's ruling, the decision could be appealed to a specialist independent tribunal of experts known as a rent assessment committee.

Control and regulation are about the management of rent increases. Under control, specific properties, identified by reference to their rateable values, had their rents frozen, with allowances made for improvements and local tax increases. Over time the controlled rent became fixed at a level that is significantly below that which would be set by market forces. In particular locations this discouraged new investment, leading to existing landlords withdrawing from the market bringing about an 'informal economy' of illegal arrangements (such as 'key money'). Control was more stringent during wartime periods (after 1915 and 1939) when it was recognised that free markets had to be abandoned because normal supply activities became distorted due to construction resources and labour being diverted into the building of munitions factories and other projects associated with the war effort. At the time, control was regarded as temporary and designed to protect tenants from the inflation brought about by wartime disruptions in supply and immediate post-war shortages. After the first world war, however, the system was largely maintained and all except the grandest of houses remained subject to control, although exceptions began to be made – for example for vacant properties. After the second world war the restrictions remained until the 1957 Rent Act when the more valuable houses were released from control. Sitting tenants in less valuable properties continued to have their rents controlled until they moved, leading to a gradual decline in numbers.[22] In Great Britain all remaining controlled tenancies were finally converted to regulated tenancies by the Housing Act 1980.

The Conservative government's relaxation of rent control was primarily intended as a measure to bring about more investment in the sub-standard stock (Kemp, 2004, p39). However, in some parts of the country the period which followed the lifting of controls in 1957 was characterised by the harassing and eviction of tenants by what the press termed 'slum' or 'bully-boy' landlords and has since been termed *Rachmanism* (after the activities of Peter Rachman, a petty criminal and slum landlord operating in west London). The 1957 legislation allowed for capital gains to be realised as landlords either sold or demolished the vacated dwellings. Contrary to the legislators' intentions, this hastened disinvestment in private accommodation and some 300,000 dwellings were lost to the sector between 1958 and 1964.[23] In addition, the findings of the Milner Holland Committee's Inquiry into the problems of housing in London led to a high profile public commitment by the 1964 Labour government to reintroduce controls. This they did through the Rent Act 1965.

---

22   The Rent Act 1957 decontrolled some 5 million dwellings. These included dwellings above a certain rateable value, with regional variations, all vacated dwellings, all new unfurnished dwellings and all properties with a resident landlord.
23   Balchin and Kieve, (1977) *Urban Land Economics*, p194.

Regulated tenancies and fair rents

In Great Britain[24] the current system of regulation (as opposed to control) originates from the Rent Act of 1965. The act introduced the concept of the 'fair rent' for most private sector tenancies which had been released from control by the 1957 act and coverage was extended to include furnished lettings without a resident landlord by the Rent Act 1974. Fair rents were extended to housing association tenancies by the Housing Finance Act 1972. The Rent Act 1977 consolidated all these measures but this framework has subsequently been almost completely dismantled by the Housing Act 1988 so that now the regulatory regime of fair rent tenancies only applies to lettings which were created before 1989.

Fair rents were introduced in the wake of the 1965 Milner Holland Report. The system was designed to balance the proprietary interests of landlords and tenants and, in particular, sought to overcome the disincentive effects on investment that resulted from rent control. Rent control involves market abandonment while rent regulation involves market modification. The idea behind a fair rent is that rent officers should regulate arrangements between landlords and tenants by fixing a rent that relates to the market without abandoning the tenant to the vagaries of unrestrained market forces (see Kemp, 2004, p45).

The so-called 'fairness' of a fair rent stems from its apparent similarity, in the minds of the civil servant who designed it, to the market ideal of a *marginal cost price rent* (see page 419). That is, it is designed to reflect the rent that would be charged in the area in question if conditions of perfect competition prevailed (i.e. if there were no shortages and thus no super-normal profits).

Fair rents are set by independent agents of central government known as 'rent officers'. In England The Rent Service, formerly the Rent Officer Service, became an executive agency of government in November 1999.[25] The creation of the agency did not alter the rent officers' status – they still remain independent statutory officers responsible for making 'fair rent' valuations, valuing local private sector rents for housing benefit, and advising local authorities about the effects of rent on housing renovation grants. The agency only operates in England, as in Scotland and Wales the equivalent service is part of the civil service within the respective devolved administrations. Rent officers are required to set rents that ignore the personal circumstances of both tenants and landlords. Furthermore, the rents they set must assume that the properties are not in short supply; so that the rent must not include any element that reflects the dwelling's scarcity. They must, however, take into account other market factors including the property's age, location, character and state of repair. Fair rents are registered and remain fixed for a period of two years (in Scotland three years). Either party can appeal to a rent assessment committee if they wish to challenge the rent officer's decision.

---

24   See note above for the situation in Northern Ireland.
25   Originally within the Department of Environment, Transport and the Regions, subsequently the ODPM and from April 2004 departmental responsibility was transferred to the DWP.

A fair rent may consist of two elements: one relating to rights of occupancy (i.e. pure rent) and the other to service charges – that are assessed on the basis of their value to the tenant rather than on the costs of provision.

A fair rent is not a *controlled rent* in that it is not simply frozen within bands set by rateable values.[26] It is not a *welfare rent* in that it is not determined by reference to the personal circumstances of the tenant. It is not a *real market rent* because, although it does take account of the property's character, location, age, and condition, it ignores any price effect resulting from shortages or surpluses. It is an *administrative* arrangement that seeks to 'square the circle' by regulating rents in a way that would produce a similar outcome to that which would occur in an unregulated, perfectly competitive market.

The 1980 Housing Act extended the fair rent regime by converting all remaining controlled tenancies into regulated tenancies. The legislation also sought to encourage the growth of private landlordism by lowering the fair rent registration period from three to two years and by introducing two new forms of tenancy that gave landlords repossession rights after fixed terms. New protected shorthold tenancies allowed landlords to let vacant dwellings for terms ranging from one to five years. The act also allowed landlords, under certain conditions, to let dwellings under new assured tenancy agreements. Assured tenancies simply borrowed, with modifications, the arrangements for letting commercial properties under the Landlord and Tenant Act 1954 and applied it to residential properties. Following the Housing Act 1988 assured tenancies became the main mechanism of deregulation of the sector[27] (see below).

Policy towards reviving the sector

Reasons for decline

Since the mid-1980s there has been considerable debate about both the political desirability and practical possibility of reviving the private rented sector to a point where it could once again play a significant role as a provider of housing for people on average or below average incomes.[28]

There is evidence to suggest that the decline in private landlordism has an international dimension. In many developed countries the decline has occurred as an inevitable result of long-term political, social and commercial forces. Michael Harloe's study of private renting in Germany, Holland, France, Denmark and the

---

26 Rateable values were used to set thresholds above which properties are excluded from fair rent regulation and to set rent levels for the remaining controlled tenancies between 1957–1980.

27 The model for security remained the same but specific legislation was cast for the residential sector rather than borrowing from the machinery of the Landlord and Tenant Act 1954.

28 See in particular the writings of Best, R., Crook, A.D.H., Eversley, D., Gibb. K, Harloe, M., and Kemp, P.A.

United States found that, by the mid-1980s, despite attempts to ease the impact of restrictive legislation, a widespread and powerful amalgamation of political and economic circumstances was restricting the tenure to a 'marginal' and 'problematic' role.[29]

In Britain, as elsewhere, it is clear that the decline in private landlordism is in large part explained by long-run social and economic restructuring. Over the last 80 years, many new investment opportunities have emerged to compete with residential property provision and at the same time, saving and investment mechanisms have become more sophisticated and accessible. During the same period the state's commitment to the provision of various forms of social rented housing has expanded, and this commitment carried with it a range of fiscal support measures that were denied to the private landlord. Fiscal support has also reinforced the preference for home-ownership that began to emerge in the inter-war period and developed at a pace after 1950. By the 1980s most commentators were arguing that, in combination, these forces have become so powerful that it is not possible to reverse the historical trend towards decline by a simple process of deregulation, and that any government wishing to attract substantial amounts of private money into the sector will need to provide positive incentives to potential investors.

A key problem associated with the development of a residential portfolio relates to what might be termed the 'funding issue'.[30] Historically, lenders have viewed residential investment as a business activity and as a result, landlords tend to pay higher interest charges than those available in the owner-occupation market. Recognition that funding issues could be inhibiting general growth in the sector led to the launch of the 'buy to let' scheme in 1996. This is a scheme initiated by the Association of Residential Letting Agents and a number of mortgage providers that is designed to provide preferential loans to landlords so as to encourage wider investment and participation in the market. The preferential interest rates are granted subject to specific requirements relating to such things as maximum loan to value ratios, minimum rent to interest ratios, minimum capital values and loans, and detailed criteria regarding unacceptable or ineligible properties and letting arrangements. Buy to let had (by the end of 2004) attracted £52.2 billion in mortgages and surveys suggested landlords 'have a long-term interest in the market'.[31]

Other sector-specific investment schemes are being developed by individual lenders and groups of lenders.[32] The success of such schemes will depend, to a large extent, on general investment opportunities in the economy. In the final analysis, all housing investment has to compete for funds with the full range of other enterprises.

---

29   Harloe, M., (1985), *Private Rented Housing in the United States and Europe*, Croom Helm.
30   This phrase is taken from John Mansfield, *Inside Housing*, January 15 1999.
31   Council of Mortgage Lenders, press release 14 February 2005.
32   For example, in 1998 Aichisons, an Oxfordshire agent, co-ordinated the launch of the Residential Investment Centre, adding a further six institutions willing to provide funds for residential investment purposes.

Recent policy initiatives

Governments have found it politically difficult to provide direct subsidy to private landlords[33] and have therefore relied on policies of deregulation coupled with indirect subsidies in the form of tax breaks when they have wanted to stimulate the sector. The Conservative administrations of the 1980s and 1990s were ideologically predisposed in favour of private renting and their attempts to breathe new life into the sector involved the application of two contrasting, but mutually reinforcing, pressures for growth. One involved improved incentives targeted at landlords in the form of deregulation measures and tax breaks. The other took the form of reduced support for their competitors in the social sector and involved cutting back financial subsidies and legislative protection for municipal housing and housing associations which had the effect of narrowing the fiscal advantage.

By the mid-1980s, research and informed opinion indicated[34] that an effective strategy for reviving the sector needed to have the following interrelated features:

- clarity about the sector's future specific contribution towards satisfying housing need and demand;
- further deregulation needed to be realised;
- the introduction of fiscal incentives to encourage new investment;
- a greater degree of tenure neutrality with respect to fiscal policy in general;
- the introduction of measures designed to ease the management burden.

The role of private renting

How the sector is to be supported will depend to a large extent on an understanding of the part we wish it to play in the fulfilment of overall housing policy. Recognition of the fact that the decline in private renting is in part an inevitable consequence of wider structural changes in society has resulted in a general consensus that, in the foreseeable future, it will continue to play only a limited role compared with owner-occupation and social renting. The current debate is not about whether it should replace one of the existing primary tenure arrangements so much as whether, in the future, it should or could play a more prominent role. Arguably, the most important role that private renting could play would be to provide a greater degree of flexibility. Many argue that it is well-suited to offer accommodation to certain groups at certain points in their housing careers including the provision of a temporary stop-gap to those seeking long-term housing solutions in other tenures.

---

33 However, see sections below on local authority section 28 grants and tenure neutrality.
34 See, for example, the various submissions to the Inquiry into British Housing chaired by the Duke of Edinburgh and published as *Report* (1985), *The Evidence* (1985), and *Supplement* (1986), NFHA.

The need for more rented accommodation is clearly indicated by recent projections of household growth that show a probable increase of between three and four million households in England alone in the period 1996 to 2021.[35] This growth will result from falling death rates, net inward migration and new household formation through increased divorce and marital separation rates. New housing demand for relatively short stay accommodation is likely to arise from the increasing need for mobility that will result from the gradual restructuring of the labour market in a way that weakens job security and gives a greater prominence to short-term contracts. These trends point to a particular need for more single-person dwellings that are both affordable and immediately accessible. Expected patterns of internal migration indicate that in some areas, such as London and some Northern conurbations (especially Greater Manchester) shortages of suitable accommodation to rent by the young, the single and the occupationally mobile may be very pronounced.

The present government's commitment to promote a healthy private rented housing sector was restated in the 2000 housing green paper, which said that, *'Through its flexibility and speed of access, it can also help to oil the wheels of the housing and labour markets'*.[36]

Deregulation

An early priority of the Conservative administration elected in 1979 was to begin dismantling the provisions of the Rent Acts. Fair rents were being set at levels well below those that would have prevailed in a free market and tenants also had a significant degree of security of tenure. Such restrictions were seen by many to be inhibiting the growth of private renting and throughout the 1980s pressure grew for a less tightly-controlled system that would redress the balance of proprietary interests. The idea was to allow landlords to charge market value rents and to repossess their properties more easily. The 1980 Housing Act allowed certain landlords to let newly-built residential property on assured tenancies with fewer contractual restrictions or to let existing or new dwellings as Rent Act protected 'shorthold' tenancies with a guaranteed right to possession at the end of a fixed-term.[37] The effect of the new *assured* tenancy agreements was, however, limited by the requirement for the dwellings to be purpose-built (new or substantially renovated with letting in mind) and owned by an organisation approved by the

---

35 Alan Holmans, (1995), 'The Rising Number of Households Requiring Homes – The National and Regional Picture', in Wilcox, S., *Housing Finance Review 1995/96*, Joseph Rowntree Foundation, pp17-24. Also Wilcox, 1999, p66.
36 Department of Environment, Transport and the Regions/Department of Social Security, April 2000, para. 5.1, p44.
37 This is sometimes referred to as the 'notice-only ground' as possession was guaranteed provided the landlord served the tenant with a notice of their intention to take back the tenancy at the end of the fixed term. The notice had to be served within certain time limits before the end of the fixed term so that the tenant had a minimum warning period.

Secretary of State. Protected shorthold tenancies also failed to prove popular, partly because they were still subject to rent regulation and partly because the administrative procedures for setting them up and terminating them were complicated.

The 1987 housing white paper marks the point when the government decided to breathe new life into private renting. As a result the sector was substantially deregulated by the Housing Act 1988, which sought to allow market forces and landlord-tenant negotiations to be the guiding influence on rent levels and security of tenure. The expansion of assured and assured shorthold tenancies was intended to make the sector more attractive to investors. After the 1988 Act rents rose.[38] The largest increases were in the furnished part of the sector, where net rents, after deduction of housing benefit, doubled between 1989 and 1993.[39] In unfurnished accommodation immediately prior to the reforms rents were lower, on average, than housing associations. By 1993, however, they were, on average, double those of housing associations.

The Housing Act 1988 reformed the structure of the independent rented sector.[40] It established *assured tenancies* as the main form of letting for the use of private landlords and housing associations alike. Its measures constituted a significant degree of deregulation and, in establishing the new arrangements, existing Rent Act *regulated tenancies* were to be phased out as the property became vacant. In this way, although all regulated tenancies retained their security of tenure and regulated rents, from January 1989, all new tenancy agreements were now assumed to be *assured* or *assured shorthold.*[41]

The provisions of an assured tenancy agreement are specifically designed to enhance the *proprietary investment interests* of the landlord while, at the same time, maintaining a degree of security of tenure which is regarded as a key proprietary *consumption interest* of the tenant. Under the reformed arrangements, rents and duration of tenancies are negotiated as in a free market, but the tenant, as well as enjoying security of tenure during the contract period, has the right to a statutory periodic tenancy at the end of that period. On the tenant's death their spouse has an automatic right to take over the assured tenancy.

---

38 Average rents rose across the board and it was not simply a matter of deregulated rents increasing the average. Rents also increased for the remaining regulated 'fair rent' tenancies – partly because the improved evidence base of open market rents on which rent officers could base their valuations. As a result of the rapid increases in the regulated fair rent sector in 1999 the Labour government introduced restrictions on the rate that registered fair rents could be increased relative to the retail price index. See also Kemp, 2004, Chapter 5.
39 Office for National Statistics, *Social Trends 25*, 1995, p179.
40 A term used in the 1987 white paper to describe the wider rented sector outside public ownership that includes both private landlords and housing associations.
41 The legislation does not allow an assured tenancy to be imposed on an existing protected tenant. A protected tenancy was simply the contractual tenancy set up within the remit of the Rent Act. Once the contractual period ended the statutory tenancy came into being; both protected and statutory tenancies were regulated.

To encourage private landlords to meet the increasing demand for short-term lets, the 1988 legislation allowed for a variant of the assured agreement called an *assured shorthold tenancy*, in Scotland called *short assured tenancies*. These arrangements allow for fixed-term tenancies that must not be less than six months duration. A tenant has the right to apply for a rent determination by a rent assessment committee if they think the contractual rent is significantly out of line with that being charged for similar properties in the locality. During the term of the tenancy, a landlord can seek repossession on one of a number of specified bases (e.g. rent arrears), and at the end of the term has an absolute right to repossess the property. In England and Wales the Housing Act 1996 made *assured shorthold* the 'normal' or 'default' tenancy arrangement: that is, unless an assured tenancy is specifically agreed, then the arrangement is assumed to be on a shorthold basis. The act further enhanced the proprietary interests of landlords by modifying the mandatory rent arrears ground for possession by reducing the minimum required debt from the equivalent of 13 weeks rent to 8 weeks rent.

Regulation, deregulation and better regulation

Industry representatives have always maintained that the pre-1989 system of regulated rents and tenant security was a powerful factor in the decline of the sector. There now appears to be a degree of political consensus that the current balance of rights between the landlord and the tenant is about right and any moves to restore the previous position may frighten off potential investors.[42] Some tenants' groups have argued that the current balance of rights does not allow them to enforce their statutory rights for fear that their tenancy will not be renewed at the end of the fixed period. The 2002 Shelter Commission on private renting[43] suggested that the flexibility of the current arrangements, whereby security can be negotiated for any period provided it is for at least six months, is an advantage which has not yet been fully appreciated by potential investors. The commission thought that there was potential for this advantage to be exploited more fully by developing a variety of rental 'products' – in effect niche markets – such as letting for longer periods to tenants who have proven to be a low risk. At present many investors insist on letting on six month assured shortholds. This may reflect an 'immaturity' in the UK residential sector whereby investors are still sensitive about re-regulation. This immaturity is not reflected in the letting of commercial property which is worth more tenanted than untenanted.

There is also a degree of consensus among potential investors that the persistent poor image of the private landlord (see Rachmanism above) is also a disincentive to invest. There is acknowledgement that at the bottom end of the market there is a need to improve standards. Joint CIH/BPF research as to the prospects for better regulation of the sector[44] found that there is general industry support for regulation

42 Crook, A. and Kemp, P. (1999) *Financial Institutions and Private Rented Housing*, Joseph Rowntree Foundation.
43 *Private Renting: A New Settlement* – A commission on standards and supply, Shelter/JRF, 2002.
44 *Chains or Challenges?* CIH/BPF, 2001.

targeted at the worst properties and poorest standards of management. In the remainder of the sector, self-regulation and the demands of the market are thought to be sufficient to drive up standards. The research also found that there was support for introducing a requirement that managers should be 'fit and proper persons', provided a clear definition can be set. Support for such targeted regulation (largely directed at HMOs, see above) is consistent with guidelines drawn up by the government's Better Regulation Task Force (BRTF).[45] The BRTF considers that regulation should not be viewed as problematic provided that it is a rational and proportionate response to the risks and their consequences.

To some extent the poor standards of management which exist are due to the predominance of small non-professional landlords which has led some to describe the sector as a 'cottage industry'.[46] The result is that the majority of landlords do not have the professional skills that would be expected from larger corporate bodies. This partly explains the interest of governments in trying to attract more corporate investment into the sector by the use of fiscal incentives.

Fiscal incentives

An established feature of the British tax system has been to encourage business investment by the provision of tax allowances and exemptions, commonly referred to as 'tax breaks'. In comparison with most other business activities, landlords have been treated ungenerously with respect to tax breaks and this is sometimes pointed to as an historical explanation of the relative lack of enthusiasm for investment in rented housing.

In the UK the Inland Revenue takes what is known as a 'rental business' approach to tax assessment. Under these arrangements, profits from UK land or property are treated for tax purposes as 'earnings' arising from a business activity. Tax liability is based on commercial accounts drawn up in accordance with accounting principles. This means that landlords with a portfolio of properties are assessed on earnings and expenditures that are lumped together so that expenses on one property can be deducted from the receipts of another – so long as the properties are let on commercial terms, and not cheaply to friends or relatives. It also means that a trading loss can be carried over into subsequent tax years and set off against future tax liabilities.

Income and corporation tax
Private individuals (sole traders) and business partnerships are subject to income tax, whilst companies pay corporation tax on their profits – the equivalent of income tax for corporations. In both cases different sources of income are assessed differently with their own exemptions, allowances and rates of tax. These rules are set out in *six schedules* of the Income and Corporation Taxes Act 1988. Landlords

---

45 Cabinet Office, 2000. See also note 38 above.
46 Shelter/JRF, 2002, p19.

are taxed under 'Schedule A' that covers rent and other income generated from any interest or ownership of real property.

Allowable revenue expenses. A landlord is allowed to offset certain revenue expenses against their liable income so long as these are incurred wholly and exclusively for business purposes. These revenue allowances include ordinary expenditure on maintenance, repairs, insurance and management costs. The costs of major repairs to reinstate a worn out or dilapidated asset are usually deductible as revenue expenditure but extensive alterations to a building that amount to the reconstruction of the property are counted as capital expenditure and therefore are not allowed as an ordinary revenue business expense. The cost of servicing a loan taken out to acquire the property is regarded as a revenue expense and is therefore allowable.

Capital allowances. It is a general income tax principle that you cannot deduct capital expenses in computing your taxable income. This means, for example, that in calculating taxable profits, a landlord cannot deduct the purchase price of the property being let or the amount of any depreciation or any loss incurred in selling the property. This rule applies to all business activities not just rental businesses. Despite this general principle, in some cases capital expenditure on a property (but not the land) may qualify for capital allowances. A capital allowance effectively enables the business to claim further deductions in calculating its taxable rental profit.

Some industrial and commercial businesses can deduct a percentage of the property's overall capital value to allow for the asset's depreciation; however, this is not permitted in the case of residential accommodation. Although there are no capital allowances for the cost or depreciation of residential property, the costs of maintaining plant and machinery such as lifts and heating systems can be allowed for, and a 'wear and tear' depreciation allowance may be due for such items as fridges, freezers, furniture, furnishings, etc. that are supplied with the accommodation.

Capital gains tax
Unlike owner-occupiers, private landlords are not exempt from capital gains tax when they sell the dwellings they have been letting. Furthermore, unless they are dealing in furnished holiday lettings, landlords of residential properties do not benefit from the various types of capital gains tax relief that are available to other traders. This means, for example, they cannot enjoy the benefit of roll-over or retirement relief which would normally apply when the owner sells on their business.

The owner-occupier landlord and the rent-a-room scheme
There is a long tradition of people letting out rooms in their own homes. The lodger was a common feature of working-class domestic life in the Victorian and Edwardian periods. Lodgers do not have security under the Housing and Rent

Acts and can be evicted without a court order if they share facilities with their landlord.

To encourage this kind of informal letting arrangement in 1992 the government introduced a tax allowance that allows home-owners to let out spare rooms and pay no tax on any rent received up to the value of the allowance.[47] In practice, the scheme is administered by the claimant simply ticking a box on his or her tax return. Landlords can elect for the excess to be taxed in full or, alternatively, they can apply for normal income tax rules for the whole income less allowable expenses. The scheme has no implications for capital gains liabilities. Advisors usually argue that it would be sensible to draw up clear agreements about payment of council tax and other household expenses. Furthermore, insurance companies should be informed about the arrangements or cover may be deemed to be invalid.

Section 28 capital grants
Section 28 of the Local Government Act 1988 allows for the provision of production subsidies by giving local authorities discretionary powers to award capital grants to investors in new or refurbished private housing for rent. The grant must come from the authority's own resources and the risk and ownership must be lodged in the private sector. This provision is little used in practice.

Tax breaks: BES, HITs and tax transparent vehicles

The Business Expansion Scheme (BES)
In the late 1980s the government considered that deregulation was not sufficient to 'kick-start' the sector back to life and the BES was introduced to reinforce the other incentives. Rather than introduce a new package of tax breaks they utilised the machinery of the existing Business Expansion Scheme which was originally designed to encourage individuals to invest in high risk venture companies which lacked sufficient capital to fulfil their growth potential. In July 1988, the BES was extended to include investment in companies letting housing on assured tenancies. It allowed individuals to invest up to £40,000 a year in a BES housing company and claim income tax relief at their marginal rate. Capital gains tax was also exempted so long as the shares were held for a minimum of five years, after which it was assumed the company would be profitable and trading on the stock market. The opportunity to invest in BES incentives ended in December 1993 so that by the end of 1998 the scheme had effectively come to an end.

The first two years of the scheme attracted over £500 million of investment in residential letting companies, producing around 10,000 dwellings, two-thirds of which were newly-built. However, the five year minimum holding period meant that investors were able to withdraw from the sector at the end of that term and realise the growth in the property's value. Most commercial investors did so. Although the scheme raised over £3 billion in investment only around one-quarter

---

47 This figure currently stands at £4,250 p.a. (since April 1997).

of this was by 'entrepreneurial' companies, much of the rest was by companies linked to housing associations, universities and building societies, which saw the scheme as a way to increase their stock on cheaper terms than conventional private loans (Kemp, 2004, p58).

In the 1990s the Conservative government sought to attract investment from the financial institutions which previously had shown little interest in residential accommodation. The vehicle by which it was hoped to stimulate investment was through a new type of financial intermediary introduced by the Finance Act 1996 known as a Housing Investment Trust.

Housing investment trusts (HITs)

An investment trust is a company whose objective is to collect and reinvest the money capital of its shareholders in a spread of equities and other securities with a view of generating an investment income. Unlike ordinary trading companies, the money capital raised by its own share issues is reinvested in the share capital of other organisations. In this way, it acts as an intermediary between those wishing to invest money capital and those needing to raise money capital for commercial ventures. A housing investment trust is a type of investment trust which allows a qualifying company to establish a portfolio of residential properties within a maximum purchase price.[48] The dwellings must be let on assured tenancies and at least three-quarters of the stock let at any one time. In return for operating within these rules the trust will qualify for the (lower) small companies' rate of corporation tax on rental income and exemption from capital gains tax on any capital appreciation.

Running a HIT requires both fund management and property management, making them more complicated than an ordinary investment trust. The fund managers are also required to invest all funds in qualifying properties within two years. Overall the procedures required to set up a HIT are considerably more complex than those associated with investment in equities, making them unattractive to investors.

The lessons from the BES and HITs

Although BES and HITs are not currently playing a significant part in the provision of private renting, the debate that surrounds such fiscal experiments remains important. BES proved that it was politically acceptable to subsidise private landlords. Housing investment trusts were first proposed in the 1995 housing white paper, which envisaged an expanded role for the private rented sector through the creation of a new type of housing agency that would allow investors to buy shares (encouraged by significant tax breaks) and thereby generate the funds needed to create new homes for rent.

HITs were intended to attract pension and insurance funds which have the sort of 'serious' money that could make a real difference to the sector and become a

---

48   Set at £125,000 in Greater London and £85,000 elsewhere.

permanent feature housing investment rather than the BES experiment which was viewed as a short-term 'pump-priming' exercise. By financing housing provision through the market for equities, a system is created whereby the overall supply of funds becomes permanent but the individual investor is able to liquidise the investment if the need arises. HITs provide investors with a vehicle to invest in the sector at arms length – enjoying the benefits of buying and selling shares in housing without the risks of having to own property directly or get involved with managing tenants.

The demise of HITs

From the start there were some doubts about the effectiveness of the tax concessions offered by HITs. Pension funds and insurance companies already benefit from tax concessions on their investments. Furthermore, the potential tax advantages were significantly reduced by the in-coming Labour government in 1997 which brought in measures designed to close corporate tax 'loopholes' and prevent investment trusts reclaiming the bulk of the tax they pay on dividends.

Despite the potential benefits of HITs there were early indications that they would not be a success. One explanation is the poor reputation that private rented housing has among investors which has meant that there is no recent tradition in Britain of investing in residential property partly because the memory of earlier rent control still lingers. More importantly, HITs were viewed by investors as far too complex and not sufficiently 'tax transparent'.[49] The property investment limits were also probably a disincentive as they were relatively low in comparison with average house prices. Research by Crook and Kemp[50] found that no HITs were established in the five-year period after their introduction. By the end of the 1990s the industry view was that HITs would not work nor would a tweaking of the model be sufficient to attract investment. What was needed was a completely new model not a 'HITs mark II'.[51]

Despite the closing of tax loopholes the Labour administration signalled its willingness to consider the role of tax incentives in encouraging investment in the housing green paper. However, further proposals were not discussed until the publication of the *2004 Pre-Budget Report*.

The Pre-Budget Report 2004, REITs and tax transparent vehicles

The *2004 Pre-Budget Report* revived the idea of fiscal incentives and acknowledged that a 'tax transparent' vehicle would improve liquidity and provide access to property for long-term savings. It announced that the government intended to issue a consultation paper on '*the most appropriate*

---

49 Crook, A. and Kemp, P., 1999.
50 Crook, A. *et al.*, (2002) *Investment returns in the Private Rented Sector*, British Property Federation.
51 *ibid* see also Department of Environment, Transport and the Regions /Department of Social Security, April 2000, p47.

structure for tax transparent property investment trusts[52] as recommended in the interim report of the Barker Review on housing supply (see Chapter 7). This suggests that the government is anxious to learn from the failure of HITs and consider the views of the industry to develop a vehicle which more precisely suits their needs.

The concept of tax transparency is an idea that has been borrowed from established property investment vehicles which operate successfully in other countries such as Australia and the USA where the vehicles are known as Real Estate Investment Trusts (REITs). Tax transparency is more subtle than tax relief – the idea is that money flowing through the vehicle (i.e. the business) is not taxed; instead shareholders pay tax at their own marginal rate. This avoids the position whereby the investor's money is taxed twice, once in the business and once again when they receive their dividend.

REITs like HITs are a form of investment trust whereby the majority of funds must be invested in property and the majority of any income generated must be paid out in shareholder dividends – the exact proportion varies from country to country but is within the range of 70-90 per cent. However, unlike HITs, there is no requirement to invest exclusively in residential property or – worse from the point of view of investors – in residential property let on assured tenancies. This allows investors to build up a portfolio of property, perhaps including residential property, which spreads their risks.

The Pre-Budget Report also indicated that the government was considering one other area that may help stimulate investment in the private rented sector – that of personal savings and investments for retirement. At present an individual making savings in a pension scheme benefits from tax relief. However, if instead they choose to save for their retirement by buying property and letting it then this does not attract tax relief. The government indicated that it is considering the options for a more flexible system of saving for retirement in which the saver can benefit from tax incentives regardless of their chosen vehicle for investment.

Whatever the method favoured by the government for increasing investment in the private rented sector there are some doubts as to whether fiscal incentives will increase the overall supply of housing. Rather it can be argued they will simply result in a change in the balance between each sector. The success of the buy to let market has led to complaints from aspiring owner-occupiers that they have been priced out of markets by investors buying up property to rent.[53] Further there is evidence to suggest that REITs do not stimulate an increase in investment in property (let alone residential property), but rather investors defer until gains can be made. This was the experience in Australia where REITs failed to attract much

---

52 Cm 6042, *Pre-Budget Report*, December 2003, paras. 1.21 and 3.111, HM Treasury.
53 BBC News Online, 28 May 2003 'Cost of renting 'increases''.

---

investment for 20 years until the property market collapsed and prime real estate became available at knock down prices.[54]

Tenure neutrality

The introduction of tenure neutrality into fiscal arrangements is seen by many as a key feature of any strategy for reviving the private rented sector. The argument here is that the sector's revival is inhibited by the lack of a 'level playing field' and unless and until private landlords are allowed to operate under fiscal arrangements that are equivalent to those facing other providers, they will be unable to play their full and appropriate part in the housing system.

This argument emphasises the need to reform the system of housing taxes and subsidies in ways that do not unduly privilege or penalise one form of tenure in comparison with the others. One approach would be to take away the current concessions given to owner-occupiers (Chapters 6 and 7). The withdrawal of mortgage interest tax relief to owner-occupiers in 2000 has helped in this respect. Further equalisation measures might prove to be politically difficult. However, some commentators have argued for the extension of subsidies and incentives for other tenures to be available to the private rented sector.

The Housing Act 2004[55] made a small step in this direction with new powers which allow the government to give grant aid to bodies other than registered social landlords to acquire, develop or improve housing for letting or for low-cost home-ownership.[56] The advocates of this kind of tenure neutral subsidy[57] argue that its extension to the private sector will not necessarily prove expensive to the Exchequer or work to the disadvantage of tenants. They argue that the cost to the Exchequer would be modest because the sector is relatively small and if it grew at the expense of the owner-occupied sector, the additional cost would be zero as owner-occupiers already benefit from such subsidies. Furthermore, if the private sector grew at the expense of the public sector, the public purse may actually make savings. To avoid exploitation of tenants, private landlords might have to agree to submit to regular rigorous inspection and or regulation in return for the grant aid.[58] This, however, would in itself require extra public expenditure.

---

54 Crowe, S. of UBS speaking at the University of Cambridge: Forum on Tax Transparency and Alternative Investment Vehicles for Listed Property Companies in the UK, 15 January 2004.

55 These new powers, which took effect in February 2005, are contained in sections 27A and 27B of the Housing Act 1996, as inserted by the Housing Act 2004, s220. Under the powers private landlords can invest in new stock, which either they choose to manage or contract out the management to an agent such as a housing association.

56 See Chapter 15 for more details. In practice this is unlikely to mean an increase in subsidy but rather that private bodies will be competing with registered social landlords for the same limited pot of money.

57 For a clear summary of these arguments see Halifax Building Society, *Viewpoint*, spring 1992.

58 Under the new Housing Act powers (in note 56 above) payment of grant may be subject to conditions similar to those imposed by the Housing Corporation on registered social landlords.

Summary

There is currently much debate about the need to revive private renting as a means of responding to the changing nature of employment. According to the housing green paper the government believes that the sector is performing 'below its true potential'. This is important for three reasons.

1. For many people there is no alternative to private renting at some stage in their lives (e.g. students and young workers).
2. In some areas social rented housing is in short supply and many low-income households are forced into renting privately.
3. Private renting has a potential to be flexible and responsive and thereby able to act effectively as a stepping-stone to other tenure arrangements.

A policy to revive the sector will need a multiple strategy that combines deregulation with positive fiscal incentives and/or the provision of a low-cost management service, and/or a move to tenure neutrality.

Further reading

Crook, A. and Kemp, P., *Financial Institutions and Private Rented Housing*, JRF, 1999.

DETR/Department for Social Security, *Quality and Choice: A Decent Home for All*: *The Housing Green Paper*, April 2000, Chapter 5.

Kemp, P., *Private Renting in Transition*, CIH, 2004.

Rugg, J. and Rhodes, D., *Chains or Challenges?: The prospects for better regulation of the private rented sector*, CIH/BPF, 2000.

Shelter, *Private Renting: A New Settlement – A Commission on Standards and Supply*, Shelter, 2002.

CHAPTER 19:
Financial support measures for the vulnerable

Housing benefit, tax credits, pension credits, 'Supporting People', and income support for mortgage interest

Introduction

In this chapter we will look at the financial support and benefit provisions that are available to help households who find it difficult to meet their housing expenses or who are in some other way 'at risk'. We will distinguish between the assistance given to tenants and that available to owner-occupiers. We will see that, while the support arrangements for renters and owners are quite different, when the current schemes for both these types of support were originally devised they shared a common operational rationale: that is, eligibility to both is determined by reference to a common poverty baseline.[1] This baseline is defined in terms of entitlement to income support (IS), jobseeker's allowance (JSA) or the pension credit (PC).[2] The point to be made is that these baseline allowances in IS/JSA/PC

---

1   Until April 2003 the method of establishing this baseline was common to the calculation of income support, income-based jobseeker's allowance (JSA-IB), housing benefit and council tax benefit. However with the introduction of the child tax credit, working tax credit, and from October 2003, pension credits, this common means of assessment has been disrupted. From April 2004 (after a transitional period) income support and JSA-IB no longer includes allowances for children; instead help is given through the new child tax credits which are ignored as income in the calculation of those benefits, whereas they continue to be included in the calculation of housing benefit and council tax benefit but child tax credit will count in full as income. Where the claimant qualifies for income support in their own right (i.e. ignoring their children) they are assessed as being entitled to the maximum rate of child tax credit. Further complications arose from the introduction of the pension credit in October 2003. The pension credit consists of two elements: the guarantee credit which replaces income support for the over 60s; and the savings credit, a new allowance designed to give credit for those with modest savings or other private income. The allowances in housing benefit are higher than the allowances for the guarantee credit to take account of the savings credit. In spite of these changes the basic principle holds true that those who receive income support or its replacement for pensioners, the guarantee credit, are assumed to have too low an income to be able to contribute towards their housing costs.
2   Throughout this chapter references to income support include references to income-based jobseeker's allowance and the guarantee credit of pension credit. For a short description of the differences between jobseeker's allowance (JSA) and income support see note 4 below. For a description of the pension credit see note 1 above and the main text.

---

are intended to help with general living expenses *excluding* those associated with housing. Assistance with housing-specific expenses is provided by housing benefit for those who rent and by income support for mortgage interest (ISMI), for those who own.

Over the years there has been a degree of confusion about how to finance housing-related support services provided for vulnerable groups such as the frail elderly and people with mental health problems. These arrangements have also recently been reformed and from April 2003 have been replaced by a new system of support known as 'Supporting People' which is described in outline later in this chapter.

The reader should be aware that much of the content of this chapter is necessarily technical and descriptive. What is more, many of the arrangements are currently under review. Those with a general interest in housing finance may find it helpful to concentrate on the 'overview' principles and to regard the detail as reference material. What follows is intended to provide both a description and an analysis of current arrangements that will provide a clear point of departure for those who wish to follow the unfolding debate about how best to support vulnerable people so that they can be secure and active citizens.

The system of housing benefit

The basics: an overview

Housing benefit provides weekly means-tested assistance to low-income households to help them pay their rent. It is a housing-tied social security payment that takes the form of a 'rebate' to council tenants and an 'allowance' to housing association and private tenants. It currently provides rebates for over 1.8 million council tenants and allowances for over 1.9 million housing association and private tenants. It should be thought of as a demand-side 'consumption' subsidy designed to augment the real incomes of eligible claimants so that they are able to acquire access to a form of housing that is deemed to be appropriate to their needs.

Housing benefit helps almost 3.8 million households in Great Britain meet the costs of renting their homes. The largest group of recipients is the elderly who account for over 40 per cent of the total. Lone parents and the long-term sick and disabled both account for around 20 per cent each of the total caseload. The remaining 15 per cent include: the unemployed, short-term sick, those in work on low incomes (other than lone parents), widows and widowers, and refugees. Given the prominence of the current debate about 'social exclusion', it is an important social fact that the majority of claimants are dependent upon other social security benefits for the main source of income. Nearly one-half of claimants live in council housing, just under one-third rent from a registered social landlord, and just under one-fifth rent from a private landlord.

Housing benefit provides a supplement to real income that is related to the claimant's actual or notional housing costs and which will meet some proportion (up to 100 per cent) of those costs. Rebates for council tenants are deducted from the rent bill whilst rent allowances to private tenants are normally made by cheque which can be paid to the tenant or direct to the landlord (the decision is normally the tenant's). For private sector or housing association rent allowance claims, the benefit is paid in arrears either to the claimant or directly to the landlord.[3] Although, broadly speaking, it is the size of the rent that determines the level of benefit, this can be reduced for rent allowance cases if either the rent or the accommodation is deemed to be excessive. However, from November 2003 a new system of housing benefit for private tenants in which the eligible costs are based on a locally-determined flat-rate allowance instead of the actual costs is being trialed in nine local authority 'pathfinder' areas.[4] Following the pathfinders it is intended that these reforms for the private sector tenants will be rolled-out nationally in 2007 or 2008 and will replace the current scheme based on actual costs. The government also intends to pilot[5] a flat-rate allowance scheme for social sector tenants in a number of authorities expected during 2006 or 2007. Further details of the workings of both these arrangements are given below but hereafter the current scheme based on actual costs will be referred to for convenience as 'the 1988 scheme'.

The principle of the 1988 scheme is that claimants who receive income support/ JSA /PC[6] or who have incomes that are lower than these benefits, are entitled,

---

3   From October 1996 housing benefit rent allowances are paid two weekly in arrears to the claimant or four weekly in arrears where payment is made direct to the landlord.

4   A further nine authorities will trial the new scheme in 2005 to test elements of its administration and provide an opportunity to 'adopt best practice in implementation before the system is introduced nationally' which is expected in 2007 or 2008.

5   The language is significant. A pathfinder implies that the reforms already have government approval and will eventually be rolled out once the best course to achieve this has been identified whereas a 'pilot' implies a more fundamental assessment of whether the idea should be adopted at all.

6   From October 1996 unemployment benefit and income support were replaced by the jobseeker's allowance (JSA). Unemployment benefit was a flat-rate payment paid on the basis of the claimant's national insurance record regardless of income whilst income support was a means-tested benefit paid to unemployed claimants if their income, including any unemployment benefit, was below the state minimum. These two benefits were merged in to JSA. Consequently there are two types of JSA, 'income based' for those with incomes that are lower than the income support level, and 'contributions based' for those who qualify for a flat-rate benefit payment based on their national insurance contributions regardless of income. The system works to define the qualifying poverty benchmark for those needing help because of unemployment on the same basis as income support claimants. This means that they receive the same amount of income augmentation and access to other underlying benefits including housing benefit as they would if they were on income support. The only practical difference is that claimants on JSA are required to actively seek work and if they fail to do so they suffer a loss of benefit. From October 2003 the pension credit replaces income support for persons aged at least 60 (see note 1 and main text for details). Throughout this chapter references to income support include entitlement to income-based jobseeker's allowance and the pension credit.

---

with certain exceptions, to assistance equivalent to a cash allowance that would cover the whole of their eligible rent. These claimants are also entitled to a rebate on up to 100 per cent of their council tax.[7] Where the claimant's total income is higher than their income support allowance the amount of benefit entitlement is reduced according to a formula, referred to as the 'taper'. The taper reduces the maximum benefit payable by a fixed percentage for every £1 of additional income over the income support level. Detailed calculations of housing benefit entitlement can be complex because the system deals with people in a wide variety of circumstances and housed in different sectors of rented housing.

Housing benefit is administered by those local authorities that have responsibilities for providing housing services – i.e. district, metropolitan, London borough, and unitary councils (see Chapter 8 for a brief description of the structure of local government). The cost, however, is met by central government via the Department for Work and Pensions (DWP).[8]

During the early 1990s DWP expenditure rocketed as government policy shifted its emphasis away from supply-side, general 'bricks-and-mortar' subsidies towards demand-side, targeted 'personal' assistance. DWP statistics show that between the time that the current arrangements were established in 1988 and the mid-1990s, the number of housing benefit claimants increased from four million to 4.7 million and expenditure ballooned from less than £4 billion to more than £11 billion (1996/97). More recently, though, expenditure has levelled off at about £12 billion and the number of claimants fallen back to 3.7 million (2003/04, figures for Great Britain).

The principle: satisfying merit needs

The main structure of the 1988 scheme was established following a series of reforms in the mid-1980s and is designed to help low-income households to consume an 'adequate' level of housing service. This minimum level of service can be thought of as a *merit need*. By this we mean that, for economic and humanitarian reasons, society has decided that a certain level of housing should be available to all irrespective of their ability to pay. The intention is that those whose incomes are too low to give them access to this minimum level should qualify for some form of assistance. Given its purpose, the following question of principle arises: 'Is housing benefit an aspect of housing finance or social security finance?'

---

7   The last Conservative Budget restricted council tax benefit so that claimants with property in bands F, G and H have their benefit restricted to that of band E, from April 1998. This was implemented by the in-coming Labour government but eventually abolished in April 2004.
8   Between 1990 and 2004 funding for expenditure on rent rebates was largely paid for by the ODPM (and its predecessors) as part of the overall HRA subsidy calculation (see note 27). Five per cent of the cost had to be met by local government itself although some account was taken of this in the calculation of its Revenue Support Grant.

Throughout this book we have made the point that the best way of appreciating the nature and scope of housing finance is to understand the purposes to which financial resources are put. These are summarised in simple diagrammatic form in Figure 2.1 (Chapter 2). Reference to this diagram indicates that, along with *provision* and *management*, *redistribution* might be considered to be one of the functions of the system of housing finance. However, it must be stressed that, unlike provision and management, redistribution should not be regarded as a primary function of the system. As the chapters so far have made clear, housing finance is primarily concerned with the provision and use of the capital and revenue resources that enable residential property to be produced and managed. Redistribution is concerned with income augmentation and, as such, is arguably more a matter of welfare policy than of housing finance. The main reason for redistributing real incomes is to help low-income households meet those financial outgoings that are necessary to enjoy some agreed minimum standard of housing provision.

Economists have developed the concept of merit needs to help explain why the state may intervene to provide certain goods and services directly or to redistribute disposable incomes so as to increase the consumption of certain goods and services provided by the market. It is argued that some things are so central to a civilised life or to the general national interest that, even if an unregulated free market system *could* provide them, the state *should* nevertheless involve itself to ensure that a sufficient quantity of an appropriate quality at an affordable price is, in fact, provided. In contemporary Britain, for example, there is a general consensus that education, medical treatment and shelter are so crucial to the maintenance of a worthwhile life and an effective economy, that all citizens, including those with little means, should have access to some minimum level of schooling, health care, and accommodation. Without state involvement there is no doubt that the market would provide facilities in these areas, but the problem is that such provision may not be sufficient to meet all needs, or be of an appropriate standard or type, or be in the right place, or be of a price that all in need could afford. In other words, without state involvement, it is likely that there would be a degree of *under-consumption* of these 'merit goods and services': under-consumption that is, in comparison with that which society regards as being necessary and appropriate for the needs of a modern, advanced economy.

The history: from 'discretionary rebates' to 'mandatory benefits'

For many years local authorities have had the power to implement rent rebate arrangements. The Housing Act 1930 empowered councils to remit the rents of their own poorer tenants but did not require them to do so or provide any Exchequer assistance. Therefore any authority exercising its power to provide rent rebates funded them by either: imposing higher rents on its better off tenants; using its general housing subsidy for that purpose; transferring monies from the rate fund, or by a combination of these methods.

The lack of funding together with the administrative complexity involved in operating a scheme meant that not many were established. Indeed, the very idea was unpopular with many councillors and better off tenants who feared that such schemes would attract the 'wrong type' of tenant onto their estates. After 1936, when each authority was required to operate a unified Housing Revenue Account, rent-pooling became practicable. For most authorities rent-pooling became the preferred way of providing affordable dwellings for poorer tenants.

Rent-pooling operated as an internal quasi-market and allowed housing managers to make use of the significant rent differentials that existed between newly-built dwellings with relatively high historic debt costs and older dwellings which were relatively low. It is important to understand that the differences in rents were primarily the result of differential historic costs rather than of differential utilities. That is, an older dwelling had a lower burden of debt but as a 'home' it would have functioned as adequately as a newer property. The existence of these differentials allowed the local authority landlord to allocate the older, cheaper stock to its poorer tenants without providing them with a significantly inferior home. In this way, allocating officers were able to give low-income households access to council housing without the provision of a scheme of rent rebates.

From the 1960s onwards, however, the arguments in favour of rebates began to gain prominence. Many Conservative politicians were ideologically opposed to *bricks-and-mortar* subsidies that produced housing at sub-market rents for everyone irrespective of need. Rather than provision in kind, they favoured welfare arrangements, such as rent rebates: they saw these as offering a way of raising rents towards market levels and, at the same time, targeting scarce public funds at those in greatest housing need. These ideas were increasingly articulated in Conservative party circles and they had a significant influence on the drafting of the bill that eventually became the Housing Finance Act 1972.

The 1972 legislation introduced into the public sector the concept of 'fair rents' together with a system of deficit subsidies and rent rebates and allowances. The legislation's intention was simultaneously to raise rents and reduce general housing subsidy. A national rent rebates scheme was introduced in recognition of the need to provide assistance to low-income tenants to help bridge the gap between 'fair rents' and their ability to pay them. As well as rebates to council tenants, authorities were required to set up rent allowance schemes for private sector and housing association tenants living in their areas. Running in parallel with these arrangements was a system of rate rebates, which was introduced by the Rating Act 1966, administered by the Department of Health and Social Security. The DHSS also provided a separate scheme for help with rent by including the whole of the charge in the calculation of entitlement to supplementary benefit, a claim for which disqualified the tenant from claiming a rent rebate/allowance under the local authority scheme. Since the method of calculating supplementary benefit was somewhat different from that for rent rebates, those who qualified for both had the problem of calculating which of the two generated, for them, the most assistance (the so-called 'better off problem').

In 1981, the Department of the Environment published a consultation paper[9] that pointed to the need to reform the entire system by creating a unified housing benefit to be administered by one authority. The administrative arrangements were made by the Social Security and Housing Benefits Act 1982, but a properly unified system was not introduced until 1988.

More radical reform came with the 1986 Social Security Act, the provisions of which were implemented in 1988 ('the 1988 scheme'). Along with housing benefit, the act introduced major reforms to all the main means-tested benefits. Supplementary benefit was replaced with income support and family income supplement was replaced with family credit, which was paid to families with children where one or both parents worked at least 16 hours a week. Family credit was designed to boost the income of families in low-paid employment up to a maximum amount which was dependant on family size, and was payable where the family income was no greater than a fixed threshold (£81.95, April 1999). If the income was more than this the maximum benefit was tapered away. However, for low-paid families in rented housing it was possible for the claimant to be entitled to both family credit and housing benefit, the former counting as income for the latter. The result was that over a range of income the tapers overlapped resulting in a very high overall rate of withdrawal. The high withdrawal rates acted as a severe work disincentive, something that the in-coming Labour government was determined to address as part of its welfare reform agenda.

The introduction of the community charge (poll tax) in 1990 saw the end of an integrated housing benefit that dealt with both rent and local tax. Community charge benefit was introduced as a separate benefit requiring a separate claim. When the community charge was replaced in 1993 by the council tax this split continued with community charge benefit being replaced with council tax benefit.[10]

Housing and other benefits under the Labour government

Reform was announced in the 1998 Budget, which resulted in more generous child allowances in income support, housing benefit and council tax benefit as well as the introduction of the working families' tax credit (WFTC) in 1999. WFTC was essentially a more generous version of family credit but was paid as an earned income tax credit, delivered through the income tax system. These changes were in line with the Labour government's philosophy of weakening the 'dependency culture' by linking, wherever possible, the receipt of benefit with employment.[11]

---

9   *Assistance with Housing Costs*, Department of Environment, 1981.
10   Community charge benefit was a separate benefit requiring, strictly, a separate claim although, in practice, authorities usually assessed both benefits from a single claim form. Technically, a claim for one was not a claim for the other. When council tax benefit replaced the community charge benefit, this arrangement continued.
11   Despite its attractiveness to ministers, the reform might be said to have the drawback of confusing the tax system, which is designed to collect revenue, with the welfare system, which is designed to disperse collected revenues to the less well off.

A further objective was to end the situation in which one department of state (the DWP) distributes support to people on low incomes whilst another (the Inland Revenue) charges taxes.

However, this new arrangement turned out to be only a step towards more radical reform. The Tax Credits Act 2002 (implemented in stages between 2003-05) marked the end of the unified structure of means-tested benefits created by the 1988 reforms, leaving only housing (and council tax benefit) intact. The Tax Credits Act was part of the Labour government's wider welfare reforms designed to reinforce the message that people under pension age should normally be expected to support themselves through work. The reforms were also intended to progress the government's target to abolish child poverty by 2020.

To achieve this all the various systems of means-tested support for children paid to parents whether unemployed or in work were combined into a single system of means-tested child support payable regardless of employment status – the child tax credit (CTC). Child tax credits combine all the child allowances previously available through the income tax system (including WFTC) with those from income support. From 2005 income support and jobseeker's allowance will take account only of the adults in the household while disregarding any income from child tax credits. Where the parent is entitled to income support/JSA/PC in their own right the maximum CTC is awarded.

To reinforce work incentives, the in-work (adult) elements previously payable through WFTC and disabled person's tax credit together with payments under the New Deal 50 plus programme (for people aged at least 50 starting back to work) were combined to form the new working tax credit (WTC). WTC will be payable to disabled workers and families with children working at least 16 hours a week or to others aged at least 25 working 30 hours or more.

Working families with children will be assessed for CTC and WTC together. The maximum amount of CTC and WTC payable is then tapered away as income rises above a set threshold; WTC is reduced first until none is payable, and then CTC. Where the parents are not in work, CTC is reduced at the same rate but starting at an income at which their entitlement to WTC would disappear if they were in work.

Although the new tax credits are modelled on their predecessors (WFTC and family credit) there are some important differences. These arise from the fact that they are (negative) payments of tax. Income is calculated gross annually (i.e. before tax and national insurance), based on income in the previous tax year, with items of income treated in the same way as they are for income tax. One result is that where the claimant has capital only the income generated from that capital will count. There is no longer a tariff income (see below) or absolute capital limit. Together these add up to a significant break from the 1988 scheme of means-tested benefits with a universal assessment of (weekly) income.

The new terminology, 'working tax credit', has been consciously thought through. It is symbolic of the government's political commitment to shift the poverty debate away from notions of *unemployment, dependency* and *benefit* towards notions of *work, independence* and *taxation*. It reflects a political consensus that relief from tax is more in line with a policy of 'welfare to work' than is the payment of benefits.

The new payments are also intentionally more generous. One of the calculated consequences is that tax credits will boost incomes to such an extent that most families will no longer qualify for housing benefit. The effect will be to 'float off' claimants from the worst excesses of the poverty trap which apply when the tapers from housing, family and in-work benefits overlap resulting in very high marginal rates of withdrawal (see later in this chapter).

The workings of the housing benefit scheme

Claiming housing benefit

Under current arrangements, housing benefit can be claimed in one of two ways, depending on whether or not the applicant is in receipt of income support /JSA/ PC. Entitlement to one of these benefits establishes an official definition of 'poverty' and, in so doing, sets a minimum baseline that is used to administer a range of entitlements including housing benefit. Where claimants receive income support they may qualify for full housing benefit and in such cases the appropriate DWP office notifies the local authority, who arrange to pay housing benefit from the date income support commences. Claimants not in receipt of income support have to apply directly to their local authority that then calculates the amount of housing benefit to which they are entitled. Payments cannot predate the application unless 'good cause' can be shown as to why the claim was not made earlier.[12]

Determining eligibility

From their inception in the Tudor period, all poverty relief measures have had to address the issue of eligibility. Eligibility has always been tested against qualifying criteria relating to residency, need, and income.[13]

---

12 The 'good cause' must have lasted throughout the relevant period. For a comprehensive explanation as to what is accepted as a good cause see *Claim in Time: Time Limits in Social Security Law*, Third Edition, Martin Partington, LAG, 1994.

13 Early Poor Law rules were designed to restrict relief to the 'deserving poor' of the parish. In the Victorian period, all but the destitute were discouraged from claiming help by restricting relief for able-bodied people to a place in a harsh and stigmatising parish workhouse. After the Second World War, the responsibility for provision moved from the parish to the welfare state and, as a result, national rather than local residency qualifications were applied. The welfare state culture also brought with it an attitude shift away from the idea that benefits are a form of charity for the deserving poor, towards the idea that they are a form of social security entitlement, available to all citizens if and when they need it.

Claimants with the appropriate residency qualifications will have their entitlement calculated against criteria that are guided by notions of *reasonableness* and *appropriateness*. These criteria are translated into rather complex, and constantly changing, regulations that are designed to prevent landlords exploiting the system by charging 'excessive' rents and claimants from exploiting the system by living in accommodation that is 'unnecessarily' lavish and expensive.

In this context, 'reasonableness' is judged by considering whether or not the rents they are seeking help with are reasonable when compared with local rent levels. If the claimant is a council or housing association tenant the rent is normally accepted as being reasonable.[14] The eligible rent establishes the maximum amount of benefit that can be paid. What proportion of this maximum is judged to be appropriate for the claimant to receive will depend on the household's circumstances. These circumstances are judged by reference to household needs, income and savings.

Reasonableness and eligible rent

Housing benefit is paid on the *eligible rent*, which may well differ from the actual rent charged by the landlord. Eligible rent comprises the basic rent for the dwelling together with service charges which, from April 2003, are only eligible if they relate to: the landlord's furniture, services in communal areas or maintaining the fabric of the dwelling. From April 2003 government assistance with other housing-related support charges is provided through the 'Supporting People' programme (see below).

Unreasonable or 'excessive' rents are not supported by the scheme. The eligible rent has to be 'reasonable' in comparison with local rent levels and housing benefit will not contribute to any part of rent that is judged to be significantly in excess of what would be expected in an open market. It is possible for a particular asking rent to be judged unreasonable even though it is well below the average: for example, if the dwelling was in a very poor state of repair or yet to be modernised with no bathroom. In addition, although the rent may be at the market rate, it may nevertheless be exceptionally high because the property is of a luxury standard at the top end of the market, in which case it will also be deemed unreasonable and benefit will be restricted.

Appropriateness and eligible rent

The rent also has to be 'appropriate' to the particular circumstances of the claimant to be eligible. The size of the dwelling is seen as a relevant criterion for

---

14 The benefit authority must refer a housing association rent to the rent officer if they consider the rent to be unreasonably high or the property unreasonably large for the claimant's household. In practice it is rare for authorities to conclude that the size or rent of the property is unreasonable. In cases where a referral is made the rent officer's assessment will be binding – see main text below for how these are calculated. In theory a council rent can be restricted if it is unreasonable but in practice this never happens.

all claims referred to the rent officer. Where a family is deemed to be over-accommodated the rent officer will set a notional market rent for accommodation which would be of the appropriate size, known as a size-related rent. Together with the restrictions as to whether the rent is judged unreasonable or excessive, these valuations constitute what is known as the claim-related rent.

The rules about what is judged to be appropriate do not just take account of whether the claimant is over-accommodated. They also imply a judgement about what range of the market of appropriately-sized accommodation it is appropriate for the state to cover for people claiming benefit. These rules were first introduced in January 1996 as part of a series of changes attempting to stem the growing housing benefit bill. The objective was to create an incentive for claimants to seek out and negotiate less expensive accommodation which meets their requirements, for example by accepting a two bedroom flat instead of a house, or a property in a less popular area.

Under this arrangement, in addition to assessing the market rents for individual properties and any size-related rent, The Rent Service[15] has to advise the local authority of the *local reference rent* (LRR) if the actual rent is higher. The LRR represents the maximum rent that can be covered by benefit. It is calculated as the mid-point of a range of rents charged for dwellings in a locality which are both reasonable and of the appropriate size. In other words, since 1996, housing benefit is granted in full (100 per cent of rent) only up to a median market average[16] for an appropriately-sized dwelling in the locality.

These rules are particularly stringent with respect to young, single people. From October 1996 the regulations were further tightened to assume that young, single people only need to occupy bed-sit accommodation. These rules mean that, for the under 25s, the maximum rent is restricted to a figure that equates to the mid-point of the range of normal market rents for shared accommodation (i.e. with separate bedroom and shared kitchen/ bathroom) – known as the *single room rent* (SRR). In effect this means that the government now regards a 'bed-sit' rent as the limit of support that it is reasonable to give to young people, although the rule was slightly relaxed from July 2001 to include rooms in a shared house. Further benefit restrictions apply to 16 and 17 year olds who, whilst entitled to housing

---

15 The Rent Service, formerly the Rent Officer Service, was established as an Executive Agency of the Department of the Environment, Transport and the Regions (now ODPM) in 1999. The service only operates in England. In Scotland and Wales the work of rent officers is a function of the civil service in their respective devolved administrations. In all cases rent officers have independent statutory status.

16 The LRR equates to the 'trimmed' median average: that is, the mid-point of an 'appropriate' spread of rents for that property type ignoring any exceptionally high or low rents. For example, in some areas there may be a relatively large number of luxurious dwellings let to wealthy people for very high rents. In such circumstances a trimmed rather than a true average is used to fix the LRR.

benefit on the same terms as others aged under 25, can only claim income support or jobseeker's allowance whilst out of work in very limited circumstances.[17]

There is evidence that these rules have caused a shortage of accommodation for this age group as some landlords now discriminate against the under 25s.[18] Critics argue that this restriction, together with the rules for jobseeker's allowance, aggravate problems of homelessness, child prostitution, and drug abuse, and is encouraging begging on the streets. The 1996 Budget proposed to extend the SRR to all single claimants under the age of 60.[19] However, the idea was abandoned by the in-coming Labour government in 1997.

The maximum rent rule

We have seen that eligible rent is restricted to what is reasonable and appropriate and that where rent fails any of these tests the rent officer will make a valuation which will restrict the rent. It is important to understand that for a particular claim a rent may fail more than one test and in this case the eligible rent will be restricted to the lowest of all the rent officer valuations (whether this is the local reference rent or otherwise). In addition, in spite of any rent officer restriction, the authority has discretionary powers to restrict the rent still further.

The overall effect of all of these rules is that housing benefit may well not cover the actual rent so that for some households the assistance does not meet their full rent outgoings even if they are on income support. It should be noted, however, that claimants whose rents are restricted may be eligible for help to meet any shortfall through the separate, cash-limited, discretionary housing payments scheme.

Appropriateness and income

In addition to the rules about whether the rent is appropriate, the amount of benefit paid also has to be judged appropriate by reference to what the claimant can afford to contribute towards the rent. To determine this, an assessment is made of the income needed by the household to meet their (assumed) basic living expenses (i.e. non-housing costs) and this is compared with the household's assessed

---

17 The change disqualifying most 16 and 17 year olds from income support was introduced in September 1988. In October 1996 on the introduction of JSA, the rules were consolidated and re-codified for the unemployed. Some in this age group can still qualify, but not those, generally, who just leave school without a job. Those with physical impairments or who are estranged from their parents whilst completing their secondary education, are two examples of those who still qualify.

18 DETR (1999) *Housing Benefit and the Private Rented Sector*, p72.

19 Among others, this reform would have affected the consumption interests of that growing group of people whose marriages have broken down. Although it would not have applied to an individual who is a lone parent, it would have affected the entitlement of some quarter of a million claimants.

income. The assumed level of basic living expenses varies according to household size, together with any qualifying special needs, and is called 'the applicable amount'. The applicable amount varies according to whether the claimant is single, part of a couple or a lone parent, together with allowances for each child. Additional allowances apply if the tenant or their partner is: aged 60 or over, disabled or a carer, and for each disabled child in the household. Where the claimant is single a lower rate of allowance applies if they are aged under 25.

The applicable amount is compared with the household's assessed income to determine the amount it is considered reasonable for that family to contribute towards the rent. The family's appropriate contribution is determined by a fixed percentage of their income that is in excess of their assumed basic living expenses (i.e. non-housing needs) – their applicable amount. Ordinarily, the benefit payable will simply be their maximum rent less their assessed contribution. However, where there are other adults in the household excluding the claimant's dependants, such as their adult children, it is assumed that they will be contributing to the rent.

Anyone regarded as a member of the household who is not the claimant's partner or a dependant child will be a *'non-dependant'*. In such cases 'non-dependant charges' are deducted from the claimant's maximum rent. Deductions are made on the basis of a sliding scale[20] except in certain circumstances, e.g. where the claimant is blind. The total deductions may be sufficiently high so as to wipe out the claimant's entitlement to benefit completely. All benefit will be lost, even if the claimant's income is assessed as being insufficient to contribute to the rent, if the total non-dependant charges exceed the maximum rent. Obviously these deductions result in considerable savings to the Exchequer. Throughout the 1990s when benefit expenditure was increasing rapidly, the temptation for government to increase these charges each year by more than inflation proved irresistible. These rules only apply to household members. Special rules cover multiple households living in the same property such as boarders, sub-tenants, and others who pay their rent separately.

If any rent remains after non-dependant charges have been deducted from the maximum rent, an assessment is made of the claimant's ability to make a contribution towards the remainder. To assess the claimant's contribution a comparison is made between the income they require to cover their non-housing costs, their applicable amount, and their actual income. If their assessed income is less than or equal to their applicable amount then they are deemed to have insufficient income to be able to contribute and so will receive the *maximum benefit* (i.e. the maximum rent less any non-dependant charges). If the claimant's income assessment exceeds their applicable amount their maximum benefit is progressively reduced. In other words, the higher the household's income, the lower its award.

---

20   The amount currently deducted varies from £7.40 a week to £47.75 a week for a non-dependant earning £322 per week or more (2005/06).

Income support, income-based JSA and pension credit claimants paid the guarantee element. Claimants in receipt of these benefits are assumed to have no income (i.e. zero). The result is that their assessed income will always be less than their applicable amount, automatically qualifying them to maximum benefit. The means-test is carried out by the DWP when the claim is made for the income support/JSA/ pension credit, since these benefits are themselves means-tested. All other claimants not entitled to these benefits have their means-test carried out by the local authority. The point we need to emphasise here is that income support is not intended to cover outgoings related to rent or council tax charges. The need for *income support/JSA* provides access to further benefits related to these outgoings. These parallel benefits are *housing benefit* and *council tax benefit* administered by local councils.

All other claimants except those awarded pension credit. For claimants who do not receive income support an assessment is made of their capital and income which is available to contribute towards their rent. This assessment takes the form of a means-test carried out through the application form. If the claimant's weekly disposable income is equal to, or less than, the eligible costs, they will receive the maximum benefit, i.e. the maximum rent less any non-dependant charges.

Claimants with capital (which includes savings) are assessed by reference to upper and lower limits. Where the value of the capital is more than the upper limit (currently £16,000) they are not entitled to housing benefit. Capital is valued the same way as for income support.[21] Capital valued at less than the lower limit (currently £6,000 for claimants aged at least 60 or £3,000 in any other case) is disregarded. All income earned by that capital and savings is also disregarded; however, each block of capital between the lower and upper limits is assumed to produce a nominal £1 per week which is carried forward to the income assessment. A block is each £500 (or any remainder) of capital where the claimant is aged at least 60, or £250 in any other case. This assumed income is known as the tariff. From April 2006 the lower capital limit and the tariff for claimants aged under 60 will be aligned with those for people aged 60 and over.

The income assessment includes net earnings from employment, other benefit entitlements (including pensions) and other unearned income, including any tariff from capital. Earned income is assessed on the aggregated earnings of the claimant and partner net of income tax, national insurance and half of any contributions made to a pension scheme. To give some incentive to work a (small) fixed amount of the net earnings is ignored; this is referred to as the 'earnings disregard'. The current earnings disregard is £5 a week for single people and somewhat more for

---

21 However, for working age claimants claiming income support or income-based JSA the savings limit is £8,000 rather than £16,000. Working age claimants with savings between £8,000 and £16,000 have to apply directly to the local authority. There is no upper savings limit for pension credit claimants who qualify for the guarantee credit who will be entitled to the maximum housing benefit. Pension credit claimants who qualify for the savings credit only (without the guarantee credit) are still subject to the upper capital limit of £16,000 and a tariff on savings between £6,000 and £16,000. This mismatch in the capital rules results in an anomaly sometimes referred to as 'the cliff face' (see main text).

other categories of claimant.[22] In certain circumstances further disregards apply if the claimant works at least 30 hours per week or where by taking work the claimant cannot avoid incurring childcare costs.[23] Most unearned income, including income from other social security benefits, counts in full.[24]

If the claimant's income, including any tariff from capital, exceeds their applicable amount, then their maximum benefit is progressively reduced at a rate of 65p for each £1 of income in excess of the applicable amount (65 per cent). So for example, if a claimant were paying rent at £70 per week, and his or her income exceeded the applicable amount by £20, the housing benefit payable would be £57, after a deduction of £13 had been made, representing 65 per cent of the £20 excess. If income exceeded the allowance by £110, this would be the point when no benefit would be paid, as the 65 per cent deduction exceeds the rent level itself. These deductions, called the taper, are akin to a high marginal rate of income tax and, as such, create a problem referred to as the 'poverty trap' (see below).

Calculating entitlement: Housing benefit and the pension credit

Since the 1998 Budget the government has been pursuing a strategy of targeting benefit increases on families and pensioners. More recently this has been reflected in changes in administration designed to meet the different needs of working age claimants and those who have retired. In effect the administration of all DWP benefits has been split into two halves: the 'Jobcentre Plus' which acts as the claim gateway for people of working age, and the Pensions Service for others.

The first stage in this strategy was to up-rate the income support allowances for claimants aged 60 and over in line with increases in earnings (or with prices if higher). The effect is that over time the income support level ratcheted up at a greater rate than state pensions. Since income support is used to calculate housing benefit needs, the levels are reflected in the housing benefit allowances. In the second stage, from April 2001 the government doubled the lower capital threshold for means-tested benefits from £3,000 to £6,000 for persons aged over 60.

Finally, from October 2003, they introduced the pension credit, a new means-tested benefit to top up the state pension. The pension credit is made up of two elements: the guarantee credit and the savings credit. The guarantee credit simply replaces income support for people aged 60 or over but with changes to rules

---

22 Earned income disregards are £25 for lone parents, £20 for the disabled and carers and £10 for a couple.

23 Some claimants can claim what is known as 'the child care disregard'. Working lone parents or couples where both are working at least 16 hours, and paying for child care, are able to have those child care costs deducted (up to a maximum amount) from their earned income (including any working tax credit). The 30 hours work disregard (worth £14.50 in 2005/06) and childcare disregard are both in addition to the standard disregard.

24 The main exception being attendance allowance and disability living allowance which are fully disregarded. The first £10 of any war pension and £15 of maintenance received from a former partner are also disregarded.

about the treatment of capital. First, the tariff rate was halved from £1 for each £250 capital to £1 for each £500. Second, the upper savings limit was lifted completely. The first of these changes was mirrored in the housing benefit calculation whilst the second was not. This has resulted in an anomaly whereby a claimant entitled to the guarantee credit with over £16,000 capital will receive the maximum housing benefit, whereas a claimant with a similar amount of savings but with a slightly higher income such that they do not qualify for any guarantee credit will be disqualified altogether. This anomaly has been called the 'cliff face' and introduces a new benefit trap.

The savings credit is a completely novel innovation in the benefits system. It rewards claimants aged 65+ who have accumulated an income from pension(s) (including additional state pension) or capital (based on the tariff) which is greater than the basic state pension. Any additional income will accumulate a credit at a rate of 60p for each £1 of income above the basic state pension up to a maximum level when the claimant's income is equal to the guarantee credit.[25] Where the claimant's total income from their pensions is above the guarantee credit any accumulated credit will taper away at a rate of 40p for each £1 in excess. To ensure that all claimants entitled to the savings credit gained by its full value when it was introduced, the housing benefit allowances for all claimants aged over 65 were increased by the amount of the maximum award of savings credit. Where the claimant is entitled to the savings credit the local authority is obliged to use the Pensions Service assessment of income and capital in the calculation of housing benefit.[26]

The cumulative effect of these changes is in effect to produce two different versions of housing benefit – one for people of working age and another (more generous) version for pensioners.

Issues about housing benefit

The 'poverty trap'

All means-tested benefits tend to create a *poverty trap* when entitlement is withdrawn as earnings increase. The withdrawal acts as a disincentive to seek work-related advancement. The *real income effect* of an increase in earned income is diminished by a combination of deductions and withdrawals. The deductions

---

25 At its introduction in October 2003 the maximum amount of savings credit was £14.79 for a single person and £19.20 for a couple. These relatively modest amounts are expected to be ratcheted up over time since the amount depends upon the difference between the basic state pension and the basic pension credit guarantee (i.e. the income support level for pensioners). The Labour government has a policy of increasing the pension guarantee by earnings instead of general prices (as used for the basic state pension). As earnings rise faster the difference between the pension guarantee and the state pension will also grow faster than prices resulting in a jacking up of the maximum over time.

26 Although certain adjustments are made to these figures, most notably the amount of the savings credit itself is included as income.

include income tax and national insurance contributions. The withdrawals include working tax credit or child tax credit, housing benefit, and council tax benefit.[27]

The statutory deductions, combined with the tapering off of benefit entitlements, create the so-called 'poverty trap' by diminishing the effect of any increases in earned income. The loss of benefit resulting from the withdrawal acts as a kind of 'poor person's income tax' and is pernicious insofar as the overall marginal 'withdrawal rate' is high in comparison with the real income tax rates of average and high earners. In the extreme case, the overall rate of withdrawal is as high as 95.5 per cent resulting in net real income of only 4.5p for every extra £1 earned from work.

However, following the introduction of working families tax credit in 1999 the number of households caught in this deep trap[28] fell significantly since the income of most working families was boosted to such an extent that they were beyond the reach of housing benefit altogether (often referred to as being 'floated off').[29] Floating off reduces the overall rate of withdrawal since only one taper applies. This policy was deliberate and was carried forward in the tax credit reforms of 2003. One other option would have been to reduce the housing benefit taper, but over the range of incomes where the tapers from other benefits overlap, a relatively large reduction in the housing benefit taper would have only a very small effect on the overall rate of withdrawal. The main beneficiaries of such an approach would be non-working households with only a very small incentive effect for those in work. The alternative would be to include a housing costs element within the calculation of the tax credit, instead of housing benefit, avoiding an overlapping taper altogether. The only problem with this approach is finding a satisfactory method of calculating housing costs which reflects local circumstances but which is convenient and simple enough for administrators to use on a national basis (tax credits being administered nationally rather than locally). This problem would be easier to resolve if the reforms from the pathfinder scheme to pay housing benefit on a flat-rate allowance were carried forward (see below).

---

27 The housing benefit taper is set at 65 per cent of marginal net income in 1998 and the council tax benefit taper at 20 per cent, giving a combined withdrawal effect of 85p for every £1 earned above the applicable amount.

28 Academics often refer to the 'depth' and 'width' of a trap. A deep trap is one with a very high rate of withdrawal. The width is the range of incomes over which the withdrawal applies. An intractable problem is the appropriate balance between the two: reducing the depth (i.e. steepness of the taper) will inevitably be at the expense of extending its width and vice-versa.

29 Prior to the introduction of WFTC, the number of families facing the highest marginal rates in excess of 90 per cent where withdrawals from tax, national insurance, WFTC, housing benefit and council tax benefit ran concurrently, was estimated to be 130,000; whereas after the reforms it was expected to apply to just 20,000. Likewise the numbers facing marginal rates in excess of 70 per cent fell from 740,000 to 260,000. However, this was inevitably at the expense of extending the numbers of households facing at least some benefit withdrawal. The reduced depth has been at the expense of increasing the width (see note 28) in the 60 per cent plus range. HM Treasury Pre-Budget Report 1998: *The Modernisation of Britain's Tax and Benefit System*, Number 3, p16.

In addition to the poverty trap the additional costs associated with moving off benefit and into work produce further disincentives. In an attempt to lessen the disincentive effect, extended payments were introduced in 1996 whereby housing benefit (and council tax benefit) continues to be paid at the same rate during the first four weeks of work. This effectively eases the transition into employment by smoothing over the gap created by payment of wages or salary in arrears. It also guards against interruptions in benefit should the job fall through for some reason. The qualifying rules have since been extended to include long-term sick or disabled people starting work after a period of incapacity for work through sickness or disability, and lone parents as well as unemployed claimants 'signing on'. The rules were also relaxed to make it easier to start work by avoiding the need for a separate claim. As an additional incentive to encourage lone parents back into employment they are also entitled to two weeks' income support when starting work.

Housing benefit and public expenditure

Although reasonableness and appropriateness are meant to be the underlying principles of the assessment regulations, it is clear that many of the eligibility restrictions have been partly motivated by the Treasury's desire to cap the growing bill for housing benefit.[30]

The cost of housing benefit falls on the Exchequer. Expenditure on rent allowances is reimbursed at 100 per cent by central government in the form of subsidy. The administration costs, as against the benefit payments, are reimbursed partly in the form of a specific grant.[31] Central government can penalise authorities deemed to be operating the system in a way that is judged to be inefficient by limiting or withdrawing grant.

Housing benefit, because it can offer tenants' greater purchasing power in the rented housing market, will widen choice and stimulate consumption. In the late 1980s ministers seemed enthusiastic to push the rents for social housing upwards towards market levels (see discussions in Chapters 4 and 12). At that time around one-third of tenants in social housing were on income support and entitled to maximum housing benefit whilst two-thirds of social housing tenants[32] received

---

30 Social security expenditure dwarfs all other expenditure categories. This means that it is always under pressure to be controlled. In particular, governments always have an eye on the fastest rising item within the social security budget at any one time. Hence, state pension reforms in the 1980s, housing benefit in the mid-1990s, and disability benefits in the late 1990s.

31 Since April 2004, subsidy for rent rebates is no longer part of HRA subsidy, as it was before in England and Wales (see Chapter 12).

32 The current proportions are that around two-fifths of social sector tenants are on income support while three-fifths receive some amount of benefit. The lower proportion receiving any benefit probably reflects the numbers of working claimants who have been floated off by tax credits.

some level of housing benefit. In 1989-90 the cost of this support was £4.24 billion. The government realised that their social sector housing finance reforms together with private rented sector rent deregulation would result in higher rents but they argued that tenants on low income would be protected by housing benefit. Their justification was that switching subsidies from bricks-and-mortar to people would be more efficient because resources would be better targeted on those who really needed them.

The higher rents in all sectors were brought in on the back of housing benefit. By the mid-1990s, the annual bill for housing benefit had topped £10 billion, or 12 per cent of the social security budget. It was estimated that, if the system were not revised, then this would rise to 15 per cent by 1998. Eventually, the growing benefit bill brought about a change in government thinking. As the Conservative government's housing reforms added more and more to the consumption costs of social housing, the assumption that housing benefit should 'take the strain' was challenged. In 1994, the Department of Environment's chief economist, Norman Glass told the Harry Simpson lecture that *'there is now a real issue about how much further the process of reducing the disparity between social rents and market rents should continue'*.[33] This statement signalled a change in policy (see Chapters 12 and 14).

It was clear that the savings made by cutting capital grants had brought about higher demands on social security expenditure. In any one year, the cuts in general housing grant were more than the additional benefit paid out, bringing a net saving to the Exchequer. However, while the cutting of a capital grant represents a one-off saving, the resultant addition to revenue expenditure is re-occurring and there comes a point at which the accumulated revenue costs outweigh the initial capital savings, so that over time the policy adds to public expenditure. There was a failure to calculate the displacement costs from one department of state to another and to calculate the longer-term revenue consequences of short-run capital cuts. Such a policy might be termed disconnected short-termism. It is a basic principle of financial management that current capital decisions have future revenue consequences (refer to Chapter 1).

By the mid-1990s the additional expenditure on housing benefit led the government to change its housing policy in two ways. First, it relaxed its ideological commitment to put upward pressure on social housing rent levels. Second, it began to bring in measures to restrict the eligibility criteria for housing benefit claimants. In 1994 the chancellor announced plans to introduce a cap on the rents eligible for housing benefit in an attempt to control its burgeoning cost to the Exchequer. This and other measures designed to limit eligibility to benefit were described above.

The Labour government's Comprehensive Spending Review sought to address the question of disconnected short-termism by requiring the various spending

---

33   Reported in *Roof*, Nov/Dec 1994, p22.

departments to cross-reference the revenue consequences of their spending plans. However, interrelated problems of social security have proved to be particularly complicated, and were not resolved by the time the review was published in the summer of 1998.

Housing benefit and devolution

Unlike housing policy in general, responsibility for housing benefit remains UK-wide and is determined in Whitehall. (Strictly speaking, the Northern Ireland administration has a measure of autonomy over benefit policy, but in practice it maintains a scheme which is essentially the same as that for the rest of Britain.) This inconsistency has not so far been of tremendous importance. But as will be explained, the government is now developing new approaches to housing benefit which relate closely to its policies on rents. Rents policy is a devolved matter. Not only that, but in Scotland especially social sector landlords have regarded it as a local matter and rents vary widely. As explained in Chapter 12, while there is an overall 'affordability' policy applying to Scottish social sector rents, there are not the same enforcement mechanisms that apply in England and Wales.

Changes to housing benefit policy tend to be influenced strongly by English housing policy, particularly in the social sector. But more far reaching reforms, now being developed, could have radically different effects in the devolved administrations, and particularly in Scotland.[34]

The pressure for more radical reforms

As we have seen, the frequent changes made to housing benefit during the 1990s tended to be ad hoc and motivated by the aim of controlling the growth in expenditure. The almost constant stream of changes piled complexity onto an already complex scheme making it increasingly *'difficult to administer to acceptable standards'*.[35] By the end of the decade there was a consensus in the social housing movement that simplification and help to authorities to improve administration were the most urgent priorities for reform.[36]

By 1999 housing benefit cost the Exchequer over £11 billion per year, £750 million of which was estimated to be lost through fraud and error. Given the scale of this expenditure together with the breakdown in administration it was an obvious target for reform. Government proposals for major structural change were

---

34 For fuller development of this argument see Wilcox, S. (2002) 'Border Tensions: devolution, rents and housing benefit' in Wilcox, S., *UK Housing Review 2002/03*, CIH/CML, Coventry and London.

35 House of Commons Social Security Committee Sixth Report: *Housing Benefit*. Volume I paragraph 25. HC 385-I (2000).

36 *The Crisis in Housing Benefit and how to respond to it*. CIH Briefing paper, November 2000.

---

first floated in the 2000 housing green paper. In the same year, the report of the parliamentary Social Security Committee provided further weight to these arguments and highlighted the need for simplification to aid the failing administration.

Both publications discussed the merits of basing the payment of benefit on the full rent, a feature that is almost unique to the British social security system and one which had been subject to much academic criticism. It is argued that the structure of the 1988 scheme provides no incentive for the tenant to take an interest in their rent, since any increase in rent will be matched by a corresponding increase in benefit, leaving the tenant with no extra to pay. Consequently, there is no incentive to shop around for accommodation that is more reasonably priced or which more closely matches their needs. Some also argued the lack of incentive is exacerbated by the normal method of payment which is direct to the landlord. The result is often a belief that many tenants on benefit do not pay rent and that responsibility for the transaction is purely a matter between the benefit administrators and the landlord.

Amongst the reform options discussed in the green paper to tackle these problems the one most favoured by academics and housing experts was that benefit should only be paid on a fixed proportion of the rent, say 80 per cent, leaving the tenant to pay the rest out of their own pocket. Tenants on low incomes would be compensated by including a fixed allowance in their income support based on 20 per cent of average rent levels, maintaining the incentive to shop around for more reasonably priced accommodation, thereby saving money from the public purse. The presumption that benefit would be paid to the landlord would also be reversed to help reinforce the tenant's responsibility for the rent.[37]

The government published its proposals for reform in November 2002 in its paper *Building Choice and responsibility: a radical agenda for housing benefit,* the contents of which were decidedly more radical than those of the green paper. They proposed the end of direct payments to landlords,[38] but instead of benefit being based on the actual rent as in the existing (1988) scheme or a fixed proportion of it as favoured in the green paper, it proposed that it would be based on a locally-determined flat-rate allowance, to be known as the 'local housing allowance'. Both of these proposals were to be demonstrated in a number of 'pathfinder' areas for private rented sector tenants only but with the intention to pilot[39] a parallel scheme for social sector tenants as soon as 'conditions allow'.

---

37   The arguments are set out fully in Kemp, P. (2000) *Shopping Incentives and Housing Benefit Reform*, CIH/JRF, Coventry.

38   Direct payments would still be available where the claimant is on direct payments of income support for rent arrears or where the authority considers that either: the claimant 'will have difficulty managing his affairs' or 'it is improbable that they will pay their rent'.

39   The distinction between a 'pilot' and a 'pathfinder' is important. A pathfinder implies that the government is committed to the principle and will roll-out the policy once the best way of implementing it has been found. A pilot is a more fundamental appraisal which includes the possibility that the policy will be abandoned if it proves unworkable.

Between November 2003 and February 2004 nine local authority pathfinder projects were established to trial a flat-rate allowance for private rented sector claims. A further nine were added between April and July 2005. In these areas, the flat-rate allowance is based on the local reference rent for an appropriately-sized dwelling but with the modification that the localities used and the levels of rent for each size of dwelling will be published by The Rent Service in advance. Those whose rents are currently restricted to a level below the local reference rent will gain while all others will continue to be paid at the same rate (because their rents would be restricted to the local reference rent in any case). The pathfinders are likely to run for two years and the results will be evaluated. Following evaluation and after refinements from any lessons learned it is expected that these reforms for private rented sector claims will be rolled-out nationally in 2007 or 2008.

At the time of writing it is too early to draw any conclusions as to the behavioural effects but critics have suggested that the end of direct payments will result in an increase in rent arrears and that landlords will simply raise their rents to the level of the flat-rate allowance. Others have claimed that tenants will 'down-market' and become concentrated in the poorest accommodation in overcrowded conditions so that they can pocket the excess allowance, allowing money intended for housing to leak away.

A number of social sector pilots are expected to commence sometime in 2006 or 2007. The pilots are likely to be selected from those authorities where local conditions are such that rent convergence resulting from the rent restructuring programme (Chapter 12) will be met early. The exact details of the social sector local housing allowance are yet to be determined but it is most likely to be based on the mid-point of (restructured) social sector rents for an appropriately-sized dwelling. Undoubtedly one effect will be to make tenants on benefit more price conscious than under the existing scheme in which the whole of any additional marginal cost of more expensive (and popular) housing is met by benefit. It may also provide an incentive for the more efficient use of stock.

The social sector pilots will also be evaluated and if judged to be a success the reforms will be rolled-out nationally, although this may not be possible until rent restructuring is complete. Following rent restructuring, it is likely that controls on rents will be lifted. However, given that two-thirds of social sector tenants are on benefit, landlords will be reluctant to increase rents at a rate faster than any rise in the local housing allowance. In effect the control mechanism for rents will be through the housing benefit system. Therefore the mechanism by which the local housing allowance is up-rated post rent restructuring will be crucial. One option is through an inflation-based formula. The attractiveness to the Treasury of such an approach is adopted is obvious – the housing benefit budget will no longer be driven by rent inflation making planning for future expenditure more predictable. Overall government spending on housing benefit will become more like a fixed budget than a purely demand-led programme.

Arguably the introduction of a flat-rate allowance may assist the introduction of a universal housing allowance covering all tenures. A housing allowance based on actual costs would subsidise those on high incomes if their housing costs were correspondingly high; whereas a flat-rate allowance automatically disqualifies unreasonable costs thus avoiding the possibility that it would be payable at unacceptably high levels of income and so controlling expenditure. It would also make it easier to administer the benefit centrally, allowing the reform to be accommodated within the system of tax credits. Including a housing costs element within the tax credit calculation would also avoid the problem of very high marginal tax rates which apply when housing benefit and tax credits are withdrawn concurrently – thus improving work incentives. However, there may still be a need for a separate, residual housing allowance scheme – similar to housing benefit – for those who are unable to work or who have retired.

Funding support services and Supporting People

Since the growth of the housing association movement in the mid-1960s social landlords have concentrated a significant proportion of their resources on the development of 'sheltered housing' and other innovative forms of provision to provide for the 'special needs' of a wide range of vulnerable people. Such schemes often provide support services as an integral part of the accommodation package. The range of provision includes such groups as the frail elderly, those with mental health problems, ex-offenders, the young 'at risk', homeless, victims of domestic violence, and those recovering from drug addiction, all of whom require support in order to be able to sustain their tenancy, foster independent living and maintain a reasonable quality of life. The support services vary in scope and intensity and include general counselling and advice, assistance with administrative affairs, services provided by wardens, life skills coaching and liaison work with other agencies and individuals responsible for the person's welfare.

One particularly difficult problem for administrators of housing benefit was the lack of clarity about the extent to which service charges for such housing-related support could be met by benefit. In August 1997 a crisis was precipitated by a series of high profile court cases which disqualified nearly all support charges from being covered by housing benefit. The court's decision put under threat the viability of many supported housing projects. The government acted quickly to introduce temporary regulations which reversed the court's ruling for existing projects while it conducted a review of the funding arrangements for supported housing.

The conclusions of the review and the government's proposals for reform were published in late 1998. Following a period of consultation the government announced that it would introduce a new system of funding support services –

known as 'Supporting People' – from April 2003. In working towards the new arrangements for a transitional period from 2000 to 2003 the housing benefit regulations were amended to make clear that support charges were to be allowed but would have to be separately identified and accounted for from the rest of the rent. The separate accounting would allow the government to calculate how much money would be needed to be transferred to the new Supporting People pot in April 2003, to ensure that existing levels of service could be maintained.

In addition to service charge income, costs were also paid for by a mixture of cross-subsidy from the rents of other tenants, local taxation and through various special grants from a variety of public sources.[40] However, this system had a number of weaknesses:

- The various funding streams overlapped and there was no clear mechanism to reflect a strategic view of the needs of the area. Instead decisions were often influenced by the funding streams available.
- To access services an individual would have to move to an appropriate scheme.[41] These arrangements were not sufficiently flexible to provide 'floating support' for potential users in their own home.
- The true costs of the service were hidden from users and were not sufficiently transparent.
- Where service charges were met through housing benefit there was no effective mechanism for ensuring the charge was reasonable and the services were of an acceptable quality.
- High service charges extended the range of the poverty trap and were therefore a disincentive to work.

The new Supporting People arrangements which came into effect in April 2003 replaced these disparate funding streams with a single pot which is administered by local authorities.

The money is distributed as grants according to the strategic needs of the area. Ordinarily grants are made to landlords on three-year contracts to provide specific support services for a specified number of residents in a particular scheme. The grant compensates the landlord for not levying support charges. Instead the local authority levies a variable charge according to the resident's income via a separate means-test. So, for example, a resident on income support will be assessed as having a zero charge. Any income collected in charges can be used by the authority to fund other services.

---

40 The complex of funding sources included for example (in England) Supported Housing Management Grant provided by the Housing Corporation; Probation Accommodation Grant funded jointly by the Home Office and the ODPM and grants for resettlement hostels paid by the DWP under s29 of the Jobseeker's Act 1995.

41 They would have to move to a housing project which has been subsidised by one of the various government grants or move into rented housing (including subsidised rented housing) and receive help through housing benefit with the charges.

Projects which aim to bring about independent living within two years (such as the young homeless) are exempt from a charge. The vast majority of these residents would be on income support and so very little income would be generated. The majority of these residents will also be of working age so the lower overall charge will help to improve work incentives and assist transition to independent living.

For most residents the net effect on what they pay is much the same as before. The advantage of the new system is that money for new projects can be allocated more strategically. The contracting arrangements make it easier to plan the budget and influence the quality of the services. For the Treasury there is the added attraction that an element of a demand-led budget (housing benefit) has effectively been transferred to a cash-limited system.

This advantage became particularly apparent in 2004 when the government announced a cash-limit to Supporting People which means that the fund will grow more slowly than inflation, following criticisms about escalating costs and inefficiency. Providers have argued that the fund is now unlikely to be sufficient to support a full range of services and that cuts – particularly in 'unpopular' areas like working with people with drug dependency – are inevitable.

Income support for mortgage interest

The social security legislation of the 1980s that established the modern housing benefit system specifically excluded owner-occupiers from entitlement. At the time, the idea of a unified housing allowance embracing all tenures had been considered, but the inclusion of home-owners would have involved a radical restructuring, or even the abandonment, of mortgage interest tax relief to finance it. At a time when the creation of a 'property-owning democracy' was at the heart of the government's housing policy ambitions, such an idea was considered to be politically unacceptable.

However, it was recognised that there needed to be a safety net which stabilised circumstances and enabled owners to remain in their home when their earnings were interrupted by sickness or unemployment. The safety net takes the form of income support for mortgage interest (ISMI).

Assistance for mortgagors in difficulties with their repayments has been a long-standing feature of the UK housing system. This form of income augmentation dates back to the immediate post-war period and the introduction of national assistance (1948) when owner-occupation began to gain prominence. The scheme operates to provide assistance in maintaining mortgage loans up to a maximum limit (currently fixed at £100,000) to borrowers who have limited savings (currently £8,000 or below) and who have lost their income from work due to redundancy, accident, illness, or retirement. A key feature of the scheme is that only the interest element of the outstanding loan, calculated on a standard rate, is covered. Crucially, however, no assistance is available to those who cannot afford to keep up their mortgage because of low wages. In fact, any claimant who works 16 hours or more per week, or where their partner works 24 or more hours is automatically barred from any assistance with ISMI.[42] As a result, those who start back into low-paid work after a period of unemployment may find that, after paying their housing costs, their disposable income is less than when they were on benefit. This is referred to as the 'employment trap'.

Rules of entitlement

1. *Part-time work.* If a claimant works for more than 16 hours a week, or their partner works more than 24 hours a week, all entitlement to ISMI is withdrawn.

2. *Savings.* Except in the case of claimants aged over 60 who are also in receipt of the pension credit guarantee (who are entitled to the maximum help), claimants whose assessed capital is in excess of £8,000 are excluded from benefit. For all other claimants with capital between £3,000 and £8,000 a tariff is carried forward into the claimant's assessment of income. The tariff is calculated in the same way as for housing benefit.[43]

3. *Predetermination.* From May 1994, regulations have excluded from assistance any increase in housing costs resulting from new loans taken out whilst the claimant is in receipt of income support.

4. *Deferred payments.* With the exception of pensioners, claiming the pension credit help with housing costs is deferred during a waiting period. For all other claimants, waiting periods were introduced in October 1995. Before their introduction, eligibility for ISMI was tied strictly to eligibility for income support. The length of the waiting period depends on whether the mortgage was taken out before or after the 1995 rule changes. Existing borrowers get no help at all for the first two months of claim, up to 50 per cent of their interest for the next four months, and up to 100 per cent of their interest thereafter.[44]

---

42 Although they may be entitled to working tax credit, WTC has no specific housing costs related element but it may provide the claimant with a greater income than when out of work if the amount of eligible interest under ISMI is relatively modest.

43 If the DWP is of the view that someone previously had savings but has deliberately spent or disposed of them in order to bring them below the limit then they can still be treated as if they still possess it. This is called 'the notional capital rule'. The rule only applies if the DWP can show that the motivation for disposing of the capital was to qualify for benefit.

44 Strictly speaking, ISMI does not pay full or half of mortgage interest, but includes this as a need element in the person's IS/JSA calculation. So, for example, if the claimant does not qualify for IS on a standard calculation (i.e. excluding housing costs), their housing costs may help them to qualify. The total IS they receive will be the difference between their eligible housing costs and any income in excess of their total needs excluding housing costs. Therefore, it may not cover the full 100 per cent of the mortgage interest.

Those with post-1995 mortgages get no help for the first nine months (39 weeks) and thereafter (from week 40) up to 100 per cent of their interest can be met through ISMI. For reasons of cost, administrative simplicity and to provide an incentive to claimants to ensure they are being charged a competitive rate, all payments covered by the scheme are calculated on a standard rate of interest rather than the actual rate.[45] In this way the DWP does not look at the actual payments being charged and match them but, after the waiting period, pays a rate pegged to the Bank of England base rate.

The waiting period is calculated, not from the point at which income support/JSA is received, but from the point at which the claimant becomes unemployed or incapable of work. This provision was introduced so as not to penalise the thrifty behaviour of those who saved prior to their financial difficulties.

5. *Eligible interest.* Subject to approval, claimants may be able to have the interest on certain repair and improvement loans met. To qualify for support, the repair or improvement has to be shown to be necessary to maintain the home in a habitable condition. Only specified works approved by DWP regulations qualify. The list includes, amongst other things: provision of a bath and necessary plumbing and hot water, home insulation, and correcting unsafe structural defects. Loans for approved repairs and improvements can be taken out whilst the claimant is already on ISMI, unlike ordinary loans where restrictions apply. Regulations prevent the assistance being used to service non-mortgage debts such as buildings insurance and endowments. Any charges that are related to any second mortgages do not qualify as 'eligible' expenses for ISMI purposes.

It is possible to receive help with more than one mortgage. If a second mortgage has been taken out to repay the original mortgage, that element of the latter which is repaying the original loan is eligible interest. A mortgage taken out for purposes other than acquiring an interest in a dwelling is not eligible.

The mortgage interest liability may be considered to be excessive and capped if the accommodation is considered to be unnecessarily large for the claimant. Restrictions also apply if the property is in an area that is considered to be too expensive compared with other areas in which suitable accommodation is available or if the housing costs are unreasonable when compared with other accommodation in the area.

---

45 Since November 2004 this has been set at the Bank of England base rate plus 1.58 per cent. Prior to November 2004 it was based on a weighted average of the published rates of the top 20 building societies.

6. *Non-dependant charges.* As with housing benefit, a deduction will be made from ISMI if a claimant has a 'non dependant' living with them. It is assumed that such a person (e.g. adult child), is making a contribution to the running costs of the home. The amount deducted will depend on the age, income and working status of the relative.

7. *Right to buy transferees.* Council and housing association tenants on secure tenancies who become owner-occupiers for the first time whilst on income support have their ISMI tied to the amount of rent used to calculate their housing benefit when they were renting. This measure is designed to ensure that a degree of equity exists between housing benefit and ISMI in order not damage the government's commitment to expand owner-occupation (see discussion below) but also to prevent abuse and control costs whereby a claimant could simply opt for the subsidy which was worth the most.

8. *Direct payments.* Since 1992, the system has operated by making direct payments to lenders.

Differences between housing benefit and ISMI: a question of horizontal equity

As we have intimated, ISMI to owner-occupiers is in some respects equivalent to the housing benefit paid to augment the incomes of poorer households in the private and social rented sectors. However, in contrast with housing benefit, ISMI is restricted to those who are out of work and are in receipt of either income support, income-based JSA or the pension credit guarantee. ISMI is always paid direct to the lender[46] and is administered by the local offices of the DWP.[47]

As explained above, income support entitlement is withdrawn if or when the claimant starts work of 16 hours or more per week. Under present arrangements, a further question of horizontal equity[48] arises because, in such circumstances, owner-occupiers lose their entitlements to ISMI while claimants who rent their homes can continue to seek help with their housing costs via housing benefit. This anomaly is known as 'the employment trap' (see below).

To overcome the horizontal inequity that exists between tenants and owners, the Chartered Institute of Housing argues the need to create a common system of

---

46 The principle of direct payments to lenders was established in July 1992. In return, lenders' organisations introduced a voluntary agreement not to repossess the home if ISMI was being met in full on the mortgage interest obligation. However, this agreement has somewhat broken down following the changes introduced in 1995 which fixed the payment according to a standard rate of interest, although regulations still require payments to be made direct.
47 By contrast, housing benefit is administered by local authorities acting as agents of the DWP.
48 For an explanation of the notion of horizontal equity see pp41-42.

'housing credit' to apply across both tenures.[49] It could be argued that a housing credit system could be used to weaken the disincentive effects of the employment and poverty traps by incorporating provisions that would allow claimants in both tenures to continue to receive support whilst in work. Work incentives could also be improved by establishing an earned income disregard that is more generous than that currently applied to housing benefit claimants and extending it to ISMI claimants. Further reforms would integrate working tax credit and housing benefit into a 'housing credit' scheme with a single calculation and a common taper. A unified tax credit scheme which included a housing costs element would avoid the problem of concurrent tapers applying over a range of income with the consequent very high withdrawal rates which occur when tax credits, housing benefit and council tax benefit are all in payment and are withdrawn as income increases.[50]

ISMI and the 'employment trap'

The government's Social Security Advisory Committee highlighted the nature of the ISMI 'employment trap':

> 'If the partner's work of 16 hours or more precludes either of them claiming income support but the partner's earnings are insufficient to maintain them both and pay the mortgage, the only sensible course of action is for the partner to cease work so that income support may be claimed.' (Social Security Advisory Committee, 1994)[51]

In a limited way the government has addressed the issue of work disincentives through the family credit and its successor the child tax credit/working tax credit schemes, and through the jobseeker's allowance. However, in CTC/WTC (and its predecessor schemes) claimants cannot claim help with mortgage costs and, although the JSA does permit claimants to work less than 16 hours a week,[52] earning more than £5 will cause benefit to be reduced by £1 for every £1 earned – a marginal withdrawal rate of 100 per cent. In addition there were a number of other disincentives to taking up employment in the original scheme, particularly temporary jobs. First, except for very short periods in work where the two claims for ISMI would be 'linked,' a claimant taking a temporary job would need to serve their full waiting period again (of 40 weeks) before re-qualifying for ISMI. Second, unlike housing benefit, there was no system of extended payments to smooth the transition into work. Following recommendations in the housing green paper the linking arrangement was extended to 52 weeks (having previously been extended from the original four weeks to 12) and extended payments were introduced from April 2001.

---

49   Alison Barker, 'Housing credit "would be fair to homeowners"', in *Public Finance*, 31 January 1997, p4.
50   Wilcox, S. (1998), *Unfinished Business*, Chartered Institute of Housing, p17.
51   From Department of the Environment, *A Foot on the Ladder, A Study of Households on the Margins of Renting and Owning a Home*, HMSO 1994. para.2.9. Although since 1996 partners of claimants have been able to work up to 24 hours before entitlement is lost.
52   If it is the partner who is working, then the limit is 24 hours.

ISMI and public expenditure

Owner-occupation expanded rapidly during the 1980s and this, together with subsequent downturn in employment and job security, meant that the cost to the DWP expenditure rose sharply from £286 million in 1988 to a peak of £1,210 million in 1993.[53] These rising costs caused the government to alter the arrangements.

Under the old system, claimants received half the interest paid for the first 16 weeks of claim and full interest after that. Following an announcement in the 1994 Budget, in October 1995 the government made cuts to ISMI payments. The public expenditure savings are largely achieved by deferring the support to those who qualify (see above). Official estimates at the time predicted savings in ISMI of some £200 million. However this figure failed to make any overall cost-benefit analysis of the changes, such as the consequences of higher levels of homelessness that might result from the new rules. Currently, of those who have their homes repossessed, some 60 per cent end up in the public sector. As a result there is an unforeseen fiscal consequence: once the former owners move into rented housing they become eligible for housing benefit and thus are potentially an added burden on the public purse. In this way, via a process of repossession, measures designed to save public expenditure simply relocate its incidence and, in the process, create personal misery, as well as additional work for advice workers and housing practitioners.

Two political motivations appear to have been behind the change in rules outlined above. The first was a concern about rising public expenditure and the second was the desire to encourage personal responsibility and increase private sector involvement in the provision of cover.

Ministers justified the restrictions on the assumption that new borrowers would turn to private insurance for cover and, as the insurance market expanded in response to the new climate, the price would fall.[54] But private insurance operates in a free market and competition between lenders is likely to result in differential charges for different categories of risk. Only about 40 per cent of ISMI recipients are unemployed[55] and the rest are people with financial difficulties resulting from marital breakdown, disablement, an accident, or illness. Because some groups are more likely to be at risk from unemployment or sickness, competitive insurance companies will charge higher premiums for those claimants considered to be a higher risk.

Mortgage payment protection insurance differs significantly from the income support system (ISMI). Eligibility for the latter depends on the size of the loan, the

---

53 *UK Housing Review 2004/05*, Table 110, CIH/JRF/CML, 2004.
54 *Roof Briefing*, December 1994.
55 Ibid.

value of the mortgagor's savings and whether they have a partner who is economically active. ISMI will cover only the interest element after the waiting period has expired. In contrast, private insurers will normally cover the full mortgage obligation including repayment of principal and any endowment premium – they may also cover payment of associated insurances. However, private insurers tend to limit their liabilities with a variety of restrictive clauses and by reducing future benefits if the numbers of claims rises significantly. It should also be noted that the whole idea of 'insurance' is to restrict cover to unforeseeable risks such as sudden disability or redundancy and not to apply to changes which reflect some degree of personal choice such as retirement, the winding up of a self-employed business or withdrawal from the labour market to look after children. Most insurance agreements would also exclude loss of income resulting from voluntary redundancy, resignation and dismissal (as does ISMI).

The realities of private payment protection are that insurance companies will use 'credit scoring' techniques to protect themselves from high risk agreements and, as a result, some groups will be excluded from private cover altogether such as the seriously ill and the elderly, whilst others such as those in insecure employment will be charged higher premiums. Mortgage insurance currently costs about £3 per £100 of monthly repayment, but costs are likely to be higher during periods of high unemployment.[56] The typical policy pays nothing for the first few months and then only covers the full premium for a fixed period (typically 12 months). Private insurance cover tends to be regressive in that it usually charges higher premiums for those at greatest risk (e.g. the elderly and those in low-paid, insecure employment). In this way the reforms are likely to create a socially divisive, two-tier system of private coverage.

Another concern is that some individuals may be vulnerable to pressure selling and being sold inappropriate products. As former welfare claimants assume the role of private customers they will have to rely heavily on the industry's voluntary code of practice and the industry-funded Insurance Ombudsman Bureau that operates a voluntary scheme to deal with complaints. Evidence from Citizens Advice[57] has shown that many of their clients have purchased cover only to discover that when they needed to make a claim they had been paying premiums for a policy from which they could never benefit. Others had fallen foul of rigid qualifying conditions that could make it almost impossible to lodge a successful claim.[58] Furthermore, Citizens Advice argues that exclusion clauses in many policies prevent some claimants from participating in government retraining schemes without losing their entitlements.

In response to criticisms about private insurance, the Council of Mortgage Lenders and the Association of British Insurers introduced a new scheme in 1999.

---

56 In the mid to late 1990s costs were typically £7 per £100 of monthly benefit.
57 *Dispossessed* (1993) and *Security at Risk* (1995).
58 Ann Abraham, chief executive NACAB, letter to *Inside Housing*, 26 April 1996.

Their scheme lays down minimum standards such as policies that will pay out within 60 days and provide cover for a minimum of 12 months. Automatic exclusion clauses will not be included so that each claim will be treated individually. The success of such a scheme will largely depend on how potential clients judge the relationship between the cost, how much extra will be added to the monthly mortgage repayments, and the protection benefits received. Herein lies a dilemma: the scheme, which could add an extra £50 or £60 a month to the mortgage costs of a household, may seem relatively unattractive to someone in secure employment with entitlement to generous sickness payments. Therefore the scheme may attract a disproportionate number of people in insecure employment who are more likely to make a claim. This will keep the unit costs high and thereby limit the scheme's market appeal. The scheme may also be flawed in another way. One of the most common reasons people have for getting into difficulty with their mortgage repayments is relationship breakdown, and it would appear that the proposals do not provide cover for this eventuality. More recently the attractiveness of these products has been diminished somewhat by the growing popularity of 'flexible' mortgages in which the customer can opt to pay more during times of relative prosperity or take a 'payment holiday' at times when their income suffers a downturn. Flexible mortgages may yet prove to be more competitive and provide better coverage than a traditional product with insurance.

A private, voluntary, self-regulating, unsubsidised scheme is always more likely to exclude the most vulnerable or be too expensive for those who face the highest risks to join. A compulsory, universal scheme would be more affordable and encourage insurers to extend the product range. It would, however, need to be underwritten by public funds.

Summary

Under the 1988 housing benefit scheme rents for housing association and local authority tenants are normally accepted as reasonable for benefit purposes. In contrast, for private sector tenants the total amount of housing benefit is fixed by reference to local rent levels. Within this ceiling, the support given to any particular household is determined by a means-test that compares their income and savings with their assumed needs. Claimants receiving income support are entitled to maximum housing benefit which is calculated as the maximum eligible rent less any non-dependant deductions. The housing benefit for other claimants is based on a calculation that compares how much their income exceeds their applicable amount (i.e. income support level) and reduces their maximum benefit by 65 per cent of this excess.

During the 1990s in response to Exchequer concerns about the rising cost of housing benefit, the eligibility rules were tightened, but this only served to make the scheme more complex and difficult to administer. More recently the introduction of tax and pension credits designed to improve incentives to work and save have been driving technical changes to the calculation of housing benefit. These changes have disrupted the common means of assessment which was the principal feature of the 1988 social security reforms and have introduced new anomalies which may prove to be unsustainable.

The other major feature of the 1988 scheme was that benefit was based on actual housing costs. The weakness of this is that it gives tenants no incentive to take an interest in their rent. Therefore reforms which apply to private rented claims are being trialed in which benefit is calculated on a locally-determined flat-rate allowance which is based on the local reference rent. In the longer term, a flat-rate system will make it easier to introduce a universal housing allowance covering all tenures. This would also help to remove the employment trap for home-owners and to tackle the excessively high rates of withdrawal faced by those on housing benefit and tax credits as they improve their earnings.

Further reading

DETR/Social Security, *Quality and Choice: A Decent Home for All*, The Housing Green Paper, April 2000, Chapters 5 and 11.

Kemp, P., *'Shopping Incentives' and Housing Benefit Reform*, CIH/JRF, 2000.

Wilcox, S., *Unfinished Business: Housing Costs and the Reform of Welfare*, CIH/CML/LGA/NHF and JRF, 1998.

Zebedee, J., Ward, M. and Lister, S., *Guide to Housing Benefit and Council Tax Benefit*, CIH/Shelter (updated annually).

BIBLIOGRAPHY

Note: Where possible the location of the publishing house has been included, but this has not been achieved in all cases.

General publications

Anderson, J. and Ricci, M., (Eds), (1990), *Society and Social Science,* The Open University: Milton Keynes.

Atrill, P., (2003), *Financial Management for Non-specialists,* Prentice Hall.

Balchin, P. N. and Kieve, J. L., (1977), *Urban Land Economics*, Macmillan: London and Basingstoke.

Baldry, D., (1998), 'The evaluation of risk management in public sector capital projects', in *International Journal of Project Management*, Vol.16, No.1 pp35-41, Pergamon.

Barker, A., (1997), 'Housing credit "would be fair to homeowners" ' in *Public Finance,* 31, January 1997.

Blackaby, B. and Chahal, K., (2001), *Black and Minority Ethnic Housing Strategies,* CIH: Coventry.

Blackaby, B., (2004), *Community Cohesion and Housing: A good practice guide,* CIII: Coventry.

Bovaird, E., Harloe, M. and Whitehead, C., (1985), 'Private Rented Housing: Its Current Role' in *Journal of Social Policy,* 14(1).

Bradshaw, J., (1972), 'The Taxonomy of Social Need', in McLachlan, G., (Ed), *Problems and Progress in Medical Care*, 7th series, Nuffield Provincial Hospitals Trust, OUP.

Bramley, G. and Morgan, J., (1998), 'Low Cost Home Ownership Initiatives in the UK', in *Housing Studies*, Vol.13, No.4 pp567-586.

Brown, T. and Passmore, J., (1998), *Housing and Anti-Poverty Strategies*, CIH/JRF: Coventry.

Button, F., (1993), *Best Practice for Better Borrowing*, NFHA: London.

Carey, S., (1995), *Private Rented Housing in England 1993/94,* HMSO: London.

Chaplin, R., Jones, M., Martin, S., Pryke, M., Royce, C., Saw, P., Whitehead, C., and Yang, J.H., (1995), *Rents and Risk: Investing in Housing Associations,* JRF: York.

Chartered Institute of Housing, (1997), *Sustainable Home Ownership: New Policies for a New Government*, CIH: Coventry.

Chartered Institute of Housing, (1997), *Good Practice Briefing No.7 – Local Housing Strategies,* April 1997, CIH: Coventry.

Chartered Institute of Housing, (1997), *Good Practice Briefing No.11 – Rents and Service Charges*, December 1997, CIH: Coventry.

Chartered Institute of Housing, (2000), *The Crisis in Housing Benefit and how to respond to it,* Good Practice Briefing, CIH: Coventry.

Chartered Institute of Housing/Local Government Association briefing, (prepared by Bob Blackaby), (2001), *Modernising the Legal Basis for Local Authorities' Strategic Housing Role,* CIH/LGA: Coventry and London.

Chartered Institute of Housing (NI), (2001), *Large Scale Voluntary Transfer and the NIHE,* CIH: Belfast.

Chartered Institute of Housing/Royal Town Planning Institute, (2003), *Planning for Housing: the potential for Sustainable Communities,* CIH/RTPI: Coventry and London.

Chartered Institute of Housing/Local Government Association/Royal Town Planning Institute, (2004), *Intelligent Approaches to Housing – Achieving better integration in planning for housing,* CIH/LGA/RTPI: Coventry and London.

Chartered Institute of Public Finance and Accountancy, (1995), *Financial Reporting in Local Government: Capital,* CIPFA: London.

Chartered Institute of Public Finance and Accountancy, (2003), *The Prudential Code for Capital Finance in Local Authorities,* CIPFA: London.

Citizens Advice Bureaux, (1993), *Dispossessed,* National Association of Citizens Advice Bureaux.

Citizens Advice Bureaux, (1995), *Security at Risk,* National Association of Citizens Advice Bureaux.

Citizens Advice Bureaux, (1998), *Unsafe Deposit: CAB clients' experience of rental deposits,* National Association of Citizens Advice Bureaux.

Commission on Social Justice, (1994), *Social Justice: Strategies for National Renewal,* The Report of the Commission on Social Justice, Vintage: London.

Coopers and Lybrand, (1996), *Consensus for Change – Public Borrowing Rules, Housing Investment and the City,* CIH: Coventry.

Cope, H., (1990), *Housing Associations: Policy and Practice,* Macmillan: Basingstoke and London.

Council of Mortgage Lenders, *Housing Finance,* CML's journal, CML: London.

Council of Mortgage Lenders, (2005), *Buy-to-let growth is slowing down,* press release, 14 February 2005, CML: London.

Crook, A. and Kemp, P., (1999), *Financial Institutions and Private Rented Housing,* JRF: York.

Crook, A., Kemp, P., Barnes, Y., and Ward, J., (2002), *Investment returns in the Private Rented Sector,* British Property Federation.

Denman, D. and Prodano, S., (1972), *Land Use: An Introduction to Proprietary Land Use Analysis,* George Allen and Unwin: London.

Denman, D., (1978), *The Place of Property,* Geographical Publications Ltd.

Down, D. and Green, H., (1996), *Housing in England 1994-95,* HMSO: London.

Drury, C., (2002), *Management Accounting for Business Decisions,* Thompson.

Duncan, P. and Thomas, S., (2001), *Neighbourhood Management: A Good Practice Guide,* CIH: Coventry.

England, M., (1997), *The Tenants' Guide to Housing Finance,* London Housing Unit.

Flynn, N., (1997), *Public Sector Management (3rd edition),* Prentice Hall/Harvester Wheatsheaf: Hemel Hempstead.

Ford, J., (2000), 'MPPI take-up and retention: the current evidence', in *Housing Finance* No.45, February 2000, pp45-51.

Forrest, R., Murie, A. and Williams, P., (1990), *Home Ownership: Differentiation and Fragmentation,* Unwin Hyman: London.

Freeman, A., Holmans, A. and Whitehead, C., (1999), *Evaluating Housing Affordability – Policy Options and New Directions*, LGA: London for the CIH, LGA and NHF.

Garnett, D., (1994a), *The Theory and Practice of Cost-Benefit Analysis*, Faculty of the Built Environment Working Paper WP31, UWE: Bristol.

Garnett, D., (1994b), *To Redevelop or Rehabilitate? A CBA Approach to Decision Making*, Faculty of the Built Environment Working Paper WP32, UWE: Bristol.

Garnett. D., (1995), 'Multiple rationality Analysis: An Approach to Reconciling the Competing Interests Associated with Housing Renewal Schemes'. Paper given to the Commonwealth Association of Surveying and Land Economy and the International Federation of Surveyors: *Sustainable Development: Counting the Cost – Maximising the Value*, Harare, Zimbabwe, August 1995. Copies available from the author, UWE Bristol.

Garnett, D., (1996), *Building Obsolescence*, UWE: Bristol.

Garnett, D., (1999), 'Absent Voices: Accommodating the Interests of Future Generations Through Multiple Rationality Analysis', in the *International Journal of Sustainable Development*, Vol.2, No.4.

Gibb, K. and Munro, M., (1991), *Housing Finance in the UK: An Introduction*, Macmillan: Basingstoke and London.

Gibson, M. and Langstaff, M., (1982), *Introduction to Urban Renewal*, Hutchinson.

Goss, S. and Blackaby, R., (1998), *Designing Local Housing Strategies – A Good Practice Guide*, CIH: Coventry.

Gray, D., (1999), *What's it all about? Registered social landlord accounts explained*, NHF: London.

HACAS Consulting, (1999), *Housing Associations – A Viable Financial Future?* (Eds Lupton, M. and Perry, J.), CIH: Coventry.

HACAS Chapman Hendy, (2002), *Beyond Bricks and Mortar – Bringing Regeneration into Stock Transfer*, CIH:Coventry.

HACAS Chapman Hendy, (2003), *Empowering Communities – the Community Gateway Model*, CIH: Coventry.

Harloe, M., (1985), *Private Rented Housing in the United States and Europe*, Croom Helm: London.

Harriott, S. and Matthews, L., (2004), *Introducing Social Housing*, CIH: Coventry.

Hawksworth, J. and Wilcox, S., (1995), *Challenging the Conventions: Public Borrowing Rules and Housing Investment*, CIH/Coopers and Lybrand: Coventry.

Holmans, A., (1995), 'The Rising Number of Households Requiring Homes – The National and Regional Picture' in Wilcox, S., (1995), *Housing Finance Review 1995/96*, Joseph Rowntree Foundation: York.

Holmans, A., (2000), 'Owner-occupied households: recent trends in England and the USA, Australia, Canada and New Zealand', in *Housing Finance*, No.45, February 2000, pp30-35.

Holmes, R. and Marshall, D., (1996), *Property Profiling and Data Collection for Housing repairs and Improvements*, Construction Papers 61 and 62, (Ed. Harlow, P.), Chartered Institute of Building.

Kemp, P., (2000), *'Shopping Incentives' and Housing Benefit Reform*, CIH/JRF: Coventry and York.

Kemp, P., (2004), *Private Renting in Transition*, CIH: Coventry.

King, P., (2001), *Understanding Housing Finance*, Routledge: London.

Local Government Association, (2004), *RSG Settlement 2004/5 (England): Guide*, produced annually by the LGA: London.

Lowndes, V., (1997), 'Change in Public Service Management: New Institutions and New Management Regimes', in *Local Government Studies*, Vol.23, No.2, Summer 1997.

Lowry, I. S., 'Filtering and Housing Standards: A Conceptual Analysis', in *Land Economics*, 1960, pp362-370.

Mackay, C. and Williamson, A., (2001), 'Housing Associations in Ireland, North and South' in Paris, C., (2001), *Housing in Northern Ireland*, CIH: Coventry.

Mackintosh, S., Malpass, P., and Garnett, D., (1988), *Most Peoples' Dream: A Study of Home Ownership and the Management of Maintenance of Older Low Cost Housing*, NAB: London.

Malpass, P., (1990), *Reshaping Housing Policy: Subsidies, Rents and Residualisation*, Routledge: London and New York.

Malpass, P., (Ed), (1997), *Ownership, Control and Accountability: The New Governance of Housing* (Housing Policy and Practice Series), CIH: Coventry.

Marsh, A. and Mullins, D., (Eds), (1998), *Housing and Public Policy: Citizenship, Choice and Control*, OUP: Buckingham.

Marshall, D., (1996), 'Condition Surveys for Housing Associations: Some potential pitfalls and a survey of client experience' in *CIOB Construction Papers No. 68*.

Meen, G., (1994), *The Impact of Higher Rents*, Housing Research 109, Joseph Rowntree Foundation: York.

Mew, H., Robinson, C., Humphrey, A., Kafka, E., Oliver, R. and Bose, S., (2003), *Housing in England 2001/2002: A report of the 2001/2002 Survey of English Housing*, The Stationery Office: Norwich.

Moody, G., (1996), *Boosting Housing Investment through Capital Receipts*, CIH: Coventry.

Graham Moody Associates, (1998), *Council Housing – Financing the Future*, CIH: Coventry.

Moore, C. M., (1987), *Group Techniques for Idea Building*, Sage Publications.

Mullins, D., (1998), 'More choice in Social Rented Housing' in Marsh, A. and Mullins, D., (Eds), (1998), *Housing and Public Policy: Citizenship, Choice and Control*, OUP: Buckingham.

National Federation of ALMOs, (2004), *Guidance on Arms Length Management of Local Authority Housing – 2004 edition*, HouseMark.

National Federation of Housing Associations, (1985 and 1986), *Inquiry into British Housing*, The Report (1985), the Evidence (1985) and the Supplement (1986), NFHA: London.

National Federation of Housing Associations/Rowntree Foundation, (1990), *Paying for Rented Housing, Research Report 12*, NFHA: London.

National Housing Federation, (1996), *Financial Planning: a practical guide*, NHF: London.

National Housing Federation, (1997), *Reinvestment Strategies: A Good Practice Guide*, NHF: London.

National Housing Federation, (1997), *Rents, resources and risks: the new balancing act*, NHF: London.

National Housing Federation, (1998), *Private Finance Loans Monitoring Bulletin*, NHF: London.

National Housing Federation, (1999), *Statement of Recommended Practice (SORP): Accounting by registered social landlords*, NHF: London.

National Housing Federation, (1999), *Living with risk: An overview of risk for registered social landlords*, NHF: London.

National Housing Federation, (2002), *Neighbourhood Funding Streams 2002 – At a glance guide*, NHF: London.

National Housing Forum, (1998), *Regionalism, Devolution and Social Housing*, NHF: London.

Nettlefold, J.S., (1908), *Practical Housing*, Garden City Press: Letchworth.

Oxley, M, and Smith, J., (1996), *A European Perspective of Housing Investment in the UK*, Avebury.

Paris, C., (2001), *Housing in Northern Ireland*, CIH: Coventry.

Partington, M., (1994), *Claim in Time: Time Limits in Social Security Law*, Third Edition, LAG: London.

Pawson, H., (2004) 'Reviewing Stock Transfer' in Wilcox, S., (2004) *UK Housing Review 2004/2005*, CIH/CML: Coventry and London.

Perry, J., (2004), 'Full Speed Ahead' in *Inside Housing*, 14 May 2004.

Pike, E.R., (1966), *Human documents of the Industrial Revolution in Britain*, Allen & Unwin: London.

Quilgars, D., (1999), 'High and dry down Acacia Avenue', in *Roof*, March/April 1999, pp45-51.

Ratcliffe, P., (2001), *Breaking down barriers: improving Asian access to social rented housing*, CIH: Coventry.

Rauta, I. and Pickering, A., (1992), *Private Renting in England in 1990*, HMSO: London.

Rugg, J. and Rhodes, D., (2001), *Chains or Challenges?: the prospects for better regulation of the private rented sector*, CIH/BPF: Coventry.

Saunders, P., (1990), *A Nation of Home Owners*, Unwin Hyman: London.

Scottish Foundation of Housing Associations, (2002), *Developing Affordable Rents*, SFHA: Edinburgh.

Shelter/JRF Commission of Private Renting, (2002), *Private Renting: A New Settlement*, Shelter: London.

Sillett, J., (2004), *Housing: The Right to Choose*, Local Government Information Unit: London.

Sim, D., (Ed), (2004), *Housing and Public Policy in Post-Devolution Scotland*, CIH: Coventry.

Smith, J., (2004), 'Understanding demand for home-ownership: aspirations, risks and rewards', in *Housing Finance,* No. 62, summer 2004.

Spalding, J., (1983), *The Future Constitution and Powers of Building Societies,* known as the John Spalding Report, Building Societies' Association: London.

Stewart, J. and Stoker, G., (Eds), (1995), *Local Government in the 1990s*, Macmillan: London.

Taylor, M., and Wilcox, S., (2004), 'The Funding and Affordability of Social Housing' in Sim, D., (Ed) (2004), *Housing and Public Policy in Post-Devolution Scotland,* CIH: Coventry.

Timmins, N., (2001), *The Five Giants – A biography of the welfare state,* Harper Collins: London.

Travers, A., (2004), 'The Ex-Files' in *Public Finance,* 30 July 2004.

Walker, D, and Brombley, G., (1995), 'Briefing' on rental securitisation in *Inside Housing,* 17 February 1995.

Whitehead, C. and Kleinman, M., (1992), *Review of Housing Needs Assessment,* Housing Corporation: London.

Wilcox, S., Bramley, G., Ferguson, A., Perry, J., and Woods, C., (1993), *Local Housing Companies: New opportunities for council housing,* JRF/CIH: York and Coventry.

Wilcox, S., (1995), *Housing Finance Review 1995/96*, Joseph Rowntree Foundation: York.

Wilcox, S., (1996), *Housing Finance Review 1996/97*, Joseph Rowntree Foundation: York.

Wilcox, S., (1997), *Housing Finance Review 1997/98*, Joseph Rowntree Foundation: York.

Wilcox, S., (1998), *Unfinished Business: Housing costs and the reform of welfare benefits*, CIH: Coventry.

Wilcox, S., (1999), *Housing Finance Review 1999/2000*, Joseph Rowntree Foundation, Chartered Institute of Housing and the Council of Mortgage Lenders: York, Coventry and London.

Wilcox, S., (2002), 'Border Tensions – Devolution, rents and housing benefit' in *UK Housing Review 2002/2003,* CIH/CML: Coventry and London.

Wilcox, S., (2002), *UK Housing Review 2002/2003,* CIH/CML: Coventry and London.

Wilcox, S., (2003), *UK Housing Review 2003/2004,* CIH/CML: Coventry and London.

Wilcox, S., (2003) Another Fine Mess' in Wilcox, S., (2003), *UK Housing Review 2003/2004,* CIH/CML: Coventry and London.

Wilcox, S., (2004) *UK Housing Review 2004/2005,* CIH/CML: Coventry and London.

Wild, D., (1996), 'Unsafe as Houses', in *Public Finance*, 29 November 1996.

Williams, P, (2002), 'Stand and Deliver! – Tackling the housing challenges in post-devolution Wales' in Wilcox, S., (2002), *UK Housing Review 2002/2003,* CIH/CML: Coventry and London.

Zebedee, J, Ward, M. and Lister, S., *Guide to Housing Benefit and Council Tax Benefit,* updated annually, CIH/Shelter: Coventry and London.

Official publications

Audit Commission, *Housing after Transfer: the Local Authority Role,* Audit Commission: London, December 2002.

Audit Commission, *A Modern Approach to Inspecting Services,* Audit Commission: London, 2004.

Building Economic Development Committee, *Ways to Better Housing*, NEDO, 1986.

Cabinet Office, *A New Commitment to Neighbourhood Renewal: National Strategy and Action Plan,* Cabinet Office: London, 2001.

Committee on Standards in Public Life, *Second Report of the Committee on Standards in Public Life: Local public spending bodies,* Cm3270, The Stationery Office, May 1996.

Communities Scotland, *Memorandum of Understanding,* Communities Scotland: Edinburgh, 2001.

Communities Scotland, *Performance Standards for Social Landlords and Homelessness Functions,* Communities Scotland: Edinburgh, 2001.

Communities Scotland, *Better Communities in Scotland: closing the gap,* Communities Scotland: Edinburgh, 2002.

Communities Scotland, *Option Appraisal – Guidance for Local Authorities,* Communities Scotland: Edinburgh, 2004.

Communities Scotland, *Strategic Housing Investment in Scotland,* Communities Scotland: Edinburgh, 2004.

Department of the Environment, *Fair Deal for Housing,* White Paper, Cm4728, HMSO, July 1971.

Department of the Environment, *Housing Policy: A Consultative Document,* Green Paper, CM6851, HMSO, 1977.

Department of the Environment, *Assistance with Housing Costs,* HMSO, 1981.

Department of the Environment, *Housing: The Government's Proposals*, Cm214, HMSO, 1987.

Department of the Environment, *Local Government in England and Wales: Capital Expenditure and Finance,* Consultation paper, DoE, 1988.

Department of the Environment, *A New Financial Regime for Local Authority Housing in England and Wales,* HMSO, 1988.

Department of the Environment, *A Foot on the Ladder: A study of households on the margins of renting and owning a home,* HMSO, 1994,

Department of the Environment, *Evaluating Large Scale Voluntary Transfers of Local Authority Housing*, HMSO 1995.

Department of the Environment, Transport and the Regions, *Modern Local Government, In Touch with the People* (White Paper), Cm4014, 1998.

Department of the Environment, Transport and the Regions, *Modernising local government: Local democracy and community leadership*, Cm6646, 1998.

Department of the Environment, Transport and the Regions, *Modernising local government: Capital finance,* Cm7257, 1998.

Department of the Environment, Transport and the Regions, *Rethinking Construction,* Report of the Construction Task Force, Egan Report, 1998.

Department of the Environment, Transport and the Regions, *Towards an Urban Renaissance*, The Report of the Urban Task Force, Chaired by Lord Rogers of Riverside, 1999.

Department of the Environment, Transport and the Regions (with the Department for Social Security), *Quality and Choice: A Decent Home for All*, The Housing Green Paper, HMSO, April 2000.

Department for the Environment, Local Government and the Regions, *Strong Local Leadership - Quality Public Services,* White paper, Cm5327, HMSO, December 2001.

Department for the Environment, Local Government and the Regions, *Business plans for council housing: guidance,* HMSO, 2002.

Department of the Environment and the Welsh Office, *Our Future Homes,* The White Paper on Housing Policies, Cm2901, June 1995.

Department of Health and Social Security, *Inequalities in Health,* Chaired by Sir Douglas Black, 1980.

Department of Social Security, *Supporting People: a new policy and funding framework for support services,* DSS, 1998.

Department of Trade and Industry, *Social Enterprise: a strategy for success,* DTI, July 2002.

Department of Work and Pensions, *Housing Benefit Direct,* newsletter from the DWP: London.

Department of Work and Pensions, *Building choice and responsibility: a radical agenda for housing benefit,* DWP, 2002.

House of Commons Social Security Select Committee, *Housing Benefit,* Volume 1, House of Commons, HC 385-1, 2000,

HM Treasury, *Building Societies: A New Framework,* Green Paper, Cm9316, HMSO, 1984,

HM Treasury, *Better Accounting for the Taxpayer's Money,* White Paper, Cm2929, July 1995.

HM Treasury, *Public Expenditure: Statistical Analyses 1996-97* Cm3201, London: HMSO, 1996.

HM Treasury, *Modern Public Services: Investing in reform,* The Comprehensive Spending Review, Cm4011, 1998.

HM Treasury, *The Modernisation of Britain's Tax and Benefit System,* Pre-Budget News Release Number 3, 17 March 1998.

HM Treasury, *Stability and Investment for the Long Term,* Economic and Fiscal Strategy Report, Cm3978, June 1998.

HM Treasury, *Review of Housing Supply: Securing Our Future Housing Needs,* known as the Interim Report Analysis of Barker Review after its author, Kate Barker, HMSO: Norwich, December 2003.

HM Treasury, *The Pre-Budget Report, The strength to take the long-term decisions for Britain: Seizing the opportunities of the global recovery,* December 2003.

HM Treasury, *Review of Housing Supply: Delivering Stability: Securing Our Future Housing Needs,* known as the Final Report of Barker Review after its author, Kate Barker, HMSO: Norwich, March 2004.

HM Treasury, *Public Expenditure Statistical Analysis 2004,* Cm6201.

HM Treasury, *The UK Mortgage Market: Taking a longer-term view,* known as the Miles Report, HMSO: Norwich, March 2004.

HM Treasury, *Economic and Fiscal Strategy Report 2004, (the Budget),* HMSO: Norwich, March 2004.

HM Treasury, *Releasing Resources to the Frontline: Independent Review of Public Sector Efficiency,* Known as the Gershon Report after chair, Sir Peter Gershon, HMSO: Norwich, July 2004.

Housing Corporation, *Best Value for registered social landlords.* Guidance Note, Housing Corporation, February 1999.

Housing Corporation, *Regulatory Code and Guidance: The way forward, our approach to regulation,* Housing Corporation, 2002.

Housing Corporation, *Partnering through the ADP,* policy paper, Housing Corporation, July 2002.

Housing Corporation, *Scheme Development Standards (fifth edition),* Housing Corporation, April 2003.

Housing Corporation, *Reinventing Investment,* policy paper, Housing Corporation, October 2003.

Housing Corporation and National Housing Federation, *Global Accounts and Sector Analysis of Housing Associations 2003,* compiled by Gordon Ibbotson and Richard Peck at FSMD based on the HC database, annual publication, Housing Corporation and National Housing Federation: London.

London Research Centre, *Housing Benefit and the Private Rented Sector,* DETR, 1999.

Low Cost Home Ownership Task Force, *A home of my own,* report from the Task Force chaired by Baroness Dean, Housing Corporation: London, November 2003.

Ministry of Housing and Local Government, *Houses: The Next Step,* CM8996, HMSO, November 1953.

Ministry of National Insurance, *Social Insurance and Allied Services,* known as the Beveridge Report after its chair, Sir William Beveridge, HMSO, Cm6404, November 1942.

National Audit Office, *Modernising Construction,* The Stationery Office: London, 2001.

National Audit Office, *Improving Social Housing Through Transfer,* Report by the Comptroller and Auditor General, The Stationery Office: London, 2003.

NEDO, *Changing Work Patterns,* A report by the IMS, HMSO, 1986.

Northern Ireland Housing Executive, *The Northern Ireland Housing Market – Review and Prospects 2004-2007,* NIHE: Belfast.

Office of the Deputy Prime Minister, *Housing Signpost,* regular newsletter, ODPM.

Office of the Deputy Prime Minister, *Housing Revenue Account Manual,* regular annual publication from the ODPM: London.

Office of the Deputy Prime Minister, *Survey of English Housing,* Continuous survey started in 1993 by the DoE, now ODPM publication compiled by the National Centre for Social Research.

Office of the Deputy Prime Minister, *The Way Forward for Housing,* ODPM, December 2000.

Office of the Deputy Prime Minister, *The Way Forward for Housing Capital Finance,* ODPM, August 2002.

Office of the Deputy Prime Minister, *A Guide to Social Rent Reforms in the Local Authority Sector,* ODPM, 2002.

Office of the Deputy Prime Minister, *Sustainable Communities: Building for the future,* ODPM, February 2003.

Office of the Deputy Prime Minister, *Review of the delivery of the Decent Homes target for social housing – PSA Plus Review,* ODPM, February 2003.

Office of the Deputy Prime Minister, *The Decent Homes Target Implementation plan,* HMSO, June 2003.

Office of the Deputy Prime Minister, *Local Authority Housing Finance – A Guide to the New Arrangements,* ODPM, 2003.

Office of the Deputy Prime Minister, *Support for Local Authority Capital Investment – A Consultation Document,* ODPM, 2003.

Office of the Deputy Prime Minister, *Guidance on Arms length Management of Local Authority Housing,* ODPM, 2003.

Office of the Deputy Prime Minister, *The Allocation of Management and Maintenance Allowances with HRA Subsidy,* ODPM, July 2003.

Office of the Deputy Prime Minister, *Housing Private Finance – A Tenant's Guide,* ODPM, November 2003.

Office of the Deputy Prime Minister, *The Future of Local Government – Developing a 10-year vision,* ODPM, 2004.

Office of the Deputy Prime Minister, *Delivering Decent Homes,* ODPM press release 2004/0115, 5 May 2004.

Office of the Deputy Prime Minister, *Fifth Report of the ODPM Housing, Planning, Local Government and Regions Committee,* ODPM, 7 May 2004.

Office of the Deputy Prime Minister, *Balance of Funding Review,* HMSO, July 2004.

Office of the Deputy Prime Minister, *Resource accounting in the Housing Revenue Account: consultation paper,* ODPM, 2004.

Office of the Deputy Prime Minister, *Three Year Review of Rent Restructuring,* ODPM, 2004.

Office of the Deputy Prime Minister, *Housing Revenue Account Manual,* ODPM, 2004.

Office of the Deputy Prime Minister, *Sustainable Communities: Homes for All: A five-year plan from the Office of the ODPM,* ODPM, January 2005.

Office of the Deputy Prime Minister/Welsh Assembly Government, *Park Homes Site Licensing: Proposals for Reform,* ODPM, January 2005.

Office of the Deputy Prime Minister/Stephens, M., Whitehead, C. and Munro, M., *Lessons from the past, challenges for the future for housing policy: An evaluation of English Housing Policy 1975-2000,* ODPM, February 2005.

Office of the Deputy Prime Minister, *Social Housing Efficiency: a discussion paper,* ODP, March 2005.

Office for National Statistics, *Social Trends,* annual biography of the nation, The Stationery Office: Norwich.

Office for National Statistics, *Living in Britain 2002: General Household Survey,* The Stationery Office: Norwich, 2004.

Scottish Executive, *Scottish Public Finance Manual,* regular publication from the Scottish Executive: Edinburgh.

Scottish Office, *Investing in Modernisation – An Agenda for Scotland's Housing*, The Scottish Housing Green Paper, HMSO, February 1999.

Social Exclusion Unit (SEU), *Bringing Britain Together: A national strategy for neighbourhood renewal,* Cm4045, HMSO: London, 1998.

Social Exclusion Unit (SEU), *Report of Policy Action Team 4: Neighbourhood Management,* part of the national Strategy for Neighbourhood Renewal, SEU: London, 2002.

Strategy Unit, *Private Action, Public Benefit,* Cabinet Office, September 2002.

Topic index

Notes:
1. The index covers the main text but not introductions to chapters, summaries or (in most cases) footnotes.
2. Acts of parliament are only included if they are referred to more than once in the text.
3. Proper names (e.g. of organisations) are generally only included if they are referred to more than once in the main text.

Chartered Institute of Housing

retail price index (RPI), 41, 221, 286-287, 351
revenue contributions to capital outlay
 (RCCO), 186, 198-199, 292-293
revenue deficit funding and grants, 344-345,
 349-350, 354, 356
revenue expenditure and revenue income,
 13-16, 152-153, 198-199, 263-265, **279-
 294**, 320, 335-337, **349-350**
Revenue Support Grant (RSG), 192, 194, 254,
 264-271, 273, 441
right to buy (RTB), 40, 55, 68, 90, 101, **110-
 112**, 113-116, 121, **124-127**, 140, 187, 192,
 196, 198, 204, 216, 235, 297, 386, 465
right to acquire (RTA), 112-113, 337
ring-fenced accounts, 168-169, 180, 198, 269,
 272, 274-276, 283, 289
risk management and risk mapping, 320, 390,
 394-403
rough sleepers, 255, 271
rural home ownership grant, 116

Schedule A tax, 106, 152-153, 417, 431
Scotland, policy differences in, 111, 115-116,
 125-126, 148, 174, 176, 191, 193, 195,
 198, 202, 208, 210, 213, 215, 222, 232,
 243-244, 261, 278-279, 284, 301, 308-309,
 457
Scottish Executive, 70-72, 90, 92, 189, 194,
 208, 216, 220, 245, 265, 301, 308, 325
Scottish Housing Quality Standard (SHQS),
 92, **210-212**, 213, 232
Scottish Parliament, 70-73, 82, 97, 165, 185,
 308, 321
searches, 148
second homes, 74
securitisation, 146, 239-240, 385
sensitivity analysis, 373, 394, 402-403
service charges (for services to leaseholders or
 tenants), 49, 122, 126, 200, 280, 282, 286,
 343, 353-355, 424, 447, 460-462
service charges (costs of servicing a loan or
 debt), 47, 48, 51, 107, 159, 168, 263-264,
 273, 277-280, 284, **292-293**, 320, 334,
 342-343, 345-346, 372, 382, 385
shared appreciation mortgages, 145
sinking funds, 29, 47, 122, 336, 344, 346, 404
single capital pot, 201, 260, 338
single regeneration budget (SRB), 256-258
single room rent (SRR), 448-449

shared ownership, 107, 116, 123, 127-128,
 304, 336, 378
slum clearance, 73, 169, 245, 259-260
social exclusion/inclusion, 185, 202, 206, 244,
 256-258, 300, 307, 348, 439
Social Exclusion Unit, 69, 72, 257-258
social fund, 81
Social Housing Grant (SHG), 54, 58, 95, 320-
 321, 326-330, 332, **334-335**, 338, 345, 351,
 378, 388
special needs, 33, 57-58, 165, 202, 255, 353-
 355, 450, 460-462
Special Needs Management Allowance
 (SNMA), 355
specific grants, 268, 270-271, 455
specified capital grant (SCG), 193-194, 202
spending reviews (*see also* Comprehensive
 Spending Review), 69, 75, **81-84**, 87, 97,
 175, 187, 190-192, 206, 208, 224, 230,
 259, 268-269, 273, 312, 456
staircasing, 115-116, 128, 142
stamp duty, 78, 122, **149-150**
starter homes *and* starter home initiative,
 116-117
statement of recommended practice (SORP),
 314, 343, 352, 376-379, 404
stock condition surveys, 225, 243, 405
stock retention, 215-216, 232, 234-236, 238-
 240
stock transfer, 194, 205, 208, **215-223**, 230,
 236, 244, 256-257, 271, 301, 309-310, 351,
 373, 381, 383, 392
stock transfer levy, 219, 222
strategic and enabling role (of local authority),
 32, 72, 165, 179-180, 225-226, **242-262**,
 327
subsidy, 15, 26, 40, **54-62**, 67, 73, 76, 90-91,
 94-95, 104, 106-108, 111, 128, 152-154,
 159, 186-187, 192-194, 198, 235, 237-239,
 261, **263-298**, 329-330, 382, 426, 436, 439,
 442-443, 455, 465
supply estimates and supply expenditure, 86-
 87, 97
supply-side subsidies, 17, 61-62, 67, 441
supported borrowing *see* borrowing support
Supported Capital Expenditure (SCE), 187,
 192, 201-203, 292
Supporting People, 122, 244, 252-253, 255,
 270, 282, **352-355**, 439, 447, **460-462**

Aster Group – sponsors of Housing Finance

Aster Group has assets approaching £350 million, a turnover of nearly £50 million and employs more than 400 staff. It is the parent company of a number of high-performing not-for-profit organisations operating in central southern and south-west England that provide affordable housing for rent and purchase, care and support and property services. It is a Housing Corporation 'lead investor' and provides development and other services for group companies and partners.

Sarsen Housing Association was formed in 1995 and provides management and maintenance services for around 5,500 homes in south-west England, which includes working on behalf of other housing associations, local authorities and private landlords.

Formed in 2000, **Testway Housing** is one of the best performing social housing providers in the country, owning over 5,000 homes. Testway has gained national recognition for its estate management, community involvement initiatives and communications activities.

With a particular focus and expertise in care and support, **Ridgeway Community Housing Association** provides 'extra care' housing for older residents and works with a number of partners to provide support for customers with special needs. Ridgeway also includes a domiciliary care provider, a Lifeline service; and four Care and Repair home improvement agencies.

Aster Property Management is responsible for managing the Group's commercial activities, maintaining and repairing homes owned by Aster Group companies and also providing property maintenance services to other organisations and private homes. It also provides homes for rent in the private sector and offers leasehold management services.